John Henry Newman

Sean Gaynor

13/9/2015. Knock

THE 'MAKING OF MEN'

The 'Making of Men'

The *Idea* and reality of Newman's university in Oxford and Dublin

Paul Shrimpton

GRACEWING

First published in England in 2014
by
Gracewing
2 Southern Avenue
Leominster
Herefordshire HR6 0QF
United Kingdom
www.gracewing.co.uk

© 2014 Paul Shrimpton

ISBN 978 085244 824 3

Typeset by Gracewing

Cover design by Bernardita Peña Hurtado

For Philip and Jane

and for Benedict, Thomas and Liliyana

CONTENTS

FOREWORD

'**N**OW FROM FIRST to last, education [...] has been my line', wrote John Henry Newman in his private journal in 1863.[1] This may well seem surprising since we would normally think of Newman as a theologian rather than an educationist, even though Newman's *Idea of a university* has long been recognized as the one classic work on university education. Nevertheless, Paul Shrimpton has already shown us in his admirable *A Catholic Eton? Newman's Oratory School* (2005) the extent to which Newman threw himself into the daily, mundane business of running a school. In this new book he turns his attention to Newman's work as the founder and first president of the Catholic University of Ireland.

As a young Fellow and tutor of Oriel College, Oxford, Newman had been actively involved in trying to introduce, albeit in vain, the kind of individual tutorial system for which Oxford is now known. In Dublin his ambition was to combine the best of the collegiate, tutorial system of Oxford with the continental professorial system, such as that of the Catholic University of Louvain.

Newman's letters reveal in great detail his extraordinary administrative and practical abilities, talents not normally associated with academics and thinkers. Paul Shrimpton makes full use of these and other unpublished materials to show how Newman was much more than the author of *The idea of a university*. However, his research also effectively supplements that work by revealing the extent of Newman's vision of what a 'holistic' university education should mean in practice.

This excellent study is an important and timely contribution to the contemporary debate about the purpose and function of universities. As a work of original research, it is in addition a valuable addition to Newman studies.

Ian Ker

Note

1. *John Henry Newman: autobiographical writings* (London, 1956), p. 259.

PREFACE

T HIS IS NOT just another book about John Henry Newman and education, based on his classic *The idea of a university*, but a book about the thinking, acting, organising Newman who helped to reform Oxford University and who saw into being every aspect of the Catholic University Dublin as its founding rector.

Nor is this book based on the lectures or essays that make up the *Idea*; instead it is based on Newman's vast correspondence and memoranda concerning the two universities, on the letters, diaries and memoirs of those he worked with, on accounts ledgers, buttery records, punishments books, timetables, rules and regulations, prospectuses, minute books, reports of all types, and a host of other documents. By combining a forensic use of primary sources with a contextual account of the changing university story—the microscopic with the macroscopic—I have tried to show Newman's educational endeavours in the full context of the times, and hence in a new light. What emerges from this story is a picture of a Christian humanist and man of action, capable not just of academic speculation but of taking on a large educational project and of delineating what a university *ought* to look like if it is to foster human flourishing in the full Aristotelian sense.

During the nine years I have worked on this book it has been gratifying to see how interest in Newman's educational ideas continues to grow, as evidenced by the publications of Alasdair MacIntyre, Stefan Collini and Mike Higton, to name just three, as well as references in the speeches and writings of Pope Benedict XVI—who, of course, beatified Newman in 2010. But accounts of, or commentaries on, Newman's contribution to education in Dublin almost universally dismiss his practical achievements; and it is this assumption that this book questions and, as it turns out, largely refutes. The task of rebutting specific misinterpretations of Newman's Dublin years would have been an endless one, as most commentators have been wide of the mark when reflecting on Newman's practice of education. I have refrained from pointing out their errors: Newman's actions, I think, speak for themselves.

My professional experience in teaching and in running a student residence has given me a distinct advantage in writing about Newman's educational endeavours, compared with someone who is 'merely' an academic. Four years working as assistant director (i.e. warden) of the student residence Netherhall House in London and twenty-eight years at the chalk-face at Magdalen College School in Oxford—for twelve of those years having a key role in students' progress to university in general and Oxford and Cambridge in particular—have heightened my pastoral sensitivities and alerted me to so much that is special in Newman. His ways of dealings with the aspirations as well as the waywardness of youth have the ring of truth that anyone involved with the rising generation 24/7 will recognise.

I feel privileged to have had this opportunity to write about such a towering figure, one whose reputation is second to none in the field of higher education. Blessed John Henry has taught me a great deal about human nature over the years, and I only hope that my own shortcomings have not distorted the portrait I have tried to give of one of history's great 'makers of men'.

Paul Shrimpton
Grandpont House, Oxford
9 October 2014

ACKNOWLEDGEMENTS

IN WRITING THIS book I have drawn on primary material in three archives – the Birmingham Oratory, University College Dublin and Archbishop's House Dublin – and I am grateful to the archivists and librarians at each of them for their generous help and suggestions. I also wish to thank the librarians at the Bodleian Library Oxford who have assisted me over the last nine years.

I am grateful to the Master and Governors of Magdalen College School Oxford for granting me study leave in June 2007 so that I could make the first of two archival visits to Dublin.

I am immensely grateful to my two main readers, Dr Peter Damian Grint and Edward Short, who have both provided invaluable editorial assistance and taken such a keen interest in my project. Peter—Fr Peter, as of 4 May 2013—forced me to write with greater clarity and to explain what needed explaining more fully, and covered my drafts with (electronic) red ink as befits someone who has worked in academic publishing in Oxford for over a decade; he continued to assist me even after moving to Rome. Edward, too, helped me from overseas, in his case from New York; he read through a mature draft of the book, unpicking and challenging my every loose statement and dubious sounding paraphrase of Newman's prose, and in that way forced me to sharpen my arguments. He also contributed very helpful suggestions as to what I had *not* said and needed saying. Obviously, all the infelicities and errors that remain in the text are my very own, not theirs.

I owe thanks to all those who have assisted me in obtaining images for use in the plate section, particularly John Briody, and to Jonathan Henry who helped prepare the images for publication.

Naturally, I wish to thank the Fathers of the Birmingham Oratory for their kindness in granting me access to their archive and for permission to reproduce material from the collections held there.

I feel honoured that Dr Ian Ker has taken an interest in my project and offered to write the Foreword; he also read the final draft and provided me with some telling observations. I have learned more about Newman from him than anyone else.

Lastly, I wish to thank Tom Longford, Rev Dr Paul Haffner and the rest of the Gracewing team for all their support and willingness to prepare this book for publication.

ABBREVIATIONS

AW	*John Henry Newman: autobiographical writings*
BOA	Birmingham Oratory archives
CUG	*Catholic University Gazette*
DDA	Dublin Diocesan archives
DIB	*Dictionary of Irish biography*
DP	Dublin Papers [BOA, C.7.3]
HS	*Historical sketches*
LD	*The letters and diaries of John Henry Newman*
MC	*My campaign in Ireland*
NU	*Newman's university: idea and reality*
ODNB	*Oxford dictionary of national biography*
Report and Evidence (1853)	*Report and evidence upon the recommendations of Her Majesty's commissioners for inquiring into the state of the University of Oxford, presented to the Board of Heads of Houses and Proctors*
Robertson Report	*Report of the Royal Commission on university education in Ireland, 1902–3*
Royal Commission Queen's Colleges (1858)	*Report of Her Majesty's commissioners appointed to inquire into the progress and condition of the Queen's Colleges at Belfast, Cork, and Galway: with minutes of evidence, documents, and tables and returns*

Royal Commission Cambridge (1852) — *Report of Her Majesty's commissioners appointed to inquire into the state, discipline, studies and revenues of the University and colleges of Cambridge: together with the evidence, and an appendix*

Royal Commission Oxford (1852) — *Report of Her Majesty's commissioners appointed to inquire into the state, discipline, studies and revenues of the University and colleges of Oxford: together with the evidence, and an appendix*

Royal Commission Trinity (1853) — *Report of Her Majesty's commissioners appointed to enquire into the state, discipline, studies and revenues of the University of Dublin and of Trinity College, together with appendices, containing evidence, suggestions, and correspondence*

Spec. coll. — Special collection

UCDA — University College Dublin archives

ILLUSTRATIONS

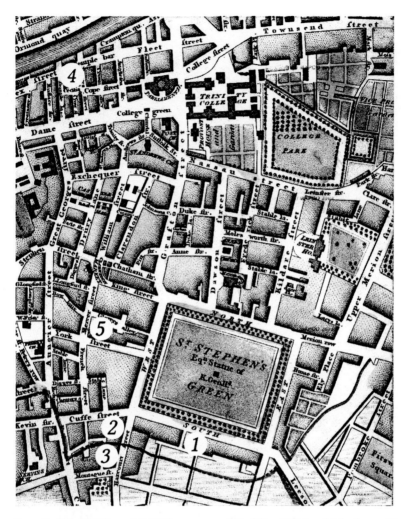

Detail of the William M. Wilson map of Dublin, 1798, which shows St Stephen's Green and, to the north, Trinity College. Maps of the 1850s are virtually identical to this one.

1. St Patrick's House, 86 St Stephen's Green
2. St Mary's House, 6 Harcourt Street
3. St Laurence's House, 16–17 Harcourt Street
4. Catholic University Medical School, Cecilia Street
5. St Luke's Medical House, York Street

INTRODUCTION

J OHN HENRY NEWMAN famously declared that if he 'had to choose between a so-called University, which dispensed with residence and tutorial superintendence, and gave its degrees to any person who passed an examination in a wide range of subjects, and a University which had no professors or examinations at all, but merely brought a number of young men together for three or four years', as Oxford used to do at the end of the eighteenth century, then he would have no hesitation in opting for 'that University which did nothing, over that which exacted of its members an acquaintance with every science under the sun'. He explained that he was not saying which was *morally* the better, because it was obvious that 'compulsory study must be a good and idleness an intolerable mischief', but rather which 'was the better discipline of the intellect': that is, which was 'the more successful in training, moulding, enlarging the mind, which sent out men the more fitted for their secular duties, which produced better public men, men of the world, men whose names would descend to posterity'.[1]

This is a provocative and challenging opinion, especially given Newman's fame for occupying the academic high ground, and it is encapsulated in just one sentence in his classic text, *The idea of a university*. The *Idea* has been described by a leading historian of university education as 'unquestionably the single most important treatise in the English language on the nature and meaning of higher education',[2] and is endlessly cited, typically by those who take a high view of a university education and see Newman as the most inspiring advocate of a liberal education. Yet the *Idea* is incomplete, and even those familiar with Newman's thinking are apt to overlook the fact that it was not intended to be a systematic or exhaustive treatment of a subject—and that indeed key elements of his thinking barely feature in it, or are missing altogether. Certainly a different note is struck every now and then when he digresses from his main purpose, as when he challenges his listeners and readers with the paradox just cited; these scattered references provide strong hints about a key idea that he did *not* develop in the *Idea*—about the pastoral dimension of a university education.

Newman made the same point more succinctly in a private letter written in 1873, in which he stated that, broadly speaking, 'a residence without Examinations comes nearer to the idea of a University Education than examinations without residence'. He went on to say that 'University Education has, properly speaking, no equivalent; what is most like an equivalent in its effect, is for a youth to be well read, well travelled, and well introduced', though this was 'not the result of a system'.[3] Remarks such as these make it clear that Newman had a very broad conception of what he meant by the word 'education', and that he resisted the tendency, common then as now, to reduce its meaning and narrow its scope.[4] While it is true that he was involved in educational ventures of all kinds throughout his long life (1801–90) and that he constantly reflected on and wrote about education, he did not consider it something confined to its more formal moments or institutional settings. This attitude to education colours all of Newman's involvement in the university world, and it had an ancient source.

Human flourishing: an Aristotelian tradition

Like many other original thinkers, Newman was heavily influenced by the works of Aristotle, particularly the *Nicomachean ethics*. Newman not only learnt from Aristotle's explanations, but from the questions he asked and the way in which he argued. In grappling with the fundamental questions of human existence, Aristotle argues that happiness is the reward of virtue; that the good life, the fulfilled life, is made possible by developing positive traits or strengths of character called virtues; and that discernment in these matters is easier to the extent that a person is virtuous. These insights of the great pagan philosopher—for Newman was a natural Aristotelian—strengthened Newman's understanding of the human person and orientated him in his educational endeavours. By Aristotle's criteria, the public recognition of Newman's holiness through his beatification is not marginal to any assessment of the wisdom of Newman's educational thinking; rather, it suggests he is eminently suited to advising on the conditions for the attainment of that very Aristotelian concept of human flourishing, particularly in its university setting.

The philosophy of Aristotle has inspired Alasdair MacIntyre to challenge contemporary modern and post-modern culture—the so-called Enlightenment project—and led to a revival of virtue ethics. MacIntyre has changed the landscape of philosophical inquiry by re-establishing the importance of virtue and re-evaluating the influence of social and cultural traditions on the way we think and understand. He has progressively argued for and articulated a revival of Aristotelian (and Thomistic) accounts of rationality and conduct, in response to what he sees as the uprooted and fragmented condition of post-Enlightenment philosophy. In his works he has alluded to, but not enlarged upon, his 'massive debt' [5] to Newman; but in a lecture series entitled 'God, philosophy, universities' delivered at the University of Notre Dame in 2006 he explained his indebtedness.[6] In the published version of these lectures,[7] MacIntyre assigns a pivotal role to Newman and his foundation of the Catholic University in Ireland in the history of what he calls the 'Catholic philosophic tradition'.

In *God, philosophy, universities* (2009) MacIntyre attempts to sketch (and defend) a tradition in which a confident faith in God is compatible with a robust form of intellectual inquiry, even one which questions the Church's formulations about God. His selective history takes in Augustine, Boethius, and Jewish and Islamic thinkers—all drawing on the genius of Aristotle—who contributed to the emergence of the university and the Catholic philosophical tradition in the twelfth and thirteenth centuries. Aquinas considered philosophy an independent form of inquiry, though one guided by faith, and this enabled him to develop a comprehensive formulation of the way in which God is to be conceived as the source of intelligibility for the created world. This provided a philosophical basis for the university enterprise and helps to put Newman's contribution into context and to explain his line of action.

In a chapter called 'The Catholic absence from and return to philosophy, 1700–1850', MacIntyre describes the aridity of teaching in Catholic institutions in this period and the absence of dialogue between Catholic philosophers and the seminal thinkers in the development of modern philosophy. 'Where philosophy flourished, Catholic faith was absent. Where the Catholic faith was sustained, philosophy failed to flourish.'[8] Most of the influential thinkers of the period were anti-Catholic and regarded the Church as the bastion of superstition and discredited beliefs; and their arguments appeared to be borne out by the fact that secular learning flourished precisely where Catholic claims were seldom advanced or heard. MacIntyre explains that the loss was to the inhabitants both of cultures where the intellectual claims of the Catholic faith were not articulated, and of cultures where Catholic intellectual formation did not interact with the modern critiques of Christian theism. For Catholics, encounters with the major thinkers of the time were effectively postponed—and they did not occur until Catholic universities once again became institutions central to enquiry and debate, as in the Middle Ages.

The new forms of university life that appeared in Protestant Europe and post-Revolutionary France from the end of the eight-

eenth century had, according to MacIntyre, three common characteristics: theology was marginalised or abandoned; philosophy
became just one subject among many; and each subject claimed
autonomy for itself. The resulting fragmentation of knowledge and
understanding and the disappearance of any sense of underlying
unity meant that the modern university embodied attitudes that were
deeply at odds with a Catholic view of knowledge and the world.
According to the Catholic view, each subject area contributes to
knowledge of the whole; theology gives this knowledge a unity; and
a central task of philosophy is to integrate the theological understanding of the world with that provided by secular subjects. Such
an integrated view of reality was completely foreign to the modern
universities; yet they were the ones driving research, making new
discoveries and integrating them into their own (autonomous) fields
of knowledge to become starting points for further inquiry.

From all this Catholics were either excluded or self-excluded, as
the new universities were either Protestant or secular. In 1834 the
Belgian bishops took the bold initiative of refounding a Catholic
university at Louvain; but although Louvain was to flourish once
again, its leaders were not yet ready to react to the intellectual
condition of Catholics in a culture that was so alien and inimical to
Catholic thought. That reaction came from a remarkable and
unexpected event: the Irish bishops' invitation to Newman to
establish a Catholic University in Ireland. The story of what ensued
is important not only for the modern university, Catholic or
otherwise, but also for the revival of Catholic philosophy. Why was
this? For MacIntyre, it is due to,

> the extraordinary quality of Newman's mind, character, and
> intelligence. This was someone of high intellectual powers,
> of notable integrity, someone well aware of the claims of the
> Enlightenment, a reader of Hume and Gibbon, someone who
> understood what was at issue in contemporary philosophical

debate, someone with a distinctively modern sensibility and
literary style, who, at a time when Catholicism seemed to be
intellectually impoverished and unable to come to terms with
the claims made in the name of secular reason, had identified
himself with the Catholic faith.[9]

This description is useful in explaining why Newman is someone
who speaks to the modern world and why he has so much to offer.
His insights into the human condition and his interest in the world
around him lend his words and example the quality of a great
Christian humanist.

This was a theme picked up by Pope Benedict XVI during his
visit to Britain in September 2010 which culminated in Newman's
beatification at Birmingham. He spoke of the 'modernity of his
existence, [...] his great culture, [...] and his constant quest for
the truth' as the three elements which give Newman 'an exceptional
greatness for our time' and make him 'a figure of Doctor of the
Church for us'.[10]

Perennial problems, modern solutions

The prevailing view of Newman's time in Ireland is that it was
wasted, except for the happy accident that it gave the world an
educational classic.[11] But I do not believe this to be the case. On
the contrary, I maintain that it is important to examine Newman's
theory and practice *together*, to use all the available sources and fill
out the vision contained in the *Idea* by extending it into the pastoral
dimension, and to see how that vision was translated into a reality
by its originator, first at Oxford (long before the *Idea* was written)
and later in Dublin. Only by doing so is it possible to appreciate
Newman's vision for the university in its entirety.

The fact that the Catholic University failed to prosper might
imply that the vision was faulty, or that theory was translated into
practice without taking the circumstances into account, or that

Newman was a poor administrator—or any combination of these. But there is an alternative, very simple and plausible explanation: that the obstacles were so great that the Catholic University was almost certain to fail from the outset. If this is the case, the story of how Newman sought to translate educational theory to plans on paper, and plans on paper to a living institution, takes on an importance that should not be underestimated. When he was made a cardinal, twenty years after leaving Dublin, one of the official addresses he received came from the then rector and senate of the Catholic University. After thanking Newman for having 'devoted his best and most valued energies of many years' as 'Joint-Founder of the Catholic University', the address goes on to remark (prophetically) that,

> we feel assured that the plan for the higher education and the system of University government which you initiated and organized, will, centuries hence, be studied by all who may have to legislate for Catholic education, as among the most precious of the documents which they shall possess to inform and guide them.[12]

The *Idea* and its various editions have given rise to a sprawling secondary literature, but most commentaries overlook Newman's other educational writings; some forget that he was an Oxford Fellow for over twenty years, that he was the founding rector of the Catholic University in Ireland, and that he later established the first Catholic public school in England; and that in all these he made important *practical* contributions to the development of education. The one major in-depth study of the university Newman established in Ireland is Fergal McGrath's *Newman's university: idea and reality* (1951). This impressive piece of scholarship has acted as the definitive work on the Catholic University for over sixty years, yet it has some serious drawbacks. Two-thirds of McGrath's study is spent examining the background to the foundation and the immediate build-up to it, while Newman's previous educational activity in Oxford is ignored. Despite his attention to detail, McGrath does not really convey what day-to-day life at the Catholic University was like; and there is only a summary sketch of what happened to the University after Newman's departure. My intention is to develop McGrath's work in three ways: by using the archival material he could not locate or was unaware of; by extending his study to take into account both Newman's university career at Oxford and the fortunes of the Catholic University after his departure from Dublin; and by providing a fuller account of the life of the University during Newman's rectorate (1854–58), with emphasis on the pastoral dimension.

There are several good reasons for a book on the pastoral purpose of a university along the lines of Newman's vision. Firstly, it is important to redress the lopsided coverage of Newman's views on higher education caused by an over-emphasis on the *Idea*. A masterpiece it may be, but there is a good case for saying it should be accompanied by a *caveat lector*. Secondly, there is an urgent need for a vision like Newman's to fill the educational vacuum that currently exists in discussions about the purpose of a university. Although it may not be obvious to those outside the walls of academia, to those within it is all too apparent that economic considerations have become the dominant driving force and that much has been sacrificed in the relentless drive for 'efficiency'. The current obsession with targets has aggravated this trend, as the inevitable consequence of institutions focussing on the measurable is the neglect of what is not measurable—which is often closely related to the original raison d'être of the institution concerned. Thirdly, the time is long overdue to address one particular manifestation of the impoverishment of university life: the shameful neglect of its pastoral dimension—that is, of everything that goes on outside lecture hall, laboratory and library. These matters are no longer regarded as the concern of academics, not least because of the pressure they are under to meet their targets; university administrators often have very different priorities, such as fending off anticipated litigation or boosting an 'output' figure for a university ranking-table. These three points are worth developing briefly, because they will alert the reader to what is so special in what Newman has to offer.

To explain the first reason we need to ask, Why does the *Idea* give a misleading impression of Newman's educational vision and where do its deficiencies lie? Certainly, Newman uses the *Idea* to identify many of the central functions of a university and to give lasting literary form to an argument which still captivates readers and inspires reflections on what a university ought to be. But the book was never meant to be an exhaustive account of his educational ideas, as the manner in which it came about will show. It comprises two parts: a series of lectures delivered in 1852 to prepare the ground for the opening of the Catholic University; and occasional lectures given at the University while he was rector. They were published individually at first, then in two separate collections in the 1850s, and only in 1873 were they were brought together (after heavy editing) under the title by which they are now known. His third collection of articles on education, also written in the 1850s, was not included.[13]

Undoubtedly Newman's enduring influence in education is almost entirely due to the *Idea*, but it is easy to forget that the purpose of the lectures was *not* to inspire or guide future generations, but the much more immediate task of winning over his audience to the type of university he was about to set up. The historical context is vital for understanding why Newman developed the arguments he did, as they were composed to deal with the particular problems he faced. Some of these problems still exist, others do not; more importantly, Newman did not address matters upon which there was then general agreement, but which have since become thorny questions. In composing the *Idea*, he dwelt extensively on what he considered was the essence of the university, not its fully functioning state and pastoral well-being. One of the 'problems' of the *Idea* lies in its idealism: if it inspires some readers, it has the opposite effect on others. They may admire the high ideals, but they simultaneously dismiss them on account of their perceived impracticality.[14] This negative reaction is less likely to occur when Newman is seen in action and working on a practical level.

The second reason, that Newman provides a much-needed educational vision for today, is hardly contentious, because it is generally recognised that the *Idea* provides an attractive alternative to the shapeless, relativistic and uninspiring alternatives of contemporary universities. The concept of a university as an institution of unique purpose has all but dissolved, and contemporary universities increasingly function as performance-oriented, heavily bureaucratic, entrepreneurial organisations committed to a narrowly economic conception of human excellence. Just as Newman battled in his own day against dangerous trends within education, so others fight in our own times for similar causes. The recent output of literature which draws attention to and explores the loss of direction at the modern university is indicative of a loss of a coherent vision. In attempting to recover a sense of purpose, several of these modern critiques use the *Idea* as a key point of reference,[15] and some use Newman as the pivotal figure in their analysis.[16] It is unsurprising that his educational vision, with the pastoral idea at its root, is an ideal foil to the schemes of modern-day planners, since the bureaucratic is the enemy of *caritas*, the engine of true education.

The third reason for this book—to address the neglect of the pastoral dimension of the university—is not such an obvious one, and requires elaboration. In 2005 there appeared a collection of essays about the predicament of higher education called *Declining by degrees: higher education at risk*, interesting not least for its foreword by the North American novelist Tom Wolfe.[17] Wolfe ridicules the superficiality of East Coast society in the United States and its obsession with getting its offspring into Ivy League universities without for a moment reflecting on what those universities might do to their sons and daughters. 'I have never met a single parent—not one—who has ever shown the slightest curiosity about what happens to them once they get here or what they may have become by the time they graduate', he recalls telling a group of seniors at Harvard, shortly after the publication of *The bonfire of vanities* in 1987; nearly two decades later he could still say he had 'never heard a single parent speculate about what value might be added by those four undergraduate years, other than the bachelor's degree itself, which is an essential punch on the ticket for starting off in any upscale [i.e. well-paid] career'.[18] A similar obsession about 'getting in' exists in Britain, where the equivalent promised land is Oxbridge (or, to a lesser extent, the Russell Group universities). Few have been the voices who dared to ask, as John Finnis did in Oxford in 1981, 'Does the university corrupt youth?'[19]

In the United States, parents and their offspring who are concerned about what actually takes place on university campuses and whether conditions really *do* favour human flourishing can opt for one of the hundreds of faith-based colleges or universities.[20] Otherwise, they simply have to take their chance at the secular universities, where the prevailing aspiration is to have a 'good time' and do just enough work to see themselves into a well-remunerated career. Without the countercultural support provided by family and friends, the typical university student satirised by Wolfe is likely to graduate emotionally scarred and ill-prepared to form a strong marriage, bring up children or offer selfless service to country and society.

Whether in Britain or the United States, concern about suitable residential conditions is not on the agenda for most students or parents; few bother to consider which arrangements might be most conducive to human flourishing, let alone where they might be found. There was a time when religious or charitable organisations saw the provision of student accommodation and oversight as a mission worth undertaking and a service worth providing; but nowadays attention is directed at welfare activities which are deemed to be more deserving: the collapse is both one of supply and of demand.

The wisdom of generations and the experience of life seem to have been set aside. For centuries that part of the life-cycle between childhood and adulthood (from approximately fifteen to twenty-five) has traditionally been designated as the third of the seven ages of man, and the one which parents and educators regarded as the most dangerous. For the Tudor schoolmaster Roger Ascham that period was 'the most dangerous tyme of all a man's life, and most slipperie to stay well in';[21] for the Georgian legal codifier Sir William Blackstone it was the 'awkward interval'.[22] Today's world, by contrast, is blasé to the point of being irresponsible about the 'third age', and yet in some respects the predicament of today's students is more precarious than it ever was: most live away from home and inhabit an artificial world of opportunities and attractions, with few demands on them other than the academic, and belong to a society where there are rights aplenty, but few duties. For an age which supposedly worships authenticity, there is a surprising amount of (unconscious) compliance with the dictates of the prevailing culture; and since the prevailing moral norms are minimal, there are few limits to self-indulgence other than the regard of one's friends and the size of one's bank overdraft.

Looking back on his own passage through this unnatural state, Newman referred to it as 'the dangerous season of my Undergraduate residence'.[23] At Oxford he witnessed at first hand the consequences of that intoxicating mix of freedom and virtually no responsibility, and realised that formative living depended on the previous acquisition of good habits and on wise oversight by the authorities. Throughout his life Newman was preoccupied with the 'problem' of human freedom, and in particular how it played out in a person's formative years. In all his educational ventures he grappled with how best to negotiate that delicate and gradual process of launching the young person into the world, how to pitch demands and expectations with just that right mixture of freedom and restraint. He was acutely aware of the need to avoid excessive regulation and oversight on the one hand, and neglect on the other. In Newman's age as in our own, well-meaning but counterproductive over-protectiveness at the various stages of education was as common as gross neglect; and then, as now, this was particularly evident at that crucial moment of transition from school to university. Yet there is one marked difference between Newman's time and our own: then it was taken for granted that universities acted *in loco parentis*, but once the age of majority was lowered from twenty-one to eighteen, this ceased to be the case. This minor social revolution occurred in Britain in 1969, accelerating a process which had been going on for decades: its effects have been momentous though largely unrecognised.

The relationship between teacher and taught has changed in countless other ways, especially in recent years. Over the thirty-year period 1975–2005, the number of freshmen in the United States expecting their university years to bring better job prospects quadrupled from 20% to 80%, while during the same period the number who anticipated that it would help them develop a philosophy of life dropped from 80% to 20%. In both the UK and the US, ideas about the market place have deeply affected universities, with such obvious manifestations as the disappearance of idealism and the rise of the undisguised pursuit of material well-being. As one commentator puts it, students are 'treated like pampered consumers whose preferences must be *satisfied*, not as acolytes whose preferences are being *formed* in the process of being educated': for the current generation of undergraduates, 'monasticism is out and hedonism is in'.[24]

The reason Newman is invoked so frequently in debates about the modern university is that he has much to say, about both its general failings and its pastoral shortcomings. Just as the nineteenth-century journalist R. H. Hutton saw Newman's writings as a bracing antidote to the influential fallacies of the age's approved sages,[25] so contemporary observers regard them as a stimulating antidote to the nostrums of today's academics and administrators and those responsible for the direction and well-being of higher education. A university administrator, lecturer, researcher, rector and educator of public opinion, Newman can address all involved as equals. Above all, when he reminds academics that teaching rather than research is the central function of a university, he anticipates the situation described by the gentleman scholar G. M. Young, that by the 1860s and 1870s England had marched 'through the gateway of the Competitive Examination [...] out into the Waste Land of Experts each knowing so much about so little that he can neither be contradicted nor is worth contradicting'.[26] Specialisation and obsession with research and publication are not only present today but more accentuated than ever—which is why Newman's advice is so prescient and of such pressing interest. Newman has something to say not only to the modern-day research university, but to the liberal arts college, the institute of technology, the medical school, and all the other permutations of higher education. He also gives hope to those pursuing the prospects of a liberal arts college—or indeed a Catholic university—in Britain today. Much can be learnt, therefore, not just from the *Idea* but from Newman's practical engagement in education: by seeing how he approached the task, adapted to circumstances, and reacted to crises; what he aspired to in the long run and what he settled for in short term; even how he dealt with student misdemeanours or their quirky dietary requirements.

Methodology

Newman lived and thought at a particular moment in history and it is therefore essential to appreciate his historical context and background in order to understand his actions. His schemes for dealing with university students need to be seen within the context of the developing university, the cultural and social setting in which he was working, and the contemporary outlook of the Church to which he belonged. This requires a broadly chronological contextual analysis. By way of example, some knowledge of the educational situation in Ireland is essential for understanding the dynamics of the Catholic University, but the directly political problems in Ireland, which dominate many accounts of the University, including McGrath's, have limited bearing on Newman's educational scheme and therefore do not need extensive treatment; they are, besides, amply described elsewhere.

The sources for undertaking a study of Newman's pastoral idea of a university are plentiful. Published studies include the major biographies and academic studies of Newman, institutional histories of Oxford and the Catholic University, and histories of Britain and Ireland.[27] Published primary sources are equally abundant: Newman's vast correspondence is contained in thirty-two volumes, to which must be added some forty volumes of his writings across a range of disciplines. Newman's educational ideas weave in and out of his correspondence and sermons, and it is often impossible to separate the educationalist from the philosopher or theologian; nor are all his published educational works easy to access.[28] As regards unpublished material, the archive at the Birmingham Oratory contains most of Newman's correspondence, together with many thousands of related letters to him or between third parties, all his unpublished sermons, and papers and memoranda related to, *inter alia*, Oxford and the Catholic University. The archive was closed to visitors in 2003 following the unexpected death of the archivist, and seems likely to remain so for some time.[29] Two other archives which are essential for researching the Catholic University are those of University College Dublin—the Catholic University's successor—and of the Archdiocese of Dublin. These contain items such as letter-books, ledgers, prospectuses, circulars, annual reports, student registers, minute books for various committees, and records of disciplinary offences. By combining material from these three archives with the printed sources, it has been possible to piece together the story of the Catholic University in a way which has not been done before and to bring to life the university that Newman established.

At the same time this book is more than an institutional study, as it incorporates this research within a key strand of Newman's thinking on education: his pastoral concept of the university. It so happens that his development of this concept can be told as a story, and one well worth the telling. In it we see not so much Newman the thinker, but Newman the man of action.

Chapter 1 starts with Newman the schoolboy, before moving on to his Oxford period (1817–46), first as undergraduate, then as Fellow, clergyman, tutor, examiner, Tractarian and scholar. The ups and downs of his own educational formation helped him develop the main strands of his educational ideas by his mid-twenties, and he was able to apply them by reforming the teaching system at the college which was leading the intellectual recovery of Oxford. Newman's contribution to the revitalisation of Oxford and his leading part in the Oxford Movement ensure his place in the history of a university which was at the intellectual heart of an expanding empire and an industrial world power. The maturation of Newman's ideas was not interrupted by his reception into the Catholic Church, and it found new expression in his vocation to the priesthood and the Oratory of St Philip Neri.

The call to found a Catholic University in Ireland and Newman's response to it, are dealt with in Chapter 2. Here the Dublin lectures, which lie at the heart of the *Idea*, are seen in their original context and in their bearing on the new university, before the chapter examines how Newman's paper plans evolved in response to real-life events. Chapter 3 uses some of Newman's least known writings to locate his vision for the pastoral well-being of students within the competing models for higher education in the period. Newman was conversant with many of the rival systems for teaching and living arrangements, as well as the overall priorities aimed at by their proponents, and it is against this background that his vision can be appreciated for its originality. The chronological approach is resumed in Chapter 4, which explains how Newman nurtured the Catholic University into being and formed it during its first two years, before the story is interrupted again to allow Chapter 5 to examine life at the University: student and professorial life; academic, cultural and spiritual life. Chapter 6 tells the tale of Newman's last two years in Dublin and Chapter 7 examines the fortunes of his legacy in Dublin during the decades after his departure; it finishes with the various attempts involving Newman to allow Catholics to study at Oxford.

As Arnold Toynbee remarked, the fate of a society always depends on its creative minority. Newman belonged to this minority: his ideas are capable of changing the way we live and think, with important ramifications in particular for the world of the university. As MacIntyre comments, reading him we are confronted with arguments, engaged with insights, and challenged. But a further element to the encounter is Newman himself, who is concerned for his readers and anxious that his words might make them better able to see things as they are. He speaks to us with moral and spiritual urgency, determined that neither habit, familiarity, nor prejudice will prevent us from being open to the truth, including the truth about ourselves. Reading Newman complacently, in order to find only what confirms our existing way of thinking and feeling, is to miss the profoundly interpersonal challenge which he intends. This challenge may influence, surprise, or even upset us. Because he inhabits the same modernity as ourselves, he speaks to our own time in ways which are designed to inform and transform us. This influence unites intellectual, moral and spiritual considerations in ways which are inseparable from the call to conversion.[30]

Notes

1   *The idea of a university: defined and illustrated* (London, 1873; 1907), p. 145.
2   S. Rothblatt, 'An Oxonian "idea" of a university: J. H. Newman and "well-being"', *The history of the University of Oxford*, vol. vi, ed. M. G. Brock & M. C. Curthoys (Oxford, 1997), p. 287.
3   Newman to Northcote, 23 February 1872, *LD*, vol. xxvi, p. 25.
4   When speaking of education, Newman would sometimes add expressions such as 'in the larger sense' to emphasise his use of the word (*Idea of a university*, p. 170; memorandum, 21 January 1863, *MC*, p. 259; *Historical sketches*, vol. iii (London, 1872; 1909), p. 6). The concept of *paedeia* is central to Newman's thinking, embracing the total development of the human person. See J. Arthur & G. Nicholls, *John Henry Newman. Continuum library of education thought*, vol. xviii (London, 2007), p. 90.
5   *Whose justice? Which rationality?* (London, 1988), p. 354.
6   I am grateful to Brian Boyd for lending me his notes of the five lectures of this course which were about Newman and the Catholic University, and for his willingness to discuss them with me.
7   *God, philosophy, universities: a selective history of the Catholic philosophical tradition* (Maryland, 2009). Although Newman and MacIntyre share a common mentor in Aristotle and although they both use his rich concept of human flourishing, it is not always easy to distinguish what Newman thinks from what MacIntyre thinks, with the risk that MacIntyre may use Newman's thoughts to serve his own ends. Nevertheless, despite this risk and MacIntyre's broad-brush approach to the history of ideas, this book is full of insights in the way it uses Newman's arguments.
8   MacIntyre, *God, philosophy, universities*, p. 133.

9   MacIntyre, *God, philosophy, universities*, pp. 137–8.
10   *Benedict XVI and Blessed John Henry Newman. The state visit 2010: the official record* (London, 2010), p. 45.
11   Wilfrid Ward's two-volume biography, *The life of John Henry, Cardinal Newman* (London, 1912), regards the Catholic University as a trial which broke his spirit and an utter failure. In *Newman's university* (London, 1951) Fergal McGrath pictures Newman as a tired man struggling valiantly against the odds and the tide of history, giving him the air of a tragic figure disillusioned by opposition and intrigue. Ward, and to a lesser extent McGrath, consider that the enterprise was compromised by the narrowness of Newman's views, his oversensitivity and reserve, and his preference for speculative rather than active work. By contrast, the biographies of Newman by Ian Ker and Meriol Trevor bring out the man of action and show how much was achieved despite the almost insuperable difficulties that the Catholic University had to wrestle with.
12   B. Woodlock, Address from the rector and senate of the Catholic University of Ireland, 12 May 1879, *MC*, p. 414; reprinted in *LD*, vol. xxxii, p. 393.
13   Newman referred to his *three* works on university education in his Advertisement to the 1859 edition of the Dublin lectures; two of them coalesced to form the *Idea of a university*, but the third, *Office and work of universities* (1856), was published separately and is now rarely read (see the *Idea of a university*, ed. I. T. Ker (Oxford, 1976), pp. xxxvi–xxxvii; *The rise and progress of universities and Benedictine essays*, ed. M. K. Tillman (Leominster, 2001), pp. xxviii–xxix).
14   Roy Jenkins, a former Chancellor of Oxford University, confessed that the *Idea* left him dazzled but intellectually unsatisfied. 'Newman had mostly held me spellbound in the grip of his prose, but he had convinced me neither that he had a practical plan for an Irish university in the 1850s or that he had left guidelines of great relevance for a university of any nationality or any or no faith today' ('Newman and the Idea of a university', *Newman: a man for our time*, ed. D. Brown (London, 1990), p. 155).
15   Examples include: D. Maskell & I. Robinson, *The new idea of a university* (2001); G. Graham, *Universities: the recovery of an idea* (2002); S. Collini, *What are universities for?* (2012); M. Higton, *A theology of higher education* (2012), as well as MacIntyre's *God, philosophy, universities* (2009).
16   Newman is the pivotal figure in Jaroslav Pelikan's *The idea of the university: a re-examination* (1992) and in Sheldon Rothblatt's *The modern university and its discontents: the fate of Newman's legacies in Britain and America* (1997).
17   The previous year Wolfe had illustrated the effects of the malaise at univer-

sities in his novel *I am Charlotte Simmonds*, which paints a depressing picture of a student's depraved and aimless life at an elite North American university.

[18]   *Declining by degrees; higher education at risk*, ed. R. H. Hersh & J. Merrow (New York, 2005), pp. x–xi.

[19]   This is the title of a paper he read at Grandpont House, Oxford on 28 October 1981. Stanley Hauerwas nuances the idea in a paper entitled 'How Christian universities contribute to the corruption of youth', arguing that 'the university simply reinforces the corruption that has already begun. Quite simply, the university underwrites the assumption that morality is something we create through individual choice rather than it being the shaping of our lives through disciplined discovery of the good.' (*Christian existence today: essays on church, world and living between* (Durham, North Carolina, 1988), p. 247).

[20]   One of the few attempts to research these colleges and universities and their impact on national life is Naomi Riley's *God on the quad: how religious colleges and the missionary generation are changing America* (2005). This is a study of twenty institutions which aim to educate their students in a strong religious philosophy, whether Baptist, Catholic, Evangelical Protestant, Mormon or Orthodox Jewish.

[21]   *The schoolmaster* (1570; Ithaca, 1967), p. 205.

[22]   *Commentaries on the laws of England*, vol. i (New York, 1827), p. 205.

[23]   Newman to Greaves, 27 February 1828, *LD*, vol. ii, p. 58.

[24]   D. L. Kirp, 'This little student went to market', *Declining by degrees,* pp. 116, 118.

[25]   E. Short, *Newman and his contemporaries* (London, 2011), p. 303.

[26]   G. M. Young, *Victorian England: portrait of an age* (London, 1936), p. 160.

[27]   Most of the works consulted are listed in the bibliography.

[28]   Among the rare items are *My campaign in Ireland, Catholic University reports and other papers*, which was published privately after Newman's death, and the *Catholic University Gazette*, the journal edited by Newman.

[29]   It is unlikely that researchers will be able to regain access until a replacement has been found and the papers properly catalogued. However, in May 2013 it was announced that about 200,000 items in the Newman archive were to be digitised and that the process was expected to take about three years. Meanwhile Newman scholars can make use of the microfilm copies of archival material kept at the library of Yale University.

[30]   See MacIntyre, 'Newman: education, conscience, and faith today', article on the website <www.newmancause.co.uk>.

1 EALING, OXFORD AND BIRMINGHAM

IT IS A commonplace that, when setting up schools of learning, educational founders and planners have drawn extensively from their own experiences. This was certainly true of Newman, because he frequently reflected on his own education and in the process learnt both from what was sound and inspiring and from what was ill-judged or deficient. His experiences were stored up for future years (as were all his school and college notebooks, which he kept throughout life), and the lessons learnt were brought to bear in a lifetime at the 'chalk-face'. It is noteworthy that when Newman was invited to establish a university in Dublin, he was in his early fifties and had spent most of his life immersed in education: firstly as a schoolboy and student; then as a tutor, lecturer, examiner, dean of discipline and researcher; as an Anglican clergyman, spiritual guide and preacher; and, latterly, as a seminarian and Catholic priest. He was thus able to draw on the wealth of nearly half a century's experience in order to map out his vision of a university that would promote human flourishing in general, and intellectual development in particular.

In many ways the world Newman inhabited was unlike our own, and it requires an effort of the imagination to transport ourselves back into the early and middle decades of the nineteenth century; unless we do so, much of what Newman did and said will appear in an historical vacuum and as a consequence will lose much of its instructive power. The very vocabulary of education needs to be put into context, for words such as 'tutor', 'lecture' and even 'education' itself take on different connotations in different historical periods—and indeed may even be used in several ways at any one point in time. That said, human nature remains essentially unchanged, and the insights of men of genius into its traits and idiosyncrasies have a timeless quality about them. In Newman's case his understanding of the human condition reveals itself by the way he set about the task of educating young men and creating the conditions which would favour the formation of character.

Schoolboy and undergraduate

John Henry Newman was born in London on 21 February 1801, the eldest of six children. He received a stimulating pre-school education in the secure and happy surroundings of the family home in London, and he imbibed a thorough knowledge and love of Scripture from his mother, his grandmother, and his aunt Elizabeth. His religious upbringing was of a standard non-doctrinal, non-sacramental, Bible-reading Anglicanism. At the age of seven he was sent to Ealing School, a large, successful private boarding establishment, quite unlike the great public schools of England: it had first-class facilities, a homely atmosphere, a broad curriculum, specialist teachers and small classes.[1] Newman excelled in his studies and participated enthusiastically in school life, acting in Latin plays, winning prizes for speeches, taking part in debates, learning to play the violin, writing musical compositions, leading a boys' society, and editing six different school magazines. He also enjoyed reading the eighteenth-century essayists and poets, and attempted to imitate their style in poems, satires and historical romances; and he devoured the novels of Walter Scott. By contrast, he had no interest in outdoor or sporting activities other than walking and riding. His eldest sister describes the adolescent John Henry as 'a very philosophical young gentleman' and, though shy and sensitive, 'always full of thought and never at a loss for an answer'.[2]

Newman's lifelong stress on the role of personal influence in education can be traced back to his formative schooldays at Ealing, where he was befriended by Dr George Nicholas, the scholarly headmaster, and deeply influenced by the sermons, conversations and suggested reading of the Rev. Walter Mayers, the senior classics master and a devout evangelical. In the aftermath of the collapse of his father's bank in March 1816, Newman spent the summer vacation at school, where he was thrown into the company of Mayers, and during this time he fell seriously ill. That autumn he experienced the religious conversion that he regarded as the most momentous event of his life and from which he emerged as a believing Christian.[3] The occasion was not unlike two other later crises which followed the same general pattern: a period of expanding intellectual powers and self-confidence which was then checked by some sharp affliction—in this instance, the humiliation and upheaval involved in the loss of the family home and business. Newman interpreted the affair as God's chastisement for intellectual pride, as the precocious fifteen-year-old had begun to dabble in the writings of the deists Tom Paine and Voltaire and the religious sceptic David Hume, and to toy with the 'arguments for infidelity'.[4]

Going up to Trinity College, Oxford at the tender age of sixteen was a chastening experience for the earnest young man of Calvinist leanings, who found himself among sixty undergraduates, all of them older than himself, not over-studious and given to enjoying life. Within a week of arriving, at the tail-end of the academic year 1816/17, his preconceptions of Oxford were shattered when he attended a wine party and found himself in the company of undergraduates who enthusiastically set about getting drunk. As Newman would later say, it was the support of Walter Mayers which helped him through 'the dangerous season of my Undergraduate residence',[5] by warning him not to associate with those who were dissipated and instead to seek out select friends—and by urging him to face up to the dangers of residence at Oxford and endure the 'ridicule of the world'.[6] Far from the world of student high jinks and outdoor pursuits, Newman spent his first year buried in books, lectures and private devotions.[7] For someone who would later be admired for his capacity for friendship, it might seem surprising that Newman made few college friends and that he found only one soul-mate in Trinity, his fellow undergraduate John Bowden, with whom he stuck up an intimate friendship; but the composition of the student body goes some way to explaining Newman's small friendship circle.[8]

At the time, undergraduates lived in college during the academic year and, if they sought to complete their degree, remained in residence for between three and five years. On arrival most freshmen would have been seventeen years old, some eighteen, and a few sixteen or nineteen. As a college Trinity was known as a 'gentlemanly' establishment, which meant it had a sprinkling of undergraduates classed as 'noblemen' and a good proportion —about a third—of 'gentlemen commoners', young men from aristocratic backgrounds who paid higher fees, enjoyed certain privileges and wore distinctive academic dress.[9] Ranking above the 'commoners' (who ate at the 'common tables'), the gentlemen-commoners often treated Oxford as little more than a finishing school, and many did not even bother taking their degrees. On arriving at the University, most of them would have joined 'sets' or social groups which operated through existing ties of school or family networks, or else were formed afresh through common interests, such as hunting or rowing—or drinking or gambling.

The students of the 1810s would have reached university by a variety of routes. A good proportion came from the 'great' schools of England, those that later developed into the Victorian 'public schools'. But before the reforms of the 1820s and 1830s, these schools were unruly institutions where bullying was rife and living conditions primitive; they trembled on the edge of anarchy, as headmasters and their few assistants resorted to flogging on a large scale in their struggle to maintain control. Many upper-class parents regarded them as 'nurseries of vice', and turned instead to private tutors. For parents of more limited means, the realistic alternatives included the grammar schools, which accepted boarding as well as day pupils, and the hundreds of small private establishments dotted around the country where Anglican clerics supplemented their income by teaching. In the absence of any established pattern of education, parents often tried a combination of home tutoring, private establishment, local grammar school, and public school, either for a particular child or for their different children. A vast (and lucrative) private education market supplied tuition to match need—and 'need' could also include general oversight, where this was felt to be lacking at school. Whether operating on a domestic basis or otherwise, the role of the private tutor was assumed to cover the education of the whole person: physical, intellectual, social and moral; and since the moulding of a child's character required authority over him, the tutor was granted standing so that he could act *in loco parentis*. In times when the age of majority was twenty-one, the private tutors of wealthy young men would follow their charges to university, or else a new private tutor would be engaged.[10] Though Newman did not enjoy the luxury of a private tutor, he was supported at Trinity by the guidance and encouragement of Walter Mayers, as well as that of his parents.

Like so many parents and well-meaning critics or moralists at the time, Mayers 'feared the strength of an undergraduate peer culture thoroughly dominated by an unprecedented hedonism manifested by a far more interesting and diverse world of recreation, comfort and intellectual interests than had existed before'.[11] Well-wishers pronounced on the wisdom of choosing companions of a suitable moral character and the advisability of avoiding whatever might lead into physical or moral dissipation, in much the same way that Evelyn Waugh's 'cousin Jasper' subjected Charles Ryder to similar admonitions. Their strictures might be given added weight when accompanied by the warning that decadent behaviour would risk plunging the family into debt or shame. But at the same time warnings were tempered, if not compromised, by encouragement not to give offence and not to be over-scrupulous in mixing with those who might be in a position to advance career prospects later in life or to bestow patronage. The dons were trapped in a similar dilemma, as those seeking career advancement outside the University needed to cultivate links and play the sycophant to students with the right connections. This conflict of interest existed at the great schools as well as the Oxbridge colleges, and it led to an institutional culture of arbitrary discipline and uneven application of rules, where infringements were 'winked at' provided signs of deference to authority were shown. Some Oxford colleges were known to favour brains, others wealth, some had a reputation for strictness, others for laxity, but everywhere exceptions abounded. Given that students received such mixed messages on how to behave, it is not surprising that there was an uneven quality to student life and confusion on the part of both students and their parents.

On commencing his university studies an Oxford undergraduate was assigned to one of the official tutors in his college. In the case of Newman he was assigned to the junior of Trinity's two tutors, the Rev. Thomas Short, who as soon as he realised he had a genuine scholar on his hands lent Newman a book and invited him to breakfast. Dr Short had recently returned to Trinity after four years teaching at Rugby School,[12] where he had been second master, and though no great scholar himself was a patient and exacting teacher. He was alive to the spirit of reform that was gradually spreading from one reluctant college to another in the wake of Oxford's New Examination Statute (1800), which had introduced the honours degree and given an incentive to both teachers and taught. In a bid to raise academic standards at Trinity, Short oversaw a tightening of discipline and the introduction of open scholarships. Newman described the measures to his mother: 'There are lamentations in every corner of the increasing rigour; it is laughable, but it is delightful, to hear the groans of the oppressed.'[13] By dint of hard reading in term and out, and careful preparation for his end-of-term college exams, Newman landed one of the new scholarships in May 1818. This achievement occurred towards the end of his first year of residence and marked a new phase of his undergraduate career.

Buoyed up by his academic successes, Newman began to blossom, and—though he later chided himself for living the life of a dilettante—indulged a broad range of interests. Without stinting on his reading of classical authors, supplemented by the study of mathematical texts, logic and Scripture, he took up the works of Gibbon and Locke, entered himself for university prizes, attended concerts, studied manuals and tried experiments in chemistry, and attended lectures in the newly-emerging science of geology. At a time when student activities were migrating from locations in town into the colleges, which were becoming the natural home for sport, dining and drinking, debating, politics and literature, Newman played first violin in a music club at St John's College and co-founded the Trinity College Book Society for the dissemination of modern novels (such as *Ivanhoe*). With his friend John Bowden, he composed a verse romance called *Bartholomew's Eve*, which they had printed (250 copies in two instalments, November 1818 and February 1819), and started a periodical. Appearing just two years after the first truly undergraduate magazine, *The Undergraduate* ran to six numbers and enjoyed a brief popularity, until the cover of anonymity was blown in March 1819 and the editors abandoned the enterprise. The reason for closing it down was that they had voiced dissatisfaction with academic arrangements, such as the pedantic donnish concern with detail and the exclusive devotion to ancient authors in the proscribed course of reading. One of the two editors (almost certainly Bowden) enquired whether the dons enjoyed the 'sulky homage of the sneering Undergraduate' or whether the 'reverence of arbitrary rule' was capable of inspiring undergraduate affection.[14]

In an introductory piece in the first issue, written in the style of Johnson, Newman describes the different classes of 'gownsmen' that existed at the time and from which the periodical intended to draw its readership. Distinguishing between those 'who make business their pleasure and those who make pleasure their business', that is, between the 'reading' and the 'non-reading' man, Newman explained that it was only necessary to enumerate the latter, since 'Study like truth has one appearance; idleness like falsehood takes innumerable.' The idlers were styled under five headings: the Revilers, who openly attacked study; the Valetudinarians, who would study if their health permitted, and instead devoted their waking hours to 'the chase and the water'; the Philosophers, who simply 'do not see the *good* of it'; the Procrastinators, who 'big with industrious resolutions', deceive themselves and put off the evil moment; and the Quacks who 'conceal their total neglect of study' by means of imposing words, and instead spent their time promenading in the streets, lounging in shops, on social visits or on the tennis court.[15]

It is important to recall that Oxford was still in the process of rousing itself from over a century of academic torpor. The main reason the students spent most of their time socialising and in outdoor pursuits was that, for the majority of them, there were few incentives to work. The main academic incursion into their leisure-time was the requirement to attend 'college lectures' (i.e. classes) for two or three hours a day. During these a college tutor would typically oversee a group of up to fifteen students translating Latin and Greek texts, to which he might add a commentary of a grammatical, historical or philosophical nature. It was an unwieldy system, as the tutors were expected to tackle too many subjects and the pace was reduced by the presence of many backward and idle students. In consequence, a parallel, semi-official system had emerged, in which private coaches were engaged by serious students for individual or small-group tuition, or else engaged (as 'cram coaches') by idle students in a last-minute attempt to salvage a degree. In student parlance, the private coach was either a 'class-coach' or a 'pass-coach', the former indicating that everyone who aimed at honours was virtually obliged to supplement the regular college instruction with that of a private tutor.

In his first year Newman had made enquiries about engaging a private tutor, and had dropped the matter on account of the expense, but on winning a Trinity scholarship he now had a guaranteed income of £60 p.a.[16] So in October 1818, at the start of his second year, he and Bowden engaged the services of James Ogle, who had recently graduated from Trinity with a First in mathematics and, like other private coaches, was combining tutoring with his own reading until he succeeded in gaining a fellowship. The two undergraduates were tutored by him in mathematics for two hours a day until February 1819, when Ogle became a 'public' tutor[17] at Trinity, after which he could only give them one hour a day. Not being *au fait* with the private-tutor system, Newman did not continue the extra tuition into his third year.[18]

The third and final period of Newman's undergraduate existence began in April 1819 when he set himself the ambitious goal of seeking honours in both classics and mathematics, and as a consequence dropped his unrelated studies and focussed on his exams. Hard reading became the order of the day, and in the six-month approach to Finals he was averaging twelve hours of study a day. He teamed up with Bowden to establish a study regime that ensured that revision was never passive: several subjects were kept on the go at any one time, to avoid staleness, and they constantly reviewed topics by means of written summaries and oral exercises. Newman filled notebook after notebook with mathematical problems, chronologies, abstracts, summaries—and summaries of his summaries. But as December 1820 approached he became unnerved by the thought that an academic triumph would pave the way for pride, and, weakened by mental exhaustion, he began to panic, so much so that when the (public and essentially oral) exams began he was nervous in the extreme and broke down. Instead of the double First predicted for him, the outcome was a bare pass in classics and not even that in mathematics.

Newman later attributed his failure to a lack of tutorial guidance which left him, young and inexperienced as he was, almost entirely to his own devices. Not that Newman blamed his tutors or the college, far from it; for the rest of his life he remembered them with great affection.[19] Years later he came to realise that 'at that time the very idea of study was new' and that just a handful of colleges had adjusted to the demands of the honours system; only they possessed the real tutors, shared the tradition, and—crucially—supplied the examiners.[20] Oriel, Balliol and Christ Church belonged to this charmed inner circle, but Trinity did not. Instead of concentrating on a restricted corpus of texts and preparing for an exam that required ready translation by sight and quick answers to factual questions, Newman had laboured to acquire depth of understanding by analysing texts and studying commentaries. The whole episode taught Newman some valuable educational lessons, not least the need for a prescribed academic routine, structured learning and individual guidance. But in the event Newman's 'toilsome years' were not without profit: in 1822, against all the odds, his talents were recognised by Oriel, the leading college of its day, which awarded him one of its coveted fellowships.

Fellow, clergyman and tutor

In the early part of the nineteenth century Oxford talent was said to
flow Orielwards, and its common room became home to the academic talent of the day. The college's pre-eminence had come about
by a combination of strong leadership and the absence of restrictions
on its fellowships, which enabled it to attract the best minds. The
dominating tone at Oriel was set by a group known as the Noetics,
who sought to provide a defence of Christianity against deists and
rationalist Unitarians, and to shore up the Anglican Church against
intellectual assaults by raising academic standards at Oxford, which
together with Cambridge functioned as a national seminary. Drawing
heavily on the works of Aristotle, the Noetics contended that truth
should be pursued by means of reasoned argument, fearless commentary on all aspects of society, and a dialectical style of argument which
manifested itself in constant cross-questioning. The Oriel common
room, described by some as 'a wholesome intellectual ferment',[21] by
others as exhibiting 'a morbid intellectual restlessness',[22] created a
new conception of academic life in Oxford. Though it became a
standing joke that its famous teapot was the centre of its inspiration,
as it was always ready and replaced the half-gallon flagon of wine that
was usual in most common rooms, it characterised its seriousness of
purpose. Newman was entranced by the scholarship he found there
and the daily interaction of mind with mind, and saw in it a pattern
of university life that he was later to idealise in prose.

It was from the Fellows of Oriel that Newman received the sort
of education that was sorely missing at Trinity (and indeed at most
colleges). He had arrived during the college's golden years, when
the provost was Edward Copleston, widely regarded as 'the representative man of university culture',[23] who had defended Oxford
to brilliant effect in 1810 against attacks from the *Edinburgh Review*
and over the following two decades inspired an intellectual renaissance in Oriel and Oxford in general. The great teacher of his day,

Copleston had developed a rigorous catechetical style of teaching and was the first to live out what became the Oxford ideal, *multum, non multa*.[24] His abiding claim that 'to *exercise* the mind of the student is the business of education, rather than to pour in knowledge'[25] influenced Newman profoundly, as it did countless others. But since Newman was too much in awe of Copleston, the task of drawing the timid young graduate out of his shell was entrusted to Richard Whately, who took Newman walking and riding over the summer of 1822, and conversed with him at length. If Copleston was the founder of the Noetics, Whately became their leading light in the mid-1820s when they were the dominant intellectual movement in Oxford; he it was who ensured that the *Ethics* and *Rhetoric* were the leading class-books and thereby became responsible for the deep Aristotelian bent of Oxford minds. As Newman recounts, Whately 'was the first person who opened my mind, that is, who gave it ideas and principles to cogitate on'[26] and taught him to think for himself. Known for his challenge to students, 'Shall I form your mind, or cram you for a First?',[27] Whately enlisted Newman's assistance in rewriting his textbook, *Elements of logic*, which became the standard work on logic for the next two decades.

In June 1824 Newman was ordained a deacon of the Church of England and took up the curacy of St Clement's, a working-class parish adjoining the University, and a year later was ordained an Anglican priest. Through this undertaking Newman came under the influence of another Oriel Fellow and leading Noetic, Edward Hawkins, who was vicar of the University Church; during the long vacation of 1824, when they found themselves together at Oriel and virtually alone, Hawkins became a keen and able adviser to Newman on parochial matters. While Newman was inspired by Whately's originality, he learnt the importance of precision from Hawkins. Newman recorded his intellectual debt by saying that Hawkins 'was the first who taught me to weigh my words and to be

cautious in my statements'.[28] Twelve years apart, they were like
pupil and tutor rather than colleagues, and never more so than
when Hawkins carefully checked through Newman's first sermons
and gave him helpful criticism. It was by means of his arguments
and illustrations from Scripture that Hawkins weaned Newman
away from his simple Calvinism, although the process was quick-
ened by Newman's exposure to parish life, which helped him see
that the standard Calvinist division of Christians between 'real' and
'nominal' was untenable.

It should be noted that at the time some two-thirds of Oxford
graduates proceeded to Holy Orders[29] and a still greater proportion
of dons did so, resigning their fellowships in order to marry or to
take up a living. Though this did not necessarily translate into 'a
deeper engagement with ordinary people's pastoral and spiritual
affairs',[30] in Newman's case it did, and a month before he was
ordained deacon he actively sought out parish work. Once installed
he began visiting his parishioners assiduously, took his preaching
seriously, set up a Sunday school for children and saw to improvements of the church building, all of which greatly boosted church
attendance. In a sermon preached to the parishioners of St Clement's shortly before his twenty-fifth birthday, Newman shows that
he had thought deeply about the nature and purpose of education,
and that he had already discerned in outline many of his key
educational principles.

Taking as his text 'knowledge puffeth up, but charity edifieth'
(1 Corinthians 8:1), words of St Paul addressed to the Christians
at the flourishing city of Corinth, Newman explained that, living
among a highly civilised people, the Christians there fell into the
error of 'preferring *knowledge* to that warm and spiritual *charity* or
love', gifts to graces, the powers of the intellect to moral excellence.
Newman pointed out that he and his congregation were living in
parallel times, and warned that the error of exalting human knowl-

edge over Christian love or piety would lead to the mistake 'of supposing, that in proportion as men know more, they will be *better men in a moral point of view*', and that a good education is a remedy for the world's evil. Instead, 'All education should be conducted on this principle—that it is a means towards an end, and that end is *Christian holiness*'.[31] Moreover,

> the object of education is to *write the divine law upon the heart* [...] to prepare the heart for the gospel of Christ—it is to lead us to correct views of our own state and knowledge of our own hearts—it is to train us and win us over to habits of practical godliness, to accustom us to deny ourselves, to govern our passions, to fix our affections on God, and to trust Him with a humble and implicit faith.[32]

It was therefore 'an error to suppose that the end of education is merely to fit persons for their respective stations in life', since in that way 'education is robbed of its religious character, and made the mere instrument of worldly ambition'. True, education concerned 'the temporal callings of men, but it does not rest there'. The purpose of education was that people might so fulfil their respective occupations 'as to make them the means of spiritual profit to their souls—we are preparing their souls, that their worldly trades and professions may affect them as they ought, may be the instruments of good to them [...] preparing them to do good in their generation'. He also drew out some of the practical consequences of overlooking 'the real end of educating', such as the tendency 'to store their minds with many precepts and much information', attempting to do a great deal in a short time, and trying to educate 'by mechanism', instead of taking children separately and addressing them 'almost one by one'.[33]

At the time of preaching this sermon Newman was not only combining his Oriel fellowship with parochial duties, but acting as tutor and dean of the dozen undergraduates at Alban Hall, an independent academic hall owned by Merton College, giving most of the lectures, setting weekly compositions, and dining with them three times a week. The previous year, when Whately was appointed principal of Alban Hall, Newman had accepted the invitation to be his vice-principal, since he had begun to think his calling might be for college rather than parish work.[34] Now, in January 1826, after nine months of official tutoring at Alban Hall, his mind was made up, and when offered a tutorship at Oriel he accepted. Not only did he resign from Alban Hall, but he also gave up the curacy of St Clement's, justifying his decision on the grounds that the tutorship was a spiritual office and a way of fulfilling his Anglican ordination vows. What might appear as an excuse for merely indulging academic inclinations was, in Newman's case, the result of several years of discernment, coupled with a conviction that the seventeenth-century idea of the college tutor could be revived. In the Laudian statutes of 1636,[35] which were still in force, the role of the tutor was more associated with pastoral care than with secular instruction; and although the tutor's main task had become that of a college lecturer, enough of the old associations lingered on to convince most people that the task should continue to be undertaken by unmarried clergymen.

There is no doubt that Newman gained a great deal from his short stint in a parish: above all, it enabled him to develop his 'practical intelligence' and to see the limitations of the rationalism that he had encountered in the Oriel common room. Surrounded in College by academics infatuated by the claims of the intellect, Newman was helped by his parish work to acquire a more critical understanding of the merely intellectual; and this prepared the ground for his eventual rift with the Noetics. Though Newman was at first entranced by the arguments of the Noetics, he later came to draw a contrast between the 'civilisation of intellect' and the 'civilisation of conscience', seeing the latter as his aim.[36]

Just as Newman had shown impressive commitment to parish work, so he showed an equal dedication on entering into the tutorship. Before a month had elapsed he became worried by the 'considerable profligacy' among the undergraduates, many of whom were 'men of family', and by the lack of 'direct religious instruction' for them, and in his zeal he set about doing battle with the privileged young men whom he considered to be the ruin of the place.[37] Though he had previously dealt with some of the University's most idle men at Alban Hall, then regarded as Oxford's Botany Bay, at Oriel he came up against a set of gentlemen-commoners who were notoriously rowdy. By all accounts his first year in office was a stormy one, as Newman set about reforming with a vigour born partly of principle and partly of inexperience. Despite the resistance he encountered, which took the form of gossip and the occasional student prank, Newman stuck resolutely to his task. And, though the college authorities did not support his efforts to tame the unruly or his attempts to eliminate abuses in chapel, he succeeded in winning over the studious element by his unstinting application as a tutor.

Newman had five years' experience under his belt when he took on the college tutorship, having joined the ranks of the private tutors in 1821, after taking Finals, in order to support himself. At first he had struggled to attract tutees on account of his poor degree, but once he landed the Oriel fellowship he had more than he could handle.[38] Prior to acting as vice-principal of Alban Hall, he had been the private tutor of a dozen or so undergraduates, some of whom 'read' with him during vacations. By the time he became a college tutor at Oriel in 1826, he realised that the use of the private tutor system in parallel with the college lectures was what explained the success of colleges like Oriel, but he disliked the arrangement and as a college tutor sought to make it redundant. In the tutorial system then operating at Oriel, each student was assigned to a tutor who in theory was supposed to oversee his work, arrange the distribution of his lectures, assist him in his difficulties, and oversee his religious instruction: but this was far from the reality. The students were usually divided by subject according to their needs and assigned their college lectures irrespective of who their tutor was; and the normal relation between tutor and undergraduate was distant and largely nominal. A month after undertaking the tuition, Newman remarked: 'I think the Tutors see too little of the men'.[39] He was more scathing when, looking back years later, he described how, in the Oxford of his day,

> things went on for the most part by mere routine, and form took the place of earnestness. I have experienced a state of things, in which teachers were cut off from the taught as by an insurmountable barrier; when neither party entered into the thoughts of the other; when each lived by and in itself; when the tutor was supposed to fulfil his duty, if he trotted on like a squirrel in his cage, if at a certain hour he was in a certain room, or in hall, or in chapel, as it might be; and the pupil did his duty too, if he was careful to meet his tutor in that same room, or hall, or chapel, at the same certain hour; and when neither the one nor the other dreamed of seeing each other out of lecture, out of chapel, out of academical gown. I have known places where a stiff manner, a pompous voice, coldness and condescension, were the teacher's attributes, and where he neither knew, nor wished to know, and avowed he did not wish to know, the private irregularities of the youths committed to his charge.[40]

Rather than collaborate with this dismal state of affairs, Newman set about his duties in a very different fashion. To the more disciplined and promising students he offered 'his sympathy and help in College work',[41] and he laid it down as his rule that he would give without charge whatever additional instruction was necessary for those of his pupils who wished to read for an honours degree.

Declaring that the system of private tutors brought students unnecessary expense, he undertook to combine in his own person the teaching offices of public tutor and private. But that was not all: he also assumed into his role as college tutor the pastoral responsibility that, at the time, was an additional function of the private tutor, and this rendered Newman's approach more potent still. He read with his pupils, walked with them, breakfasted and dined with them,[42] and (in Newman's own words) 'cultivated relations, not only of intimacy, but of friendship, and almost of equality, putting off, as much as might be, the martinet manner then in fashion with College Tutors, and seeking them in outdoor exercise, on evenings, and in Vacation'.[43] Within two years he acquired 'such a devoted body of pupils as Oxford had never seen', at least since the Middle Ages, according to his tutee Thomas Mozley, who likened him to 'a father, or an elder and affectionate brother'.[44]

In Newman the undergraduates found a teacher who took the trouble to master his subject matter, by entering into it not just with his intellect but with his whole personality, giving life to the matter under consideration rather than merely conveying it by rote and rule. However dull the material might be—such as the logic they had to cover—Newman had the knack of breathing life into it. From the testimony of his pupils we know that he challenged each of them to think for himself, to understand what he was reading, and to articulate his ideas; to compare and contrast, to challenge and contradict, to reduce an argument to its simplest form, to test it against historical examples, to recast it in his own words or in a different style, and to make comparisons with the present day. Further evidence of the method Newman employed comes from the notes he made for lecturing and examining. His copy of the *Ethics*, for example, is interleaved with numerous sheets containing points for elucidation and questions intended to serve as the basis for class discussion. On moral virtue, he asks:

How can we say that a person by doing just actions *becomes* just, is he not just already—a person who performs grammatical or musical actions is a grammarian or musician? Your second answer declares the arts not to be analogous to the moral virtues; as long as it suited your purpose they were so—how do you reconcile this? What are the three tests of a virtuous action? What thing *alone* is requisite for the possession of one of the arts? Is this same thing of *much* avail in the moral virtues?[45]

The ideal that Newman aspired to as a lecturer appears in a novel he wrote two decades after scribbling these lecture notes. There he describes a 'capital tutor' at Oxford who 'knew his subject so thoroughly' that some of his lectures were 'a masterly, minute running commentary on the text, quite exhausting it'. Nevertheless, the tutor 'never loaded his lectures; everything he said had a meaning and was wanted'.[46]

In the Easter sermon of 1827, during the termly service at which it was customary to take Communion, Newman spoke to the Oriel undergraduates of his responsibility for their welfare: 'Account of us as thinking much and deeply of your eternal interests, as watching over your souls as those who must give account.'[47] Seen in the context of the mood of the time, these sentiments were not particularly unusual, for among the families of the lesser gentry, clergy and professional classes there was a growing eagerness to find educational settings which were conducive to moral growth. In both schools and universities, parents sought measures that would protect their sons against the indolent habits of a dissolute aristocracy; and an additional advantage of employing a private tutor was that he could oversee his charge and act *in loco parentis*. In absorbing this role into the college tutorship along with the academic coaching—or, rather, bringing it back to life—Newman found himself overwhelmed,[48] and the strain of it all seems to have contributed to a second breakdown in November 1827 while acting as University Examiner in classics. The direct cause of the collapse was the vast amount of preparation he undertook in 'getting up' all the main texts. But the straw which broke the camel's back was the news that Copleston had got a bishopric and that Oriel would need a new provost, for suddenly Newman found his mind racing with anticipations of what this might mean for the college.

In the elections for the new provost Newman backed his former mentor Edward Hawkins over John Keble, as he thought Hawkins showed greater promise of enforcing college discipline, which was vital for the continued reformation of the college along the lines Newman envisaged. In January 1828 Hawkins was elected provost and Robert Wilberforce took over the vacant tutorship, joining the senior tutor Joseph Dornford, Newman, and Hurrell Froude, who had become a tutor the previous term. These two changes meant that as a tutor Newman was now second to senior, and no longer isolated but supported by two like-minded men, who shared his view that secular education could, if conducted properly, become 'a pastoral cure'. The younger tutors were in perfect harmony with Newman's interpretation of the Laudian statutes, which stressed the pastoral role of tutors and maintained (as Newman put it) that 'a Tutor was not a mere academical Policeman, or Constable, but a moral and religious guardian of the youths committed to him'.[49] They joined Newman in offering the more deserving pupils as much time and attention as the best private tutors; and in doing so the Oriel tutors provided 'the germ of the modern tutorial system' at Oxford.[50]

In working out their educational views in the tutorial context, the three tutors were unwittingly providing the germ of a very different plant: the Oxford Movement. Their contribution to the preamble of the Movement effectively took up the line begun by Keble, who during his Oriel tutorship (1817–23) had come to

regard the office 'as a species of pastoral care'. As an Oriel undergraduate, Froude had been tutored by Keble, and later he and
Wilberforce attended the reading parties Keble had organised
during several long vacations in the early 1820s, and there experienced the new form of relationship between student and don that
Keble had established. What exactly this new relationship
amounted to is unclear, but certainly when Froude and Wilberforce
joined Newman in successive terms, they were already thinking
along very similar lines. It seems that Froude had absorbed from
Keble something else besides the pastoral dimension of the tutorship, something which he called 'ethos'. This incorporated the idea
that the search for religious truth could not be separated from the
pursuit of goodness, that intellectual training in theology could not
be dissociated from religious and moral formation.[51] Though
Newman was unfamiliar with the concept of ethos before Froude
expounded it to him, the idea was latent in his mind, as can be seen
from the careful records Newman kept of his pupils, both public
and private, which included occasional allusions to their spiritual
progress.[52]

In the absence of any system for religious training at Oxford,
Froude, Newman and Wilberforce made use of the great heathen
treatise on morals, Aristotle's *Ethics*, as the basis for a course in
ethical studies through reflection and discussion on the motives
and principles of action and on the formation of moral habits and
character.[53] They also made use of Bishop Butler's *Analogy of
religion* (1736), the authoritative modern text complementing the
Ethics. Butler, like Aristotle, held that moral goodness facilitates
decisions about what is right and wrong in particular cases; that to
be practically wise in discerning the good to aim at and the means
to achieve it, a person should be—or strive to be—virtuous. Man
has a perfectible nature and its improvement is achieved by the
gaining of sound habits which in turn result from good actions.

Once developed, these virtues act as security against disordered inclinations and passions, and strengthen the will in its search for truth. In stressing that uprightness was more important than intellectual ability for judging moral and religious truth, the three Oriel tutors (and, earlier, Keble) sought to instil in the minds of their students the moral temper or character which was to become emblematic of the Oxford Movement.[54]

A glimpse of Newman's teaching style can be gained from the surviving fragments of two student essays, which have evidently been preserved because they contain Newman's comments at the end. In both cases Newman provides the student with two types of advice: about essay writing in general, and about how the student has dealt with the particular title given him. It seems that, since essay writing was a relatively recent innovation, Newman felt obliged to offer extended advice on the art of composing to a set theme. He tells one of the two students that when he writes an essay, he should 'endeavour to be in *earnest*', that he is not expected to keep to truisms, that he need not be 'dull or grave—release yourself from the notion. In writing, you should aim at saying on your subject, just what you would say, supposing you were obliged in society to talk upon it.' Not that the subject in question was likely to arise in discussion with friends, 'but you can fancy yourself thrown among older people, and *forced to give* your opinion. You would be obliged to say something, & though you might feel awkward, would clearly comprehend what *was* required of you' —and, equally, what was not. To accomplish this would require an effort at first, but the student was told that he would gradually improve and acquire the facility. The other student had been given a subject which ended with the phrase 'make the best of events, when they come, whatever they are'. He was advised, 'Never take a thesis as an *abstract* proposition but try to examine *how far* it is true in life—and try to recollect what instances you have known of it—i.e. though it be true, do not at once assume it to be so—then consider the effects of it—whether good or not.'[55] Both students were offered advice on how they might have approached their subject more incisively by means of further questions that could have been addressed and which would lead on to useful distinctions, telling comparisons and, overall, a deeper analysis.

A third fragment survives which contains Newman's comments on, not an essay, but what appears to be a student's 'declamation' to be read out in hall, on a theme set by the provost. Though it is unclear what the actual theme was, Newman's 'corrections' include a commentary which speaks volumes about his own understanding of the formative role of Oxford. In the commentary the student is upbraided for not entering fully into the provost's view (as expounded by Newman), and given the following advice:

> This University intends, (as far as the time of a student's residence allows) *to form his character*, religious, moral, & social—i.e. to make him a Christian & a gentleman. Towards making him both, it is a great step to make him a scholar & a man of literary taste—or rather, *while* making him such, right feelings & principles may be instilled into him.[56]

These broader educational objectives come to the surface in the brief records Newman kept on his tutorial pupils, where it is clear that he had in mind more than the mere mastery of texts or intellectual progress. To monitor pupils on a university course where there were few set texts and reading was tailored to individual needs, Newman kept a record of the reading he set his pupils, the plan of study he devised for each of them and how they coped with it, the warnings they received from him and the provost, and how they performed in exams. But there is more, because throughout Newman intersperses comments on academic ability with shrewd character descriptions. Thus, Neve was 'a man of some ability' who 'has idled time'; Wykeham was 'frank and honest', but '*very* backward'; Perkins had

'Good abilities, but has been spoilt'; Marriott showed a 'want of scholarship', but was 'not wanting in sense'. Newman was honest enough to record instances where his first estimation proved unsound: about Osborn he wrote 'fear idle', but a term later, 'judged hastily and harshly' and 'one of the best'; Stevens was at first sight 'A wretched scholar—deficient in everything', but the following term Newman records 'takes much pain—seems well disposed [...] How rash my judgements!'[57]

Also clear from the notes is that Newman took stock of each student and adjusted his demands accordingly. Those who were academically able or well-grounded were not allowed to coast unchallenged or to idle their time away, while weaker students were coaxed along and offered support. Forbes, for example, 'takes pains—seems to need encouragement'; while Houblon arrived as 'a very poor scholar', but a term later Newman records that 'he certainly has taken pains this term', and eventually he gained his degree. In those instances where the chemistry of affinity and friendship led to a greater bonding, Newman would exert himself further. He found Mozley to be a promising scholar with a 'clear and elegant mind' and 'a deep thinker', and 'walked with him'. Mozley made fine progress but in his fourth term Newman records that 'His bad habits of delay etc are quite grievous. After many remonstrances was obliged to impose him [i.e. give him an additional written assignment], wh[ich] he took well—I must not spoil him.' A term later, Newman notes that he 'seems in mind and habits much improved'. Not all students felt comfortable with the close attention Newman offered them: in the case of Phillipps, a private pupil, Newman records that, 'having reason to suppose he represented it as a bore, I dropt it. I must be cautious.' The patience and paternal instincts of Newman are evident in his dealings with the ups and downs of undergraduate life. Perkins 'did several things imprudently' and was 'idlish' and noisy, 'Yet I like him', Newman notes, 'and think he will turn out well'. After Perkins had been spoken to severely at 'collections' (the formal end-of-year meeting with the head of house at which reports about progress and behaviour were read out and discussed), Newman 'warned him most seriously as a friend'. At one time Newman felt obliged to 'confine' two students: Tucker, whom he thought careless and rude, though 'I like him too'; and Money, for a 'direct disobedience'.[58]

Newman could be sternly demanding of his pupils, especially if he saw they were wasting their talents and could take a strong reprimand. On one occasion he reproached Henry Wilberforce, a younger brother of Robert, for wasting two terms. Henry was told that 'if you feel ashamed of yourself for having wasted time, some permanent good may ensue and you may be induced to correct a bad habit'; Newman hoped that his feelings of self-reproach would be lasting, as 'you have not done your duty like an honest man and a Christian'. After his scolding, Henry was given detailed advice about what he should be reading in preparation for his exams, and warned: 'Beware of repenting indeed of idleness in the evening, but waking next morning thoughtless and careless about it'.[59]

Two letters survive which Newman wrote to parents of his tutees. One is addressed to the father of Edward Stewart, a 'sharp youth, and very fair scholar', who was good-hearted and had 'a large Eton acquaintance'. By his second year, Newman feared he had 'been led astray in no sl[igh]t degree',[60] and though Edward was spoken to severely at collections in his seventh and eighth terms, Newman was uncertain whether he intended to mend his ways. The letter to his father was penned in the son's second year and occasioned by the fact that Stewart senior had been unable to see Newman when he called at Oxford, in all likelihood at the start of term when dropping off his eighteen-year-old son. To make up for this missed opportunity, Newman sent a lengthy report, which begins by stating that Edward had given a 'very favourable impres-

sion both of his disposition and attainments'. However, Newman
went on to say:

> I think it right to tell you that I am not without apprehension
> as to his persevering in the honourable and praiseworthy
> conduct with which he has commenced his College resi-
> dence. He is apparently a young man of open heart and
> warm feelings—and as he has a large school acquaintance,
> he is of necessity brought in contact with numerous individ-
> uals, who [if] he is wanting to himself will be very likely to
> spoil him. I feel so much interested in him, I earnestly hope
> this may not be the case—and hope [I] need not apologize
> for the freedom with which I have laid before you my
> opinion of it.[61]

This letter not only shows that Newman took his pastoral responsibilities seriously but that he saw them as shared with, if not
delegated from, parents.

The second parental letter concerns Henry Lee Warner, a weak
scholar who was warned at collections in Lent Term 1828 that he
would be leaving if he did not watch out. The following January,
Newman wrote to comment on 'the marked improvement' which
had taken place in Henry's 'conduct since I last felt it my duty to
address [him] on the subject. I then stated my persuasion that there
was much in his character calculated to secure the approbation and
esteem of those who knew him, if he chose to exert himself.' The
rest of the letter deserves to be quoted in full as it vividly conveys
Newman's sense of the tutorial role and how he conceived it within
the college.

> I am truly happy to say that he has shown his good sense
> and resolution since in rousing himself from the indolent
> habits to which he was then giving way, and has discovered
> an energy of mind the apparent absence of which was the
> principal defect of his character. This improvement has

been consistent and progressive since Easter last; I doubt
not it will continue; and that, when we part with him in the
ordinary course of the University system, we shall retain a
pleasant memory of his connexion with the College and he
on his part will feel the benefit of his residence among us.
You will understand me as expressing my personal feelings—the Provost and my Colleagues are aware of my
intention of writing to you, and as far as they are acquainted
with your Son's conduct take the same view of it as myself,
but it is obvious that I am able, as your Son's Tutor, to speak
more explicitly on the subject than others who have had
fewer opportunities of observing him.[62]

In giving the impression that harmony reigned between the authorities at Oriel, the letter disguises the vastly different approaches to
college discipline adopted by Newman and the old guard. For
Newman, university was a place of transition from boyhood to
adulthood and therefore entailed responsibilities for the maturing
individual, as well as greater freedom. While providing an emanci-
patory experience, college life brought with it the baggage of rituals,
disciplinary restrictions, spatial constraints, domestic requirements,
academic duties, a daily timetable, and shared living, all of which
served a formative purpose. At one and the same time tutors needed
to be kindly to their charges and understanding, while remaining
firm, demanding and unyielding. This degree of formative attention
to the needs of students, which involved considerable give and take,
was not part of the repertoire of other Fellows; and its absence
explains why Newman was annoyed at the favour shown the
gentlemen-commoners in high quarters at Oriel, and manifested
his disapproval both to those who favoured and to those who were
favoured. His high-minded stance inevitably grated with those who
adhered to the old order and gave rise to tensions.

While it is true that a few other college tutors recognised the
pastoral dimension of their office, none of them went anything like

as far as the Oriel three in applying and developing it, to the extent that their approach was regarded as highly unconventional, if not revolutionary. No longer isolated among Noetics, but joined by two other Tractarians-in-the-making, Newman set about reforming the college with characteristic energy and purpose. Commenting in February 1829 on the accomplishments of the preceding year, Newman outlined the changes to a former Oriel Fellow:

> We have gone through the year famously, packed off our lumber, parted with spoilt goods, washed and darned when we could, and imported several new articles of approved quality. Indeed the College is so altered that you would hardly know it again. The tangible improvements of system have been, first the diminishing the Gentlemen Commoners from 20 to 8 or 9—Then the dismissal of the Incurables —Then the rejecting unprepared Candidates for admission—the number is awful, some twice. Then the giving chance vacancies to well recommended and picked men. Then the introduction of paper work into the Collection-examination. Then the refusing testimonials to unworthy applicants. Then the revival of a Chapel Sermon at the Sacrament—Then the announcement of a prize for Greek Composition.[63]

The purpose of introducing written papers for the (unofficial) college exams was to provide the sort of essay question that required organised knowledge and original thought rather than merely factual knowledge, and it reflected Newman's preference for *subjects* and a broader philosophical approach rather than an emphasis on *books* and a narrowly textual method. During the summer of 1828 he made a similar proposal for the University exams and sent it to the eight other examiners who served with him;[64] two years later the Examination Statute was revised along these lines. (Whether there was a causal relationship is not clear.) A separate reform he proposed for Oriel was that there should be a coordinated start to the academic year, and that instead of freshmen arriving throughout the year, as they did in other colleges, they should begin together.[65]

Hawkins generally approved of these initiatives and backed up his tutors, but in Lent Term 1829 Newman introduced his most important and far-reaching reform, which involved a major change to the lecture system. The plan effectively made official what three of the four tutors had been doing unofficially: as Newman summarised it, the 'bad men' were left in large classes (according to the existing system) while 'the better sort' were placed in small classes and 'principally with their own tutors quite familiarly and chattingly'.[66] In practice, the plan distinguished between subjects requiring a more intimate or personal setting, such as those with a high moral content or where grounding was required to prepare for lectures, and those subjects where the class size was irrelevant. The guiding aim was to give each tutor control over and responsibility for his own pupils.

The new system was instituted in January 1829, but on this occasion the tutors did not inform the provost of their initiative. When he learnt of it at Easter, he instructed the tutors to revert to the old system, but they objected and argued their corner; only when the senior tutor refused to continue acting against the wishes of the provost did the matter come into the open. The quarrel which ensued was fiercely contested, but in the end Hawkins had his way and in June 1830 he effectively dismissed the three younger tutors, by depriving them of pupils. Much ink has been spilt on the affair, about the causes, what was at stake, and how to interpret the outcome. The dispute concerned the tutors' role—strictly disciplinary in the provost's view, fully pastoral in theirs—but a number of other interconnected issues came into play, such as the weakening of the provost's control over the undergraduate curriculum and the shift in responsibility from the tutors as a body to the tutors as individuals. On a practical level Hawkins was uneasy with what he saw as the proselytising influence of his tutors and feared that the college might lose its connections with wealthy families. The dispute was also affected by the personalities involved: Hawkins had become over-jealous of his authority and autocratic in his management of the college, while Newman, for his part, had begun to show 'an unbecoming truculence and insubordination'[67]—and made a serious error of judgement (as he admitted afterwards) in keeping Hawkins in the dark. Yet the key issue at play in the dispute is still very much with us today: in his opposition to the three tutors Hawkins personified an impoverished view of education, one which pays only lip service to its pastoral dimension and to the close interaction of students and teachers.

In chronicling the events it is all too easy to repeat the version Newman supplied in the *Apologia*, which was written over thirty years after the row and smoothes away the angularities. The lengthy memorandum that he wrote in 1830 reveals a number of things about the provost that Newman charitably passed over in the *Apologia*: that Hawkins was not a 'man of parts'; that he was 'an eminently unpractical man';[68] that he did not try to enter into the views of others; that he was intent on maintaining the status quo; and he had refused to answer Newman directly. It is important to stress that Newman shows no animus against Hawkins in his memorandum; he was, after all, instrumental in securing the provostship for Hawkins. The portrait he paints emerges from the facts of the situation, not from bitterness or resentment; and it is clear from the memorandum that Newman sincerely wished that Hawkins had behaved more creditably.[69]

To judge by the number of Firsts gained by Oriel before, during and after the operation of the plan, it is clear that Newman's system was the most effective.[70] Moreover, the tutorial dispute signalled the end of Oriel's reputation and the start of its decline.[71] In the long term the Oxford system moved in the general direction indicated by Newman (though not for the same reasons), so that undergraduate teaching would eventually take place either in the lecture or in the tutorial or small class. In one sense, Newman's plan to give more time to the industrious student was an extension into tuition of the principle already recognised in the two-tier system of pass and honours degrees. But the issue for Newman was that he regarded the tutorial office as a pastoral one, so that it would be weakened if he was made a lecturer on books instead of a teacher of men. Newman was convinced that, unless the teacher threw himself heart and soul into his work, the outcome would be unreal and hollow. Although his major innovation was discontinued by Hawkins, it indicates the drift of Newman's educational methodology, which he would later implement more fully in Dublin.

A decade before the tutorial row, Newman had composed a ditty on Oriel for *The Undergraduate*, which included a stanza which is unconsciously prophetic of his future work:

As we all have the good of the college at heart,
The men are divided and each has a part;
The lecture we give to the general stock,
But each has besides a particular flock;
And them we are gratis to superintend,
And act as a sort of tutorial friend.[72]

Devastated though Newman was by the loss of the tutorial office, he submitted to the outcome and, for 'the good of the college', assumed a different 'part'. He had already succeeded Hawkins as vicar of St Mary's, the University Church—a living in the gift of Oriel, not a University post—and that position was to give him an influence that would extend beyond, not just Oriel, but the University. After his pupils had dried up, he acted as pro-proctor for the University and in 1831–32 was a Select Preacher. In the summer of 1832, Newman joined Froude and his father on a cruise in the Mediterranean. On his return, the Oriel Fellows elected Newman as dean (and thereby vice-provost), and for two years he oversaw college discipline. The post also meant he was responsible for assigning subjects for declamations and the weekly themes that all undergraduates were expected to write, and for looking over them and selecting which were to be read in hall.

Tractarian, scholar and preacher

Freed from his tutorial duties, Newman was able to devote more time to private study, preaching at St Mary's, and contributing to what was to become a national debate on education and religion. Along with Hurrell Froude and John Keble, he was one of the founders of the Tractarian (or Oxford) Movement and its leading exponent and apologist in the 1830s. Named after the *Tracts for the times*, which they wrote and distributed to clergy and others throughout the country, the Tractarians sought to revive features of the Church of England which they thought had been obscured by Protestantism and the Enlightenment: its apostolic roots, its sacramental nature, and its spiritual independence from the State. The *Tracts* were intended to reform the Established Church, which they viewed as one of the three branches of the one true Church, and defend it against liberalism. In reviving interest in the Church Fathers and writing about Catholic practices on the European mainland, the Movement eventually inspired changes that began to reverse some of those made at the Reformation.

Although the Oxford Movement was essentially a religious movement, it had an educational dimension to it, as the Tractarians were convinced that education was a religious activity and therefore involved religious principles. In this sense, Newman's campaigning at the University and national level can be viewed as the working out, on a larger stage, of the principles that governed his involvement in the tutorial dispute at Oriel. A major national grievance at the time came from the growing number of non-Anglicans who found themselves excluded from the two ancient universities by the religious test barriers there, which were originally devised to exclude Catholics.[73] The needs of these Dissenters were partially met by the foundation in 1828 of London University, modelled not on Oxford or Cambridge but on Edinburgh and the German universities, and established as a secular institution. This entailed a double violation of Newman's principles: its professorial method of teaching and non-residential character emphasised the imparting of knowledge, rather than the forming of minds, while the non-sectarian stance meant removing religious instruction, which for Newman lay at the heart of education.[74] Only the second drawback was obviated when King's College was founded in 1831 by the Established Church, and then only partially, because its non-residential arrangements limited the scope of religious influence.

After a long period of Tory rule, the incoming Whig administration presented the reforming Liberals with the opportunity to challenge vested interests, and in 1832, the great year of reform, post-Enlightenment ideas of progress were in the air; it seemed, finally, as if the umbilical cord between church and state had been severed.[75] In educational matters it was becoming fashionable to speak of the improvement of society as a goal to be achieved, not by nurturing virtue and training the will, but by nourishing the intellect and increasing access to knowledge. Seen against this backdrop, the loyalties of Newman and his fellow Tractarians ran counter to the spirit of the age, and seemed to illustrate the conviction that Oxford was the 'home of lost causes' and 'impossible loyalties'.[76] In 1834 a Bill was introduced in Parliament to remove the religious tests at Oxford and Cambridge, triggering a pamphlet war that lasted for two years. The first pamphlet was written by Newman, and it argued that religion was so much part of the very fabric of an Oxford education, with its daily routine of morning and evening chapel, that to admit Dissenters would destroy the whole.

> Each tutor knows all his pupils personally, with more or less intimacy according to the dispositions of each party, &c.; but still, in many cases, with an intimacy bordering on friendship. The tutor is often the means of forming his pupils' minds, of setting up a standard of thought and judgement in his society, and that, of course, in accordance with, or rather based upon, the doctrines of the church.[77]

After this Newman left to others the task of penning the pamphlets, and joined Edward Pusey and William Sewell on the committee that ran the campaign, using the structures that had recently been put in place for distributing the *Tracts*.

Largely thanks to the united front it put up, Oxford was able to see off calls for reform inspired by Whig influence outside the University, but shortly after the Bill's defeat in Parliament,[78] bitter controversy erupted within the University over proposals to replace subscription to the Thirty-Nine Articles with a Declaration of Conformity. The battle over the reform of the religious tests raged for a decade, pitting liberal reformers against the rising Tractarian party, each side arguing for a set of beliefs which concerned the whole spirit and method of education. This is not the place to chart the involvement of Newman and the Tractarians in the complicated and protracted dispute, but it is worth emphasising that, though the Tractarians were determined to infuse a religious spirit into education, they were deeply intellectual and in no sense minded to turn the University into a simple seminary.[79] Far from undervaluing academic values, they enriched and deepened Oxford's collegiate life.[80] This applied above all to Newman, and it helps to explain why he was widely regarded during these years as 'the greatest force both morally and intellectually in the University'.[81]

The influence Newman exerted derived in great measure from his preaching at the University Church of St Mary the Virgin. As a preacher, he avoided the then-usual oratorical devices of the pulpit and instead addressed his congregation in a 'low, soft, but strangely thrilling voice' which 'left unforgettable memories with many of his listeners'.[82] His way of exploring old themes in new ways, his deep insights into Scripture, his ability to develop a single theme over forty-five minutes using simple but delightful English, his shrewd psychology and his knack of penetrating the hearts of his listeners and revealing to them their self-deception, vanity and mediocrity—all this contributed to make him one of the great preachers of his time, and enabled him to inspire many Anglicans to live out their Christianity in an authentic and profound way. His parochial sermons incorporated and elaborated on key ideas of the Movement and were almost as central to it as the *Tracts*, though they deliberately avoided controversial questions. In his University sermons (in fact lectures in all but name), on the other hand, Newman grappled with fundamental matters such as the role and working of conscience, the nature of religious belief, the development of Christian doctrine, and the relation between faith and reason, themes on which he has made a major contribution to Christian thinking. In printed form,[83] the sermons reached countless others, and in this way the reverberations of the Movement were eventually felt at the level of Anglican parish life throughout the country. Prominent though Newman's role was among the Tractarians, it needs to be seen as part of a wider phenomenon, since the Movement was the work of many and took on various forms. Among those influenced at Oxford were several hundred who would follow (or, in some cases, precede) him into the Catholic Church, and out of this number came the handful who would join him in 'transporting' Oxford to Dublin.

What lay at the heart of the Oxford Movement for its originators, Froude, Keble and Newman (all of whom had once been tutors at Oriel), what indeed provides the key for understanding the Tractarians, is their dominant theological temper and intellectual character, which can almost be summed up as a hunger for holiness.[84] It was grounded in Aristotle's *Ethics*, interpreted and supplemented by Butler's *Analogy*, and developed in original ways by each of the former tutors. United by bonds of friendship and intellectual affinity, they saw Oxford as the depository of a Catholic ethos and a stronghold against the assaults of liberalism. The Tractarians thought that the University should aim to nurture men through the study of those disciplines dealing with the moral virtues, whereas the liberal reformers wanted to make 'knowledge, rather than moral discipline the object of our studies, and to cultivate rather the habit of bold and irreverent inquiry', instead of those virtues attuned to the pursuit and reverence of truth.[85] While utilitarian thinking led to over-emphasis on the intellect and neglect of the moral dimension of the person, the Tractarians placed equal if not greater emphasis on raising moral and religious standards, understood as the 'intertwined combination of sound belief and right conduct'.[86] In refuting the critics of Oxford, Sewell wrote:

> We [...] do not consider the communication of knowledge as the chief design of our post, or the grand end of education [...] We are [...] entrusted with the care of the young [...] and our consideration is to form and fashion and bring them to that model of human nature, which in our conscience we think is perfection.[87]

On a pastoral level, the Tractarians were concerned to prevent the University from degenerating into an exam factory on the style of some French or Prussian academy, where students lived in lodgings outside its precincts and had little personal contact with professors, with the resulting loss of corporate identity.

Although Newman no longer exerted a direct influence as a tutor after 1831, his influence on the University's tutorial system seems to have grown rather than declined. The explanation for this surprising turn of events forms part of the story of the Oxford Movement, which spread in grass-roots fashion to the junior men of the University through the more personalised form of tuition initiated by the Oriel tutors and continued by their tutees, immediate successors and followers. The largely oral character of Oxford academic tradition at the time meant that the new approach was discussed among tutors and students and subject to cross-pollination and development out of sight of the general public. It was undoubtedly fostered by the inter-collegiate dining club which Newman founded in April 1828 with the aim of bringing young academics together—mainly tutors—and which met fortnightly until 1833.[88] While the spread of Tractarian ideals and principles was readily fostered by what Newman called 'the force of personal influence and congeniality of thought',[89] the educational value of the new tutor–pupil relationship was prized by many who were unsympathetic to the Tractarian cause; and during the decades after Newman's dismissal a growing number of tutors came to regard their office as a pastoral one—given impetus in 1837 when the Hebdomadal Board re-enacted the section of the Laudian Code on the tutor's moral and religious responsibilities—as well as prizing it as an ideal way of nurturing scholarly endeavour.[90] Valued as an intellectual training, individualised tutorial instruction eventually became the norm at Oxford—and to this day this ideal sets it and Cambridge apart from the rest of the educational world.[91]

Newman's sway over Oxford in the 1830s cannot be attributed to his preaching alone, but owed a great deal to his personal magnetism, which created a discipleship among those around him. He captivated an idealistic and serious-minded younger generation in the University who reacted against the academic conservatism and religious laxity of the time, and was idolised by undergraduates who hung on his words and even imitated his gait and gestures.[92] J. A. Froude, the brother of the leading Tractarian Hurrell Froude, has left his impressions of the man who inspired such devotion:

> Newman's mind was world-wide. He was interested in everything which was going on in science, in politics, in literature. Nothing was too large for him, nothing too trivial, if it threw light upon the central question, what really man was, and what was his destiny. [...] He seemed always to be better informed on common topics of conversation than anyone else who was present. He was never condescending with us, never didactic or authoritative; but what he said carried conviction along with it. When we were wrong he knew why we were wrong, and excused our mistakes to ourselves while he set us right. Perhaps his supreme merit as a talker was that he never tried to be witty or to say striking things. [...] He was lightness itself—the lightness of elastic strength—and he was interesting because [....] he had something real to say.[93]

What is particularly striking about this recollection is that it comes from an historian who had once been under the sway of Newman and the Tractarians, before rejecting Christianity; nevertheless, he understood the virtues in Newman and never ceased to respect them.

However much the Tractarians shared in common, we should not assume that they were able to imitate the subtle manner in which Newman managed to combine his educational role with that of Christian pastor. Writing of himself in the third person, Newman records that he 'set before himself in the Tutorial work the aim of gaining souls to God' and that when he became vicar of St Mary's in 1828, the 'hold he had acquired over them led to their following him on to sacred ground, and receiving direct religious instruction from his sermons'.[94] And yet the undergraduates he met at the teas he gave on Monday evenings between 1837 and 1841 recount that he never used the occasions to press his own religious views;[95] indeed J. A. Froude and others relate that Newman spoke about all the subjects of the day *except* the religious controversies, and that he put everyone at ease. One undergraduate who breakfasted weekly with Newman was able to calm the fears of an anxious relative by declaring that Newman never talked to him about Tractarianism; instead he urged him 'to diversify my reading, to take exercise, and to get as much practical knowledge and cheerful society as I can'.[96] The rapport Newman established with students was achieved not by ingratiating them, but by appealing to their higher natures and opening up prospects. Young men warmed to his simplicity of manner, which was quite at odds with the donnish demeanour of the time, and the great interest he took in everything around him. His sympathy and feeling for the rising prospects and promise of youth can be felt in many of his letters and sermons, and evidently attracted young men to him.[97]

During the 1830s, just when the liberal reformers were intent on revising college statutes and urging Oxford to sort itself out, Newman's preoccupation at Oriel was in promoting a return to the spirit of its fourteenth-century founder, to a time when provost and Fellows lived together in a simple, frugal fashion, devoting themselves not to contemplation, like monks; nor to preaching, like friars; but to study and to using their knowledge in the service of God.[98] As Hawkins was by this stage opposed to Newman's every move in college, the nearest Newman could come to re-establishing the ancient College of St Mary (as Oriel was originally known) as a society of graduates involved in advanced study was the private initiative that he and Pusey inaugurated in 1836. It began in a house taken by Pusey, where three or four graduates pursuing theological studies were taken in rent-free; by the time Newman took it over two years later the young men were collaborating in the *Library of the Fathers* and other similar projects. But the experiment failed to flourish, as the young graduates moved into colleges once they gained fellowships, and besides, as Tractarianism was becoming a bar to their academic prospects, in July 1840 Newman closed the house down. That year also marked the end of his heavy journalistic responsibility as editor of the Tractarian periodical the *British Critic*, which he had undertaken since 1838.

The patristic studies undertaken at the 'house for young writers' reflected a fascination with the Church Fathers of the first millennium among the Tractarians. From the late 1820s onwards Newman had immersed himself in patristic research, and in studying the Alexandrian Fathers, particularly Clement and Origen, he was struck by the way they attempted to deepen their understanding of Christianity by drawing from their own education in the pagan classics. The synthesis of philosophy, science and pagan literature with Christian Revelation developed gradually over the centuries, and this fusing of the liberal arts with Christian learning provided the foundation for medieval culture. Newman's mind resonated with the approach of Clement and Origen in using the intellectual training provided by the pagan classics to enhance the assimilation of Christian learning and promote a deeper understanding of religious truths. Here he found a lesson which confirmed him in his respect for the classical tradition.

In January 1841, on the occasion of the opening of a public 'reading room' at Tamworth by Sir Robert Peel, Newman entered into educational controversy by ridiculing the belief that secular knowledge could lead to virtue and knowledge of God; and he challenged the utilitarian attitudes that Peel espoused by arguing that education ought not to be confused with vocational training. Later that year, Newman's *Tract 90* appeared. The controversy it caused led to its condemnation by the Anglican bishops, an outcome which shattered Newman's hopes of confirming the

Catholic credentials of the Established Church. Retiring from active involvement in Oxford life, he moved to the parish of Littlemore on the outskirts of Oxford, and there established a semi-monastic 'college' where he and his companions devoted themselves to prayer and study. Despite his long-held wish 'to live and die a fellow of Oriel',[99] he resigned his fellowship and six days later, on 9 October 1845, was received into the Catholic Church.

Catholic and Oratorian

No sooner had Newman become a Catholic than he put himself forward for the priesthood and was sent to train at the College of Propaganda Fide in Rome. Searching for a way of combining the advantages of the religious life with the secular priesthood, Newman discerned a calling to follow the Rule of the Oratory of St Philip Neri, which had been established in the sixteenth century. The Oratorian Rule enables secular priests to undertake parochial duties in large towns and cities, while benefiting from community life, and can be adapted to particular circumstances and local needs in order that each Oratory house—which is independent—can develop its own style. On 30 May 1847 Newman was ordained a priest and in December he returned to England with several other convert friends from Oxford to set up the first English Oratory of St Philip Neri, in Birmingham, with Newman as its superior. To their Brief of Institution, the Pope added on his own initiative that the Oratory should work especially 'among those in the higher ranks, the more learned and generally among the more educated'.[100] This added phrase was to guide Newman in his educational ventures.

The effect of personal influence in the task of evangelising culture was one characteristic that attracted Newman to St Philip Neri, and it reinforced its importance for him. Besides sharing his sense of fun and aversion to pomposity, Newman saw in the work of St Philip— and his understanding of the spirit of the Renaissance—a revival of the truly humanistic nature of the Church. He was attracted to St Philip because he 'carried out the Church into the world and aimed to bring under her light yoke as many men as he could possibly reach'; and he saw in the saint a model from whom one could learn to bring the laity into taking a more active part in the mission of the Church, as the people St Philip gathered around himself 'had little or nothing to do with ecclesiastical matters [...] and they freely admitted laymen into their fellowship'. Newman says of him that 'it was his mission to save men, not from, but in, the world'.[101]

After a temporary stay at Oscott, six miles north-east of Birmingham, the Oratorians established themselves in a former gin distillery in the city centre, where they combined study and writing with running a mission (i.e. a parish). There they organised catechism classes, gave lectures twice a week, and worked mainly with the Irish poor. Similar work awaited them in 1852, when the Oratory moved to permanent, purpose-built premises at Edgbaston, a suburb to the south-east of Birmingham; there they soon found themselves caring for a large and growing parish, also characterised by urban poverty. Within the parish the Oratory looked after orphanages, poor schools and a workhouse, and they even tried to start a hospital for the poor. As superior of the Oratory, Newman was not only responsible for overseeing these endeavours but for the well-being of his fellow Oratorian priests and lay brothers. The running of the Oratory itself involved many domestic tasks: those of librarian, sacristan, music master, novice master and treasurer (this last complicated because each Oratorian priest retained his own property). The task of overseeing the growth and harmony of this small community was not a merely *a* good work that he undertook, but his central and abiding concern as a Catholic priest. Everything else that he undertook, even the establishment and running of a new university, had to play second fiddle to his calling as an Oratorian.

Newman's responsibilities as superior brought him endless worries and consumed a great deal of his time and energies. No sooner had the Oratorians returned from Rome and established themselves at Maryvale, in Birmingham, than Newman's bishop asked him to accept as Oratorians a group of seventeen converts led by Willam Faber. This unexpected addition to the six original Oratorians completely changed the chemistry of the Oratory and placed together two leaders with contrasting—even incompatible—characters; and if that were not enough, Faber's idea of an Oratory was markedly different from Newman's. The solution to the tensions that ensued was to allow Faber to begin an Oratory in London, where it soon acquired a markedly Italianate and Ultramontane reputation. The two Oratories developed in quite different ways, and this was particularly so in their approach to educational work, to the extent that Newman's emphasis on it was held by Faber to be a departure from the intentions of the founder. Relations between the two Oratories, and indeed between their provosts, were strained from the beginning, and disputes about interpretations of St Philip's Rule simmered for over a decade.

Besides throwing the original Oratory off balance, the accession of Faber's converts brought responsibility for maintaining a property called St Wilfrid's, near Cheadle in Cheshire. Interestingly, one of the two educational schemes Newman devised for making use of it aimed to meet the recognised need of something 'for Catholic lay students, when they have completed the ordinary school course, which should be to them what Oxford and Cambridge are to Protestant boys from Eton and Harrow'. The draft prospectus for the proposed New College at St Wilfrid's gave prominence to ancient, classical and modern languages, as well as mathematics and general literature, and listed nine staff, all converts from Oxford and Cambridge and all but one Oratorians.[102] But the plan petered out because the London Oratorians would not commit themselves to it.

Nevertheless, Newman was constantly on the lookout for ways in which the Birmingham Oratory could put into operation the Pope's intention for them to work with the more educated classes. This was somewhat problematic as they were located in an industrial city where the vast majority of Catholics were uneducated and living in poverty, but Newman was content to bide his time and wait for the openings he knew would come. Meanwhile he set aside time to guide those who sought his help by letter or by visiting him in person at the Oratory; he composed, delivered and published lectures to assist his fellow Catholics and those who contemplated following him into the Catholic Church;[103] and he turned his hand to further studies and writing. In all this Newman was trying to help form the next generation of lay faithful by encouraging them to take a full part in the world, to defend their beliefs and to spread them. He wanted the laity to wake up and become an active force both within the Church and in the world; but for this they needed to be trained and educated, a task that he saw himself called to undertake after his conversion in 1845. As he himself put it, 'from first to last, education, in this large sense of the word, has been my line'.[104]

Newman revisited his student days in Oxford when composing *Loss and gain: the story of a convert* (1848), which was among the first of the genre of university novels—and the first to directly link the protagonist's personal growth to a university experience.[105] The picture Newman paints of Oxford is a self-contained learning environment inhabited by earnest young men who are forming their life views, casting them into words, putting them on an intellectual basis, and testing them out on others. In describing how students mature both morally and intellectually, Newman draws the distinction between those who come to form a coherent 'view'[106] and those who come to acquire an insubstantial 'viewiness',[107] which perhaps remains with them all their lives.

> When, then, men for the first time look upon the world of politics or religion, all that they find there meets their mind's eye as a landscape addresses itself for the first time to a person who has just gained his bodily sight. One thing is as far off as another; there is no perspective. The connection of fact with fact, truth with truth, the bearing of fact upon truth, and truth upon fact, what leads to what, what are points primary and what secondary—all this they have yet to learn. It is all a new science to them, and they do not even know their ignorance of it.[108]

Some students develop a comprehensive perspective of the landscape of life by painstakingly piecing together fragments of vision, experience and action, and thereby construe a coherent picture of the world which gives them the possibility of living a coherent life. Others 'have no consistency in their arguments'; they argue one way today, and another the next. 'Their lines of argument diverge; nothing comes to a point; there is no one centre in which their minds sits, on which their judgment of men and things proceeds.'[109]

Though Newman's hero is less well-read and knowledgeable than a college friend, the friend turns out to be too quick to form a view, impatient to reduce things to a system and over-fond of argument, and ends up as glib and superficial; it is instead the protagonist who acquires a consistent and true view of things by means of patient questioning, the careful sifting of facts and discernment of principles, a refusal to take intellectual short-cuts or to make do with simplistic explanations. Implicit in the story is that what makes this process possible is the residential nature of a university which provides for such formative opportunities outside the lecture hall; by means of the collegiate structure and the human scale of domestic arrangements, the right conditions are provided for the flourishing of the individual student through the companionship and friendship nurtured there.

Though Newman kept himself busy with academic projects and pastoral duties in the early 1850s, he was ready to throw himself into the service of the Church in some more substantial project, although he naturally did not wish to engage in work which was incompatible with his Oratorian calling. He was ideally suited for involvement in an educational venture, and at fifty and in good health he had much to offer. However, he did not expect to be called across St George's Channel for a project as audacious as the establishment of a Catholic University.

Notes

[1]   P. Shrimpton, *A Catholic Eton? Newman's Oratory School* (Leominster, 2005), p. 170.

[2]   [H. Mozley], *Family adventures* (London, 1852), pp. 17, 46.

[3]   Although Newman became what might loosely speaking be termed a Calvinistic Evangelical, his was 'quite unlike the standard form of Evangelical conversion, of conviction of sinfulness and the sensation of transforming release by divine deliverance from it'; instead, he saw it as a personal call to holiness, rather than an assurance of salvation freeing him from the need to obey the moral law, and adopted a more doctrinal form of Christianity (S. Gilley, 'Life and writings', *The Cambridge companion to John Henry Newman*, ed. I. Ker & T. Merrigan (Cambridge, 2009), p. 2).

[4]   A. D. Culler, *Imperial intellect: a study of Newman's educational idea* (New Haven, 1955), p. 4.

[5]   Newman to Greaves, 27 February 1828, *LD*, vol. ii, p. 58.

[6]   Mayers to Newman, 16 June 1817, *LD*, vol. i, p. 36n.

[7]   What these devotions were can be deduced from an article he wrote for *The Christian Observer* entitled 'Hints to religious students at College' (October 1822, pp. 623–6). In the course of suggesting that the religious student should not leave his devotions to the end of the day, he mentions spending half an hour each evening on prayer, meditation, self-examination and the reading of Scripture.

[8]   Nevertheless, while he was at Trinity, Newman corresponded regularly with several school friends from Ealing.

[9]   At Trinity the gentlemen commoners were denied the right to dine at high

table in 1809, shortly before Newman arrived, though they were compensated for this loss with the provision of their own common room (C. Hopkins, *Trinity. 400 years of an Oxford college community* (Oxford, 2005), pp. 203, 206). However, the practice of gentlemen commoners dining at high table persisted at Oriel during Newman's time there.

10 In *Liberal education; or, a practical treatise on the methods of acquiring useful and polite learning*, vol. ii (London, 1781; 1795, pp. 87–8) the headmaster Vicesimus Knox recommends that a 'private tutor of character' be engaged 'to inspect his pupil not only in the hours of study, but also amusement', because a 'faithful tutor, who will thus condescend to watch the moral conduct of his pupil will be far more desirable than a man of genius and learning, who will only attend to literary improvement'.

11 Rothblatt, *The modern university and its discontents*, p. 311.

12 In 1828 Short was beaten to the headmastership of Rugby by one vote, the victor being Dr Thomas Arnold.

13 Newman to Mrs Newman, 28 November 1817, *LD*, vol. i, p. 48.

14 *The Undergraduate* 5 (10 March 1819), p. 37.

15 *The Undergraduate* 1 (8 February 1819), pp. 4–7. Other contemporary descriptions divide the undergraduate body into 'fast', 'slow' and 'reading men'; or into 'sinners', 'smilers' and 'saints'.

16 Besides the Trinity scholarship, which lasted for nine years, Newman received a generous allowance of £320 from his father between December 1816 and the summer of 1818 (*LD*, vol. i, pp. 54–6).

17 The term 'public' tutor meant the official or college tutor, as opposed to a private tutor.

18 The terms for tuition with Ogle were £50 for the academic year until the change of hours in February, when they were reduced to £30. By contrast, college tuition was three guineas a term.

19 While Thomas Short won Newman's respect, the college dean, Morgan Kinsey, inspired affection and treated him 'with the familiar kindness of an elder brother'. Newman was also grateful to his private tutor, James Ogle, as well as the senior tutor, John Wilson, who had seen him for between two and five hours a day in his final term.

20 Newman's memoir, 13 June 1874, *AW*, p. 51.

21 M. Pattison, *Memoirs* (London, 1885; 1969), p. 79.

22 T. Mozley, *Reminiscences: chiefly of Oriel College and the Oxford Movement*, vol. i (London, 1882), p. 20.

[23]   Pattison, *Memoirs*, p. 8.

[24]   One meaning of the Latin (often given in the form, *non multa, sed multum*) is 'much, not many', though the looser translation 'depth, not breadth' gives the sense better. The fuller form of the Latin proverb is *multum non multa scire sapientis est*, which can be translated as 'it is wise to know something deeply, rather than to know many things'.

[25]   Copleston to J. Penrose, [1810], quoted in W. J. Copleston, *Memoir of Edward Copleston* (London, 1851), p. 38.

[26]   Newman to Monsell, 10 October 1852, *LD*, vol. xv, p. 176.

[27]   Culler, *Imperial intellect*, p. 39.

[28]   *Apologia pro vita sua* (London, 1865; 1908), p. 8.

[29]   J. M. Sanderson, *The universities in the nineteenth century* (London, 1975), p. 2. The figures furnished by Sanderson give a slightly unrepresentative picture of the composition of the student body because they exclude those who left without taking a degree, whereas they include everyone bound for the Church as graduation was effectively a professional qualification for entry.

[30]   Arthur & Nicholls, *John Henry Newman*, p. 19.

[31]   'On some popular mistakes as to the object of education', sermon preached on 8 January 1826 at St Clement's Oxford, BOA; reproduced in Arthur & Nicholls, *John Henry Newman*, pp. 206–7.

[32]   'On some popular mistakes as to the object of education' (with variants introduced when the sermon was preached a second time on 27 August 1826), BOA.

[33]   'On some popular mistakes as to the object of education', 27 August 1826, BOA. Here Newman is speaking of education from a *supernatural* viewpoint, so there is no contradiction with his earlier claim that (from a natural viewpoint) the purpose of education is to train the mind.

[34]   In 1825 Newman also considered whether he might have a vocation to be a missionary. That March he dropped all idea of going into the law, having kept several terms at Lincoln's Inn since his enrolment there in November 1819.

[35]   The Laudian Code decreed that the tutor should imbue the students committed to his charge with good morals and instruct them in approved authors, above all in the rudiments of religion and the Thirty-Nine Articles. He was also to be responsible for his students' behaviour.

[36]   Short, *Newman and his contemporaries*, p. 157. Newman's contemporary R. H. Hutton states in *Cardinal Newman* (1891, p. 111) that Newman's 'denunciation of the mere religion of civilization' was trenchant as early as

1832, though Newman appears to use the expression 'religion of civilization' in this sense only once in print, in the much later *Grammar of assent*
(1870; 1898, p. 400).

37 Newman's diary, 7 May 1826, *LD*, vol. i, p. 286n.

38 Culler, *Imperial intellect*, p. 47.

39 Newman's diary, 7 May 1826, *LD*, vol. i, p. 286n.

40 *HS*, vol. iii, pp. 74–5.

41 Newman's memoir, 13 June 1874, *AW*, p. 90.

42 Newman kept a record ('Memorandum Book about College Pupils', BOA,
A6.15; reproduced in P. Lefebvre, 'John Henry Newman tuteur: tradition,
rupture, developpement 1826–1831', DEA, Ecole Doctorale des Etudes
Anglophones, Paris, 2004, pp. 158–66) of those who ate with him in his
rooms, as opposed to Hall, and it reveals that during his first three years as
a tutor he breakfasted with students 111 times. On about half these
occasions the students were his own tutees—and they were the ones who
were more likely to breakfast with him repeatedly, though never more than
once a term. In the six months from Michaelmas 1829 to Easter 1830
Newman dined privately with undergraduates on no fewer than thirty-three
occasions, that is, about twice a week on average.

43 Newman's memoir, 13 June 1874, *AW*, p. 90.

44 Mozley, *Reminiscences*, vol. i, pp. 136, 181. In fact, Tom Mozley became
Newman's brother-in-law on marrying Harriett Newman in 1836; five
months earlier, his brother John had married Jemima Newman.

45 Quoted in Culler, *Imperial intellect*, p. 76. 'How does A[ristotle] obtain his
definition of happiness—and mention the specific use of each chapter
previous to it, and how *it comes in*. lib. i' is the first of nine assignments that
Newman set Henry Wilberforce (18 January 1830, *LD*, vol. ii, pp. 189–90).
Newman lectured and tutored on the *Ethics* in Lent Term 1827 (Books i to
v); Easter 1827 (Books vi, vii, x); Michaelmas 1829 (Book i); Lent 1830
(Books vi, vii, x); Easter 1830 (Books v, viii, ix); Easter 1831 (Books i, ii, iii,
iv, vi).

46 *Loss and gain: the story of a convert* (London, 1848), p. 183. Besides its narrow
curriculum, the chief defect of the Oxford system was that many tutors
taught it as a purely literary course, rather than seeing the texts as reposi-
tories of philosophical and historical thought or as instruments to instruct
in the art of thinking.

47 Sermon preached on 15 April 1827, *Sermons, 1824–1843*, vol. i, ed. P. Murray
(Oxford, 1991), p. 341.

48   After setting himself a punishing work regime in the spring of 1827, he
     wrote to his sister Jemima, 'this has been a fagging week' (19 April 1827,
     LD, vol. ii, pp. 11–12); then a fortnight later to his mother, 'Here we are
     "all droning, droning, droning, all treading in the tutorial mill" ' (4 May
     1827, *LD*, vol. ii, p. 14). When approaching the end of his tutorship he
     commented that he would 'soon be released from my excessive engage-
     ments, which exhaust my spirits' (Newman to Golightly, 3 January 1831,
     LD, vol. ii, p. 307).

49   Newman's memoir, 13 June 1874, *AW*, p. 91.

50   M. G. Brock, 'The Oxford of Peel and Gladstone, 1800–1833', *History of
     the University of Oxford*, vol. vi, p. 61.

51   J. Pereiro, *'Ethos' and the Oxford Movement: at the heart of Tractarianism*
     (Oxford, 2008), pp. 85–7. In *Oriel College* (London, 1900, p. 197) D. W.
     Rannie describes how Froude had the 'incommunicable and inexpressible
     gift of great personal influence, which in his case took the most irresistible of
     all forms, that of impressing others with his equal pre-eminence in intellect
     and character'. Influenced by Froude's ardour and assertiveness, Rannie
     claims, Newman became a belated pupil of Keble.

52   Mozley, *Reminiscences*, vol. i, p. 210. Scattered throughout Newman's 'Mem-
     orandum Book about College Pupils' (BOA, A6.15) are references to reli-
     gious matters *before* he was joined by Froude and Wilberforce: in the entry
     for Osborn he writes 'I walked with him etc. spoke to him about Sacrament';
     for Mozley, 'hopeful in religion'; for Money, 'Well behaved'; for Marriot,
     'good religious principles'; and for Stevens, 'quite ignorant of religion' one
     term, and the next, 'seems well disposed—spoke to him about Sacra-
     ment—he had been reading Bᴾ Wilson yesterday on it'.

53   This emphasis by the Oriel tutors could be considered as an early manifes-
     tation of the revival of character formation, which began in the 1820s in
     the reformed public schools and then spread to other schools and Oxford
     and Cambridge over the next forty years (Rothblatt, *Tradition and change
     in English liberal education* (London, 1976), p. 133).

54   Pereiro, *'Ethos' and the Oxford Movement*, pp. 86–92, 103.

55   'Memorandum Book about College Pupils', BOA, A6.15.

56   'Memorandum Book about College Pupils', BOA, A6.15.

57   'Memorandum Book about College Pupils', BOA, A6.15.

58   'Memorandum Book about College Pupils', BOA, A6.15.

59   9 July 1827, LD, vol. ii, p. 23. The older Newman might have found the
     pompous tone of this letter embarrassing.

60 'Memorandum Book about College Pupils', BOA, A6.15.

61 Newman to Stewart, November 1826, *LD*, vol. i, p. 312.

62 Newman to Lee Warner, 6 January 1829, *LD*, vol. ii, pp. 113–14.

63 Newman to Rickards, 6 February 1829, *LD*, vol. ii, p. 117.

64 Culler, *Imperial intellect*, p. 77.

65 Culler, *Imperial intellect*, pp. 64–5, 118.

66 Newman to Rickards, 6 February 1829, *LD*, vol. ii, p. 117.

67 Quoted in Culler, *Imperial intellect*, p. 69, from a note by Newman dated 15 September 1850 in the Oriel Tutorship file (BOA, VC 61).

68 'The Oriel tuition', 9 July 1830, *LD*, vol. ii, p. 247.

69 'The Oriel tuition', 9 July 1830, *LD*, vol. ii, pp. 246–50.

70 Pattison, *Memoirs*, p. 88; K. C. Turpin, 'The ascendancy of Oriel', *History of the University of Oxford*, vol. vi, p. 190. The number of Firsts obtained at Oriel in the three periods 1825–29, 1829–33 and 1833–37 were two, eleven and five; nine of the eleven who gained Firsts in the middle period were pupils of Newman (Lefebvre, 'Newman tuteur', p. 111).

71 K. C. Turpin, 'The ascendancy of Oriel', *History of the University of Oxford*, vol. vi, p. 190.

72 'Letter from a Tutor [of Oriel] at Oxford, to his Friend in the Country', *The Undergraduate* 6 (20 March 1819), p. 50.

73 At Oxford, students were required to subscribe to the Thirty-Nine Articles both on matriculation and on taking a degree; at Cambridge, the tests were only required for the latter.

74 *Idea of a university*, p. 145.

75 P. Nockles, 'An academic counter-revolution: Newman and Tractarian Oxford's idea of a university', *History of universities* 10 (1991), p. 181.

76 M. Arnold, *Essays in criticism* (London, 1865), preface.

77 *British Magazine* (1 April 1834), p. 446.

78 In the summer of 1835 the Bill was passed in the Commons, but defeated in the Lords. The religious tests were eventually removed, partially in 1854, then fully in 1871.

79 For an account of these battles, see P. B. Nockles, 'Lost Causes and … impossible loyalties: the Oxford Movement and the University', *History of the University of Oxford*, vol. vi, pp. 195–267.

80 P. B. Nockles, 'Oriel and the making of John Henry Newman—his mission as college tutor', *Recusant History* 29:3 (May 2009), p. 418.

81 W. C. Lake, *Memorials of William Charles Lake, Dean of Durham* (London,

1901), p. 41.

82   I. Ker, *Newman. His life and legacy* (London, 2010), p. 13

83   Newman's parochial sermons were first published in eight volumes between 1834 and 1843 and his university sermons in one volume in 1843; they were reprinted innumerable times before the end of the nineteenth century.

84   Pereiro, *'Ethos' and the Oxford Movement*, p. 103: they called this theological temper and intellectual character 'ethos'.

85   [H. Wilberforce], *The foundation of faith assailed in Oxford* (London, 1835), pp. 8–9. A letter of Henry to his former tutor reveals that Newman was behind this pamphlet (*LD*, vol. v, p. 65n).

86   P. Nockles, 'Newman and Oxford', *John Henry Newman. In his time* (Oxford, 2007), pp. 26–7.

87   *Thoughts on the admission of Dissenters to the University of Oxford, and on the establishment of a state religion* (Oxford, 1834), p. 7.

88   Its members included J. Dornford, Froude and R. Wilberforce of Oriel; F. Oakeley and J. T. Round of Balliol; J. Garbett of Brasenose; A. P. Saunders of Christ Church; W. Falconer, W. Jacobson, R. Martin and J. Richards of Exeter; J. Awdry and H. Deane of New; H. Woodgate of St John's; and R. Walker of Wadham. Newman does not describe these meetings other than to say that they ate plain dinners (Newman's diary, 14 May 1829, *LD*, vol. ii, p. 143).

89   Newman, *Apologia pro vita sua*, p. 40.

90   The Report of the commissioners investigating Oxford makes it clear that the merging of the private and public tutor systems had not taken place by the 1850s, though it was seen by several leading academics as a highly desirable goal. Nevertheless, by 1850 undergraduates were receiving closer and more regular individual attention from their college tutors. The Lincoln College tutor Mark Pattison was a leading proponent of this attitude, and his evidence to Royal Commission in 1851 has been described as a 'sustained argument to prove the necessity in higher education of a personal relationship between the teacher and taught' (M. C. Curthoys, 'The "unreformed" colleges', *The history of the University of Oxford*, vol. vii, p. 152, quoting from J. Sparrow, *Mark Pattison and the idea of a university* (1967), p. 92).

91   Nevertheless, the modern tutorial system only emerged fully after major reforms. For the way this came about at Cambridge see Sheldon Rothblatt's *The revolution of the dons: Cambridge and society in Victorian England* (1968). For a more party-political account of the changes at Oxford see A. J. Engel's

From clergyman to don: the rise of the academic profession in nineteenth-century Oxford (1983).

92 This was not something Newman encouraged, as he always discouraged personal discipleship among his associates and the type of influence it would give rise to.

93 *Short studies on great subjects* (New York, 1883), pp. 183–6.

94 Newman's memoir, 13 June 1874, *AW*, p. 90.

95 Besides Newman, the young Oriel Fellow (1836–42) and tutor (1837–68) Charles Daman attended several of these parties. He was the author of *Ten letters introductory to college residence* (1848), which contains words of advice that are remarkably similar to those of Newman.

96 Quoted in Mozley, *Reminiscences,* vol. ii, p. 225n.

97 A good example is his famous sermon 'The Second Spring', preached on 13 July 1852. 'How beautiful is the human heart, when it puts forth its first leaves, and opens and rejoices in its spring-tide. Fair as may be the bodily form, fairer far, in its green foliage and bright blossoms, is natural virtue. It blooms in the young, like some rich flower, so delicate, so fragrant, and so dazzling. Generosity and lightness of heart and amiableness, the confiding spirit, the gentle temper, the elastic cheerfulness, the open hand, the pure affection, the noble aspiration, the heroic resolve, the romantic pursuit, the love in which self has no part.' (*Sermons preached on various occasions* (London, 1870; 1898), pp. 165–6).

98 While a tutor, Newman had begun to speak about provision at Oriel for the 'sound instruction and paternal care of Adam de Brome' (Newman to Froude, 15 August 1829, *LD*, vol. ii, p. 157).

99 Newman's memoir, 13 June 1874, *AW*, p. 63.

100 *Newman the Oratorian: his unpublished Oratorian papers,* ed. P. Murray (Dublin, 1969), p. 426.

101 'The Mission of St Philip—Part 2', sermon preached in January 1850, *Sermons preached on various occasions,* pp. 225, 239.

102 W. Buscot, *The history of Cotton College* (London, 1940), pp. 238–42.

103 These were published as *Lectures on certain difficulties felt by Anglicans in submitting to the Catholic Church* (1850) and *Lectures on the present position of Catholics in England* (1851).

104 Newman's journal, 21 January 1863, *AW*, p. 259.

105 Sheldon Rothblatt argues that *Loss and gain* was the first coming-of-age novel or *Bildungsroman* to make the university the central or primary

character in a novel ('Loss and gain: John Henry Newman in 2005', *The university and society: from Newman to the market. Conference on shaping the future of university education,* ed. A. Lavan (Dublin, 2006), p. 17).

[106] It seems that Newman gained his use of the word 'view' from Froude and that it came to be known as an Oriel term: see Culler's *Imperial intellect,* pp. 195–7.

[107] According to Mike Higton, Newman was the one who coined the term 'viewiness' (*A theology of higher education* (Oxford, 2012), p. 88 note 39) to characterize those who form 'views' on important questions without taking the trouble to investigate them properly.

[108] Newman, *Loss and gain: the story of a convert* (1848; London, 1872), p. 17.

[109] Newman, *Loss and gain,* p. 18.

2 ESTABLISHING THE CATHOLIC UNIVERSITY

THE PROSPECT OF founding a Catholic university in Ireland in the mid-nineteenth century would have been unthinkable to the vast majority of Catholics in the United Kingdom. Ironically it was the British government which provided a major incentive for Catholics to undertake the project when, in 1845, it decided to establish the secular and non-denominational Queen's Colleges at Belfast, Cork and Galway. If this was the proximate cause for the establishment of a Catholic university, the more remote and deeper one was the need to address a grievance shared by the vast majority of Irishmen: the provision of suitable higher education that Catholics could attend. Together with the resolution of the 'land question' and the disestablishment of the Irish Church, the 'university question' constituted one of the three main demands of Irish Catholics after the Catholic Emancipation Act of 1829. One manifestation of Protestant hegemony had been the monopoly of higher education—and all the possibilities it opened up—by means of Trinity College Dublin, splendidly located at the heart of the capital. Founded in 1592 as a college invested with the powers, functions and status of a university, Trinity had long been regarded as a younger sister of the two English universities, and indeed bore a strong family resemblance to Oxford.

Although Trinity became staunchly Anglican after the Restoration, by 1794 it had become politically expedient for the British government to open up its degrees to Catholics and Dissenters by removing the religious test barriers for undergraduates (although not for scholarships or fellowships). Relatively few Catholics took advantage of this relaxation, as the whole atmosphere at Trinity was permeated with Protestantism, and over time the arrangement was regarded with increasing disapproval in Catholic clerical circles. The attempt of the Peel administration to provide an alternative solution by means of the 'Godless' Queen's Colleges met with limited success, as it underestimated Catholic opposition to 'mixed' (i.e. Catholic–Protestant) education. The question of mixed education had already led to deep divisions within the Irish episcopate in the debate over the national schools, which pitted 'Castle'[1] or pro-Westminster bishops against 'patriot' ones; now, with the prospect of the Queen's Colleges, they were split again, even though rescripts from Rome in 1847 and 1850 upheld official opposition to mixed education and forbade the bishops to cooperate with the new colleges. As an alternative, Rome urged the bishops to establish a Catholic university on the model of Louvain, which had been set up successfully by the Belgian bishops in 1834.[2]

The Catholic University of Louvain was set up with the sanction of Pope Gregory XVI as a 'free university'—that is, its administration, teaching, and budget were independent of the State. The Belgian episcopate had overall control of the institution and appointed the rector, who governed with the assistance of a council, the most important members of which were the deans of the five faculties (theology, law, medicine, philosophy and letters); the professors were appointed by the bishops on the presentation of the rector and grouped into faculties, each of which elected its own dean; the rector was assisted by a vice-rector, whose special charge was the care of the students. Having begun with 86 students, Louvain had grown to 754 within twenty-five years. This rapid success owed a great deal to the favourable arrangement for granting decrees: the Belgian state recognised and convalidated the degrees awarded in all subjects except theology, which was recognised instead by Rome.

A second Louvain

In 1850 the scheme for a Catholic university in Ireland was no more than a pipe-dream. Four years of famine had ravaged Ireland and seen more than a quarter of the population starve to death or forced to emigrate to escape that fate. Threatened by ruin, landowners were evicting tenants on an unprecedented scale (over 300,000 during the period 1849–52) and this, in turn, led to mass civil unrest and a standing army of 30,000 quartered in Ireland to defend the calamitous system and crush rebellions; meanwhile the British government scarcely lifted a finger to alleviate the human disaster taking place within the United Kingdom. There can hardly have been a less propitious time for founding a university than at the end of the Great Famine. Nevertheless, the prospects for doing so changed dramatically in 1850 when the vacant primatial See of Armagh was filled by Paul Cullen, rector of the Irish College in Rome and the leading supporter of Rome's university plan. Granted the title of 'apostolic delegate' and commissioned by the Holy See to convene the first synod in Ireland for over two centuries, Cullen was Rome's choice to sort out the tempestuous Irish Church. At the synod he convened at Thurles in August 1850, the bishops voted by narrow margins—two and four votes respectively—to prohibit their clergy from holding office at the Queen's Colleges and to warn the laity strongly against attending them. Despite the divisions over whether to cooperate or not with the Queen's Colleges, Cullen managed to secure unanimous approval for a Catholic university; and a University Committee[3] was appointed to act for the bishops. The Committee, which met monthly under Cullen's chairmanship, chiefly concerned itself with fundraising by means of subscriptions and parish collections in Ireland, further collections in England, France and North America, and with investment of these funds in government stocks. By the end of 1851 the Committee had in its hands a total of £30,000, of which nearly

£23,000 was collected in Ireland: remarkably, the lion's share came not from the middle or upper classes, but from the Irish poor.[4] This uneven yield from the Irish national collection reflected a lack of enthusiasm for the project among the bishops in the wealthier areas such as Dublin, but it was also an indication of the lukewarm support for episcopal projects among the better-off laity; their apathy did not bode well for the new university which hoped to draw many of its students from their ranks.

In June 1851 the Committee formally asked Cullen to 'draw up a plan for organizing the University & report it to the Committee, associating with him whom he pleases for the purpose';[5] in fact he had already embarked on the task, having approached Newman for advice and the names of converts who could help. Evidently Cullen hoped that if he secured one of the leading Oxford converts he would enhance the university's reputation and attract English support; it would also enable him to avoid having to appoint a native Irishman, who could hardly avoid falling foul of the feuds within the Irish hierarchy.[6] Cullen already knew Newman from Rome, where he had assisted him on a number of occasions, so it was only natural that Cullen should now turn to him for advice. He told Newman: 'if you could spare time to give us a few lectures on education, you would be rendering good service to religion in Ireland'.[7] Newman duly provided Cullen with eleven names—all converts, nine from Oxford and two from Cambridge—while at the same time commenting that none of them really struck him as suitable to act as rector. In July, Cullen crossed over to England and stayed overnight with Newman en route to London, where he had a meeting with three recent converts: Henry Edward Manning, the future cardinal of Westminster; William Monsell, MP for Limerick and the future Baron Emly; and James Hope (later Hope-Scott), a Parliamentary barrister who was an expert on ecclesiastical and educational matters. After the converts had talked over the plan for the projected university—location, residential arrangements, structure and professors—they agreed that the best method of proceeding would be to refer all these matters to Newman, and that 'he should be requested to consider the best means of establishing the University' and 'frame a report for publication as the basis for all further discussions'.[8]

Cullen readily accepted their recommendation to devolve the whole matter to Newman and, confirmed in his conviction that Newman was the man with the energy, administrative skills and vision to see this highly ambitious scheme through, he broke his return journey to Dublin to offer Newman the rectorship. At first Newman declined the offer, suggesting instead that he should act as Prefect of Studies. 'What I should desire,' he told Cullen, 'is to do as much work for the University as possible with *as little absence as possible* from this place'[9]—by which he meant the fledgling Oratory at Birmingham, of which he was Provost. This concern turned out to be Newman's single most serious constraint on his involvement in the project; and it was one Cullen never learnt to come to terms with. Meanwhile Newman agreed to join two members of the University Committee, Patrick Leahy, president of the diocesan college at Thurles, and Myles O'Reilly, a prominent propagandist for educational reform, to draw up a report on the organisation of the university, assisted by T. W. Allies, an Oxford convert and friend of Newman, who was to act as secretary. The subcommittee met in Birmingham at the end of August, after which the two Irishmen travelled to London to consult Hope, Manning and Monsell.[10] After seeking the advice of others by post,[11] including the rector of Louvain Mgr Pierre de Ram[12] and the German theologian Ignaz von Döllinger, the subcommittee reconvened at Thurles in early October to complete their 'Report of the Subcommittee on the Organization of the University' for the University

Committee. On returning to Birmingham, Newman sent a copy to Hope asking him to forward his comments to Cullen.

Though the Report was ostensibly the work of three, it bears the clear mark of Newman's mind and provides the first glimpse of his intentions. The Report recommended that, like the recently founded university at Louvain, the Catholic University should be framed on the medieval model, with the lower faculty of arts leading on to the higher faculties of theology, law and medicine. A four-year BA degree in this lower faculty was considered to be best suited to the probable age and professional plans of the students—and, tellingly, to 'the development of character'.[13] The idea was to begin with the arts faculty, which would be subdivided into letters and science: within the letters division were ancient and modern languages, history, English literature, and archaeology; and within the science division, all the physical, biological and social sciences, together with mathematics, ethics, metaphysics, and philosophy of religion—and even a subsidiary school of engineering. This broad curriculum showed that Newman's mental horizons were not confined to Oxford, which had a narrowly classics-based curriculum, and that his affection for Oxford did not blind him to its educational shortcomings, which he intended to remedy in the Catholic University. The same can be said for his plans for the professoriate, which was to be set up along faculty lines. At Oxford, and indeed Trinity College Dublin too, the professors were on the periphery of the teaching system and possessed no administrative functions, though both universities would subsequently alter this state of affairs following investigations by Royal Commissions. In advance of these changes, Newman granted his professors a central role and status.

The Catholic University was to be run along the lines of Louvain: the rector and vice-rector were to be nominated by the episcopal body (i.e. the bishops); the deans of discipline, the

University secretary, bursar and other officers were to be appointed by the rector, subject to the approval of the four archbishops; the professors and lecturers were to be appointed during the first ten years by the archbishops, acting for the bishops as a whole, on the recommendation of the rector; within each division of the arts faculty the professors were to elect a dean, who would convoke and chair meetings. At these meetings the professors would discuss faculty matters and draw up programmes of study, which they would then submit for the approval of the rector. Two other bodies were proposed along the lines of Louvain: a council to advise the rector on academic matters, composed of the deans of faculties and the vice-rector; and a senate with legislative powers on such matters as the framing of statutes, composed of the rector, the vice-rector, the University secretary, the professors and, after ten years, a number of graduates appointed annually by the graduates themselves (their number not exceeding a quarter of the whole body so as not to swamp the resident body by their votes, as at Oxford). As for the students, 'They shall be interns [i.e. resident], so far as circumstances may permit'.[14]

The Report concluded by noting that during the provisional constitution of the first ten years the bishops would have the power to alter whatever went wrong, but that afterwards it was hoped that the constitution would have sufficiently matured to allow for a greater degree of self-government by the University. From the outset the rector was to have a wide scope for action and a commensurate responsibility. He was to regulate the course of studies and the duties of the professors; to devise Rules of Internal Discipline with the advice of the vice-rector and deans of discipline; to summon and preside over the council and senate; and to make a detailed annual report to the bishops on the state of the University.

Paper plans were one thing, but practicalities were another. Having all but agreed to undertake the rectorship, Newman now did his best to ensure that he was given as free a rein as possible according to his long-held principle that great things are worked out not by committees, but by individuals.[15] Knowing that the committee that would oversee his work and exercise overall control was a rather special one, being scattered around Ireland, he sought an assurance that he would be given the freedom of action he needed. He already knew from Hope that Cullen was of the opinion 'that the University should be started without statutes, or any formal constitution, and that the Rector and his assistants should govern according to their discretion, until experience had given the data for establishing it in a regular manner'.[16] With this in mind he wrote to Cullen to express his agreement that the University should be started experimentally. In his letter to Cullen, which he sent via Hope so that his friend could add his comments, Newman agreed that the rector should be subordinate to the board of archbishops, but he went on to argue that he should be 'autocrat: Two authorities will ruin the attempt'. The rector should have the power of choosing his associates, 'especially *lecturers* and *tutors*', as opposed to the professors. Once the University was set up and a system established, then after two or three years of 'an autocracy', different influences would be beneficial. After warning Cullen to brace himself for an English convert element among the teaching staff, if he were appointed, he added that the deans of discipline would be Irish, as would some of the lecturers.[17]

Hope told Cullen he agreed wholeheartedly with Newman's provisional scheme and recommended that the board leave him 'wholly unfettered during the provisional period'; since Newman's responsibilities would be great, it was only reasonable that his powers should be proportionately ample.[18] Before hearing from either Hope or Cullen, Newman wrote again to Cullen to emphasise that, though the final form of the University would be entrusted to a committee, the provisional state should be committed entirely to one person. He added that he was for beginning with very few professors and tutors, but with a good fund for scholarships and prizes to help 'the deserving students and create a sort of model set of men, who would form the nucleus of a good tradition'. This emphasis on merit and the worthy student can be traced back to Newman's days at Oriel when he fiercely opposed the unearned privileges and immunities that the gentlemen-commoners enjoyed; but an additional reason for founding bursaries to help 'the poorer and meritorious class of students' was to counter the effect of the generous scholarships made available by the British government in order to entice students into the Queen's Colleges.[19]

In a Postscript that was longer than the Report itself, two important principles were outlined. Firstly, the need for 'a perfect unity of purpose and operation' in the teaching and governing body was paramount, so as to secure the harmonious action of the professors and lecturers, 'their growth into one body, and their production of a real education for those under their care'. To this end, they needed to be guided by a working rather than by a theoretical constitution. Secondly, they needed to meet 'the actual state of the pupils, as to knowledge, and moral and intellectual training': time was needed before the University would be able to create its own atmosphere and a standard both in knowledge and of moral character. 'In the meantime it must take the youth as it finds them, and make the best of them, which entails a certain period of experimental action.'[20] With a view to beginning in January 1852, the sub-committee recommended the immediate appointment of a small number of professors and lecturers, who between them might cover the main subjects, teaching two or three each if need be, and acting as tutors at the same time. This reference to tutors, which was absent from the main Report, was dwelt on at length in the Postscript.

The proposal—undoubtedly Newman's—was to blend the 'Professorial and Tutorial systems', by arranging for the same people to undertake both teaching functions in order that students would benefit from both systems. As with his reforms of the teaching at Oriel in 1829, the question of which system to employ depended on the subject matter: lectures were more appropriate for the physical sciences; tutorials for languages. There was no need for Newman to explain why lectures were needed, especially to those on the University Committee who had known no other system of teaching, but he did think it worthwhile to point out that this method had its shortcomings: 'the work of a Professor is not sufficient by itself to form the pupil. The catechetical form of instruction and the closeness of work in a small class are needed besides.' Newman explained that, even if the professor was a man of genius and able to interest his students, what was gained from his lectures would often be very superficial. Undoubtedly, students who were academically self-motivated would be able to profit from them; but in general, if the reliance was solely on lectures, 'the result will be undisciplined and unexercised minds, with a few notions, on which they are able to show off, but without any judgment or any solid powers'.[21] Arguing in this fashion, Newman arrived at his working rule: 'that the principal making of men must be by the Tutorial system'. In this way the professor, acting as a tutor,

> on a smaller number at a time, and by the catechetical method, will be able to exert those personal influences, which are of the highest importance in the formation and tone of character among the set of students, as well as to provide that the student shall actually prepare the subject for himself, and not be a mere listener at a lecture.[22]

All the key ingredients of the Oxford tutorial ideal, as envisaged by Newman, are present here, the combination of large- and small-group teaching with individual tutorial oversight, all of it a natural development of his thinking and practice as an Oriel tutor.[23]

In a further recommendation the Report suggested that relations be established with existing schools and colleges, and that, if necessary, the University should start its own preparatory schools, not only so as to ensure a supply of applicants but also to improve the standard of secondary education. When the University Committee met on 12 November, the Report was approved and a resolution was passed—unanimously and with acclaim—that Newman should accept the rectorship. Informed that the *summum imperium* would reside with the episcopate, but that the rector would have full acting discretion, Newman accepted at once. In his reply, he asked if there were a way of putting the University 'under the patronage of our Blessed Lady, for it would be most desirable'.[24]

Newman's proposal was the expression of a long-felt devotion to the Blessed Virgin,[25] as well as having a clear theological context: Newman, indeed, sees Mary as a principal authority for accepting theology as a branch of knowledge and, no less significantly, as 'our pattern of faith',[26] making her the example at the heart of the universal knowledge of the university. It is no surprise, then, that when writing on 'The prima facie idea of a University', Newman concludes by describing it in markedly Marian terms as 'a seat of wisdom, a light of the world, a minister of the faith, an Alma Mater of the rising generation'; and it is in this context that he first announced publicly that he was placing the Catholic University 'under the patronage of the Blessed Virgin'.[27]

Three years would elapse before the university would open its doors. In the short term, however, Newman was occupied with preparing the lectures on education that Cullen had invited him to deliver.

Newman's Dublin lectures

The ten public lectures that Newman composed in 1852 are rightly considered educational masterpieces, for they have inspired debate on the nature and purpose of a university education like no other work in the English—or indeed any—language. Nevertheless they are lectures and not in any systematic form and, if read in isolation, can give a misleading impression of what he attempted to do in Dublin. The lectures were not designed to convey his pastoral vision of a university—in fact they have little to say about it explicitly—yet they do fill out much of his educational thinking, and so need to be examined. By viewing them in their context, though not in detail (space does not permit and the literature about them is vast), it will become clear how much they need to be interpreted according to the times and circumstances in which they were delivered, and why they represent only part of Newman's larger conception of education. A further difficulty is that vital distinctions are so embedded in the text that the reader can become absorbed by the magnificent prose and distracted from the underlying theme. For those prepared to give his arguments the sort of critical attentiveness they call for, the lectures prove how deeply Newman thought about such matters as the relation of college to university, teaching to personal development, and the importance of new knowledge and its limitations in the formation of the human mind.

Running through the lectures are two main arguments, both of which are still pertinent today: the need to include theology in a university; and the claim that the main business of a university is the cultivation of the intellect rather than immediate preparation for professional occupations. The first amounted to an attack on the non-denominational or secular university, and was directed at those who supported the Queen's Colleges or University College London, where theology was deliberately excluded. The second sought to place the new university on the academic high ground and to counter those who wanted to subordinate liberal education to short-term, practical, economic, political—or even religious—considerations. In the first four lectures and in part of the fifth Newman argues at some length that, since all knowledge is one and since no part can be studied fully without relation to the other parts, this implies that theology cannot be omitted without distorting the rest of the curriculum. In the fifth to the eighth lectures he looks at the nature of knowledge and shows that it can be viewed and pursued with a view to culture of the intellect or for more immediate practical purposes. The former, he argues, is a good in itself and constitutes the primary aim of a university. While all subjects tend to the cultivation of the intellect, some are particularly suited to fostering mental culture, and it is these that a university should therefore concentrate on. Universities also prepare for the professions, either directly by making provision for disciplines such as medicine and law, or indirectly by providing the best preparation through mental cultivation. In the last two lectures Newman dealt with the relation between this mental culture and religion.

Newman delivered the first five lectures to the general public in Dublin on five successive Mondays, starting on 10 May 1852; the rest were ready by the autumn, but never given. All ten were published the same year, first separately and then together in a single volume under the title *Discourses on the scope and nature of university education*. Most people are familiar with the *Discourses* as the first part of *The idea of a university: defined and illustrated*.[28] The second half of the *Idea* comprised occasional pieces composed in the period 1854–58, most of which appeared in the *Catholic University Gazette*, before they were published together in 1859 as *Lectures and essays on university subjects*. It was only in 1873 that the two parts were brought together to form *The idea of a university*. It is thus perfectly clear the *Idea* was not written as a systematic

treatise on the nature and purpose of university education, although
it has often been treated as such.

The lectures themselves were not composed as an exhaustive
exposition of their subject matter but as an exploration of a theme;
and they were written to deal with particular problems which
Newman faced in the 1850s in his attempt to win over and bring
together various factions within Irish society. One of his aims was
to fill out the idea of a university and make it appealing, because he
had heard from Robert Ornsby, one of his English friends in Dublin,
that words like 'education' and 'university' did not convey the same
ideas to Irishmen as they did to Englishmen, and that for many
Irishmen the latter term meant little more than a sort of super-
secondary school (since the only possibility for a Catholic higher
education on offer in Ireland—other than for those preparing for
the priesthood—was to stay on and pursue studies at school).
Despite a recent surge of anti-English feeling in Ireland, on account
of the British government's policy of non-intervention during and
after the Great Famine, Newman decided to use the example of
Oxford as a way to convey the fuller idea of a university, and by that
means to win over that small but influential constituency that
hankered after Trinity College Dublin. His approach to the Dublin
barristers and their like-minded friends was thus intentionally more
by reasoned argument: he appealed to English precedent rather
than on strictly Catholic grounds and the call of duty. He had been
informed by Ornsby that Catholic 'society' in Dublin was small and
on the whole pro-Castle, and that the general mind of this class was
unconsciously imbued with Protestant notions 'caused by the long
habit of conciliating Protestants by softening their faith and pre-
tending liberality'.[29] His delicate task here was to wean them off the
idea of mixed education by persuading them that he could offer
something to match Trinity College Dublin and Oxford, and which
was Catholic to boot. He set about this by basing his argument for

theology at university on the plea for true intellectual culture, which ought not to exclude any important discipline from the circle of knowledge. He also described how a faith-based university like Oxford gave a religious colouring to all the studies pursued there.

Newman was aware of the tensions within Irish society, a result of the painfully slow process of emancipation and social integration of Catholics. As the penal laws were relaxed at the end of the eighteenth century, Catholics had begun to emerge from a disadvantaged underclass; then, in 1829, the Act of Catholic Emancipation made wide-ranging concessions, granting full civil rights to Catholics and opening up most public posts to them. But emancipation also created tensions within the Catholic body, since the major concern of the hierarchy was the safeguarding of the faith and the maintenance of ecclesial order, while many lay Catholics in the professions were more preoccupied with civil concessions. This division of interests was exacerbated by British educational policy in Ireland: the introduction of the national schools in the 1840s, and the Queen's Colleges in the 1850s, led to divisions within the hierarchy itself, for leaders such as Archbishop Murray saw practical advantages in going along with the system of mixed education, while in ecclesiastical circles more closely aligned with official Church policy these developments had helped to create a climate of extreme caution, even suspicion, towards a portion of the educated laity.

Newman sought to bridge the lay–clerical divide and to win over that portion of the laity which deeply distrusted anything with clerical sponsorship; this meant that he had to convince them that he was not a puppet in the hands of the hierarchy, charged with the task of establishing a lay seminary or even a training school for commerce and the professions. In eulogising the university as the home of learning *for its own sake*, he left his listeners in no doubt as to his intentions on this score. His insistence on the place of

theology in the university curriculum undoubtedly warmed the
hearts of the clergy, but they would have been less pleased with the
fifth lecture, where he rejects the idea 'that Theology stands to
other knowledge as the soul to the body; or that the other sciences
are but its instruments'.[30]

Another split within his extended audience was along nationalist
lines: the 'Castle set' favoured collaboration with Westminster and
closer ties with Protestants, as well as the maintenance of the Union
between Ireland and Britain, while the nationalists refused to
collaborate with the British government—though the Young
Ireland nationalists *were* prepared to accept the Queen's Colleges
on the ground that their non-sectarian character would foster
political unity. On this question Newman deliberately adopted a
neutral stance and avoided all reference to Irish politics in his
lectures—as he did throughout his time in Dublin. It was not that
he was unaware of the political situation on the ground (his letters
show that he was a well-informed and incisive judge of it), but he
saw no other way of proceeding; and in the circumstances it was
certainly the wisest course of action to take.

It is important to grasp Newman's concept of knowledge, as it
paves the way for understanding one of the grand aims of a university. 'All that exists, as contemplated by the human mind, forms one
large system or complex fact, and this of course resolves itself into
an indefinite number of particular facts, which, as being portions
of a whole, have countless relations of every kind, one towards
another.' The effect of a proper university education is described
by Newman as enlargement of the mind:

> the action of a formative power, reducing to order and
> meaning the matter of our acquirements; it is a making the
> objects of our knowledge subjectively our own, or, to use a
> familiar word, it is a digestion of what we receive, into the
> substance of our previous state of thought.[31]

This organic, living knowledge, not just of things themselves, but of their mutual relations, enables the intellect to gain,

> a connected view of old and new, past and present, far and near, and which has an insight into the influence of all these one on another; without which there is no whole, and no centre. It possesses the knowledge, not only of things, but also of their mutual and true relations; knowledge, not merely considered as acquirement, but as philosophy.[32]

Acquiring this overview or 'philosophical habit of mind'[33] is one of the chief goals of a university education. By this means a lawyer, physician, geologist, or economist studying at a University,

> will just know where he and his science stand, he has come to it, as it were, from a height, he has taken a survey of all knowledge, he is kept from extravagance by the very rivalry of other studies, he has gained from them a special illumination and largeness of mind and freedom and self-possession, and he treats his own in consequence with a philosophy and a resource, which belongs not to the study itself, but to his liberal education.[34]

After composing the first five lectures, which dealt with the university from a philosophical standpoint and considered it in its essence and independently from the Church, Newman tried to anticipate objections to the sixth, 'Philosophical Knowledge its own end', by drafting several introductions so as to explain his meaning. The *direct* end of a university, he asserts, is knowledge or 'cultivation of mind', just as the *direct* end of hospitals is bodily health; neither of them is *directly* intended to make men religious. 'A University is not *ipso facto* a Church Institution', he argues; like a hospital, it 'has no direct call to make men Catholic or religious, for that is the previous and contemporaneous office of the Church'. Nevertheless the *indirect* effects of a university are religious; 'As the Church uses Hospitals religiously, so she uses Universities'. In order 'to secure its religious character, and for the morals of its members, she has ever adopted together with it, and within its precincts, Seminaries, Halls, Colleges and Monastic Establishments'.[35] What follows from this line of thinking 'is that the office of a Catholic University is to teach *faith*, and of Colleges to protect *morals*'.[36]

When the lectures were published together in one volume, the explanation had found another form in the Preface. There Newman explains that he views the university as 'a place of *teaching* universal *knowledge*', which implies that its principal object is in the first place intellectual, not moral, and in the second that it entails the diffusion of knowledge rather than its advancement. This means that, in its essence, a university is neither a seminary or centre of religious training, as this would hardly make it a 'seat of literature and science'; nor is it a research institute, because otherwise it need not have students. While claiming that 'Such is a University in its *essence*, and independently of its relation to the Church', Newman immediately points out that in practice the university 'cannot fulfil its object duly [...] without the Church's assistance'. This implies that 'the Church is necessary for its *integrity*',[37] by which he means an ease of harmonious functioning and completeness. A further qualification follows, as Newman explains that this ecclesial assistance or incorporation does not imply that the university's main characteristics are changed; the university retains the office of intellectual education, but now aided in the performance of that office by the steadying hand of the Church. Newman reminds his readers that,

> when the Church founds a University, she is not cherishing talent, genius, or knowledge, for their own sake, but for the sake of her children, with a view to their spiritual welfare and their religious influence and usefulness, with the object of training them to fill their respective posts in life better,

and of making them more intelligent, capable, active members of society.[38]

This means that when the Pope recommends to the Irish hierarchy the establishment of a Catholic university, his

> first and chief and direct object is, not science, art, profes-
> sional skill, literature, the discovery of knowledge, but some
> benefit or other, to accrue, by means of literature and
> science, to his own children; not indeed their formation on
> any narrow or fantastic type, as, for instance, that of an
> 'English Gentleman' may be called, but their exercise and
> growth in certain habits, moral or intellectual.[39]

But this does not mean that in acting like this the Church 'sacrifices Science, and, under pretence of fulfilling the duties of her mission, perverts a University to ends not its own'.[40]

In arguing that the end of a university was intellectual culture,[41] Newman was defending the university against those who burdened it with some other end, such as practical utility or religious training and morality. Following Aristotle's argument that everything has its own perfection, whether intellectual, aesthetic, moral or practical, Newman held that,

> To open the mind, to correct it, to refine it, to enable it to
> know, and to digest, master, rule, and use its knowledge, to
> give it power over its own faculties, application, flexibility,
> method, critical exactness, sagacity, resource, address, elo-
> quent expression, is an object as intelligible [...] as the
> cultivation of virtue, while, at the same time, it is absolutely
> distinct from it.[42]

In saying this he was simply inquiring what a liberal education was in itself, not what it was worth nor what use the Church made of it. It was an important distinction to draw because Newman was faced by two dominant outlooks, each of which showed a marked tendency to use the university as a vehicle for something other than its primary end, and thus tended to distort the education that was imparted. Besides their obsession with 'useful knowledge', the intellectual descendants of John Locke—such as his pupil Lord Shaftesbury, the *Edinburgh Review* circle, the utilitarian Jeremy Bentham, and politicians like Lord Brougham and Sir Robert Peel—held that education alone was needed to make the public moral, and religious teaching was thereby redundant; ecclesiastics, on the other hand, had a tendency to be interested in education only insofar as it ministered to religion and the Church.[43] Newman dealt with both tendencies by defending what he maintained was the proper business of a university:

> Its direct business is not to steel the soul against temptation or to console it in affliction, any more than to set the loom in motion, or to direct the steam carriage; be it ever so much the means or the condition of both material and moral advancement, still, taken by and in itself, it as little mends our hearts as it improves our temporal circumstances.[44]

The educational theories of Locke and his intellectual descendants were widely influential in Newman's time, and Newman set himself to expose and refute them. He notes of Locke that he 'preceded the Edinburgh Reviewers in condemning the ordinary subjects in which boys are instructed at school, on the ground that they are not needed by them in after life'; and that 'he distinctly limits utility in education to its bearing on the future profession or trade of the pupil, that is, he scorns the idea of any education of the intellect'.[45] As for the *Edinburgh Review*'s attack on Oxford, it was based on the idea that the university 'should be set to rights on the basis of the philosophy of Utility; a philosophy,' he adds, not without irony, 'as they seem to have thought, which needed but to be proclaimed in order to be embraced'.[46] And when he turns to Brougham, Newman sees him as having had a major role 'in effecting the public recognition in these Islands of the principle of separating secular and religious knowledge', leading to the absurd assertion that 'Religion is not knowledge, has nothing whatever to do with knowledge, and is excluded from a University course of instruction, not simply because the exclusion cannot be helped, from political or social obstacles, but because it has no business there at all, because it is to be considered a taste, sentiment, opinion, and nothing more'.[47] Brougham was one of the leading 'patrons of society' who had helped to establish University College London in 1826 as an institution 'free' of religion and offering 'useful' knowledge.

The Dublin lectures are thus, in a general sense, a refutation of the arguments of these contemporary thinkers and politicians, and in this they bear a relation to Newman's satirical letters to *The Times* in 1841, occasioned by the opening of the Tamworth Reading Room. In his opening address, Sir Robert Peel had suggested that reading would not only lead people to appreciate the wonders of Creation, but also make them good and virtuous citizens. Newman probed the fallacy here: Peel was implicitly replacing religion with secular knowledge when he asserted (in Newman's words) that 'Useful Knowledge is the great instrument of education. It is the parent of virtue, the nurse of religion; it exalts man to his highest perfection, and is the sufficient scope of his most earnest exertions.' Newman took issue with the idea that 'a man "in becoming wiser will become better" ', because it was based on an inadequate account of the relationship between knowledge and virtue—based, that is, on a false understanding of human nature; in Peel's account, there was no place for conscience or moral development. And he advised Peel: 'If virtue be a mastery over the mind, if its end be action, if its perfection be inward order, harmony, and peace, we must seek it in graver and holier places than in Libraries and Reading-rooms'.[48]

Like Bentham and Brougham, Peel held that religion should be excluded from education, as it was simply a source of controversy and division. Newman countered by arguing that without the aid of religion, knowledge alone was utterly incapable of achieving what Peel claimed for it. History showed that the 'apprehension of the unseen is the only known principle capable of subduing moral evil, educating the multitude, and organizing society; and that, whereas man is born for action, action flows not from inferences, but from impressions,—not from reasonings, but from Faith'. Therefore, Newman argued, 'Christianity, and nothing short of it, must be made the element and principle of all education. Where it has been laid as the first stone, and acknowledged as the governing spirit, it will take up into itself, assimilate, and give a character to literature and science.' Otherwise, 'if in education we begin with nature before grace, with evidences before faith, with science before conscience, with poetry before practice, we shall be doing much the same as if we were to indulge the appetites and passions, and turn a deaf ear to the reason'.[49] A decade later, in the *Idea*, Newman developed his case for denominational education by arguing that theology was necessary in order to acquire a philosophical view: 'Religious truth is not only a portion, but a condition of general knowledge. To blot it out is nothing short, if I may so speak, of unravelling the web of university teaching.'[50]

Another weakness that Newman exposed was in the training of virtues. From his pastoral experience he knew that moral improvement was not simply a result of learning facts or grasping intellectual principles, but was instead something intimately concerned with the will and conscience. In this he discerned 'a chief error of the day' (which is still with us today): the idea, proposed by the proponents of 'useful knowledge',

> that our true excellence comes not from within, but from without; not wrought out through personal struggles and

sufferings, but following upon a passive exposure to influences over which we have no control. They will countenance the theory that diversion is the instrument of
improvement, and excitement the condition of right action;
and whereas diversions cease to be diversions if they are
constant, and excitements by their very nature have a crisis
and run through a course, they will tend to make novelty
ever in request, and will set the great teachers of morals
upon the incessant search after stimulants and sedatives.[51]

In arguing that knowledge was as distinct from morality as it was
from utility, Newman was not denying that benefits would accrue
from intellectual activity pursued for its own sake; this becomes
clear when he writes of the effects and indirect benefits of a
university education. 'If then a practical end must be assigned to a
University course, I say it is that of training good members of
society. Its art is the art of social life, and its end is fitness for the
world.'[52] This amounts to saying that intellectual virtues are substantial goods which are inseparable from their economic and social
usefulness, even if this usefulness is not their main aim. Newman's
attitude is summed up in his working principle that 'though the
useful is not always good, the good is always useful'.[53] Likewise,
while maintaining the *theoretical* autonomy of knowledge from
morality, Newman maintains that *in practice* a link exists between
them and that there is no clear division between the natural and
supernatural orders: 'We attain to heaven by using this world well,
though it is to pass away; we perfect our nature, not by undoing it,
but by adding to it what is more than nature, and directing it
towards aims higher than its own.'[54] In both cases education entails
benefits which extend beyond the purely intellectual.

Having made his case that the great object of a Catholic university is to make its students into something, whether 'gentlemen' or
something else, Newman goes on to examine whether his concep-

tion answers 'the *sort of benefit*' which the Holy See had in mind
when recommending the establishment of a Catholic university. In
analysing what precisely it was that Catholics wished from a
university—to put themselves on a level with Protestants and to
further the cause of Catholic emancipation—Newman identifies
its main advantage as culture of the intellect or mind. 'Our desid-
eratum is, not the manners and habits of gentlemen', which can be
supplied by various means besides a university, 'but the force, the
steadiness, the comprehensiveness and the versatility of intellect,
the command over our own powers, the instinctive just estimate of
things as they pass before us', which is usually gained only with
'much effort and the exercise of years'. This is what Newman calls
'real cultivation of mind'. He does not deny that a university
education also fosters 'the characteristic excellences of a gentleman', as a liberal education at university manifests itself 'in a
courtesy, propriety, and polish of word and action, which is beautiful in itself, and acceptable to others; but it does much more. It
brings the mind into form'.[55]

To bring out his meaning, Newman compares the lively banter
of teenagers with the conversation of adults of unformed minds.
Teenage boys who have not yet gained 'a foundation for the
intellect to build upon', who have 'no discriminating convictions,
and no grasp of consequences', will be found to 'talk at random
[…] and cannot help being flippant' because they 'are merely
dazzled by phenomena, instead of perceiving things as they are'.
This is not dissimilar, says Newman, to the idle conversation of
adults who converse on weighty matters in an equally shallow
manner. Among the intellectual infirmities that he lists are those of
(unconscious) self-contradiction; the inability to see difficulties in
difficult subjects; mental obstinacy and prejudice; and the intem-
perate holding of opinions. When the intellect has been 'properly
trained and formed to have a connected view or grasp of things', it

results in 'good sense, sobriety of thought, reasonableness, candour, self-command, and steadiness of view'. In some it might develop the habits of business and the power of influencing people; in others, the talent of intellectual research. But in all 'it will be a faculty of entering with comparative ease into any subject of thought, and of taking up with aptitude any science or profession'.[56] Newman develops this line of reasoning as follows:

> It is the education which gives a man a clear conscious view of his own opinions and judgments, a truth in developing them, an eloquence in expressing them, and a force in urging them. It teaches him to see things as they are, to go right to the point, to disentangle a skein of thought, to detect what is sophistical, and to discard what is irrelevant.[57]

In contrast to those who regarded knowledge as involving merely an acquisition or a method, Newman viewed it as a personal possession and a habit of mind, which is why he insisted that 'education is a higher word [than instruction]; it implies an action upon our mental nature, and the formation of a character; it is something individual and permanent'.[58]

Possibly the most famous part of the *Idea* is that which contains Newman's celebrated portrait of the gentleman. To modern ears, 'gentleman' is a word with (negative) associations of snobbishness and privilege, but for Newman it connoted the model citizen of Athens, the man who exemplified natural or human virtues. Nevertheless, Newman had an ambivalent attitude to the figure of the gentleman, as he was at one and the same time both the best product of a liberal education and an imperfect being—at least when compared with the *beau ideal* of a specifically Christian education. In one of the most dramatic shifts in the *Idea*, Newman concludes his lengthy delineation of the excellences and charms of this attractive figure[59] by showing how it falls short of that higher form of excellence which results from grace: sanctity.

Knowledge is one thing, virtue is another; good sense is not conscience, refinement is not humility, nor is largeness and justness of view faith. Philosophy, however enlightened, however profound, gives no command over the passions, no influential motives, no vivifying principles. Liberal Education makes not the Christian, not the Catholic, but the gentleman.[60]

It is because the Dublin lectures are about the *essence* of a university, not about its fully functioning existence, that they contain a great deal about the intellectual formation of the individual at university, but relatively little about character formation itself and the benefits of residential student life. The main exception occurs in the seventh lecture, where Newman extols the advantages of a residential university by dwelling on the mutual education that takes place there.

> When a multitude of young men, keen, open-hearted, sympathetic, and observant, as young men are, come together and freely mix with each other, they are sure to learn one from another, even if there be no one to teach them; the conversation of all is a series of lectures to each, and they gain for themselves new ideas and views, fresh matter of thought, and distinct principles for judging and acting, day by day.

This goes some way to explaining his preference for a residential university without formal teaching (other than tutorials) over a non-residential university with lectures and exams: the former provided the setting for a deeper formation. Part of this unofficial educative experience comes about from the very mix of students, for life at university 'is seeing the world on a small field with little trouble; for the pupils or students come from very different places, and with widely different notions, and there is much to generalise, much to adjust, much to eliminate'.[61]

Between the Idea *and the reality*

Three years were to elapse between Newman being named rector and the university opening its doors. After the initial flurry of public activity and the head of steam built up by Newman's lectures, the extended period of apparent inactivity which followed suggested to most observers that the university project was just one more abortive attempt at ameliorating the Irish condition. Yet there were good reasons for the delay. One major obstacle to the establishment of a university in Dublin disappeared in February 1852 when Daniel Murray, the archbishop, died. Not only had he favoured compromise with the government over the Queen's Colleges and been lukewarm about the projected Catholic university, but he had discouraged fundraising and only attended the first of the University Committee meetings, even though they took place on his doorstep. When Rome chose to fill the vacant seat by transferring Cullen to Dublin, the prospect of starting the university in Dublin suddenly became a practical possibility. On Newman's side, delay was inevitable as he was caught up in a libel action brought by the apostate Dominican, Giacinto Achilli, who served Newman a writ for criminal libel in October 1851 on account of a piece Newman had written about him. Newman interrupted the Dublin lectures in order to stand trial in London in June 1852, but the final verdict was reached only in January 1853, when Newman was fined £100 and costs (and lectured by the judge about his moral deterioration). The protracted legal proceedings and the threat of imprisonment gave Newman a great deal of anxiety, as well as a large quantity of work. Although the costs were considerable—around £12,000 —friends and admirers around the world rallied to his side and defrayed the expenses.

In the months following the Dublin lectures Newman plied Cullen with requests for information and decisions, and passed on his own views and wishes, but he was generally met with either silence or else notification of decisions already taken. Cullen's procrastination and peremptoriness are characteristics that historians have noted and that have contributed to unfair representations of the prelate, picturing him as a narrow, sectarian figure when compared with the liberal English convert. In fact, as far as education was concerned, the two shared a good deal of common ground: both saw the vital importance of education for the nation; viewed the separation of religion and secular learning as a calamity; and anticipated the dangers of a secular education.

Since Archbishop Cullen is the other main protagonist in the story of the foundation of the Catholic University, it is worth taking a brief look at his background. Paul Cullen had received a fine classical education at Carlow College for three years before leaving, at the age of seventeen, for the College of Propaganda Fide in Rome, where after eight years of theological studies he was ordained to the priesthood. After lecturing in Rome for three further years, he was appointed rector of the Irish College, one of the many national halls of residence for students studying for the priesthood at the Roman universities, where he was responsible for the priestly formation and general welfare of the students; at the same time he also acted as an agent for the Roman authorities in their dealings with the Irish hierarchy. During his twenty-nine years in Rome, Cullen seems to have acquired all the instincts of an Italian ecclesiastic—including the time-honoured Roman habit of procrastination. In Rome, too, he witnessed the involvement of students in the political upheavals that took place in 1848, and from that time on saw the Young Ireland movement as a sinister counterpart to the Young Italy one, fearing the Young Irelanders would attempt to import a similarly anti-religious republicanism onto Irish soil.

From October 1852 to early 1854 Cullen systematically ignored his newly appointed rector, and all Newman could do was to sound out other members of the University Committee for news of progress or decisions. In fact Cullen had more than his share of difficulties with the University project, and was trying to walk a tightrope in his dealings with the Irish episcopate over the matter. Most troublesome of them was the Archbishop of Tuam, John MacHale, who argued vehemently that the body of bishops, and it alone, had the right to set up and govern the Catholic University; from February 1852 he objected to everything the University Committee proposed and did his level best to block its decisions.[62] The first modern bishop to be educated entirely in Ireland, McHale was by the mid-1840s the most popular man in Ireland after Daniel O'Connell. A political radical and an uncompromising champion of the poor and underprivileged, McHale combined his stand on social justice with a commitment to cultural and political nationalism. On account of his pugnacious and confrontational tactics in his dealings with the representatives of British rule, he was widely known as the 'Lion of the West'.

At a time when Cullen could count on the support of only seven of the twenty-eight bishops, MacHale spread the view that Cullen was attempting to control the Committee—as indeed he undoubtedly was.[63] But Cullen knew that the episcopate as a whole was too unwieldy a body for setting up a university, and that a committee was needed instead—a view Newman undoubtedly shared. Furthermore, at a time of strong anti-English feeling, MacHale's objection to the appointment of Englishmen caused problems for Cullen, since Newman had stipulated that 'I *must* have men I know about me'[64]—by which he meant Englishmen. In particular, Newman wanted an Englishman for his vice-rector, but this would have been inflammatory for Irish public opinion.

Though it is true that MacHale wanted the bishops to have exclusive control of the university, while Cullen was happy to allow laymen onto the University Committee, their differences were less than they seemed, for Cullen too was strongly of the opinion that the control of education was the prerogative of the clergy. In this he differed markedly from Newman, who wanted 'to make the laity a substantive power in the University',[65] though at first there were few indications of the divide. At the time there was a widespread assumption within Catholic (and indeed Church of Ireland and Anglican) circles, that teaching ought on the whole to be entrusted to clergymen, although this view was now being challenged.[66] In his wish to appoint lay staff at the University, Newman could be said to be in the vanguard of this movement. Certainly he sensed that not a few laymen—and not only the anticlericals—were unhappy with the old state of affairs and eager to see it change. Indeed, a priest on the University Committee had told him, 'The public does not give us priests credit for ability to fit young men for the world, and certain I am that the word and example of a pious layman will always be less suspected and more efficacious with boys than those of an equally pious priest.'[67] Another unspoken difference at the outset concerned the interpretation of official pronouncements as to *who* the university was principally aimed at—a matter confused by the documents themselves, which sometimes stressed one line, sometimes the other. The English contingent (including Newman) saw the university as an 'imperial venture' intended to provide a liberal education for the whole of the Catholic English-speaking world; understandably, the Irish viewed it in more local terms, as answering national and more immediate, practical needs.

Another reason for Cullen's silence was his preoccupation with dissension among the hierarchy over Irish nationalism and the thorny issue of the limits of clerical involvement in the political question. The newly-formed Tenant League, set up to champion security of tenure and a fair rent for the workers on the land, received widespread support from both clergy and laity, but the country became sharply divided by the two factions within it: those who advocated an independent political movement and those who argued for an alliance with one of the major political parties —which, in practice, meant the Whigs. Besides splitting the country, the division caused dissension within the ranks of the Catholic clergy, pitting Cullen against MacHale. By opposing clerical involvement in nationalist politics, Cullen earned the dislike of journalists and nationalist leaders alike. In addition, Cullen's leading role in Ireland, and his profile as a model Ultramontane at a time when a process of centralisation was taking place within the Catholic Church, brought a negative reaction from clergy and laity alike, and it was aggravated by his autocratic style of government and unwillingness to confide in others.

Exasperated with the slowness and ineffectualness of the University Committee, and unaware how divided the episcopal body had become, the rector-in-waiting was left watching anxiously from across St George's Channel, awaiting a summons. On the question of how to begin the university, a majority of the Committee favoured a well-staffed professoriate and imposing buildings as a means of exciting interest and showing the intent to match the foundations of Trinity and the Queen's University (the degree-awarding body erected in 1850 for the three Queen's Colleges). In a minority were those favouring a modest start, but they included Cullen and Newman, as well as Hope.

On a visit to Ireland in August 1852, Newman heard that Cullen had begun looking for a site, and this prompted him to draw up a memorandum 'as to the best mode of starting the University', which he entitled 'The Statement of August 14th 1852'. Although Newman eventually decided against sending it to Cullen, and instead sent a brief note, the document provides a crucial insight into the development of Newman's plans; among other points it contains a fully worked-out scheme for accommodating the students in small lodging houses and shows Newman's fertility of mind in devising a solution for the particular need in question. But as he foresaw that the scheme was running ahead of itself and stood to complicate the lives of both Cullen and the Committee, he divulged its contents only to his English friends, whose advice he sought (and whose interest he hoped to awaken).

In July 1852 Newman had explained to Cullen that, since the vice-rector needed to be someone who saw things from the same point of view as the rector, and since Newman could think of no-one suitable at the time, it was better not to appoint. But two months later—without any warning—Cullen appointed James Taylor as vice-rector.[68] In the event, Taylor, a former president of Carlow College, acted as the general secretary of the University Committee and left before the University got going. Another of Cullen's abrupt actions occurred in February 1853, when he saw to it that the University Committee chose 86 St Stephen's Green as the site for the University and purchased it for the grand sum of £3500. Besides his surprise at not being consulted, Newman was forced to rethink his plans, because until then he had assumed that the location would be on the outskirts of Dublin, 'out of the glare of the town'.[69] Like everyone else involved in the university project, Newman was wary about a city location because of the dangers it presented to student life; having a clear perception of the difficulties of a university situated in a capital, he now had to consider how to meet them. He wanted to provide for the students' legitimate enjoyment of the recreations of the town; but because of the proximity to theatres he intended to find a way of meeting the difficulty rather than impose a blanket prohibition on the students, and to this end he considered licensing a theatre for them.[70]

Stirred into action by the purchase of 86 St Stephen's Green, Newman jotted down his thoughts in a memorandum that shows how his mind was getting to grips with practicalities and turning over ideas for the day-to-day working of the University. This document is valuable both for what came to fruition in Newman's time and for what was abandoned, and illustrates the way Newman went about turning grand ideals into a workable scheme. Among the 'objects to be kept in view' in devising a plan for the University, Newman noted the need to unite 'indulgent or at least gentle discipline with moral and religious results' in a way which would 'combine authority with influence'. This meant that the plan should 'so consult for the natural course of the ideas, purposes, needs, pursuits and acts of the youthful mind, i.e. its habits and ways, as to lead it to concur and co-operate with the principles and precepts of education which wisdom and experience [...] lay down'.[71] A separate object concerned providing a stimulus for study, other than the incentive of professional gain, since at the outset the university would be unable to award degrees. As a new institution, it needed to have a good number of prizes in order to attract students, as well as encourage academic endeavour.

'The University being for the sake of its students, as its final end',[72] Newman noted down nearly two dozen matters that needed to be resolved, all of which related to their studies and daily life. He divided the students into two categories, interns and externs, with the intention of excluding the externs from scholarships, posts, and even (when they became available) degrees, except during the initial provisional phase. Interns would live in a house presided over by a married tutor, if they were fifteen years of age or under, or by a dean with a tutor or tutors, if above. When of age, students would transfer from a tutor's to a dean's house, and might also change their tutor; Newman anticipated that the tutors' houses would be dearer than the deans' houses, but in both cases they would contain a maximum of twenty students. (This is the only reference that Newman makes to students as young as fifteen; in all other documents the youngest age he considers is sixteen, the age at which he himself entered Oxford.[73]) Though the deans' houses would vary in comfort (and expense), thereby catering for the different classes of student, the discipline would be the same in all. Each house was to have a small chapel where students were to attend Mass every morning, night prayers, and evening benediction on Sundays, Thursdays, and major feast days. Students were to attend lectures every day except Sundays, Thursdays and feast days, and to dine at home every day but Thursday. Other than those living at home (the care of whom would require separate consideration), externs were to spend their day under a dean and tutor, and to attend Mass at the dean's chapel every morning, without being considered a member of a house.

As in the plan Newman had devised at Oriel, tutors were to select the lectures for their students, prepare them for these lectures, question them about their content afterwards, and prepare them for the university exams. To this end, professors were to provide abstracts of their lectures for the benefit of tutors and students. Lectures were to last one hour, to take place between 9 am and 2 pm, and would start with a verse from the *Gloria* or the *Veni Creator*. They were to be supplemented by evening lectures on 'lighter' subjects such as poetry, the fine arts, natural history, chemistry, physics and music. Newman envisaged that the deans would be middle-aged men, while the tutors would be young men who had lately taken their degrees, just like the private tutors at Oxford, and be licensed to combine the roles of public and private tutor; but rather than having their students assigned to them, it might be better (Newman thought) to allow the student to choose his tutor. One of the tutor's tasks was to ensure that students did not attend lectures unless they had demonstrated that they had an elementary knowledge of the subject concerned, not only so that they were able to benefit, but also that they did not slow down the pace of the lecture. As for exams, Newman thought they should be frequent—so as to avoid idleness—and partly oral, partly written.

It is evident from his notes that Newman toyed with the idea of each student going on a retreat for one or two days at the beginning of each academic year, and then to Confession and Communion: 'This too will be the proof that the student is a Catholic'. He also envisaged the establishment of student confraternities, each with its own altar, as a means of fostering piety. Other matters addressed include making provision for a library; a museum, whose keepers would be professors of the physical science department; an exhibition room for paintings and sculptures, under the professor of fine arts; a debating society; a proper cricket ground; and facilities for recreations as diverse as rowing and billiards. Excerpts copied out of the 1852 *Report* by the Oxford University commissioners show that the expenses of a student who lived 'sparingly and never mixed in society' amounted to £64 over twenty-six weeks, not including groceries, wine, books, travel and clothes (which would vary according to their social background). Interestingly, when considering the catering arrangements, Newman thought of splitting up the tables, as in a restaurant, rather than having them form one long table as in an Oxbridge dining hall, so that students could invite their friends to breakfast or dinner. But he knew that, no matter what the arrangements were, the *genius loci* (or 'spirit of the place') would ultimately depend 'mainly on the intercourse of students with each other'.[74]

One of the main objectives of the Royal Commission investigating Oxford during the period 1850–52 was to find ways in which the University could be opened up to the larger public by reducing unnecessary expenses. To this end, the commissioners examined the students' living expenses and academic fees (including private tuition), as well as costs arising from their own extravagance —which they exaggerated in their report—and they recorded the comment that 'A parent who paid less than £600 for his son's degree had reason to congratulate himself.'[75] Newman studied the *Report* carefully, as it provided him with a wonderful opportunity to update himself on the state of Oxford and acquaint himself with the dons' most recent suggestions for reform; and he pored over the voluminous response it produced, the *Report and evidence upon the recommendations of Her Majesty's commissioners for inquiring into the state of the University of Oxford, presented to the Board of Heads of Houses and Proctors* (1853). Compiled by Oxford academics, this document examined the commissioners' four suggestions for the extension of the University by means of a greater variety of living arrangements,[76] and strongly urged against any attempt to annul the obligation for students to belong to a college.

Summoned at last

Finally, in October 1853 Newman was summoned to Ireland by the University Committee, 'at his earliest convenience, to assume his functions as rector and to take such measures as may be necessary for the opening of the university'.[77] On 3 November 1853, after delivering an address in Liverpool, he paid an overnight visit to Dublin where he met the University Committee at 86 St Stephen's Green. In a crucial meeting with Cullen he conceded that no permanent appointments to professorships would be made, but gained the key point of having the nomination of the tutors. Right away he wrote to his four first choices, as well as to three others to act as reserves. He also began working on the format of the projected *Catholic University Gazette*, which he hoped to launch in January 1854. For 'extraordinary professors', men of international fame whom he hoped would give occasional lectures so as to attract students even from abroad, he began negotiations to engage Orestes Brownson and Ignaz von Döllinger. The former was a famous North American convert, pugnacious owner-editor of the controversial *Brownson's Review*, which criticised the North American bishops (and Newman, too); the latter was a well-known professor of church history at the University of Munich (later excommunicated for his liberal theology).

While Newman was pleased with the Committee's (private) decision to give him the go-ahead, he foresaw that there would be difficulties in dealing with the highest ecclesiastical authorities while only being a priest: 'both in liberty of speech and opportunity of access to such dignitaries, he was within very restricted limits'.[78] Aware of this handicap, Cullen had planned to give him an outward sign of recognition by asking the bishops to make Newman a vicar-general to each of them (following the precedent of the rector of Louvain), but the poor relations between the bishops now ruled that out.

Since there was no official act inviting him to Dublin, Newman asked Cullen to admit him to his duties publicly so as to provide a warrant for his activity. This was important not just for himself but for the university, since a lack of public recognition could entail a misconception of what a university was—a public body which needed a public act to set it up—and suggest instead that the goal was a private college. Newman even thought of offering to resign as a way of forcing the bishops to act, since he was unwilling to wait another year or two in order to begin; besides, he had all but engaged tutors and so needed approval to confirm the appointments. An unexpected boost occurred in late January 1854 when Cardinal Wiseman told him that he could make use of the information that he would soon be made a titular bishop. Once the news got out, Newman became the recipient of congratulations and gifts. But over the following months all mention of the intended bishopric was dropped by those in the know, and Newman was left to infer a change of mind from their silence and finally to conclude that the bishopric had been indefinitely shelved.[79]

But before this evaporation of his expectations, Newman had returned to Ireland and embarked on a tour of the country to visit the bishops and to make enquiries about the state of the colleges and schools, as well as to advertise the projected university. The tour began on 18 February but, after less than a month and with only six bishops seen, the worst winter in decades caused it to be cut short. Newman encountered largely negative reactions to the prospect of a Catholic university from the clergy he met on the tour; though he was greeted everywhere with welcoming hospitality, he could not but notice a general expectation of failure about the enterprise.[80] In Dublin, John Curtis, the Provincial of the Irish Jesuits, told him that the class of students required for a university did not exist in Ireland; his advice was to go to Cullen and 'say, "Don't attempt the University—give up the idea" '.[81] As for the laity, the few willing to consider the university project at all were decidedly gloomy about it. Peers such as the Earl of Fingall, the Earl of Kenmare and Viscount Castlerosse refused even to give their names as honorary members (i.e. patrons) of the Catholic University, while the Dublin lawyers were lukewarm at best and justified their position by claiming consistency with the bishops' previous policy of toleration of mixed education in the national schools negotiations of the 1840s. The two members of the University Committee who (unofficially) represented the wealthier landed gentry, Michael Errington and James More O'Ferrall, were despondent about the University's prospects. The latter showed Newman a letter from his brother Richard, a politician and colonial administrator, which prophesied that the 'Protestant party will endeavour to raise a cry in which many Catholics are disposed to join, that the new University is got up for the purpose of placing Catholic education entirely in the hands of the Clergy and for the exclusion of the Laity from all interference'.[82]

Undeterred by the pessimism and faintheartedness he found everywhere, Newman soldiered on, but he was becoming ever more aware that the Irish situation was a far cry from what had existed at

Louvain.[83] What they needed at Dublin, he felt, was an 'external manifestation' in the form of lecturers and professors, and, at the same time, 'the beginning of an inward and real *formation*'. The latter required just 'a few persons who thoroughly understand each other, and whom I entirely know; who can quickly and without show be bringing into shape the students who come to us'. The dedication of these few would compensate for the prevailing apathy. 'We must feel our way—and get over a mass of prejudice and opposition. No rule can do this—but the zeal, energy and prudence of the individuals employed in the work.'[84]

On the day Newman returned to England the long-awaited Brief of Pius IX was issued. Previous papal Briefs had confirmed the decrees of the Synod of Thurles and formally approved the foundation of the Catholic University (23 March 1852), and had congratulated the bishops on their decision and urged immediate action (25 March 1852). The Brief of 20 March 1854 formally appointed Newman as rector and ordered the Irish bishops to meet in synod within three months, under the presidency of Archbishop Cullen, to decide on the measures necessary for the immediate opening of the University. The Brief contained two guiding principles for the foundation: it stressed that the Catholic religion should be 'the soul of the whole educational system'; and it urged that the teaching staff should not only give the students good example by their lives, but should 'make it their earnest endeavour to mould the characters of their pupils to piety, good conduct and all the virtues', as well as giving secular instruction in conformity with the Church's teaching.[85]

Rather than spurring Newman on in his task, the Brief forced him to think carefully about whether the line he had adopted in his Dublin lectures might be inconsistent with the two principles enunciated in the papal pronouncement, and therefore whether his ideas were at odds with those of the Holy See. He had, after all, argued that in essence a university was concerned with imparting a liberal education and that its aim was not, strictly speaking, a directly moral one. After a good deal of reflection he came to the conclusion that the apparent disparities between the papal Brief and his lectures came about partly because of the different approaches taken (on account of their different concerns) and partly because of language used (due to their different cultural backgrounds), and hence that they were not in fact inconsistent. Indeed, regarding the first question Newman had stated in his final lecture that,

> it is no sufficient security for the Catholicity of a University, even that the whole of Catholic theology should be professed in it, unless the Church breathes her pure and unearthly spirit into it, and fashions and moulds its organization, and watches over its teaching, and knits together its pupils, and superintends its action.[86]

On the second question, about moral formation and training at a Catholic university, the apparent discrepancy can be resolved by observing that in the lectures Newman was treating of a faith-based university in the abstract, while the Pope was dealing with a Catholic university in practice. Though Newman's metaphysical distinction separated liberal knowledge from moral formation, this did not imply that the university's essential task of securing mental culture precluded the overall end of education including moral formation and training. Arguing from history, Newman contended in the Preface to the *Idea* that it was subsidiary bodies within the university, such as colleges and halls, that were the chief promoters of morality.[87]

A more minor observation which unsettled Newman's mind concerned the variations in nomenclature for the new institution, for in the Brief and the accompanying letter to Cullen the term *universitas* (used eight times) is occasionally substituted by the terms *lyceum* (three times) and *gymnasium* (twice)—though Newman seems to have overlooked the implied equivalence in the phrase *Lycaeum seu Universitas*. He was anxious that the phrasing might have the effect of limiting or modifying his idea of a university, a fear derived in part from considering the effect the text might have on Irish ecclesiastics in encouraging them to think in terms of a college.

Newman received a copy of the Brief on 15 April and not long afterwards set off for Dublin, where he remained until the bishops had finished their synod. Prior to the meeting, he submitted to the bishops his blueprint for the university in a second major memorandum.[88] The memorandum describes the structure of the academic course, which was to extend over seven years, in three stages, each complete in itself and entitling the successful candidate to a qualification. Those entering the university, typically (for the Irish) at the age of 16, became 'students' and began two years of study, covering such subjects as classics, mathematics, logic and history, at the end of which they sat an exam to become a 'scholar'. Most students would finish their liberal studies at this stage, and many might enter into business or else a professional school such as law or medicine. Those who stayed on for a further two years for the degree of 'bachelor' would study courses in subjects such as modern history, economics and metaphysics. After this, only those would continue who aimed at the degree of masters in arts or science, or a doctorate in theology, law or medicine, each of which meant another three years. This outline underwent minor modification over the following months, but essentially remained unchanged during Newman's time in Dublin. The course content had a remarkably modern feel for its time, and showed that Newman was not wedded to the classics-based curriculum of Oxford; it is however striking to see how closely it followed the medieval liberal arts course—probably not by accident, given Newman's intimate knowledge of the medieval university.

The synod began on 18 May and lasted for several days, after which the bishops' deliberations were published as decrees. These may be summarised briefly as follows: a university was to be established over which the bishops would exercise the *supremum ius*; its administration, according to statutes approved by the hierarchy, would be entrusted to a rector; the rector was to have powers to undertake measures for the well-being and progress of the university; the rector was to submit to the bishops an annual report on the condition of the university; the rector was empowered to propose the professors, but their appointment was to lie with the bishops; the rector had the right to set up houses of residence, to appoint deans to take charge of them, and to lay down the regulations for their government; the bishops were to proceed immediately to determine the rules for the administration of the university; there was to be an annual collection in Ireland for the university; professors and students were urged to adhere strongly to the Catholic faith.[89] The decrees reserved considerable powers to the hierarchy, but no more than at Louvain.

Overall the decrees closely matched Newman's memorandum of April 1854, and only on one point was he disappointed: that he was not given the appointment of the vice-rector. He also noted that they made no reference to a *lyceum* or *gymnasium*, only to a *universitas* (and, for variety, an *academia*). After modifications, the decrees were sanctioned by Propaganda Fide and confirmed by the Pope. Rome also expressed its pleasure that the university should be placed under the patronage of the Blessed Virgin, under the title *Sedes Sapientiae*.[90]

Newman returned to England after the episcopal synod, then crossed over to Dublin just over a week later, on 3 June, for his installation as rector. Two days earlier he announced in the first number of the *Catholic University Gazette*[91] that the University would open later that year on 3 November. There were barely five months to prepare for this and all he had to boast of was one empty building. His inauguration as rector ushered in a period of frantic activity in which he penned up to twenty letters a day. These letters are another source for filling out the vision he held, as are the historical articles he wrote in the *Gazette*; together they help to round out the picture of the university presented in the Dublin lectures.

Notes

[1]   Dublin Castle was the administrative seat of the British government in Ireland.

[2]   A university had been founded at Louvain in 1425 and it flourished until the French Revolutionary Wars, which resulted in the Netherlands coming under French rule and the university being suppressed. It was reopened as a state university in 1816, but in 1830 Belgium seceded from the Netherlands and in 1834 the Belgian bishops founded a Catholic university in Mechlin; the following year it moved to Louvain, where the state university had been closed, and it was renamed the Catholic University of Louvain. The new university took over the buildings of the ancient one. There had been a strong Irish connection with the old Louvain and during the sixteenth, seventeenth and eighteenth centuries Ireland supplied the university with around 1200 students, most of whom belonged to one of the four Irish colleges at Louvain, three religious and one secular.

[3]   The Committee comprised the four archbishops and one other bishop from the four provinces, each of whom had the right to co-opt one priest and one layman.

[4]   The nationwide collection in March 1851 brought in £22,840. That same year £3100 was collected in England and £4735 in the United States. John Coolahan has pointed out that 'unlike England there was no tradition among the Irish landowning classes of public service towards education' (*Irish education: its history and structure* (Dublin, 1981), pp. 19–20).

[5]   Minute Book of the Catholic University Committee, 26 June 1851, UCDA, CU1.

6   Initially Cullen thought that, as a priest should be rector, 'we hope that the vice Rector will be one of the University of Oxford converts and a layman' (Cullen to Kirby, 18 March 1851, quoted in E. Larkin, *The making of the Roman Catholic Church in Ireland, 1850–1860* (Chapel Hill, 1980), p. 121); then he reasoned that 'If Dr Newman could be persuaded to come, he would at once give a name and fame to the good work' (Cullen to Kirby, 16 April 1851, quoted in C. Barr, *Paul Cullen, John Henry Newman, and the Catholic University of Ireland, 1845–1865* (Leominster, 2003), p. 64).

7   Cullen to Newman, 15 April 1851, *LD*, vol. xiv, p. 257n.

8   'Memorandum on the subjects discussed at a meeting of several gentlemen with the Primate relating to the establishment of a Catholic University in Ireland', 13 July 1851 [misdated 1852], DDA, Cullen Papers, 45/3/6. Despite the advantage of a Dublin location for subjects like law and medicine, Hope, Manning and O'Ferrall were of the opinion that a location such as Thurles would be better 'to avoid the corrupting influence of a large town'; they also thought that the collegiate system should be adopted. James More O'Ferrall was one of the members of the University Committee.

9   Newman to Cullen, 23 July 1851, *LD*, vol. xiv, p. 316.

10   A list of thirty-two questions in Newman's 'Memorandum on the University of Louvain', [1851] (*LD*, vol. xxxii, pp. 49–50) deals with, *inter alia*, the living arrangements and religious customs. 'Are they collected in *lodging houses*, or are they their own master? What recreations are provided for students? Are there University walks or pleasure grounds, places for games etc.? Have the students ever a *retreat* by obligation, e.g. at the beginning of the year? To what religious duties or observances are they invited? Do they perform with their auditors any religious act whatever before commencing or at ending the Lecture—e.g. saying "In Nomine etc" or Hail Mary?'

11   Newman obtained pamphlets and reports from Louvain, and had questions answered about the arrangements there: the power of rector, whether the system was provisional, the proportion of lay students, and whether the professors were laymen. The notes he took between August and October 1851 are preserved in the 'Louvain University working and routine file' (BOA, C.6.3).

12   Mgr de Ram was the rector of Louvain from its re-foundation in 1834 until his death in 1865; he was a successful administrator who managed to combine his office with his own academic research as an historian. In April 1853 Newman sent his fellow Oratorian Ambrose St John to Louvain to meet de Ram and his assistants so as to learn about the university there.

For the 'Additional questions' that St John was to ask about the functioning of the university church, see *LD*, vol. xv, p. 357n.

13   'Report on the Organization of the Catholic University of Ireland', October 1851, *MC*, p. 77.

14   'Report on the Organization of the Catholic University of Ireland', October 1851, *MC*, p. 80.

15   *Idea of a university*, p. 142.

16   Hope to Newman, 24 July 1851, quoted in *AW*, p. 281.

17   Newman to Cullen, 11 October 1851 (via Hope), *LD*, vol. xiv, pp. 382–3.

18   Hope to Cullen, 13 October 1851, DDA, Cullen Papers.

19   Newman to Cullen, 14 October 1851, *LD*, vol. xiv, p. 389. From the outset, the three Queen's Colleges each offered forty-five junior scholarships worth £30 p.a., and there was the promise of senior ones worth £50 p.a. to follow. During the period 1851–58 the average annual number of matriculations between them was 134.

20   'Report on the Organization of the Catholic University of Ireland', October 1851, *MC*, pp. 82–3.

21   Newman develops his thinking on lectures and how to profit from them in 'Discipline of Mind', a public lecture he delivered in November 1858 (*Idea of a university*, pp. 480–504).

22   'Report on the Organization of the Catholic University of Ireland', October 1851, *MC*, pp. 84–5. In one of his Oxford University sermons Newman voiced one of the key ideas shared by the three Tractarian tutors at Oriel: that truth is preserved and communicated 'not by books, not by argument, nor by temporal power, but by the personal influence of such men [...] who are at once the teachers and patterns of it'. He spoke of 'God's noiseless work', that is, of the effect of unconscious holiness on others ('Personal influence, the means of propagating the truth', sermon preached on 22 January 1832, *Fifteen sermons preached before the University of Oxford* (London, 1871), pp. 91–2, 96). This sermon is considered by some scholars to mark the beginning of the Oxford Movement (P. Nockles, 'A house divided: Oriel in the era of the Oxford Movement, 1833–1860', *Oriel College: a history*, ed. J. Catto, (Oxford, 2013), p. 328).

23   Several Oxford tutors thought along the same lines as Newman and articulated their views to the commissioners investigating Oxford. A. H. Clough of Oriel spoke convincingly of the deficiencies of the professorial system and the need of the tutorial, especially for the discipline of the student's mind. Lectures lead to students catching the flame of intellectual ardour, he maintained, but

the effects are transient; eager rather than steady studies result. 'For chastening and correcting, for sobering and undeceiving, the undersoil cultivation which brings more than the mere spontaneous growth, some closer than Professorial contact is needed; needed by the clever, who go beyond, as much by the dull who fall behind.' Benjamin Jowett of Balliol proposed that by a division of labour—Latin and Greek taught by the tutor, ethics and logic by the professor—they would end up 'acting in connexion with each other' (*Royal Commission Oxford* (1852), pp. 99, 214).

[24] Newman to Cullen, 16 November 1851, *LD*, vol. xiv, p. 426.

[25] 'My College was St Mary's, and my Church; and when I went to Littlemore, there, by my own previous disposition, our Blessed Lady was waiting for me. Nor did she do nothing for me in that low habitation' (Newman to H. Wilberforce, 12 January 1848, *LD*, vol. xii, pp. 153–4).

[26] 'The theory of developments in religious doctrine', *Fifteen sermons*, p. 313.

[27] *CUG* 2 (8 June 1854); 'What is a university?', *HS*, vol. iii, p. 16.

[28] The fifth lecture was omitted in the abridged 1859 edition of the *Discourses*, which involved over 800 textual changes, and from the *Idea of a university*, which retained most of these alterations to the text. Further editions of the *Idea* appeared, concluding with the ninth edition of 1889, a year before Newman's death. For an authoritative introduction to and commentary on the *Idea*, see Ian Ker's critical edition (1976). Unless otherwise stated, the citations from the *Idea* come from the first edition of 1873.

[29] Ornsby to Newman, 16 April 1852, quoted in *NU*, p. 145. As early as 1848 Archbishop MacHale had remarked that he believed the proposed university would fail, precisely because 'Our high Catholics are rotten to the heart's core, and our middle Catholics are fast corrupting in the same manner, by love of self and place' (quoted in W. E. Stockley, *Newman, Education and Ireland* (London, [1933]), pp. 101–2).

[30] *Discourses on the scope and nature of university education* (Dublin, 1852), p. 152.

[31] *Idea of a university*, pp. 45, 134.

[32] *Idea of a university*, p. 134.

[33] *Idea of a university*, p. 51. Angelo Bottone explores this elusive concept at length in *The philosophical habit of mind: rhetoric and person in John Henry Newman's Dublin writings* (Bucharest, 2010).

[34] *Idea of a university*, pp. 166–7.

[35] First draft of an Introduction to Discourse VI, 16 July 1852, sent to J. B. Dalgairns on 21 July 1852, *LD*, vol. xv, pp. 131–2. In the article 'Architec-

tural description of the University Church', the author—either Newman or Ornsby—asserts that 'the University is, we may again repeat, a secular institution, yet partaking of a religious character' (*CUG* 51 (3 April 1856), p. 60).

36   Second draft of an Introduction to Discourse VI, sent to J. B. Dalgairns on 23 July 1852, *LD*, vol. xv, p. 134. The Introduction was published with Discourse VI on 18 August 1852, but was removed when the *Discourses* were published in a single volume on 2 February 1853.

37   Preface, *Idea of a university*, p. ix. The fact that Newman used exactly the same words in his university sketch 'Professors and tutors' (*HS*, vol. iii, p. 183) demonstrates his awareness of their importance.

38   Preface, *Idea of a university*, p. xii.

39   Preface, *Idea of a university*, p. xi.

40   Preface, *Idea of a university*, p. xii. Newman generally uses the word 'science' to mean 'academic discipline' rather than its restricted, modern sense.

41   We should bear in mind that Newman's idea of knowledge and intellectual culture is not at all the same as Matthew Arnold's. When Newman speaks of 'intellectual culture' he means 'the culture of the intellect', that by which the intellect is 'generally exercised in order to its perfect state' (*Idea of a university*, p. 165). By contrast Matthew Arnold—who gave the word 'culture' its modern sense—sees it as 'a pursuit of our total perfection by means of getting to know [...] the best which has been thought and said in the world' (*Culture and anarchy: an essay in political and social criticism* (London, 1869), p. xviii). For Newman, therefore, a liberal education is about learning how to think, whereas for Arnold it is something similar to a 'great books' programme. Having rejected religion as the highest expression of civilised values, Arnold had high hopes that culture could act in its stead as a transformative influence on industrial civilisation, while Newman rejected (and ridiculed) the idea that learning could by itself redeem a fallen world. See also I. Ker's *The achievement of John Henry Newman* (London, 1990), p. 9; 'Newman's *Idea of a university*. A guide for the contemporary University?', *The idea of a university*, ed. D. Smith & A. K. Langslow (London, 1999), pp. 21–2.

42   *Idea of a university*, pp. 122–3.

43   This tendency manifested itself in an extreme form in the writings of the French priest Jean Gaume, whose *Le Ver rongeur des société modernes, ou Paganisme dans l'éducation* (1851) ignited a lively controversy in France; it appeared in English as *Paganism in education* (1852). Gaume argued that

the revival of interest in pagan antiquity during the Renaissance had paved the way for the Revolution and other social ills; he wanted pagan authors (who had been taught in the Catholic colleges for three centuries) largely excluded from the curriculum and replaced by Christian ones. The Gaume controversy had just begun when Newman started his Dublin lectures, and he spoke out clearly against the new theory: while acknowledging the opinable nature of the question, he felt that 'the Church's true policy is not to aim at the exclusion of Literature from Secular Schools, but at her own admission into them. […] She fears no knowledge, but she purifies all; she represses no element of our nature, but cultivates the whole.' (*Idea of a university*, pp. 233–4).

44   *Idea of a university*, p. 120.

45   *Idea of a university*, pp. 158, 159.

46   *Idea of a university*, p. 154.

47   *Idea of a university*, pp. 29, 32.

48   'The Tamworth reading room', *Discussions and arguments* (London, 1872), pp. 255, 258, 268.

49   'The Tamworth reading room', *Discussions and arguments*, pp. 304, 274–5.

50   *Idea of a university*, p. 70.

51   'The Tamworth reading room', *Discussions and arguments*, p. 266. This passage is almost certainly inspired by Edward Copleston, an important influence on Newman for a number of his educational ideas: Copleston had written, '*things made easy* appear to me to defeat the end of education' (Copleston to J. Penrose, [1810], quoted in Copleston, *Memoir of Edward Copleston*, p. 38).

52   *Idea of a university*, p. 177.

53   *Idea of a university*, p. 164.

54   *Idea of a university*, p. 123.

55   *Idea of a university*, pp. xiv, xvi.

56   *Idea of a university*, pp. xvi–xviii.

57   *Idea of a university*, p. 178. This passage is quoted more extensively in Appendix I. Newman's point is illustrated succinctly by the former Prime Minister Harold Macmillan, who recalled a classics lecturer at Oxford who began his second-year lecture course by reminding them, that, apart from the few who would become teachers or dons, 'nothing that you will learn in the course of your studies will be of the slightest use to you in after life—save only this—that if you work hard and intelligently you should be

able to detect *when a man is talking rot*, and that, in my view is the main, if not the sole purpose of education' ('Oxford Remembered', *The Times*, 18 October 1975).

[58] *Idea of a university*, p. 114.

[59] See Appendix II for this well-known description of the gentleman. Philip Mason's *The English gentleman: the rise and fall of an ideal* (London, 1982) gives a good description of Newman's gentleman.

[60] *Idea of a university*, p. 120.

[61] *Idea of a university*, pp. 146–7.

[62] At the first meeting of the Catholic University Committee in October 1851 MacHale objected to the eight bishops on it being in a minority, and argued that responsibility for the University should be vested in the bishops as a body. After opposing Cullen's policy at the committee's third meeting, in January 1852, MacHale wrote to explain his opposition, arguing that the committee was 'only provisionally established and for preparatory arrangements'. When he refused to sign the petition to the Pope asking for a Brief to authorise the erection of the Catholic University, Cullen sent the petition to Rome without his signature (Larkin, *The making of the Roman Catholic Church*, pp. 124, 130–4).

[63] During the years 1852–56 a struggle was going on between the two archbishops, Cullen and MacHale. At the outset, MacHale was able to count on the support of nine of the twenty-eight bishops, and Cullen on seven. By 1856 Cullen had gained dominance, but it came at a cost to his reputation and health (Larkin, *The making of the Roman Catholic Church*, pp. xvi, 150).

[64] Newman to Allies, 19 April 1852, *LD*, vol. xv, p. 72.

[65] Memorandum, 25 November 1870, *AW*, p. 327.

[66] The Royal Commission investigating Trinity College Dublin recommended that the obligation for Fellows to take orders be abolished, but in the event the measure was diluted and the number of lay fellowships was merely increased from three to five (R. B. McDowell & D. A. Webb, *Trinity College Dublin 1592–1952: an academic history* (Cambridge, 1952), p. 217). Likewise, the proportion of lay fellowships was slightly increased at Oxford.

[67] Cooper to Newman, 10 October 1852, quoted in *AW*, p. 288.

[68] Years later Newman commented: 'It is plain from what took place in 1852 etc that Dr Cullen's idea of a Vice Rector from the first was, not as an official who would represent me but one who would represent the Archbishop against me, as a regulator of my movements' (*LD*, vol. xviii, p. 221n). See also the comment in his memorandum, 25 November 1870, *AW*, p. 294.

69 *MC*, p. xx.
70 There was a widespread view at the time that the theatre was liable to corrupt youth. Undergraduate theatricals, which had been banned at Oxford in the seventeenth century, revived in the 1860s, but they took place outside the city until the ban was lifted in the 1880s. The advent of the railway threatened to bring the metropolis and its attractions within reach of Oxford students, and before it opened in 1844 the University succeeded in winning substantial rights of search and enquiry. On account of its location in Dublin and its largely non-residential student population, Trinity had long been unable to restrict student access to the theatre.
71 'Memorandum relating to the Catholic University', 19 February 1853, BOA, A.3.8.
72 'Memorandum relating to the Catholic University', 19 February 1853, BOA, A.3.8.
73 At the time, students in Scotland began their university studies at fifteen or sixteen; the University of London similarly fixed its minimum age for entry at fifteen when it opened in 1828.
74 'Memorandum relating to the Catholic University', 19 February 1853, BOA, A.3.8.
75 *Royal Commission Oxford* (1852), p. 33. The commissioners estimated that the cost of a degree for a frugal student was £370 (*ibid.*, p. 33).
76 The four new forms of residence proposed were: unattached lodgings, affiliated halls, independent halls and private halls.
77 Minute Book of the Catholic University Committee, 21 October 1853, UCDA, CU1.
78 *MC*, p. xli.
79 At the time everyone—the Pope included—thought the idea to be a good one, as it would facilitate Newman's dealings with the Irish bishops; but on Cullen's recommendation the prospect was at first postponed, until the University was started, then effectively dropped by the summer of 1855 (though most people did not realise this until later). Cullen's argument for the postponement was that the time was not right and that it might cause opposition.
80 The Bishop of Limerick, John Ryan, an honest bluff man, allowed Newman to enter his name on the University books on the firm understanding that he should not 'be supposed to prophecy any thing but failure' (Memorandum, 25 November 1870, *AW*, p. 324).
81 Curtis told Newman that the middle class were too poor, the gentleman

class sent their sons to Trinity to study law, and the upper class sent their sons to England or the Continent (University journal, 8 February 1854, BOA, A34.2; reproduced in *AW*, p. 323).

[82]   R. M. O'Ferrall to J. M. O'Ferrall, 5 May 1854, *LD*, vol. xvi, p. 128n.

[83]   Though Newman had made a careful study of Louvain, it is unclear whether the Irish bishops knew much about the Catholic University there; Irish students had not studied there for over sixty years and Louvain now was remote from Irish circumstances. Although it had been reconstituted, Louvain had an ancient tradition and buildings ready to occupy when it was re-established. While it was under the authority of the Belgian bishops, all its exams (except for those in theology) were tied into the State's university system, which meant that students sat state exams as well as university exams and that the university could confer degrees. In 1845 about one third of Belgian students attended Louvain; the rest attended one of the other three universities, two of which were state universities.

[84]   Newman to Wiseman, 23 January 1854, *LD*, vol. xv, pp. 27–8.

[85]   Brief to the archbishops and bishops of Ireland, 20 March 1854, *MC*, p. lxxxi (trans. *NU*, p. 273).

[86]   *Idea of a university*, p. 216. The consistency of his approach with the Church's traditional teaching on the essential unity of religious and secular knowledge was brought out much more clearly in 'The Tamworth Reading Room'. There Newman states: 'Where Revealed Truth has given the aim and direction to Knowledge, Knowledge of all kinds will minister to Revealed Truth' (*Discussions and arguments*, p. 274).

[87]   Arguing first in a strictly philosophical sense, then on the basis of historical fact, Newman wrote: '*I do not think that a University has to do with morals.* [...] Nor do I think that the Church on the whole employs a University for morals, (except as *teaching* them, but *that* comes under faith) but I think she uses small bodies in the Universities, Colleges and Halls, etc etc. as the preservative of *morals*, more naturally. In short, as a Bishop's jurisdiction *foro exteriore* is to a priest's over his penitent in *foro interiore*, in an analogous way is the University to the College. [...] The University takes care of faith in fullest sense—the College of morals' (Newman to Moriarty, 23 July 1852, *LD*, vol. xv, pp. 136–7).

[88]   The substance of this memorandum, dated 29 April 1854, can be found in *MC*, pp. 93–100.

[89]   *Ex decretis conventûs episcoporum Hiberniae*, 18 May 1854, *MC*, pp. 88–91. For a summary of the thirteen decrees, see *NU*, pp. 296–7.

90   Newman arranged for a statue of the Blessed Virgin to be displayed in
     University House, with the invocation 'Sedes Sapientiae, ora pro nobis' on
     its pedestal; the statue was still in place in 1901 (*St Stephen's. A record of
     university life* 1 (1 June 1901, p. 4)). The seal of the Catholic University, as
     reproduced in the commemorative pamphlet *Catholic University of Ireland.
     Centenary celebrations. Catalogue of the exhibition* (Dublin: [1954]), shows
     an image of the Blessed Virgin standing and holding an open book,
     surrounded by the legend *Sedes Sapientiae, ora pro nobis*. It bears some
     resemblance to the seal of the Catholic University of Louvain, which is
     based on a fifteenth-century wooden carving from the nearby church of St
     Peter's; this *sedes sapientiae* image shows the Virgin enthroned with the
     Child sitting in her lap.
91   Newman prefaced his articles in the *Gazette* with the words 'Sedes Sapien-
     tiae, ora pro nobis'.

3 SEARCHING FOR AN EDUCATIONAL *VIA MEDIA*

THE SUMMONS TO Ireland in October 1853 marked the moment when Newman could finally begin to set in motion the scheme he had been nurturing since July 1851, when he had been offered the rectorship. His vision for the Catholic University was well defined from the first moment and was only modified during the foundational period in order to meet the needs and the constraints—financial and other—of the situation. But what, precisely, was Newman's vision? It is important for us to examine it in more detail and to compare it with other contemporary conceptions of the university; and also to see how he intended to implement his ideas in practice. Fortunately Newman outlined both his vision and his plans in a handful of documents which he composed in the foundational years, including several written shortly after the University opened.

It is worth emphasizing that Newman did not give the Irish bishops the university they *wanted*, but the university he thought they *needed*;[1] that is to say, he believed he had been entrusted with the mission of setting up not just a new university but a new *kind* of university, and this was why he needed to be given a free hand for the task. By a happy coincidence, the new foundation brought together an original mind and a rare educational opportunity. When we consider Newman's scheme within the mid-nineteenth century world of higher education, it becomes easier to identify the overall purpose of the institution he helped to establish, and at the same time to assess his achievement. On account of the novelty of the Catholic University, as well as the mind behind it, it may be said that the arguments and explanations that Newman gave to justify his choices form part of the foundational process, and that these are no less important for assessing the institution's worth than the structures he put in place.

The university landscape at the time was in a state of change, with advocates for several competing versions of higher education. Some universities educated principally for the professions; others emphasised the advance of knowledge and research; and there were a few—like Oxford and Cambridge—which aimed to form well-rounded individuals for leadership in Church and State. There were rival teaching methods, too, in the lecture, the tutorial and the seminar, the selection of which depended on the overall purpose embraced by the institution. It is in this context that we can understand the significance of Newman's decision to imitate the collegiate system of Oxford, grafting it onto the university structure of Louvain, and in that way to 'combine the distinctive features and strengths of both'.[2] His choice had nothing to do with a conjectured 'emotional attachment' to Oxford; nor can it be argued that he lacked knowledge of other university systems. Rather, both his choice of university system and the way he implemented it are illustrative of his pastoral vision of education. He went to great lengths to explain his idea and, in order to win over the general public to his way of thinking, wrote a series of articles—or, as he called them, 'sketches'—on the history of the university. Published together under various titles, these 'university sketches' contain an extended argument for the collegiate system and the tutorial method of teaching. This collection is little known today, largely because Newman had to write the sketches hastily and had no time for polishing them up. But in our age, when the mission of forming the individual has been all but squeezed out of the modern university, these writings of Newman help to fill out the vision he describes so elegantly in the *Idea* and are as potent a challenge to those who work in education now as they were in his time.

The short memorandum that Newman prepared for the synod of bishops in 1854 is another key document, useful for the manner in which it combines clearness of principle with workable practice. It shows that while Newman saw the need of delineating the great principles of education, he was also quite prepared to admit that education involves 'questions not merely of immutable truth, but of practice and expedience'. Rather than feel constrained by the principles he had so eloquently described in the Dublin lectures, he was ruthless in the way he went about applying them in practice—as indeed he indicates in the first lecture:

> It is no principle with sensible men, of whatever cast of opinion, to do always what is abstractedly the best. Where no direct duty forbids, we may be obliged to do, as being best under the circumstances, what we murmur and rise against, while we do it. We see that to attempt more is to effect less; that we must accept so much, or gain nothing; and so perforce we reconcile ourselves to what we would have far otherwise, if we could.[3]

This rule of thumb goes some way towards explaining why Newman did not feel constrained to follow existing educational models—or his own high principles—and instead devised new arrangements which borrowed from various traditions, so long as they could be fused into a coherent whole. In Oxford he had challenged the existing system in a number of ways, and been regarded by the college authorities as over-strict and needlessly demanding on the students; in Dublin he was to find he would be accused of precisely the opposite, that is, of being lax and easy-going.

Rival concepts of the university and its purpose

In current studies of the nature and function of higher education, it is noteworthy that while there is a general consensus about what the overall aims of the university *are*, there is a marked lack of unanimity as to their relative importance. The same was true in the mid-nineteenth century, only then the differences were more sharply defined, as the rival versions of a university appeared to be mutually exclusive possibilities—unlike the present day, when several theoretically incompatible approaches are in practice combined in a single institution. By the end of the nineteenth century, most lists of the overall objectives of a university would have included, in one form or another, the following four ends: the preservation and diffusion of culture, and the raising of the cultural level of society; preparation for the professions and the higher branches of commerce and industry; the advance of knowledge and research of every kind; and the development or maturation of the individual student, including what is required for social living. With the exception of research, these ends are also to be found in Newman's memorandum for the bishops' synod, where he declares that the object of the Catholic University was to provide for Catholic education 'in a large sense of the word "education" ', and then proceeds to draw out in ten points what this 'large sense' encompasses.

1. To provide means of finishing the education of young men of rank, fortune, or expectations, with a view of putting them on a level with Protestants of the same description.

2. To provide a professional education for students of law and medicine, and a liberal education for youths destined to mercantile and similar pursuits, as far as their time will admit it.

3. To develop the talents of promising youths in the lower classes of the community.

4. To form a school of theology and canon law suited to the needs of a class of students who may be required to carry on those sciences beyond the point of attainment ordinarily sufficient for parochial duty.

5. To provide a series of sound and philosophical defences of Catholicity and Revelation, in answer to the infidel tracts and arguments which threaten to be our most serious opponents in the era now commencing.

6. To create a national Catholic literature.

7. To provide school books, and generally books of instruction, for the Catholics of the United Kingdom, and of the British Empire, and of the United States.

8. To raise the standard, and systematize the teaching, and encourage the efforts, of the schools already so ably and zealously conducted throughout the country.

9. To give a Catholic tone to society in the great towns.

10. To respond to the growing importance of Ireland, arising from its geographical position, as the medium of intercourse between the East and the West, and the centre of the Catholicism of the English tongue, with Great Britain, Malta (perhaps Turkey or Egypt), and India, on one side of it, and North America, and Australia, on the other.[4]

At the time of writing this memorandum, Newman feared that the bishops were contemplating merely a college rather than a full university.[5] Besides contending that a college was not attractive to students from overseas (or, indeed, to someone like himself as prospective rector), he was concerned that there might be an excessive emphasis on guidance and personal training, and troubled at the prospect of an *a priori* restriction of the curriculum. As Newman understood them, the 'college' and the 'university' were educational worlds apart, and he feared that the authorities might be content to fall back on the tried and tested idea of the college.

At root what was involved were attitudes to the post-Enlightenment era. The age in which they lived was no longer one in which scientific enquirers went about their task with unquestioning reverence for God, but one where many were openly hostile to organized religion; the tide of scientific and philosophic thought was now running hard against traditional Christian teachings, and the resounding triumphs of scientific progress in all fields threatened to make the claims of religion superfluous and promise a new world order. New forms of government in the wake of the French Revolution had led to wide-scale questioning of authority and civil unrest. In this clash of ideas, the tendency of many Catholics was to adopt a fortress mentality, retreating from the world and from the confusion of ideas and practices found there—and an example of this was the temptation to abandon the goal of founding a university for the safer option of a college.

Such an approach was unthinkable for Newman. In the address he wrote for the Catholic University in 1855 on 'Christianity and Scientific Investigation' he balances the claims of revealed religion and natural knowledge, and explains that a university,

> is pledged to admit, without fear, without prejudice, without compromise, all comers, if they come in the name of Truth; to adjust views, and experiences, and habits of mind the most independent and dissimilar; and to give full play to thought and erudition in their most original forms, and their most intense expressions, and in their most ample circuit.[6]

The university man 'who believes Revelation with that absolute faith which is the prerogative of a Catholic, is not the nervous creature who startles at every sudden sound, and is fluttered by every strange or novel appearance which meets his eyes'. Rather than live in a state of apprehension, 'he laughs at the idea, that any thing can be discovered by any other scientific method, which can contradict any one of the dogmas of his religion'.[7]

In an age when the field of human knowledge was widening at an unprecedented rate and newly-formed disciplines were rapidly gaining in status and scholarly depth and rigour, universities had to consider how much of the new knowledge to embrace. In the second edition of the *Discourses*, published in 1859, Newman inserted a passage which makes his position clear: 'It is a great point then to enlarge the range of studies, which a University professes, even for the sake of the students; and, though they cannot pursue every subject which is open to them, they will be the gainers by living among those and under those, who represent the whole circle.' The great benefit of a university was that it brought together in one place learned men from different disciplines who, through dialogue and for the sake of peace, were forced to adjust the claims and relations of their respective subjects, and in this way 'learn to respect, to consult, to aid each other. Thus is created a pure and clear atmosphere of thought, which the student also breathes, though in his own case he only pursues a few sciences out of the multitude.'[8]

This aim was to be achieved principally through the faculty of arts (which included mathematics), within which Newman intended to include some of the emerging disciplines, such as economics. Separate from this, he aimed to set up practical or technical schools such as engineering, mining and agriculture, which would use and develop the material resources of Ireland, as well as a school of Irish language and history, an astronomical observatory, and science laboratories—'institutions which will have their value intrinsically, whether students are present or not'. While it is clear that Newman saw research as having its part to play in the university, he stressed that the *primary* function of a university is to teach rather than to undertake research. But he was careful not to draw the line too closely. In his address 'Christianity and Scientific Investigation' he says that a university is the 'high protecting power of all knowledge and science, of fact and principle, of inquiry and discovery, of experiment and speculation; it maps out the territory of the intellect, and sees that the boundaries of each province are religiously respected, and that there is neither encroachment nor surrender on any side'.[9] Elsewhere he writes, 'A professor is not to be overburdened with lectures, that he may have time for the steady pursuit and thorough mastery of his department of science or learning'.[10] Overall, however, he felt that the proper home of research lay outside the university, albeit in institutions closely connected with it.[11]

While Newman made a certain provision for research, others such as Pusey insisted that the formation of the mind should be given not only pride of place but an absolute monopoly in university life:

> The object of Universities is […] not how to advance science, not how to make new discoveries, not to form new schools of mental philosophy, not to invent new modes of analysis, not to produce works in medicine, Jurisprudence or even Theology, but to form minds religiously, morally, intellectually. It would be a perversion of our institutions to turn the University into a forcing-house for intellect.[12]

This way of thinking represented just one of several competing views in the debate about the different university traditions and their merits. In France, the Napoleonic universities emphasised preparation for service to the State; in the German states primacy was often given to research. In England, the old idea of producing cultured individuals was being challenged by the new utilitarian emphasis on science and economics, a contest which pitted Oxford and Cambridge against London and Edinburgh. In the United States, both the English and German strands were taken up and developed.

Intellectual distinction, as measured by original research, was definitely *not* the primary mission of an English university in Newman's undergraduate years at Oxford, where there was little academic output beyond the publication of general articles and text books. Teaching was the main function, and it was conducted with the aim of producing an elite class of well-formed individuals who would go on to occupy positions of leadership in Church and State. Moral superintendence was thus a critical aspect of the functions of the English university. Generally the dons were clergymen with a clerical, not a university, career in mind: the best place to be intellectually creative was outside university, at one of the royal academies or scientific institutes. Only in the 1860s were there signs of a separation of academics into two types: the good college man, devoted to his charges; and the dedicated scholar or scientist. A decade earlier, when pressure for research was just beginning to mount—and long before it had been raised to the level of an ideology—Newman insisted in his lectures on the central teaching function of the university and the wider emphasis on character development.

The Oxbridge pastoral conception of teaching was centred on the student and on transmission of received values from teacher to taught, made into a living reality in the college and the tutorial. The theory and practice of a liberal education drew from classical traditions, which placed great emphasis on social and moral qualities such as courage, loyalty, nobility, self-sacrifice and wisdom. Likewise, in the early part of the nineteenth century, intellectual life was definitely not considered to be the only life worth nurturing—in fact, creativity and originality were viewed with something like suspicion—and success was measured not just by exams, but by personal development and manifested in truly civilised behaviour. Equally, if not more, important was the human dimension, such as friendships and personal qualities. For the leading Oxford Tractarians, the pursuit of knowledge without an accompanying pursuit of virtue was likely to lead to egotism and intellectual pride. But even if it did not, the all-consuming quest for intellectual betterment was prone to encourage students to become asocial and emotionally unbalanced.

Few in the 1850s would have guessed that within a century the German research university, rather than the Oxbridge collegiate one, would become the generally accepted model in England. Unlike Oxford and Cambridge, where there was an institutional tradition of acting *in loco parentis*, in the German universities there was no official concern with the private or personal lives of undergraduates, and no need, desire, or opportunity to develop the wider civic sense of responsibility that was so conspicuous in much of the English-speaking world. Central to the German idea of a university was the concept of *Bildung*, which emphasised the self-formation or self-realisation of the individual student in gaining a mastery of cultural or scientific knowledge; insofar as the researcher was interested in teaching, it was more because of the subject taught than the student. Poor staffing ratios and the lack of advice and counseling meant that undergraduates had been left to look after themselves. The lack of a corporate university identity was compensated for in the 1820s and 1830s by the creation of organised student confraternities, whose members were bound together with elaborate rituals and corporate discipline, reinforced by pledges of honour. Little known in Britain even today, these new student confraternities were certainly unknown to Newman.

A 'phantasia of life'

In setting up a university on Irish soil, Newman's main task was not so much to persuade the Irish of the merits of his particular version of the university, as to argue the case for establishing a university at all and to convince people that it was both feasible and worthwhile. Ireland had never had a proper university until the foundation of Trinity, and even afterwards there was neither the means nor the will to start a university for Catholics. Irishmen who sought a university education had to travel to the Continent, where a number of universities (including Louvain) had Irish colleges. The rural nature of Ireland's economy and the almost complete absence of Catholics from public life and the professions, owing to the penal laws, meant that the majority of Irish-speaking Catholics had no interest in university education—and especially not in a university in the English-speaking Pale of Dublin, the only part of the country where the alien immigrants had resisted assimilation and instead created their own Anglo-Irish culture.

However erudite Newman's exposition of the nature and purpose of the university, however well thought out philosophically, the new university would not succeed unless it managed to recruit a sufficient number of students; in practice, this meant that there needed to be some form of marketing campaign. Newman undertook this task personally. He saw to advertising and explaining the arrangements for the projected university; he announced academic appointments and broadcast the names of eminent men who lent their names as supporters of the enterprise; he provided arguments about the benefits of enrolling so as to persuade young men to come forward; he disabused the public about what the university was not; and he demonstrated the need of a university for both the Catholic population of Ireland and, more generally, the English-speaking Catholic world. Newman was particularly suited for this task of arousing, challenging and educating public opinion about the prospects of the university, owing to his experience as a pamphleteer and leader of the Tractarian Movement.

Since 1849 the prospect of a Catholic university had produced papal rescripts, episcopal synods, national collections and pastoral letters to the faithful, but little in the way of concrete results, and by 1854 a general feeling had set in that the delay in starting foretold yet another national failure.[13] What was needed now was action

—and evidence of action. Since the printed word was the only effective way of reaching sizeable audiences, it was principally this means that Newman used to undertake the promotion of the university. He did so by bringing out a weekly periodical called the *Catholic University Gazette*, which he edited from 1 June 1854, the eve of his installation as rector, until the end of the calendar year. This meant that by the time the University actually opened, five months later, he had been able to use nearly two dozen issues for his purposes. In a memorandum entitled 'What I aimed at', he explains that the *Gazette* would 'contain a record of the University proceedings, would be a medium of intelligence between its governing body and members, would give a phantasia of life to it in the eyes of strangers, and would indoctrinate [i.e. teach] the Irish public in the idea of a University'.[14]

Besides notices about university regulations and proceedings, the eight-page *Gazette* featured leading articles by Newman that were intended to familiarize people with the idea of a university education by presenting snapshots of it in different historical eras. Newman's aim was to reach out to a public which had practically no knowledge of what a university consisted of, no feel for higher education, and little exposure to university graduates. Except for the few who could aspire to a career in medicine or law and undertake the extensive training this involved, Irish Catholics had little conception of why anyone should need—or want—to prolong their studies and postpone the start of gainful employment. In the minds of most Catholics, university education was associated with the ruling Protestant class; it was coloured by images, not of the industrious medieval scholar burning the midnight oil in a spartan garret, but of high-spirited exploits of privileged young men of means, for whom university was often a mere finishing school.[15] It was a world apart, even for the Dubliners who had it on their doorsteps.

By means of the *Gazette*, Newman also sought to impress upon his readership the fact that responsible people down the ages took care to provide suitable living conditions and paternal oversight for the young scholar living away from home. At the same time he illustrated the need for a different kind of discipline over the student than that exercised by the home tutor or schoolmaster. In doing so, he was unwittingly addressing a concern he only fully appreciated towards the end of his rectorate, when he had come to realise the extent to which Irish Catholics failed to see the need for a gradation of liberties as the young man approached adulthood—what might be termed a progressive 'education in freedom'. The right mixture of liberty and restraint was scarcely possible either at the colleges run by religious orders or at the seminary colleges which compensated for the absence of tertiary education by offering extra courses for those of university age. Undoubtedly these makeshift arrangements were better than nothing, but for Newman they were no substitute for an 'education in freedom' in a university setting.

Of the twenty-nine articles Newman wrote for the *Gazette* in 1854, twenty were the historical snapshots in which he tells the tale of the organic growth and development of the university. Though these essays[16]—sometimes known as *University sketches*[17]—are far less well known than the Dublin lectures, Newman scholars have argued that they are vital for a full understanding of Newman's educational views.[18] In the preface to a recent edition of the sketches, Katherine Tillman explains that in them Newman is searching for the university's 'living *image* in memory and imagination, in its historical development, and in its real, institutional embodiments'. While the 'bare and necessary idea' of a university is an abstract, ahistorical and static notion of what a university is in its essence, for Newman the image is the concrete, historical and living embodiment of the idea (however imperfectly derived from it) at a given time and place. The university *'whole and entire'* is,

Tillman says, both image and idea taken together.[19] Indeed, it was never Newman's intention for the Dublin lectures to be taken in isolation from what he saw as three companion volumes on university education: the Dublin lectures (1852); the occasional lectures and essays (1859); and the university sketches (1856).[20] While only the first two constitute the *Idea*, all three examine the idea of a university: the first as the idea *defined*, the second as the idea *illustrated*, and third as the idea *lived out* in history.

In the university sketches Newman employs images to bring home ideas and enable them to be grasped more readily, giving them greater force by appealing to his readers' imagination. The device of a 'sketch' also allows Newman the liberty to select from the (limited) sources at his disposal just those traits that he wished to draw out and illustrate. The sketches are not intended to be historically rigorous essays about the development of the university, but a work of historical imagination where, as Tillman puts it, 'fact gives way to enchanting description and embellished story-telling'.[21] Composed in an age when the writing of history was frequently used to instruct or edify, the historical purpose of the sketches is subordinated to the didactic function of opening minds to the world of the university.[22]

Besides filling out his image of the university, Newman used the sketches to explain (particularly for the benefit of the Irish) why he had chosen to imitate the Oxbridge collegiate arrangement. For nearly fifty years the Oxbridge system had been the subject of an educational battle, in which proponents of the professorial and tutorial systems argued about which university teaching arrangement was superior. It broke out in 1808 when the *Edinburgh Review*, the mouthpiece of the University of Edinburgh, made the case for the professorial system, claiming that this system had been used in medieval times. The debate was rekindled in the late 1820s by the discussion surrounding the new university in London; it was then taken up at Cambridge, and lately had been debated at Oxford. Essentially the question was whether a university should be conducted on the professorial system, as at Edinburgh and London, or on the collegiate system, as at Oxford and Cambridge.

The professorial university was geared towards the transmission of knowledge and preparation for the professions, as well as the expansion of knowledge through research, but provision for residential living was not viewed as an essential part of its mission. The collegiate foundations of a medieval university, on the other hand, contributed to the stability of society and religion by nurturing upright citizens through the study of classical literature with the aid of a tutor. An Oxbridge college was a place of residence where a student would find himself under the guidance and instruction of college tutors and others who would oversee his personal interests, both moral and intellectual. Oxford in particular was essentially a teaching university, with a highly traditional curriculum and virtually no fame for research, although this was beginning to change in the 1840s. By contrast, Edinburgh had been an international centre of intellectual ferment and research for over a century: its vibrant arts faculty was staffed by specialist lecturers and continually expanding into new disciplines; its medical faculty was among the foremost in Europe. Although many Englishmen—at least before the Oxbridge reforms—sent their sons north of the border for a university education, there was considerable caution in most Anglican circles about Edinburgh's free-thinking atmosphere and lack of collegiate discipline.

The debate about the nature and purpose of a university is one that must have fascinated many observers in Britain at a time when the two sets of arguments would have appeared as closely matched and the outcome uncertain; and it is an equally engaging question for present-day educationalists who trace back the origins of the modern university to the mid-nineteenth century. Although Oxford and Cambridge shared a common medieval parentage with their Continental siblings, by the eve of the French Revolution the sole two English universities looked more like distant cousins owing to their idiosyncratic developments in the early modern period. One major difference was that the English universities were controlled by the colleges rather than by the academic departments or faculties; another that the humanities curriculum (which included mathematics) had not been eroded at the expense of the higher faculties of theology and law (and medicine, where it existed), but instead constituted the staple diet of the student. While at other universities the standard teaching method was the hour-long lecture to large groups, with little attention being given to individual needs and ability, at the English universities the practice of small-group tuition based around directed private study had become the predominant form of instruction. Thus the Oxbridge colleges effectively constituted the university once teaching had been transferred to the colleges after the Reformation.[23]

Partly on account of the liberal curriculum and partly because the colleges acted *in loco parentis* in promoting good discipline as well as good learning, the upper classes in England patronised the universities in large numbers, sending their sons to Oxford and Cambridge rather than to private tutors or academies, as their counterparts did on the European mainland. Thus the English universities trained the elite of the nation as a whole, rather than just those bound for the professions. During the turmoil of the Revolutionary period, the majority of universities on the Continent were closed or replaced by professional schools. Although many of the universities outside France were restored after 1815, the rejuvenation was not along the lines of the *status quo ante*; instead there was widespread absorption of the Napoleonic system of professional schools, together with the emergence of a new type of university: the research university. Effectively, an ideological shift in the *conception* of the university had taken place.

In the late Middle Ages universities were centres of both teaching and research, but in the course of the sixteenth and seventeenth centuries they by and large ceased being centres of active inquiry; so when sustained research in the natural sciences began to take off in the second half of the seventeenth century, its institutional locus was not the university but the academy. 'By the eighteenth century, it was universally accepted that the university was a teaching institution *tout court*.'[24] But this arrangement was challenged by the new German model, inspired by Wilhelm von Humboldt at Berlin, which reinstated research by orientating the university towards the advance of knowledge.

A less wholesome effect of the Revolutionary period was the disappearance of many smaller universities and the dramatic increase of student populations in the larger cities. Most of the students from outlying towns were left to find their own accommodation, and, being unsupervised outside the lecture-room, were unprotected from the temptations of city life. The growth of radical student politics was evident everywhere, and in 1848 students were conspicuously present at the barricades and working for the overthrow of regimes across Europe.

It is possible to distinguish four groupings of the university species in the early 1850s: the traditional ones surviving on the periphery of Europe, foremost among which was Edinburgh; the restored universities in central Europe, restructured but bereft of identity and weakened by state interference; the nationalised French universités; and the emerging German Humboldtian research universities (which as a model of the university came to dominate in the twentieth century)[25]—yet this view of the educational landscape was only partially visible to Newman. The universities he knew best were Oxford and Cambridge, but these were institutional anomalies, even after half a century of reform. Aware that they stood on the threshold of even greater reform (with the appointment of a Royal Commission in 1850 to inquire into their discipline, studies and revenues), he was fully acquainted with how they had generally resisted the educational ideas emanating from French and German thinkers, and, closer to home, fended off the demands of Whigs and radicals for reform along utilitarian lines. While Newman was familiar with the historical development of the university in Europe, he seems to have had little intimate knowledge of the emerging models on the continental mainland, particularly the German one.[26] But to the extent that his Irish readership was even further removed from developments on the continent, the task of persuading his reading public of his decision to ignore the prevailing fashions and adopt a reformed version of the Oxbridge system was all the more straightforward.

The professorial system and its limitations

In the university sketches Newman starts the story of the 'university' with its precarious beginnings in the academies of Athens, before moving on to Rome. From the forerunners of the university in the schools of Athens and Rome, he charts its survival in times of war and destruction, its cultivation in the monasteries, its protection by the popes, its great flowering in the Middle Ages and its struggle for survival in later times. As the concept of the university changes over time, Newman discerns some of the characteristic features in each of its developments, what he calls an adumbration of the pattern or 'an anticipation of its type'.[27] Like the living ideas of 'state' and 'church', the university idea survives and develops, and continually adapts according to circumstances.

In telling the story of the historical development of the university project, Newman uses the device of attributing change to the shifting fortunes of two rival powers, which he calls 'influence' and 'discipline' or 'system' (or 'law').[28] The tension between these opposing forces is a key idea in Newman's educational thinking and therefore one that guided him in the creation of the Catholic University; absent from the *Idea*, the tension acts as a *leitmotif* in the university sketches. Beginning with Athens, Newman examines the moving forces behind academic institutions in order to discern what gave rise to their periods of growth, reform or decay. Taking 'influence' and 'system' to be the two great principles governing the conduct of human affairs, he observes that, in order of time, influence comes before system. This is the course of history: 'it begins with the poet and ends in the policeman'. The same is true of the history of universities: 'they begin in Influence and end in System'. The first teachers were like preachers or missionaries, who attracted disciples by means of personal influence—which Newman describes as the absence of rule, 'the action of personality, the intercourse of soul with soul, the play of mind upon mind'. But individual action is fickle and unreliable, and it needs the steadying hand of system to preserve the gains made. Thus 'a University has been embodied in a constitution, it has exerted authority, it has been protected by rights and privileges, it has enforced discipline'. This pattern of development has recurred in both ancient and medieval times. What 'zeal began, power and wisdom completed: private enterprise came first, national and governmental recognition followed; [...] the Athenian created, the Imperialist organized and consolidated'.[29]

Newman goes on to say that influence exerts itself primarily through the professorial system, while discipline does so through the collegiate system (or its equivalent); the university, considered as a whole, is the proper sphere of action for influence, the college for discipline. Having approached the central question in terms of influence and law, 'the two moving powers which carry the world',[30] Newman arrives at his compromise solution of running the two systems together. In his view neither was complete without the other. Natural rivals of one another and disposed to usurp each other's rights, the forces of influence and discipline in fact had to act in harmony, as each needed the other. Hence, for Newman, 'It would seem as if a University seated and living in Colleges, would be a perfect institution, as possessing excellences of opposite kinds.'[31]

This was the conclusion which the royal commissioners reached after investigating Oxford in 1850–52. They thought that by combining the two systems, the professorial system could become 'the crown and completion of the Tutorial': it would answer the need for lecturers in the new academic disciplines, it would promote the writing of text books by Oxford men (instead of the University having to rely on those by foreign professors), and it would encourage tutors to stay on by providing a goal for them. Unlike the universities abroad, where the professorial system had been adopted not from choice but from necessity, Oxford's wealth gave it 'the means of combining the two, and of carrying out the spirit of each more perfectly.'[32]

These ideas were welcomed by many Oxford academics, but were met with outright opposition by others; and although both responses feature in the *Report and Evidence* (1853) upon the commissioners' recommendations, the latter looms larger. Pusey devoted over a third of his 173-page submission to what he identifies as the great question of the commissioners' *Report*: the two rival systems, professorial and tutorial. He argued that the recommendations had a tendency to destroy the collegiate system 'and with it the formation of minds', and added that he was confirmed in his opinion by his eighteen months spent in Gottingen, Berlin and Bonn, where he had witnessed the absence of moral training and discipline in the professorial system. Since 'The *formation* of the mind, not the *information* conveyed is the main object of education', he rejected the commissioners' recommendations.[33]

Not long after the first of Newman's sketches appeared in the *Gazette*, the first academic appointments at the Catholic University were announced in its pages.[34] But the advertising of prominent names produced a response Newman had not anticipated: he was criticised for placing too much emphasis on the recruitment of high-calibre professors, and for neglecting the need of order, system and rule. In a sketch originally entitled 'Objections answered',[35] Newman interrupts the flow of his history to answer the charge and explain his reasoning. He points out that, since the University was starting without state patronage, it had to create the demand, and great minds were to be the instruments of this. He acknowledges that in advocating the professorial system he appeared to be acting against the line he had adopted at Oxford, where he had argued that knowledge without principle opened up the way to heresy. What were so many eloquent and attractive masters in the history of the Church, like Arius, but forerunners of those dangerous contemporary Germans, 'a set of clever charlatans, or subtle sophists, who aim at originality, show, and popularity, at the expense of truth?'[36] To place such men at the centre of a university would probably lead to disorder.

In grappling with this dilemma Newman made his own original contribution to the question by employing the Aristotelian distinction between the *essence* of something and its *integrity*. The essence of an object refers to what is necessary for its nature, whereas its integrity (*eudemonia*) refers to what is required for its harmonious functioning or well-being; it is a gift added to its nature. Without it that nature is indeed complete, and can act and fulfill its end, though not with ease. For Newman, the essence of a university consists in the communication of knowledge, in lecturers and students, in the professorial system; but the influence of professors

alone is insufficient for its well-being, for a rich and full life and all
that the term *eudemonia* connotes. 'For its sure and comfortable
existence we must look to law, rule, order; to religion, from which
law proceeds; to the collegiate system, in which it is embodied'.[37]

In the sketch called 'Professorial and Tutorial Systems' Newman
argues that 'Colleges are to be accounted the maintainers of order,
and Universities the centres of movement', and he insists on
upholding the principle in spite of the countless instances history
could throw up of professors who lacked personal weight and
persuasiveness, and of colleges which become neglectful of moral
and religious discipline. This separation of functions had only been
referred to once in the *Idea* (in the Preface), and there Newman
makes a different distinction, arguing that a University was in
essence a place of teaching and that it carried out its function
independently of its relation to the Church. In practice, however,
it was unable to fulfill its purpose properly without the aid of the
Church, since the Church was necessary for its *integrity*. In the
university sketches Newman was able to develop the theme at
greater length. Here he argues that 'Colleges are the direct and
special instruments, which the Church *uses* in a University, for the
attainment of her sacred objects'. By combining the two antitheses,
university–college and professor–tutor, Newman arrives at his
conclusion: 'The Professorial system fulfils the strict idea of a
University, and is sufficient for its *being*, but it is not sufficient for
its *well-being*. Colleges constitute the *integrity* of a University.'[38]

The collegiate system

Leaving aside the philosophical arguments of the lectures, Newman
now leads the reader to 'the real state of the case': the historical
pattern of events. He asks his audience to undertake a leap of the
imagination and to picture a few learned men arriving at a great city
where, after obtaining the sanction of the local bishop, they set up a

school of learning. Whether or not they are priests, Newman takes his aspiring dons to be earnest and principled men who are set on their work and not over-concerned with their own comfort. Attracted by their learning, zeal and eloquence, pupils arrive from near and far, but they experience difficulty in finding board and lodging. Whether they live alone in attics or basements, or share lodgings with others, they are exposed to trials which would test even those with the greatest self-command or devotion to learning; the vast majority would be unsettled when thrown out of their normal routine and would suffer 'when withdrawn from the eye of those who know them, or from the scrutiny of public opinion'. Newman asks his readers what it must be like for young men 'of unformed minds, so little weaned from the world that their very studies are perhaps the result of their ambition, and who are under no definite obligation to be better than their neighbours, only bound by that general Christian profession', to move into lodgings which are ill-suited to their needs. 'The excitement of novelty or emulation does not last long; and then the mind is commonly left a prey to its enemies, even when there is no disarrangement of daily life'.[39]

In such circumstances it would be fanciful to expect the academics to exercise control over their pupils, even if they had any jurisdiction, or to imagine that they could bring their personal influence to bear upon any great number of them, or that they could do much more than deliver lectures and meet their pupils during normal working hours. The very popularity of such an academy would in all likelihood lead gradually to the formation of a 'mob of lawless youths', much like the rioters at Athens he had described in an earlier sketch. Such a state of affairs would arise even if the students were comfortably off—and would be all the worse if they happened to be wealthy. To these almost certain disorders, Newman adds that of the academic carried away by his own success; not only the taught but the teacher, too, has his perils, since 'there are in his path such enemies as the pride of intellect, the aberrations of reasoning, and the intoxication of applause. The very advantages of his position are his temptation.'[40] The superiority of oral instruction over books in communicating knowledge increases the risk that the speaker might become puffed up with the popularity of his own eloquence and that the hearer might be carried away by his fascination with the speaker. Both dangers are inherent in a professorial system. The cosmopolitan nature of the university gives rise to another disorder, since the young converge there from countries which have different traditions and which have often been at enmity with one other; it is only to be expected that hostilities would exist and break out in conflicts, and that these might draw in third parties such as the townsfolk, the university authorities or even the Church. If this seemed too like a tale from the distant past, Newman reminds his readers that duels and party skirmishes were not uncommon even then in the German universities, and that town-and-gown rows were not yet matters of history in Oxford.

These considerations were intended to show that the thirst for knowledge and the opportunity of satisfying it, though they constitute the real life of a university, are not sufficient to enable it to reach its ultimate end, unless they are 'surrounded by influences of a different sort, which have no pretension indeed to be the essence of a University, but are conservative of that essence'.[41] For these influences Newman turns to the Church. He proposes that the real wisdom is, as the Apostle James says (James 3:17), that which comes down from above, and is marked chiefly by purity and peacefulness. 'These may be called the three vital principles of the Christian student, faith, chastity, love; because their contraries, viz., unbelief or heresy, impurity, and enmity, are just the three great sins against God, ourselves, and our neighbour, which are the death of the soul.'[42] These are the chief dangers of the professorial system;

and just as its deficiencies are obvious, so—Newman argues—is its remedy, insofar as human nature admits of one.

> I have been saying that regularity, rule, respect for others, the eye of friends and acquaintances, the absence from temptation, external restraints generally, are of first importance in protecting us against ourselves. When a boy leaves his home, when a peasant leaves his country, his faith and morals are in great danger, both because he is in the world, and also because he is among strangers. The remedy, then, of the perils which a University presents to the student, is to create within it homes, 'altera Trojæ Pergama', such as those, or better than those, which he has left behind. Small communities must be set up within its precincts, where his better thoughts will find countenance, and his good resolutions support; where his waywardness will be restrained, his heedlessness forewarned, and his prospective deviations anticipated.[43]

Newman points out that the received wisdom of lawgivers and founders has long been to 'find a safe outlet for natural impulses and sentiments, which are sure to be found in their subjects, and which are hurtful only in excess; and to direct, and moderate, and variously influence what they cannot extinguish'. This was traditionally achieved by dividing up the student body to make it more manageable and at the same time to provide a safe channel for national, provincial, or political feelings, and allow a wholesome rivalry. Such student societies tended to promote an 'honourable emulation' and stimulate academic exertion, while also changing a selfish feeling of pride into a concern for the reputation of the society. Patriotic sentiments, too, would find their outlets in national or regional colleges or halls, and, thanks to a 'salutary organization', the love of one's country, while not losing its intensity, would become 'purer, more civilized, and more religious'.[44]

Newman defines the term 'college' to mean a body of men not merely living together in one dwelling, but belonging to a single establishment; it suggests a foundation invested with authority, public recognition and an endowment. The buildings housing this quasi-family ought thus to be of a prominent character so as to reflect its official status, for they became 'the enduring habitation of an enduring body'. It is a household which 'involves the same virtuous and paternal discipline which is proper to a family and home'. Being a domestic establishment in which teachers and taught live together as one family, the college 'is all, and does all, which is implied in the name of home'. Young men leave the family home to find another—a home from home; because they do not know the world and so are easily discouraged by the difficulties of life; because they still have to learn how to cope with the temptations of the world; because they have not yet learned *how to learn*. Ideally, the 'collegiate home' assumes the characteristics of the family home, and thus becomes 'the shrine of our best affections, the bosom of our fondest recollections, a spell upon our after life, a stay for world-weary mind and soul'.[45] There is no contradiction between these homely images and the disciplinary role Newman gives to the college, because by 'discipline' he means not an externally imposed code of behaviour but the discipline of a regular and ordered personal and social life, a *self*-discipline that is intellectual, moral and religious. In this way college would take over where family leaves off by providing a place of refuge and companionship, and also prayer and instruction.[46]

Arguably, the loftiest conception of the collegiate residence appears, not in the university sketches but in the *Idea*, on the dedication page, where Newman quotes a well-known phrase from the Gospel, *Hospes eram, et collegistis me* (Matthew 25:34). The phrase is usually translated along the lines 'I was a stranger and you gave me shelter', and at first glance appears to refer to those mentioned in the dedication that follows, to 'his many friends and benefactors, living and dead, at home and abroad', who had come to his aid during the Achilli trial; it could also be taken as referring to his Irish hosts who had welcomed the stranger from England. But a third interpretation is also possible: by situating the phrase in a university context, Newman could be giving it a meaning along the lines of 'I was a student and you "colleged" me'—*collegistis* being cognate with *collegium* (college)—and thereby a completely different emphasis. Seen in this light, the task of caring for students in halls of residence takes on an importance that approximates it to nothing less than one of the seven corporal works of mercy.[47]

Newman explains that attempts to meet the needs of the non-priestly 'clerk' in the twelfth or thirteenth century led to the formation of rudimentary halls or boarding houses kept by professors. As Newman had already indicated, a parallel custom had existed in Athens, 'where there was a great deal of rivalry and canvassing between the Professorial housekeepers, each eager to obtain as many lodgers as possible';[48] a similar situation arose and had to be checked at Paris in the thirteenth century. Newman's depiction of the spartan conditions in an era before endowments for poor scholars existed provides a graphic illustration of the student's dire need for suitable living conditions. Yet when colleges and scholarships were endowed for poor scholars, the benefactors were concerned as much to minimise the moral dangers the young were exposed to, when away from home and without guardians, as to address their basic physical needs.

The influx of sons of the nobility and gentry to Oxford in the fourteenth century resulted in several colleges becoming the preserve of the wealthy, to the detriment of the university. Eventually the colleges became all-powerful, but this 'antagonism of the Collegiate to the University principle only occurred after the Colleges had first rendered signal service to the University, not just by completing it in those points where the University was weak, but even corroborating it in those in which it was strong'. In particular, the colleges helped give the university vigour and stability when there was a large influx of foreigners. During this period, the colleges as a whole catered for all ranks and classes of the community, not just the poor scholars; and they gradually became more suited to the study of the liberal arts, rather than the learned professions. Seeing the colleges as 'hardly more than the Nations formally established and endowed',[49] Newman envisaged that at the Catholic University the collegiate houses would differ from each other so as to cater for different levels of society, and that there would be separate houses for such national groupings as the English or the South Americans. In the sixteenth century, when statutes were introduced at Oxford to bring the wandering poor scholars within the walls of the colleges, the onus of teaching shifted from the university to the colleges, as the teachers of grammar, rhetoric and philosophy began to teach mainly within the colleges. This change also had ramifications for the Catholic University, because Newman intended his collegiate establishments to imitate the Oxbridge colleges by undertaking a teaching role.

In one of the most powerful passages in the sketches Newman describes the ties of loyalty and friendship that can develop in a college setting. Imagine, he says, what it is like for the future landowner, statesman, lawyer or clergyman who enters an Oxford college; he goes to university when the mind is most impressionable and the affections are warmest, when associations are made for life, when character is most open and the feelings of reverence most powerful. There he forms friendships and spends his happiest days; whatever he achieves academically during his time at college, when he looks back in later years, he finds himself bound by ties of gratitude to the memories of college life.

> He has received favours from the Fellows, he has dined with
> the Warden or Provost; he has unconsciously imbibed to the
> full the beauty and the music of the place. The routine of
> duties and observances, the preachings and the examinations
> and the lectures, the dresses and the ceremonies, the officials
> whom he feared, the buildings or gardens that he admired,
> rest upon his mind and his heart, and the shade of the past
> becomes a sort of shrine to which he makes continual silent
> offerings of attachment and devotion. It is a second home, not
> so tender, but more noble and majestic and authoritative.[50]

The former undergraduate will keep up some connection with his college for the rest of his life, and will readily revisit the scene of his undergraduate years, where 'he gazes on old faces, revives old friendships, awakens old reminiscences', and then returns home renewed with the memories of his youth.[51]

Whether or not late medieval Oxford attained the healthy balance between university and college that Newman imagines is beside the point; his sketches were a work of historical imagination intended to portray a picture of student life that was as reassuring to the Irish ecclesiastic as it was attractive to the Dublin lawyer. Newman was unable, however, to point to any *contemporary* instance which illustrated the benefits of the university–college alliance, only to examples which manifested the 'two antagonistic evils, of naked Universities and naked Colleges'. The great seats of learning on the European mainland and in Scotland illustrated the need of colleges to complete the university, while Oxford and Cambridge illustrated the need of a university to give life to the assemblage of colleges.[52]

Having identified the drawbacks of a university without colleges, Newman used two other sketches to describe the English situation, 'where the action of the University is suspended, and the Colleges have supreme and sovereign authority'.[53] The consequences of this extraordinary situation were disastrous for the colleges, since it isolated them from the beneficial influence of public opinion. In the eighteenth century the colleges 'became shamefully indolent and inactive', and were in no sense any longer places of education, but for the most part mere clubs where the members did little but amuse themselves. The authorities generally neglected the young men confided to them, allowing them instead to follow their own whims; indeed, in so far as the authorities influenced the students, it was often through bad example. The one power which could have exerted a natural authority over them was the university—but the university was only a name, powerless to act. To his description of the decay of Oxford—a state not unfamiliar to the Irish who knew something of the eighteenth-century decadence at Trinity College, Dublin—Newman adds that 'the critical evil' of powerlessness of the university still existed at Oxford and Cambridge. Nevertheless, great reforms had been brought about by persistent lobbying and by 'improving the tone and enlightening the minds of their members'.[54]

Newman also explains the defects of the English situation in terms of influence and discipline. In the professorial university the influence of the celebrity lecturer could somehow make up for the lack of an academic system, but in the collegiate university 'the system cannot in any sort dispense with personal influence. With influence there is life, without it there is none; if influence is deprived of its due position, it will not by those means be got rid of, it will only break out irregularly, dangerously'. In his experience 'An academical system without the personal influence of teachers upon pupils, is an arctic winter; it will create an ice-bound, petrified, cast-iron University, and nothing else.' Newman called this state of affairs 'the reign of Law without Influence, System without Personality'. Many Oxford undergraduates of his generation had been content with this state of things because it gave them the illusion of freedom, but there were others who had aimed at higher things, both intellectual and moral. Searching for those who would exert that influence upon them, they gravitated to where they 'saw a little more profession of strictness and distinctness of creed, a little more intellect, principle, and devotion, than was ordinary'. Thus 'a whole class of teachers gradually arose, unrecognised by its authorities, and rivals to the teachers whom it furnished, and gained the hearts and became the guides of the youthful generation, who found no sympathy where they had a claim for it'. In a few years this new generation found itself in public office, and then, 'from the memory of their own past discomfort, they tried to mend matters, and to unite Rule and Influence together, which had been so long severed, and [...] they claimed from their pupils for themselves that personal attachment which in their own pupillage they were not invited to bestow'.[55]

Newman's description is of course too rosy to be realistic, if it is supposed to represent Oxford as a whole, for in the 1850s the system of private and public tutors working in tandem was, if anything, more firmly established than it had been in the 1820s. The Oxford commissioners learned that it was difficult for college authorities to gain the confidence of their pupils, and that without this their influence was necessarily slight (though there was a great difference between a strict college and a lax hall), while the private tutors often became the friends and advisers of the students. Generally it was not possible for college tutors to associate with undergraduates, which meant that the character of the young men must be formed chiefly through their dealings with their fellow students or their private tutors. The commissioners took up the suggestion of two Oriel tutors, A. H. Clough and Henry Vaughan, that the private and public tutorial roles should be merged together—precisely what Froude, Newman and Wilberforce had attempted at Oriel in the 1820s. This, they suggested, could be achieved by relieving the tutors of the professorial dimension of their work (i.e. their lecturing duties); then they would have more time for individual superintendence and gain a better idea of what their pupils knew, and in this way the private tutors would be superseded by college tutors. Moreover, 'their relations with their pupils would become more intimate and confidential if they were less complicated and multifarious'.[56] This solution had been spelt out by Newman in 1840, when he found himself agreeing in principle with the Hebdomadal Board over its (failed) attempts to bring back the professorial system.[57]

'Hospes eram, et collegistis me'

It was no simple task for Newman to translate his vision into a living institution, for he faced a wide range of obstacles: an absence of a university tradition among Irish Catholics and little appreciation of the purpose of a liberal education; a complete lack of experience in dealing with students *qua* students; serious financial constraints; a population which was dispirited and with little faith in new ventures; deep divisions between clergy and the educated laity, manifested in clerical highhandedness and lay anticlericalism; and a generous dose of anti-English feeling. Though these difficulties severely hampered his plans and meant that the university which emerged bore only a limited likeness to his ideal, the plans are instructive for historians of education because they present a clear picture of how Newman managed to adapt his principles to the Irish situation of the mid-1850s.

One of the key principles which runs through all Newman's university papers was his concern that young students living away from home should find a home from home at the crucial juncture in life between childhood and adulthood. This, like other working rules that guided Newman in setting up the Catholic University, is not easily deduced from any blow-by-blow account of life at the

University during his rectorship. These principles emerge more distinctly from his university papers and private correspondence, which record the way his plans evolved and thereby reveal what was of fundamental importance to him and what was marginal. There are six key documents that effectively contain the essence of Newman's evolving plan and they were written in six successive years: the 'Report on the Organization of the Catholic University of Ireland' (October 1851) which he co-wrote with Leahy and O'Reilly; his first major memorandum about the university project, 'The Statement of August 14th 1852';[58] a memorandum written when 86 St Stephen's Green was acquired (February 1853); the memorandum composed (29 April 1854) for the episcopal synod; the annual Report for 1854–55 (completed in October 1855); and the 'Scheme of Rules and Regulations' (submitted to the University Council in April 1856). All of these are foundational documents, including the last two, because they distilled Newman's earlier thoughts about the University and gave them lasting literary expression.

The centrality of the lodging houses in Newman's scheme of education is evident in all these documents and shows that Newman had a clear vision of his aims from the outset. Knowing he was operating under severe constraints in pioneering a Catholic university in a cultural environment that was foreign to him, in this matter as in others he adopted a flexible approach when translating his ideas into practical arrangements. After the first sketch of 1851, the details were gradually filled in, and occasionally some were erased or altered—but none of the modifications he was forced to make altered his overall conception. The published Report for 1854–55 was, in fact, the first occasion the public were able to read about the system of lodging houses—and this included the bishops, since the memorandum of April 1854 did not descend to detail.[59] The story of how the lodging houses worked out in practice and how the problems that arose were faced will be left to the following chapters.

It was in his Statement of 14 August 1852 that Newman first explained in detail the plans for residential arrangements that he had been nurturing since he had been invited to join the university project.[60] After acknowledging that the University's first priority was a central building with rooms for offices, lectures and exams, he turns immediately to the residential question. Beginning with practical considerations, he argues that it was preferable not to gather all the students into one building, because they would be unable to acquire one large enough, and, even if they could, they would be unable to estimate how many students would come. Moreover, every student would need at least one room for himself, which meant that even a very large house would have to be 'cut up badly' to provide a good number of decent-sized rooms—and, besides, the process of adapting one would be expensive.

> But I have a far stronger and a moral reason for disliking large houses. *The only way* to hinder the disorder incident upon a University in a town is to do what they were forced to do at Oxford and other Universities in the middle ages—to open *Inns* or *Halls*, as they were called (which, when endowed, became Colleges). We shall be as bad as Trinity [College Dublin], unless we do the same—and here we can let our apparent difficulty be an excuse for what is a direct and substantive benefit. We shall seem to be forced by necessity into a number of what will seem like lodging-houses, but which will really be separate organized establishments in and under the University.[61]

Newman envisaged lodging houses which would hold up to twenty students each, presided over by a dean (or 'dean of twenties'), each with its own private chapel and a chaplain, one or two lecturers, and resident tutors. 'Thus there would be some sort of governing body in each house, or what would ultimately become such.' If possible, each residence would also have two or three scholars, who would act as 'a sort of medium between the governing body and the independent [i.e. ordinary] students. This, however, would be the gradual work of time; and need not be talked about at first ('lodging-houses' alone would be talked of at first).'[62] Nevertheless, Newman foresaw that some of these lodging houses would eventually become inns, halls, or hostels (all names used in the Middle Ages) and that, naturally, one of them would be called St Patrick's.

Newman considered such a plan 'to be *indispensable* for discipline—the experience of ages has shown it'—but it had another great advantage besides making the large body of students manageable: 'it will introduce a spirit of emulation, an *esprit de corps*'. Furthermore, as in the Middle Ages, the plan could interest different parts of the country in the undertaking, since each diocese could have its own hall, for priests or laity or both; and it would also be a useful way of getting scholarships founded. Religious orders, too, could have their own establishments; and so could the bishops; or, indeed a faculty, like theology. Newman did not flesh out the scheme further and instead rounded off his outline with a clear demand: 'I am mentioning, I repeat, not what can be done at once, but what is to be aimed at; and I mention it now, because it must be aimed at from the first, and a false step now may render the whole project simply impracticable.'[63]

Three years later, when the first academic year had run its course, Newman was able to inform the bishops about what had actually taken shape, as well as what he hoped to see in the future. What is clear from his Report for 1854–55 is that the arrangements were virtually identical to those contained in the Statement and outlined in the memorandum of 1854 to the bishops; however, not all the aims from the lengthy memorandum of February 1853 were incorporated, as some of these were intended for a later day. The first annual Report explained that when a student was admitted to the University, he 'is at once put under discipline, and he is required to join himself to some particular House or Community, of which he becomes a member'. Each house was under the rule of a dean, assisted by a number of tutors, each had its own chapel and common table, and each a working-day timetable that ran approximately as follows: Mass at 8 am, followed by breakfast; attendance at lectures from 9 am to 1 or 2 pm; dinner at 5 pm; and the students' presence indoors by a fixed hour in the evening, which varied according to the time of year. Each house was to be 'independent of the University in all money matters', though it was anticipated that there would be exceptions to this rule at the beginning. Furthermore, 'all the Houses, both as regards superiors and subjects, would be under the supreme jurisdiction of the University, the dean and tutors being in every case appointed by the rector, and subject to his visitation and interposition'.[64]

It was one thing for Newman to assume that the Oxbridge model was capable of being replanted on Irish soil, but would it in fact meet the different needs there? In the Oxbridge system, the only way of becoming a member of the university was by first being accepted by a college; so where would this leave Irish students who expected to live at home or with friends of the family? Newman's solution was that,

> it should be in the power of the Dean or President, under sanction of the Rector, to permit young men to live at the houses of their parents or friends, if they wish it; but in the case of such externs, their home, or abode, whatever it is, must be considered as a licensed lodging house, or rather as an integral part of the academical domicile; so that the young men so situated are as simply [i.e. completely] under the jurisdiction of the Dean as if they resided under his roof.[65]

No doubt the bishops appreciated the need to organize suitable living arrangements, but they may have wondered why there was so much emphasis in the Report on the scheme of lodging houses. It was probably because Newman realized that all the bishops had to go on were their own individual experiences as seminarians, either in Ireland or abroad in Lisbon, Paris, Rome or Salamanca.[66] So in order to win them over to his line of thinking, he embarked on a lengthy analysis of the problem they faced.

The houses, he told them, were on principle small and numerous, as they were intended for 'the enforcement of discipline upon young men, who are at a very anxious time of life, and come to us under very anxious circumstances'.[67] In dealing with young men who were at the least docile age in life, he laid down (in the Scheme of Rules and Regulations) his guiding principle 'that the young for the most part cannot be driven, but, on the other hand, are open to persuasion and to the influence of kindness and personal attachment; and that, in consequence, they are to be kept straight by indirect contrivances rather than by authoritative enactments and naked prohibitions'. Since there was nothing 'more perilous to the soul than the sudden transition from restraint to liberty', university residences were entrusted with the momentous task of launching the young man into the world. The worst they could do was to continue the discipline of school, because this would not prepare the student to be his own master; by failing to recognise this, the authorities would be letting slip a very special opportunity. Instead, they had to treat the weak like a mother or 'Alma Mater, who inspires affection while she whispers truth; who enlists imagination, taste, and ambition on the side of duty; who seeks to impress hearts with noble and heavenly maxims at the age when they are most susceptible, and to win and subdue them when they are most impetuous and self-willed'. At the same time, Newman was under no illusions about how difficult it would be for the university authorities 'to maintain a persevering, gentle oversight', while laying down the law—and enforcing it.[68]

It was Newman's view that, by itself, the formal discipline of a university was defective and hence in need of personal influence for completeness. He proposed to meet the difficulty of securing university discipline (a subject close to episcopal hearts) in a number of different ways, but principally by means of the lodging houses; the intellectual atmosphere nurtured in them; and the tutorial system. These were not separate strategies but part of an organic whole rooted in the central conception of residence. The scheme for lodging the students in small communities ensured that no great number would live together. 'A large College of lay students will be found impenetrable and unmanageable by even the most vigilant authorities. Personal influence requires personal acquaintance, and the minute labour of a discretionary rule is too fatiguing to be exercised on a large number.'[69]

Newman also considered it of great importance to create among the students a healthy intellectual atmosphere, which once begun would be carried on by tradition. 'It is scarcely too much to say that one-half of the education which young people receive is derived from the tradition of the place of education. The genius loci, if I may so speak, is the instructor most readily admitted and most affectionately remembered.' The authorities were unable to create it directly, but they were in a position to foster and influence it; one important means of doing so was by the establishment of generous scholarships, to be given away in open competition.[70] Newman maintained (perhaps somewhat optimistically) that often,

> the most studious are the best principled and most reli-
> giously minded of the young men; at least a certain share of
> self-command, good sense, and correctness in deportment
> they must have; and, by bringing them forward in the way
> I am proposing, the respect due to successful talent comes

in aid of order and virtue, and they become the centre of influence, who are likely to use influence well.[71]

It ought to be a condition, Newman argued, that those receiving scholarships should be resident members of a lodging-house; that they should exercise certain collegiate functions, such as acting as sacristan, serving at Mass, or assisting the professors and tutors in the distribution of lecture lists; that they should have certain small privileges, such as eating at a separate table in the refectory, admittance to the library, privileged access to the dean's and tutors' rooms, and their special confidence;

> and thus, without having a shadow of jurisdiction over the rest, they would constitute a middle party between the superiors and the students, break the force of their collisions, and act as an indirect and spontaneous channel of communicating to the students many an important lesson and truth, which they would not receive, if administered to them from the mouth of a superior.[72]

It is useful to dwell for a moment on the *genius loci*, as Newman felt that everything in a long-established institution was influenced by this intangible but all-important power. It has been described as combining 'in itself the power of discipline with the power of influence, for though its ways were secret and indirect and personal, it had all the authority of law and all the consistency of a living idea'.[73] Newman's audience would have been familiar with the concept from the Dublin lecture in which he describes how a youthful community naturally gives birth to a living teaching, which in course of time takes the shape of a self-perpetuating tradition 'which haunts the home where it has been born, and which imbues and forms, more or less, and one by one, every individual who is successively brought under its shadow'. It constituted 'a sort of self-education', and was clearly visible in the academic institutions of Protestant England.

> A characteristic tone of thought, a recognized standard of
> judgment is found in them, which, as developed in the
> individual who is submitted to it, becomes a twofold source
> of strength to him, both from the distinct stamp it impresses
> on his mind, and from the bond of union which it creates
> between him and others.[74]

Leaving aside the question of whether the standards and principles
of any one particular ethical atmosphere were true or false, there was
no disputing that here was a real teaching—and hence its importance
for the Catholic University. Since it was starting without the aid of
this tradition, Newman deliberated about how to substitute for this
'invisible teacher', as well as how to grow it from seed. Two means
at his disposal—and for making good the university's discipline
—were the lodging houses and the scholars; a third was the tutors.

Tutors: the 'real working men'

While conceding that, 'from the nature of the case, some years must
pass before the objects I wish them to answer can be really carried
into effect', Newman expected much from the influence of the
tutors. Ideally they would be young men, not more than two or
three years older than their pupils, who had recently finished their
own course of studies at the University and gained honours in their
exams, or else were (or had recently been) holders of scholarships.
They would be,

> half companions, half advisers of their pupils, that is, of the
> students; and while their formal office would be that of
> preparing them for the Professors' Lectures, and the Exam-
> inations [...], they would be thrown together with them in
> their amusements and recreations; and, gaining their confi-
> dence from their almost parity of age, and their having so
> lately been what the others are still, they may be expected

> to exercise a salutary influence over them, and will often
> know more about them than anyone else.[75]

This description of the role of the tutor has similarities with the Arnoldian role of the school prefect: in both cases a beneficial influence was to be exerted by those who were a little older (and wiser); tutors, like prefects, were to be chosen for their academic and personal qualities; they were to act as intermediaries or buffers between the authorities and the rest of the student population; and they were to be rewarded with certain privileges.

In the 'Report on the Organization of the Catholic University of Ireland' (October 1851) Newman had announced his intention to combine the professorial and tutorial systems, adding that 'the principal making of men must be by the Tutorial system'.[76] A year later, in the Statement, he explained that at Oxford the 'real working men were, not the Professors, but the Tutors', and that he wished this to be the case at Dublin as well. Being 'young men who go through the drudgery of preparing the students for examination, and see that they profit by the Professors' Lectures', the tutors needed to live alongside their pupils; at the same time, together with the lecturers, they would assist the rector and form 'the working and influential portion of the University' and thus would be 'the practical managers of the whole'.[77] For this reason, Newman had insisted that *he*, as rector, must be the one to appoint them. To gain his point he explained in the memorandum of April 1854 that, since his preferred system of young tutors was impractical at the beginning, as the tutors were supposed to be students who had passed exams and of several years' standing, *pro tem* the tutorial work should be committed to three or four older academics, who would also carry out tasks necessary for the commencement of the University, such as organising the plan of studies and compiling a list of set texts and the course of reading to be recommended to the students.

As early as August 1852 Newman explained to a potential tutor that he aimed at getting a number of good tutors '*who will be the real strength of the institution*',[78] and the following summer he began to sound out other convert friends and acquaintances; when he received the summons to Dublin in October 1853 he had already lined up interested parties and made several tentative offers. That Newman lavished great care on his choice of tutors in the months leading up to the opening of the University—shown by the number of letters on this matter—indicates that he considered their selection to be of vital importance to the whole enterprise. It is evident, too, from the content of this correspondence which shows that he had a precise idea of what he wanted and that he was ambitious in his stipulation of the necessary qualities. Though the university needed an 'external manifestation' of lecturers and professors to satisfy, *inter alia*, public expectations, for its inner, working life it required something less conspicuous—namely tutors or 'catechists'. For 'the beginning of an inward and real *formation*', the University needed,

> a few persons who thoroughly understand each other, and whom I entirely know; who can quickly and without show be bringing into shape the students who come to us. [...] We must *feel our* way—and get over a mass of prejudice and opposition. *No rules* can do this—but the zeal, energy and prudence of the individuals employed in the work.[79]

Once he was summoned to Dublin, Newman sought to engage four tutors who would form the basis of the system: 'They will have nothing to do with discipline, but be as much as possible the *friends* of their charge. They will not be responsible for their conduct, but for their intellectual proficiency'.[80] He expected them 'to gain the confidence and intimacy of the young men—and, in this way, to smooth the Dean's work', hence the insistence that they ought to have nothing to do with discipline, 'for else, good bye to the confidence I speak of'.[81] Though their task might involve only three hours of formal contact time a day, the tutors were expected to live in so that they could spend more time in the company of their students. The people Newman had in mind were therefore young unmarried men who aspired to academic positions; they had to be capable of working with one another, as well as with Newman, and of winning the trust of the undergraduates. Since they were to be the equivalent of the Oxford private tutors, Newman intended to recruit them from the pool of talented Oxbridge converts: besides being *au fait* with the tutorial system, these men were more likely to fall in with Newman's view that the students should be required 'to read a few books well rather than many imperfectly, i.e. cultivate taste, imagination, judgement, rather than a smattering of a great many authors'.[82]

In weighing up the merits of experience against youth and availability, Newman opted for the former, and before the year was out four people had accepted his offer of a tutorship at £200 and two more at £100. One of the four was James Stewart (aged thirty-seven), who had been schooled in Aberdeen before attending Trinity College, Cambridge. He had become an Anglican curate in the diocese of Durham and second master of a grammar school, then a tutor and curate in Suffolk; after becoming a Catholic in 1849 he had taught for three years in Mauritius, before returning to England to tutor again.[83] He was highly qualified for the role Newman had in mind, and during the three days he and Newman spent together at Birmingham in June 1853 they talked at length about the future university. Another first choice for Newman was Robert Ornsby (aged thirty-four), who had gained a First at Lincoln College, Oxford and gone on to become a Fellow and lecturer in rhetoric at Trinity College, as well as Master of the Schools (a university post). Like Stewart, he had been a curate before his conversion. He was married, working as assistant editor of *The*

Tablet, and based in Dublin, from where he had been advising Newman about Ireland. Cullen was uneasy about both these appointments, but especially Stewart's, because he felt that the Irish antipathy towards the Scots was even greater than that towards the English. Both men were to combine tutoring with full lectureships, one in Latin and Greek language, the other in classical literature, while neither resided in a collegiate house (Ornsby, because he was married), though they each took in one or two student lodgers.[84]

Though what the University really needed was a team of young, single tutors, most of the suitable Oxbridge converts Newman knew well were older and married, and this explains why he offered tutorships to Henry Wilberforce (aged forty-seven), the fourth and youngest son of the 'emancipator' (and the younger brother of Robert, who had been a tutor with Newman at Oriel), Edward Thompson (aged forty-one) and James Northcote (aged thirty-three), all of whom had first-rate credentials. The former two accepted, but Northcote declined.[85] Rather than pressure Northcote into accepting, Newman held back when he saw the initial response, because he felt that the enterprise was so 'important that all should begin con amore'.[86] A problem the three of them shared was that they had literary or scholastic ambitions and children to feed—though Newman held out the prospect of lectureships on top of the tutorship.

The only unmarried man to be offered a tutorship was the convert priest William Penny (aged forty-one), who was appointed as a tutor in mathematics and logic at £100 with board and lodgings. Educated at Westminster School and Christ Church, Oxford, he had stayed with Newman at Littlemore and become an Oratorian, but he found himself unsuited to community life and left the Oratory, though remaining a friend of Newman. The other lower-paid tutor was Thomas Scratton (aged thirty-three), an Oxford convert who had also tried his vocation at the Birmingham Oratory.

After offering him the tutorship Newman had doubts about whether he would be popular as a tutor, and also whether he would get on with the other tutors; so, since he had enough tutors, he withdrew the offer and offered Scratton instead the post of Secretary of the University, which he accepted. In engaging these various men to 'work the Tuition province, i.e. all the *internal* business of the University as distinct from Lecturers and Professors',[87] Newman intended to rely heavily on their ability to shoulder the weight of the institution. At one point he considered including the tutors' general reports in the *Gazette* so as to give their role greater standing, but like many of his ideas it did not come about.

The general public was not privy to Newman's private correspondence or to his working documents about the University, yet they too needed to be informed about tutorial arrangements, not least because parents of potential students, benefactors and other well-wishers were anxious to know what academic system Newman was intending to adopt. It was in the sketch in the *Gazette* which describes the advantages of collegiate living that Newman found the opportunity to advertise and explain the benefits of the tutorial system. In 'Professorial and Tutorial systems' he emphasizes that, while much is conferred by the college as a second home, the student gains still more by signing up for tutorial supervision since it complements the education imparted at lectures. While the college was the main setting for general discipline (in the wider sense of 'training'), the college tutorial was the ideal vehicle for the student's *intellectual* discipline:

> his diligence will be steadily stimulated; he will be kept up to his aim; his progress will be ascertained, and his week's work, like a labourer's, measured. It is not easy for a young man to determine for himself whether he has mastered what he has been taught; a careful catechetical training, and a jealous scrutiny into his power of expressing himself and of

turning his knowledge to account, will be necessary, if he is really to profit from the able Professors whom he is attending; and all this he will gain from the College Tutor.[88]

Towards the end of the Catholic University's second academic year, Newman judged that he was ready to commit himself to a summary of the tutorial system in his proposed Scheme of Rules and Regulations. After outlining the tutor's role as an assistant to the dean of a house, Newman clarifies that the tutor's duty was 'certainly the moral, but more directly the intellectual care of his pupils, of which he relieves the Head'.[89] As originally envisaged, his chief work was to prepare his pupils for the lectures and examinations. Newman then turns to the heart of the tutor's task, explaining at length how it would require adaptation.

Newman hoped that the tutor would adjust himself to the needs of each student and cater not just for those who were able and studious, but also for those who showed little love of learning, or had not developed study habits, or were backward, and select their course of reading and recommend the lectures they were to attend and the books and subjects they were to present for examination. The tutor needed to oversee the reading of the more promising students by starting them off with advice, explaining the difficult passages, testing them now and again, bringing to their attention points they might overlook, helping them with summaries and generally keeping an eye on them. Different tactics were required for the backward, who would need support to remedy their shortcomings and make the most of their lectures, and for the idle, who would need to be kept on their toes and confronted with their lack of diligence in the run-up to exams. All this would demand of the tutor 'a sustained solicitude, and a mind devoted to his charge'.[90]

Newman enlarged on the possibilities of the tutor's role by suggesting that the way to a young man's heart lay through his studies, particularly in the case of the more able. Feeling grateful to the person who takes an interest in the things which are at that moment nearest to his heart, the student opens up to his tutor and from the books before them the two are,

> led into conversation, speculation, discussion: there is the intercourse of mind with mind, with an intimacy and sincerity which can only be when none others are present. Obscurities of thought, difficulties in philosophy, perplexities of faith, are confidentially brought out, sifted, and solved; and a pagan poet or theorist may thus become the occasion of Christian advancement.[91]

In this way the tutor forms the pupil's opinions and becomes the friend, perhaps the guide, of his life after university. Newman's lofty conception of the 'serious importance' and 'really interesting nature' of the tutor's office for the well-being of the university are captured in the following words:

> In this idea of a College Tutor, we see that union of intellectual and moral influence, the separation of which is the evil of the age. Men are accustomed to go to the Church for religious training, but to the world for the cultivation both of their hard reason and their susceptible imagination. A Catholic University will but half remedy this evil, if it aims only at professorial, not at private teaching. Where is the private teaching, there will be the real influence.[92]

Newman's idea of the tutor's role touches on much that makes him special as an educational thinker—and much that is characteristic of him as a person: his recognition of the importance of education for the development of young people; his love of his fellow human beings; his *caritas*; his stress on the formative value of personal influence; his appreciation for the personal element in the process of understanding and embracing knowledge and faith; his patience with human weakness in the fitful process of maturation; his grasp of the obligations and rewards of the universal; his insistence on the practical. In particular, Newman held that moral and religious truths were best communicated and most likely to stir the heart by the power of personal influence, and that tutorials should be conducted on this basis. These views were not the outcome of research or reading, but rather the result of many years in education, during which he had tried to live out his high ideals and to observe critically and ponder on what he saw around him.

Operating the lodging houses

If little has been said so far about the lodging houses themselves, other than the fact that Archbishop Cullen purchased 86 St Stephen's Green in February 1853, this is because nothing further happened for a year, other than naming the building University House. In February 1854 Newman began to put in motion building works to convert the top two stories of No. 86 into student bedrooms, the basement into a dining room and kitchens, and the rooms on the ground and first floors into lecture rooms, offices, a library and a temporary chapel. He took no action to acquire other collegiate houses until August, though he now needed to consider who to appoint as deans.

Newman hoped the collegiate houses would be run by young or middle-aged Irish priests, because he thought the deans should be familiar with Ireland and its ways. However, he was willing to make an exception to this working rule in the case of Fr Henry Marshall, an Oxford-educated English convert who was working in Ireland and very popular with the Irish, being greatly admired for his wit: Newman invited him to become a dean, on condition he could recruit twenty young men for his house. However, when Cullen found out he intervened and told Newman to take Fr Michael Flannery instead.[93] Like Marshall, Flannery was a priest in his mid-thirties; he had taught moral theology for six years at the missionary seminary of All Hallows before becoming vicar general of the diocese of Killaloe. Flannery's appointment was essentially an act of Cullen's which Newman felt bound to accept, and it was to give rise to considerable problems later. Flannery had called on Newman in March asking for a post at the University, and Newman had offered him the deanship of University House on the same condition he offered Marshall: that he gather the young men for it. After Cullen intervened, this important condition was waived. There was also confusion about his terms, as Newman offered Flannery £100 for the post, whereas the University Committee had proposed that the two deans of discipline be paid £150, probably based on an assumption by Leahy that his duties would be similar to those of the dean of a seminary.

Newman had envisaged that the 'nations' would reside in separate collegiate houses, so when the Archbishop of New York told Newman he hoped to send between 60 and 120 students within a year or two, Newman anticipated that they would reside in a house of their own;[94] likewise, when the first South American arrived, Newman thought they might have to consider establishing a South American house. Although neither North nor South Americans materialised in any numbers, the collegiate houses did develop along different lines; but they did so largely for financial reasons. At first Newman estimated that the fees ought to be around £100 p.a. Three months before opening, Newman was minded to fix the fees for University House at between £40 and £50, though, as he commented to a friend, 'it will be in every sense a rough place—it must be so'.[95] From Newman's breakdown of the finances given below, it can be seen that the 'pension' included lecture fees and private tuition, as well as remuneration for the board of the dean and tutors.

Expenses of a Student in the University House

N.B. The University takes upon itself the Rent, Taxes, and House Porter of the University House.

The Students take on themselves Laundress, and the Grocer and Chandler.

The Dean and Tutors take on themselves firing in addition (I think we shall be able to give them this in.)[96]

1. Dinner, (as by Mr M. O R[eilly]'s calculation) per week	£11.80
2. Breakfast (minus tea and sugar)	£1.60
3. Supper (2/3 of Breakfast)	£1.00
TOTAL	£14.20 say £15.00
Board 38 weeks at 15/–	£28.10
Firing 30 weeks at 3/–	£4.10
Attendance for 38 [weeks] at 15/ a month for 9 months: £6.15—say £7	£7.00
Tuition from two Tutors	£4.00
Share in Dean and Two Tutor's board viz £28.10s x 3 ÷ 15 (3 being the Dean and Two Tutors and 15 the number of students)	£6.00
TOTAL	£50.00

The fees for University House were announced in the *Gazette* (28 September 1854) as fifty guineas, 'including board, lodging, firing, servants, public lectures, and private tuition'—but even this sum was strongly objected to. Being the only collegiate house founded by the University, it was expected to offer the lowest fees, since it was felt that if a student's expenses were low it would encourage the laity of Ireland to take advantage of the education offered. Newman had argued that to lower the rate further would make the

University foot the bill; but others maintained that since the University was intended for the special benefit of Ireland, and since the contributions came mainly from Ireland, it was appropriate that Irish youths should receive some benefit in a reduction of their maintenance costs. Newman accepted the argument, and a fortnight after the first announcement the fees were lowered to forty guineas. In fact, the expenses of University House worked out at around £80 per head, largely because it filled up only gradually during the first year, from five to thirteen.

The lodging houses and the tutorial arrangements formed an integral part of the University, and their place within the whole can be seen from the Scheme of Rules and Regulations. There Newman lays down that each collegiate house was to be presided over by a dean, who would enforce the necessary discipline and, being in most cases a priest, would serve the community chapel. The dean would be assisted by one or more tutors, as he preferred, or else could combine the office of tutor with his own. He was 'bound to rule and guide the students committed to his charge with firmness and tenderness, and to minister to the best of his power to their religious and intellectual advancement'.[97] Newman summarised the dean's overall responsibilities as follows:

> The Heads of Houses are charged with the moral and intellectual advancement of the Students of their Houses, who are strictly committed to them as *pupilli,* and are under their tutelage. They are responsible for their religious and correct deportment, for their observance of the Rules both of the House and of the University, and for their acquitting themselves adequately both before the Professors and the Examiners.[98]

Changes in the houses, such as the appointment of deans and tutors, required the agreement of the rector; and, where extreme measures were called for, he alone had power to dissolve a house.

In line with standard practice, collegiate heads and tutors were barred from being examiners so as to avoid any conflict of interest.

Any priest or graduate of the University could, with the rector's permission and the approval of the Archbishop of Dublin, set up and run a collegiate house, which would then become an integral part of the University; all the houses were obliged to be self-supporting, though the rector was at liberty to offer financial assistance in special cases (as with University House). The dean need not actually run the house himself, as he could appoint a sub-dean to do so; in either case he was at liberty to appoint a bursar and a chaplain if needed, as well as residential and non-residential tutors—all with the rector's consent. In each instance the chaplain was to reside in the house and be a priest approved by the archbishop; in matters of discipline he came under the jurisdiction of the vice-rector—which effectively meant that the vice-rector had to be a priest, too. Each student was to submit the name of his confessor to his dean at the start of the year; and, besides frequenting the sacraments, the student was expected to attend 'such devotions as his Head [i.e. the dean] appoints for him'.[99] This last stipulation of Newman's certainly has the ring of a seminary about it, but in all likelihood it would have varied in its interpretation according to the dean in question.

The students who were attached to a house but living outside—the externs—could reside only in a dwelling approved by the rector, and they had to be indoors by 10 pm; besides their academic commitments, they were expected to attend High Mass in the University Church and to observe their religious duties in exactly the same way as the interns. Their general welfare was the responsibility of the vice-rector. Each week the professors were to submit a record of attendance and conduct of the students at lectures: to the vice-rector for externs, and to heads of house for interns. Being responsible for the discipline of the University, the vice-rector (with the rector's consent) had power to interfere with the internal administration of the houses; to remove an intern from a house, at the initiative of the dean; to give them leave of absence; and to award honours or punishments for their conduct. The five levels of lighter punishments ranged from a simple admonition to a fine; the three heavier, from loss of a term to expulsion.

Although Newman envisaged that discipline—understood in the wider sense—would be underpinned chiefly by the lodging houses, the *genius loci*, and the tutorial system, he saw other means that would also supply that much-needed personal influence and bolster university discipline: the professors; the university sermons; the sacraments (particularly Confession) and spiritual activities (such as confraternities and devotions); and—surprisingly per-haps—academic dress. Though he did not want to burden the professoriate with an officially-recognised pastoral function, he nevertheless hoped that 'the Professors will without effort, and almost spontaneously, draw around them such young men as, from a turn for a particular study, or in other ways, are open to their influence'. A similar absence of compulsion is evident in Newman's attitude towards the university sermons. While maintaining that they would be of 'incalculable benefit', he thought their influence would be undermined if they were made compulsory for students; instead he hoped that through provision of seating and the attrac-tion of good preachers it would 'become a fashion, or rather a rule of the place, to attend the University Church'. In this way, he hoped that 'through the divine blessing, their hearts will receive indelible impressions'.[100]

To complement the provision at the collegiate houses for the students' spiritual needs, Newman wanted the University Church to supply confessionals, at least one religious confraternity, and the opportunity for the cultivation of particular devotions. In a private letter he wrote, 'we hope to act upon the young men, instead of using strict *rules of* discipline—which in a University is impossible. To bring out my idea of a University fully, I must establish some confraternity or the like to *win* young minds instead of driving them.' He explained that this would require priests not connected to the University 'to act on the University men'.[101] The academic gown he expected them to wear in church and also—as at Oxford—during lectures, at dinner and on other formal occasions, whether of a religious or secular nature. Since the wearing or carrying of a gown would identify a student, he felt it 'would much subserve the cause of discipline'.[102] Nevertheless he did not act on this particular idea: the introduction of academic dress was the result of a petition addressed to the rector in 1855 and signed by forty-one students (at that time virtually the entire student body of the University).

Preparations for 3 November

Much of Newman's time in the run-up to 3 November 1854 was spent in negotiating academic appointments. There was no shortage of candidates to put themselves forward, and, as might be expected, there was great variety in the ability, level of experience, flexibility, salary expectations, and motivation of these men. Active members of the University Committee eagerly recommended people for different posts, or else proposed them on the basis of their general merits. Newman availed himself of all this advice, but also took care to sound out those who had not volunteered information before taking up references and interviewing interested parties. There was no official mechanism for making appointments or for fixing salaries, so Newman had to be guided by his own good sense and the advice of others. He was constrained by the limited funds available and by the need to avoid incurring Cullen's displeasure—though when he did meet with his disapproval he showed he could fight his corner. Aware of Newman's insistence on having men about him whom he knew and who were familiar with the

Oxbridge system, Cullen was nevertheless minded to see that the majority of positions went to Irishmen so as to pacify anti-English feelings in Ireland; he was also determined to keep those with strong nationalist tendencies out of the University, although he did not always have his own way in this.

In his task of setting up the University, Newman had to steer a path between doing too little and doing too much. On the one hand, he saw that the University needed to appoint Catholics with 'professorial merit or fame', as these attributes were 'the very life of a University which has to make its way without secular patronage'.[103] On the other, neither he nor anyone else had any idea how many students were intending to enroll, and so he needed to be careful not to engage too many staff. In the event he erred on the side of appointing too many—perhaps consciously, as he wanted to lay the foundation of academic institutions which were 'useful in themselves and attractive to the public',[104] while ensuring that the main teaching posts for the arts course were filled in advance of the opening of the University (and advertised as such). For the professorships and lectureships Newman aimed to appoint men with a national or international reputation, the most promising he could attract; and he accomplished this task virtually single-handedly.

The task of attracting distinguished academics was not straightforward, as the University was an experimental and therefore risky venture. Certainly Newman had to face the suspicion of those who thought he was a pawn of the episcopate, or were doubtful of plans that might be changed or superseded, or were unconvinced that he could honour the pledges he had made. As he himself put it, 'It seemed unreasonable to ask men of name to commit themselves at once to our intellectual, social, and moral responsibilities, and to undertake new and untried engagements which might dispossess them of old and sure ones.' Yet he was gratified by the number who were prepared to risk their careers for the project, and heartened to discover 'so many generous, high-minded, and zealous men to share my labours'.[105] The one quality he considered essential for the enterprise was enthusiasm, and it is this characteristic which explains why these academics were willing to accept provisional promises of employment, meagre salaries,[106] postponements of duties, and alterations of their terms and conditions—even changes of the subjects which they were to lecture in! Another was their fascination and love for Newman.

Newman was boldly imaginative in the way he utilized the talent available and in the way he encouraged potential staff to involve themselves in the new subject areas that were just beginning to open up. When his efforts to establish an astronomical observatory came to nothing,[107] he took up the idea of setting up a meteorological observatory instead, but was frustrated by the lack of funds available. At a time when little science was being carried out inside universities in the United Kingdom,[108] he was determined to establish a faculty of science in Dublin. He was equally determined to set up a medical school and to attract leading practitioners to lecture there.

Though Newman's 'University Journal' catalogues all these negotiations, it contains not one mention of the anticipated influx of students. But the announcement that the University was to open on 3 November was only made public the previous May, and from this fact it can only be presumed that Newman was less concerned with what the size of the initial intake might be than with ensuring that the University was in a state to welcome them and undertake its pastoral responsibilities. That said, Newman did all he could to advertise the University among his English friends; and his hopes that some would cross St George's Channel for their education led to a burst of house-hunting over the summer, in anticipation of their arrival. Only on 27 October did Newman take up residence at 6 Harcourt Street, just off St Stephen's Green, which was to be his base in Dublin for the next four years.

Notes

1 I owe this insight to Alasdair MacIntyre from a lecture he gave at Notre Dame University on 1 November 2006 in the series 'God, philosophy, universities' (from the lecture notes of Brian Boyd).

2 I. Ker, 'Newman the teacher', *Newman and education*, ed. M. Davies (Rugley, 1980), p. 38. See also Ker, 'Newman's *Idea of a university*', pp. 15–16.

3 *Idea of a university*, pp. 8–9.

4 Memorandum, 29 April 1854, *MC*, pp. 93–4.

5 In the Report for the Year 1854–55 (*MC*, p. 7) Newman explains that 'a College is a domestic establishment or community, in which teachers and taught live together as one family', while 'a University is a collection of Professors and Schools [i.e. faculties], independent of each other, though united under one Head and by one code of laws'. A college is self-contained and has little or no direct bearing upon society at large, while a university is open to everyone and assumes a public character.

6 *Idea of a university*, p. 458.

7 *Idea of a university*, p. 466.

8 *The scope and nature of university education* (London, 1859), pp. 138–9. In this way the student is able to grasp the 'great outlines of knowledge, the principles on which it rests, the scale of its parts, its lights and its shades, its great points and its little', even though they do not form part of his immediate studies (*Idea of a university*, p. 101).

9 *Idea of a university*', p. 459.

10 He adds: 'Nor are his duties confined to the lecture hall: in this day, especially, he may be quite as usefully employed with his pen as with his tongue' ('Scheme of Rules and Regulations submitted to the Council in April 1856', *MC*, pp. 96, 110–11). A copy of this document at the Birmingham Oratory contains in the margins the phrase 'Professors to write books' (Culler, *Imperial intellect*, p. 311).

11 In distinguishing between the tasks of teaching and researching, Newman argues in the *Idea of a university* (p. xiii) that the capacities for undertaking both are not commonly found in one and the same person, since research demands isolation and concentration, and teaching an external involvement. For his fuller thoughts on the matter see pp. xii–xiv. For an explanation of Newman's approach to research see I. Ker, 'Newman's *Idea of a university*', pp. 12–16.

12 E. B. Pusey, *Collegiate and professorial teaching and discipline* (Oxford, 1854),
    pp. 215–16. Pusey's evidence to the Royal Commission investigating Oxford
    was the largest contribution to the *Report and Evidence* (1853) produced by
    the university in answer to the commissioners, whose recommendations
    were inspired by the German university system. Pusey had first-hand knowl-
    edge of the German system, having studied theology at three German
    universities during the summer of 1825 and the academic year 1826/27
    (*ODNB*).

13 An Irish priest collecting for the University in the United States wrote from
    Baltimore on 15 November 1852: 'Many intimate to us their fears that it
    will be like other Irish projects—a failure' (quoted in *NU*, p. 188); Ambrose
    St John similarly reported from Ireland that it was commonly assumed that
    the university project, like so many others, would come to nothing (St John
    to Newman, 19 September 1853, *LD*, vol. xv, p. 426n). The Report of the
    University Committee, presented to the bishops in May 1853, stated that
    'after so long a period of inaction' it was necessary 'to act with promptitude,
    on account of the diffidence which has been produced in the Public Mind,
    and which now has to be counteracted by redoubled energy on the part of
    the promoters and friends of the University' (quoted in *NU*, p. 251).

14 *MC*, pp. 294–5.

15 W. M. Thackeray's novel *Pendennis* (1849) describes the lifestyle of a
    fashionable 'young buck' at Oxford and his extravagant spending habits
    and pastimes, which included horse-driving and hounds, as well as books,
    art, furniture and clothes. That this was not merely satirical fiction can be
    seen from the mention of the same habits in the *Royal Commission Oxford*
    (1852, p. 24).

16 The essays were published together as *Office and work of universities* (with
    an alternative subtitle, *University teaching, considered in a series of historical
    sketches*) in 1856, then—more appropriately—as the *Rise and progress of
    universities* in 1872, and finally they came to form the first and major part
    of *Historical sketches*, vol. iii (1872, pp. 1–251).

17 This title appears to have been used for the first time by the publisher
    George Sampson in his printing of *University sketches* (London, 1902).

18 In his preface to *University sketches. Text of 1856* (Dublin, [1952], p. vii)
    Michael Tierney argues that the sketches form 'a very important part of a
    coherent body of thought'. In *NU* (p. 319) Fergal McGrath goes so far as
    to assert that they are as valuable as the *Idea*, if not more so.

19 Newman, *The rise and progress*, ed. M. K. Tillman, pp. xxiii–xxiv, xxviii.

20 In the advertisement to the second edition of the *Discourses* (1859), Newman refers to 'his two other volumes on University Teaching': two of them coalesced to form the *Idea of a university*, but the third, *Office and work of universities* (1856), was published separately.

21 Newman, *Rise and progress*, ed. Tillman, p. xxxvii.

22 This overriding aim has been overlooked by those who fault the sketches for the misconceptions they contain, such as misreadings of historical developments. It was inevitable that Newman should have committed blunders in his ambitious history of the university over two and a half millennia, written at a time when scholars were just beginning to turn their attention to the subject.

23 For a fuller overview of the situation, see L. W. B. Brockliss, 'The European university in the age of revolution, 1789–1850', *The history of the University of Oxford*, vol. vi, pp. 77–145.

24 Brockliss, 'The European University in the age of Revolution, 1789–1850', *The history of the University of Oxford*, vol. vi, p. 104.

25 Brockliss, 'The European University in the age of Revolution, 1789–1850', *The history of the University of Oxford*, vol. vi, p. 125. The French concept of Université was of a network of discrete faculties formed into a single administration under government control.

26 When the Birmingham Oratory archives reopen it will be possible to reassess this assertion. Peter le Page Renouf, a professor at the Catholic University, was sent by Newman on a fact-finding tour to the universities at Louvain and Bonn—and may have visited Friburg and Tübingen as well (Renouf to his sister, July 1855, *The letters of Peter le Page Renouf (1822–1897)*, vol. iii, ed. K. J. Cathcart (Dublin, 2003), pp. 17–18). Renouf challenged Newman's assertion that the German system established 'that the Professors should also be private Tutors', telling Newman, 'I know nothing about universities where this is the case. I should rather say that the tutorial element, if it ever existed in German universities, has utterly disappeared' (28 June 1858, *ibid.*, p. 58). Certainly Sir John Acton considered that 'the merits of the German system [were] never clearly understood, I think, by Newman' (Acton to Renouf, 30 May 1863, *ibid.*, p. 182). But neither did Acton have any first-hand knowledge of the Oxbridge system, as he told Renouf: 'I have always trusted to the professorial system to make Catholics some day superior to Oxford and Cambridge men—at which all my Oxford friends laugh' (11 December 1862, *ibid.*, p. 157). See also Acton's letter to Renouf on 8 June 1863 (*ibid.*, p. 187).

27 *HS*, vol. iii, p. 100.

28 It would seem that Newman took the idea from Samuel Taylor Coleridge, who argues in *On the constitution of the Church and State* (London, 1830, pp. 18–28) that healthy institutions needed to incorporate both the principle of progress and the principle of permanence.

29 *HS*, vol. iii, pp. 77–8, 88.

30 *HS*, vol. iii, pp. 72–3. Faced with the difficulty of explaining the pagan origins of the university, which did not include theology, one solution was to argue that the integrity of the university was given by the medieval institution of the college; another was to argue in terms of discipline and influence.

31 *HS*, vol. iii, p. 229. Newman was not the first to make this claim. The Scottish philosopher Sir William Hamilton had argued previously that 'the statutory combination of the Professorial and Tutorial systems […] is implied in the constitution of a perfect university'. However, this statement was nuanced by the assertion that 'A tutorial system in subordination to a professorial we regard as affording *the condition of an absolutely perfect University*' ('On the state of the English universities, with more especial reference to Oxford', 1831, *Discussions on philosophy and literature, education and university reform* (London, 1853) pp. 417, 448).

32 *Royal Commission Oxford* (1852), pp. 95–6, 99–100.

33 *Report and Evidence* (1853), p. 64 (in *Report*); pp. 5, 9, 40–1 (in *Evidence*). In the *Evidence* (pp. 44–50, 254) Mark Pattison of Lincoln College argued strongly in favour of the tutorial system and against the professorial: he told the *Royal Commission Oxford* (1852, p. 45) that 'the mischief of the Professorial System is that it implies a different idea of Education; that it aims at, and is the readiest and easiest way to, a very inferior stamp of mental cultivation, but a cultivation, which from its showy, available, marketable character, is really an object of ambition in an age like the present.' Roland Muckleston of Worcester thought that 'sacrificing the Tutorial System to the Professorial' was 'a scheme which involves a change from catechetical teaching to oral lectures; which abolishes moral superintendence in furtherance of objects merely intellectual, which is un-English in its principle', and that it would fail in its objectives (*Evidence*, p. 254). Frederick Meyrick of Trinity compared the two systems and used the example of Leipzig to argue against the professorial system (*Evidence*, pp. 275–83).

34 *CUG* 5 (29 June 1854).

35 The sketch, which originally appeared in *CUG* 9 (27 July 1854), was renamed 'Discipline and Influence' in *HS*.

36   *HS,* vol. iii, pp. 72–3.

37   *HS,* vol. iii, p. 74.

38   *HS,* vol. iii, pp. 182–3. The sketch 'Professorial and Tutorial Systems' in *CUG* 10 (3 August 1854) was named 'Professors and Tutors' in *HS.* The Church's role in Newman's scheme will be explained more fully later in this chapter. See pp. 130–1, 153, 157–9.

39   *HS,* vol. iii, pp. 183–4.

40   *HS,* vol. iii, p. 185. In another sketch, Newman uses the case of Abelard in Paris to illustrate both the strength and weakness of the professorial system: 'its power to collect students, and its impotence to preserve and edify them' (*ibid.,* p. 192).

41   *HS,* vol. iii, pp. 188–9.

42   *HS,* vol. iii, p. 189.

43   *HS,* vol. iii, pp. 189–90. The expression *altera Trojæ Pergama,* a classical allusion culled from Virgil's *Aeneid* (Book 3, lines 86–7), effectively means 'another Troy' or 'a home from home'.

44   *HS,* vol. iii, p. 190.

45   *HS,* vol. iii, pp. 213–15. Originally entitled 'Colleges the correction of the deficiencies of the University principle' (*CUG* 27 (30 November 1854)), the definitive title of this sketch is 'Colleges the corrective of universities: Oxford'.

46   For a description of collegiate life at Oxford in terms of homely intimacy, it is hard to find a better one than that of Sir David Lindsay Keir, Master of Balliol, which though half a century old is still up to date: 'Every true Oxford man would agree that the essence of Oxford is college life. To have one's own rooms, on one's own staircase, making one's friendships with undergraduates and dons, to have meals together, to drop into one's JCR, read in one's College Library, worship in one's College chapel, to play on one's own field or row from one's own boathouse […] It is on this intimacy of daily life that an Oxford education is based. From this it derives its unique value. A College is more than a hostel; it is more than just a private society of teachers and pupils, it is a household, a very large one, of course, but a household all the same. There is nothing quite like it and its Cambridge counterpart in the whole world.' (*Balliol College Record,* 1960, p. 5).

47   The seven traditional corporal works of mercy are: to feed the hungry; to give drink to the thirsty; to clothe the naked; to shelter the homeless; to visit the sick; to visit the imprisoned; and to bury the dead.

48   *HS,* vol. iii, p. 221.

49   *HS*, vol. iii, pp. 223, 226. This was a hypothesis of Newman's, based on a
     misinterpretation of the historian Anthony à Wood, which has not been
     borne out by later research.

50   *HS*, vol. iii, p. 234.

51   *HS*, vol. iii, pp. 234–5.

52   The diminished role of the university at Oxford in this period meant that it
     only oversaw minor tasks such as collecting (university) fees, publishing
     academic calendars, setting (university) exams, awarding degrees and execut-
     ing some disciplinary powers.

53   *HS*, vol. iii, p. 229. Originally 'Abuses of the Collegiate System' (*CUG* 29 (14
     December 1854)), in *HS* the sketch bears the title 'Abuses of the Colleges:
     Oxford'. This sketch, Newman's last, is noteworthy principally because it was
     here that he brings out most fully the complementary roles of university and
     college. See Appendix III for the frequently quoted passage which is unsur-
     passed as an articulation of the university–college principle.

54   *HS*, vol. iii, pp. 235–6.

55   *HS*, vol. iii, pp. 75–6.

56   *Royal Commission Oxford* (1852), pp. 22, 26, 88, 100–1, 212. The two
     systems were also in operation at Cambridge, where it was estimated that
     £50,000 p.a. was spent on private tutors (*ibid.*, p. 89).

57   Newman told a former Oriel tutor that the college tutors were overworked
     and that the professors 'could take from them advantageously many
     departments of general education—and then the Tutors would be more
     strictly guardians and formers of the Pupils' minds' (Newman to Rickards,
     7 February 1840, *LD*, vol. vii, p. 232).

58   Written as a letter to Cullen, but *not* sent, this document was effectively a
     memorandum which summarised Newman's ideas at the time. It was not
     unusual for Newman to act in this way: as on other occasions, the document
     served as a means for helping him sort out his ideas, as Newman found that
     he thought best with a pen in his hand, and it also helped him discuss them
     confidentially with his friends.

59   A measure of the importance of the Report for 1854–55 is that Newman
     arranged for it to be translated into Italian and printed (Newman to St John,
     4 April 1856, *LD*, vol. xvii, p. 204).

60   Culler (*Imperial intellect*, p. 165) claims that Newman's collegiate plans for
     the Catholic University were largely the outcome of discussions he had had
     with Froude and Pusey in the 1830s, but he provides no evidence to back
     up his assertion.

61 Newman to Cullen, 14 August 1852 (not sent), *MC*, pp. 271–2. By 'large houses', Newman means large institutional buildings that could accommodate around a hundred students.

62 Newman to Cullen, 14 August 1852 (not sent), *MC*, p. 272.

63 Newman to Cullen, 14 August 1852 (not sent), *MC*, p. 273.

64 Report for the Year 1854–55, 13 October 1855, *MC*, pp. 33–4.

65 Report for the Year 1854–55, 13 October 1855, *MC*, pp. 33–4.

66 The schemes for the Queen's Colleges had made provision for Catholic halls of residence, though none had been set up. Priests had been appointed deans of residences at Cork and Galway, and one was about to be appointed at Belfast when the Synod of Thurles took place and the hierarchy decided against these arrangements. The Catholic deans of residences were to have the 'moral care and spiritual care' of their students and were allowed to give religious teaching to them in lecture rooms set aside for this purpose. (*Royal Commission Queen's Colleges* (1858), pp. 12–13; *NU*, pp. 65–6).

67 Report for the Year 1854–55, 13 October 1855, *MC*, p. 35.

68 'Scheme of Rules and Regulations', 1856, *MC*, pp. 114–17. This was eventually incorporated into, and published as, *Constitution and statutes of the Catholic University of Ireland*, 29 June 1869 (DDA, 45/5/V(4)). A longer extract from the Rules and Regulations on how to manage students is given in Appendix IV.

69 Report for the Year 1854–55, 13 October 1855, *MC*, p. 39. Newman's thinking on discipline had the support of precedent at Louvain, because there—as a long-standing member of the Catholic University Committee told him—the 'main point on which it seems to be an example to be studied is the discipline. It being perhaps the only example of one combining freedom in the students with the safeguard of Catholic Morality' (M. O'Reilly to Newman, 2 April 1855, BOA, Louvain routine and working file, C.6.3).

70 To modern ears there is nothing particularly novel about the idea of open competition, but at the time it was an innovatory practice. It saw the old order of privilege and sponsorship giving way to meritocracy, typified by such legislation as the India Act (1853), which opened up appointments to the India civil service. At Oxford, reformers in the 1850s battled to open up scholarships, exhibitions and bursaries to ordinary students without ties of kin, school, geographical location or parental status.

71 Report for the Year 1854–55, 13 October 1855, *MC*, pp. 39–40.

72 Report for the Year 1854–55, 13 October 1855, *MC*, p. 40. There is more than an echo here of the prefect system introduced by Thomas Arnold at

Rugby which played a key part in reforming the public-school system. During the middle decades of the nineteenth century it gradually became accepted that character training was enhanced by a delegation of authority to the boys themselves and that, besides instilling virtues, self-government had two practical advantages: it made the headmaster's job easier, and it prevented rebellion by uniting some of the most influential boys with the masters. Though theologically at odds with Arnold's latitudinarianism, Newman clearly admired his use of surrogate authority and employed it himself.

[73] Culler, *Imperial intellect*, p. 166.

[74] *Idea of a university*, p. 147

[75] Report for the Year 1854–55, 13 October 1855, *MC*, pp. 41–2.

[76] *MC*, p. 85.

[77] Newman to Cullen, 14 August 1852 (not sent), *MC*, pp. 276–7.

[78] Newman to Thompson, 26 August 1852, *LD*, vol. xv, p. 156.

[79] Newman to Wiseman, 23 January 1854, *LD*, vol. xvi, pp. 27–8.

[80] Newman to H. Wilberforce, 23 November 1853, *LD*, vol. xv, p. 485.

[81] Newman to Dunne, 28 July 1854, *LD*, vol. xvi, p. 207.

[82] Newman to Paley, 20 May 1854, *LD*, vol. xvi, pp. 137–8.

[83] To support his application for a tutorship and lectureship, Stewart compiled a twenty-page printed booklet of testimonials (BOA, DP 25, Testimonials, applications and salaries of professorship).

[84] When warned that his plan for lodging houses would 'awaken jealousies' involving those he appointed, Newman attempted to pre-empt this possibility by suggesting to Ornsby that 'if you set yourself up there previously, you would escape the jealousy, yet would be available' (Newman to Ornsby, 7 March 1853, *LD*, vol. xv, p. 324).

[85] Wilberforce resigned from the tutorship in April 1854, and Thompson pulled out when he found his health was suffering, and was replaced by the Irishman David Dunne.

[86] Newman to Thompson, 7 September 1853, *LD*, vol. xv, p. 419. He also protested against Henry Wilberforce 'taking *things to help me*. It will not be enough, however affectionate the motive—you must do things *con amore*, or not at all. I shall be ruined if people come forward to help me—they must come forward to help the object as a τέλος τελειότατον [an end in itself]. You will love me and serve me best, by not thinking of me, and measuring your actions by your zeal for the cause.' (23 November 1853, *LD*, vol. xv, p. 484).

87   Newman to Stewart, 6 December 1853, *LD*, vol. xv, p. 489.

88   *HS*, vol. iii, p. 190. Henry Vaughan proposed to the Oxford commissioners a similar arrangement: the tutor would begin the work which the professor would take up and complete, as this would free the tutor for personal acquaintance with his pupils, while the professor would be freed from the drawbacks which destroyed his advantages in the Scottish and German universities, and 'will be enabled to work more profitably from having an audience better suited to receive his instructions' (*Royal Commission Oxford* (1852), p. 100).

89   'Scheme of Rules and Regulations', 1856, *MC*, p. 117.

90   'Scheme of Rules and Regulations', 1856, *MC*, p. 119.

91   'Scheme of Rules and Regulations', 1856, *MC*, p. 119.

92   'Scheme of Rules and Regulations', 1856, *MC*, p. 120. A longer description of the role of the tutor is given in Appendix V. In *NU* (p. 386) McGrath comments that the passage about the duties of tutors is 'not so much worthy of note' as that about the duties of professors, a remark which reflects his own educational background and lack of appreciation of the tutorial system.

93   In May, Marshall had attended an unruly public meeting in Dublin to protest against the British government's decision to carry out an investigation of Catholic convents, and he made such a strong speech that Cullen banned him for preaching for six months. The ban was rescinded when Marshall published an apology and promised to abstain from politics (Larkin, *The making of the Roman Catholic Church*, pp. 245–6).

94   Newman to H. Wilberforce, 12 July 1854, *LD*, vol. xvi, p. 196. John Hughes, the first Archbishop of New York and the leading Catholic Irishman in the United States, had called on Newman at Birmingham in 1846, and in 1853 had arranged for a collection to be made to meet the costs of Newman's Achilli trial. Hughes was very optimistic as to the money and students that would flow to the Catholic University from the United States, and he invited Newman to cross the Atlantic for a lecture tour before the term opened in November. It is likely that Newman decided against the tour because he could not afford the two months such a trip would require; he had earlier considered touring major cities of North America, from New York to New Orleans, even though he dreaded the inconvenience such a trip would cause him (Newman to Flanagan, 9 February; Newman to Stanton, 28 February: *LD*, vol. xvi, pp. 40, 65; Cullen to Newman, 14 November 1854, *Paul Cullen and his contemporaries: with their letters from 1820–1902*, ed. P. MacSuibhne, vol. iii (Naas, 1965), p. 198). The Bishop

of Boston, John Fitzpatrick, passed through Birmingham on 21 July 1854 and Newman may well have spoken to him about the University.

95   Newman to Ryder, 17 August 1854, *LD*, vol. xvi, p. 221.
96   23 September 1854, *LD*, vol. xvi, p. 256n. Firing refers to the cost of heating the building.
97   'Scheme of Rules and Regulations', *MC*, p. 104.
98   'Scheme of Rules and Regulations', *MC*, p. 114.
99   'Scheme of Rules and Regulations', *MC*, p. 120.
100 Report for the Year 1854–55, 13 October 1855, *MC*, p. 42.
101 Newman to Wenham, 24 November 1856, *LD*, vol. xxxii, p. 161.
102 Report for the Year 1854–55, 13 October 1855, *MC*, p. 43.
103 Report for the Year 1854–55, 13 October 1855, *MC*, p. 16.
104 Report for the Year 1854–55, 13 October 1855, *MC*, p. 11.
105 Report for the Year 1854–55, 13 October 1855, *MC*, p. 17.
106 The average salary at the Catholic University was £185 and the maximum £300, whereas at Louvain the minimum salary for a professor was £500 (*MC*, p. 153). The average income for a tutor at Trinity was £650 (McDowell & Webb, *Trinity College Dublin*, p. 179). Not everyone was sympathetic to the financial constraints that Newman was operating under, and on one occasion he exclaimed: 'It pains me to find how people are making money the first thing in the University' (Newman to Scratton, 23 April 1855, *LD*, vol. xvi, p. 446).
107 Newman approached his Tractarian friend Manuel Johnson, the director of the Radcliffe Observatory at Oxford, for advice about setting up an observatory and for recommendations of Catholic astronomical observers.
108 There were around six hundred mechanics institutes in England at the time. Owens College, Manchester opened in 1851 as a centre for science; in advance of both Oxford and Cambridge, London University opened a faculty of science in 1859.

4 THE UNIVERSITY OPENS

THROUGHOUT THE SUMMER of 1854 Newman was immersed in overseeing all the practical business of setting up the University so as to be ready to open in November. Yet he did not allow the daily demands on his attention to obscure what was of paramount importance for the nascent university: that there should be 'a perfect unity of purpose and operation'. He knew that it was one thing to appoint a number of professors with different titles and subjects of study, and another to cultivate 'the harmonious action of these, their growth into one body, and their production of a real Education for those under their care'. He was anxious to achieve this harmony and to lay solid foundations for the future, aware that the first few months would prove crucial. He also considered it vital that the University should adjust itself quickly to the level of 'knowledge, and moral and intellectual training' of the first pupils. Time would be required before the University could create its own atmosphere and establish its own standards of knowledge and moral character. 'In the meantime', he insisted, 'it must take the youth as it finds them, and make the best of them.'[1]

Education makes the man

The official inauguration of the Catholic University had in fact taken place in May 1854, when the Irish bishops had assembled to decide on the measures necessary for starting the University that autumn. On Pentecost Sunday, at the end of High Mass at the pro-cathedral in Marlborough Street, Dublin, Newman had been sworn in as rector. In the crowded church and in the presence of Archbishop Cullen and other dignitaries, Newman made his profession of faith and solemnly pledged obedience to the Irish bishops in all his endeavours to secure the success of the University. The actual opening of the University on Friday, 3rd November, was by contrast a very subdued affair; the bishops were all in Rome when, without fanfare or ceremony, the classical and mathematical schools were opened, and with them the Catholic University. Entrance exams were conducted by the vice-rector (Patrick Leahy), the Professor of Classical Literature (Robert Ornsby) and the Lecturer in Logic (David Dunne); and the young men tackled a Latin composition, answered several questions on paper, and were interviewed individually. Seventeen were successful, and they began their studies on Monday 6th, after attending a soirée the rector had organised for them at the University House the previous evening.[2]

Some of Newman's words to the students on the evening of 5th November have survived, thanks to Ornsby, who appreciated the historical significance of the occasion and devoted several pages to the meeting in his memoir of the first term.[3] From Ornsby's description we know that, besides Newman and the students, the others present were the dean of the house (Michael Flannery) and the three academics, including himself. It was a solemn affair, as Newman's intention was to set his stamp on the foundation from the very first moment, and to inspire the young men with his high ideal of what a university should be. He had already delivered lofty speeches and addresses to assembled clerics and dignitaries; now, for the first time, he would address those for whom the University was actually intended.

They assembled in the refectory; the list of names was read out by Dunne, and then the students were introduced individually to Newman and Flannery. Newman's opening words to the students acknowledged that they had come to the University to prepare for the professions and callings they intended to follow, whether the law, medicine, engineering, or something else; but he added that, while whatever they learned would certainly have a bearing on those professions, there was another, more important, reason for their coming to the University. They could learn their profession at other places, but there was something they would learn better at the University than anywhere else, and this was the subject on which he intended to dwell. To illustrate his point he told them a story about a mother and her son: the mother had been widowed and left with few means to provide for her children. One of them, a young man, was offered a job which was well below his expectations, and was inclined to reject it; but his mother persuaded him to rethink, arguing 'that it is not the place makes the man, but the man makes the place'. What she meant, Newman explained, was that if a man was 'well educated, of cultivated mind, well principled, and gentleman-like', wherever he found himself he would be valued for what he *was*, without a thought about his trade or profession, provided it was an honest one. 'A gentleman carries his own recommendation with him.' He might be poor, he might be obliged to take up a humble trade, but that was beside the point: 'he will adorn his place, he will render himself and his place respectable, if he has these personal recommendations'. On the other hand, if he was without these qualities he might occupy a high position and command great wealth, 'yet in a little while the world will find him out, and pass him by and think little of him, or even ridicule him'. There was, Newman argued, a great truth contained in the idea,

> that there is an education necessary and desirable over and above that which may be called professional. Professions differ, and what is an education for one youth is not the education for another; but there is one kind of education which all should have in common, and which is distinct from the education which is given to fit each for his profession. It is the education which made the man; it does not make physicians, surgeons, or engineers, or soldiers, or bankers,

or merchants, but it makes men. It is that education which
enables the man to adorn the place, instead of the place
adorning the man. And this is the education for which you
especially come to the University—it is to be made men.[4]

Newman then tried to explain 'what it is to be a *man*, as distinct
from having a profession', and to do this he took up the mother's
words to her son again. Supposing that the son was in fact well-
educated, though not well off or in a good job, he would come
across all sorts of people through work, the family circle, or society
at large. Few would care what his job was; what they would
see—and what would impress them—would be what he was
personally. At first they might simply notice that he seemed
well-behaved; then, knowing him better, they might comment on
his modesty, on his mature sense of judgement, on how his conversation showed that he had thought and reflected. Then, as time
went by, able men would take notice of him and say: 'A very
clear-headed man that—he is a man whose opinion I should go by
if I were in difficulty. He has a great sobriety and soundness of
understanding; he takes very sound views of things.' And so, as the
young man grew older, he would gradually become the centre of a
wide circle of people who relied on his judgment; and he might
become one of those who 'sway the current of affairs, public and
private'. Such a person would be in a position to do great deal of
good, particularly if he were a religious person.

Just as a strong man will make a better soldier than a weak one,
so a man thus strong in intellect, thus cultivated and formed, will
be able to do a great deal for God and the Church, for his creator,
his Lord and Saviour, and for his Christian brethren, which another
man could not do.[5]

On the other hand, someone who had grown up 'without
learning to be a real man' would be a boy all through his life—and
there was no lack of examples. 'They have no opinion, no view, no

resource; they are not fond of reading or thinking, they cannot amuse themselves; their only amusement is going out of doors for it'. Since they have no opinion, no-one would think of asking them for it; when they are with friends they have nothing to converse about, and their conversation is likely to be empty. 'Hence they get tired of themselves and of each other, and go out for amusements, and then, perhaps, get into bad amusements, because they have no resources.'

> Gentlemen, if I am called upon to state the difference between a boy and a real man, I should say this—that a boy lives on what is without and around him; the one depends upon others for instruction and amusement, the other is able in great measure to depend upon himself. You come here to learn to pass from the state of boys to the state of men.[6]

The education they would receive at the Catholic University was something that would fit them for every situation they might meet with in life. A man might, in the course of time, face adversity; but if he had a cultivated mind, he would act under these changed circumstances with dignity and decorum. Or again, if sudden successes were to come his way, he would act calmly and as he ought to; he would not be like those who come into a great fortune, do not know how to spend it wisely, and throw their opportunities away. A well-trained mind will act with decorum; it will not be thrown off balance by any of the changes of life, but will make the best of all circumstances and conduct itself exactly as it should.

Newman went on to explain what a university was. Catholics in Ireland had been barred from university, owing to the circumstances; but now the Holy See thought it was time to remedy the situation, and make available to Irish and other English-speaking Catholics that higher education which until now the Protestants had monopolised. Since it was the nature of a university to gather people from all quarters, they would meet with men from a variety of backgrounds, and thus would add to each other's knowledge. Speaking of the discipline that was characteristic of a university, he reminded them that they were no longer boys, but verging on manhood; children were ruled largely by fear, but this was no longer the case with them; they were, by and large, their own masters. The university authorities would take them for intelligent youths, would have confidence in them, and take them at their word, and hoped to be met by a similar spirit of confidence. Newman alluded to the Romans putting on their *toga virilis,* and quoted the passage of St Paul (1 Corinthians 13:11) about putting aside childish things. Though in one sense they were always children—children of their Heavenly Father—and would be foolish to forget it, they should now feel that manhood had arrived and endeavour to show a manliness of mind. They must begin well, and then a *genius loci,* a good general character and spirit, would reign over the University.

Turning to practical matters, Newman explained that the choice of the start of term, St Malachy's Day (3 November), was partly from devotion to the saint who was much honoured in Ireland, and partly because it was the time of year when colleges generally opened, which would give them a long vacation stretching from August to October inclusive. He spoke of the qualifications—and sang the praises—of the vice-rector, the deans and the professors. As for the normal working-day routine, lectures would take place in the morning and then they would be free from lunch until dinner at 5 pm, after which their timetable would be settled by the deans. He finished by speaking of their numbers—there were only fifteen present—with which he was pleased, though more might have been expected. If they lived to be old, they would look back with pleasure to St Malachy's Day 1854, when they had taken part in the founding of the University, which would by then be great; and the fewness of the numbers with which they began would form a happy contrast with the great numbers of later years. Newman wound up the proceedings by reciting Shakespeare's rousing speech of Henry V on the eve of the battle of Agincourt.

Establishing the academic routine

A young man joining the Catholic University in 1854 would have found a small institution at the heart of Georgian Dublin, operating out of a central building which looked out across St Stephen's Green. Just half a mile away from the bulk and splendour of Trinity College, the University would have appeared as a tiny, almost domestic, establishment, for all its ambitions. The young Catholic might even have shared these ambitions and dared to believe that this little institution would one day challenge that long-established emblem of Protestant hegemony, buoyed up in his hopes by the sight of teaching staff from the heart of the English establishment. Feelings of optimism would have been reinforced by the gradual growth in student numbers over the year. During the first term the numbers on the lecture list rose from seventeen to twenty-seven; further additions over the Christmas vacation meant that the Lent term began with thirty-seven, and, despite several departures over the Easter vacation, the summer term began with forty. In total, around sixty were on the University books during that first year, though there was a fair amount of coming and going. In addition to those who matriculated there were some others who only attended the 'evening display lectures', which were advertised in the press and aimed at attracting new students.[7]

On the first day of Michaelmas Term, the students attended lectures in classics and mathematics at University House, and, two days later, began lectures in modern languages. The earliest surviving lecture list comes from the second term and it shows that the young men would have been kept hard at it with lectures and classes.[8] There were daily lectures in classics and mathematics at 10 am, 11 am and

12 noon, and language classes in French between noon and 2 pm; these were followed by an hour of Italian twice a week. Evening lectures took place every weekday at 8 pm, on French, Sacred Scripture, Spanish poetry, Irish literature or classical literature, and occasionally these were followed at 9 pm by lectures in Italian or geography. During the summer term there were few evening lectures but, to compensate, lectures were introduced on Saturday mornings at 10 am, 11 am and noon. During the first year most of the evening display lectures (which were open to the general public, including women) took the form of inaugural lectures, the first of which was given by Newman on Thursday, 9th November, 'On the place held by the Faculty of Arts in the University Course'.[9]

These heavyweight lectures came at the end of a working day which included at least four hours of contact time in classes or lectures. But this was not all. Besides the official University exams, which were due to take place at the end of the second and fourth years—the scholar's and licentiate[10] exams respectively—Newman ensured that the students were kept up to the mark with regular testing at the end of every term. During the first year, these 'terminal exams' took place on 21–22 December, 26–30 March and 16–19 July, and were presided over by the rector himself. The length of time set aside for examining—eleven days that first year—is a measure of the importance Newman attached to the task. He had always done so; among his many contributions to education, one that is rarely recognised is that he was an examiner[11] all his adult life, whether at Oxford, Dublin or, later, at the Oratory School in Birmingham. One of the reforms he had undertaken at Oxford was to introduce written work[12] into the termly college exams at Oriel; and as an Oxford University examiner he had sought to ensure that examining was made more rigorous. In the months prior to the opening of the Catholic University he had immersed himself in all the details of the entrance exams, which were devised by three of the lecturers.[13] While he strongly disliked cramming and superficial learning, he maintained that regular tests had a specific use in training the intellect: 'they impart self-confidence, they serve to bring home to a youth what he knows and what he does not, they teach him to bring out his knowledge and to express his meaning clearly'.[14] For this reason he felt that at Dublin, 'The Examination system is the key to the whole University Course, and the Examiners should be as formal Officers of the University as Professors.'[15]

Nearly all the first students were interns, residing in three collegiate houses.[16] The largest of them was University House, the splendid town-house that had been purchased in 1853 and which doubled as the main university building. A second collegiate house was formed within an existing seminary school located nearby at 16–17 Harcourt Street, a Georgian mansion once owned by the Earl of Clonmel. St Laurence O'Toole's Seminary and Catholic Day School[17]—as it was styled in *Battersby's Catholic Directory*—catered for local boys living at home and boarders intended for the priesthood, and was run by the recently ordained James Quinn. In 1854 the older boys were enrolled as members of the University and, under the deanship of Quinn, formed a collegiate house known as Dr Quinn's House which shared the same premises as the school. The third residence, 6 Harcourt Street, was the Rector's House, and here Newman presided as dean (as well as rector). That such fine buildings should be associated with an impoverished new institution might seem surprising, but it should be remembered that until the Act of Union (1800) Dublin was a European city which boasted fine buildings and a thriving social life; after 1800, decline set in and fifty years later there were plenty of large properties on the market at reasonable prices.

Ironically, the first name entered in the University Register is that of Daniel O'Connell, grandson of the 'liberator',[18] who on account of his ancestry was awarded a scholarship which enabled him to reside at University House and attend lectures free of charge for four years. As the majority of students at University House were Irish, it soon became officially recognised as an endowed house for the natives of Ireland with the right to 'present' to it those who passed the entrance exams and fulfilled the other requirements. As a consequence it was renamed St Patrick's House; Dr Quinn's House, meanwhile, became St Laurence's and the Rector's became St Mary's.

St Laurence's was at that time the principal school in the centre of Dublin, rivalling the only older foundation, St Francis Xavier's. It was staffed mainly by scholarly secular priests, with some assistance from laymen. The president, James Quinn, had studied under Paul Cullen at Rome, where he had completed a doctorate. On returning to Dublin, he had pleaded forcefully for the establishment of a secondary school there, and soon found himself in charge of St Laurence's; though of delicate health, he had thrown himself into the task, and revived a nearby elementary school at Arran Quay to act as a feeder, employing the same staff for both. The senior school advertised itself as one for 'ecclesiastical boarders' and for day boys preparing for the professions and business 'in the shortest possible time' at thirty guineas p.a. Both the lay boys and the clerical boarders were given a classical education, supplemented by modern languages, drawing and music.

In 1854 Quinn was assisted by two other priests, able scholars from the Irish College in Rome; the chief lay assistant was David Dunne (aged twenty-four), who had also studied for the priesthood and completed a doctorate at the Irish College, though he remained a layman. Dunne's teaching role at the school was drastically reduced in November 1854 when he became Lecturer in Logic at the Catholic University and a tutor—but at St Patrick's, not St Laurence's; and in 1855 two more priests joined St Laurence's, Matthew Quinn (a younger brother of James), and Robert Dunne (the younger brother of David). The arrangements for students at

St Laurence's were quite unlike those at St Mary's and St Patrick's, for a number of reasons: the premises and some of its resident staff were shared with a school; the lay boys lived at home, and continued to do so after matriculating at the University; the domestic regime was that of a junior seminary; and the strictness of discipline was along the lines of what the staff would have experienced at the Irish College in Rome. Having joined the Irish College at the age of seventeen, Quinn had experienced a very different kind of education from that of Newman. Though dealings between them were generally warm, due to their generous natures, they had vastly different outlooks and priorities, and indeed inhabited different educational worlds. Yet rarely did Quinn complain about Newman, or about what he thought was the undue English influence on the University and the negative effect this would have on the institution: and to Newman he said nothing at all.[19]

St Mary's lay between the other two collegiate houses, being 50 yards from St Laurence's and about 400 yards from St Patrick's, but the physical proximity of the houses did not signify any other closeness. St Laurence's catered mainly for local students who lived at home; St Patrick's was almost entirely residential and its inmates hailed from beyond the Pale of Dublin; St Mary's was predominantly patronised by students from overseas. The three houses differed, too, in the strata of society from which they drew their students. But above all they differed in the way they operated, largely on account of the character and background of the deans. Newman had anticipated that the houses would be a disparate set of establishments, though he was to find to his cost that maintaining the peace between them and ensuring that the University dealt with them equitably was to exercise his powers of diplomacy to the limit. He may have had an inkling of the difficulties that lay ahead of him on account of the collegiate houses, when he confided to a friend shortly before the University opened: 'There will be a great many small local jealousies, which I must not mind; and I must get my friends to pray that I may have, not only the gift of wisdom, but of tranquillity.'[20]

Newman and St Mary's

Shortly before Newman was appointed to the rectorship of the Catholic University in November 1851, he indicated his intention to involve himself at various levels of the new institution, and not just as its head. His remark to his friend George Ryder that 'I mean to be Chancellor, Rector, Provost, Professor, Tutor all at once, and no one else any thing' may have been a quip, but he was in fact anticipating the need to turn his hand to many different tasks. He ought to have added at least two other titles to his repertoire, those of dean and student recruitment officer, as he undertook these too. Joking apart, he expressed to Ryder his hope that his sons might go to Dublin and 'prove themselves some of the first fruits and flowers of the University'.[21] In like manner he used every connection he had to drum up support for the University from the English constituency and beyond, urging friends to assist the enterprise by recommending students for it.

As the opening of the University approached, Newman began to consider whether he could form an English house with seven or eight sons of his friends or other contacts. By opening up the Rector's House to students he thought he could help solve one of the 'actual difficulties—viz the necessity of beginning with *several* houses for different classes of students'.[22] By adapting his own house, he thought he might be able to attract young men of the higher classes, and by this means help to advertise the University. It is clear that as late as July 1854 Newman had no intention of acting as dean, since at the time he was instructing an agent to find him a suitable house which would also have room for a dean, two tutors and five students, as well as servants. As the building was expected to furnish a chapel and a common room for the students, it needed to be of a decent size; and besides, as Newman emphasised, 'A number of persons living together of different ages and pursuits require a large house.'[23] Towards the end of October, after a number of properties had been inspected, Newman decided to rent 6 Harcourt Street and to furnish it at his own expense. It was at this stage, with mounting costs and a lower than anticipated number of students entering the University, that Newman decided to shoulder the task of dean himself.

Although Newman had anticipated receiving mainly sons of Englishmen of the professional classes, he found himself overseeing a cosmopolitan household with considerable social éclat. By the end of the first term the student body comprised two Englishmen (plus another who was an extern), two Scottish cousins of noble blood, two Irishmen (one of them a baronet), and two titled Frenchmen. No wonder Newman could say, 'we have quite a galaxy of high people in this house'.[24] They were not only a diverse group by nationality, but also by age, ranging from fourteen to twenty-one years old.[25] To Newman it seemed that the appeal of an English education might be catching on overseas, and he hoped to reap the benefit. During the first term he created extra rooms in his house to meet demand, and over the Christmas vacation completed the process of converting the stables into a chapel, at a total cost of £300. At Christmas 1854, it looked as though more rooms would be needed for French, Belgian and Polish youths—a prospect which struck Newman as being like a revival of the medieval state of affairs.

But all these developments brought their troubles and worries, and if friends in Dublin were spared the details, the Birmingham Oratorians were most certainly not. The letters Newman sent home describe the petty problems he had to face, such as dealing with servants who arrived late or who forgot to lock up properly. On one occasion Newman had to stay up until midnight waiting for the caretaker to return—'Don't mention all this. 'Tis the cares of house-keeping', he told the Oratorians.[26] Then there were difficulties with the domestic staff and ensuring that they were able to cook and serve dinner properly. At one point, after seven weeks of substandard cooking and cleaning, Newman informed the cook and her sister that they were to leave, whereupon 'she changed her cooking so marvellously, that it seems a fright does good', and her sister became 'a pattern of clean dusting'.[27] One of the lecturers Newman appointed, the poet Aubrey de Vere,[28] has recorded his impressions of the rector's domestic role: 'I was pained by the very humble labours to which Newman seemed so willingly to subject himself. It appeared strange that he should carve for thirty hungry youths, or sit listening to the eloquent visitors [...] Such work should have fallen on subordinates, but their salaries it was impossible to provide.'[29]

It was partly to help resolve a problem at the Oratory that Newman arranged for Thomas Godwin, an Oratorian lay-brother who supervised the servants, to leave Birmingham and work at St Mary's as caretaker and general factotum. He was chronically disorganised and forgetful, and his carelessness led to the other servants taking liberties; but he became something of an institution in the house, 'singing in the kitchen with astonishing compass and volume'.[30] In spite of the lack of college plate and the other paraphernalia of an Oxford college, and with only a few silver-plated spoons and forks, Newman somehow managed to maintain a semblance of 'high table' in the midst of this amiable anarchy —though guests were surprised when Godwin joined in the conversation whilst serving at table. Many years later Godwin reflected on his happy times at St Mary's, likening the residence to a beehive. 'Little do the outer world know how beautifully the family was managed', he recalled. 'I can see the Father sitting in his little room receiving first this one and then the other, directing, guiding, calling each by their names as if he were their very

Father'.[31] Besides speaking to the students, Newman received a constant stream of visitors, most of whom were connected with the University. John Hungerford Pollen, the newly-appointed Professor of Fine Arts, remembered his first visit, when after dinner he, Newman and one of the lecturers retired to the drawing room, where the three Oxford graduates chatted merrily over port and biscuits about their university days. Pollen had been a Fellow of Merton College and a popular senior proctor of Oxford University (1851/52), before forfeiting his fellowship on becoming a Catholic. Though he had not met Newman before, Pollen found him charming and simple, despite all his worries.[32]

For the first time, at the age of fifty-three, Newman found himself keeping house and overseeing the servants and all the domestic finances—and these were made more complicated by Newman's wish to accommodate the residents' needs. Not all the rooms he could offer were equally comfortable, and only the oldest students were guaranteed a single room and a fireplace; the youngest were forced to share rooms, which were divided in two with a screen. Newman's budget for the thirty-eight-week year shows that he intended to balance the books by contributing £300 himself.[33]

Anticipated receipts for 9 months:

5 at £100;	1 at £80;	own at £300	£1000

Anticipated expenditure:

Current expenses/month of £72 x 9 months	£648
Rent	£110
Board wages	£13
	£771

Although the average fee was more than £80, he found himself in the red at the end of the year, and each year the deficit increased slightly—and this was in spite of Newman's personally undertaking the duties of dean, chaplain and tutor. It should be added that, unlike the other houses, Newman gave wine at dinner, and in some instances paid for extra tuition; he also factored into his calculations a cost for wear and tear on furniture and fittings.[34] By way of explaining the large difference in fees between his house and St Patrick's (£42), Newman placed a notice in the *Gazette* (12 October 1854) which stated that the availability of more expensive residential arrangements would not divide the student body as regards 'academic advantages, social equality, and unity of discipline'.

To a parent who complained about the fees, Newman replied, 'I do not know what advantage I have in the arrangement [of running St Mary's], except the feeling that I am promoting a great Catholic work. […] young men […] are extravagant in coal, in candles, in washing, all of which are included in the £100. They give a great deal of trouble merely from thoughtlessness.'[35] If he were a Protestant clergyman in England, he added, he would have charged £300 instead. The fact is that he could have easily distanced himself from the residences and the problems they threw up: yet it was typical of Newman that he wished to deal with individuals rather than remain aloof in academic and administrative isolation. He took on the deanship of St Mary's not on a whim, but to ensure that the pastoral units of the University functioned along the lines he had mapped out.

To understand the part Newman expected the collegiate houses to play, it is very helpful to take a closed look at how he ran St Mary's and dealt with each of its students. From what at first sight might seem to be jumble of disconnected facts and anecdotes, patterns will emerge which shed light on Newman's ability to turn theory into practice.

One of the two Irish residents was the baronet Sir Reginald Barnewall (aged seventeen), who belonged to an old Anglo-Irish family which had lost most of its estates on account of remaining Catholic. He was a sociable country gentleman, tall and thin, and also delicate; he required a breakfast of boiled milk with thick slices of bread soaked in it. The posthumous son of the ninth baronet, he had been anxious to leave the society of his elderly relations; initially an extern and coming daily to Newman's house, he decided after a fortnight to become an intern of St Mary's, and he proved to be a good student, devout, and in possession of sharp wits. In January 1855 St Mary's welcomed its second Irishman, Ernest O'Meagher, whose family lived in Paris after the recent loss of his Spanish mother. His father had at first thought of sending him to Oxford, where the religious test barriers for the BA degree had just been removed, but instead he opted for the Catholic University.

A more curious instance of paternal influence brought St Mary's one of its two French students, when Newman appointed to a lectureship in French literature Peter le Page Renouf, who was of an old Guernsey family and an Oxford convert. After a period of teaching and study at Oscott College, Renouf had become private tutor to Louis, the son of the comte de Vaulchier, while continuing his own studies; when Renouf responded enthusiastically to New-man's invitation to take up an academic post, the comte insisted that Renouf should take Louis with him. Renouf not only continued to act as tutor for Louis de Vaulchier but slept in the same room (the back drawing-room), as the boy was of delicate health and suffered from nervous attacks. Besides his teaching role (which entailed taking the French class and giving a lecture a day), Renouf acted as the main humanities tutor for St Mary's. Newman had hoped Renouf might also substitute for him as dean in his absence, but discovered that he was too impractical. The other Frenchman in the house was Charles de la Pasture, second son of the marquise de la Pasture; he joined St Mary's from Downside School, near Bath, and remained at the University for three years.

Among the first Englishmen to join the University were two sons of George Ryder, who had been receiving spiritual direction from Newman in Birmingham. Harry, the eldest, entered St Mary's the first term, and his brother Lisle, a godson of Newman's, arrived at St Patrick's the following term. The other Englishman living at St Mary's was Victor Duke (aged nineteen), who before moving to Dublin had been tutored at the Birmingham Oratory along with Harry and Lisle. Victor was one of eight children of an Oxford convert who was a doctor at St Leonards, Sussex, and he remained at St Mary's for two years before trying his vocation at the Birmingham Oratory. Another son of an English convert to join St Mary's was Henry Bowden (the nephew of Newman's best friend at Oxford), but in his case it was as an extern. He had been educated at Eton (where he had been in the football and cricket XIs), and had become a Catholic shortly after leaving. From October 1853 he had been a private pupil of Robert Ornsby, and then in 1854, his last year in Dublin, he was enrolled at the new university while lodging with the Ornsbys at Kingstown.

Lord Ralph Kerr, the third son of the seventh Marquis of Lothian, had become a Catholic in January 1854 and spent the rest of the year at the Birmingham Oratory, before moving to Dublin. His cousin, Francis Kerr, the third son of Lord Henry Kerr, had become a Catholic when just twelve years old and had also been tutored at Birmingham, where he would have remained but for Newman persuading his father to send him to St Mary's. On account of his age—fourteen—he was considered as an extern 'accidentally lodging with Newman', paying the reduced fee of £60. Newman knew only too well that he had undertaken a delicate task in caring for the youth, and for this reason he arranged for him to share a room with Charles de la Pasture. Newman wrote regularly to his father to keep him abreast of the ups and downs of the young lad's progress. At one point the boy was worried that his head was shrinking, and Newman could do little more than listen. Of greater concern was his propensity to waste money. When Newman heard how he had bought a book in a 'foolish extravagant way', after borrowing the money off a servant, he advised his father to provide Francis with an allowance which would make him careful and 'pinch' him. Besides the 'pension' and pocket money, he told his father that there were only three necessary expenses: clothes, travelling and books. Although de Vaulchier managed on £7 a year, Newman admitted to Lord Henry Kerr that he had been 'ambitious to bring the expenses of some youths four or five years older than Francis, within £20 a year'.[36] Three days later further details emerged: Frank had borrowed nearly £3 off Newman and his servant for needless expenses: 7/- on bookshelves, 2/3 on a parcel, 2/- on a volume by Horace, 2/- on a devotional book, 3/6 on a necktie, 5/- on a knife and scissors, and 1/- on crape for his hat; then another £1 on skating for a fortnight and cabs; and a further £1 on a subscription to a circulating library, old-fashioned religious books, and two pipes (both of which he gave away). Newman asked Frank to declare his bills and put everything on paper so that he could send them home to his father.[37] As if this were not enough, a long letter followed detailing Frank's encounters with an expensive Dublin tailor.[38] But besides letters occasioned by Frank's spending, there were others to his father of a more standard nature, containing reports about his academic progress and exam performances, vacation reading, and news about his health and recreational activities.[39]

There is every indication that Newman thoroughly enjoyed his first two terms at the helm of St Mary's. Though he acknowledged that 'my real and anxious work is beginning, for I have a houseful of eight youths' and no-one with whom to share the responsibility, he told the mother of Henry Bowden that the young men were all behaving themselves. The 'French Viscount, Irish Baronet and Lord Ralph Kerr are three of the most amiable innocent youths you can fancy, and if I can keep them so, will be a great gain for us—but you may fancy it is a great anxiety.'[40] It is telling that when Archbishop Cullen enquired from Rome about how the University was progressing Newman responded not about its governance or student numbers, but with a pastoral account of the small collegiate house he was overseeing: everything was going well, he told Cullen, and he felt fortunate in his set of youths.[41] And when a priest friend of Newman asked after the University, he too was told about St Mary's: 'if they did not go on to my entire satisfaction, I should get rid of them without a scruple. Many of them are as devout and innocent as novices, and all of them are gentlemen.'[42] This did not, of course, mean that St Mary's had all the best students, because, as Newman knew, St Patrick's had many excellent youths too. Neither does it imply presumption on Newman's part. In fact he asked the Bishop of Southwark to commend his own and all the young men to the patronage of the Virgin Mary:

> They are a very good set, and, judging from their way of going on, (I am speaking of them all, 30 or 40 of them altogether) I do trust they are in a state of grace, and going on hopefully. Of my own in particular I speak with great confidence—and consider that of the many blessings with which we have been favoured here, the greatest is the set of youths who make up my own house. Alas, youths are so changeable, that I must not boast, yet it can't be wrong in saying it in thanksgiving, that I could not ask a more religious innocent set of fellows than I have. And it is most important, for, as you know, the Irish love rank and that sort of thing, and the example of youths, such as those of whom I have charge, being attentive to their duties, gentle and modest, has great influence on the whole body. Their minds are occupied with reading, and they are making progress in their studies.[43]

Asked if he had news about the University for the Pope, Newman instructed Lord Kerr to inform the pontiff that the Blessed Sacrament was now reserved at St Mary's.[44] In fact, from January 1855 onwards Mass was said there daily and attended by several of the residents. Those who did attend regularly, like Louis de Vaulchier, Reginald Barnewall and Ralph Kerr, were also diligent enough to get an hour's reading in between Mass and breakfast. But there was less of the model student about the others, and as the year wore on they began to show their true colours. The regime of lectures, classes and tutorials seems to have kept the young men busy during term, but once the end-of-term exams were over and the three-week Easter vacation arrived, those who chose to remain at St Mary's rather than stay with friends were inclined to take things easy, to Newman's horror. 'Ralph K[err] *must* be idle, Francis [Kerr] *is*, Frederick Thynne *wishes to be* idle, and Reg[inald Barnewall], if not idle, loves amusement, and these four somewhat frighten me',[45] he reported to Birmingham. He was relieved when the summer term began and the idle time was over. The previous term he had commented: 'I should be very jealous of any youth I took into my house—and should be afraid of any beautiful snake getting among us'.[46] But the arrival of the eldest son of the convert Lord Charles Thynne was one such, and four weeks into the term Newman complained, 'He has already begun corrupting my youths'.[47] Besides being idle, he evidently managed to disgrace himself and was removed from St Mary's on 24 May, after which he stayed at Pollen's[48] as an extern until his father collected him four days later. After a short spell at the Birmingham Oratory, where they found 'he was quite like an Eton boy and exhibits nothing bad',[49] he obtained an Army commission.

A different problem erupted a few weeks later when Frank Kerr and Harry Ryder caught scarlet fever, which Newman blamed on their frequent and 'imprudent' swimming in the Liffey. They remained with Newman at St Mary's while the others were farmed out to University staff: Barnewall, de la Pasture, Duke and O'Meagher to Scratton; Renouf and de Vaulchier to Pollen; and, when he recovered, Frank Kerr to Ornsby—not Scratton, as Newman feared he would be idle there—then later to Stewart. Newman made time to visit the sick students each day and cheer them up, and helped nurse them back to health; and on their road to recovery, he even went out riding with them.[50] The lecturer Aubrey de Vere, who had also caught scarlet fever, never forgot the way Newman cared for him when ill. 'In spite of countless other engagements', he records, 'every day Newman found time to sit by my bedside occasionally, and delight me by his conversation.'[51]

Over the summer of 1855 Newman had an unpleasant exchange of letters with the father of the two Ryder boys. Lisle, the younger of the two, was a moody and wilful teenager who been in the habit of lying in bed in the mornings at St Patrick's. Being a friend of the boy and his confessor, Newman decided to talk to him about the matter; but, when his laziness persisted, his father sent Lisle such a harsh letter that Newman pleaded for leniency towards the boy —which led the father to accuse Newman of double standards. The added complication was that the elder brother, Harry, whom Newman had looked after so assiduously during his illness and protracted convalescence, thought he had a vocation to be an Oratorian—but his father was set against it. After accusing Newman of coming between him and his sons, the father withdrew them from the University; Lisle was sent to Ushaw College in England, while Harry entered the English College at Rome.[52]

Being the 'aristocracy' of the new University, the residents of St Mary's were, according to de Vaulchier, 'rather scoffed at' by outsiders; he recounts that the life they led under Newman was as near to Oxford life as he dared allow it, and that it was generally known that the Irish bishops strongly disapproved. The students of

St Mary's were regular in attending lectures, but 'were allowed to come and go according to our fancy. Leave was only asked when we missed dinner, or wanted to go out at night', although Newman did ensure that if they went out after dinner they never went alone.[53] The other two houses did not enjoy this degree of liberty, and as a consequence there was gossip about Newman's students. De Vaulchier recalled that Newman was 'consistently kind to me',[54] though in his memoirs he emphasised that it was to the resident tutor, Renouf, that the residents referred all their difficulties, whether about their studies or other matters. Renouf seems to have shouldered the bulk of the tutorial burden at St Mary's, as the mathematics tutor, William Penny, lived at St Patrick's, but Newman lent a hand with the tutoring when he could. Writing to defend Newman's reputation as a Latinist after his death, Charles de la Pasture recalled, 'I learnt more as to the writing of Latin from a few classes given privately to the men of his own house by Newman as its tutor than I did from a longer course' of lectures under the two professors of Latin, Ornsby and Stewart. He added, 'to read the Greek tragedians in the same manner with Newman was, indeed, a classical treat I love to recall'.[55] Newman also oversaw Victor Duke, Harry Ryder and Ralph Kerr in their preparations for the scholar's exam, advising them to choose their Latin and Greek set texts carefully from those listed in the *Gazette* (14 December 1854).[56]

It is clear that whatever spare time Newman had at his disposal he would spend with his charges; when he travelled to and from Birmingham at the beginning and end of term, he usually did so in the company of English students; and when accepting invitations to dinner at institutions such as Clongowes Wood, the Jesuit school outside Dublin, or the missionary college of All Hallows, he was in the habit of taking a student with him. He encouraged the students to play musical instruments by organising lessons for them, and arranged for a singing master to visit twice a week, with the aim of practising for sung vespers and Mass. Despite his own lack of interest in any form of organised sport, Newman encouraged the students to row, as he considered it a healthy recreation as well as a cheap one, and in the spring of 1855 he saw to it that the University was provided with a cricket pitch. To this end he instructed the University Secretary 'to preside at a Committee of "men" (you will then be αναξ ανδρων [Lord among men]) to choose a cricketing ground', and to ensure that Henry Bowden, who had played cricket for Eton in 1852, was present,[57] and to look into the ground behind University House. But Scratton thought it inadvisable to have a cricket field which was overlooked by houses, as he thought the students were 'rather a rough lot' and would not do the University credit, so he looked elsewhere instead.[58]

During the summer of 1855 the stables at the back of University House were converted into a billiard room for the University. This was not a sop to student whims but a carefully considered response to a problem that had developed during the first academic year, when the students took to the tables in nearby Dawson's Lane, at what was regarded as the great billiards place in Dublin. Though it was kept by a good Catholic who professed to keep a strict eye on the students, and though priests played there in private, the danger for the students was that they were likely to form undesirable acquaintances there and become involved in betting. Rather than simply issue a ban on frequenting the place, Newman sought to acquire a table for the University with the intention of formally licensing a 'keeper' and then forbidding the young men to go elsewhere, but the expense and want of a room delayed the plan. Although Newman knew it 'won't quite answer the purpose, for *the youths wish to see play*', he decided to push ahead over the first summer vacation using a loan of £160 from the University.[59] Upon completion an announcement appeared in the *Gazette* to the effect that a spacious room had been set up 'to serve as a billiard room, for the recreation of the students', and that it was open from noon until 5 pm under the care of 'a respectable and efficient marker, who has orders to prevent all gaming and betting'.[60]

Though no student records survive of social life at St Mary's, the personal recollections of the caretaker Thomas Godwin suggest it was a lively household. Two decades after Newman's departure he could still remember 'the jolly recreations which might be termed musicals or extempore plays or charades' that took place at St Mary's. Evidently Godwin was a fixture at these innocent amusements, for he was carried upstairs bodily by the students to sing or to play the cello or double bass at their regular gatherings. Though Newman absented himself from these student socials, we know he took a great interest in them, because afterwards he plied Godwin with questions about them.[61]

While the greater part of student life outside the lecture room centred around the collegiate houses, as Newman had intended, there was one activity which cut across the collegiate system and drew from the University as a whole. This was the Historical, Literary, and Aesthetical Society, which first met on 9 March 1856 and survives to this day as the Literary and Historical Society, or L&H. It functioned partly as a debating society, but also as a medium for the delivery of papers and as an outlet for student journalism. So distinctive and influential was this student society that a section of the next chapter is devoted to its origins and early life.

Academic oversight and the expansion of the University

On 16 July 1855, at the end of the first academic year, there began two days of examining for the scholar's degree in University House.[62] Besides the two examiners, one internal (Professor Edmund O'Reilly, an Irish priest who had lectured at Maynooth for over a decade) and one external (Edward Walford, a former scholar of Balliol College, Oxford), there were also present the rector, the Archbishop of Dublin and various other clerics. One by one, the students braved this formidable array and at the end of the second day a handwritten notice in Latin confirmed that ten of them were successful.[63] The next batch sat the scholar's exam in mid-November, and a third group were processed in March 1856; the external examiners on these occasions were, respectively, the Professor of Natural Philosophy from Queen's College, Galway and a classicist from Trinity College, Dublin. The presence of these visiting examiners was intended to lend weight to the Catholic University exams, which was all the more needed in the absence of any public recognition, and the names and qualifications of both the internal and external examiners were paraded for this very purpose. Examiners were also assembled for the annual awarding of four scholarships, two each in classics and mathematics. In November 1854 all four were awarded, but a year later only one applicant was deemed worthy of a scholarship. Following Newman's guidelines, the successful candidates had to reside in one of the collegiate houses.

The final day of internal exams in the summer term of 1855 marked the beginning of the long vacation, and the students were told that if they wished 'to keep the ensuing Session', they must be present at Mass on the morning of 3 November. As a spur to academic endeavour over the summer, Newman announced that seven prizes of five guineas each were open for competition: an essay in English comparing the views of named classical authors; a translation into English of a passage from Virgil; a Greek exercise; a composition in Latin describing the death of Alexander the Great; an account in English of the conversion of Ireland; knowledge of MacLaurin's account of Newton's discoveries; and knowledge of conic sections geometrically illustrated. The first five were to be submitted to the rector on return after the summer, candidates being 'bound in honour to offer only what is bona fide the result of their own labour'; the latter two were to be decided by examination at the beginning of November.[64] The students were warned that prizes would not be awarded if entries failed to reach a minimum standard.

During that first year other developments took place which the undergraduates would not have been aware of. At the end of the first term, it became common knowledge that the Pope had ratified the University statutes (which were based on the Louvain statutes) enacted by the bishops the preceding May and approved their adoption for six years, but that a significant change had been introduced. As a result of private lobbying, Cullen had ensured that the overall control of the University resided with the four archbishops, rather than with the episcopal body as a whole, and that he had the casting vote as apostolic delegate. When MacHale heard that he had been outmanoeuvred by Cullen he was furious, and from this point onwards set himself completely against Cullen and the University.[65] News of the disagreement, and the hardening of attitudes it produced, was a reminder to Newman that he and the University were caught up in a complicated web of intrigues and battles. A second important development—or setback—was Newman's failed attempt to relieve himself of some of the financial administration of the University by establishing a lay finance committee. He told Cullen, who had just returned from Rome, where he had been for nine months, that 'some soreness exists on the part of the educated and upper class through Ireland on the ground that they are allowed so little share in the management of the money matters of the University. I think they would have joined us before now, if they had been more definitely recognised'.[66] Among the letters Newman received on the subject was one from a lay member of the University Committee, who complained that 'the tendency is to make the University a close borough of clergymen and a clerical College', and pointed out that this had not been the intention of those who had assisted Newman at the start.[67]

Newman's request for greater lay involvement was turned down on this and later occasions.[68]

In October 1855 Newman presented the Irish bishops with an official resumé of the first academic year in his Report for the Year 1854–55; but for a much briefer, unofficial gloss on the state of affairs, it is useful to read the letters he wrote, such as his entertaining account to the mother of Henry Bowden, the extern attached to St Mary's.

> We are getting on with the University as well as we possibly can. It is swimming against the stream, to move at all—still we are in motion. The great point is to set up things—That we are doing. The medical schools will begin in October—the Church is building—and an Institution for Physical Science in course of formation. It will be years before the system takes root, but my work will be ended when I have made a beginning. Four years are now gone since I have been engaged upon it—the Holy Father has given me leave for two years more —and, as you may think, I shall be heartily glad when they are at an end. A Rector ought to be a more showy, bustling man than I am, in order to impress the world that we are great people. This is one of our great wants. I feel it vividly—but it is difficult to find the man who is this with other qualifications too. […] I ought to dine out every day, and of course I don't dine out at all. I ought to mix in literary society and talk about new gasses and the price of labour—whereas I can't recollect what I once knew, much less get up a whole lot of new subjects—I ought to behave condescendingly to others, whereas they are condescending to me—and I ought above all to be 20 years younger, and take it up as the work of my life. But since my qualifications are not those, all I can do is to attempt to get together a number of clever men, and set them to do what is not in my own line.[69]

The start of the second academic year had a buzz about it. Not only were there thirteen new students in the arts faculty, with four more arriving after the start of term, but there were around forty others entering the new medical school. Over the summer of 1854 Newman had pulled off the greatest coup of his rectorate by purchasing the Cecilia Street Medical School, which been running since 1837 and was recognised by the Royal College of Surgeons in Ireland. In 1854, after two of its most able staff departed, the proprietor decided to sell up, and when the fully-equipped premises came onto the market, Newman empowered Andrew Ellis, who had been Professor of Surgery at Cecilia Street since 1837, to purchase the school, which he did for £1500. The transaction was carried out without the proprietor realising he was effectively selling to Catholics (which he would not have done, if he had known), and without the knowledge—let alone the approval—of the archbishops. But Newman was unable to staff the medical school at short notice, which meant that the opening was delayed until the start of the second academic year. Dissection work began on 1 October 1855, and on 2 November the school was formally opened with an inaugural address from Ellis, the dean of the new faculty and Professor of Surgery. However, most of the forty-three who enrolled that year were non-matriculated students who were not subject to the University rules. Newman hoped that eventually the majority of the medical students would want to benefit from the two-year arts course, and to entice them to do so he arranged that those with two year's standing were remitted the fees, which were £2 2s per medical course. By taking this measure Newman hoped the University would eventually possess 'a school of medical practitioners, who do not merely avail themselves of our classes, but are identified with Alma Mater as her children and her servants, and who will go out into the wide world as specimens and patterns of a discipline which is at once Catholic and professional'.[70]

The school's instant success was a consequence of the medical situation in Dublin, where only ten out of sixty-two medical officers in hospitals were Catholic, and only two out of forty-nine medical lecturers. Overall, this meant that only twelve out of 111 medics in positions of trust and authority were Catholic. The opening of the medical school was something of a gamble, because it began without any official recognition, but at the end of the first term the recognition was forthcoming and with that the success of the school was guaranteed. It proved to be the healthiest institution attached to the University, and continued to thrive until its absorption into the National University of Ireland in 1909.[71] Besides addressing the immediate need for the training of Catholic doctors in Ireland, Newman's enthusiasm for the project arose from his anticipation of the profession's growing importance. He reminded the Irish bishops that,

> Medicine and Surgery, considered as Arts, are confronted, at the great eras of human life, at birth and at death, with a higher teaching, and are forced, whether they will or no, into co-operation or collision with Theology; so again the Practitioner himself is the constant companion, for good or for evil, of the daily ministrations of religion, the most valuable support, or the most painful embarrassment, of the parish priest.[72]

But medicine also had to be considered as a science, and here the Catholic University Medical School had its own part to play. Any study, when pursued exclusively, tended from the very constitution of the human mind to close itself against truths which lay beyond its range; and, unless the claims of revealed religion were recognised in the arts faculty (which at the time included science), they would be regarded as disproved, merely because they were beyond the reach of its investigations. In like manner,

> the presence, though not the interference, of Theology is necessary in the lecture-halls and theatres of Medical, as of other Science, by way of rescuing scientific teaching, what-

ever be its subject-matter, from a narrowness of mind, of which indifference to religion is only one specimen. The Catholic University, then, will have done a great service to Medical Students, if it secures them against the risk of forgetting the existence of theological truth, and its independence of the teaching of Philosophy and Science.[73]

Besides medicine, the other school to open in November 1855 was that of engineering, with lectures in mathematics, geometry, natural philosophy (i.e. physics) and technical drawing.[74] Newman had hoped that the engineering school would combine academic residence with practical studies and field work, but initially the University had to settle for less.[75] Though lacking official recognition, the course provided a suitable preparation for the entrance exams of the College of Military Engineering at Woolwich, and within three years two of the University's engineering students were successful. The fees were identical to those of the medical faculty, with the carrot of free lecture courses for those who had passed through the two-year preparatory arts course. Newman was not only intent on setting up schools of medicine[76] and engineering, but anxious to do the same for chemistry and physics: indeed, his longer-term plan was to set up the premier institution of physical science in the United Kingdom.[77] W. K. Sullivan, perhaps Ireland's most renowned scientist at the time, was appointed Professor of Chemistry and Dean of the Faculty of Science in November 1855, and was charged with acquiring the books and apparatus that would be needed to begin, together with the Professor of Natural Philosophy, Henry Hennessy (coincidentally Sullivan's brother-in-law), appointed the previous year.[78] Already a member of the Irish Academy on account of his contributions to science, Hennessy was shortly afterwards elected to the Royal Society and produced many valuable and original papers while at the Catholic University.

As with the other schools, Newman gave guidance and authorised major decisions, and this involved him in many petty problems
which cumulatively absorbed much of his time and made endless
demands on his reserves of diplomacy. The medical school in
particular was a drain on his time because he had to encourage
doctors to join the concern, negotiate rates of pay, resolve rival
claims for titles, forge links with hospitals, and so on.

Despite Newman's best efforts, he was unable to set up a Faculty
of Law for November 1854. He had approached several leading
lawyers, but without success: Thomas O'Hagan QC (the future Lord
Chancellor of Ireland) was offered any lectureship he wanted and
was asked to recommend men from the Irish Bar; George Bowyer,
Liberal MP for Dundalk, agreed to give a course of lectures; Myles
O'Reilly agreed to lecture on jurisprudence; and John Pigot, son of
Chief Baron Pigot, conditionally agreed to be Professor or Lecturer
in Real Property. The practical difficulty the University faced was
the premium on attending Trinity or the Queen's Colleges, which
shortened the time needed for the Bar by two years. Despite this
obstacle, Newman still hoped that it might be possible to establish
a law faculty, though he failed to see it come about during his
rectorship;[79] in the absence of any alternative, Catholics studying
for the Bar continued to go to Trinity. Newman had initially been
keen to start the University with a Faculty of Theology, but he
changed his mind once he realised there would be no demand at the
outset. In the event Cullen's strong wish to see theology given
prominence meant that in November 1856 the chair of dogmatic
theology was added to that of sacred scripture, and soon afterwards
one in canon law. Newman regarded the theology faculty as being
in the bishops' hands—if not entirely in Cullen's—and he was
reluctant to get involved in paying salaries.[80] Although the Catholic
University had no theology students itself, some forty external

students (all either seminarians or priests) attended lectures given by the theology faculty at a parish house in the city.[81]

The rector was also anxious to see the system of collegiate houses expand. When the second academic year started, a new collegiate house was opened along the lines of St Laurence's. Two of the day-pupils (both 'intended' for the priesthood) from the Academy of St Mary of Mount Carmel, the Carmelite secondary school in Lower Dominick Street, entered the University in November 1855 and they were joined by a further seven the following January; they formed the House of Our Lady of Mount Carmel under the deanship of Fr Thomas Bennet, Provincial of the Order of Calced Carmelites and a vice-president of the missionary seminary of All Hallows. Bennet was one of the first graduates of the University of Louvain, where he would have seen a rudimentary collegiate structure in operation, but the Carmelite house contributed no other students until 1863 even though it remained affiliated to the University. Both his house and James Quinn's were ideally placed to draw students from the locality, and by the end of the second academic year Newman was quite optimistic as he felt the two schools were 'working' Dublin well. The second academic year saw provision at St Patrick's expand from fifteen to twenty-seven places when the adjacent house, No. 87, was acquired for the University and a passage linking Nos 86 and 87 was constructed.

There was also the prospect of a fifth collegiate house. After the purchase of the medical school in Cecilia Street, Newman turned his mind to providing a lodging house where the trainee medics could be offered rooms at a reasonable rate 'and exempted from the various inconveniences, material and moral, which befall them in a great city'. Starting with a simple lodging house to provide them with basic needs at a reasonable cost, with 'the higher object of removing them from the temptations which surround young men who are thrown without protection on a large town', he hoped it might develop into a university residence for medical students.[82] The lodging house was advertised in the *Gazette* (18 September 1854) as receiving the sanction of the University, but without a formal connection—which meant that its residents were not subject to its rules or barred from attending lectures at other medical schools in Dublin. Even though the charge was a modest £7 per quarter (reduced to £6 in the *Gazette* of 12 October 1854), there was insufficient demand and the scheme was temporarily shelved. Nevertheless, it shows Newman's constant concern for residential living conditions.

The support the collegiate houses received from the University was more than a moral one, as it assisted each of them with a yearly contribution of £50. To this was added a sum proportional to the number of residential students: £100 each year when there were above five; £150 when above twelve; and £200 when above twenty. The purpose of these grants was to reinforce a key element of Newman's organic plan for the teaching university, the provision of suitable tutors in the collegiate houses. When the University opened, however, there were not nearly enough tutors and over the next four years Newman found it difficult to implement his plan the way he had intended. When the University opened William Penny doubled up as the mathematical tutor at both St Patrick's and St Mary's; during the first academic year he was the only resident tutor at Patrick's, then he was joined in the second by David Dunne, the classical tutor of St Patrick's, who had been living at St Laurence's during the first year.[83] For the first two academic years the (resident) classical tutor at St Mary's was Renouf; he was joined in the second year by William Scott, a former Fellow of Brasenose College, Oxford, who had become a Catholic in 1854. The University Calendars list tutors only for St Patrick's and St Mary's, not for St Laurence's and Our Lady of Mount Carmel, and from this omission and their precarious existence as collegiate houses it may be assumed that neither of the latter properly entered into Newman's system.[84]

During the second year most of the academic lectures took place at 10 am, 11 am and noon, with supplementary ones following on at 1 pm in subjects that now included modern history, German language and literature, and (after Christmas) political economy.[85] Evenings seem to have been abandoned not only for the student lectures but also for the free public lectures, which now took place at 3 pm.[86] The library, which had been started the previous year, began to attract gifts and large bequests of books and the University Secretary took on the task of cataloguing them and acting as librarian.[87] Despite all this activity, University matters almost disappear from Newman's correspondence in the Michaelmas Term of 1855: but there was a reason for this. Throughout Newman's rectorate, the Catholic University and the Birmingham Oratory competed for his presence; and just as there were critical periods when the University needed his undivided attention, so there were times when the Oratory required his steadying hand. Early in 1855 the Birmingham Oratory had been unsettled by an Oratorian who had returned (temporarily) from the London Oratory and considered that the Birmingham house lacked the spirit of St Philip Neri, the founder. After separating a few years earlier the two oratories had developed along very different lines, and misunderstandings and differing interpretations of the Rule of St Philip caused relations between them to deteriorate.[88] When the London house petitioned Rome for a change in the Rule—without consulting Newman—it threatened to alter the *modus vivendi* in Birmingham. To protect the Rule he had brought into England and to safeguard the spirit of the Birmingham house, Newman eventually decided to resolve the matter in Rome, and during his visit there (26 December 1855 to 11 February 1856) Patrick Leahy the vice-rector was left in charge of the University—the only occasion 'in which a Vice Rector was a reality', Newman commented at the time.[89]

Congregation business naturally dominated the visit, but Newman did take the opportunity to speak to the Pope and the Roman curia about the University. It would seem that the Roman authorities encouraged Newman to foster the development of the Catholic University along the lines of the University of Louvain, because from Rome he wrote to the rector of Louvain proposing the name of an Oxford convert who could act as 'official correspondent' between the two institutions, so as 'to draw the lines closer still'.[90] The model of Louvain had been used as a blueprint for the organisation of the University in the 'Report on the Organization of the Catholic University of Ireland' (October 1851); and in fact one of its key components, the Council, had recently gathered for its first weekly meeting on 12 November 1855. It was chiefly an advisory body for the rector, though on important matters a two-thirds vote could prevent the rector from acting. The Council comprised the deans of faculties, following the Louvain model, in contrast to the Hebdomadal Board at Oxford, which was composed of heads of house, to the exclusion of the professoriate.

In contrast to the Council, the Senate was invested with legislative powers; it was 'the representative of the collective University' to the outside world 'in all matters of religion and morals', not just intellectual. 'Its presence is the presence of the University, and its acts are University acts.'[91] Having received only the unofficial approval of the bishops, the Senate was convoked for the first time on 14 July 1856 in the University Church, following the medieval custom (as revived by Louvain). For Newman, this was 'almost the coming into constitutional existence of the University'.[92] It met again two days later for its first public assembly, during which, in the presence of the Archbishop of Dublin (who presided), other bishops, the University authorities, students and the general public,

Newman distributed prizes to the medics who had passed their first-year exams. After speeches from Newman and the archbishop, Newman dissolved the Senate.[93]

A separate instrument of government, the Council of the Faculty of Arts and Philosophy (the only fully-formed faculty other than the medical one), was launched in June 1856. The bulk of the matriculated students belonged to the arts faculty and, as they included virtually all the residents of the collegiate houses, their fortunes were interlinked. The relationship was closer still on two other counts: the guiding role of the tutors, who assigned to each student the lectures he was to attend; and the system by which the lecturers sent the heads of house a weekly report of student attendance and conduct at their lectures. In practice the complementary teaching roles of faculty and collegiate house meant that decisions arrived at by one party had to be transmitted via Newman to the other. Inevitably points of contention arose over the dovetailing of the tutorial and professorial systems, though the first matter that needed resolving concerned the exam system. In Michaelmas 1856 Newman introduced a proposal to make the terminal exams collegiate-based, to be set by the tutors, as at Oxford, instead of being university-based and overseen by the lecturers. The faculty opposed the change and were unanimous in their wish to continue the current system, in which each lecturer set his own exam. After consulting with the deans of houses, Newman gave way and dropped the proposal.[94] At the end of that term the arts faculty lodged a strong objection to the deans' practice of dispensing from lectures those who were preparing for exams. Newman upheld their complaint; he also approved their recommendation to display exam marks in the entrance hall of University House.

One of the first tasks the arts faculty undertook was that of devising the conditions for 'keeping term', and a printed provisional version was ready for the start of the third academic year (though Newman did not rush to approve it).

Provisional Conditions of Keeping Term

1. Attendance at the terminal examination.
2. Attendance at least at four-fifths of each set of lectures assigned to the student at the commencement of term.
3. In the case of interns, residence during the entire term.
4. Externs must present themselves to the Vice-Rector on the first day of term.
5. The passing of the entrance exam with the remainder of the term to reckon as a term.
6. Sickness allowed as an excuse on the certificate of the Heads of Houses in the case of interns, or of the Vice-Rector in the case of externs.
7. The Rector may, in special circumstances, grant dispensations.
8. Misconduct may be punished by the loss of term, at the discretion of the Rector.
9. Heads of Houses may establish bye-laws with regard to the keeping of terms by their respective students, subject to the above general rules, under the approbation of the Rector.

Of the Session [academic year]

1. A Session consists of three terms.
2. During the entire course two '*grace terms*' may be allowed at the discretion of the Rector; a payment of five pounds for each of these terms being made to the University chest.[95]

These rules were designed to ensure that the faculty and the collegiate houses worked in closer harmony, and also to tighten up on academic discipline, raise standards, and encourage hard work. They also enabled the arts faculty to discuss exam results as a matter of standard business, and to decide which students should be 'allowed their terms'.

Only after Newman's departure did the system of tutors assigning students their lectures became a point of dispute, whereas during his four-year rectorship the problems that arose seem to have been resolved with just a little fine-tuning. This was largely on account of the familiarity of the first lecturers and tutors with the division of labour operating at Cambridge and Oxford. On the one occasion the faculty were concerned about the lecture choices the students were permitted, and they petitioned Newman to instruct the heads of house to see to it that the lectures of their students were so arranged as to include at least one set of lectures on a Greek or Latin author. Unfortunately, no personal accounts survive of how tutorials were conducted at the Catholic University, so it is unclear how they contributed in practice to the overall process of personal formation. In the absence of any direct data on the tutorials, the only information about their operation comes from the practical indications that Newman gave prospective tutors: as he explained to an Oxford friend who had recommended someone as a tutor, the work,

> is more of influence than of instruction. But at the same time influence is gained *through* the reputation of scholarship etc, and the very duty which comes on a Tutor is to do that which the pupil cannot do for himself, e.g. to explain difficulties in the works read in lecture, and to give aid in the higher classics, or to cram for examinations.[96]

Changes at St Mary's

In November 1855, at the start of the second academic year, there were three new residents at St Mary's, all of whom had attended Ushaw College, where the majority were preparing for the priesthood: two Englishmen, Augustus and Henry Bethell, aged eighteen and twenty, and a Trinidadian called Joseph Farfan, aged twenty-one. Henry, the elder of the Bethells, had become a Catholic while at Eton, after which he had transferred to Oscott College, where—unlike Ushaw—only a small proportion were 'church' boys. Augustus had also become a Catholic as a boy, and shortly before arriving in Dublin told Newman that he thought he had a vocation to the priesthood and that he was ready to begin his training. This presented Newman with a problem. As he told his mother, 'the having young men at all in my house and under my care is a great anxiety to me. I have very good boys, whom I trust and whom I love—but youth is always impulsive and changeable—and I am never without fear and misgivings about them.' The difficulty was immeasurably greater in the case of a young man with a priestly vocation, because of the risk that he might lose it by 'mixing with others, *unless* he lives by rules and is very careful'. He explained he needed to know Augustus well in order to make the right demands on him, neither too much nor too little, and that he intended to lay down rules for his conduct.[97] It was 'an anxious thing to have charge of a youth with a vocation',[98] he told Mrs Bethell the following year, since it was awkward for someone aged eighteen to receive the tonsure when surrounded by lay youths.

As a result of these additions St Mary's was full to capacity—and indeed Newman felt he could have filled a much larger house. Unfortunately, little has survived of life at St Mary's in its fourth term beyond a couple of letters from Newman to Lord Henry Kerr, the father of young Frank. In the first Newman promises to keep the boy 'tight to his work', explaining that he now had French classes three times a week, and would later begin drawing—adding that his fees would be raised to £100.[99] The workload does not appear to have satisfied Lord Henry, as in a second letter Newman agreed to arrange for Frank to have an additional hour a day with a private tutor, which would help him overcome his 'natural languor'.[100]

When Newman travelled to Rome in December 1855 to resolve the dispute between the two English Oratories, one of the Birmingham Oratorians substituted at St Mary's during Newman's four-week absence. The task fell to the only Irishman at the Oratory, John Flanagan, who came from a well-known and well-heeled Dublin family and had lived an active social life—making a name for himself in the hunting field—before he discerned his priestly vocation. During Newman's absence he acted as chaplain and confessor, while William Penny said Mass for the house at 8 am. The instructions Newman left for Flanagan reveal that, during the two short intervals when neither of them was present at St Mary's, the Blessed Sacrament was to be under the care of the student Victor Duke, who was thinking about the priesthood. Like the other Oratorians, Flanagan had been kept up to date with developments in Dublin, and so was able to continue the negotiations which Newman had begun over the expansion of the residence to the house next door, which was occupied by a hairdresser and a shop. The plans under consideration involved renting either the whole house or else just the upper two stories, and constructing a linking passageway between the buildings.

On his return to Dublin, Newman found that scarlet fever had struck again, and though it soon went, it was not long before most of the house were down with whooping cough. During his absence an additional student had been accepted at St Mary's, joining the University from Oscott. William O'Shea, the only son of a Limerick solicitor, proved to be a bad influence on the others and a source of difficulties in the house. Newman felt he had to go, and go he did that summer, transferring to Trinity College, Dublin.[101] Unfortunately, Newman also lost three good residents that summer, and this seems to have shattered his expectations that he could use the surplus from the residence to pay for the expansion of St Mary's. This was all the more frustrating as he had now laid out £600 from his own pocket on furniture and improvements to the house. All these worries, which were in addition to his primary concerns as rector of the University (and as superior of the Birmingham Oratory), caused Newman to exclaim, 'My youths, through O'Shea, are giving me trouble—and I don't know how I can possibly stand another year'.[102]

Another local loss was William Scott, who had been a resident tutor that year—'a capital one', according to Newman; he had been poached by Ornsby, who had persuaded Scott to join him and his student lodgers. All these pressures were contributory factors to the change confirmed on 11 May 1856: Newman was to step down as dean of St Mary's at the end of the second academic year, and his place was to be taken by William Penny (who was replaced by Scott as resident tutor at St Patrick's). Newman knew Penny well from his years at Littlemore and the Birmingham Oratory, but no sooner had he arranged the handover than he began to worry about the bad example his replacement was giving. For one thing, Penny liked whisky; so did the residents, and Newman had gone to some trouble to ensure they did not bring spirits into the house. Then Penny was prone to postponing the morning Mass. 'Considering the very idea of a Dean is regularity, this is provoking—but what can one do?', he wrote home.[103]

By the start of the third academic year Newman had formalised the procedure for Irishmen who wished to enter a collegiate house. As the arrangements for entrance show, he was keen to set high standards and determined not simply to take anyone who applied.

> The Candidate for entrance in any Collegiate House of the University,
>
> 1. Presents himself to the Dean of the House, and gives him the recommendatory letters from the Superiors of his School, or the persons who had last the care of his education.

2. He proceeds with a paper of recommendation from the Dean to one of the Examiners to undergo the entrance examination.

3. This paper, countersigned by the Examiner, in token of his having satisfied the examination, he presents to the Secretary, and at the same time pays his Entrance Fee and half year payments in advance both to the University and Collegiate House.

4. In the Rector's presence he promises to obey the Authorities both of the University and his House, and to observe the University Rules and Statutes.

N.B. In the case of Externs the Vice-Rector takes the place of the Dean.[104]

As St Mary's catered mainly for students living outside Ireland, few of the applicants were seen or tested prior to arrival, and instead references had to be relied upon—but these could be problematic. In September 1856 Newman accepted into St Mary's a nephew of Count Zamoyski, whose family was living in France, exiled from Austrian Poland. Intelligence arrived in advance from the brother of Scratton (the University Secretary) who had met the Zamoyski boys at the Royal Agricultural College, Cirencester: one was a 'steady industrious fellow' and 'quite a gentleman'; the other 'a dissipated looking fellow who looks like he might turn out *fast*'.[105] Newman told Scratton, 'I fear ours is the crooked Z';[106] and he wrote home flippantly, 'Young Zamoyski is coming—so, I suppose we shall soon be as lax and disreputable as Ch[rist] Ch[urch, Oxford].' He was also expecting two sons of the ninth Prince de Ligne:[107] 'Renouf is to tutorize the two boys, and Anderdon to confess them. I to feed them. The drawing room to lodge them.'[108] The eldest of the de Lignes, Charles, was aged eighteen and turned out to be 'a very nice fellow'; the younger, Edouard was sixteen. Newman realised that accepting young aristocrats was a gamble: 'Foreigners don't come to the Catholic University for degrees. They will make the University fashionable. I trust they will not make it dissolute.'[109]

Another aristocratic addition to St Mary's was Henry Fraser, aged eighteen, who arrived with his father, the eleventh Lord Lovat. The surname Martin does not reveal the provenance of the only other newcomer, nor does the University Register (from which he is missing), but he can hardly have come from a poor background as all the new arrivals began paying fees of £110 (plus the entrance fee). Along with de Vaulchier, de la Pasture, Barnewall and the two Bethells, this brought the total number of interns at St Mary's to ten. Joining Penny and Renouf as tutor was the priest William Anderdon, a convert who had studied at King's College London and then Oxford. Newman still resided at St Mary's when in Dublin, and though he was no longer dean he wrote, firmly, 'This House is still mine, with the youths in it'.[110] And indeed he continued to deal with applications to St Mary's and some of its administration.

Newman's fears about aristocratic influence at St Mary's began to come true in his final year in residence. Towards the end he realised that most of the residents were 'in a precious stew' as regards their academic work, 'and trying to make up'. With Penny as dean and with all the other concerns that year, he had—he felt—not managed to exercise a proper oversight over the residence. The results of the unhappy state of affairs were evident to him, though not the origins. Now, towards the end of the third academic year, he had to plan ahead for the following year when his successor would probably find himself alone. 'Zamoyski *must* go', he decided, and 'as to the two Princes, I would keep them if I dare'.[111] He did his best to persuade Scratton to take Etienne Zamoyski as a lodger, but the prospect was hardly attractive, and in the end the de Lignes and Zamoyski returned after the long vacation. That summer St Mary's lost two of its most reliable residents, Barnewall and de Vaulchier, and with the latter went his tutor, Renouf; the loss of continuity did not bode well. But not all the changes at St Mary's were for the worse, as among the newer residents were students like the Bethell brothers who undoubtedly exerted a steadying influence in the house. They also influenced the Historical, Literary, and Aesthetical Society for the better. Despite Newman's intermittent presence in Dublin, the club was thriving and it counted all the 'fast' set among its members; presiding over them, in its second and third years respectively, were Henry and Augustus Bethell.

Notes

[1]   'Report on the Organization of the Catholic University of Ireland', October 1851, *MC*, pp. 82–3.

[2]   Though the number admitted on 3 November was seventeen, it had risen to twenty by Monday, 6th November, when lectures began (Student register, 1854–79, UCDA, CU6).

[3]   Ornsby, 'The Autumn Term, 1854', *CUG* 43 (1 February 1855); reprinted in *MC*, pp. 319–24.

[4]   Address to the students on the opening of the University, November 1854, *MC*, pp. 314–15.

[5]   Address to the students on the opening of the University, November 1854, *MC*, pp. 315–17.

[6]   Address to the students on the opening of the University, November 1854, *MC*, pp. 317–18.

[7]   Newman records in his University Journal a conversation which he had with the Jesuit Provincial of Ireland on 8 February 1854, in which he was warned that no young men would want to attend his proposed evening classes. The warning was a response to Newman's suggestion that there would be 'a class of students answering to the day-pupils of King's College, London' as well as 'the class who frequent Mechanic's Institutes' (quoted in *NU*, p. 252). Referring to this incident in his address to the evening class in November 1858, he recounted how wise men had told him, 'There is no class of persons in Ireland who *need* a University'. In answer to those who asked, 'who will fill its lecture-rooms?', he had said, 'We will give lectures in the evening, we will fill our classes with the young men of Dublin' (*Idea of a university*, p. 480).

8   This was in line with Newman's conviction that 'It is a great thing to have a routine prescribed, in which the student is obliged to move, without choice of his own' (Newman's memoir, 13 June 1874, *AW*, p. 52).

9   Newman's inaugural lecture was published as 'Christianity and Letters' in the *Idea of a university* (pp. 249–67). He was followed by the vice-rector on 'The Church and the Bible'; Robert Ornsby on 'The Utility of Classical Studies'; Peter le Page Renouf (Professor of Ancient History) on 'The Literary History of France'; Denis MacCarthy (Professor of Poetry and English Literature) on 'The Nature and Meaning of Poetry'; Augustus Marani (Professor of Italian and Spanish) on 'The Origin and Rise of the Italian Language and Literature'; and T. W. Allies (Professor of Modern History) on 'The Object and the Idea of the Philosophy of History'.

10   After taking advice from counsel, Newman decided not to use the titles 'BA' and 'MA' for degrees as that was deemed to be illegal. Among the supporters and staff of the University, opinion was evenly divided about whether or not to defy the British government: the Young Irelanders wished to push ahead; others preferred to wait for a charter. On account of the lack of unanimity Newman adopted the more cautious approach, even though Rome had given the University permission to award degrees.

11   The role of the examiner in the days of oral exams was, if carried out diligently, an exacting one, and required the person to become thoroughly acquainted with the material being examined. A conscientious examiner could have a great influence on the way in which the set books were studied.

12   Newman spoke about the importance of written work in his address 'Literature', arguing that writing simultaneously develops and disciplines the personality, of which it is a reflection. 'The throng and succession of ideas, thoughts, feelings, imaginations, aspirations, which pass within him, the abstractions, the juxtapositions, the comparisons, the discriminations, the conceptions, which are so original in him, his views of external things, his judgments upon life, manners, and history, the exercises of his wit, of his humour, of his depth, of his sagacity, all these innumerable and incessant creations, the very pulsation and throbbing of his intellect, does he image forth, to all does he give utterance, in a corresponding language, which is as multiform as this inward mental action itself and analogous to it, the faithful expression of his intense personality, attending on his own inward world of thought as its very shadow: so that we might as well say that one man's shadow is another's as that the style of a really gifted mind can belong to any but himself. It follows him about *as* a shadow. His thought and feeling are

personal, and so his language is personal.' (*Idea of a university*, p. 276).

13 The requirements for the entrance exam included Latin and Greek constru-
ing and parsing (one book in each); translation into Latin; Greek and Roman
history; elementary geography; the first book of Euclid; the rules of arithmetic, proportion, fractions, decimals and square roots; St Matthew's Gospel
and an approved catechism (*MC*, pp. 130–5).

14 Newman to Northcote, 23 February 1872, *LD*, vol. xxvi, p. 26. On the other
hand, Newman thought that exams by themselves were likely only to
'promote cramming and create prigs' (*ibid.*).

15 Newman to MacDermott, 21 August 1858, *LD*, vol. xviii, p. 445. On leaving
the University in 1858 Newman noted: 'The Examiner System has never
been formed—I ought to write a paper on it'; and he allocated £350 for 'a
good staff of Examiners' in his budget for 1858/59 ('University annual
expenses', 11 November 1858, *LD*, vol. xviii, pp. 585–6). The University
calendar for that year listed W. H. Scott as the Public Examiner.

16 The University Secretary states that two of these houses were only affiliated
to the University at the start of the second term (13 January 1855, University
transactions 1854–80, UCDA, CU10), though the first twenty students
entered in the University Register (UCDA, CU6) are listed as coming from
the three houses: nine from University House, ten from Dr Quinn's House
and one from the Rector's House.

17 Named after St Laurence O'Toole, the twelfth-century Archbishop of
Dublin, the school was opened in 1850 and within three years had twenty-
seven boarders and forty-three day boys.

18 The irony is all the more piquant given not only the university's aim of
transcending the nationalism that O'Connell represented, but also Newman's own opinion of O'Connell, of whom he wrote in the *Apologia* (p.
123): 'I had an unspeakable aversion to the policy and acts of Mr.
O'Connell because, as I thought, he associated himself with men of all
religions and no religion against the Anglican Church, and advanced
Catholicism by violence and intrigue.' In another irony of history, Newman's house, 6 Harcourt Street, later became the headquarters of the Irish
Republican Party Sinn Féin.

19 See D. Kerr, 'Dr Quinn's School and the Catholic University, 1850–67', *Irish
Ecclesiastical History* 108 (1967), pp. 89–101.

20 Newman to Dodsworth, 18 August 1854, *LD*, vol. xvi, p. 225.

21 Newman to Ryder, 15 October 1851, *LD*, vol. xiv, p. 394.

22 Newman to H. Wilberforce, 5 July 1854, *LD*, vol. xvi, p. 188.

23 Newman to Ornsby, 21 July 1854, *LD*, vol. xvi, p. 204.

24 Newman to de Lisle, 7 May 1855, *LD*, vol. xvi, p. 462.

25 The ages of the students in Newman's house were: fourteen, fifteen, sixteen, seventeen (four of them), eighteen and twenty-one.

26 Newman to Flanagan, 3 December 1854, *LD*, vol. xvi, p. 312.

27 Newman to Flanagan, 13 March 1855, *LD*, vol. xvi, p. 410.

28 Though known as a poet, de Vere was appointed Professor of Political and Social Science. After the potato blight stuck for a second time in 1846, he and his three brothers had thrown themselves into the organisation of famine relief schemes, encouraged fellow landlords to commit resources, and helped to supervise and regulate the process of emigration. Out of this came his study of the Anglo-Irish political economy, *English misrule and Irish misdeeds* (1848), where he called for systematic emigration from a rural society that was uneconomic, as well as the redevelopment of agriculture along efficient lines.

29 A. de Vere, *Recollections of Aubrey de Vere* (New York, 1897), p. 266.

30 Newman to St John, 27 October 1854, *LD*, vol. xvi, p. 283.

31 Godwin to an unnamed Oratorian, 1879, quoted in M. Trevor, *Newman: light in winter* (London, 1962), p. 64.

32 Pollen to Maria La Primaudaye, 13 May 1855, quoted in A. Pollen, *John Hungerford Pollen, 1820–1902* (London, 1912), p. 253.

33 Newman to Flanagan, March 1855, *LD*, vol. xvi, p. 339.

34 Newman was to make it University policy that every dean should furnish the rector with an inventory of the University furniture in his house, and that the dean 'also provides each of his inmates every term with a list of the articles of furniture lent him by the University, inspects their condition at the end of it, and charges on him the expense of misuse' (Rules and Regulations, quoted in *The Tablet* (23 August 1856), p. 539).

35 Newman to O'Meagher, 3 December 1854, *LD*, vol. xvi, p. 314.

36 Newman to Kerr, 2 March 1855, *LD*, vol. xvi, pp. 397–8.

37 Newman to Kerr, 5 March 1855, *LD*, vol. xvi, p. 403.

38 The commissioners investigating Oxford University identified 'extravagant expenditure' as one of the three besetting ills of the undergraduates (*Royal Commission Oxford* (1852), p. 23).

39 Newman to Kerr, 25 July 1855, *LD*, vol. xvi, pp. 512–13.

40 Newman to Mrs Bowden, 11 January 1855, *LD*, vol. xvi, p. 347.

41 Newman to Cullen, 23 February 1855, *LD*, vol. xvi, p. 389. Newman also

wrote about his house to Francis Kenrick, Archbishop of Baltimore, who had passed through Dublin during the Christmas holidays (when Newman was in Birmingham) on his way home from Rome, and told him that he hoped one day to have American students too (Newman to Kenrick, 11 January 1855, *LD*, vol. xvi, p. 348).

[42] Newman to Walker, 8 January 1855, *LD*, vol. xvi, p. 345.

[43] Newman to Grant, 20 March 1855, *LD*, vol. xvi, p. 420.

[44] Newman to Kerr, 30 January 1855, *LD*, vol. xvi, p. 370.

[45] Newman to Bowles, 17 April 1855, *LD*, vol. xvi, p. 442.

[46] Newman to Walker, 23 February 1855, *LD*, vol. xvi, p. 390.

[47] Newman to Flanagan, 24 May 1855, *LD*, vol. xvi, p. 469.

[48] Pollen was someone Newman could rely on and at one stage he had three students in his charge. One was Henry Bowden, who, several years earlier, had stayed with a relative at Oxford and been invited to Merton by Pollen, then the Senior Proctor. Bowden described Pollen's 'cheery friendliness and utter absence of "donnishness" ', despite their difference in age, and how he accompanied Pollen on his rounds with the bulldogs (university police); 'his chumminess and chaff made me feel half Proctor, half bull-dog myself'. At the Catholic University 'his cheerful hope and buoyancy were of immense help in what were to many, young and old, very difficult times'. Seeing that his young friends required 'recreations', Pollen used to go with them to the races (Memoir of Bowden, 10 April 1910, quoted in Pollen, *John Hungerford Pollen*, pp. 219, 254–5).

[49] Darnell to Newman, 13 June 1855, *LD*, vol. xvi, p. 470n.

[50] That June, Lady Henry Kerr wrote to thank Newman for his kindness in looking after Francis during his illness. The Countess de la Pasture expressed her thanks for the measures Newman had taken in dealing with the outbreak, remarking that three of her cousins had died from scarlet fever that spring (BOA, DP 29).

[51] De Vere, *Recollections*, p. 268.

[52] Harry did later become an Oratorian, despite his father's opposition. For further details of the affair see *LD*, vol. xvi, p. 524; vol. xvii, pp. 409–10, 418.

[53] *The life work of Sir Peter le Page Renouf*, ed. W. H. Rylands, G. Maspero & E. Neville, vol. iv (Paris, 1907), pp. l–li.

[54] De Vaulchier to Newman, 9 May 1861, *LD*, vol. xvi, p. 626n.

[55] Charles de la Pasture to the editor, *The Tablet* 114:3618 (11 September 1909), p. 416.

56 Newman to St John, 17 December 1854, *LD*, vol. xvi, p. 326.

57 Newman to Scratton, [28 April 1855], *LD*, vol. xvi, p. 455. Newman's reference to 'Lord among men' was Homer's title for Agamemnon.

58 Scratton to Newman, 9 May 1855, Scratton's letter book, p. 217, UCDA, CU11.

59 Newman to Flanagan, [June 1855], *LD*, vol. xvi, p. 496. Cullen complained that Newman had spent 'a very large sum on billiards', and that while such things might be done at Oxford, 'here it is really too bad for us to throw away the money of the poor on such trifles' (Cullen to Kirby, 15 January 1856, quoted in Barr, *Paul Cullen*, p. 145). In fact, a second-hand billiard table was acquired and the billiard room made a handsome profit of £20 in 1857/58.

60 *CUG* 46 (1 November 1855). Student gambling was a serious problem in the mid-nineteenth century. In their report (*Royal Commission Oxford* (1852), pp. 22–3) the Oxford commissioners commented on the recent disciplinary improvements as regards drunkenness and rioting, but recorded that much needed to be done in the areas of 'sensual vice', gambling and extravagant expenditure.

61 Godwin to an unnamed Oratorian, 1879, quoted in *Light in winter*, pp. 64–5.

62 Candidates were obliged to present Latin and one other subject from philosophy, criticism, geography, chronology, mathematics, logic and physical science, as well as either Greek or a modern language. In classics there was no prescribed syllabus; candidates presented books by one author, such as four books of the *Iliad* or the *Odyssey*, four plays by Euripides, five books of Livy, or six books of the *Aeneid*. Recommended text books in philosophy included Fénelon's *Evidence of the existence of God* (trans. 1779), Wiseman's *Twelve lectures on the connexion between science and revealed religion* (1836) and Schlegel's *Philosophy of history* (trans. 1835); in criticism, Burke's *On the sublime and beautiful* (1801), Copleston's *Praelectiones* (1813) and Keble's *Praelectiones* (1842); in geography, Adams's *Summary of geography and history both ancient and modern* (1794; 1824); in chronology, Clinton's *Fasti Hellenici* (1824; 1851); in mathematics, the six books of Euclid, algebra up to quadratic equations and some trigonometry; in logic, Murray's *Compendium of logic* (1852); and in physical science, Arnott's *Elements of physics* (1827), Whewell's *History of the inductive sciences* (1837), and Herschell's *Outlines of astronomy* (1849). (*MC*, pp. 135–8).

[63] University transactions 1854–80, p. 20, UCDA, CU10.

[64] University transactions 1854–80, p. 21, UCDA, CU10.

[65] Larkin, *The making of the Roman Catholic Church*, pp. 246, 248–9, 252, 261–2. When Cullen wrote to Newman to inform him that the Pope had approved the regulations that the bishops had submitted, he omitted to say that changes had been made (on account of his unilateral recommendations). He did, however, tell Newman that MacHale had done everything he could in Rome to prevent the regulations being confirmed (20 December 1854, *LD*, vol. xvi, pp. 339–40n).

[66] Newman to Cullen, 26 July 1855, *LD*, vol. xvi, pp. 514–15. In a draft of this letter (p. 514n) he expressed himself more strongly, writing that he had reason to believe that 'a strong opinion and much soreness exist on the subject [of a lay committee to manage the University accounts] among the laity of the educated class, and we shall not gain the names of the Catholic gentry, till the money matters of the University are in their hands'. It was not until 8 September that Cullen replied.

[67] J. M. O'Ferrall to Newman, 17 December 1854, *LD*, vol. xvi, p. 515n. A 'close borough' means one having the right of sending a member to Parliament, whose nomination is in the hands of a single person.

[68] A sub-committee had been set up by the University Committee in October 1853 to represent it, especially in financial matters, and it comprised Cullen, Patrick Leahy, Michael Errington, James More O'Ferrall and Myles O'Reilly. It met only once, on 4 October 1855; when invited to attend, O'Ferrall did not know that the committee existed (*LD*, vol. xvi, p. 539n).

[69] Newman to Mrs Bowden, 31 August 1855, *LD*, vol. xvi, p. 535.

[70] Report for the Year 1855–56, *MC*, p. 67.

[71] The story of the medical school is told in F. O. C. Meenan's *Cecilia Street: the Catholic University Medical School, 1855–1931* (Dublin, 1987).

[72] Report for the Year 1855–56, *MC*, p. 66.

[73] Report for the Year 1855–56, *MC*, p. 66.

[74] Newman appointed Terence Flanagan as Professor of Civil Engineering. He had worked on several railway projects in England, Belgium and Portugal, and was the brother of the Oratorian priest John Flanagan.

[75] Glasgow and Manchester were the main centres of scientific engineering in Britain, the first chair being founded at the former in 1840; engineering was institutionalised at Manchester with the foundation of Owens College in 1851. University College, London created the second chair of (civil) engineering in 1841, and the subject also had permanence at King's College, where it

had been introduced in 1838. An ambitious course in engineering was introduced in Durham in 1838, but it struggled to get going and by 1851 had no students. At Edinburgh engineering began to take off in the 1850s and in 1868 a chair was established. Engineering became an examinable subject at Cambridge from 1865, a decade before the foundation of the first chair in mechanism and applied mechanics; it was not until 1894 that an engineering laboratory was opened. The first professor of engineering at Oxford was appointed in 1908. (See R. A. Buchanan, 'The rise of scientific engineering in Britain', *British Journal for the History of Science* 18:2 (July 1985), pp. 218–33). At Trinity College Dublin an engineering school was established in 1841 with a chair in civil engineering; the students had to complete the first year of the undergraduate humanities course before they could study for a diploma in engineering (McDowell & Webb, *Trinity College Dublin*, pp. 180–5).

[76] During the third academic year Newman was able to purchase the medical library of the rector of Munich University, comprising some five thousand books, scientific papers and journals. The negotiations were undertaken by Renouf who visited Munich in the summer of 1856.

[77] When in Rome in 1856, Newman was urged to further to the best of his power the interests of physical science at the University (Newman to Cullen, 17 June 1858, *LD*, vol. xviii, p. 385).

[78] During the third year, a chemistry laboratory was set up along the lines of German university laboratories, intended for three types of student: those undertaking purely scientific research; those needing chemistry for practical purposes, such as agriculture, mining, metallurgy, bleaching, brewing, sugar-boiling and paper-making; and for the medical students. A complete set of lectures in physics was given that year, but the Faculty of Science as a whole had not got under way properly; as a preliminary for doing so, the dean had contacted universities in Austria, Belgium and France about their arrangements for teaching science, and the feedback had been used to design a scheme of study for the Catholic University. Science scholarships had been awarded that year, but with mixed results. (Report for the year 1856–57, *MC*, pp. 174, 177–8; Report of the Dean of the Faculty of Science for the year 1856–57, *MC*, pp. 206–7).

[79] Newman hoped that John O'Hagan, a barrister who had been educated at Trinity, would combine his lectureship in political economy with one in law; O'Hagan acted as dean of the faculty of law when the University Council first met in November 1855. Three years later, on his 'University

annual expenses' (11 November 1858) Newman allocated £100 for jurisprudence, to be taught by O'Hagan, with the comment that the arrangement 'has not yet come into effect, though it ought to settled at once. I heartily and earnestly wish it carried out' (enclosed with Newman to Anderdon, 16 November 1858, *LD*, vol. xviii, p. 584).

80   Edmund O'Reilly, Professor of Dogmatic Theology, did not draw his salary, but Patrick Leahy and Laurence Forde, Professor of Canon Law, did. Being the vice-rector, Leahy was entitled to part of his salary anyway. See *LD*, vol. xviii, p. 158n for the dispute about Forde's salary.

81   L. McKenna, 'The Catholic University of Ireland', *Irish Ecclesiastical Record* 31: 723 (March 1928), p. 236. Newman thought the faculty should be established close to the seminary college All Hallows, and that the lectures should form an advanced course, 'beyond the routine of a Seminary course'; O'Reilly disagreed, proposing instead a regular course for those preparing for the priesthood (Newman to O'Reilly, 27 April 1855; O'Reilly to Newman, 30 April 1855, *LD*, vol. xvi, p. 453).

82   Report for the Year 1854–55, *MC*, pp. 21, 54.

83   Newman regarded this division of interests between two houses as unhealthy, and his request for Cullen to grant Dunne permission to transfer to St Patrick's was eventually granted.

84   It is possible that some of the tuition may have been shared out to James Stewart or Robert Ornsby, as they were both originally engaged as tutors, as well as professors, but there is no evidence to confirm this.

85   Taught then as a blend of economics, political science and sociology, the subject was ironically described by Newman as the 'study of wealth'. He was very aware of the importance of this emerging discipline, for when he took over the editorship of the *British Critic* in 1838, there was a dramatic change in tone in its coverage of political and social matters. As Simon Skinner has argued, Oriel was the 'single most important tributary of that stream of clerical political thought in the early nineteenth century now designated "Christian economics" '; the ideas emanating from its common room—Noetic and Tractarian—gave rise to two 'diverse and ultimately antithetical schools of thought': laissez-faire attitudes and their paternalist counter-culture ('Oriel to Olive Twist: Noetics and Tractarians at large', *Oriel College: a history*, pp. 379, 407).

86   As Newman remarked in his address to the evening class in November 1858, the evening classes were suspended 'only because the singularly inclement season which ensued, and the want of publicity and interest

incident to a new undertaking, made them premature' ('Discipline of mind', *Idea of a university*, p. 481).

87 The University received the library of the recently deceased Archbishop of Dublin, Daniel Murray, another collection of around five hundred books from a recently deceased priest, Michael Dillon, and a collection of publications 'on various scientific subjects' written by academics at Louvain. James Hope-Scott, who had already given the University an anonymous donation of £5000, presented the library with 192 volumes on civil and canon law; Robert Wilberforce gave eight volumes of Luther's works and twenty-nine on French ecclesiastical assemblies, and his brother Henry presented others. The Special Collection of the UCD library contains a three-volume subject catalogue for the Catholic University that Scratton began in 1858.

88 Among other points of difference, one matter of contention concerned the hearing of nuns' confessions.

89 *LD*, vol. xvii, 99n.

90 Newman to de Ram, [after 4 February] 1856, *LD*, vol. xvii, p. 144. The person Newman proposed was David Lewis, a former Fellow of Jesus College, Oxford now living in Brussels, whom he had shortlisted in 1851 as a possible lecturer and tutor for the Catholic University.

91 'Scheme of Rules and Regulations submitted to the Council in April 1856', *MC*, p. 108.

92 Newman to Holmes, 14 July 1856, *LD*, vol. xvii, p. 323.

93 University transactions 1854–80, pp. 45–6, UCDA, CU10.

94 See *LD*, vol. xvii, p. 537n; Minutes of the Council of the Faculty of Philosophy and Letters [i.e. Arts and Philosophy], 4, 5 & 11 December 1857, UCDA, CU4; Newman's memorandum, n.d., BOA, C.6.26/209.

95 University transactions 1854–80, p. 53, UCDA, CU10.

96 Newman to Allies, 6 November 1857, *LD*, vol. xviii, p. 164.

97 Newman to Mrs Bethell, 27 August 1855. *LD*, vol. xxxii, pp. 114–15.

98 Newman to Mrs Bethell, 11 April 1856, *LD*, vol. xvii, p. 217. Augustus tried his vocation at the Birmingham Oratory, but left and became a secular priest.

99 Newman to H. Kerr, 15 November 1855, *LD*, vol. xvii, p. 62.

100 Newman to H. Kerr, 28 November 1855, *LD*, vol. xvii, p. 77.

101 In 1867 O'Shea married Catherine, the youngest daughter of Rev. Sir John Page Wood. He became MP for County Clare in 1880 and got to know

Parnell. So did his wife, who divorced him in 1890 in a scandal which brought Parnell's political career to an end (*ODNB*).

[102] Newman to Flanagan, 26 April 1856, *LD*, vol. xvii, p. 226.

[103] Newman to Flanagan, 10 June 1856, *LD*, vol. xvii, p. 257.

[104] 'Directions to Candidates for Entrance', University transactions 1854–80, p. 52, UCDA, CU10.

[105] Scratton to Newman, 8 October 1856, *LD*, vol. xvii, p. 402n.

[106] Newman to Scratton, 9 October 1856, *LD*, vol. xvii, p. 402.

[107] At the time Prince de Ligne was president of the Belgian Senate and dubbed by Peel as the greatest financier in Europe.

[108] Newman to Flanagan, 19 November 1856, *LD*, vol. xvii, p. 453.

[109] Newman to Monsell, 24 November 1856, *LD*, vol. xvii, p. 459.

[110] Newman to Hope-Scott, 28 March 1857, *LD*, vol. xvii, p. 549.

[111] Newman to St John, 29 June 1857, *LD*, vol. xviii, pp. 68–9.

1. Oriel College chapel and hall, 1836

Newman's rooms are in the corner of the quadrangle on the first floor, adjoining the chapel. He turned the large closet above the chapel door into his own private chapel; it now features stained glass windows about his life.

*2. Oriel College and the spire of the University Church
of St Mary the Virgin, 1829*

3. Interior of the University Church of St Mary the Virgin, 1834

Newman was vicar of St Mary's from 1828 to 1843 and from this pulpit delivered many of his famous sermons. The University Church could hold a congregation of up to a thousand.

4. John Henry Newman preaching at the University Church of St Mary the Virgin

5. *A college lecture, from* The adventures of Mr Verdant Green *(1853)*

This is perhaps the only contemporary image of a 'college lecture', which brought together students of widely differing abilities and educational backgrounds. It reflects the ineffectiveness of college teaching, and it was to counteract this inefficiency that Newman and two other Oriel tutors sought to combine the roles of the private and college tutor. As a result they provided the germ of the modern tutorial system at Oxford.

6. A wine party, from The adventures of Mr Verdant Green *(1853)*

Each of the collegiate houses at the Catholic University organised parties for its own dozen or so residents, at which wine was allowed, but not spirits. Speeches and toasts were made, stories and jokes were told, and the songs they sung had their own college choruses.

7. *University House, No. 86 St Stephen's Green*

The ground floor, *piano nobile* and basement rooms of No. 86 were used as offices and lecture rooms of the Catholic University; the two upper stories comprised St Patrick's House which catered for Irish students. No. 86 was built in 1765 for the notorious anti-Catholic MP Richard Chapell Whaley, nicknamed 'Burn Chapel' Whaley on account of his harassment of Catholics, and inherited by his son, the no less notorious Tom 'Buck' Whaley.

8. The Bishops' Room, University House

The original Catholic University Committee used this room for its
meetings, hence its name. It was here, too, that students came one by
one for their 'collections', when in the presence of the whole professoriate
and the rector, they listened to reports about their progress and
behaviour read out by their lecturers and head of house; this was followed
by a public interview with the rector, Newman.

9. *Opening of the University Church on 1 May 1856*

Defying the vogue for the Gothic style, Newman chose the form of a Byzantine basilica for the University Church; it had the merits of functional beauty (being best for the acoustics and sight), lower cost (as most of the decoration was internal), suitability for the use of Irish marble, and relative harmony with the surrounding Georgian buildings. When it was opened, the altar and baldachino were unfinished.

10. Main altar of the University Church

In the centre of the alabaster altar frontal is the outline of a Byzantine cross; Christ in Glory appears in the middle surrounded by the four Evangelists and the doctors Ambrose, Augustine, Gregory and Jerome. The priest shown is wearing a Roman chasuble, the kind that would have been worn in Newman's time.

11. Bust of Newman in the Catholic University Church

This bust of Newman was made by Sir Thomas Farrell and set in a niche half-way down the nave in 1892, two years after Newman's death. It shows Newman as he would have looked while rector of the Catholic University (1854–58).

12. Paul Cullen, co-founder of the Catholic University

Archbishop Cullen was the main force in the Irish hierarchy behind the foundation of the Catholic University and it was he who asked Newman to be the founding rector and gave him ample scope for his work. Cullen was created the first cardinal of Ireland in 1866.

13. James Quinn, dean of St Laurence's House, c. 1862

James Quinn was dean of St Laurence's House from 1854 until 1859, when he was consecrated the first Bishop of Brisbane. His episcopate was marked by disputes arising from his authoritarian style and a tendency to micro-manage his diocese.

14. *Aubrey de Vere, 1868, Professor of Political and Social Science*

15. William Monsell, 1st Baron Emly, c. 1865, political adviser to the Catholic University

16. *Robert Spencer Lyons, Professor of Physiology and Pathology*

17. Eugene O'Curry, 1857, Professor of Irish History and Archaeology

18. Detail of the Certificate of the Catholic University Medical School

The Medical School in Cecilia Street was acquired in 1854 and received its first students in October 1855. It soon became the most successful part of the Catholic University, and when it was absorbed into University College Dublin in 1909 it was the largest medical school in Ireland. The building, which lies at the junction of Cecilia Street and Dame Street, still exists.

19. Design for the new buildings of the Catholic University

J. J. McCarthy, the builder of many Irish churches who was known as the 'Irish Pugin', was appointed Professor of Architecture by Newman in 1857. At the start of Bartholomew Woodlock's rectorship McCarthy was asked to design the buildings for the new site in the north of Dublin. The foundation stone was laid in 1862 in a ceremony which attracted a crowd of one hundred thousand but the building was never started. By contrast, Newman's policy was to start small and grow gradually.

5 THE LIVING UNIVERSITY

TO UNDERSTAND THE Catholic University as a living community rather than a mere proposition on paper, it is helpful to look at daily life in this small, bustling institution, and in particular to consider five key aspects: what life was like for a student residing in a collegiate house; how Newman led his team of academics; how the professoriate taught their young charges; what was the character of the main student society; and finally how Newman and his staff worked to advance the students' spiritual lives, above all through the University Church.

Recollections of St Patrick's

Few descriptions have survived of collegiate life during Newman's rectorship, but of those that do there is one that provides a rounded picture of the institution on St Stephen's Green: a lengthy account written by John Augustus O'Shea after an interval of forty-five years. On leaving the Catholic University in 1859, O'Shea became a well-known journalist, first as the Paris correspondent of *The Irishman*, then as a special correspondent of the London *Standard* for the period 1869–94. In his two-volume memoir *Roundabout recollections* (1892) he devotes a whole chapter to the Catholic University and provides a colourful picture of the three years he spent at St Patrick's House. Some allowance has to be made for a blurring of facts, given the time that had elapsed since his student days as well as his tendency to romanticise the exploits of his youth, but despite these two drawbacks the account succeeds in conveying the atmosphere of a collegiate house—and of the University, too.

Like other Irishmen who came to the University from beyond the Pale of Dublin, O'Shea never forgot the imposing mansion in

St Stephen's Green where the University was housed. Half a century later he had no difficulty in picturing the spacious rooms with their oak doors, stone balconies and large gracious windows, the melancholy lion *couchant* over the Doric entrance portico, and its broad flight of stairs—though he omits to mention the back stairs used by the students to get to their rooms on the upper floors.[1] Built at a time when Ireland had a substantial aristocracy, it had been the home of the notorious anti-Catholic MP Richard Chapell Whaley, nicknamed 'Burn Chapel' Whaley on account of his harassment of Catholics, and then of his son, the no less notorious Tom 'Buck' Whaley, who had used it for meetings of the dissolute Hell-Fire Club. O'Shea naturally stressed that there was no association between St Patrick's and the antics of the leading Dublin buck and his set of revelling, reckless men of means; in his opinion, 86 St Stephen's Green was the equivalent of a Roman palazzo or a French hôtel.

O'Shea mentions the collegiate houses of St Mary's and St Laurence's, as well as St Luke's, which opened for medical students in the autumn of 1857, but he makes no reference to the Carmelite house—presumably because its impact on the University was negligible. For O'Shea, St Mary's was the 'swell' house, since it was 'a sort of fellow-commoner's preserve' and contained all the 'personages'. The residents of St Patrick's looked up to those from St Mary's, but looked down on St Laurence's, which they 'patronisingly regarded as a mere upper school, and not an orthodox college'.[2] It was common knowledge among them that Newman had framed the Catholic University on the model of Oxford —O'Shea does not so much as mention Louvain—and that a good number of the teaching staff had come from the two ancient English universities, in some cases having forfeited their positions on becoming Catholics. The reputation of these and other learned men among the lecturers and professors certainly reached the students and made the University attractive to them.

On his arrival at St Patrick's, the sixteen-year-old from county Tipperary found that one of the older students, James Molloy, exercised great influence over his juniors on account of his sporting prowess. This short, stout 'pocket Hercules' was captain of the house cricket XI, the stroke of their champion rowing VIII, and a natural sprinter. He was musical too, and he press-ganged O'Shea into working the organ pumps for him for up to two hours a day, for five weeks; this 'gymnastic torture' was supposedly in aid of getting O'Shea fit to act as long-stop in the vital cricket match against Skimmary's (as St Mary's was known), and to row 'bow' for the house VIII—but, as O'Shea relates, his training did not prevent him from catching an 'ignominious crab'[3] in a crucial race. O'Shea's willingness 'to fight for the honour of the house'[4] conveys the healthy sporting rivalry that was undoubtedly engendered by the collegiate system, and which involved most, if not all, of the residents. St Patrick's had use of a boathouse at Ringsend,[5] where the Dodder empties into the Liffey, and training usually involved rowing out to Pigeon House Fort, on the south side of Dublin Bay. There they bathed off the spit leading up to the lighthouse, had a brisk game of ball, and then demolished a hearty lunch. If the wind was up, they might set up sail, and glide across the bay to Dollymount.

No surprise that close friendships were forged and that O'Shea should recall grateful memories of 'the pure-minded high-spirited array of youths in old St Stephen's Green, who neither drank nor lied, diced nor swore, but bore the gentlemanly escutcheon aloft and pure'.[6] Among other fellow residents, he remembers Daniel O'Connell, grandson of the 'liberator', bold of heart and boyish in looks, whose recklessness led to an early death while yachting outside Kingstown Harbour; Hugh Patrick MacDermot, 'red prince' of Curlew, later solicitor-general, and then attorney-general, of Ireland;

big brawny Michael Green, who fought in the Irish brigade at the Battle of Spoleto, winning a Papal honour, and later became a barrister and legal-commissioner under the Land Act; J. B. Dillon, a medical student who became a well-known lawyer; Charles Dawson, who was elected mayor of Dublin in 1882 and 1883; and George Errington, who became a Liberal MP and was used by the British government as an unofficial envoy to the Vatican in the 1880s.

The one genuine scholar among them, Augustus Henry Keane, was a small fellow whom they regarded as 'a cyclopædia on two legs': he was a keen philologist and orientalist, with a (student) reputation for rivalling Robert Ornsby in Greek and Peter le Page Renouf in hieroglyphics, and he later became Professor of Hindustani at University College, London. In general, however, there was more interest in football and the latest cricket match at Lord's than academic matters. Though without a sports ground, the residents of St Patrick's had the run of St Stephen's Green[7] for exercise and they shared a cricket pitch at Rathmines with the other houses. Billiards they played (thanks to Newman) in their own back yard, and not a few were anxious for fame with the cue; one of the science professors played with them, and was full of theories about angles of incidence and reflection, but he lost to the best of the students (who, as O'Shea notes, had rather more time for practice). On one occasion the residents engaged a 'bruiser'—probably unofficially—to give them lessons in the noble art of boxing. Mental sparring, on the other hand, was publicly encouraged and sponsored by the Historical, Literary, and Aesthetical Society, which in O'Shea's time met on Monday evenings in one of the basement rooms of No. 86.

O'Shea's recollection that the student body contained a large proportion of foreigners, mostly French or Belgian, some of them aristocrats, tallies with the roll-call of St Mary's. Less clear is his assertion that the colleges[8] feeding the Catholic University were mainly English (Stonyhurst, Oscott, Downside and St Edmund's

Ware) rather than Irish (such as Tullabeg and Clongowes Wood).[9] His recollection that the students differed in race, nation and party shows that in its early days the University attracted students from near and far, as Newman had hoped it would. Moreover, there was harmony between the 'nations', and little if any student antagonism towards the Englishmen on the staff[10]—quite the opposite, in fact, if we are to take O'Shea's recollections as typical. Among the most respected and liked was the shy English priest William Penny, whom he describes as 'most muscular of Christians, profound connoisseur of tobacco pipes and kindliest of beings'.[11] An athlete during his undergraduate days at Oxford, Penny took a lively interest in the sports and pastimes of the Catholic University students, acting as umpire in their rowing trials and making himself available for coaching and training. His gift of £50 towards mathematics books for the University library shows that he was, like the majority of the teaching staff, fully dedicated to the enterprise. Penny's availability and standing among the students were undoubtedly contributory factors that led Newman to appoint him as his successor at St Mary's.

House 'entertainments' were part and parcel of life at St Patrick's, and show the residents in another light. O'Shea recalls a wine party one evening to celebrate the prize one of their number had been awarded, when speeches and toasts were made, stories and jokes were told—all to loud applause—and the songs they sung had their own college choruses.[12] The noise eventually woke the University chaplain, William Anderdon, whose room was beneath the party, and after a gentle reprimand the students dispersed. (Curiously, O'Shea makes no mention of the dean, Michael Flannery, on this occasion—or, indeed, in any other context.) St Patrick's night (17 March) was deemed a gala occasion and the residents were left to enjoy themselves without the restraining presence of the authorities. O'Shea recalls a memorable after-dinner speech when those present were assured that St Patrick's Day had been celebrated in the Church since the time of Moses. The equivalent event at St Laurence's, the celebration organised to mark the feast of St Laurence O'Toole (14 November), seems to have been a more formal affair, as among its guests in 1856 were the archbishop and several professors.

Youthful high spirits also manifested themselves in pranks, some of which were played upon one of the University's most able professors, James Robertson. Born in London of Scottish parents, Robertson had studied philosophy and history on the Continent, and translated Schlegel's *Philosophy of history* (1835) and Möhler's *Symbolism* (1843); amiable and gracious, he was stooped, sallow in complexion and gaunt—and rather unkindly nicknamed 'death's head' on this account. He was also excessively short-sighted, and this the students exploited. It became a game to see how many times they could greet him in the street; and in his history lectures, which were rich in scholarship, there were occasions when they hid under the tables, then reappeared, to disconcert him. But, as Robertson was also the 'essence of politeness' and a masterly lecturer, they went no further in their antics.[13]

At the end of the academic year the students were required to attend an 'inquiry into progress and behaviour' which, as at Oxford, was called a 'collection'. They were solemn affairs—and meant to be. The students were summoned one by one into the boardroom in University House, at the end of which seated behind a table were the rector, the deans and the entire teaching staff. The victim was provided with a chair. The dean read out a report on conduct and attendance at chapels, then the lecturers gave their verdict in turns. Being good-natured, most of them refrained from being severe; but O'Shea remembers all too well the time when he was hauled over the coals. James Stewart declared he was not without brains in classics, but idle; David Dunne reported that he had no 'bias' for logic, and that he was inattentive on occasions; Augustus Marani complained about his high spirits during the lectures on modern languages. At this point Newman asked O'Shea to explain himself. The ordeal finished with Newman counselling him to make better use of his time, adding, as O'Shea recalled: 'Alas! every day you live you will have less temptation to indulge in careless joyous waste of opportunity; but the opportunity, once lost, may never present itself again.'[14]

O'Shea's recollections bear out Newman's opinion that, for most students, the threat of exams is the chief inducement to study. Exams at the Catholic University were internal, termly affairs, except for the public exams: the scholar's exam at the end of the second year, the inceptor's exam at the end of the third year; and the licentiate exam at the end of the fourth year. O'Shea describes how, in the days leading up to the exams, 'It was quite common, then, in the mid hours of the night, to see martyrs to indolence stewing away in their room, with pots of green tea before them, wet towels round their aching brows and their feet in hot water, in the delusion that they were assisting exhausted nature.'[15]

O'Shea rounds off his memories with a portrait of the rector himself. He recalls Newman's striking figure as he walked with short rapid steps from Harcourt Street to St Stephen's Green, 'tenuous and angular, his head bent forward, his ascetic features shrouded in meditation, and his keen eyes looking neither to the right nor to the left, but introspectively, as it were, with a contemplativeness far removed from things of the thoroughfare'. Newman dressed in a clerical frock-coat and knee breaches, and usually carried an umbrella. He was regarded by students, remarks O'Shea, with 'a sort of awestruck worship';[16] they were proud of him, yet felt they could not rise to his level; he was too cold, dry and self-contained for their youthful minds. They preferred ardour to argumentation; Wiseman's *Fabiola*, with its florid images, vivid character sketches and rhythmic rhetoric, to Newman's *Callista*.[17] When Newman preached, the University Church was invariably packed, but, says O'Shea, the young men were not generally carried away by his sermons. The language, of course, was polished, the thoughts elevated, the reasoning flawless, but the sermons suffered from one fatal drawback: they were read. Irish youths were accustomed to listening to priests who preached *ex tempore* and with passion; a discourse read from a manuscript might be more lucid and logical, but for them it lacked life.[18]

Caring for the Common Room

Naturally the academic staff at the Catholic University saw Newman in a different light, and this was particularly the case for those who had known him at Oxford and witnessed his influence as an energetic Tractarian leader. Tom Arnold, the younger son of the famous headmaster of Rugby School, joined the University for the third academic session as a tutor and Professor of English Literature, and left his impressions of Newman in his memoirs: 'The air of deep abstraction with which he used to glide along the streets of Oxford was now in great measure exchanged for the look of preoccupation and anxiety about temporal affairs, which the features of a man to whom business was neither habitual nor congenial would naturally assume under the new circumstances'.[19] But, this aside, he thought Newman was quite as vigorous as at Oxford. During his first term in Dublin, Arnold told his wife that there was an immense amount of 'mere business' connected with the office of rector which should have been undertaken by others. Newman's mind was too refined and polished for such work; it was like 'cutting blocks with razors'.[20] Although Newman showed consummate skill and efficiency in establishing the University, Arnold reckoned that the genius for command did not come naturally to him; 'with an intellect that seems to grasp all combinations, to fathom the secret springs of action in all men with whom he has to deal, and almost intuitively to perceive all the possible courses of proceeding under any given circumstance, he is deficient in that force of the intrepid will, which marks the born ruler of men'. Moreover, he sensed that Newman's affections were centred on the Birmingham Oratory, where his thoughts were 'ever gravitating'.[21]

As one might expect from the son of England's foremost reforming headmaster and from someone who had reorganised the educational system of Tasmania, Arnold in his recollections brings out the organiser in Newman. The poet Aubrey de Vere, on the other hand, saw more of the pastor in him. De Vere had first encountered Newman in Oxford in 1838, then at Littlemore in the early 1840s, and a year before his own conversion to Catholicism in 1851 had attended Newman's *Lectures on certain difficulties felt by Anglicans*. What impressed him in 1856 was the patience with which Newman bore his trials, his kindness and his delightful conversation—and the contrast between the humble houses bearing the name 'Catholic University' and the monumental buildings of Trinity College, de Vere's own *alma mater*.[22] The poet discerned in Newman 'a very human personality', whose sensitivity exposed its subject to sorrows, cares and anxieties. Living at close quarters with Newman at St Mary's, de Vere found not coldness but such a complete absence of convention that the force of his personality made an immediate impact. There was nothing of the aloof intellectual about him, but rather sweet gravity, simple manners and plain speech. The Irishman detected in Newman 'a quick sympathy and fierce moods before injustice', and it reminded him of Edmund Burke. He saw in Newman 'a tenderness marked by a smile of magical sweetness, but a sweetness that had in it nothing of softness'. There was 'a decided severity in his face, that severity which enables a man alike to exact from others, and himself to render, whatever painful service or sacrifice justice may claim'. This severity, together with his reputation, could be daunting for

those who found themselves in Newman's presence and it sometimes gave the impression of coldness on Newman's part. But for
de Vere, who got to know him well, he came to recognise a
combination 'of dauntless courage with profound thoughtfulness'
and to appreciate what he summed up as that 'rare union of the
contemplative mind and the heroic soul'.[23]

Someone who met Newman for the first time in Dublin and
instantly took to him was John Hungerford Pollen, a former Fellow
and senior proctor at Oxford who had become a Catholic in 1852,
and a man of great energy and humour. He was apprehensive on
meeting Newman, but, as he reported to his fiancée, he found that
Newman was 'most kind, ever so nice, and full of fun'[24]—a remark
which shows a different side to Newman's character than that
encountered by de Vere. On their arrival in their new home in
Dublin, Pollen and his bride found a note of welcome from
Newman: 'May it be an auspicious messenger, crowned with
flowers and dressed in its best'.[25]

Newman was a gregarious, clubbable man who delighted in being
with people. The affection and loyalty he inspired was shown above
all in the spontaneous reaction of his colleagues, who, on hearing in
1858 that he intended to leave the Catholic University, pleaded with
him to remain. On that occasion, David Dunne told Newman that
'from the first moment of my connexion with the University I have
looked up to you rather as a father than a superior'.[26]

The lecturers and professors at the Catholic University were all
too aware of the onerous task Newman had taken on in attempting
to set up the institution almost single-handedly. They knew from
personal experience that virtually every aspect of life at the University came into being through his hands. Besides overseeing academic affairs, the financial administration, the launching of new
faculties and schools, editing the *Gazette*, delivering lectures each
term and preaching sermons, Newman also acted as the academic

and moral conscience of the University. Despite all the administrative pressures bearing down on him, he managed to give priority to his dealings with the academic staff. This emphasis resonated with his abiding concern for the pastoral well-being of the University, because if its main task was to 'make men', then the makers of men themselves needed to be encouraged, reassured and given direction.

As the University grew and the number of staff increased, so did the task of dealing with them. This was why towards the end of the second academic session Newman introduced weekly evening soirées for the academic staff, when tea was served in the library of University House. In his Report for the Year 1855–56 he was able to inform the bishops about the 'good understanding and fellow-feeling and mutual sympathy' that prevailed among the teaching staff. In fact, this aspect of the nascent university was a top priority for him: 'There is no surer indication and instrument of success in an institution', he told the bishops, 'than an *esprit de corps*: and without it there can be no real life at all.'[27] Newman's private correspondence with friends outside the University confirms what he thought about his team of fellow workers and the way they pulled together. 'We have hitherto been in most perfect harmony',[28] he told Hope-Scott, the loyal and trusted friend he usually turned to for advice.

Undoubtedly the project of establishing a Catholic university inspired many Irishmen, but it fired up the Oxbridge converts with a zeal that was almost missionary.[29] In sounding out the motives of those hoping to join the University staff, Newman made it absolutely clear that he did not want them to undertake work there simply out of a desire to please him. Instead, as he told Peter le Page Renouf, 'We must begin all con amore, with zeal to do a great work as the first motive.'[30] Renouf's reply makes it is clear that he immediately grasped the apostolic nature of the venture, and on that score accepted the offer to take his part in it.[31] Enquiring about a position at the University, Arnold had told Newman he was anxious for employment, 'if it were possible, in the service of the Church' with the expectation that he would be able 'to do some plain useful work';[32] and after ten days at the University he wrote home excitedly about the 'very interesting experiment'.[33] Although he had been drawn to the University project by the magnetism of Newman, he was not for abandoning it during Newman's last term, when prospects looked less promising. Instead, he told Newman that it was 'worth submitting to much privation' for the Catholic University, 'even on mere chance that our hopes may one day be realized', because he felt that the University could still come to something, if they all put their shoulders to the wheel.[34]

When it came to handling the academics and getting the best out of them, Newman was well-placed to harness and drive his team, and this both because the men were largely his appointments, and because his own talents were such that he had their utmost respect. He told the Bishop of Kerry, who had helped him select the Irish lecturers, 'I have the utmost confidence in them. [...] the difficulty of ruling them only arises from the existence of zeal and talent, pulling, as is natural, in the course of time, in various directions'.[35] Newman's broad range of academic interests no doubt eased his task, because it helped him to enter into each person's area of speciality and even to suggest new lines of investigation. One of the more remarkable instances of this was the way he dealt with Eugene O'Curry. On the first occasion they met, O'Curry showed Newman the catalogues of Irish manuscripts that he had been unable to get published and as a result Newman offered him a professorship in archaeology and Irish history—and agreed to print the catalogues into the bargain. After attending O'Curry's groundbreaking lectures on the manuscript sources of ancient Irish history, Newman not only agreed to publish them but had a font of Irish type cast for the purpose. The University thus provided valuable assistance to Irish Studies when the foundations of the discipline were being laid.[36]

Another striking instance of the way Newman dealt with the academic staff is the way he treated Pollen, who was talent-spotted by Newman and launched into a career as an architect. At a turning-point in his life, when Pollen had resigned his Anglican curacy to become a Catholic, Newman boldly entrusted the gifted amateur artist not only with a chair in Fine Arts but the commission to build the University Church. (In later years Pollen worked with and befriended the Pre-Raphaelites Edward Burne-Jones, J. E. Millais and D. G. Rosetti.) Pollen's memoirs record that Newman was emphatic in his advice to the professors that they should focus on their special fields of research, whatever they might be: 'to cultivate them thoroughly; to make quite sure of the ground; to be in no hurry to put forward new conclusions, to keep them back perhaps for considerable intervals; to look at them all round, to reconsider them from time to time'. He had the knack of drawing out what each professor had to say on his own proper subject in easy conversation. 'He encouraged you to put your conclusions into terms; to see what they looked like from various sides; to reconsider, prune or develop as might be required.' Besides working alongside Newman, Pollen found that relaxing with him in conversation, 'listening to talk that was never didactic and never dull', was refreshing after the day's toil.[37] Moreover, despite the many difficulties pressing round him, Newman injected a spirit of optimism into the whole enterprise and gave orientation to them all.

Pollen has left on record that under Newman there was no dissension among the staff and that all was harmony; he talked freely and vividly with his Irish friends, and keenly appreciated their wit and genius. 'Father Newman enjoyed a wide popularity among the priests of Ireland. In them he saw the courage, the constancy of a whole nation of confessors for the Faith; a nation to whom a debt of justice was due; a debt of which he desired earnestly to discharge his share.'[38] Was the harmony in the common room despite the English presence or, perhaps, because of it? Bishop Moriarty thought the latter. Ireland, he felt, lacked 'the spirit and traditions of University teaching' that were needed to create a university. 'We must depend on England where the old fire was hidden', he told Newman. Despite 'all our national vanity and touchiness and Anti-Englishness', he considered that 'Irishmen will more easily unite in submission to what is English. There is too much party spirit amongst us to submit to each other—an Englishman in abstracto is the best centre of unity we can have.'[39]

The faculty members of the Catholic University would have imbibed Newman's views on education through their reading of the *Discourses*, the university sketches, and his other articles in the *Gazette*. Among the latter, several deal with methods of teaching and learning, and there Newman analyses and even satirizes some of the educational theories of his time. In the days before formal professional training, the reading of these articles and the conversations arising from them would have served the function of lectures and seminars on the art of teaching and the psychology of learning. The academics would have learnt what Newman meant by superficial knowledge when reading 'The Entrance Examination a trial of accuracy', which describes an oral exam in Latin and Greek and illustrates the importance of the principle of 'really know what you say you know'.[40] The article conveys Newman's view that precise and accurate reading, rather than merely wide reading, is the key to educational progress; it encapsulates the approach that Newman championed against those who urged a superficial omniscience.[41] Another article, 'On Latin composition', concludes with a classic statement of Newman's education theory:

The great moral I would press upon you is this, that in learning to write Latin, as in all learning, you must not trust to books, but only make use of them; not hang like a dead weight upon your teacher, but catch some of his life; handle what is given to you, not as a formula, but as a pattern to copy and as a capital to improve; throw your heart and mind into what you are about, and thus unite the separate advantages of being tutored and of being self-taught,—self-taught, yet without oddities, and tutorized, yet without conventionalities.[42]

To put this theory into practice Newman had to rely on those he had appointed, whether they were lecturers, tutors or examiners, to enter into his way of thinking, to give it some practical expression, and even to embody it. Using his position as rector—talking with the professors informally, delivering the occasional lecture, and presiding at the internal examinations and collections—Newman was able to explain his meaning and teach by example.[43] From the official reports of the lecturers, from their correspondence with Newman, and from the minutes of faculty meetings, it is evident that they were one with him (and, in this instance, with the age) in placing great store on competitive examinations. In fact, their annual reports to the rector reveal a sense of frustration and disappointment at the general backwardness and lack of application of the students. In his departmental report David Dunne complained of the 'general indisposition to study, frequently degenerating into idleness'. Amongst those who had profited *least* from his lectures were a number of able students, some of whom were scholars, and their general inattention and negligence had interfered with the progress of others. A different obstacle to progress was 'the *absence of a tradition'*—not a *traditio docens* (a tradition of teaching), but a *traditio docta* (a tradition of the taught), which would animate, guide and assist the students.

Placing before the Student the example of the long list who have preceded him, pursuing the same course, treading in the same path, in which he now finds himself, telling him what and how they studied, what helps they used, what methods they followed, their defects, the origin of their failures, the cause and measure of their success, appealing to his judgment through his feeling and imagination and sense of honour: such a tradition, embodying in its practice the history of the body to which he belongs, does for the Student what no Professor can ever do.[44]

Comments such as this are revealing, since they illustrate the extent to which the lecturers and tutors shared Newman's educational thinking in the manner in which they tackled their students' deficiencies.

Under Newman's inspiration the Catholic University was ahead of the times in the way academics took an interest in the students and their activities, as it was not until the 1860s and 1870s that this new attitude to students and their needs became the norm in Oxbridge colleges. In the late 1850s dons such as Oscar Browning founded the Politics Society and Dante Society at King's College, Cambridge, and took college men to the theatre in London and on trips to Italy, but this was the exception. It was during the 1860s and 1870s that a new class of Oxbridge don emerged, someone who had a professional interest in scholarship, who made university teaching his career, and who wanted to revive the college as a place of close relations between teachers and taught. He saw himself as acting *in loco parentis* and viewed the college as a surrogate family which sought to mould its members through admiration and loyalty rather than fear and regulations. This new attitude to students and teaching had practical ramifications. These dons gave parties to introduce junior and senior members of the college to each other; they opened their rooms to students and made themselves available for serious and informal conversation; they took an interest in student sport; they adopted a kind rather than aloof attitude to students; they preferred an internalised discipline rather than one enforced by means of formal restraints; they encouraged students to open up to them; and they favoured the more studious students and were ambitious for their success. Above all, they wanted a vital, alert and energetic student body.[45]

Looking after for the learning environment

Summarising the faculty reports that constituted the bulk of the Report for the Year 1856–57, Newman explained to the bishops that the third academic year had seen a general improvement in the attitude and demeanour of the students, expressed in their greater attentiveness at and preparation for lectures, and their greater proficiency in examinations. But despite the greater diligence shown, the professors were unanimous in complaining about the serious lack of grounding of those entering the University, particularly in classical languages, history and science, to the extent that the students frequently lacked the preparation necessary to profit from the lecturers; this meant that the lecturers had either to run remedial courses or to lower their sights. The absence of able students who could set high standards went some way to explaining this state of affairs, as did the youthfulness of the students, which was more keenly felt in a subject like philosophy where defective training in logic and lack of intellectual discipline were more clearly exposed.[46] But the disappointment of the lecturers can also be put down to their own ambitions, a consequence of Newman's success in attracting a highly educated common room.[47]

The lack of grounding at school was a difficulty that Newman had anticipated. A year before the University opened he had told Ornsby, 'One special idea I have (of course all this secret) is to try to get an influence over the principal schools and colleges in Ireland—we *depend* on them, and unless they send us well trained youths, we can do nothing'.[48] Orsnby later remarked that the 'terrible deficiency of solid school education is an ανηνμτον νακον [unending evil]'.[49] Newman addressed the problem of student supply in 1856 by appointing a committee consisting of Edward Butler, David Dunne and Michael Flannery to look into the matter; their proposal called for a system of affiliation of Irish schools to the University to increase its influence over them and to raise standards.[50]

The problem was that the middle of the century had been a period of transition for secondary schools in Ireland, the National System having effectively destroyed the old classical academies without providing any substitutes, while the new schools and colleges were only just beginning to appear. Officials at the Queen's Colleges blamed their low numbers on the difficulty of boys acquiring a classical education, and when the *Report* on the Queen's Colleges appeared in 1858 it suggested that this was 'the most powerful cause of preventing the youth in Ireland availing themselves of the advantages held out by the Queen's Colleges'.[51] It was complaints from the Queen's Colleges about the deficiencies of the secondary schools which led to a commission being set up to inquire into the state of all the endowed schools of Ireland.[52]

In the long term it was hoped that the Catholic University would act as a catalyst to the raising of school standards, but in the short term Newman was forced to consider ways to accelerate this process and to compensate for the academic deficiencies of school leavers. One solution at hand was to adapt the content of the *Gazette* for this purpose. So when Ornsby took over the editorship in January 1855, it was announced that the *Gazette* would be expanded and feature articles dealing with universities both at home and abroad; with school education insofar as it prepared for university; and with practical suggestions for those in, or preparing for, university. The change of editorship was not announced, but attentive readers observed the change in style and the circulation dipped during 1855.[53] Nevertheless the content was largely determined by Newman, who fed Ornsby with ideas and relied on him to work them out.

In an article entitled 'The Gazette', Newman explained to its readers that its aim was to tell parents, guardians, clergy, educators of youth, and students themselves, what this Catholic University 'is actually *doing*, what it *means*, what sort of training it expects from those who come to it, and what advantages it holds out to its students'. Crucially, it added: 'We tell parents that for the interests of their sons, University education is one of the most momentous questions they can think of', since society was changing and would in the future give leading positions of influence to those who had reaped the benefits not merely of school education, but of university education—and these were 'widely different things'.[54]

In tackling the lack of educational training among Catholic youth, Newman penned a series of articles[55] on what nowadays would be called study techniques and revision skills, and in this way attempted to provide guidance to the student who read the *Gazette* and to those who advised and taught him. Some of the articles touched on strategies for mastering particular subjects, such as 'On Latin composition' and 'The study of geometry', while others were of a more general nature: two about techniques for improving one's memory, two on how to profit from reading, one on time management, and another on the purpose of lectures. There was even one on the wishful thinking and self-indulgence—such as the tendency to dabble—that students are prone to, and the need for them to follow a prescribed routine and avoid caprice. The fact that Newman was prepared to grapple with such matters illustrates his determination to meet the practical needs of the student who lacked basic training and orientation.[56] Ornsby seems to have used Newman's ideas on study habits for three lectures he delivered at the Catholic Institute in Liverpool on the art of academic self-improvement, and these lectures were also published in the *Gazette*.

Just as Newman had no qualms about the *Gazette* featuring articles on study skills, so he had no hesitation in using its pages to provide up-to-date information on the employment opportunities that were opening up to Catholics as a result of changes taking place in British society in the 1850s. The gradual acceptance in society of those who were not members of the Established Church and the rise of a meritocracy were reflected in new legislation which opened up positions to all educated subjects of the Crown, as exemplified by the India Act (1853) which opened up to competition appointments to the India civil service. The *Gazette* reproduced details of the new exam regulations, and when it was announced that the East India Company's administrative training college at Haileybury was to have its monopoly on employment in India broken up, the implications for the Catholic University were spelt out. The practical effect of the selection procedures, Newman predicted, would be that places would fall mainly into the hands of university graduates, since the commissioners would favour those who had received a liberal education; furthermore, the University was well placed to benefit, since the assessment principles coincided closely with those for the scholar's degree at the Catholic University, even though the degree had no public recognition.[57]

During the summer of 1854 Newman had sought the advice of William Monsell, MP for Limerick, about the advisability of requesting official recognition of the University's degrees. Monsell, who from 1855 would hold various offices in the Liberal government, agreed with Newman that 'it would be unwise now to moot in any way the question of a charter':

> Until the University exists it will not be recognized. To recognize it at any time will be unpopular and therefore its recognition will be avoided even by our friends as long as it can be with decency. When it becomes a power, and shows signs of being a permanent one, it will be indecent to ignore it, but not till then. It would be unwise to commit the Government to hostility towards it.[58]

Confirmed in his assessment of the political situation, Newman worked to the principle that until the University had established itself in the public eye, it must make do without degrees and do the best it could with organs like the *Gazette* to further its cause.

The articles in the *Gazette* about existing universities were not only intended to inform students and the educated public about the various traditions that existed and to inspire them with such examples, but to highlight key features of the Catholic University and demonstrate that it aspired to match best practice elsewhere. Some of the articles were lifeless accounts of remote institutions; even the pieces on the University of Louvain served little purpose besides paying homage to the foundation whose example the Catholic University had been invited to follow. By contrast, other articles were inspired and pertinent. In one entitled 'University and King's Colleges in London', Newman dwells on the importance of a residential collegiate university and repeats his main educational objection to the newly-founded colleges of London University: that neither college nor university aimed at the 'philosophical idea of education, which was fulfilled in the old Universities'. In a stinging contrast, he remarks that Oxford and Cambridge,

> were emphatically places of *residence* for those who came to them, the residence of many years: the University was an *Alma Mater*, and College was a *Society*. But a University which is scarcely more than a board of Examiners and an apparatus for Degrees, and a College which is but a collection of lecture-halls, open to young men who need never see each other or their professors elsewhere, in no way rise to the height of the ancient idea, of which they usurp the title.[59]

In May 1855 Newman and Ornsby hit upon a new way of explaining the role of the Oxbridge private tutor, through reproducing in the *Gazette* extracts from Charles Bristed's *Five years in an English university* (1852). Bristed's account of life at Trinity College, Cambridge had been intended to provide his fellow North Americans with an accurate depiction of university life there and to counter the image evoked by fictional works such as the widely-read *Adventures of Mr Verdant Green, an Oxford freshman* (which first appeared in serialized form in the *Illustrated London News* in 1851).[60] Bristed's was one of the earliest accounts to provide detailed descriptions of the academic lifestyle of the serious student and, more importantly, to explain the role of the tutor. The tutorials Bristed described lasted an hour, and comprised the reading of a classical author the student had prepared beforehand, tackling an unseen passage, and working through mathematical problems. Intended to inform a North American public uninitiated in the mysteries of the tutorial system, Bristed's account was well suited for Irish consumption.

Ornsby had himself been a popular private tutor for four or five years at Oxford in the 1840s, and in two articles entitled 'The University of Cambridge' he describes how the teaching was left to private tutors at the two ancient universities. Thrown upon his own resources, the student naturally turned for guidance and sympathy to those who had recently distinguished themselves in their BA exams and remained in college in the hope of obtaining a fellowship. Two or three years older than their pupils, they were ideally placed to impart 'the best rules and cautions' for exam success; they were the undergraduates' 'saints', though as yet not 'canonized' with a fellowship. The influence these officially unrecognised teachers exercised was great, since they became the students' 'advisers, confidants, and real instructors'. Moreover, they were 'the very seat of that academical tradition and sentiment' which made the university what it was; they were 'the oracles of the rising generation', who would in time carry the country forward. Nevertheless, Ornsby noted, for all the similarities between the two universities, there were some notable differences: among other points, at Oxford the tutors tended to be either of the Puseyite or Arnoldian parties, whereas at Cambridge they were not conspicuous for 'a moral and religious bearing'.[61]

The passages from Bristed that were selected for the *Gazette* provided readers with a picture of university life that was busy and purposeful, all the more so as they focused on the society of the private tutors. Besides bringing their specialist subjects up to a higher level in their bid for a fellowship, these graduate students had to undertake wide reading for a general paper and were equally ambitious in their private reading. This select breed of scholars had other common traits: they took regular, daily exercise; they lived frugal lives; and they were serious in the views they espoused. These characteristics, as well as the warm comradeship of graduate society, are conveyed by Bristed's description of an animated dinner party—a description that offsets the more forbidding elements of their academic asceticism, and was chosen as it would appeal to the young Irishman thinking of applying to the Catholic University. Bristed relates that the private tutor at Trinity College, Cambridge took pupils in proportion to his reputation, usually about five or six pupils a day, giving to each an hour and charging according to the ability to pay: on average £7 per term for tuition on alternate days, but half that amount for the sizars,[62] and more for noblemen and fellow-commoners (the equivalent of the Oxford gentlemen-commoners). The relationship between tutor and pupil was 'usually of the most familiar kind', and if they became friends, as often happened, it could be 'very free and easy'. Bristed had provided an example of a tutorial dialogue (written out in the form of a play) involving a pair of pupils translating with a tutor; and Ornsby justified the inclusion of these dialogues by the need to convey to the reader the 'habits of mind and external developments of character' of the student, as well as the way in which the 'real and laborious teaching' at Cambridge was conducted with 'an utter familiarity and a reckless gaiety'.[63]

Ornsby's two articles no doubt helped to clarify what it was that Newman was attempting in Dublin. Another article examined the *Report* (1855) of the Royal Commission of inquiry into the seminary at Maynooth and took up two of the commissioners' criticisms: that the large numbers in the two residential houses 'precludes any effective supervision or attention to the formation of individual character, and [...] tends to engender something of the unsettled or turbulent spirit which characterizes a multitude'; and that there was a lack of intermingling between teachers and students outside classes which led to 'the absence of affectionate relations between the young men and the heads of the College, and of paternal influence'.[64] To combat the latter, one Maynooth professor made reference to the paternal system of discipline introduced by Thomas Arnold at Rugby School. A separate *Gazette* article dwelt on the striking differences between English and other universities by providing extracts from the *Quarterly Review* of June 1827; it explained that only in England did the pre-professional education consume the whole of the university course.

In the absence of evidence, it is hard to know if these and other articles from the *Gazette* had any direct effect on student life. Certainly there was intense interest among the professoriate and through them the articles would have exerted an influence on the learning environment at the Catholic University. A separate publication called *Atlantis, a register of literature and science conducted by members of the Catholic University,* was launched in January 1858 as a biannual journal for the scholarly output of the teaching staff. As a heavyweight academic journal under the editorship of W. K. Sullivan, Dean of the Faculty of Science, *Atlantis* provided an outlet for those academics who had few students to challenge and excite them, and it served to raise the academic tone of the University and set its sights high.[65]

As we know from Newman's writings, this emphasis on academic matters did not come at the expense of the broader aim of educating for human excellence, though it is hard to come by direct evidence to confirm this. Instead we have to rely on his Dublin writings if we want to fill in the gaps and capture the working characteristics with which he sought to inform the University, such as its ethical atmosphere, its attitude to the world, and its approach to social education. In applying the concept of integrity not just to the person, as Aristotle had done, but to the university, Newman asked himself, How can a university have a rich and full life? What needs to be put in place to foster both corporate and individual well-being? For Newman this was not just about intellectual flourishing, but also a moral question. He was concerned about how the student should live and how the university should be structured to make such living possible so as to provide an integral formation. He followed Aristotle in holding that 'it is impossible, or at least not easy, to perform praiseworthy actions without external means',[66] and that training was necessary to develop moral and intellectual virtues. Hence genuine human flourishing at university required the assistance of the moral and religious discipline of the collegiate house (or its equivalent) and the personal influence of tutors (or their equivalent). Newman knew that intellectual and moral virtues were best developed in a community which embodied such an educational ideal, as attendance at such places and the influence of its teachers would furnish the students with correct principles of thought and action.

For his time, Newman's approach to university education represented a marked shift in emphasis for Catholics. One instance of this was the stress he placed on preparing young men to play their part in society. In his Dublin lectures he had asked why we bother to educate and cultivate the intellect, if not to prepare for the world—and then he drew out the consequences:

> If then a University is a direct preparation for this world, let it be what it professes. It is not a Convent, it is not a Seminary; it is a place to fit men of the world for the world. We cannot possibly keep them from plunging into the world, with all its ways and principles and maxims, when their time comes; but we can prepare them against what is inevitable; and it is not the way to learn to swim in troubled waters, never to have gone into them.[67]

Applying this new attitude of facing the world to the study of literature meant that there should in principle be no ban on secular literature, since cutting out 'all broad manifestations of the natural man' would only leave those manifestations waiting for the students at the doors of the lecture room, where they would meet him 'in all the charm of novelty'. Newman confronted his clerical audience with the consequences of a heavy-handed censorship: 'Today a pupil, tomorrow a member of the great world: today confined to the Lives of the Saints, tomorrow thrown upon Babel'. By refusing the student the masters of human thought because of their incidental errors, he would be left without any rule for discriminating the precious from the base, truth from falsehood. And where would that leave him?

> [Y]ou have made him free of its newspapers, its reviews, its magazines, its novels, its controversial pamphlets, of its Parliamentary debates, its law proceedings, its platform speeches, its songs, its drama, its theatre, of its enveloping, stifling atmosphere of death. You have succeeded but in this,—in making the world his University.[68]

In practice, of course, Newman was well aware of the need to reconcile his words with 'the obedience which a University owes to the Rules of the Index of Prohibited Books, (in which Rules

Catholic Universities are recognized as in some sense officials of the Sacred Congregation)'.[69] He asked O'Reilly, the Professor of Dogmatic Theology, to enquire with Cullen as to how the University could proceed, and received Cullen's 'sanction for quietly availing ourselves and our lecture rooms of books which though prohibited, are not like Gibbon, decidedly dangerous, and are necessary for the intended professions of our students'.[70] Though ready to allow some books on the Index to be read, Cullen thought that permissions should be given without making a fuss and attracting attention. Newman also corresponded with O'Reilly about whether Protestant books such as Butler's *Analogy* could be set for the examination in the philosophy of religion; but Cullen was unhappy with such books appearing on an official university list and being regarded as the substantive matter of an examination. Newman's response was to suggest that Protestant works could be studied precisely as needing correction and subject to criticism.[71]

In the first of his university sketches Newman identified some of the social virtues which contribute to forming the gentleman: 'the carriage, gait, address, gestures, voice; the ease, the self-possession, the courtesy, the power of conversing, the talent of not offending; the lofty principle, the delicacy of thought, the happiness of expression, the taste and propriety, the generosity and forbearance, the candour and consideration, the openness of hand'. Some were natural endowments, some were found at all levels of society, some were a direct precept of Christianity; but certainly 'the full assemblage of them, bound up in the unity of an individual character', could not be learned from books. They were to be acquired where they were found: in highly civilized society. It was only reasonable that 'you cannot learn to converse till you have the world to converse with; you cannot unlearn your natural bashfulness, or awkwardness, or stiffness, or other besetting deformity, till you serve your time in some school of manners'.[72]

The Historical, Literary, and Aesthetical Society

It was one of Newman's most firmly held convictions that sound living conditions and a healthy atmosphere were a necessary condition for the student body to flourish and to be continually 'educating itself'. Whether student interests expressed themselves in more organised or purposeful ways, as in drama, music or sport, or whether they surfaced in more informal settings, such as at mealtimes and social gatherings, education in the sense of personal development was continually taking place. Though it is hard to pin down the precise nature of this activity and assess its formative value, this 'unofficial' side to university education had, for Newman, an incalculable worth.[73]

Between the formal daily round of lectures and tutorials and informal moments of relaxation and amusement, student enthusiasms—Newman thought—should find outlets in semi-formal settings, such as the Historical, Literary, and Aesthetical Society.[74] The society was entirely Newman's creation, and he was busy drafting a set of rules for what he termed a 'debating society' a few months before the University began.[75] The existence of such a society today would hardly appear noteworthy, but in the mid-nineteenth century there was something novel about it—though perhaps less so in Dublin, where Trinity College's Historical Society (founded in 1770) boasts of being the oldest student society in the world,[76] just as its Philosophical Society (founded in 1853) claims to be the oldest paper-reading undergraduate society in the world.[77]

It would be natural to assume that Newman borrowed the idea of a debating society from Trinity, but this is not the case. The idea of a debating society along the lines of the Historical, Literary, and Aesthetical Society was in fact his own, as can be seen from an unpublished article he wrote in 1819 for *The Undergraduate*, the student newspaper he and John Bowden founded and edited at

Oxford. In this article, written before the Oxford Union was founded,[78] he proposed the establishment of a debating society for Oxford undergraduates which should meet fortnightly to debate matters covering 'the whole range of history, poetry and the fine arts, indeed nothing should be excluded but the politics of the last 100 years'. Gathering its members from all the colleges and halls of Oxford, 'it would be a school for the future senator or lawyer, it would enlarge and refine the mind, it would be a most agreeable relaxation after the toils of the day'.[79] The significance of the article—and indeed of *The Undergraduate* itself—is that it reflects a general dissatisfaction with the Oxford that existed in Newman's time; more importantly, it testifies to Newman's long-held conviction that a great part of the process of education—if it is to be a *real* education—should lie outside the official academic routine. Given that a debating society was one of his most consistent interests, it comes as no surprise that it was a pet scheme of his rectorship.

Although the establishment of a debating society might appear to be an uncontentious move, in the mid-1850s when Catholic Ireland was almost without a public platform it was, as Newman well knew, a very delicate matter. He was well aware of the dangers involved in setting up a debating society, for it was not long after one had been established at Oxford that he felt obliged to criticise it as an example of the dangers of 'unbridled speculations and sophistical reasonings'.[80] When the Historical, Literary, and Aesthetical Society was launched the situation in Ireland could hardly have been less ideal: it was a gloomy time for the country, and the prevailing political atmosphere among Catholics was one of confusion, division and defeat.[81] Moreover, it was inevitable that Irish students coming to Dublin should bring with them the passions of the agrarian struggle and of the first steps towards self-government. More generally, in the charged atmosphere of post-famine Ireland, any public manifestation of political loyalties was viewed with suspicion; and among the clergy there was an assumption that students at the Catholic University should be seen—the more the better—but not heard. Lying behind their attitude lurked a fear that the public airing of student enthusiasms would prejudice the fortunes of the University, particularly its chance of securing a charter.

The name of the Historical, Literary, and Aesthetical Society reflected the content of the society's early meetings and the contemporary taste for literary composition and criticism.[82] In line with Newman's wish to keep politics at bay, he insisted (as in his 1819 article) on the rule that 'No member may introduce the subject of British politics of the last fifty years'.[83] The founding of the Historical Society at Trinity had been both an expression of and a catalyst for the awakening desire for political freedom in Ireland, and from its inception the society showed itself to be at the forefront of political thought; from the 1790s into the 1830s its meetings were punctuated with inflammatory speeches fuelled by the growth of Irish nationalism and self-determination, despite the ban on debating current political topics.[84] All the more reason for Newman to insist on a total ban on current politics at the Catholic University, and his actions accorded with the assurances he gave Cullen (in the context of employing Young Irelanders at the University) that 'I trust most earnestly that *politics* will not come into the University [...] I feel deeply that we shall be ruined, if we let *politics* in'.[85]

The first meeting of the Historical, Literary, and Aesthetical Society took place on 9 March 1856 in the basement of University House and was presided over by Newman. Among those present was one of the University's first seventeen students, Thomas Maunsell of St Laurence's House, who served on the society's first committee.[86] Other than Maunsell's brief recollection of this meeting, nothing is known about the society's first (short) session and how Newman got it off the ground, but a good deal is known about the second session of 1856/57, when the society's president[87] was Henry Bethell. Henry would certainly have been a member from the start and it is likely that the society became fully established during his presidency, as he was the ideal person to set it up along the lines envisaged by Newman. Not just his schooling (he had been educated at Eton until he left shortly after becoming a Catholic) but his family background would have prepared him for leadership in a student society, since his uncle, Sir Richard Bethell, had just become attorney-general and was soon to reach the Woolsack as Lord Westbury. Henry was also one of the Catholic University's most able students, winning prizes for English verse and criticism and a government-sponsored award that was much publicised by the University.

Much would have depended on Henry—and the previous president, if there was one—for Newman to launch the ambitious enterprise that the Historical, Literary, and Aesthetical Society undoubtedly was, both in terms of its range of activities and in its makeup as a society run entirely by students. Although originating from the rector, it had no official sponsorship—as the minutes of the arts faculty make clear when referring to it as 'a private society of the students'.[88] It is difficult to imagine the rule-book being entirely the work of a twenty-year-old student, and in the absence of any other records it may be conjectured that the general outline came from collaboration between Henry Bethell and Newman, and that the details were filled in by Henry and other students. In the preface, dated 1 December 1856, Henry explains that the subjects adopted for meetings were chosen not for their own sake but for the 'opportunities they afford for the cultivation of taste, and the development of the imaginative and inventive powers of the mind'. Meetings were intended principally 'to afford opportunity for the display of original thought—for the exercise of criticism—and for the removal of all difficulties in the way of extempore speaking, and English Composition'. This statement of intent was followed by the more down-to-earth exhortation that 'Nothing more is required from any member than a courageous determination to think for himself; to express his ideas as well as he is able; and to listen with interest to the opinions and thoughts of others, submitted to his criticism.'[89]

After describing the duties and responsibilities of the president, vice-president and secretary, the rule-book states that the 'council' (the governing body of the society) was to meet at least fortnightly, while the various committees were to convene each week for a minimum of three hours—finishing when their work was done. Each literary meeting or debate was to be presided over by a chairman, a role undertaken by *all* members of the society in turn. The chairman was to sum up the business of the meeting within an hour of starting, or after ninety minutes in the case of debates; to call upon members for papers, compositions and speeches; to maintain order and determine who was to speak first; to exercise his right to call upon any member to contribute, if no one volunteered to criticize a literary composition or to speak in a debate; to sum up the argument in a debate and announce which side he considered was 'proved'; and to write up his notes in a report book. In cases of disorderly conduct, he was to report the names of the guilty parties to the president or the council.

Evidently the society demanded a significant investment of time, not only from the society officers, but from all its members. The real workhorses, however, were the three 'reviewers', one each for the departments of history, literature and rhetoric, and aesthetics, poetry and romance. They were elected annually and their main task was that of editing the society's termly review, for which they were responsible to the council. They had to review and examine all the contributions submitted for meetings and to return rejected items (ignoring anonymous ones), and to write the leading articles in the review on the 'progress of taste in the three departments, as evinced by members'.[90] To this end they needed to pay close attention to the papers, compositions and speeches. If there was a shortage of articles for the review they could (giving ten day's notice) demand poetry or articles from *any* member. To make their task easier, they were allowed to ask for select pieces to be preserved in the society album, called the 'gem-book', obliging members to transcribe their own work into it and to sign at the bottom. The reviewers also played a part in debates by choosing the motion they thought best from those proposed by the main speakers, two on each side; in the absence of any suitable proposal, they could impose one of their own choosing.

In 1856/57 the society had twenty-three members, besides the six officers[91] (and honorary members).[92] Ordinary members of the society had to be students at the Catholic University, and were admitted by ballot (a vote of one-third could blackball entry) and on payment of the half-crown entry fee; expulsion required the consent of three-quarters of the society. Members were obliged to attend a minimum of two literary meetings a month, the interns doing so in cap and gown, and to gain admittance they had to arrive not more than fifteen minutes late. Rule 7, governing ordinary membership, stipulated that 'No member may cover his head, eat, smoke, whistle, sing, use a cane or umbrella, wear top-boots, a mackintosh, a dressing gown, or slippers, at any meeting.' Nor were they allowed to read a book during meetings, unless it was the rule-book. An elaborate system of fines ensured that the rules were kept to, each breach having its price, whether for lateness, failure to produce a paper or composition, inability to meet the deadlines for copying work into the gem-book, and, of course, for 'introducing forbidden politics' (for which the fine was a hefty 5/–).

The frequency of meetings is not referred to in the rule-book, but once the society was launched there were on alternate weeks either debates on previously advertised topics or else the reading of papers and compositions followed by discussion. The rules for the literary meetings stipulated that papers were to come before compositions. By a 'paper' was meant a factual presentation lasting a minimum of fifteen minutes, while a 'composition' was a purely imaginative work, which, if prose, had to fill four sides of closely written script and, if poetry, had to last a minimum of thirty lines. No one was dispensed from writing and reading a paper; but if members felt incapable of composition they could substitute for it by simply reading a piece of verse. In the time remaining, any member was allowed to criticise the style or substance of a presentation, or even the way it was read, but the authors of the presentation always had the right to respond to any objection—and to have the last word. Allowances were made for students from non-English speaking countries by allowing them to read in any modern language, but for everyone else quotations from another language had to be followed by a translation.

The topics for debates were supposed to be historical, literary or aesthetic questions, and could not repeat topics covered in previous papers. The two leading speakers on each side were allowed up to twenty minutes each and could use only notes, the reading of written speeches being forbidden; all other interventions were limited to ten minutes and no-one could speak a second time until everyone else had had their turn. Friends could only be 'introduced' to meetings once a term, on St Catherine's day (25 November), the anniversary of the society's foundation (9 March), and the feast of St Philip Neri (26 May); but guests could also be introduced by reviewers of meetings, the chairman of a literary meeting, leading speakers at debates, and readers of papers or compositions.

At 7 pm on Monday, 26th January 1857 Henry Bethell gave his inaugural address, on the subject of 'Taste and genius', in which he laid down a theory of taste based on the notion of innate ideas. Afterwards the vote of thanks was proposed and seconded by two lecturers from the Catholic University Medical School. There were twenty-five other meetings during the 1856/57 session; papers were given by both students and lecturers, while the lecturers prudently abstained from delivering compositions; debates were entirely student affairs. (Whether this feat of organisation was repeated when the younger Bethell took over the presidency for the 1857/58 session is unclear.) The themes of literary meetings were announced in the press, but not the debates, and for the second half of the 1856/57 session ran as follows:[93]

Feby. 9th	Paper: 'The Identity of Origin and the Varieties of the Human Race' English Verse Essay Paper: 'The Formation of Alphabets as Illustrated by Egyptian Hieroglyphics'
Feby. 25th	Paper: 'Dryden and Swift' English Verse Essay
Mar. 23rd	Paper: 'The Influence of Ireland upon Anglo Saxon Literature' English Verse Essay
May 18th	Paper: 'Richelieu and Mazarin' A verse composition
Jun. 15th	Paper: 'The Life and Writings of Silvio Pellico'
Jul. 16th	Lecture: 'The Student Life and the Principles of Success'

Proceedings were sometimes reported in the press, particularly the nationalist press. Less is known about the debates; the earliest recorded motion comes from 1858 when the question debated was, 'Which was the greater man, Julius Caesar or Napoleon?'

In his *Roundabout recollections* O'Shea relates that debate topics were 'scrupulously stale', as all nineteenth-century themes were forbidden; yet, he says, they 'managed to galvanise the dry bones of the past into spasmodic semblance of vitality'. This meant that they were at liberty to discuss the suppression of the Knights Templar, the policies of the Duke of Alba, or to compare Augustan literature with literature from the reign of Queen Anne—but not to meddle with the Union: 'It was preserved ground, and the season was a close season all the year round for us.' This was the rector's wish, 'and his desire was law'. With hindsight O'Shea conceded that this was probably a wise decision, because there were many dormant elements that might have stirred into 'discordant wakefulness'.[94] Towards the end of his university days the fifty-year ban on politics was lifted and the academics began to take a greater part in proceedings, perhaps for the purpose of ensuring that debates did not disintegrate into political wrangling.

In spite of the ban there was, according to O'Shea, plenty of fire and scholarship in the speeches: any false erudition was dealt with mercilessly and factual errors and unsound arguments were pounced upon and ridiculed—but all was conducted in good spirits and without squabbling. On one occasion the young Count Zamoyski enraged the society by arriving in boots and scarlet coat fresh from hunting with the Ward Union. He was reprimanded as a point of order, and a rule was passed forbidding such 'outrageous behaviour'. Zamoyski had his revenge at the next meeting by appearing in Polish military uniform, and only escaped censure on this occasion because he had the graciousness to leave off his spurs!

There is no doubt that Newman saw the Historical, Literary, and Aesthetical Society as a great instrument for rounding out the education imparted at the Catholic University and for preparing students for the world of work. This was the practical working out of some lines from his Dublin lectures, where he had countered the claims of the educational utilitarians of his day and dwelt on the practical benefits of a liberal education:

the man who has learned to think and to reason and to compare and to discriminate and to analyze, who has refined his taste, and formed his judgement, and sharpened his mental vision, will not at once be a lawyer, [...] a man of business, or a soldier, or an engineer but he will be placed in that state of intellect in which he can take up any of these sciences or callings [...] with an ease, a grace, a versatility, and a success, to which another is a stranger.[95]

Spiritual oversight and the University Church

Undoubtedly the spiritual health of the University was one of Newman's main concerns, although it would be a mistake to think of it as something separate from his desire for the intellectual vitality of the University and for the all-round development of its students, as if these three aims were incompatible. Unfortunately there are large gaps in the evidence surviving about the spiritual side of university life, which makes it hard to judge how successful the systems were that Newman put in place for aiding spiritual development. It was laid down that all those residing in the collegiate houses should receive 'spiritual direction', usually from the dean or chaplain of the house, and that they should go to confession regularly with one or the other of them, but in the absence of personal memoirs it is unclear what precisely 'spiritual direction' entailed; it must in any case have varied according to the dean of the house. At St Mary's, at least, the students seem to have gone to Newman for confession, though they were free to choose another confessor. There is, however, more evidence for religious *instruction* at the University. At the beginning it had been anticipated that this instruction would take place principally by means of lectures, though it appears that only three took place in the entire first session: they were given during the summer term by Dr Leahy, the vice-rector, who lectured on Old Testament themes. Little else seems to have happened until Michaelmas Term 1855, when William Penny started acting as University Catechist in Creed and Scripture. Thereafter all interns were required to attend the catechetical instructions he gave four evenings a week, as well as the course of lectures he gave on the Roman Catechism at 10 am on Sundays, before High Mass.

It was not until June 1856 that Newman decided on the arrangements for religious instruction. After considerable thought, he set out his proposal in a (private) 'Letter of the Rector to the Dean of the Faculty of Philosophy and Letters on the Introduction of Religious Teaching into the Schools of that Faculty'.[96] Before attempting to justify the place of religious instruction in the arts faculty by appealing to 'some intelligible principle', Newman noted that there were two common approaches in Catholic institutions. The majority, out of a zeal for theology, felt that the subject of religion should be confined to the theology faculty rather than be admitted to the lecture-rooms of philosophy and letters, where it would suffer from 'the superficial treatment of lay-professors, and the superficial reception of young minds'. On the other hand, a minority favoured the subject being given 'unlimited extension in the province of Letters', which meant replacing classical literature by the Scriptures and works of the Church Fathers, and teaching scholastic theology to one and all. Rather than adopt either system, Newman proposed a mid-position in which the subject of religion was admitted into the arts faculty, but operated within fixed limits so as to prevent it becoming an intrusion.[97] In this way no student would go through the academic course without any direct teaching of a religious character; furthermore, religious knowledge would form part of the subject matter for the exams for the scholar's and licentiate degrees.[98]

Taking as evident that 'youths, who are prepared in a Catholic University for the general duties of a secular life, or for the secular professions, should not leave it without some knowledge of religion', the question to address was, What should the University teach, and how much? Newman noted that, 'as the mind is enlarged and cultivated generally, it is capable, or rather is desirous and has need, of fuller religious information'; this meant that a knowledge of Christianity sufficient for an incoming student would not suffice for one about to leave. Rather than sharpen and refine the young intellects and then simply leave them to exercise their new powers on the most sacred of subjects, at the risk of making mistakes, the University—Newman felt—was under an obligation to feed these minds with divine truth as they gained in appetite and capacity for knowledge. He concluded that 'if the subject of religion is to have a real place in their course of study, it must enter into the *examinations* in which that course results; for nothing will be found to impress and occupy their minds, but such matters as they have to present to their Examiners'.[99]

The introduction of religion into what Newman called the 'secular schools' need not entail any sacrifice of principle or consistency, he argued. The subject of religion was to be treated simply as a branch of knowledge: just as students studied general history, literature and philosophy, so they ought to have 'a parallel knowledge of religion' and study sacred history, Biblical literature and Christian philosophy. The objection to doing this was that a little knowledge of religion was a dangerous thing and that the risk of error was serious—but Newman judged that the argument only really applied to doctrine itself. Church history was important for the young Catholic, as he was bound to mix with educated Protestants of his own age and would 'find them conversant with the outlines and the characteristics of sacred and ecclesiastical history as well as profane': it was desirable that he should be able to keep up a conversation with them and that he should know as well as they 'the great primitive divisions of Christianity, its polity, its luminaries, its acts, and its fortunes; its great eras and its course to this day'. He should have some idea of the early spread of Christianity; the Fathers and their works; the Christological controversies and heresies; the religious orders; the Crusades. 'He should be able to say what the Holy See has done for learning and science; the place which these islands hold in the literary history of the dark age; what part the Church had, and how its highest interests fared, in the revival of letters'. However ambitious all this might seem, he thought it important to map out the range of knowledge they ought to encourage in the lecture and examination halls. Similarly, just as students were encouraged to study classical literature, so they should be 'invited to acquaint themselves with some general facts about the canon of Holy Scripture, its history, the Jewish canon, St Jerome, the Protestant Bible; again, about the languages of Scripture, the contents of its separate books, their authors, and their versions'.[100]

As for theology itself, where the real danger of error lay, Newman recommended that the authorities exclude from the arts faculty 'the teaching *in extenso* of pure dogma', and confine coverage to a broad knowledge of doctrinal subjects as contained in catechisms of the Church and in the writings of the *lay* faithful. 'I would have them apply their minds to such religious topics as laymen actually do treat, and are thought praiseworthy in treating.' Newman clarifies this important point by explaining that he refers to 'Christian knowledge in what may be called its secular aspect, as it is practically useful in the intercourse of life and in general conversation; and I would encourage it as it bears upon the history, literature, and philosophy of Christianity'. The University authorities needed to realise that their students were going out into a world not of professed Catholics, but of 'inveterate, often bitter, commonly contemptuous Protestants', who had been versed in the doctrines and arguments of Protestantism. Newman hoped the University would be able to help its students grasp what the difference was between the Church and a sect, between ecclesiastical and civil authority, what the Church claims for itself of necessity and what it can dispense with, what it can grant and what it cannot. Their students needed to know how to answer questions commonly asked of Catholics: whether the celibacy of the clergy was a matter of faith or Church discipline; whether the Pope, by appointing a hierarchy, was interfering with the prerogatives of the monarch;[101] whether, and in what sense, Catholics consider Protestants to be heretics; whether Catholics deny the reality of natural virtue, and what worth they assign to it.[102]

Such questions as these, which might crop up in conversations, often did not require sophisticated arguments, but just a few pertinent words stating facts. 'Half the controversies which go on in the world arise from ignorance of the facts of the case; half the prejudices against Catholicity lie in the misinformation of the prejudiced parties. Candid persons are set right, and enemies silenced, by the mere statement of what it is that we believe.' What was not satisfactory was for a Catholic to say, I leave it to the theologians, or, I will ask a priest. Instead a Catholic ought to gratify the curiosity of even those who speak against Catholicism by giving them information, because it was generally the case that 'such mere information will really be an argument also'. Newman recalled the story of three Tractarian friends of his, all clergymen, who were touring Ireland in the late 1820s and on one occasion found themselves with a boy aged thirteen, who was acting as their guide. Amusing themselves by putting religious questions to the young Catholic, they soon found themselves silenced by his replies—not by refined theological arguments, but merely by his knowing and understanding the answers in his catechism.[103]

This was not to say that argument itself was out of place for laymen moving in the world. Theologians viewed Revelation from within, philosophers from without—'and the office of delineating it externally is most gracefully performed by laymen'. In the first age of the Church, laymen figured prominently among its apologists; in the present age, too, some of the most able defenders of the Church—men like Chateaubriand, De Maistre and Montalembert—were laymen.[104] If the University confined itself to the external contemplation of religion, then the range of reading would be sufficiently wide and as valuable 'in its practical application as it is liberal in character'. Besides the 'evidences' of Christianity, Newman thought it was particularly useful to include the four 'notes' (One, Holy, Catholic, Apostolic) of the Church. But, whatever the reading recommended to the students, it was vital that it was accompanied by explanations from older, wiser minds.[105]

It would have been inconceivable that Newman would have overlooked the importance of preaching when planning for the intellectual, moral and religious training of the students. This was why he had intended from the start to establish a University Church in Dublin which (besides being the natural setting for preaching) would, as at Oxford, be 'the place for all the high occasional ceremonies in which the University is visibly represented', such as degree ceremonies, formal lectures and public acts. The University Church would be an invaluable instrument 'in inculcating a loyal and generous devotion to the Church in the breasts of the young',[106] and would serve to 'maintain and symbolize that great principle in which we glory as our characteristic, the union of Science with Religion'.[107] Before the University opened, Newman had hoped ultimately to make the University Church and the collegiate houses into a personal diocese, either with the rector as its bishop, or else with the Archbishop of Dublin as its bishop and the rector as its vicar apostolic.[108] Though this remained an idea on paper, his ambitious thinking conveys the conception he had of his new pastoral responsibility.

Once St Mary's House had acquired its own domestic chapel in January 1855, Newman turned his attention to the needs of the University and began to explore the possibility of sharing a church with a local parish, but negotiations had hardly got going when the plan collapsed. The obstacles he faced caused Newman to change his mind and he opted instead for a purpose-built University Church. Despite the difficulty of finding a suitable site, Newman managed to acquire the lease of a small piece of land behind 87 St Stephen's Green, adjacent to University House. He was not deterred by the limited space available as he considered that university sermons were best suited to a church where the preacher was not distanced from the congregation.

Newman was determined to see the project through himself, just as he had been when building a parish church at Littlemore in 1835, and took upon himself the entire expense of building and furnishing the church.[109] Defying the vogue for the Gothic style, Newman chose the form of a Byzantine basilica, which had the merits of functional beauty (being best for the acoustics and sight), lower cost (as most of the decoration was internal), suitability for the use of Irish marble, and relative harmony with the surrounding Georgian buildings. The basic design of the church and its decoration was decided on by Newman, and its execution and interpretation entrusted to Pollen, the Professor of Fine Arts. Newman worked closely with him on the plans and the construction, and used his stay in Rome at Christmas 1856 to commission copies of a set of tapestries designed for the Sistine Chapel by Raphael. Just ten months after Pollen had set to work, the University Church was opened on Ascension Thursday, 1st May 1856 with a pontifical High Mass celebrated by Archbishop Cullen. The church was so much to Newman's liking that he described it as 'the most beautiful one in the three kingdoms'.[110] Measuring one hundred feet in length, thirty-six feet in breadth and forty high, it contained an ante-chapel and a spacious, aisle-less nave laid out on the plan of a plain basilica, and was decorated internally with coloured Irish marble columns; the ornate apse featured a scene depicting a vine rising from a field of birds and animals up to groups of saints, who surrounded Mary, *Sedes sapientiae*, in their midst. Pollen's first architectural commission met Newman's aspirations fully, and was generally acclaimed by all who visited. For the students who frequented the church, it was a powerful symbol of what the Catholic University represented.[111]

Priests not just from Dublin but from all over Ireland were invited to preach there, Newman's only stipulations being that they were to avoid political topics and to abide by the forty-minute time-limit.[112] O'Shea recalls the painful occasion when one preacher began with an 'extravagant eulogy' of the Catholic University and its head, before sounding off with an 'elaborate tirade' against Trinity College and its founder (Elizabeth I) of 'odious memory';[113] all that the students could see of Newman was that he had buried his head in his hands, while the academic staff looked on suitably embarrassed.

The University Church soon had its own chaplain, the Oxford convert William Anderdon, who was assisted by several priests from St Laurence's. O'Shea recalls that Anderdon was liked by everyone and that he was a great success in the pulpit: evidently Newman had chosen a chaplain who was genuinely zealous and capable of making a profound impression on the students. According to O'Shea, Anderdon never used fear nor ranted, but instead in his soothing voice 'coaxed worldly folk to thoughts of the upper things'.[114] As for the preaching of Newman himself, Tom Arnold found the Dublin sermons even more inspiring than those he had heard in Oxford; four decades later he could still remember one of them clearly. One of the students from St Laurence's House was William Walsh, who later became Archbishop of Dublin, and he remembers that the sermons 'were read by Newman in a clear musical voice, unimpassioned, and well modulated, and that they were listened to with rapt attention by fashionable and cultured congregations'.[115]

The Sunday after the Church opened was undoubtedly a moving occasion for Newman, because for the first time he would have looked down from the pulpit at the few dozen students from his university attired in academic dress. No doubt there were a good number of parents present too, as well as academic staff, though the largest contingent would have been the fashionable element of Catholic Dublin who had come to hear the famous Oxford convert preach. Though student numbers were boosted by a group from Trinity College, the student body was nevertheless a minority in the congregation of just over a thousand. As it was the feast day of St Monica, the mother of the intellectual convert St Augustine, Newman used the occasion to consider her as a type of the Church, ever solicitous for the return of its clever sons, who had rushed out into the world and were now spiritually dead. A chief task of the Catholic University, Newman explained to the congregation, was to shoulder this responsibility of the Church in caring for her student family. More generally, part of the University's special office was to receive from parental hands those who were leaving home, and to live up to and delight in its well-known designation as *alma mater*. But it was to Mary, the greatest of mothers, not to Monica, that the university turned to for its pattern as *Mater amabilis* and *Causa nostræ lætitiæ*, as well as *Sedes sapientiæ*. Like Mary, the University 'is able to confute and put right those who would set knowledge against itself, and would make truth contradict truth, and would persuade the world that, to be religious, you must be ignorant, and to be intellectual, you must be unbelieving'.[116]

At a time when the voices of revolution and intellectual scepticism were in the air, Newman resisted the temptation to flee the world for the security of the Church, and he used this first university sermon in Dublin to speak about an alternative approach. But before proposing a remedy, he sought to get to the heart of the problem. Ever since the Fall, man had lost dominion over himself and found 'separate powers warring in his own breast—appetite, passion, secular ambition, intellect, and conscience, and trying severally to get possession of him'. When he looks outside himself he sees these powers 'embodied on a grand scale' in the world: the reign of passion and appetite, the reign of brute strength and material power, but also the reign of intellect and the reign of virtue. The confusion this produces in a young person in his formative years is a serious matter, and 'what makes it worse is that that these various faculties and powers of the human mind have so long been separated from each other, so long cultivated and developed each by itself, that it comes to be taken for granted that they cannot be united'. This unconscious acceptance of the disunity of the human faculties makes people assume that 'because some men follow duty, others pleasure, others glory, and others intellect, one of these things must exclude the other; that duty cannot be pleasant, that virtue cannot be intellectual, that goodness cannot be great, that conscientiousness cannot be heroic'.[117] Moreover, it is often the case that good men are not attractive, while bad men are, so that in adolescence,

> not only is the soul plagued and tormented by the thousand temptations which rise up within it, but it is exposed more-over to the sophistry of the Evil One, whispering that duty and religion are very right indeed, admirable, supernatural,—who doubts it?—but that, somehow or other, religious people are commonly either very dull or very tiresome: nay, that religion itself after all is more suitable to women and children, who live at home, than to men.[118]

Newman paints for his congregation a detailed picture of the protracted process undergone by the young Christian who descends gradually into infidelity. Starting with the stirrings of intellectual rebellion and the indulgence of an unhealthy curiosity, there follow deeds, words and thoughts which, instead of uniting knowledge and religion, set them against each other. The young Christian is led by bad company to 'that miserable tone of conversation,—hinting and suggesting evil, jesting, bantering on the subject of sin, supplying fuel for the inflammable imagination', with the danger that 'from bad thoughts and bad words proceed bad deeds'.[119] He feels a growing distaste for good, and from hearing or reading opinions directly against religion, the young man unconsciously slips into a state of doubt, then he finds the thinking of unbelievers ever more congenial, until the day comes when he realises he has lost his faith.

Rather than place all the blame on the young man, Newman takes his part by showing that there is a good deal of truth in his delusion: his awakening intellectual faculties demand exercise and his aspirations an object, and he often does not find this exercise or object in religious circles. This is frequently the cause of his going astray, for he is not only a moral, but an intellectual being, and 'ever since the fall of man, religion is here, and philosophy is there; each has its own centres of influence, separate from the other'. The object of the Catholic Church in setting up universities, Newman declares, is 'to reunite things which were in the beginning joined together by God, and have been put asunder by man'. Others might say that the imposition of ecclesiastical supervision would tend to distort and stunt the growth of the intellect; but Newman disagreed. Nor did he envisage a compromise, as if religion must give up something and science something. Rather he wished 'the intellect to range with the utmost freedom, and religion to enjoy an equal freedom' and 'that they should be found in one and the same place, and exemplified in the same persons'.[120]

> I wish the same spots and the same individuals to be at once oracles of philosophy and shrines of devotion. It will not satisfy me, what satisfies so many, to have two independent systems, intellectual and religious, going at once side by side, by a sort of division of labour, and only accidentally brought together. It will not satisfy me, if religion is here, and science there, and young men converse with science all day, and lodge with religion in the evening. It is not touching the evil [...] if young men eat and drink and sleep in one place, and think in another: I want the same roof to contain both the intellectual and moral discipline. [...] I want the intellectual layman to be religious, and the devout ecclesiastic to be intellectual.[121]

Notes

[1]   Now known as Newman House, 86 St Stephen's Green has been restored to its former Georgian grandeur and is open to the public for guided tours. The ground floor, the *piano nobile* and the grand staircase are all decorated with rococo plasterwork by Robert West, Dublin's premier stucco artist; the back drawing-room—the boardroom where the Catholic University Committee met and other official University business was conducted—is preserved as it was in Newman's day with its mid-Victorian décor and furniture.

[2]   J. A. O'Shea, *Roundabout recollections*, vol. ii (London, 1892), p. 95.

[3]   'Catching a crab' is rowing terminology for not raising the oar out of the water in time at the end of a stroke, which completely breaks the rhythm of the boat and often brings it to a standstill.

[4]   O'Shea, *Roundabout recollections*, vol. ii, p. 99.

[5]   They may have used the club house of Pembroke Boat Club, founded in 1836, which operated from Ringsend, and which was the forerunner of the University Boat Club of TCD, founded in 1867. Subscriptions for the boat club of St Patrick's were 6/-.

6   O'Shea, *Roundabout recollections*, vol. ii, p. 100.

7   St Stephen's Green was then a plainly laid out private park, and not the attractive public garden it became twenty-five years later.

8   In the nineteenth century the term 'college' was used for institutions attached to religious communities or seminaries, and 'school' for those without such links. The term 'secular college' (or 'ecclesiastical college') was used to denote one run by the secular clergy, and 'religious college' for one run by a religious order.

9   The balance of backgrounds described by O'Shea appears to be the reverse of what it was in the University's first year. Of the thirty-eight students who matriculated during the first session, ten came from St Laurence's, seven from the Birmingham Oratory, eleven from Clongowes Wood, and one each from Thurles, Stonyhurst and Downside—leaving seven unaccounted for (Barr, *Paul Cullen*, p. 131). During the period 1854–61, twenty-seven out of the 191 students on the University books came from English schools, including six each from Oscott, Stonyhurst and Ushaw, and three from Downside (W. J. Rigney, 'Bartholomew Woodlock and the Catholic University 1861–79', Ph.D., University College Dublin, 1995, vol. i, p. 326; vol. ii, pp. 290 *et seq.*).

10 Besides lecturers in special languages, all but two of the twenty-one professors and lecturers for the academic year 1854/55 were Irish, the exceptions being Ornsby (English) and Stewart (Scottish) (Report for the Year 1854–55, MC, pp. 19–20); however, of the six tutors only one was Irish. All six of the medics engaged in 1855/56 were Irish (F. McGrath, *Newman in Dublin* (Dublin, 1969), p. 14).

11 O'Shea, *Roundabout recollections*, vol. ii, p. 96.

12 The tradition was still going strong fifty years later, as can be seen from the pages of the student magazine *St. Stephen's. A record of university life* 1–7 (June 1901–June 1902) which contains several songs in Gaelic. See also Eimar O'Duffy's *A college chorus. A collection of humorous verses by students of University College, Dublin, from the pages of 'St. Stephen's' and 'The National Student'* (Dublin, [1935]), which includes a chorus for the members of the Literary and Historical Society.

13 O'Shea, *Roundabout recollections*, vol. ii, pp. 110–11.

14 O'Shea, *Roundabout recollections*, vol. ii, pp. 120–2. It is interesting to note that Edmund O'Reilly, the Professor of Dogmatic Theology, agreed to deputise for Newman in the 1857 'terminal examinations', then pulled out when he realised how much was involved: obtaining a written report on

each student, presiding over an aural examination of each student by the lecturers, and summing up proceedings with words of praise or reprimand, as need be. He said, 'I have not self-possession or tact enough to do this in an effectual or decorous way', and explained that 'the particular kind of judicial process involved is not within my capacity' (O'Reilly to Newman, 13 December 1857, BOA, DP 44/22).

[15] O'Shea, *Roundabout recollections*, vol. ii, pp. 121–2.

[16] O'Shea, *Roundabout recollections*, vol. ii, pp. 114–15. The students of St Mary's, who encountered Newman in a domestic environment and on daily basis, appear to have had a rather less awestruck attitude towards him.

[17] Newman's second and last novel, *Callista, a tale of the third century*, was competed over the summer of 1855; he took to writing it on hearing that Wiseman had suggested that he should write a sequel to Wiseman's *Fabiola or the Church of the catacombs* (1854).

[18] O'Shea, *Roundabout recollections*, vol. ii, p. 115. As an Anglican, Newman had always written out his sermons beforehand and read them from the pulpit; on becoming a Catholic he began to preach from notes, writing them up in longer note form afterwards. See *Sermon notes of John Henry Cardinal Newman, 1849–78*, ed. Fathers of the Birmingham Oratory (London, 1914), pp. v–vi, xii–xiii. He did, however, revert to his former style on certain occasions—and the six Dublin University sermons were among these. Nevertheless, the Dublin sermons are not at all like Newman's Oxford University sermons, but more like his parish sermons there: his thoughts are very direct and matter-of-fact, and expressed in simple, plain speech. Though O'Shea may have been disappointed by the lack of oratorical fireworks, the Irish in general appreciated Newman's sermons and warmed to his style, as contemporary evidence attests.

[19] T. Arnold, *Passages in a wandering life* (London, 1900), p. 160.

[20] Arnold to Julia Arnold, 25 November 1856, *Letters of Thomas Arnold the younger, 1850–1900*, ed. J. Bertram (London, 1980), p. 84. T. W. Allies went to Dublin in December 1854 to deliver a lecture on the philosophy of history and spent five pleasant days at St Mary's, where he saw more of Newman than he had ever before. He commented, 'The whole work of the nascent University rests upon him. If he were removed at present all would go to pieces. It is the weight of his personal character, which can support and baffle the difficulties perpetually impinging, which is of so much importance' (quoted in M. H. Allies, *Thomas William Allies* (London, 1907), p. 77).

21 Arnold to Collinson, 19 September 1857, *Letters of Thomas Arnold*, p. 88. While Arnold's observations are valuable, his inference about Newman's deficiency of will-power is surely wide of the mark; Newman was fearless when his reason told him a course of action was the right course of action, regardless of the consequences.

22 De Vere, *Recollections*, pp. 256–7. Newman had been keen to appoint someone from Trinity because he thought that it was an advantage to know it well (*LD*, vol. xxxii, p. 80).

23 De Vere, *Recollections*, pp. 275, 278, 280–1.

24 Pollen to Maria La Primaudaye, 13 May 1855, quoted in Pollen, *John Hungerford Pollen*, p. 253.

25 Quoted in Trevor, *Light in winter*, p. 61.

26 Dunne to Newman, 6 November 1858, *LD*, vol. xviii, p. 502.

27 Report for the Year 1855–56, *MC*, p. 72.

28 Newman to Hope-Scott, 24 December 1857, *LD*, vol. xviii, p. 214. In 1858 Newman wrote: 'There can't be a set of men with a better spirit or more zeal' (Newman to Monsell, 9 May 1858, *LD*, vol. xviii, p. 343).

29 All the Englishman on the staff of the Catholic University were converts to Catholicism, as well as the Irishman de Vere and the Scotsman Stewart, and most (Allies, Ornsby, Pollen, Penny, Stewart and Newman himself) were former clergymen. This must have been one reason why Cullen later thought that it had been a mistake to appoint a convert as rector (Cullen to Barnabò, 18 February 1861, quoted in Barr, *Paul Cullen*, p. 237, note 4).

30 Newman to Renouf, 20 February 1854, *LD*, vol. xvi, p. 49.

31 Renouf also wrote to his parents about the appointment: 'I look upon my new vocation [...] as a call from God to do on a larger scale what every one is bound to do in his degree, to advance the spiritual Kingdom of His Son [...] that Christ may dwell in our hearts by faith, and that we may be rooted and grounded in this Love' (13 April 1854, *Letters of Renouf*, vol. iii, pp. 8–9).

32 Arnold to Newman, 23 October 1856, *Letters of Thomas Arnold*, p. 80. In a similar fashion, de Vere told a friend that he was preparing lectures 'on the *chance* of being useful', though he was not hopeful about being appointed to the University (de Vere to Monsell, 8 February 1855, quoted in Barr, *Paul Cullen*, p. 143).

33 Arnold to Julia Arnold, 14 November 1856, *Letters of Thomas Arnold*, p. 84.

34 Arnold to Newman, 1 May 1858, *Letters of Thomas Arnold*, p. 89.

35 Newman to Moriarty, 25 November 1856, *LD*, vol. xvii, p. 461.

36 O'Curry had catalogued the Irish manuscripts of the Royal Irish Academy and the British Museum in the 1840s and supported himself and his family by working on the transcription, editing and translation of Irish manuscripts. When he was appointed to the Catholic University, he possessed a virtually unparalleled knowledge of early Irish history and had recently been elected to the Irish Academy, despite his strong Catholic loyalties (*ODNB*). A chair of Irish was established at Trinity in 1840, but this was within the Divinity School and promoted and funded by Irish Evangelicals; in 1919 the appointment became a literary professorship (McDowell & Webb, *Trinity College Dublin*, pp. 190–1).

37 Pollen to Goldie, August 1890, *The Month* 507 (September 1906), pp. 317–18, 320.

38 Pollen to Goldie, August 1890, *The Month* 507 (September 1906), p. 319.

39 Moriarty to Newman, 28 November 1856, *LD*, vol. xvii, p. 461n. During the academic year 1855/56, all but six out of twenty-six academics were Irish. Three others held posts but received no remuneration: T. W. Allies, J. O'Hagan and D. MacCarthy.

40 *CUG* 4 (22 June 1854), p. 26; *Idea of a university*, p. 335.

41 In his sixth Dublin lecture Newman argued that 'the practical error of the last twenty years' was that of 'distracting and enfeebling the mind by an unmeaning profusion of subjects; of implying that a smattering in a dozen branches of study is not shallowness, which it really is, but enlargement, which it is not; [...] All things now are to be learned at once, not first one thing, then another, not one well, but many badly.' The likely result was to 'produce a generation frivolous, narrow-minded, and resourceless'; students would 'leave their place of education simply dissipated and relaxed by the multiplicity of subjects, which they have never really mastered, and so shallow as not even to know their shallowness'. The paradox was that someone who never studied at a university might well gain a more genuine education than a university graduate (*Idea of university*, pp. 142, 146, 149).

42 *CUG* 34 (18 January 1855), p. 296; *Idea of a university*, p. 371. In this last remark Newman contrasts the idiosyncratic learning styles of those who learn almost exclusively from books with the mechanical or rote learning of those who learn predominantly from teachers.

43 Archbishop Leahy's later tribute to Renouf brings out the qualities that Newman sought to foster in his common room: 'not merely of a high literary name but also of high moral worth, that necessary complement to

the Professor's teaching, which gave you sway over the minds and enabled you to form the characters of the students happily for themselves entrusted to your care. You taught by your example as much as by your words. The student saw in his Professor the Scholar, the Gentleman, the Christian —the happiest union of learning and religion' (Leahy to Renouf, 11 March 1864, *Letters of Renouf,* vol. iii, p. 273).

44 Report from the Professor of Logic, appendix to the Report for the Year 1856–57, *MC,* pp. 197–8.

45 Rothblatt, *The revolution of the dons: Cambridge and society in Victorian England* (London, 1968), pp. 227–9.

46 In the summer term of 1858 Renouf delivered an ambitious series of lectures on the history of Greek philosophy—the syllabus was published as a supplement to *Atlantis* 1:2 (July 1858)—and in the process compiled a manual of Greek philosophy. But the manual was never published, and in 1863 Renouf remarked that the University 'no longer has pupils capable of following such lectures' (Renouf to Acton, 25 January 1863, *Letters of Renouf,* p. 162).

47 See pp. 519–39 for the biographies of the academic staff Newman employed; they show the calibre of the men he managed to attract.

48 Newman to Ornsby, 24 December 1853, *LD,* vol. xxxi, pp. 41–2.

49 Ornsby to Newman, 19 November 1857, *LD,* vol. xviii, p. 203n.

50 Barr, *Paul Cullen,* p. 185.

51 *Royal Commission Queen's Colleges* (1858), p. 35. Two other obstacles were mentioned: the opposition of the Catholic Church and the fact that Trinity admitted non-residential students. As a result the Queen's Colleges were 'entirely destitute of the prestige and association which would attract those in search of a liberal education' (*ibid.*) and its students were confined to the middle classes.

52 The *Report of Her Majesty's commissioners appointed to inquire into the endowments, funds, and actual condition of all schools endowed for the purpose of education in Ireland* (1858) investigated mainly Protestant schools, as few Catholic ones had been endowed.

53 The difficulty of meeting the ambitious target he had set himself forced Ornsby to turn the *Gazette* from a weekly into a monthly publication after his first ten numbers.

54 *CUG* 46 (1 November 1855), p. 481.

55 These articles in the *Gazette* were anonymous, but their authorship was attributed to Newman by V. F. Blehl in *John Henry Newman: a bibliographical*

catalogue of his writings (Virginia, 1978).

56   Newman was doing this five years before the first Oxford manual to give practical advice on reading books, taking notes and how to benefit from tutorials, Montagu Burrow's *Pass and class. An Oxford guide-book through the course of Literae Humaniores, Mathematics, and Law and History* (Oxford, 1860).

57   See 'The throwing open of Haileybury', *CUG* 35 (18 January 1855) and also 'The Examination for the East India civil [service] appointments', *CUG* 47 (6 December 1855). Just as Macaulay's Report (1854) laid down rules for the India civil service exams, which were adopted in full, the recommendations of the Northcote–Trevelyan Report (1854) were taken up by the Civil Service Commission which was set up in 1855 to oversee open recruitment and end patronage for the home civil service. Both changes gave a new significance to the academic work of the university. At the synod of bishops in June 1856, Newman spoke about his intention to prepare students for the military academies and the home and India civil service as one of four 'immediate objects' for the University (*MC*, p. 147). The University calendar for 1858/59 gave an outline of lectures for the 'Course of study for the Civil Services', adding that the course could be tailored to suit individual need.

58   Monsell to Newman, 30 June 1854, *LD*, vol. xvi, p. 179. For a summary of Newman's policy over the advisability of petitioning for a charter, see 'What I aimed at', *MC*, pp. 301–4.

59   *CUG* 43 (3 May 1855), p. 434. Previously, Newman had objected to the scheme for London University in the fifth Dublin lecture.

60   No other book of its genre—the *Adventures* sold 100,000 copies in twenty years—was as powerful in fixing in the public mind the Oxbridge ideal of English education. The *Adventures* ignored the excesses of student life, the staple fare of so many accounts of university stories, and instead portrayed an Oxford where the official intellectual and moral influences were minimal, but where the *genius loci* and student interaction were the main forces for good (M. C. Curthoys & C. J. Day, 'The Oxford of Mr Verdant Green', *The history of the University of Oxford*, vol. vi, pp. 268–9, 286). Early in the story a clergyman advises his friend: 'It is formation of character that I regard as one of the greatest of the many great ends of a university system; and if for this reason alone, I should advise you to send your future country squire to college.' Having explained how the informal side of Oxford works, the clergyman stresses that while the advantages of social education 'come in

secondary ways, and possess the mind almost imperceptibly, yet they are of primary importance in the formation of character, and may mould it into the more perfect man' ('Cuthbert Bede', *Adventures of Mr Verdant Green* (London, 1852), p. 16).

61   'The University of Cambridge II', *CUG* 44 (7 June 1855), p. 450.

62   As at Trinity College Dublin, the sizars at Cambridge were students of limited means who paid reduced rates for meals, academic fees and lodgings in exchange for carrying out certain domestic duties.

63   'The University of Cambridge II', *CUG* 44 (7 June 1855), pp. 454, 456.

64   *Report of Her Majesty's Commission appointed to inquire into the management and government of the College of Maynooth, the discipline and course of studies pursued therein*, 1855, p. 39. The first criticism was generally accepted by the teaching staff at Maynooth, but opinion was divided on the second.

65   *Atlantis* was published biannually in 1858 and 1859, and single volumes appeared in 1860, 1862, 1863 and 1870. Each number was about 200 pages in length and included articles of a literary and scientific nature, largely the latter.

66   *HS*, vol. iii, p. 181. Here Newman is quoting from Book 1 of Aristotle's *Ethics*.

67   *Idea of a university*, p. 232. In one of his university sketches 'L'Ecole des Hautes Etudes at Paris' (*CUG* 21 (19 October, pp. 165–7)) Newman wrote about the relationship of the universities and seminaries at Paris; when it was published in the *Rise and progress of universities* (1856) he introduced ten new paragraphs at the start. The opening line began: 'No two institutions are more distinct from each other in character, than Universities and Seminaries [...] Seminaries are for the education of the clergy; Universities for the education of laymen. They are for separate purposes, and they act in separate spheres; yet, such is human infirmity, perhaps they ever will be rivals in their actual working' ('Universities and Seminaries', *HS*, vol. iii, p. 240). On the addition of the first ten paragraphs, see Blehl, *John Henry Newman: a bibliographical catalogue of his writings*, p. 89.

68   *Idea of a university*, pp. 232–4. Newman's attitude to the great anti-Catholic English writers is conveyed in a later passage: 'We may feel great repugnance to Milton or Gibbon as men; we may most seriously protest against the spirit which ever lives, and the tendency which ever operates, in every page of their writings; but there they are, an integral portion of English Literature; we cannot extinguish them; we cannot deny their power [...] They are great English authors, each breathing hatred to the Catholic

Church in his own way, each a proud and rebellious creature of God, each gifted with incomparable gifts' (*ibid.*, p. 309).

69 Newman to Butler, [19] January 1858, *LD*, vol. xviii, p. 234.

70 Newman to O'Reilly, 18 January 1858, *LD*, vol. xviii, p. 233. Newman's words summarise the content of two letters from O'Reilly to himself (both of which are quoted in Newman to Butler, [19] January 1858, *LD*, vol. xviii, p. 234).

71 In the absence of some of his letters to O'Reilly, Newman's thinking can be adduced from two letters to him from O'Reilly, dated 9 & 21 February 1858: see *LD*, vol. xviii, p. 235, note 2.

72 *HS*, vol. iii, p. 10.

73 Only occasionally, however, did Newman allude to the possibilities of this deep personal development, which were all the more effective in a residential setting. The most relevant section in the *Idea of a university* (pp. 146–7) has already been quoted on p. 80.

74 After Newman's departure it became known as the Literary and Historical Society, the last official use of 'Aesthetical' being in 1869. Today it is known more familiarly as the 'L&H' (*The centenary history of the Literary and Historical Society of University College, Dublin, 1855–1955*, ed. J. F. Meenan (Kerryman, [1956]), pp. 3–4).

75 Newman to St John, 17 February 1854, *LD*, vol. xvi, p. 48. In this letter Newman mentions that he had 'set up a debating society', a comment which led Lambert McKenna ('The Catholic University of Ireland', *Irish Ecclesiastical Record* 31:723 (March 1928), pp. 234, 245) to surmise that the society was started during Newman's stay in Ireland, between 7 February and 20 March 1854, for young men he hoped to attract to the University—but no evidence is given to support this claim.

76 The Historical Society of Trinity College Dublin sprang from two older clubs, Burke's Club, founded by Edmund Burke in 1747, and the Historical Club, founded in 1753. Its meetings took place in College and included debates and the reading of essays and poems.

77 The Dublin Philosophical Society was founded in 1843 to cater for College students who were too young to join other societies in Dublin. Two years later it was recognised by the College and became the Dublin University Philosophical Society, but as it came to be dominated by graduates the Undergraduate Philosophical Society was founded in 1853 with the College provost as its patron and protector. Two years after Newman left Dublin, the two societies merged to form the University Philosophical Society,

which continues to this day.
78 The Oxford Union was founded in 1830; a forerunner, the United Debating Society, was active 1823–25. The Cambridge Union debating society began in 1815, but was closed down in 1817 and only allowed to resume in 1821, with the proviso there was to be no discussion of political matters from the preceding twenty years (P. Searby, *A history of the University of Cambridge*, vol. iii 1750–1870 (Cambridge, 1992), p. 719).
79 Newman's enthusiasm for the scheme is conveyed in the comment: 'what an opportunity there would be for ministry and opposition, divisions of the house, and triumphings of the victorious party' ('1819 for The Undergraduate', *LD*, vol. i, pp. 63–4). The word '100' was originally 'fifty' in the manuscript (Culler, *Imperial intellect*, p. 14, which quotes from the original, contained in 'Papers relating to the *Undergraduate*' (BOA, A18.8)).
80 'Universities', *British Magazine* 5 (April 1834), p. 446.
81 In 1855 the editor of *The Tablet*, Frederick Lucas, died; he had used his publication for the cause of Irish Nationalism, supporting the Independent Irish Party and the Tenant League. That same year Ireland lost another leader of Young Irelandism, the journalist and politician Gavan Duffy, who emigrated to Australia. John Sadleir MP had been a champion of the Tenant League, but in 1853 he betrayed the Irish Nationalists and accepted a post in the Whig government; when he committed suicide in February 1856 he was found to have accumulated colossal debts. At the time Irishmen spoke of 'a paralysis of national feeling' (J. Coulson, 'Newman's idea of an educated laity—the two versions', *Theology and the university: an ecumenical investigation*, ed. J. Coulson (Baltimore, 1964), p. 48).
82 At the time there were two literary societies in Louvain: the Flemish Literary Society, which had links with the University of Louvain, and the Literary Society of the University of Louvain, which was run by professors and assisted by students (*CUG* 37 (8 February 1855), pp. 343–4; *CUG* 40 (1 March 1855), p. 384).
83 *Rules and regulations of the Historical, Literary, and Æsthetical Society* (Dublin, 1857), p. 15. When Gladstone introduced his scheme to reform Irish university education in 1873, he included 'gagging clauses' by which he sought to exclude not just theology and philosophy but even modern history (R. Shannon, *Gladstone: heroic minister, 1865–1898* (London, 1996), p. 123).
84 The Society was briefly expelled from Trinity in 1794 but readmitted on condition that no question of modern politics be debated, yet in the run-up

to the 1798 Rebellion eight members were expelled. The early years of the nineteenth century continued to be turbulent ones, and increasingly the College Board reacted to its stormy political debates with the imposition of restrictive regulations and exclusions, to such an extent that in 1815 the Society handed over its rooms and moved out of College. When it returned, in 1843, it was on the strict understanding that no subject of current politics would be debated. From then on, debates were presided over by a Fellow or the provost.

85 Newman to Cullen, 24 January 1855, *LD*, vol. xvi, p. 359. Newman's assurance is echoed in a letter that Renouf wrote to his parents on 22 January 1856: 'But we are beginning to be attacked violently, which is an additional sign of life. [...] They find that professors confine themselves strictly to *education*, & do not intend to make the university a tool for political agitation. They see in fact that nothing is to [be] made out of us for *their* purposes, and so they are becoming rabid enemies' (*Letters of Renouf*, vol. iii, p. 24).

86 Maunsell recalled the inaugural meeting when he was awarded an honorary degree by the National University of Ireland in 1915 (W. J. Treanor, 'L. & H.', *National Student* 96 (December 1945), pp. 32–3). After studying first in the Faculty of Arts, then at the Catholic University Medical School, Maunsell served as a doctor in the British Army and rose to the rank of Surgeon-General.

87 The Historical Society of Trinity did not have a president but an 'auditor'. The Historical, Literary, and Aesthetical Society did not adopt this Dublin nomenclature until shortly after Newman's departure—another indication that Newman was unaware of the workings of the Historical Society. In 1862 W. K. Sullivan became president, a title which now meant 'senior member' and having oversight.

88 Minutes of the Faculty of Philosophy and Letters, 28 December 1857, UCDA, CU 10. The remark was occasioned by a petition from the then president Augustus Bethell for the society to be allowed to set up its own library in the University Rooms. The Faculty advised Newman to turn down the request.

89 *Rules and Regulations of the Historical, Literary, and Æsthetical Society*, pp. 1–3.

90 *Rules and Regulations of the Historical, Literary, and Æsthetical Society*, p. 10.

91 These were the president, Henry Bethell; the vice-president, James Molloy; the secretary, John (or Jack) Mulholland; other council members, vicomte

Louis de Vaulchier, Augustus Bethell, Edward Maxwell. Reviewers were: in the history department, Sir Reginald Barnewall; in the literary department, James Molloy; in the aesthetic department, Henry Bethell (*Rules and Regulations of the Historical, Literary, and Æsthetical Society*, p. 19).

92 For comparison, the Trinity College commissioners were told that there were fifty-one members of the Historical Society and that they met on Wednesday evenings. The Philosophical Society had seventy members, including ten from outside the College. The only other society connected with Trinity was the University Choral Society, which was founded 1837 and linked with the College in 1838; it had 220 members (*Royal Commission Trinity* (1853), p. 84).

93 Meenan, *Centenary history*, pp. 6–7.

94 O'Shea, *Roundabout recollections*, vol. ii, pp. 103, 117–18.

95 *Idea of a university*, pp. 165–6.

96 Newman to the dean of the arts faculty, June 1856, *MC*, pp. 157–67. After some alterations, this letter became part four of 'Elementary Studies' in the *Idea of a university* (pp. 372–80) under the subtitle 'General religious knowledge'.

97 For religious instruction, Newman was able to rely on several Oxbridge graduates who had been Anglican clergymen. Newman's reliance on the laity for religious instruction can be traced back to 1827, when in referring to elementary schools he maintained that 'It seems indeed to be a fundamental mistake in a system of education, when the instructors of youth in general knowledge are not also their religious instructors.' ('On general education as connected with the Church and religion', sermon preached on 19 August 1827, BOA). Ornsby understood from Newman's letter on religious teaching that Newman was thinking of including that kind of religious teaching in the current business of such professors as Stewart and himself; but he reported that O'Reilly was 'jealous' about some parts of the letter and objected to their teaching controversial matters (Ornsby to Newman, 7 August 1857, BOA, DP 32/7).

98 Newman to the dean of the arts faculty, June 1856, *MC*, pp. 157–8. For the scholar's degree candidates were examined on the four Gospels and an advanced catechism. For a pass in the licentiate degree, candidates had to study the Acts of the Apostles and the history of the Old Testament in addition to those above, and for honours they had to choose one subject from the following: the Church; Holy Scripture; literature of religion; philosophy of religion (*MC*, pp. 137, 141–2).

99   Newman to the dean of the arts faculty, June 1856, *MC*, pp. 159–60.

100   Newman to the dean of the arts faculty, June 1856, *MC*, pp. 161–2.

101   The restoration of the Catholic hierarchy in England in 1850 and the manner in which it took place produced a strong no-popery reaction. Protestant outrage was vented from the pulpit and the press, anti-Catholic demonstrations were mounted across the country, and the allegiance of Catholics to the Crown was questioned publicly.

102   Newman to the dean of the arts faculty, June 1856, *MC*, pp. 162–4. When quoting from this letter (which had become 'General religious knowledge' in the *Idea*) in a letter to *The Rambler* (July 1859) about 'Lay students in theology', Newman adds a quotation from the theologian Victor du Buck that he received from Richard Simpson: 'My opinion is, which many others share, that at present laymen of a certain rank have more need of knowing *dogmatic* theology, ecclesiastical history, and canon law, than priests. The reason is, that in lay company the deepest and most difficult problems in those subjects are discussed. This is seldom done when any priest is present. Moreover, in your country, laymen have better opportunities than priests to correct a thousand false notions of Protestants' (*LD*, vol. xix, pp. 546–7).

103   Newman to the dean of the arts faculty, June 1856, *MC*, pp. 164–5. The anecdote is recounted in Newman to Froude, 15 August 1829, *LD*, vol. ii, p. 158; it also appears in the *Idea of a university*, p. 379.

104   Newman had recently spoken at length about the need for an educated laity in his *Lectures on the present position of Catholics in England* (1851). He told his listeners that what was needed were 'men who know their religion, who enter into it, who know just where they stand, who know what they hold, and what they do not, who know their creed so well, that they can give an account of it, who know so much of history that they can defend it. I want an intelligent, well-instructed laity; [...] I wish you to enlarge your knowledge, to cultivate your reason, to get an insight into the relation of truth to truth, to learn to view things as they are, to understand how faith and reason stand to each other' (*ibid*, pp. 390–2).

105   Newman to the dean of the arts faculty, June 1856, *MC*, pp. 165–6.

106   Substance of the memorandum read at the episcopal synod, 20 May 1854, *MC*, pp. 97–8. Newman relied on the Oratorian Richard Stanton to help him decide on arrangements for the University Church. 'Part of my plan, if I have my way, is to have rather a magnificent ceremonial; good preachers, confraternities etc.', he told him, 'and I wish to get them hot from Rome' (24 February 1853, *LD*, vol. xv, p. 311). In the process of consulting Stanton

about academic dress and the University Church, and whether they should follow Rome or Louvain, he wrote: 'I want the whole *imposing*' (12 March 1854, *LD*, vol. xvi, p. 83).

107 Report of the Year 1854–55, *MC*, p. 24. Newman considered that the University Church would 'give a unity to the various academical institutions', a unity which was also 'a unity of a religious character' (*ibid*).

108 Newman to Stanton, 12 March 1854, *LD*, vol. xxxii, p. 84. Although it is unclear how such a structure would have fitted into the canon law then in force (as the United Kingdom was regarded as mission territory, where the ordinary prescriptions of canon law did not fully apply), the 1983 *Code of canon law* makes provision for just such a 'personal diocese' in canon 372, taking up the idea in the Second Vatican Council decree on the ministry and life of priests (*Presbyterorum ordinis*, 10b); the idea of a 'personal parish' specifically for pastoral care at universities is mentioned in canons 518 and 813.

109 Having failed to borrow from the University funds the £3000 he estimated it would cost, Newman decided to pay from his own pocket, using money left over from the Achilli trial fund, in the expectation that he would recoup the outlay through collections over twenty years; but his hopes were dashed when costs rose to £5600—and then he faced soaring interest rates after the Crimea War.

110 Newman to Pollen, 9 November 1856, *LD*, vol. xvii, p. 440. This was written on the day when the Church was effectively completed, nearly eighteen months after works had started. Newman marked the occasion by celebrating the first Mass in the newly-finished Blessed Sacrament Chapel.

111 A special commemorative stamp was issued for the 150th anniversary of the University Church featuring a drawing of the apse. On the occasion of the anniversary, modern reproductions of the original wall panels (painted by two French artists and paid for by Newman) were unveiled by the Taoiseach, Mr Bertie Ahern.

112 Those invited to preach could also make use of Newman's thoughts on the subject: his open letter to Bishop Moriarty 'On the Subject of University Preaching' in the *CUG* 41 (8 March 1855, pp. 394–400) which formed the basis of his essay on 'University preaching' in the *Idea* (pp. 405–27); in response to the original letter, Ornsby wrote an article entitled 'Preaching with or without a book' (*CUG* 42 (5 April 1855), pp. 416–19).

113 O'Shea, *Roundabout recollections*, vol. ii, p. 116.

114 *Ibid.*, p. 111.

[115] P. J. Walsh, *William J. Walsh. Archbishop of Dublin* (Dublin, 1928), p. 13. The comments of Walsh and O'Shea suggest that the adult congregation found the sermons more to their liking than the student element. In all, Newman preached eight sermons at the University Church and these now form part of *Sermons preached on various occasions* (London, 1870). They were all pastoral sermons, having as a common theme the regeneration of the heart and the regaining of personal integrity.

[116] 'Intellect, the instrument of religious training', *Sermons preached on various occasions*, p. 5.

[117] *Ibid.*, pp. 7–8.

[118] *Ibid.*, p. 8.

[119] *Ibid.*, pp. 9–10.

[120] *Ibid.*, pp. 12–13.

[121] *Ibid.*, p. 13.

6 THE PROBLEMS OF KEEPING HOUSE

B Y THE TIME the Catholic University's first academic year finished, the number of students attached to the collegiate houses was forty-three. Over the first long vacation the University lost nine matriculated students and gained seventeen, taking numbers up to fifty-one. But there was more to this movement than just the arithmetic, for among those leaving were 'some of a bad style'; and within days of the new academic year Newman was able to boast: 'we have plucked [i.e. expelled] a youth this term, which has had a capital effect'.[1] It is not surprising that a disciplinary matter should have arisen so early in the life of the University, since Newman had anticipated that such problems would arise and had deliberately devised his scheme of small collegiate houses to offset them.

When Archbishop Cullen returned from Rome in the summer of 1855, after a nine months' absence from Dublin, he was keen to catch up with the news about his cherished project. The stories he heard, and the uneasiness many felt about its liberal ways, alarmed Cullen and he reported to Rome that Newman showed 'a certain ignorance of practical affairs, and has therefore permitted the introduction of things which could be very inconvenient as the years go by'; for this reason he advised a delay in the plan to make him a bishop.[2] Cullen was more explicit to Tobias Kirby, the only friend he confided in and his successor as rector of the Irish College in Rome: 'Things seem not to be going ahead in a way that can be defended'; the rector's absence from the University over the summer was unsatisfactory; the expenses incurred were very large; and,

the discipline introduced is unsuitable, certainly to this
country. The young men are allowed to go out at all hours,
to smoke, etc. and there has not been any fixed time for
study. These things make it clear that Father Newman does
not give enough attention to details. I hope that when he
returns from England it will be possible to induce him to
introduce a better system.[3]

The whole tenor of his letter shows Cullen's misapprehension of
what Newman was trying to do. The incidental problems and
apparent slack discipline were an inevitable side-effect (foreseen
though not intended) of the greater freedom Newman wanted the
students to experience. In fact, this apparent permissiveness was
very characteristic of Newman's style—he gave the same wide
berth to his Oratorians. He did not believe in smothering the young
in rules or in mapping out their day with detailed timetables, as he
meant to encourage them to take responsibility for their own
actions and to learn from their mistakes.

There was, furthermore, a certain irony to Cullen's complaint
about Newman's absence over the summer, coming from a bishop
who had spent nine months out of his own diocese: Newman had
in fact been in Ireland for forty-six consecutive weeks less six
Sundays, and was now spending the summer at the Birmingham
Oratory in order to catch up with business that had been left
pending. While there he was informed by Cullen that there were
'many complaints about the expenditure of money, and some
disciplinary matters'.[4] On this occasion, as on others, Cullen did
no more than hint to Newman about his concerns, but to Kirby in
Rome he fulminated about Newman's liberal approach to discipline
which he saw as disastrous for the students' moral formation.[5]
Having devolved so much power to Newman at the outset and been
abroad for the whole of the first academic year, Cullen appeared to
be struggling to regain control and steer the University in his own

preferred direction; his anxiety about the situation was real enough, and so acute that it contributed to the nervous breakdown he suffered in November 1855.

Cullen began by asking Newman to provide him with rules of discipline, but almost immediately changed his mind and asked Newman to draw up statutes instead. This was not at all to Newman's liking, as he thought that they 'must be the slow work of time': if Cullen insisted on having statutes immediately, Newman's recommendation was that they should simply adopt the Louvain statutes in their entirety *pro tem*.[6] But Cullen rejected this suggestion, insisting that they must have new statutes of their own,[7] and so when the new academic session began in November 1855, Newman established that the main business of the University Council's weekly meetings should be the drafting of a 'Scheme of Rules and Regulations'.[8] It turned out to be a slow business, for it was not until the following May that a printed draft was ready for Newman to circulate to the professors, lecturers, deans and tutors. In June 1856 all but two small sections[9] were unofficially approved at the bishops' synodal meeting,[10] and in July the provisional statutes were duly sanctioned by the Senate at its first meeting. They were formally ratified by the bishops at their annual meeting in the autumn, which meant that at the start of the third academic session everyone connected with the Catholic University had easy access to the *modus operandi* and rationale of Newman's scheme.

The 'Scheme of Rules and Regulations' was Newman's longest and most complete document—written with the assistance of the Council—about the working of the University. Its four main sections deal with the constitution of the Catholic University, its discipline, the academic course, and the examinations. The version presented to the bishops in June was a lengthy document which contained 'general enunciations of principle', some of which were excerpts from the articles Newman had written for the *Gazette* in

1854.[11] When this provisional version became a formal collection of statutes,[12] the 'general enunciations of principle' were omitted.[13] Despite his initial reluctance to comply with it, Cullen's request had the salutary effect of concentrating Newman's mind and of forcing him to gather his thoughts about the practical implementation of his educational ideas.

From the start of the third session, students hoping to gain admission to the Catholic University were required to read through the Rules and Regulations and to take the Form of Promise devised by Newman. The promise read: 'I A. B. promise to the Rector and Senate of this University that I will dutifully obey those who are in authority over me, and, as far as in me lies, will observe the Rules and Regulations of the place.'[14] Though there were obvious gains to having the Rules and Regulations in public circulation, Newman felt that there were also definite drawbacks, for he was all too aware that the paper proposals fell short of the living university that he was trying to nurture into existence. Moreover he feared that the rectorship and vice-rectorship might easily fall into the hands of narrow-minded men, 'who have little other idea of a University than a place for imposing fines ("not above one pound") on those who are slow at lecture and for sending out students into the Town two and two', as if they were seminarians.[15]

Newman had hoped that, by breaking the student body into manageable units, it would be possible to adopt a regime that was markedly less strict than that which prevailed at the seminaries. But this meant that there should have been a greater variety of residences than there actually was. Of the active Irish supporters of the University, there were a preponderance of men like David Moriarty (the recently appointed coadjutor Bishop of Kerry), who argued strongly for a collegiate house at around £30 or £35 p.a. so that the University could cater for students of modest means. By the end of the second academic session the University had awarded just one academic scholarship for a free place; in this instance the recipient was supposed to be a mathematical genius, but later it was found that his 'habits of intemperance' were such that they could not keep him. With this in mind, Newman asked Moriarty to consider carefully *who* it was that the modest fees (£42) at St Patrick's had in fact attracted:

> youths who had no right to come—whose fathers could afford more. They have come, have been too high-minded for discipline, though they were willing to come cheap —and have looked down on the youths of Dr Quinn's House, who in some cases actually paid more. Not a few of them have gone away, having done us no credit, and in some instances creating scandal.[16]

Newman confided to Moriarty, 'I suspect ill-conduct will be the *rule* until you improve *the Schools* and make a real testimonial from them obligatory'. He wondered what object the young men coming to the University had in mind, whether the civil service, engineering or medicine. It was important to address this question, because 'The love of learning does not seem a sufficient inducement in this day, if it is not coupled with the prospect of a livelihood.'[17] Unlike Moriarty, who looked to a revival of the age of poor scholars, Newman thought that the majority of those capable of benefiting from the University would be drawn from the wealthier classes, and that these ought to pay their way. This stance reflected a concern he personally felt: 'The difficulty which *I* feel great anxiety about is in the education of the upper class.'[18] By now Newman had become aware that the lack of grounding at school was a major obstacle for the middle-class students entering (as it was at the Queen's Colleges and even Trinity). One means Newman had at his disposal for attracting able young men who could raise the academic level was by awarding scholarships, and when in November 1855 an anonymous benefactor funded two scholarships for proficiency in classics and mathematics, Newman added two more on the part of the University—all restricted to native Irishmen. They were advertised in the *Gazette* and elsewhere, together with sample questions. As funds for scholarships were limited, Newman hoped to make them self-financing, by awarding them to students on condition that the recipients worked as assistant librarians.

This is one instance among many which shows how flexible Newman was prepared to be—and had to be, given the great need to boost student numbers. In the summer of 1855 he had allowed ten students to take the scholar's exam a year early, at the end of their first year rather than the second; this he was able to justify by a provision he had made which counted residence in the colleges in Ireland and England for any time under two years, with a certificate of good behaviour, as residence for an equal length of time at the University. This concession shows that, while arrangements were some way from his ideal of a fully residential university, he was prepared to adapt his plan to circumstances. Although the Catholic University Medical School was an instant success, its students were not matriculated and therefore not counted in student numbers. In the long run, Newman's hope was to educate aspiring medics for two years, prior to their medical studies.

To judge from life at St Mary's and St Patrick's, it would appear that success of a different sort was the pastoral well-being of the University. From small beginnings the student communities were gradually establishing themselves and creating their own traditions, though it would be a mistake to assume that St Laurence's and St Patrick's were replicas of St Mary's, if for no other reason than that neither dean had had any experience of collegiate living outside a seminary. Besides, even if they had, it was one thing to have lived in a collegiate house or seen one in operation, and quite another matter to know how to put that knowledge into practice and run a residence successfully. So it is no surprise that the two collegiate houses developed in different ways—from each other, as well as from St Mary's. The process of interpreting and adapting Newman's scheme for the collegiate houses, as outlined in the Rules and Regulations, meant that the deans discussed the scheme with the rector, its originator. The correspondence that resulted from these negotiations shows how Newman elaborated on his scheme and spelt out how it applied in different circumstances: what emerges is the generous scope Newman gave the deans and his reluctance to interfere with the day-to-day running of any house which met the basic conditions. But the letters also show that, despite Newman's flexibility, neither of the other deans was capable of entering fully into Newman's scheme.

Marked differences of opinion were apparent by 1856 and the problems they gave rise to rumbled on for as long the two deans remained in office, which in both cases meant until they were consecrated bishops: Michael Flannery was made coadjutor Bishop of Killaloe in 1858; and James Quinn Bishop of Brisbane (the first) in 1859. Despite the frustrations and annoyances endured by each party over this period, the difficulties they faced were tackled without acrimony. To a large extent they were the inevitable consequence of embarking on a grand project with wholly inadequate means; but they were also linked to the personalities involved and the particular arrangements operating at St Patrick's and St Laurence's. Flannery was virtually on his own at St Patrick's and not suited to dealing with young students; he was a hopeless organiser and showed little initiative, being unable to deal with a broken roof slate without setting off a paper trail. Quinn was proactive and a safe pair of hands, but he was steeped in a very different educational tradition to Newman; moreover, he and Newman never really hit it off.[19]

House problems at St Patrick's and St Laurence's

When the second academic year began, there were just nine students living at St Patrick's. This was something of a disappointment considering that the house was intended for native Irishmen, all the more so considering that five of them were non-natives—two were English, one Scottish, and two others foreigners who were passing through Ireland. In the hope that the University might be able to attract the 'sons of Gentlemen throughout the country',[20] Newman had seen to it that substantial improvements (costing £500) were made to the house during the first long vacation, but to no effect. He wondered whether the solution might be to set up bursaries (worth £40 p.a. for two years) in subjects that would be of special interest to the Irish, such as medicine, engineering and agriculture.

Although there was no school of agriculture,[21] the engineering school had opened for the new year,[22] and the medical school had got off to a flying start. Anxious to provide suitable accommodation for the medical students, but without funds at his disposal for doing so, Newman decided in the meantime to make use of St Patrick's, which was still losing money and unable to fill itself. He argued that since the University had laid out large sums on No. 86, it was better to get something out of it than nothing; and that if there were additional students, who received bursaries and paid a nominal sum, the house only stood to gain. His plan involved allocating ten rooms at St Patrick's for those studying the two-year arts course prior to their medical studies, and using a sum of £400 p.a. to fund ten medical bursaries whose recipients would be nominated by the ten most important ecclesiastical sees in Ireland, the remaining unfilled places being allotted by open competition. In doing this, Newman argued that he was increasing the overall number of students and laying the foundations for both the medical school and its future halls of residence. In December 1855 the Council approved this proposal, to take effect from November 1856, as well as agreeing to an increase in the fees at St Patrick's to £60 (including the £10 academic fee). By these measures, Newman effectively ensured that those who could pay their way did so, while those in need of bursaries obtained them.[23]

The shortfall of Irishmen at St Patrick's can partly be attributed to Flannery, who was unsuited to the task of running the house and uncomfortable in his role as dean. He was, in fact, still working as vicar general of the diocese of Killaloe, and because of his divided responsibilities appears to have done little to attract young Irishmen. As a result he began to feel the financial effects. In March 1856 he complained to Newman about his two tutors, Dunne and Penny, and the expense of paying them; in his opinion, they had hardly seen the students and had done them little good. Assuming that the tutors were not to Flannery's satisfaction, Newman proposed suspending their tuition work (and pay), while offering them board and lodging 'in compensation of their *charge* of the students'; and giving the tuition instead to James Stewart, the able classicist, who lived at Drumcondra. Flannery's response revealed that the problem was not the tutors but the system: he did not want his interns to pay for 'indoor tutors' or any form of tuition at all—or even for lectures. He declared his preference for the Louvain plan, where the professorial system alone operated and discipline at the two lay colleges was the responsibility of the vice-regents. What he wanted, in fact, was the equivalent of a vice-regent.[24]

Newman agreed to terminate at once the connection of Dunne and Penny with St Patrick's, as regards both tutoring and superintendence—but not immediately from the house itself, as this would attract attention and create an unnecessary fuss. Instead he suggested that the two pay board, but not lodging (as there were still vacant rooms). Offering to keep Flannery 'out of view' in the whole transaction, Newman explained, 'I consent to all this on the principle that the Ruler of a House should be left as much as possible master in it, and, as he is responsible, so should be free.' However, Newman insisted, he could not agree that the interns should pay nothing for lectures and tutoring. At Louvain students were charged £9 p.a. without private tuition; at Queen's College Cork, slightly more; and at Trinity £15 without tuition. As the Catholic University session was longer than Trinity's, as Ireland was more expensive than Belgium, and as the Catholic University fees included private tuition, Newman argued that £10 was not excessive,[25] and therefore he would require it of Flannery's students —though *pro tem* he would arrange for the University to bear the cost. Having acceded to Flannery's wishes, Newman requested him to put in writing the system he proposed to operate.[26] Flannery stated his demands: to continue as dean with his £100 plus board and lodging; for Dunne to act as vice-regent, having his board and lodging in return for taking care of the students and tutoring them; that the interns pay nothing for their tuition, Dunne undertaking the task on his professor's pay; and for Penny and the other lecturers to start paying for their board. If Dunne was unwilling to 'grind' the students, then, in Flannery's opinion, the University ought to be responsible for doing so.

It was now clear to Newman that Flannery wanted 'all the position of his office but none of its responsibility', and he welcomed the opportunity to restate clearly the principle that each collegiate house was responsible for preparing its own students for lectures and exams.[27] Indeed, he was prepared to insist besides that if someone was sub-dean (or vice-regent) and tutor, he could not at the same time be a professor. If he was paid £200 as a professor, it was to make *that* task his profession. He offered Flannery a choice: either to act as dean in the technical sense of the word, with care of discipline only, no general responsibility for his students, and no authority over the tutors; or else really to be the governor or the president of the house, 'with jurisdiction over all persons in it, with responsible care of the young men in intellectual as well as moral respects, with the duty of seeing that they have sufficient private tuition', and with a seat on the Senate.[28] They were two distinct positions and Flannery had to choose between them. Flannery opted for the latter, reassuring Newman that he was fully aware of the great responsibility of his office. Asked what tutorial arrangements he preferred, Flannery had no hesitation in expressing a preference for a residential tutor, who by being on the spot could more easily care for and supervise the students in their studies and moral development; by associating more with them, he would have greater opportunity of forming the minds and manners of his pupils, and thereby would give more assistance and moral support to the head of house. In saying this, he showed Newman that he had grasped the essence of the tutorial role, but two further stipulations indicate an unwillingness to fall in with other aspects of Newman's scheme. Flannery's request that the tutors send him weekly (rather than the standard termly) reports on the studies and general conduct of their pupils suggested he wished to hide behind his tutors, rather than engage with the students himself; and a call for 'grinding' classes at fixed hours every day, at which attendance was obligatory, indicates he was ill at ease with the flexible system of lectures and unregimented study.[29]

Fortunately, Newman was able to take Penny into St Mary's as a tutor and, a month later, to nominate him as his successor as dean. But the knock-on effect at St Patrick's was that Dunne felt overwhelmed by all the tuition he had to give there, particularly as he was tutoring the mathematics that Penny used to cover, and now he in his turn complained to Newman. Newman explained that, although there was no objection to Dunne combining the tutoring at St Patrick's with his professorship, the tutoring was entirely a matter between himself and the dean. Flannery would either have to find extra tutors, or else to undertake the tutoring himself. But

Newman did not leave matters there, although he could so easily have done so; instead he took the trouble to encourage Flannery, pointing out that the problem of finding suitable tutors at a reasonable cost was just a temporary one. Once students had passed through the system and taken their degrees, the difficulty would gradually disappear; but for the next few years 'it will require some careful management and forethought'.[30] The dean was obliged to do no more than ensure that the tutor's office was filled and his duties fulfilled. There were various ways to do this, and just one condition: that each student paid £10 p.a., independent of how many tutors there were. This was not difficult because the University gave subsidies on a sliding scale to every house for that very purpose; if St Patrick's had more than a dozen pupils then it would attract a subsidy of £150. He suggested to Flannery that he divide the tutorial work between Dunne and an external tutor such as Edward Butler (a graduate in mathematics from Trinity College Dublin), Ornsby, Scratton or Stewart. Of course, all this insistence on (and fuss about) the tutors makes no sense unless it is recalled that Newman's guiding rule was 'that the principal making of men must be by the Tutorial system'.

Towards the end of September 1856 Newman felt it was time to tell Flannery that he had heard things which made him think that Flannery wanted further assistance of a particular kind.

> Your youths reverence you as a good and holy priest; but they do not sufficiently respect you. They feel you are too good to them, and they impose on you. They want some one over them who knows the ways of boys who have not been trained in the sanctity of ecclesiastical schools. It certainly would be better if you had some one with you who would be a match for them. But the great difficulty is, that the person must not only get on well with them, but must get on with you; and I should uphold it as a great principle,

that he must be appointed by you, and under your jurisdiction as Head of the House.[31]

By reply Flannery expressed his willingness 'to improve in the management of young men', and asked Newman for practical suggestions. Aware of the shortcomings of his interns, he confessed he was unsure how to deal with them; he gave them advice, but admitted that he disliked the idea of punishing them or trying to enforce strict rules such as studying at fixed hours in their rooms, being in bed by a certain time, and not going to the rooms of others after night prayers, lest they be looked on as more adapted to an ecclesiastical seminary than a collegiate house.[32] He was happy to appoint his own tutors, but was unable to find a competent residential tutor to join Dunne—and the problem was now acute, as Dunne was engaged to be married and only willing to remain at St Patrick's for a term. Thinking it best to make the changes sooner rather than later, Newman was able to rescue the situation by securing the temporary services of the Oxford convert Tom Arnold.

Now, in late October 1856, just as the nine-month saga over St Patrick's was coming to an end and the third academic year getting under way, it was Dr Quinn's turn to strike. Out of the blue he announced that he was unable to obey the newly-approved Rules and Regulations and therefore intended to withdraw St Laurence's from the University. Although he immediately pulled back from the threat and sent in the academic fees his house owed, he asked Newman to reconsider the connection between St Laurence's and the University. He was concerned that the Rules and Regulations described the collegiate houses as 'an integral part' of the University, which meant it had disciplinary powers over them, whereas he considered his house should be independent on the grounds that it had joined the University before the statutes were passed. Newman was forced to admit that a point of ambiguity existed and he assured Quinn that the matter would be brought before the Senate; but he made it clear he was unwilling to depart from what the statutes said about the claims of the University on the separate houses.

The relationship between Quinn's house and the University was a question that dogged Newman for the rest of his rectorship. The question also gave considerable grief to Quinn, who was particularly vexed over the interrelated matters of financial support and jurisdiction. At the beginning Quinn had wanted to hand over the entire control of St Laurence's to the University, on condition that it accepted financial responsibility, but, when Newman declined to accept these terms, he had to fall in with Newman's scheme of financially independent collegiate houses, an arrangement Quinn struggled to come to terms with. Since the arrangement between St Laurence's and the University was made prior to any statutes being approved, it was therefore purely provisional: to be continued if it suited St Laurence's, otherwise dissolved. Now that the first statutes were promulgated, Quinn felt they 'operate so injuriously on St L's as to deprive it of its existence, as an independent establishment, &, in great part, of the means of subsistence'. The statutes gave the University jurisdiction over the house by empowering it to make the disciplinary alterations it deemed necessary; furthermore, by placing the externs under the jurisdiction of the vice-rector, it cut 'all obligating connection' between them and St Laurence's, though the house depended on their fees.[33] Quinn argued that the University should have no claim to jurisdiction over an establishment which existed prior to it and for which it undertook no responsibility.

One cause of Quinn's difficulties was the question of the overlapping jurisdiction over his older youths, who found themselves part of his own establishment as well as members of the University. In particular he was unhappy that the University should have jurisdiction over his church students, the bulk of whom were interns. Another source of confusion was the status of St Laurence's itself, as the house catered for schoolboys as well as students, and within each a mixture of lay and clerical—all of which presented Quinn with the daunting task of holding a line of discipline that was both consistent and appropriate. His solution was simple: to run St Laurence's with the strictness of a seminary. The clerical character of St Laurence's was the cause of yet another difficulty, that of matching a curriculum to its students. When Newman returned to Dublin in early autumn 1856, Quinn plied him with questions about the curriculum and teaching: whether there would be a full course of logic and metaphysics that coming year; whether the lecturers would teach from a textbook; whether classes would be conducted strictly in Latin; and whether there would be a full course of philosophy, as in other Catholic universities, if numbers were sufficient. These questions reflected an outlook steeped in the system of Catholic higher education that operated on the Continent, which approximated to a seminary education and relied heavily on lectures closely following textbooks or manuals.

While the question of jurisdiction had come to the fore as a result of the statutes, the difficulty which was ever-present and weighed most heavily on Quinn was the financial burden of operating St Laurence's. Essentially, he felt his house did not receive due financial assistance from the University for the labour and expense incurred in becoming a collegiate house, and which he thought he had been promised at the outset. What exactly this 'great increase in labour'[34] and additional expenditure consisted of is unclear, unless Quinn meant the teaching of theology and related subjects which the University did not yet provide. Certainly some adjustment had been made in altering the school curriculum so as to prepare pupils for the University rather than Maynooth.

What is clear is that St Laurence's was run on a shoestring: most of its pupils were unable to afford the fees for the University, and all its priests were overworked, Quinn's own health having suffered as well as that of his brother (who had broken down under the extra work and was now recovering abroad). Moreover, the priests felt that their ordinary means of subsistence was now threatened by the statutes. All this explains Quinn's exasperation and his suddenly raising the stakes by threatening to withdraw his students. In the short term Quinn suggested Newman provide financial relief by exempting the church students from academic fees and allocating more bursaries to St Laurence's.

The extent to which Newman was forced to reflect on Quinn's demands is recorded in two memoranda, which list the questions he was turning over in his mind about the connection between St Laurence's and the University: whether, considering its particular curriculum, the externs there might be considered as interns so as to secure the house greater funding; whether to allow the interns (nearly all of whom were preparing for the priesthood) free admission to the University and its lectures; whether to recognise its teachers as tutors; whether it was better for the externs to leave St Laurence's 'in order to get [an] easier life or whether they should get scholarships in the University first'; and whether there was a way St Laurence's could remain in connection with the University, but beyond its jurisdiction.[35] That autumn Newman was able to provide Quinn with immediate aid (via the Council) by ensuring that his interns who did not pay academic fees were counted in the calculation of the subsidy for tutorial provision, and by arranging a payment of £40 to look after the University High Mass. Before committing himself to any further assistance for St Laurence's, Newman felt it best to wait for the new statute which he was about to introduce and which, among many other questions, would make allowances for the peculiar set-up in Harcourt Street a few doors along from St Mary's.

In the middle of all this, unbeknownst to Newman, Cullen continued to complain to Kirby about the discipline at the University. In January 1856 he wrote: 'Dr Newman has the Oxford system in view. He wishes to leave young men to themselves. This will not do in Ireland. The people do not wish to have their children exposed to corruption, they wish to have them under discipline.'[36] The following December, after the Rules and Regulations had been promulgated, Cullen had similar misgivings: 'He appears to think the Oxford system perfect. The students must have great liberty, go hunt etc play billiards, smoke cigars, and study just as they like. I think this is not a catholic system—but perhaps it is better to say nothing.'[37] Evidently Cullen had not read the *Report* (1852) of the Oxford commissioners, as he would have realised that Newman's arrangements were a far cry from what went on there.[38]

The problems Newman faced over the collegiate houses were by no means the only ones, as he was constantly at work resolving university and other matters. A letter Newman wrote just after the third session had got under way puts the house problems into context and at the same time conveys his state of mind about the added difficulties of heading two totally different institutions in different countries:

Alas! you do not realize my work. My chattels stand about my room in the same confusion as on the night I came here three weeks ago, from my inability to find leisure for removing them to their places. My letters are a daily burden, and, did I not answer them by return of post, they would soon get my head under water and drown me. Every hour or half-hour of the day I have people calling on me. I have to entertain strangers at dinner, I have to attend Inaugural Lectures—four last week, I have to stop Professors resigning, and Houses revolting. I have to keep accounts and find money, when I have none. Besides the book I have just finished at Longman's [*Office and Work of Universities*], I have three reprinting which I am reading thro' and correcting; and I have to provide four Sermons in print by St Paul's day, that for Sunday week not having the first word written yet. I have to lecture on Latin Composition, and examine for Exhibitions [i.e. scholarships]. In ten days I rush to Birmingham for their sheer want of me—and then have to throw myself into quite a fresh world. And I have the continual pain of our [Oratorian] Fathers sighing if I am not there, and priests and professors looking black if I am not here.[39]

New forms of residence: the statute of 1857

Newman not only had to contend with problems that occurred at St Laurence's and St Patrick's, but those which affected the collegiate system as a whole. To understand his main concern about residential arrangements, it is necessary to return to June 1854 when prospective students were invited to apply to the University. On the second page of the first *Gazette* (1 June 1854) a notice had read: 'Students of the University will be located in lodging-houses under the superintendence of a Dean'. From the wording it was clear that the University was intended to be a residential establishment, a characteristic which was reinforced by an additional line, which read: 'Exceptions will be made, as cases occur, in favour of those who have the opportunity of living at home or with private persons.' Four months later, the phrase 'as cases occur' had been dropped, probably because of the number of applicants from Dublin itself. This might seem a minor point, but the question of domicile goes to the very heart of what Newman sought to establish: a university that was capable of providing each student with a deep formation, precisely because it was residential.

To ensure that a healthy atmosphere prevailed, those applying had to provide a guarantee of character, as well as proving academic competence. To this end applicants for the two-year licentiate degree were asked to produce 'testimonials of residence and good conduct for two years in an approved College'. It is also worth noting that the entrance exam was designed to test knowledge of 'the main facts and doctrines on which Christianity is established'.[40] For the purposes of joining the licentiate course, applicants were informed that the University would regard two years at their colleges (or schools), whether residential or not, on the same footing as two years passed at the University.

By the end of the first term, the number of non-resident students had grown to the point that their status needed to be formalised. The *Gazette* (7 December 1854) explained that 'externs' were of two descriptions. There were those paying £10 per session for lectures, without forming part of the University, 'that is, without being under the care of the Tutors, or being submitted to any of the examinations, or being eligible for its honours, or aiming at its degrees'; over such the University 'has no jurisdiction, and knows nothing of them out of lecture hours, and only requires that their conduct should not compromise or embarrass the authorities'. The other category were those 'who are really desirous of joining themselves to the academic body, and standing on a footing with residents'; they 'are required to unite themselves to some particular licensed establishment in the University', and doing so 'they will be altogether under the jurisdiction of the Dean of that particular establishment, and will be considered as simply members of it, accidentally lodging out in such lodgings (*e.g.* their home) as the aforesaid Dean shall sanction'.[41] The following April, Newman saw the wisdom of distinguishing the two categories, renaming the first group—those simply attending lectures—as 'auditors'.[42] It was an important distinction to make, as the externs were matriculated members of the University with their own rights and duties, whereas the auditors were not. When Newman came to write the Report for 1854–55 he described the status of the externs by stating that 'their home, or abode, whatever it is, must be considered as a licensed lodging house, or rather as an integral part of the academical domicile; so that the young men so situated are as simply under the jurisdiction of the Dean as if they resided under his roof'.[43]

In this way Newman hoped that the externs would more or less be incorporated in the collegiate houses. The plan, however, met with only partial success, and Newman had to settle for the *modus vivendi* described in the Rules and Regulations, where it stated that the extern came under the vice-rector—not the dean of his house—as regards discipline; that he should be indoors by 10 pm, attend lectures and High Mass on Sundays, and 'observe his religious duties' in the same way as an intern. The intended effect of the Rules and Regulations was to tidy up arrangements, but there remained aspects which were less than satisfactory: the absence of any collegiate life for the extern was one defect; the tenuous oversight by the (largely non-resident) vice-rector was another. In addition, the externs did not enjoy the benefit of tutorial teaching. In an attempt to persuade the existing externs to become interns, Newman pointed out to Captain Mackenzie, the person responsible for coordinating any tuition they had, that at St Patrick's students paid just £1 for entrance, £10 for lectures, and £50 for board, lodge, laundry *and* private tuition; and that, unless there were exceptional circumstances, the latter cost actually made it cheaper to be an intern than an extern.[44]

What was less than satisfactory for the externs was also problematic for the University. If the number of interns had been steadily increasing Newman might have left the question of the status of the extern to one side, but numbers were stagnant, and he was faced with the dilemma of how to attract more externs without compromising the residential character of the University. In the long vacation of 1856, just after the Rules and Regulations received provisional approval, Newman had to deal with a parent who wanted his two sons to attend the University while living at home, in Booterstown outside Dublin. According to the regulations they had to attend as auditors, rather than externs, because living outside Dublin meant they were not under the vice-rector's jurisdiction —unless the Senate exempted them.[45] But this was far from ideal and approximated to the situation at London University which Newman so strongly deplored.[46]

It was with a view to increasing student numbers and improving the situation of the externs that Newman introduced another significant change in re-defining the constituent parts of the student body. In proposing a new statute to the Senate in January 1857 about 'The position of the Heads of Houses relative to the University', Newman had to juggle with a complex situation so as to satisfy opposing needs. On the one hand, he wanted to ensure that the principal features of his vision were preserved, and right at the core of this was his conception of residential living and its formative importance. On the other hand, he had to cater for other modes of student living as best he could. By now he had been rector for seven terms and was in a position to draw upon his experience and that of others in resolving what was partly a problem of supply and demand. When he addressed the Senate on this occasion he advised them to take into account three important considerations.

In the first place, he pointed out, a head of house might find that, as time went on, the rule of the University was 'too stringent for him'. He was required to report on the conduct of his charges once a term—to the rector in the case of interns, to the vice-rector in the case of externs—and was unable on his authority alone to expel a student. He did, however, enjoy certain advantages, such as a seat in the Senate and a yearly financial grant towards his expenses, but overall he might wish to sacrifice these in return for more freedom. Secondly, it was likely that there would be some young men, particularly 'youths of expectation' or foreigners, who would find the rector's oversight of the collegiate houses 'too strong for them' and in consequence would decline to come, except as externs. 'That is, if we draw our rules too tight, they may simply break away'; and this would encourage the undesirable scenario of students coming from a distance and renting houses in town (even though they might be approved ones), a situation which was all the more likely (and dangerous) if they possessed the financial wherewithal. 'Here then we need some connexion with the University less intimate than that of a Collegiate House.' Thirdly, it was desirable to encourage the medical students to reside in University houses, but it was asking too much to require of them to submit to the discipline of a collegiate house, 'intended as it is for youths under twenty years of age'.[47]

Having consulted 'for the freedom both of Head and of Students', Newman went on to propose the introduction of two new forms of residence. The first was what he called a 'licensed house' (an unfortunately ambiguous term, given Dublin's reputation for drink), by which he meant a house:

> (1) in the possession, as tenant, of a member of the University; (2) that member must be licensed by the Rector; (3) he and his House are under the general jurisdiction of the Rector; (4) he and it are not under the jurisdiction of the Vice-Rector; (5) he has not a seat in the Council; (6) he receives no University money; (7) nor can his youths hold University Exhibitions or Burses [i.e. bursaries].[48]

In this way a young man who 'shrinks from any future strictness of the Collegiate Houses' need not become an extern, but might join a licensed house. Likewise, if a dean found his position too constrained for his purpose, he would be allowed to turn his collegiate house into a licensed one. The draft statute stated that the discipline 'is of the same character as that to which proper externs are submitted', namely the requirement to be indoors by 10 pm, attendance at lectures and High Mass, and the fulfilment of religious duties.[49] To some extent this meant in fact formalising the existing situation, for lecturers such as Ornsby and Pollen already took in student lodgers.

The second 'extension of the idea of residence' was that young men sleeping and taking their meals at home should be accounted interns so long as they were '*bonâ fide* present in some Collegiate House during the business hours of the day, say from 9 till 3', effectively placing themselves under its jurisdiction for that period of time. By 'at home' Newman meant not only living with one's parents, but with anyone acting *in loco parentis*. This second provision addressed the difficulty of defining the local limit of residence, as under the proposed statute youths living at home in Kingstown, say, were considered as interns, *provided* they attended a collegiate house during the day.[50]

The statute also addressed another grey area, namely whether students in ecclesiastical seminaries (in England, for example) could take their theology degrees at the University. Besides the other questions this involved—whether passing through the arts faculty could be dispensed with, and whether proof of 'standing' could be—the new statute meant that residence was not strictly required. In this sense it would approximate the Catholic University to the condition of Trinity College Dublin and the University of London.[51] But to ensure that there was still a bonus on residence, and to prevent the administration of the University falling into the hands of those who had never resided there and were ignorant of its traditions, Newman proposed that degrees taken by non-residents, though *bona fide* and to the outside world possessing all the advantages of a degree, were little more than honorary *within* the University. In other words, they did not qualify the person for holding office at the University, as would a degree gained after residence.

It is worth remembering the local situation in Dublin at the time, and the impact of Trinity College, which exercised an influence over Protestant education in Ireland not dissimilar to that of Oxford and Cambridge over English schooling. Despite similarities with the two English universities and the claim that Trinity was a sister foundation, there were important differences, not least on account of their locations. As Trinity was situated in the dominant Irish city, the majority of its students did not live in college. In 1830 only 20% of the 1,800 students lived in, the rest living at home, with relations or in lodgings. In 1852, when the student population had shrunk to 1,217 undergraduates, just 118 resided in college and another 518 were domiciled in Dublin, of whom over 120 resided in lodgings and not with relatives.[52] That said, about 80% of those who graduated lived in Dublin and attended lectures, because the majority of those living elsewhere failed to complete their degrees. It was generally felt that the students living outside Dublin gave Trinity a bad name and they were referred to as 'back-stairs men'; most of them lived in England, paid their fees, and only crossed St George's Channel to sit their exams in order to gain what were known as 'steamboat' degrees.[53] The prevailing student conditions in Dublin were therefore quite unlike those at Oxford and Cambridge, and they strongly influenced the provision of residential arrangements at the Catholic University.

Newman's proposed new statute of 1857 meant that the terms 'intern' and 'extern' would be replaced by 'resident' and 'non-resident' and that both types of student could obtain degrees, but that degrees were to be viewed in two ways: 'in the original aspect historically and philosophically of a licence to teach and rule in the University, and in their popular and practical aspect of a testimonial externally addressed to the world';[54] only residents would gain the former (the licence to teach and rule). It also meant that for non-residential degrees, there was nothing to be gained by living in Dublin and that since attendance was not required at lectures—only exams—students could live in England or anywhere else; and that there were three kinds of residence: collegiate halls, licensed halls (kept by members of the University), and parents' houses (or the equivalent) combined with daily presence in the collegiate halls.

The fact that none of the degrees awarded by the Catholic University—except those in medicine—were recognised by the British government was a major problem for recruitment. Newman had always been in favour of some form of affiliation (provided the necessary safeguards were in place)[55] with the degree-conferring Queen's *University*, as opposed to becoming one of the Queen's *Colleges*, but this distinction was not grasped by any Irishman he knew.[56] Although technically speaking it would place them in the position of a college, Newman argued that the situation was no different from Louvain, which was 'but a College in the eyes of the State' although it was 'bonâ fide a University' and 'recognised as such by all Catholics'. Newman thought they 'had a fair chance of getting Government to place us in the position of Louvain', but 'little chance in succeeding in gaining a State recognition of a Catholic University'; that they 'had more chance of gaining endowments from Parliament, if we came before it as claimants in the shape in which the Queen's Colleges were claimants, than if Parliament were called upon directly and distinctly to give [recognition] to a formal Catholic University'.[57] He felt that, 'if the present Government chartered and endowed us, without giving us the power of giving Degrees' they would have 'done a great deal — *you will have got the wedge in*. At a later time, you may get more.' Newman's 'only fear in this plan is that the Heads and the Professors of the University *will not* keep up the phantasia and claim of a University, which Louvain does successfully, should allow themselves to be triumphed over as if defeated, and should tamely submit to *be* a College'.[58]

The new statute of 1857 was unanimously approved at an extraordinary meeting of the arts faculty on 13 January 1857 and passed by the Senate two days later, but confusion over what it entailed as regards externs lasted for the remainder of the year or even longer.[59] In a letter to the University Secretary written in December 1857, Newman makes reference to a document entitled 'Remarks on the Statute of January 1857', mentioning that they 'have passed the Council after a careful previous examination of some months'.[60] This would suggest that the statute continued to be the subject of study, but, in the absence of this document, all that we have to go on are a few of Newman's letters to other members of the Council. Writing to Dunne, Newman explained that, in order to 'enlist Dublin more in our favor', someone submitting himself to university discipline during 'the business hours' of the day, that is, from Mass onwards, should no longer be regarded as an extern.[61] Later he asked Butler, the dean of the arts faculty, 'Could we do any thing to call attention how we consider Externs as quasi interns, if they are in a Collegiate House during the business hours of day'?[62] He emphasised that he regarded it as a matter of principle that these 'quasi interns' paid their fees *and* tuition money. By way of justifying the new statute, Newman explained that,

> we were plagued with Externs coming and going, and our not knowing whether we had jurisdiction over them or not. The difficulty of an Extern is our having jurisdiction over a person who lives at home. Why cannot he choose instead to be a Non-resident Auditor? In that case he would pay no entrance fee, but lecture money term by term, he would be able to go up to the Examinations and he would *not* be under our jurisdiction.[63]

Though it might seem that Newman was obsessed with the notion of 'jurisdiction' and laying himself open to the charge of attempting to apply a legal concept to a setting where it was inappropriate, his preoccupation was more than a legal quibble. Legally, indeed, he was on strong ground, for most of the students were minors (majority was then twenty-one years), and the University was therefore legally *in loco parentis*. But more importantly, Newman held strongly that the University undertook a grave responsibility of oversight for those who entered its doors; it acted on behalf of parents in its attentiveness to growth in virtue; it was 'an Alma Mater, knowing her children one by one, not a foundry, or a mint, or a treadmill'.[64] For someone with such an elevated understanding of the role of the university, it was not a matter of indifference whether jurisdiction could be exercised or not. This also explains why Newman had originally entertained the idea of the University and its collegiate houses being configured as a (personal) diocese.

Newman felt strongly that those who put themselves under the University's jurisdiction were entitled to a deep intellectual and moral training, which ideally included tutorial teaching. This is why, when a new classics tutor arrived at St Patrick's, Newman explained: 'If Externs make themselves quasi-interns by attaching themselves to a House then we indeed provide tuition'.[65] Scratton, the University Secretary, only grasped the implication of the new statute in November 1857, when he was in the process of charging non-residents who only attended lectures as externs, and Newman pointed out that they should be treated as auditors instead. Scratton complained that 'not *one* Professor in the whole University was at all aware of the meaning of the New Statutes when they were passed —All (I think without exception) were taken by surprise at the particular sense afterwards attached to them by the Lord Rector.'[66] Newman reminded him that the Council had approved his 'Remarks on the Statute of January 1857' and urged Scratton to act upon them. If this might appear abrupt on Newman's part, he had for some time been suffering from the Secretary's constant gossiping about him, 'bringing on me the criticism of nearly every Irish priest and layman, with all of whom he was intensely unpopular'.[67]

To judge from the reappearance of the term 'extern proper' (in the table below), Newman's efforts to encourage all externs to become quasi-interns met with only partial success. However, it should be noted that the term 'intern improper' continued to feature among the six different ways it was possible to study in the arts faculty.

Table of fees for students in the Faculty of Philosophy and Letters

	Collegiate house	Professors' money	Entrance	Total
Interns proper, in St Patrick's	50	10	1	61
Interns improper, with use of Tutor,				
1. attached to Collegiate Houses	10	10	1	21
2. in Licensed Houses e.g. Medical Lodging Houses	30	10	1	41
Externs proper	0	10	5	15
Auditors	0	10	0	10
Non-residents	fees of membership and examination			

NB Non-residents are such as, without attending the Lectures of the University, are entered and pass the Examinations.[68]

On 16 January 1857, the day after the Senate met to ratify the new statute, Newman again had to deal with Quinn, who complained (quite rightly) that he had not been given notice of the agenda, due to an oversight by Scratton.[69] Quinn registered a number of other complaints, asking once again for his house to be treated differently from the others and to be exempted from the rules affecting collegiate houses. Newman refused to budge an inch. He pointed out to Quinn that he stood to gain by the new statute, as his externs would now be counted as interns for the purposes of grant allocation; and he warned him that 'I foresee that I am pretty well at the end of those attempts to satisfy you, which are in my power'.[70] Quinn retaliated by declaring that he would now have to communicate with Cullen and that meanwhile he would cease registering students on the University books. If Quinn thought that his insistence that the University had no jurisdiction over his house would lead to Newman backing down, he miscalculated; instead it drew from Newman a robust reply: 'Most certainly I ever must and will maintain that the University ought to have jurisdiction over all its subjects.' At this juncture, having just provided Quinn with greater financial support, Newman wondered what precisely it was that Quinn objected to. If it was 'the *strictness* of the jurisdiction exercised towards Collegiate Houses', he pointed out that becoming a licensed house might provide the solution.[71] But if it was the constraints imposed on the academic curriculum by the need to follow the course of lectures proscribed by the University, he thought he had already made allowances for Quinn's young men by instructing lecturers such as Dunne (who taught logic) to teach 'in the way usual in the case of Theology Students', if that is what the students were, otherwise to teach them as 'lay-youths'.[72] In the event St Laurence's was not withdrawn from the University and no further problems were raised until the following year; but Newman did not forget about the uneasy situation there. In assessing the pros and cons of the peculiar arrangements operating at St Laurence's, he recognised that, on the one hand, 'the boys by that means melt into University Students—on the other hand they are never proper students'; and he seriously wondered whether St Laurence's should cease to be a University house.[73]

With the number of medical students set to rise to eighty for the medical school's third academic session (1857/58), there was a growing demand for a residence for them. Taking advantage of the possibilities opened up by the statute, Dr Henry Tyrrell, one of the Demonstrators in Anatomy, took the initiative and approached Newman for advice about how to proceed. Newman advised Tyrrell to write to the University trustees for aid, but meanwhile used the opportunity to encourage others to support him. Hope-Scott's offer of £150, on condition that Tyrrell was backed by the medical faculty, seems to have encouraged the archbishops to agree to set up the medical lodging (i.e. licensed) house under Tyrrell as dean. What is noteworthy is the manner in which the medical faculty supported the initiative and shared Newman's concerns for the students. In a letter the faculty sent to Newman they explained they were unanimous in their desire for a special lodging house for medics and wanted to be the first to put the idea into practice, before other people in Dublin borrowed the idea from the *Gazette* and took the credit. They wrote of the

> lamentable consequences resulting from the exposure of inexperienced youth without guidance or restraint to the moral contagion or a large city at a time when temptation is strongest and a wholesome check most needed, namely after the business hours of the day when students come together and are left to determine for themselves how and where the night shall be spent.[74]

They knew of several instances of upright students who had come to Dublin 'with a resolution to lead a regular and exemplary life' and had 'fallen within a year' and become a source of sadness to their families. The medical faculty believed that it was the special task of the Catholic University to remedy this great evil, and that upon it devolved 'the duty of demonstratively refuting the convenient but pernicious doctrine which unfortunately prevails to some extent amongst students, namely that the study of medicine necessitates and justifies a certain degree of moral laxity'. A related reason for providing a medical lodging house, they added, was that the University had the duty to provide 'a safe place of abode' for those who had finished the arts course and begun medicine, and were thereby disqualified from further residence at the collegiate houses.[75] Moreover, the faculty argued that the number of medics would increase if they managed to win the confidence of parents and guardians.[76]

A subcommittee of the medical faculty had calculated that a licensed house was viable with fifteen students paying £30 and an annual grant from the University of £133, though they had allowed a reduction of £5 as 'an inducement to come in and submit to discipline'.[77] The outcome was that the archbishops allocated £200 for its establishment and a house was purchased in York Street, very close to the medical school, and christened St Luke's. This, the first licensed hall, opened in late November 1857, a fortnight after term had begun, with fees of £30 p.a. By May 1858 its ten places were taken, and with an additional grant of £50 it was expanded to sixteen in time for the 1858/59 session, when it was oversubscribed.[78]

Originally Newman had envisaged St Mary's as a residence for English students, but in the event it had become an international house. Unwilling to abandon his original idea and eager to use every means at his disposal to solve the ever-present recruitment problem, Newman approached Pollen to ask whether something could be done to persuade Catholic men of means in England to establish an English house at the University. He pointed out that the cause would help to increase numbers at the University, as well as advertise it, and he threw out the names of a few he thought might be willing to pay the rent of an imposing house nearby.[79] A fortnight later, he had developed the idea further. 'I think the *only* way of giving the laity real power at the University, is by founding and supporting houses', because, by providing the funds, they would virtually have the presentation of the dean. He explained that he was about to pass through the Senate the statute about licensed houses, which 'would be αυτονομοι [autonomous], differing from Collegiate Houses in that they took no money from the University'. Their members would be considered, and have the privileges of, interns; their heads would be licensed, and the rector would have only the veto, rather the appointment of the dean. 'No thought is better than that of an English House', he told Pollen, and he suggested that the former Oriel tutor and convert Robert Wilberforce might be the one to head it.[80]

When nothing came of his approach to Pollen, Newman wrote to other convert friends in the hope that one of them might take up the idea of an English house. John More Capes, the editor of *The Rambler*, was open about his reluctance to back Newman's plan; he argued, 'The real thing that keeps people in England from sending either money or students is, of course, the profound distrust of Irish proceedings which is general.'[81] And yet the strange thing was that, as Newman confided to Hope-Scott, it was the Irish poor who were supporting the University, and because this was common knowledge the 'English students are taunted with getting their Professor's Lectures by means of the Irish pence'.[82] 'What I aim at', he told the Cambridge convert William Dodsworth, 'is the establishment of an English Collegiate House. *My* house is at present the English House—and I have Oxford men! don't be jealous, because it is not Cambridge as Dean and Tutor—but I want to put this on a permanent footing. What I should like to do would be to take a good house on lease, and stock it with Dean and Tutor.' He conceded that 'the difficulty is the setting off', and furthermore, that if he had not been rector, St Mary's would now be in financial trouble. 'But', he insisted, 'could I once establish a House as I propose, every thing must go well.' All the Catholic University needed for its success was 'time and to be let alone'.[83] Besides contacting convert friends, Newman tried his luck with Michael Blount, the head of an old Catholic family. Aware of the loyalty of old Catholics to the English seminary schools that had been founded on the continental mainland and relocated in England in the 1790s, he explained that in Dublin they had the rudiments of four collegiate houses already, and that there would be a fifth when a seminary was started. What he commended for Blount's consideration was a call for donations for an English collegiate house run by English trustees.[84]

By the start of the fourth academic session, Newman seems to have dropped the idea of an English house, due to the lack of any positive response. He was also becoming discouraged at finding no increase in student numbers, and confided to Pollen: 'I don't think Ireland has them'.[85] Just as the medical faculty had been the 'sheet anchor' of London University in its early days, so it seemed now to be for the Catholic University. The arts faculty was 'lame', and as it had few Irish students he threw out the idea of moving it to England, while keeping it as an integral part of the University, and having the students merely travel to Dublin for their degrees. He reckoned the plan would need £1000 from England, 'but, with lukewarm friends like Sir J. S[imeon]. and overdrained friends like Hope-Scott and [W.G.] Ward, how can one do anything'?[86]

The evening lectures which had taken place during the first academic year had been suspended for lack of interest, but in April 1858 they were started up again when the professors volunteered to take on the task themselves, in response to a petition that they be revived from a group of young men engaged in business. Although Newman feared that the plan would dissipate the energies of the professors and fail to encourage the young men to take up their studies full time, he allowed the professors to undertake voluntarily the extra work involved as 'engaging in a very charitable work'. At first he was doubtful about the scheme, fearing that it might entail the 'danger of our making ourselves mere popular lecturers', and did not hope for much more 'than the keeping them out of mischief, and inflicting one or two good principles and useful facts and historical truths on their memory'. Not that he was against the idea in principle, for he considered 'that in itself a system of such Lectures is highly desirable',[87] but he wished to distinguish between occasional lectures which 'excite or keep up an interest and reverence' for the University and those of an academic bent which affected their purpose by 'the slow, silent, penetrating, overpowering influence of patience, steadiness, routine and perseverance'.[88] During the first fortnight of evening lectures, no fewer than ninety-two young men enrolled as auditors, and there were nearly twice as many when the new academic year began in November 1858. The statute passed in January 1857 allowed the auditors to proceed to degrees, and over the years a good number availed themselves of the opportunity, though in Newman's time they were not allowed to matriculate.

Discipline wears thin

By the end of the third academic session (1856/57) there were ninety matriculated students at the Catholic University, including twenty-eight who had passed the scholar's exam, six who had passed the inceptor's exam, and two their licentiate, and around 130 attending lectures. Newman deliberately scaled down his involvement that third year—'I don't mean to be here so constantly, or to fag so hard',[89] he told a friend—and though he resided in Dublin for eight separate periods, the longest was a month. The continual journeys across St George's Channel (fifty-six crossings by the end of his rectorate) and the strain of divided responsibilities were beginning to tell on his health. He also felt that he had accomplished the task asked of him, which was to get the University going, and that the bishops needed to find a younger man to replace him.

On 3 April 1857 he took the momentous decision to resign the following November, and informed the bishops of his intention. In the negotiations which ensued, the Irish bishops asked the Birmingham Oratory to stop Newman resigning and to extend his period of release; but the Oratorians declined, pointing out that during the last six years the Catholic University had had two thirds of his time.[90] Over the summer of 1857 a compromise was reached whereby Newman and the bishops agreed to a fourth term of office, with partial residence of 'say nine weeks' in the session.[91] For the bishops, the agreement was a trial measure, which they hoped to extend; on Newman's side there was the stipulation that a vice-rector be appointed. The University had lost its (mainly non-resident) vice-rector in the summer of 1857, and finding a replacement was to prove highly problematic. Cullen was unwilling to consider a lay appointment from within the University, even though the University's statutes followed Louvain's in allowing it, and this left a small pool of priests from which to select.[92] O'Reilly was offered the job, but turned it down, after which the archbishops decided to postpone the appointment. Newman suggested that in the meantime Butler, dean of the arts faculty, be made acting vice-rector, but this proved unacceptable because of his lay status. The result was that no replacement was found.

With no vice-rector and a largely absent rector, it was hardly surprising that disciplinary problems should have arisen during Newman's fourth and final year in office (1857/58). Residing in Birmingham, Newman's only means for resolving these and other matters was to rely on third parties either to act on his behalf or to supply him with the data necessary for decision-making. The arrangement was highly unsatisfactory and damaging for the University—but for later historians Newman's carefully worded instructions and explanations are valuable records of the manner in which he handled disciplinary cases; and they provide the practical counterpart to his sensitive elaboration (in the Rules and Regulations and in the *Gazette*) of the ethos that ought to prevail at the University.

During the previous academic year St Mary's and St Patrick's had been unsettled and the students there had begun to take liberties. Once again Archbishop Cullen complained to his agent in Rome that Newman failed to discipline the students and that he allowed them to go to the theatre, balls, hunts, and rowing matches.[93]

Two major disciplinary incidents occurred in 1857/58, both of which forced Newman to take action. The first occurred in mid-December when the dean of St Patrick's brought a breach of discipline before the Council for consideration as *consilium abeundi*.[94] Newman was informed that the student James Molloy had gone to an evening party without permission, and that another student, Jack Mulholland, had bribed a servant to leave a door unlocked for his exit and a window open for him to return unobserved. On his return, Molloy had spent the night at No. 87, next door to St Patrick's. The Council's unanimous decision was not to impose on them *consilium abeundi*; but, given the grave nature of the offence, they recommended that a solemn admonition from the rector in person be added to whatever punishment was deemed appropriate.[95]

Newman had already heard of the incident and in a memorandum written before the Council's letter arrived he recorded his first thoughts on the matter, based (it seems) on statements written by the two culprits. Neither student claimed it was his first offence, he noted; Mulholland almost justified his actions, while Molloy spoke of 'an unaccountable impulse'. Since it was not clear *where* Molloy had actually spent the night and whether he had really been to a party or not, the Council needed to investigate further and question the servant: 'I decidedly think the two should receive "Consilium abeundi". The offence requires it. The example's sake requires it.' Newman had in fact been suspicious of Molloy's conduct for some time. In his first year he had upset Newman by taking advantage of permission to have his music lessons in one of the official university rooms next door to St Patrick's and turning it into a music room. (In his favour it should be pointed out that Molloy was vice-president of the Historical, Literary, and Aesthetical Society and that he showed considerable musical ability as a student, singing during the Holy Week services—and would go on to distinguish himself and make a career as a song writer.) As for Mulholland, the holder of a medical bursary, Newman was dissatisfied with his general demeanour and described him as 'weak and slippery'.[96] In O'Shea's *Recollections*, Mulholland is described as an oddity. He was a competitive billiards player and something of a fitness fanatic, having turned his bedroom into a makeshift gym by using items of furniture for his morning vaulting practice; but like Molloy he had academic interests too, acting as secretary of the Historical, Literary, and Aesthetical Society, and showing an appetite for debate, aided by his ability to bone up at short notice on any disputed issue. Though Irishmen, both had been schooled in England: Molloy at St Edmund's, Ware, and Mulholland for six years at Stonyhurst.

Newman set about resolving the matter in accordance with the Rules and Regulations, which provided (in Rule 17) for five lesser punishments at the hands of the relevant dean or the vice-rector, as well as one by the rector (rustication for a term), another by the rector and the Council (*consilium abeundi*), and a third by the Senate (expulsion). A reprimand from the rector had no place in the Rules, he told the Council, nor could it be a lesser punishment; he could only remit the matter to the dean—Flannery—while pointing out that he—Newman—was unlikely to be in Dublin until

March.[97] What he really thought of the Council's decision is conveyed in a confidential letter to the dean of the arts faculty: the Council had washed their hands of the power of the lesser punishments, invented a new punishment, and committed to Newman 'the executioner's work of administering to the culprits a reprimand. [...] Meanwhile, I fear, I fear, I fear, the *two culprits will escape*. Wait to be reprimanded by me! why the essence of good punishment is, its being *immediate*.'[98] Newman instructed Flannery that he should, in the rector's name, send both students home immediately until the start of the summer term, with loss of the intervening term.

Meanwhile Newman wrote to Molloy to explain his line of action.

> I have no wish to be severe with you or any one. It is much pleasanter to be indulgent. It gives a person in authority no trouble, and makes him popular. But you must recollect I have an account to give to my own conscience. I have ever regarded the care of young men, in whatever degree it comes upon one, as a heavy charge. At the most anxious season of life, when *their* course for time and eternity may perhaps be fixed, they come under the superintendence of the Authorities of a University. In time to come, they themselves, on whose conduct I had had to pronounce, and their companions too who had been witnesses of it might unite in thanking my memory for what at the time seemed severity, and [not] in dishonouring it for an unwise unfaithful indulgence.[99]

He said he was deeply pained at his mother's distress, which was evident in the telegram she had sent imploring that James be allowed to remain at the University. But duty had to be done. Nor was the punishment imposed decided on lightly; having heard that it was his first offence and that he wished to remain at St Patrick's, Newman told Molloy he was willing to receive any considerations Molloy could urge in his favour, and that he was willing to grant any suspension of the punishment which Flannery felt 'to be consistent with his own sense of duty'.[100]

In a similar letter to Mulholland, Newman told him he waited to hear of any extenuating circumstances and for proof of his diligence the previous term. He explained that he had no wish to be severe, that the punishment was decided on definite grounds and with deliberation, and therefore that he needed to able to justify any change. 'I have a great responsibility in having a number of men under my charge. I shall have to answer for that charge. I must not act from mere desire to please them, but in order to please Him who at present has placed them under me.' And he impressed upon Mulholland the sobering thought that it was 'commonly the case that parents have to bear their children's offences'.[101] After letters of apology to Flannery, and further exchanges between them and Newman, the two had their sentence commuted. They were to 'reside this term, but be indoors between this time and Easter every afternoon after four O clock, not asking any leave for parties etc', all on the provision 'they will accept it *in writing*.'[102] With this the episode came to an end.

A revealing postscript is that, shortly after leaving the University, Molloy wrote to Newman to ask for guidance on the theological difficulty of the presence of evil in the world and its origin. In his reply Newman thanked him for his 'affectionate letter', which was 'a recompense of my anxieties in Dublin'.[103] Several months later, in May 1860, Molloy called in at the Birmingham Oratory and stayed there three days. Mulholland, on the other hand, does not appear to have justified Newman's leniency, at least in the short run, for the arts faculty singled him out in the summer of 1858 as the one student who ought to be denied his term and temporarily prohibited from taking the scholar's exam.

The frustration that Newman experienced on account of his remoteness from the scene of action in Dublin found an outlet in his correspondence. 'I have ever acted, not by formal authority and rule, but by influence, and this power cannot be well exerted when absent',[104] he told Ornsby, one of his unofficial agents in Dublin. When Newman entrusted O'Reilly with the task of presiding at a meeting of the Senate, he and the teaching staff made such a mess of things that it brought home to Newman 'how the attempt for me to be Rector *here* of the University *there*, would break down' in a very short time. Newman had proposed that the University Council constitute a committee entrusted with certain functions by the Senate, but this proposal was rejected and instead an ad hoc committee of eleven was chosen to act during the year 1858. In so doing, the Senate contravened the rule which stipulated that nothing should be done in the University 'without the Rector's concurrence'. Newman sighed: 'A man may be an able man, an experienced man, a holy man, yet unfitted to carry on the University — and much more may he be all this, and unable to carry it *on upon another's plan and with the confidence of another'*. Without a vice-rector who understood both him and the situation it was impossible to go on. 'I *can't* govern at a distance—but I *can* commit my power *absolutely* to another, if I CAN TRUST HIM.'[105] To Hope-Scott, his long-term adviser on all matters educational, he explained:

> It is impossible [...] that I can govern 300 miles off without continual little collisions. While I am on the spot, there is a continual action and reaction between all members of the University and myself, which has hindered anything of the kind. We have hitherto been in the most perfect harmo-ny—So we are now—but I despair of its continuing if I am to act in the dark in another place.[106]

The lack of a vice-rector was another frustration and it made the likelihood of his departure at the end of the session all the greater: indeed, from February 1858 onwards Newman decided to forgo the rector's salary to indicate as much.

The prelude to the other major disciplinary affair that Newman had to face in his last year in office was the unruly behaviour of students at Trinity College. Although rioting had been a standard feature of life there in the eighteenth century, the only outbreak in the nineteenth century occurred on 12 March 1858 on the occasion of the processional entry into Dublin of Lord Eglinton, the Lord Lieutenant of Ireland. The return of the viceroy, after a change in government, was marked by a public holiday, and hundreds of students gathered at Trinity. As the procession passed by, the students threw rounds of oranges and bad eggs at the police, and eventually the superintendent of police was hit in the face. He lost his composure and ordered a charge of the mounted police, armed with swords, which was followed up by others on foot, armed with batons. In the mayhem that followed there were several serious student casualties.[107] The Trinity authorities prosecuted the police in a law suit that became a cause célèbre, though the policeman in charge was eventually acquitted. The incident was reported in the *Dublin Evening Mail* (19 March 1858), which added: 'It is, we are assured, a certain fact that the students of the Catholic University offered to make common cause with those of Trinity College in case of any further outrage on the part of the Police rendering active resistance necessary.' Cullen, who was understandably nervous, demanded an inquiry into the allegation, and after an investigation the dean of the arts faculty wrote to the *Mail* to say that it had been misinformed and that no such alliance had been made.

A few days later, on 24 March, a meeting of the Historical, Literary, and Aesthetical Society took place in the Catholic University lecture rooms, attended by several dignitaries, including the Lord Mayor and his wife. The guest speaker was the erudite but eccentric James Robertson, the butt of student pranks, who read a paper on 'The British Constitution of 1688'. Hugh MacDermot, holder of a medical bursary and a future attorney-general for

Ireland, was in the chair; Augustus Bethell, the president of society, stood at the back of the room along with a group of students, whose ranks were swelled from Trinity.

Two accounts of the behaviour at the meeting have survived: one from Dunne, which is over-sensitive; the other from Robertson himself, who in his embarrassment sought to downplay the affair. What is clear is that throughout the proceedings the students were restless, shuffling and jostling, chattering, mocking the idiosyncrasies of Robertson, creaking doors and hitting each other with knotted handkerchiefs—all of which provided amusement for the young ladies present. At the end of the paper MacDermot's words of appreciation were lost amidst the din, while in his vote of thanks the University surgeon Mr Ellis was forced to remonstrate with the students for the manner in which they received his own remarks. The Mayor looked less than pleased. The foremost disturbers, who were the worse for drink, included three externs from St Patrick's, two residents from St Mary's (Jasper White and Etienne Zamoyski), and Edward Quin, who had left St Patrick's eighteen months previously and was now at Trinity.[108]

In judging what was evidently a disgraceful disturbance, triggered by 'the influence which is so catching of the Trin. College rows', Newman attributed the real cause of the episode to the lack of a vice-rector. Less concerned with the three culprits who were externs and therefore 'not really specimens of our youths', he was troubled with White and Zamoyski, and thought 'their conduct must to be inquired into'. The best he could do at a distance was to offer his first impressions to the professors in the hope that they could improve on them. He began by noting that in the first place, since it was a private lecture at which the professors were guests, it would be difficult for the University to interfere directly:

> The Professors laid aside their Professorial gown, when they attended it, and cannot resume it to punish. It must be thrown

> on the gentlemanly feeling and good sense of the members of the Society—Who form the Committee or Governing body? they ought to make a private though distinct apology in the name of the Society to the Lord Mayor etc—and they should strike off the rioters from their lists. And one or other of them might be told confidentially that I had thoughts of suppressing the Society altogether (for it certainly *would come to that*) by way of stimulating them.[109]

If the committee did not have the power to expel members, they needed to dissolve the society, divide the assets or debts (unless there was a great loss), then form a new society in order to exclude the riotous members. 'And let them know that the University *could* expel any rioters, if *they* can't.'[110]

Secondly, 'coincident as it is with the report of their sympathising in the Trin College rows', Newman considered that it was a great opportunity to petition Cullen for a pro-vice-rector, 'under the strong apprehension that the University is going to pieces for want of one'; and he expressed his hope that the whole body of professors could be encouraged to take part in a formal request.[111]

Thirdly, Newman was pleased to have the opportunity of ending the practice he disliked—and which had given problems before—of professors lecturing in an undergraduate society. It meant, in this instance, that the student chairing the meeting was, for the duration of the meeting, the superior of Professor Robertson. He intended to ask the professors' permission to end 'this unseemly proceeding'.[112]

In line with Newman's first suggestion, the society disowned the behaviour of the six unruly members and gave them such a heavy fine that it was tantamount to expulsion; the president offered to apologise to the vice-rectoral authority (which resided in the dean of the arts faculty) and to apologise in person to the Mayor.

It was not long before the Historical, Literary, and Aesthetical Society resumed its normal business. On 3 May they listened to George Segar on 'Taste' and Charles de la Pasture reading poetry; and on 14 June to another paper by Segar, this time on 'Recreation', and poetry from James Molloy. The year was rounded off with a cricket match against a club known as the Eglintons in which the students were despatched ignominiously, though they salvaged some pride in winning the impromptu sports competition which fol-lowed.[113] Although normal service had resumed at the Historical, Literary, and Aesthetical Society, the University authorities could not ignore the affair, and two days after the disturbance, at a special meeting convened to discussed the state of studies at St Mary's, the arts faculty decided that it would draw the subject to the attention of the dean of St Mary's (i.e. William Penny) and request him 'to induce the young men to confer more frequently with their tutor'.[114]

Nor was the affair overlooked by Newman and it forced him to re-examine the question of discipline at the University. 'I cannot undertake the discipline', he told Ornsby, 'if it were merely on this account that it is not my line, and I could not exercise the office'.[115] Learning from his own bishop in Birmingham that rumours were abroad that he was unable to keep discipline, he confided to a friend in typically self-effacing manner that 'I am not in *practice* a good disciplinarian, I quite confess it. I have it as little in me to be a good schoolmaster or Dean, as to be a rider or successful chess player.' But this did not stop him feeling the need for appropriate discipline, 'for many a man approves what he cannot practise'. People seemed unaware that the University had never had a *resident* vice-rector and that according to the statutes it was the vice-rector, not the rector, who was the officer of discipline. 'Deans are too hard to be got—they are either as strict as Prefects in an Ecclesiastical Semi-nary, or they are indulgent and lax.'[116] Though such difficulties were only temporary, he felt they were serious at the start.

Besides declining to draw the rector's salary, Newman signalled his intentions by remaining in Birmingham for the duration of the summer term. It was not long before news reached him that some of the students had begun to skip dinner and dine in coffee houses. Suspecting that the lack of a vice-rector was 'ruining the University', he felt obliged to do something. 'The best rules of discipline will come to nothing', he reflected, 'unless there is some one to enforce them.' The deans needed someone to fall back upon; they needed to be able to say to their residents 'we are obliged to do so and so'. In the absence of a vice-rector, Newman proposed to the Council that they authorise a small committee to draft a set of rules, which they could impose on the deans, 'who practically acknowledge the authority of the University in their Houses'.[117] The committee included Flannery, Penny and Quinn, and the rules of discipline they drew up were effectively a graded system of penalties and fines. Only Flannery warmed to the new rules. Penny had grave misgivings about them, and Quinn was sufficiently astute to notice 'that such a system of management is not in harmony with the views which presided over the formation of the little collegiate bodies—like families'; he thought the rules imprudent and ill-adapted to their actual circumstances. In the end the Council rejected the system, and instead proposed that Newman write to the deans to insist on the observance of the Rules and Regulations.[118]

Further discontent at the collegiate houses

Although the interchange of letters between Flannery and Newman had all but dried up by the start of the third academic session, all was not well at St Patrick's, and when the long vacation of 1857 was in sight Newman reopened the question of tutorial provision there. After Arnold's departure at Christmas 1856 to take a house with his family, Flannery had ceased insisting that the residents of St Patrick's receive tuition, even though the new tutor, William Scott (who had been a resident tutor at St Mary's the previous year), was perfectly capable. Newman told Flannery that it was a matter of great concern that he felt unable to enter with 'interest or heartiness' into the regime laid down for collegiate houses, a feeling that was shown in his 'little desire or care' to secure a second tutor for the increased numbers at St Patrick's—now fourteen. This instance was 'only the expression of a state of opinion and judgement in the subject of your house, which is habitual to you'. Flannery wanted classes and compulsory lectures in his house, and sub-deans (that is, officials with 'collegiate authority') instead of tutors; he was firmly of the opinion that his house would not be in good shape until such measures were carried out. Rather than unnecessarily subject someone with responsibility, such as Flannery, to control in matters on which he had a 'definite and permanent opinion', Newman resolved that as from the following term (Michaelmas 1857) Flannery should do as he wished with his house. He should have as much freedom as Quinn, within the limits of the Rules and Regulations.[119]

Flannery's reaction to the rector's frank statement of displeasure appears to have been positive, to judge from his attempts to supplement tutorial provision in the fourth academic session, all the more necessary as Flannery had recently taken on extra administrative work as clerical secretary of the Catholic University. But Flannery's efforts to engage a temporary tutor for the Michaelmas Term gave rise to two further problems, both of which stemmed from his inability to comprehend Newman's scheme. Having the ratification of appointments, Newman pointed out that, since Flannery wanted his tutor to combine tutorial and disciplinary roles, the appointment needed to accord with Rule 13, which stated: 'The Tutor has no part in the College discipline, or any academical authority over his pupils'. If Flannery wanted to get round the rule, he needed to make his tutor 'a sort of Sub-dean and general assistant in studies' but '*without* the title of Tutor'. The second problem in Flannery's plan was that if the tutor gave compulsory, formal classes this interfered with the professorial teaching.[120] Flannery seems to have forgotten that, according to the statutes, the tutor was to correspond to 'an Oxford *Private Tutor*, and therefore could have nothing to do with discipline or private classes'. The man in question was John Kelly, a respectable elderly gentleman who had been either a schoolmaster or a domestic tutor, and was therefore of a background and age that meant he could not 'make himself a quasi-equal or associate with the young men.'[121]

Newman's hand was strengthened by a letter from the arts faculty informing him that it had ruled the proposed arrangement with Kelly as contrary to the spirit of Rule 13, pointing out the danger of 'superseding the functions of the *Professors* by those of the Tutor' if tutors were to be allowed to start conducting compulsory lectures.[122] The outcome was that Flannery was allowed to appoint Kelly, but on condition that he abided by the two provisos laid down by Newman. The following spring Flannery again found himself without a tutor, and, unable to find a residential one, sought Newman's permission to engage an external one. Newman agreed to him doing so, noting that he was not 'an uninterested witness of the deprived conditions of St Patrick's House since the Long Vacation'. And he reminded Flannery that if he had not interfered, it was precisely because it was his policy to leave tutorial arrangements in the dean's hands.[123] When offered, Arnold leapt at the opportunity to resume tutorial work at St Patrick's, though he was somewhat disappointed to discover that tuition was no longer compulsory.

A much stronger reason for leaving Flannery alone was the news which broke in November 1857 that he was to be made a bishop, which meant that he would be leaving St Patrick's. Another change on the cards was that Quinn might be appointed the vice-rector, a prospect that Newman initially favoured because it would provide him with the opportunity of separating Quinn's school from the University and letting one of the University classicists run it as a feeder school. Even if Quinn was not appointed vice-rector, Newman thought he could achieve his goal either by Quinn moving to St Patrick's with all his students or by turning St Laurence's into a pure collegiate house. Quinn himself does not seem to have entertained the possibility of becoming the vice-rector. In fact, the prospect of an energetic vice-rector arriving with his own ideas about discipline and unaware of the special circumstances at St Laurence's triggered yet another threat from Quinn about withholding students. In Newman's absence, he spoke of his grievances to Butler, Dunne, Ornsby and Stewart at a dinner he organised for the purpose in January 1858, warning them that matters had reached crisis point.

Besides his abiding worry about interference in his house (and the school) on the part of the University, Quinn's principal complaint was that St Patrick's was now effectively endowed with £400 p.a. by means of the medical bursaries. This he found grossly unfair. It meant that the deans of St Patrick's and St Mary's could reap handsome profits, due to their higher boarding fees, which the class of student attending St Laurence's could simply not afford. As it was, some of their lay boarders were supported by the priests at St Laurence's, while most of their day pupils were unable to afford the academic fees of the University.[124] Furthermore, the house was supposed to have two tutors, but could not afford them. As previous and prolonged negotiations with Newman had proved fruitless, he threatened to withdraw his students from the University unless his demands were met; if they were, Quinn held out the prospect of sending twenty new students. The lecturers listening to Quinn advised him to delay his decision and meanwhile state his claim and wait for a response. This Quinn agreed to do.

The four lecturers were convinced that Quinn was hard done by and that some financial redress was called for, particularly as St Laurence's was now drawing on its capital, and on their behalf

Ornsby sent Newman a lengthy summary of the meeting, as well their own views. From Ornsby's letter it is clear that they identified fully with Newman's conception of the University, only disagreeing among themselves about points of emphasis and the means to resolve the dispute. While they managed to talk Quinn out of his proposal for waiving academic fees, by pointing out that this would lead to an exodus of students from St Patrick's to St Laurence's, they felt that some form of subsidy was in order. Ornsby 'spoke strongly of the necessity of having a tutor qualified to prepare [students] for the more advanced lectures, because without it, practically his students don't get university education'; and he pointed out that any subsidy the University gave his house would be on condition he appointed one or two able tutors.[125]

Newman no doubt found a certain irony in Quinn's complaints about St Patrick's being comfortably off, having heard Flannery moan on several occasions that St Laurence's was in a healthy state, thanks to the profits from the school! Declining Ornsby's idea of independent arbitration over the financial position of St Laurence's, Newman passed the problem back to Ornsby, asking the arts faculty to draw up 'a general scheme for the arrangement of the relations between the University and the Collegiate Houses—and I will give it my best consideration'. Newman declared he was willing to answer 'categorical propositions' from Quinn, but no more.[126] A month later he insisted: 'I cannot directly negotiate with Dr Quinn. We fail to understand each other.'[127]

The wisdom of distancing himself from the dispute soon became apparent, as new problems emerged in the negotiations conducted by Butler, Dunne, Ornsby and Stewart. They learned that there was strong opposition from the highly-qualified priests at St Laurence's to sending more students to the University, because in altering the curriculum they had lost out on church boys, and therefore valuable income. They also objected to losing their best boys to the University, which meant they no longer taught the higher books, and lamented the fact that the University obliged them to teach their church students classics rather than the seminary course in philosophy, which they valued more highly. The prospect of engaging a tutor, who would be less-well educated than themselves and paid £100 p.a., was hard to swallow, as they worked long hours and received a mere £50 (which they contributed to the upkeep of the school). Moreover, there was a marked reluctance to allow their students the amount of freedom enjoyed elsewhere, as seen by the way St Laurence's used its students as ushers for the schoolboys.[128] No wonder that Ornsby told Newman, 'I fear his views about education and ours differ in principle'.[129]

It was clear to Newman's friends that St Laurence's would not be a serviceable collegiate house unless the school was separated off. One option Ornsby proposed was for the University to run the school as a feeder under Stewart, but, as Butler pointed out, it would need remodelling for the purpose, as 'they have the notion, so contrary to our views, of sacrificing the classics to a variety of scientific information (*badly acquired*)'.[130] Though negotiations with Quinn collapsed, they revived and eventually Quinn was able to submit demands with the backing of his fellow priests. This meant that Newman was forced to re-enter the dispute, as Quinn was providing him with two 'categorical propositions', together with the promise to send thirty students to the University the following term if his demands were met. The first requested: 'That the University should endow St L[aurence]'s House with the same amount, and for the same purposes as it has endowed St Patrick's —the endowment to be given at the rate of £10 for each student to the number of 40.'[131] Newman refused the offer, explaining that the proposition rested on a misapprehension of the state of St Patrick's and Newman's part in (what he declined to call) its 'endowment'. He explained the origin of the subsidies at St

Patrick's,[132] and assured Quinn that if he had found St Laurence's in an identical situation he would have applied the same measures; but he was unable to take the initiative in giving St Laurence's a large sum. The second proposition amounted to a request that the University advance him £6000 for the purchase of a property in Upper Leeson Street. Having himself recently failed to borrow £2000 from the University Trustees to cover his debts while building the University Church, despite the security he offered, Newman explained that he did not 'feel encouraged just now to meddle with transactions of this nature'.[133]

Newman and Quinn had reached stalemate. Quinn had not paid the University that year's entrance and academic fees for his students, but neither had the University paid him the £200 grant allocated to St Laurence's. Should they call it quits?, Newman wondered. By mid-summer, in his final months as rector, Newman began to have doubts about this tactic and wrote to his secretary:

> As to the state of Dr Quinn's youths, really it is so anoma-
> lous, that it cannot last. Are they on the *books* or not? [...]
> If they *are*, we must make an account of what Dr Quinn
> *might have* had for the youths, setting against it their
> entrance and scholarship [i.e. academic] fees. I suppose the
> balance will be in his favor. We shall pocket it, if he does not
> come to an arrangement with us.[134]

But the situation was still unresolved a year later, when Quinn left on being appointed Bishop of Brisbane.[135]

As for St Patrick's House, Newman viewed Flannery's departure as a 'great opening' which he hoped to use to install as tutor (or even dean) Thomas Pope, by repute one of the ablest unemployed converts.[136] But Newman soon realised that it was no good finding a replacement for Flannery while he remained, because of the difficulty the person would have in getting on with him. Flannery's parting words on leaving St Patrick's were to the effect that he wanted nothing more to do with the house: 'It is entirely in Dr Newman's hands.'[137]

In his final weeks as (unpaid) rector Newman assumed he would be able to leave St Patrick's under men of his own choosing, but he was overtaken by events. The academic star of St Patrick's, Augustus Keane, had just gained honours in the licentiate exam,[138] and now at the end of August 1858 he asked to be installed as tutor at St Patrick's. Keane had won a classical scholarship to the Catholic University in 1856, as well as two university prizes, and having risen through the system was therefore precisely the sort of person Newman would normally have welcomed. But there was a problem: Arnold, the acting (non-residential) tutor at St Patrick's, was unwilling to relinquish his post, being committed to the University and with a growing family to feed—they eventually had nine children. All Newman could do was to suggest to Arnold and Keane that they share the work (and pay), while pointing out that the final decision belonged to the new dean. To Keane, he suggested it would be better if he were only gradually admitted 'to the full office of House Tutor'.[139] Arnold was reluctant to divide the spoils with Keane, given his own experience and track record, but he yielded to Newman's compromise on condition that all the students were tutored.

Flannery was consecrated coadjutor Bishop of Killaloe on 5 September but only formally resigned the deanship of St Patrick's on 30 September. A week later Newman was officially informed that the archbishops had chosen Austin O'Loughlin, a former Prefect and dean of the Irish College in Paris, as dean of St Patrick's. This was startling news for Newman, because the appointment belonged to him and he had not even been consulted.[140] He had, in fact, been in the process of taking soundings for the deanships of St Mary's and St Patrick's. But as it turned out, the allocation of tutorships worked out well, because Scott left St Mary's (and became the Public Examiner for the University)[141] that summer,

Arnold took his place, and this left room for Keane, who conveniently filled the vacancy created at St Patrick's.

The demise of St Mary's

During Newman's last academic session as rector (1857/58) Penny remained as dean of St Mary's, which was full for most of the year.[142] The tutoring was shared between Penny and Scott (with some assistance from Arnold), but neither of them were up to exerting a controlling influence on the resident aristocrats, for Penny was shy and generous by nature, and Scott, the son of a Staffordshire baronet, was a gentle soul. As the year wore on, St Mary's became more unruly and in Newman's absence it became (in Arnold's words) 'a perfect bear-garden' and brought 'great discredit' on the University.[143] Newman had a good idea of what was going on thanks to Penny's regular and frank reports about the disorder at St Mary's; reading between the lines, he could see that the students were exploiting the kindness of Penny and Scott in order to live it up at balls and parties. Towards the end of May 1858 Penny told Newman that 'Some of the youths are extremely troublesome and irregular'; the princes de Ligne followed in the wake of the ring-leader, Count Zamoyski, while Jasper White tried to keep pace with them. '[T]his term [White] has strangely altered for the worse—he seldom goes to lecture, e.g. last week he appears to have been only once'.[144] On the previous Monday these four had gone to the races, returned around 8 pm, then went out (lawfully) to get dinner in town, but did not appear until midnight.

Nothing in Penny's reports would have surprised Newman, because he knew that trouble had been brewing the previous year, to the extent that he had found himself in a dilemma in negotiating with the parents of prospective residents. He had hesitated over whether to accept eighteen-year-old George Errington, the nephew of the archbishop: 'My fear is', he told Ambrose St John, 'I can't in honesty and charity take fellows, like young Errington, from Ushaw, if lax youths are my inmates.'[145] Later Newman had been concerned about the prospect of receiving the third son of Sir Robert Throckmorton, who was married to the sister of Cardinal Acton. John Throckmorton needed to prepare for the entrance exams for the Royal Military Academy at Woolwich and Newman was confident he could undertake the two-year course in one year, as a boy had recently been coached successfully for these exams while at the Catholic University.[146] 'I trust we should do justice to him', Newman told the father, but he went on to warn him ominously: 'Something must depend on a young man himself. We find it difficult to make some of our students work—though we are anxious to do so.' And he suggested John write to the other two Downside boys at St Mary's for more detailed information about the house.[147]

In the event the shenanigans at St Mary's did affect Errington for the worse, but not Throckmorton, who arrived in February 1858 and had the stimulus of a clear academic goal. The only other newcomer that year was Osmund Seager, the son of an Oxford convert and friend of Newman who had been considered as a possible lecturer and tutor for the University in 1851. Despite Osmund having been educated at the Jesuit college at Metz, Penny found him 'idle and slang in his talk' and felt he did 'much to lower the tone in the House'.[148] As for the old guard, Charles de la Pasture and Augustus Bethell continued 'the same excellent fellows that they always were'.[149] Besides the disorder in the house, Penny was faced with the financial problems of running St Mary's, which became more acute once Newman's subsidy dried up (after he decided to forgo the rector's salary). 'I have the greatest doubt whether Penny will undertake the speculation' another year, Newman confided to the University Secretary, 'or whether I could recommend him to do so.'[150] He guessed correctly, because Penny chose to revert to his former role as tutor in mathematics. Though Scott had had thoughts about taking charge of St Mary's, he decided he would be unwise to do so. If Arnold was tempted, he would certainly have dismissed the idea on account of St Mary's unruly inmates, for though he was much loved on account of his gentle nature and old-fashioned courtesy and respected as a tutor and lecturer, he had a bad stammer and lacked his father's presence: the residents would have run rings round him.

Cullen seems to have been at his wits' end as to how to resolve the lack of discipline, and he informed Rome that the University would 'collapse if some remedy is not applied'. He complained that Newman allowed the students at St Mary's to go to dances and keep horses for hunting, and that he justified this by saying there should be more liberty at the University than the secondary schools; but ordinary people objected, saying that collections for the University were not necessary to educate young men in dancing and hunting. He had spoken repeatedly about these matters to Newman, but the root of the problem was that he was wedded to Oxford practices.[151] On one of these occasions Cullen spoke to Newman for an hour and a half about his displeasure as regards the state of discipline, but to no effect: as Cullen commented to a third party, 'But then what can I do when Dr Newman just listens to me without speaking, and then says, "I will think about it", and then everything goes on just as it was before'.[152] Certainly Cullen was not alone in being scandalised that the students were allowed to go hunting, but then it should be added that field sports were not encouraged by Newman and that there was only one avid hunter at St Mary's.[153]

Over the summer of 1858 Newman failed to find a replacement for Penny, and by mid-September he had little alternative but to accept Scratton's offer to take over the administration and financial responsibility of St Mary's. Although Newman was grateful for this act of kindness, he had reservations about Scratton's ability to get on with people; and he suspected that Scratton simply hankered after greater standing and influence within the University than being the Secretary and Librarian. For his part, Scratton should have been wary, as he had received from two quarters, both friendly to the University, 'grave complaints about the idleness and general looseness, I don't mean quite immorality', of the students in general, and especially of those at St Mary's, where 'the tone is very lax and the idleness absorbing' and 'smoking all day long, and of the evening in addition given up to a kind of dissipation'.[154] Working as he did from 10 am to 4 pm in the University office, next door to St Patrick's and five minutes' walk from St Mary's, and being privy to most of the correspondence Newman received, Scratton was fully aware of the prevailing atmosphere at St Mary's. In allowing Scratton to rent the house from him, Newman gave him 'the virtual appointment of Dean and Tutors', which meant that only the rector's approval was required.[155] Though Scratton lived out at Kingstown, Newman encouraged him to undertake the tutoring in classics, and thereby to assume a recognised position at St Mary's, but Scratton declined and appointed Arnold instead. On hearing that Scratton intended to dine at St Mary's, Newman begged him to keep a low profile, though he was quickly reassured by Scratton, who stated that 'I am only "servus servorum" and intend to act as such'.[156]

Scratton's choice of dean was the University chaplain William Anderdon, who had previously stayed at St Mary's for fourteen weeks, before moving to St Patrick's 'to turn Dr Syntax for a short while' and resolve the tutorial difficulty there.[157] On paper, the team of Anderdon, Arnold and Penny looked promising, but in reality it struggled to function as one, and within weeks it was tested to breaking point. In effect, those who set the tone at St Mary's were Anderdon and Scratton, and they were intent on trying to outdo Newman by applying a new broom to the house.[158] In the words of the house manager Godwin, 'Scratton commenced to do great things, but not in the way great things are done.' On the financial front, Scratton was keen to prove that the house could be run at a profit—not least because he had agreed to split the profits equally with Anderdon—though no sooner had he taken on the responsibility than he was perplexed at how he could fill it and make it pay its way. Unlike Newman, who did not stint on home comforts and extra tuition for those who needed it, Scratton introduced economies that tested the stomachs of St Mary's; he was, according to Godwin, 'a shocking bad caterer' and bought meat that no-one could their teeth into, so that even Anderdon complained.[159]

But the crucial change at St Mary's concerned the enforcement of a new code of discipline, and to this end Scratton sought to dismiss the eccentric Godwin (along with the other domestic staff). In Scratton's view, the house manager had 'rather extravagant actions which the new regime could not tolerate' and was 'too much in the interest of the young men at the expense of the discipline of the house'.[160] He told Newman that the former lay-brother of the Oratory was 'a great obstacle to discipline in the house. Presently discipline is completely destroying the little hope we still cherish of making an University and unless Catholics are assured we are making a sweeping change in the matter it were just as well to close our doors at once.'[161] But Godwin used his influence with the returning residents (and with Newman), and managed to survive the regime change, but only at the price of restraining himself and submitting 'to the humiliation of being thought a fool'.[162]

Just before the start of term—at Cullen's suggestion—Anderdon promulgated new rules for St Mary's which tightened up the old regulations and removed exceptions. In a circular letter to parents, Anderdon explained that he wished to cultivate 'a Christian and a gentlemanly spirit' by enforcing 'proper discipline'; and that, while observing the distinction between a seminary and a university, he was determined to maintain 'such wholesome rules' as might protect the residents from the 'temptations to idleness, as well as against the graver perils, afforded by a residence in the metropolis'.[163] But the likes of Zamoyski and the younger de Ligne ensured from the outset that rules such as the ban on smoking could not be enforced while they were there, by brazenly flouting them.[164] As Anderdon later admitted, there was no malice about the two, beyond resistance to the rules, but they completely undermined the attempt to turn the house around.[165] None of these developments would have been apparent to Newman on his final, but busy visit[166] to Dublin, when he stayed at St Mary's from 26 October to 4 November, just before the start of term (and at the end of his rectorship), though he should have read something into the fact that Scratton had taken it upon himself to preside at table. During Newman's brief stay the new vice-rector[167] died, after less than a month in office, and Anderdon was made acting vice-rector, with Newman's consent.

From the start of the new session there was a concerted effort to shake the house up academically, and Scratton was soon able to boast that under Anderdon the whole University had taken a studious turn and that there were even improvements at St Mary's, though the students there bridled under the new regime.[168] A show-down at St Mary's was inevitable. It occurred on Saturday, 27th November when Count Zamoyski arrived at St Mary's in hunting pink and top boots after a day in the field, too late for dinner. Contrary to the house rules he insisted on eating in his room, and Godwin served him dinner there, as on previous occasions; but this time Zamoyski demanded wine and sent Godwin to fetch some from Scratton. When Godwin returned with Scratton's refusal and a reminder that he should not be dining in his room, Zamoyski charged down the stairs. He found Scratton in the hall, on the point of leaving for Kingstown, and there the colourfully-attired count repeated his demand on the grounds that he was providing his own meal. A second refusal from Scratton was met with aggressive language and gestures, and as Scratton was stepping outside, Zamoyski called out, 'It is too bad to speculate on our stomachs in this way', and slammed the door behind him.[169]

Re-entering the house immediately, Scratton summoned the dean, explained what had happened, and demanded that Zamoyski be sent away unless he provided an immediate and full apology. This Zamoyski refused to do, and in front of Anderdon he accused Scratton of starving him and demanded an apology of his own. After conferring with Scratton in private, Anderdon informed Zamoyski that he would have to leave the house immediately unless he apologised, pointing out that the affair might cost him his examinations; he explained that a dismissal from the house did not constitute expulsion from the University, and that Zamoyski could sit his exams as an extern, but that he would personally oppose him being granted permission to become one (because he feared the count would create as much trouble outside the house as in). As he still refused to apologise, Zamoyski was asked to leave St Mary's immediately. On hearing of Zamoyski's fate, the younger prince de Ligne rallied to his friend's side and attempted to argue his case before the dean, but Anderdon refused to listen and told de Ligne that he was free to leave with Zamoyski. Feeling honour-bound to his friend and involved in the dispute himself, de Ligne declared that, as he expected his turn would come soon, he was leaving too, and the pair of them moved into a hotel nearby.

Newman no longer held an official position at the University, but he found himself involved in the dispute and its resolution as a result of the well-intentioned, but unhelpful, actions of Ornsby. The first account of the affair to reach Newman came from his most regular correspondent at the University, but it misled Newman by implying that Zamoyski had been removed from the University without a hearing and that the regulations Newman had devised were being treated as a dead letter. From what he could tell, Ornsby thought Anderdon had acted with extreme haste in packing off a young man of respectable character, though idle, when his parents had effectively placed him under Anderdon's care. He reported that Arnold was 'disgusted with proceedings', since no man of spirit could be expected to apologise at once, and that he had tried in vain to reverse Anderdon's decision. But since it was not the time for squabbling, being barely a month after Newman's departure, Arnold and others had let the matter drop.

On hearing this news, Newman wrote back '*as the friend* of the two poor youths' to '*demand* that they [Zamoyski and de Ligne] be righted according to the statutes of the University'. He recognised that the dean had the right to remove them, but argued that 'he could not let them quit his roof till he had brought the matter before the University', whereas Anderdon had let them go without informing the Council. In unguarded confidence, Newman added that 'it was no great offence speaking against Scratton. He is no authority of the University.'[170] Besides asking Ornsby to help him remove the stigma cast on the two students, Newman wrote to the two mothers to assure them that, whatever the cause of their departure, he was certain that their sons had not done anything inconsistent with their characters as gentlemen.

When Ornsby wrote back clarifying that Zamoyski had been dismissed from St Mary's, not the University, Newman realised that this altered the situation, though still he insisted that he wanted no stigma to rest on the two young men. If asked—and he insisted his opinions were not claiming authority—he would say that the simplest way of getting out of the scrape would be for the new vice-rector to write to the two fathers to say that no sort of punishment had been inflicted on them by the University; that there was a disagreement between them and the gentleman who rented St

Mary's; and that the dean felt he could not keep them; but that the two students were hasty in not approaching the vice-rector and, instead, going away. He emphasised that he had 'never doubted Anderdon had a right to send a youth away from *his house*. But (entre nous) it *does* seem *cruel* to cast off two youths into the town'.[171] At Oxford a tutor would have written to the parents, he observed to Ornsby, and this had not been done with Zamoyski. As for Scratton, if Newman had known he had virtually moved into St Mary's and assumed the trappings of authority, he would have objected to him in the house as *lessee*—'but not as Tutor, since that was a recognised position'.[172]

But by now Newman was involved in the affair owing to two blunders committed by Ornsby. In the course of a long discussion with Anderdon, Ornsby had claimed that he was empowered by Newman to call the Council to decide the case, implying that Newman was invoking his former powers as rector; then he compounded the error by passing Newman's letter to himself (of 3 December) on to Anderdon, hoping that it would help Anderdon in summoning the Council. Instead it aggravated the situation because of the phrase 'it was no great offence speaking against Scratton'. Upset at the way Newman appeared to side with the students and not with himself or Anderdon, Scratton complained that Newman had judged the affair without a proper hearing. Zamoyski had grossly insulted him in his own house and, with the agreement of Anderdon, he had told Zamoyski he could no longer stay there. Having agreed to look after St Mary's and bear the financial risk, he regarded himself as master of the house and that the master's place was at the head of his own table. In his reply, Newman begged to differ: Scratton was merely holding the house as a trustee of the University, and this did not imply possession or occupancy. Although persuaded by Newman's explanation, Scratton declared he now wished to shut St Mary's, whatever the cost to the University.[173]

But Anderdon was not to be won over so easily. He wrote Newman a stinging letter accusing him of interference and peremptory conduct, and expressed his displeasure that Newman had not asked him for a statement of facts or an explanation. The tone of Newman's letter (to Ornsby) was hurtful to Scratton, who had met with difficulties at St Mary's and was now unwilling to continue; Anderdon shared his feelings because they had been together in an 'undertaking which certainly smiled on neither of us'.[174] He had sent a summary of the affair to Cullen, who was in Rome. Newman explained to Anderdon that all he had done was to write an unofficial letter to a non-official 'as a friend of the two youths in their parents' absence'. He had hoped Ornsby might take his part in order to assist 'in the clearing of their characters'. He now turned Anderdon's argument on its head by pointing out that Anderdon should have informed *him* of their dismissal, because the parents had originally entrusted their sons to Newman; moreover, he —Newman—was the only person who could write to Zamoyski's parents, since no-one else knew their address. Besides,

> it was not unnatural that on very first hearing the news, my
> interest in the two youths, and my sense of duty towards
> their parents, should have made me write at once and
> strongly to a friend who would interest himself in my place,
> in order to save the parents the distress of suddenly learning
> of a disgrace that had come on their children.[175]

In the event both mothers thanked Newman for breaking the news, as well as apologising for the waywardness and exuberance of their sons, and both expressed concern at how their sons' studies might be concluded. Newman also received a joint letter of apology from Zamoyski and de Ligne, thanking him for his kindness towards them. The two had remained in Dublin for a week—'no one knowing or caring', Newman observed[176]—before returning to the continental mainland. Meanwhile, Newman contacted the dean of the arts faculty to ask how they could help Zamoyski obtain his degree. Newman explained that he felt obliged to take the young man's part, for a number of reasons: firstly, as his mother's representative, 'to whom I conceive I have a *duty*'; secondly, because he thought Zamoyski had been harshly treated; and, thirdly, because a lack of hospitality had been shown him.[177] Only after prolonged and delicate diplomacy was it possible to acquire the certificate of residence from Anderdon which would enable Zamoyski to return to Dublin and sit the scholar's exam. This Zamoyski did in January, and, after paying off his debts, he then obtained permission to read for a degree at London University as a non-resident.

Though the affair could be regarded as a storm in a teacup, the details of this reveal important aspects of Newman's educational priorities. No-one familiar with the student body was unaware that Zamoyski was a difficult young man to deal with. Being idle, spoilt and moody, he required sensitive handling; but the fact that most of Newman's friends took up Zamoyski's cause indicates that they thought he was essentially a good fellow and capable of being won over. Though Newman had previously been on the point of asking Zamoyski to leave the University, his paternal instincts rose to the defence of the young man when he was in trouble. Even at the cost of being misunderstood by friends and collaborators, Newman was prepared to go to great lengths to protect the reputation of a student committed to his care, by seeing to it that his youthful excesses did not sully his good name in perpetuity. What on Newman's part might seem like needless fussiness over legal niceties turned out to be crucial in identifying the incongruity of Scratton's position, the source of much of the confusion.

Though Scratton made up with Newman and offered to continue as the lessee of St Mary's, Newman declined and insisted on taking up Scratton's original offer to surrender the house. Once it was agreed he would hand back the residence on 16 March 1859, Newman thought the only solution for St Mary's was for the University to take it over. Because it was 'one of the Houses' of the arts faculty, he wrote in his capacity as the tenant of No. 6 Harcourt Street (which at present was occupied by St Mary's) to the dean of the faculty to inform him that his—Newman's—possession of the house would terminate in November 1859. Since the house was to be closed as a University residence in March, he asked whether the University wished to rent the house from then until November, and thereafter continue the arrangement with the owner, who was favourable to the University. The alternative was for the University to make other provisions for the dean and students of St Mary's.[178] In the event, after further negotiations,[179] it was agreed to rent the house out to Scratton until November and Anderdon remained on as dean. For his part, Anderdon maintained that his line of action had proved 'experimentally to be right' and assured Cullen that St Mary's would improve, particularly as regards studies, since he had conducted strict exams there the previous term.[180]

When term began in January 1859 there were nine students at St Mary's, four interns proper and five improper,[181] with the prospect of one or two more. The healthy numbers owed something to a circular Anderdon and Scratton had sent to bishops and leading laymen in England and Scotland to encourage them 'to entrust to our charge any youth in whose moral and intellectual advancement you may be interested; and to advertise St Mary's House in the University'.[182] On the financial front Scratton discovered that the house was breaking even (even after paying the two tutors), contrary to what he originally thought, and the residence appeared to have been restored to health—but the change was only apparent: 'this house is a most wretched house and wretchedly managed', Godwin reported to Newman.[183] The departure of de

Ligne and Zamoyski had little effect: the students gradually became more unmanageable, repeatedly coming under censure. Penny, the residential tutor, blamed the unsatisfactory state of affairs on their great aversion to Anderdon and Scratton, particularly the former. By the end of term, Errington was the sole resident in the house; James Welply had decided to move out, and, if not allowed to become an extern, to transfer to Trinity; Robert Loughnan had opted to lodge with the eccentric Professor Robertson; and John Bretherton had been expelled, having obtained leave to go home but instead having gone to the races and remained two nights in Dublin. At Easter, Anderdon resigned from the deanship of St Mary's, ostensibly so that he could devote himself more fully to pastoral work at the University Church, and the new vice-rector personally took in hand what was left of St Mary's.[184] The inevitable occurred in November 1859 when, a year after the end of Newman's resignation as rector of the Catholic University,[185] St Mary's ceased to exist.

The only person who had been there all five years was none other than the house manager, Thomas Godwin, who came to regret staying on after Newman had gone. On Anderdon's departure, he described how 'he has wiped his hands today of the gents he could not get any good of'.[186] Expressing himself in down-to-earth fashion two decades later, he recalled how, once Newman had departed,

> we soon got into a mess. Mr Scratton and Mr Anderdon foolishly, silly creatures, thought they were going to manage so much better than the Father—what could I not say—let their littleness be buried. Count Yamogski [sic] soon told them what a'clock it was when he kicked in the cupboard where Mr S kept the sugar.[187]

Notes

1   Newman to Monsell, 18 November 1855, *LD*, vol. xvii, p. 70. Newman does not mention the reason for the expulsion.

2   Cullen to Barnabò, 28 July 1855 (trans.), *LD*, vol. xvi, p. 516n. This was clearly providential: had Newman been made a bishop, he would certainly not have had the opportunity to undertake many of his projects, particularly in the literary and educational realm.

3   Cullen to Kirby, [October] 1855, *LD*, vol. xvi, p. 551n. In an earlier letter (9 August 1855) Cullen told Kirby that he feared Newman had made a mess of matters at the University, because he had not bothered to consult anyone and because he did not know Ireland. Kirby relayed these observations to Barnabò (19 August) at Propaganda Fide in Rome (*Paul Cullen and his contemporaries*, vol. iii, p. 209). Writing again on 3 September, Cullen complained that Newman had 'the idea of Oxford so much before his mind, that he appears to forget how dangerous its practices are' (Barr, *Paul Cullen*, p. 144).

4   Cullen to Newman, 8 September 1855, *LD*, vol. xvi, p. 543.

5   During Cullen's tenure at the Irish College (1832–50), disciplinary matters were left to Kirby, his vice-rector. Kirby was a born disciplinarian and ensured that the seminary was run strictly and austerely, to the extent that several students wrote to their bishops complaining about ill treatment there (Barr, *Paul Cullen*, p. 145).

6   Newman to Cullen, 25 October 1855, *LD*, vol. xvii, p. 20.

7   At Cullen's request, Leahy, the University's vice-rector, had been drafting rules and regulations since August and he suggested to Cullen that they should give them a trial run (Leahy to Cullen, 6 August & 9 October 1855, DDA, Cullen papers, 45/3/VI(12 & 16)).

8   Leahy complained to Cullen that the Council did not include the deans, who were the ones who had most to do with discipline. He felt that, without rules, all was confusion within the University and that until they were made and put into effect, things would never be right. Yet, he told Cullen, Newman did not wish to be bound by rules which would in any way fetter his 'hitherto uncontrolled action'. He suggested that Cullen should ask Newman to adopt a body of rules for half a year (Leahy to Cullen, 28 November 1855, DDA, Cullen papers, 45/3/VI(19)).

9   The two sections which did not receive approval were those on the affiliation of schools to the University (which they later agreed to) and the

setting up of model and training schools.

10   Towards the end of the synod, on 26 June, Newman wrote an amusing account to Ambrose St John at the Birmingham Oratory: 'I have just come from the Synodal Meeting. I was up before the Bishops over an hour. I was perfectly cool, so much so that I longed to be attacked. [...] However, he [Archbishop MacHale] kept a dead silence, and asked no question whatever. [...] I wished the lion to attack me, I was so cool and so prepared; but you see I am not destined to be a Gérard' (*LD*, vol. xvii, p. 280).

11   Besides the main part of the document, a separate section dealt with the short-term aims of the University and its finances. Some sections of it have already been quoted in Chapter 3. See also Appendix IV.

12   The definitive *Constitution and Statutes of the Catholic University of Ireland* was approved by the bishops and published in 1869. It embodied Newman's Rules and Regulations almost verbatim.

13   This was also the case when the sections on the constitution and discipline appeared in *The Tablet* (16 & 23 August 1856).

14   Newman to Scratton, 4 October 1856, *LD*, vol. xvii, p. 397. Students matriculating at Trinity had to sign a declaration to obey the College statutes (*Royal Commission Trinity* (1853), p. 62).

15   Newman to Wilberforce, 10 June 1856, *LD*, vol. xvii, p. 259. After the publication of the Rules and Regulations the editor of *The Tablet* wrote an article attacking Cullen, and for the next three months the virtues and defects of both Cullen and the Catholic University were aired in the press.

16   Newman to Moriarty, 30 August 1856, *LD*, vol. xvii, p. 368.

17   Newman to Moriarty, 30 August 1856, *LD*, vol. xvii, p. 369. At the start of the second session Scratton had promised Newman he would in future find out the professional aspirations of students entering the University (Scratton to Newman, 6 November 1855, BOA, DP 47 (2))—quite possibly in response to a request from Newman—but it seems that he failed to see the task through.

18   Newman to Todd, 7 October 1857, *LD*, vol. xviii, p. 139. The context of this remark needs explaining: between the gentry and professional classes and the clergy there existed considerable antagonism, while the working and middle classes were much closer to the institutional Church.

19   Quinn first met Newman in Rome. They must have been on friendly terms because from May 1852 until when he acquired 6 Harcourt Street, Newman accepted Quinn's hospitality at No. 16 whenever he was in Dublin. Several years after leaving Dublin, Newman commented that he and Quinn 'did

not get on well together' (Newman to Allies, 14 June 1863, *LD*, vol. xx, p. 469). Previously Newman had commented to Ornsby (15 May 1859, *LD*, vol. xix, p. 132) that 'Dr. Q likes power and intrigue—so it seems to me'.

20   Newman to Moriarty, 9 April 1856, *LD*, vol. xvii, p. 206.

21   A school of agriculture was never opened at the Catholic University. There was one at Queen's College, Galway but the commissioners recommended closing it because it was not a success (*Royal Commission Queen's Colleges* (1858), p. 22).The Benedictines founded an agricultural college in Leopardstown near Dublin in 1867, and it was affiliated to the Catholic University for the period 1874–77; it closed down in 1888.

22   The prospectus for the Engineering School for 1855/56 describes the first-year course and the provision made for the Woolwich entrance exams (DDA, Cullen papers, 45/3/VI(27)).

23   Nevertheless, there were those on medical bursaries who struggled to pay even £20 p.a. (i.e. the £60 fees less the £40 bursary).

24   Newman, University journal, 28 March 1856, BOA, A34.2; Flannery to Newman, 30 March 1856, BOA, DP 30.

25   At Trinity, the total academic fees paid for a degree were £213, £152, £83 or £4 depending on whether the person was a nobleman, fellow-commoner, pensioner or sizar (*Royal Commission Trinity* (1853), p. 214).

26   Newman to Flannery, 29 March 1856, *LD*, vol. xvii, p. 196.

27   Newman, University journal, 28 March 1856, BOA, A34.2.

28   Newman to Flannery, 31 March 1856, *LD*, vol. xvii, p. 200.

29   Flannery to Newman, 2 April 1856, BOA, DP 30.

30   Newman to Flannery, 29 July 1856, *LD*, vol. xvii, p. 333.

31   Newman to Flannery, 27 September 1856, *LD*, vol. xvii, pp. 389–90.

32   Flannery to Newman, 29 September 1856, BOA, DP 30.

33   Quinn, memorandum, [1856], BOA, DP 31.

34   Quinn, memorandum, [1857/58], BOA, DP 31.

35   Newman, memorandum, n.d. (on reverse of Quinn to Newman, 29 October 1856); Newman, memorandum, n.d., BOA, DP 31.

36   Cullen to Kirby, 15 January 1856, quoted in Barr, *Paul Cullen*, p. 145.

37   Cullen to Kirby, 13 December 1856, quoted in Barr, *Paul Cullen*, p. 145.

38   The commissioners reported that since the 9 pm curfew was unenforceable and students' presence rarely checked at dinner, the whole day from 2 pm until midnight was effectively at their disposal; apart from Sunday chapel, the weekend was also unoccupied. Serious offences such as gambling,

fornication, or 'inveterate idleness' were punished by students being gated or rusticated. Though the tutorial system allowed many points of contact between teacher and pupil, the amount of freedom allowed great scope for idleness, extravagance and dissipation. 'The easy intercourse of College life is apt to degenerate into lounging and indolent habits, and from these the transition is sometimes rapid to gambling and vice' (*Royal Commission Oxford* (1852), pp. 20–2).

39 Newman to H. Wilberforce, 11 November 1856, *LD*, vol. xvii, pp. 444–5.
40 *CUG* 1 (1 June 1854), pp. 2, 7.
41 *CUG* 28 (7 December 1854), p. 217.
42 *CUG* 42 (5 April 1855), p. 409.
43 Report for the Year 1854–55, *MC*, pp. 33–4.
44 Newman to Mackenzie, 7 August 1856 (via Scratton), *LD*, vol. xvii, p. 343n.
45 Unavoidable, however, was the status of the non-Catholic medical students, who could only join the Catholic University as auditors.
46 See his article 'University and King's Colleges in London', *Gazette* 43 (3 May 1855).
47 Senate proceedings, 15 January 1857, *MC*, p. 338.
48 Senate proceedings, 15 January 1857, *MC*, p. 338.
49 Statute, *LD*, vol. xvii, p. 498n.
50 Senate proceedings, 15 January 1857, *MC*, p. 340.
51 The University of London effectively became an 'open' or distance-learning university in 1858, when the stipulation of attendance at affiliated institutions was dropped. The result was that only 15% of those who graduated were educated there. A campaign to turn it back into a teaching university eventually made it not just a metropolitan university, but a national and imperial one.
52 The commissioners investigating Trinity pointed out that no provision was made for this latter group and recommended that licensed halls or hostels be established for them with the same obligation to keep regular hours as those living in college (*Royal Commission Trinity* (1852), p. 63).
53 McDowell & Webb, *Trinity College Dublin*, pp. 115–17.
54 Senate proceedings, 15 January 1857, *MC*, p. 342.
55 For Newman, affiliation to a non-Catholic establishment was only possible on condition that the University was given the right of having its own examiners in subjects such as history and metaphysics, since 'examinations and examiners every where determine the reading of the students and the grinding of the Tutors. These great subjects, to secure the real knowledge

of which is one great reason for setting up a University, will either be taught and learned wrongly, or hurried over in generalities, unless we have Examiners of our own on them' (Newman to Monsell, 24 November 1856, *LD*, vol. xvii, p. 459).

56   Newman to Lyons, 4 July 1857, *LD*, vol. xviii, p. 77.

57   Newman to Woodlock, 23 February 1868, *LD*, vol. xxiv, p. 40. See also Newman to Woodlock, 11 June 1865, *LD*, vol. xxi, pp. 491–2.

58   Newman to Ornsby, 19 January 1859, *LD*, vol. xix, p. 23. Newman's main concern with this line of proceeding was that the nationalist press might raise an outcry against the plan, once made public, and scupper its chances by calling for subscriptions to cease; it was also unlikely to be supported by nationalist professors such as Robert Lyons and Eugene O'Curry. The alternative approach was give degrees out boldly and ignore the threat of prosecution, but Cullen was unlikely to allow this. Newman preferred the first plan, but thought that neither would work because of the division of Irish opinion.

59   The parent of an extern at St Patrick's interpreted the new rule to mean that his son was now deprived of the 'advantage of reading with a tutor' (precisely the reverse of what Newman intended) and protested that the new rule would either result in the externs being left entirely dependent on the lectures, putting them at a great disadvantage to the interns, or else it would encourage them to seek private—Protestant—tutors at Trinity, where almost all of them were to be found, thus defeating one of the chief objects for which the Catholic University was founded. He asked whether he could pay extra for a private tutor from the Catholic University (J. Hanly to Scratton, 14 April 1857, BOA, DP 44/13).

60   Newman to Scratton, 1 December 1857, *LD*, vol. xviii, p. 191.

61   Newman to Dunne, 1 May 1857, *LD*, vol. xviii, p. 26. This clarification was in response to Dunne's enquiry as to whether the recent statute meant that an extern living at nearby Merrion Square could avail himself of tutoring at St Patrick's by paying his £10 p.a. (Dunne to Newman, 1 May 1857, BOA, DP 44/14).

62   Newman to Butler, 15 November 1857, *LD*, vol. xviii, p. 172.

63   Newman to Butler, 19 November 1857, *LD*, vol. xviii, p. 180. Section 21 of the Rules and Regulations decreed that the Council could, under special circumstances, allow auditors to become members of the University and count the terms they had attended lectures towards the scholar's exam.

64   *Idea of a university*, pp. 144–5.

65 Newman to Scott, 28 November 1857, *LD*, vol. xviii, p. 188.

66 Scratton to Newman, 30 November 1857, *LD*, vol. xviii, p. 192n.

67 Newman to Miss Holmes, 25 May 1862, *LD*, vol. xx, p. 200. Newman came to realise that he had made a mistake in appointing Scratton. Back in 1851 he had described him to Cullen as a 'man of pleasing manners, about 30—very fond of boys and of tuition—and much given to the classics. He is made for University life' (Newman to Cullen, 28 April 1851, *LD*, vol. xiv, p. 270).

68 *The Irish Catholic University Prospectus, 1858-9* (Dublin, 1858), p. 12, UCDA, spec. coll. 34.G.2/1. In fact there were seven ways of belonging to the faculty, as auditors were allowed, in special circumstances, to reside in a collegiate house provided they submitted to the *house* regulations, as distinct from the University regulations.

69 Newman had earlier taken Scratton to task for not publishing the degree results sooner (Newman to Scratton, 25 July 1855, quoted in J. Jackson, 'John Henry Newman: the origins and application of his educational ideas', Ph.D., Leicester [?], 1968 [BOA], p. 113).

70 Newman to Quinn, 16 January 1857, *LD*, vol. xviii, p. 498.

71 Newman to Quinn, 24 January 1857, *LD*, vol. xvii, p. 509.

72 Newman to Dunne, 27 September 1856, *LD*, vol. xvii, p. 389.

73 Newman to Butler, 19 November 1857, *LD*, vol. xviii, p. 180.

74 Hayden & MacDermott (on behalf of the medical faculty) to Newman, [1857], DDA, Cullen Papers 45/3/VIII(19). While Newman had been trying for three years to set up a medical lodging house, but in vain, some Protestants had taken up the idea and set up a medical residence of their own (Newman to Leahy, 16 October, 1857, *LD*, vol. xviii, p. 62).

75 Hayden & MacDermott to Newman, [1857], DDA, Cullen Papers 45/3/VIII(19). The Trinity commissioners had suggested bringing their medical students within collegiate and religious discipline by introducing some form of tutorial control, such as by asking them to pay £2 for guardianship (*Royal Commission Trinity* (1852), p. 63).

76 The commissioners investigating the Queen's Colleges found that parents were unwilling to confide their sons to private lodging houses. To remedy the situation, they recommended halls of residence be founded at Cork and Galway (*Royal Commission Queen's Colleges* (1858), p. 30).

77 Hayden & MacDermott to Newman, [1857], DDA, Cullen Papers 45/3/VIII(19).

78 The account given in Meenan, *Cecilia Street: the Catholic University Medical*

School, 1855–1931 (p. 23) is not entirely accurate, as it states that the house only survived for one year.

79   Newman to Pollen, 29 December 1856, *LD*, vol. xvii, p. 488. Those he named were two cradle Catholics, the Duke of Norfolk and Charles Langdale, MP for Knaresborough, and four converts, Lord Charles Campden, Lord Rudolph Feilding, Sir John Simeon (who had already given money) and Pollen's brother.

80   Newman to Pollen, 10 January 1857, *LD*, vol. xvii, pp. 490–1.

81   Capes to Newman, 3 February 1857, *LD*, vol. xvii, p. 514n.

82   Newman to Hope-Scott, 28 March 1857, vol. *LD*, xvii, p. 548.

83   Newman to Dodsworth, 26 July 1857, *LD*, vol. xviii, p. 99.

84   Newman to Blount, 13 June 1857, *LD*, vol. xviii, p. 54.

85   Newman to Pollen, 17 November 1857, *LD*, vol. xviii, p. 173. Yet, a year later, Newman told the Oratorian John Flanagan, 'I really think the University is growing and will grow' (31 May 1858, *LD*, vol. xviii, p. 361).

86   Newman to Pollen, 26 November 1857, *LD*, vol. xviii, p. 187.

87   Newman to Ornsby, 20 February 1858, *LD*, vol. xviii, pp. 264–5. Though Newman was sceptical about the power of attention of those attending after a day's work, he thought it is better that young men 'should be awake or asleep in a lecture room, than in many other places which they might otherwise frequent'—and certainly better than going to Trinity.

88   'Public lectures at the University', *CUG* 42 (5 April 1855), pp. 420–2.

89   Newman to Allies, 6 July 1856, *LD*, vol. xvii, p. 311.

90   The Pope had granted Newman only three years' absence from Birmingham, which meant that by the summer of 1857 this time had elapsed. Newman had asked for seven months per year for three years (Newman to Wiseman, 5 June 1854; Newman to Walker, 8 January 1855, *LD*, vol. xvi, pp. 146, 345).

91   Newman to Leahy, 17 August 1857, *LD*, vol. xviii, p. 120.

92   For Cullen this was another example of Newman's apparent desire 'to make everything secular' (Cullen to Kirby, 8 July August 1857, quoted in Barr, *Paul Cullen*, p. 169). Newman considered that of the four priests at the University, only O'Reilly was suitable for the post of pro-vice-rector, though Quinn would have been acceptable (Newman to Leahy, 1 November 1857; Newman to H. Wilberforce, 2 November 1957, *LD*, vol. xviii, pp. 160–1). Laurence Forde, Professor of Canon Law, had been acting vice-rector during Michaelmas term 1856 and January 1857, and Cullen wanted to

appoint him, but Newman found him '*intolerable*—coarse, vulgar, unreal, and *solitary*' (Newman to St John, 16 January 1857, *LD*, vol. xvii, p. 499) and assured Leahy that he was very unpopular—'I am grieved to have to believe that even a stranger would be more popular than he'—and blocked his appointment (Newman to Leahy, [23 May] 1857, *LD*, vol. xviii, p. 47). Newman later confided to a friend that to appoint Forde vice-rector would be 'simply inadmissible. I should be a traitor to the University if I concurred in such a choice' (Newman to Monsell, 9 October 1857, *LD*, vol. xviii, p. 140).

93 Cullen to Kirby, 14 February 1857, quoted in Rigney, 'Bartholomew Woodlock', vol. i, p. 31.

94 The *consilium abeundi* (literally 'advice to leave') was a term in common usage, particularly at Germany universities, for a punishment whereby the convicted student was not formally expelled, but unofficially required to leave the university. At some institutions, re-matriculation was possible after a year; besides, a student in this position was allowed to register at any other university, as *consilium abeundi* did not carry any imputation on the morals of the student: it was generally inflicted for youthful imprudence. Expulsion, the ultimate sanction, was for more serious offences, and meant that the student could not matriculate elsewhere.

95 O'Reilly to Newman, 16 December 1857, *LD*, vol. xviii, p. 206n.

96 Newman, memorandum, 11 December 1857, *LD*, vol. xviii, pp. 206–7n. The recommendation Newman had received from the Bishop of Derry described Mulholland as a young man of excellent character who had 'attended strictly to his religious duties' (Kelly to Newman, 4 July 1856, BOA, DP 30).

97 Newman to O'Reilly, 18 December 1857, *LD*, vol. xviii, pp. 208–9.

98 Newman to Butler, 17 December 1857 (not sent), *LD*, vol. xviii, p. 206.

99 Newman to Molloy, 26 December 1857, *LD*, vol. xviii, pp. 214–15.

100 Newman to Molloy, 26 December 1857, *LD*, vol. xviii, p. 215.

101 Newman to Mulholland, 26 December 1857, *LD*, vol. xviii, p. 215.

102 Newman to Flannery, 11 January 1858, *LD*, vol. xviii, p. 227.

103 Newman to Molloy, 11 September 1859, *LD*, vol. xix, pp. 211–12.

104 Newman to Ornsby, 31 December 1857, *LD*, vol. xviii, p. 217.

105 Newman to Ornsby, 5 January 1858, *LD*, vol. xviii, pp. 220–1.

106 Newman to Hope-Scott, 24 December 1857, *LD*, vol. xviii, p. 214.

107 C. Maxwell, *A history of Trinity College, Dublin, 1591–1892* (Dublin, 1946),

pp. 241–2.

[108] Dunne to Newman, 25 March 1858, *LD*, vol. xviii, pp. 305–6n. On being asked by Bethell not to insult the Mayor, one of the externs from St Patrick's apparently replied 'that he did not give a damn for the Lord Mayor' (Meenan, *Centenary history*, p. 10).

[109] Newman to Dunne, 27 March 1858, *LD*, vol. xviii, p. 306.

[110] Newman to Dunne, 27 March 1858, *LD*, vol. xviii, p. 306.

[111] The professors wrote a memorial to the four archbishops about how damaging the lack of a vice-rector was to the University, and about how the absence of personal supervision and prompt attention was much felt when the rector was away, and created 'considerable embarrassment' ([1858], DDA, Cullen papers, 45/2/24).

[112] Newman to Dunne, 27 March 1858, *LD*, vol. xviii, p. 307.

[113] Meenan, *Centenary history*, p. 11.

[114] Minutes of the Faculty of Philosophy and Letters, 26 March 1858, UCDA, CU4.

[115] Newman to Ornsby, 30 March 1858 (draft version), *LD*, vol. xviii, p. 309n.

[116] Newman to Bellasis, 6 April 1858, *LD*, vol. xviii, p. 314.

[117] Newman to O'Reilly, 22 April 1858, *LD*, vol. xviii, p. 329.

[118] Dunne commented that one of the deans (Flannery, no doubt) was 'wholly unfit for his office' and that no greater misfortune could befall the University than his becoming vice-rector (Dunne to Newman, 31 May 1858, BOA, C.6.26/386).

[119] Newman to Flannery, 23 May 1857, *LD*, vol. xviii, pp. 45–6.

[120] Newman to Flannery, 18 November 1857 (second letter), *LD*, vol. xviii, p. 177.

[121] Note added to Newman to Flannery, 18 November 1857 (second letter), *LD*, vol. xviii, p. 177n.

[122] Newman to Flannery, 19 November 1857 (quoting from the minutes of the faculty meeting on 19 November), *LD*, vol. xviii, p. 181.

[123] Newman to Flannery, 13 May 1858, *LD*, vol. xviii, p. 346.

[124] Some boys at the school paid £10 p.a., others £6, and some attended free. Church boys generally boarded, funded by scholarships from the archbishop of Dublin.

[125] Ornsby to Newman, 4 (continued on 5) January 1858, BOA, DP 31.

[126] Newman to Ornsby 13 February 1858, *LD*, vol. xviii, p. 254.

[127] Newman to Ornsby 12 March 1858, *LD*, vol. xviii, p. 296.

128 From all accounts, the Carmelite house was even more like a seminary, since Quinn himself did not regard it as a *bona fide* collegiate house. There was a prospect that Bennet would open a new residence for students in Lower Dominick Street, but he spoke of the students being escorted to lectures; this fact alone suggests a seminary-like arrangement.

129 Ornsby to Newman, 28 March 1858, BOA, DP 31.

130 Ornsby to Newman, 28 March 1858, BOA, DP 31.

131 Quinn to Newman, 11 April 1858, BOA, DP 31.

132 When Newman arrived in Dublin in 1854 he had found the house in the possession of the University; he had furnished it for students, but soon found that it was burdened with a large annual payment. The number of students was initially insufficient to meet costs and in the first year a debt of £500 was incurred, with the likelihood that it would continue. Having had nothing to do with incurring this debt, only trying to turn it to account, Newman had argued that, if this sum had to be spent, it was better to get something for it than nothing, hence his scheme for medical bursaries, which created no further expense for the University. See pp. 298–9.

133 Newman to Quinn, 12 April 1858, *LD*, vol. xviii, pp. 318–19.

134 Newman to Scratton, 25 July 1858, *LD*, vol. xviii, pp. 423–4.

135 Newman's difficulties are put in perspective by Quinn's problems as first Bishop of Brisbane. His episcopate was marked by constant disputes arising from his authoritarian style and tendency to micro-manage his diocese; his efforts to encourage Irish immigration caused sectarian hostility, aggravated by his quip that the colony could be called 'Quinn's land' (*Australian dictionary of biography*).

136 Newman to Allies, 12 November 1857, *LD*, vol. xviii, p. 170.

137 Scratton to Newman, 23 September 1858, Letter book of University Secretary 1858–60, DDA, 106/112. Flannery threw himself into his new work as a bishop, which was considerable in the post-famine years, but within four years he was burnt out; he moved to Paris for health reasons, while his diocese was managed by three consecutive coadjutor bishops until 1891, when he died in Paris.

138 Augustus Bethell and Charles de la Pasture also gained honours in their licentiate that summer, while James Molloy gained a pass (Rigney, 'Bartholomew Woodlock', vol. ii, p. 321).

139 Newman to Keane, 31 August 1858, *LD*, vol. xviii, p. 452.

140 Leahy apologised for the mistake, saying that it had occurred through inadvertence; but later (in 1872) Newman commented that it was not an

act of inadvertence, for the reason that 'Cullen *never* considered that Deanship a mere headship of a house, but that the occupant was 'Dean of the University', and in his gift, as much as the office of Sub-rector' (*LD*, vol. xviii, p. 477n). The appointment was announced in *The Times*.

[141] Newman had heard from Renouf that the Queen's University spent about £1450 annually on examiners. He considered, 'it being an old idea of mine, of near 30 years standing, that the Examiners, at least *some* of them, should be permanent, paid well, and an influential element of a University system', whether they might deal with the lack of funds and students by 'retrenching Professors, or turning them, (if they will consent to be turned,) into Examiners' (Newman to O'Reilly, 9 July 1858, *LD*, vol. xviii, p. 404).

[142] The students at St Mary's were the younger Bethell, de la Pasture, the two princes de Ligne, Errington, Fraser, Seager, Throckmorton, White and Zamoyski.

[143] Arnold to Clough, 19 October 1858, *Letters of Thomas Arnold*, p. 92.

[144] Penny to Newman, 27 May 1858, *LD*, vol. xviii, p. 369n.

[145] Newman to St John, 29 June 1857, *LD*, vol. xviii, p. 69.

[146] In 1856 P. F. Gallwey passed the entrance exams for the College of Military Engineering at Woolwich. Adverts were placed in the Catholic press in October 1856 to the effect that pupils were prepared at the Catholic University for the entrance exams of the Royal Artillery and Royal Military Academy at Woolwich.

[147] Newman to Throckmorton 12 November 1857, *LD*, vol. xviii, p. 171. The ex-Downside pupils were Henry Fraser and Charles de la Pasture.

[148] Meenan, *Centenary history*, p. 11.

[149] Penny to Newman, 27 May 1858, *LD*, vol. xviii, p. 369n.

[150] Newman to Scratton, 16 June 1858, *LD*, vol. xviii, p. 383.

[151] Cullen to Barnabò, 31 August 1858 [trans.], *LD*, vol. xviii, p. 451n. By 1858, the struggle with MacHale had unnerved Cullen to the point that he suffered another physical and mental breakdown, which required a protracted convalescence of some seven months in Rome (*ODNB*).

[152] F. Rogers to E. Rogers, 1863 (from a dinner-table conversation with W. G. Ward), quoted in F. Rogers, *Letters of Lord Blachford*, ed. G. E. Marindin (London, 1896), p. 249.

[153] The commissioners investigating Oxford remarked that hunting was a cause of great expense, since it seldom cost less than four guineas a day, and they urged that it be brought under greater control (*Royal Commission*

Oxford (1852), p. 24).

[154] Scratton to Newman, 27 March 1858, BOA, C.6.26/357.

[155] Newman to Ornsby, 6 December 1858 (second letter), LD, vol. xviii, p. 531.

[156] Scratton to Newman, 16 September 1858, BOA, DP 29. In a letter to James Molloy two months later, however, Scratton describes himself as the 'commander in chief' of St Mary's (13 November 1858, Letter book of University Secretary 1858–60, DDA, 106/112).

[157] Anderdon to Newman, 19 October 1856, BOA, DP 30.

[158] Even before term began Godwin noticed that Anderdon and Scratton 'both seem determined to work a reformation' (Godwin to Newman, 6 October 1858, BOA, C.6.26/488).

[159] Godwin to Newman, 19 April 1859, BOA, DP 29.

[160] Scratton to Newman, 12 & 27 September 1858, BOA, DP 29.

[161] Scratton to Newman, 29 September 1858, BOA, DP 29.

[162] Godwin to Newman, 19 April 1859, BOA, DP 29.

[163] Circular letter, 18 September 1858, DDA, Cullen papers, 45/3/IX(11). One additional rule was that which required students to go to Confession monthly and to take the dean a 'billet of attendance'.

[164] Within a week of the new academic year Anderdon met with resistance to the rules from the 'foreign potentates'. Nevertheless he told Cullen of his determination that they should 'either conform or *leave*' (Anderdon to Cullen, 10 November 1858, DDA, Cullen papers, 45/3/IX(14)). Godwin reported to Newman, 'Mr Anderdon finds it very hard to manage the gents' and that all was not well: 'It is an altered house. The present cook is a specimen of every thing that is disagreeable' (26 November 1858, BOA, C.6.26).

[165] Ornsby to Newman, 5 December 1858, BOA, DP 29.

[166] Besides packing his belongings and paying farewell visits, Newman gave three inaugural lectures: 'Discipline of Mind' on 2 November, 'Literature' on 3 November, and 'Christianity and Medical Science' on 4 November. After the last, he distributed prizes and gold medals to the successful medics.

[167] This was Matthew Kelly, Professor of Ecclesiastical History at Maynooth, who had originally turned down the post on grounds of health. Newman attended his funeral at Maynooth, where he spent three nights.

[168] Scratton to Molloy, 13 November 1858, Letter book of University Secretary 1858–60, DDA, 106/112.

[169] Ornsby to Newman, 2 & 5 December 1858, BOA, DP 29.

[170] Newman to Ornsby, 3 December 1858 *LD*, vol. xviii, p. 526.

[171] Newman to Ornsby, 6 December 1858 (first letter), *LD*, vol. xviii, p. 530.

[172] Newman to Ornsby, 6 December 1858 (second letter), *LD*, vol. xviii, p. 531.

[173] Newman to Scratton, 8 December 1858; Scratton to Newman, 9 December 1858, *LD*, vol. xviii, p. 537.

[174] Anderdon to Newman, 7 December 1858, *LD*, vol. xviii, p. 535.

[175] Newman to Anderdon, 8 December 1858, *LD*, vol. xviii, p. 536.

[176] Newman to Flanagan, 5 January 1859, *LD*, vol. xix, p. 5.

[177] Newman to Stewart, 9 December 1858, *LD*, vol. xviii, p. 538.

[178] Newman to Stewart, 29 December 1858 (second letter), *LD*, vol. xviii, pp. 557–8.

[179] The arts faculty hoped Anderdon would undertake the financial responsibility of St Mary's as well as the collegiate discipline of the students, but Anderdon refused initially. Since Newman had declined to accept Scratton's offer without being backed by the faculty, they eventually agreed to the motion proposed by Arnold, and seconded by Renouf, that Scratton be allowed to do so provided that 'the *sole* charge of the discipline and government of the House is centred in the Dean, and not interfered with by any person' (Minutes of the Faculty of Philosophy and Letters, 11 & 22 January 1859, UCDA, CU4).

[180] Anderdon to Cullen, 8 January 1859, DDA, Cullen papers, 45/3/X(1).

[181] The interns proper were J. Bretherton, G. Errington, R. Loughlan and J. Welply; the quasi-interns J. Dillon, J. Hanly, Lynch, D. O'Reardon and one other.

[182] Circular letter, December 1858, Letter book of University Secretary 1858–60, DDA, 106/112. The letter seems to have attracted Loughlan from Stonyhurst and Welply from Oscott.

[183] Godwin to Newman, 10 February 1859, BOA, C.6.26/560.

[184] Anderdon to Gartlan, Palm Sunday 1859, DDA, Cullen Papers, 45/3/X (7).

[185] Technically speaking, Newman was rector until the beginning of August 1859, when the bishops formally accepted his resignation.

[186] Godwin to Newman, 19 April 1859, BOA, DP 29.

[187] Godwin to an unnamed Oratorian, 1879, quoted in Trevor, *Light in winter*, p. 65.

7 THE UNIVERSITY: CHANGE AND DECAY

A LL ACCOUNTS OF the development—or decay—of the University in the two decades after Newman's departure show that as an institution it failed to take root. But was this entirely due to the external difficulties that existed, or was it in part due to faulty design, poor management, or the pursuit of unrealistic objectives during Newman's rectorate? This question has been skipped over in most studies of the Catholic University, as no-one has taken up the task of analysing adequately the trajectory of the University after Newman's departure or of assessing the views of those involved in the enterprise as to why it did not prosper. No-one has ascertained whether Newman's structures and working principles were jettisoned immediately after his departure or allowed to wither gradually; whether they were understood and admired, or simply dismissed and quickly forgotten; whether his arrangements suited the times or whether there were others better adapted to the Irish situation; or what the professoriate thought of the changes implemented after his departure. Fortunately, there is no shortage of primary sources with which to address these questions.

Newman's departure from the Catholic University in November 1858 was a severe blow for a young institution that had depended so heavily on the inspiration and energy of its founding rector, and, as a result, over the next two decades its survival became precarious. In the short term, as the supply of overseas students dried up and the English element of the professoriate drained away, the University became solidly Irish in composition and middle- to lower-middle-class in intake.[1] Nearly three academic years were to pass before a new rector could be found, and during this time the University dwindled. The vice-rector during this *interregnum* was the elderly James Gartlan, a former rector of the moribund Irish College in Salamanca, who had arrived at the end of November 1858 and taken over from Anderdon, the temporary vice-rector. During Gartlan's first year in office there were thirty-six matriculated students in the arts faculty, but by the second year the number had dropped to below thirty, with barely twenty in residence at any one time. Gartlan was an able man, though not in good health, and on the whole acquitted himself well in what was a difficult situation, but being a stop-gap he was reluctant to take the initiative or assume responsibility for a situation that was not of his making. When a new rector was appointed in April 1861 Gartlan immediately retired; he was not replaced.[2]

The mood within the University after Newman's departure is conveyed in one of Gartlan's memoranda, which describes the problems he encountered and how he set about remedying them. In the absence of any clear authority, a restless spirit of discussion and debate had set in among the professoriate, and he realised that their attention had to be directed away from the governance of the University and back to their primary duty—teaching. To this end he stipulated that individuals must stop sending unauthorised reports about the University to the press, as they were inevitably partisan and merely fuelled the debates. In dealing with the collegiate houses, he tried to ensure that each had a tutor that could act as sub-regent to the dean, supporting him in his duties and keeping discipline. He asked for clarification on the student's daily timetable, from his rising to going to bed, and requested that each tutor fix the times of lectures to be attended by his students.[3] This desire to sort out problems by regulating timetables, and the underlying assumption that every hour of the day had to be spoken for, drew heavily from his experience in overseeing a seminary.

The appointment of the forty-two-year-old priest Bartholomew Woodlock as rector in April 1861 breathed new life into the University, and when the new academic year began, numbers in the arts faculty had risen to eighty.[4] So delighted was Cullen that he wrote to Rome to say that if Woodlock had been rector from the start 'in every probability' the University would now be competing with Trinity both in numbers and income.[5] In a similar vein he wrote to Kirby, his most trusted ally in Rome: 'Dr Woodlock is working hard for the University. He has done more in a few months than Dr. Newman did in years. He has got twice as many students as were ever in the University and I think he has got the money. [...] Dr. Newman thought to act as an oracle—he was to sit in state to do nothing and others were to work'.[6]

Woodlock was a cultured man, with a breadth of vision, considerable charm and great tact. He had just completed seven years as president of All Hallows, the seminary college for the missions, where he had shown his gifts as an administrator and a man of initiative. By 1863 he had boosted the diocesan collections for the University to break-even point, established three feeder schools, known as Catholic University Schools, and acquired ten acres of land at Drumcondra, on the north side of Dublin, as a new site for the University. But despite these early successes and the optimism they generated, the symptoms of health were only temporary. The feeder schools failed to supply the University with many students—only thirty-four entered in six years (of whom just eighteen were interns) and at a cost to the University of nearly £3000—and the announcement of a rail-route across the Drumcondra site scotched the expansion plan and led to a crushing loss of £10,000. The two losses more than offset the gains in the collections, and the report of the University Finance Committee in September 1863 recommended slashing annual expenditure from £8300 to £5000. Once teaching staff were made redundant and buildings closed, the

Catholic University effectively forfeited its claim to be a university-in-the-making, and reconciled itself to the status of a college, with the prospect of forging links with a degree-granting institution, either through affiliation or incorporation.

For fifteen years the University was kept alive by such hopes and the possibility of government recognition and support. Negotiations began with Russell's Liberal government for a supplemental charter incorporating the Catholic University as a college into an enlarged Queen's University, but these came to an end in 1866;[7] then hopes for an officially recognized Catholic University without government subsidy were extinguished when the scheme was withdrawn by Disraeli's Conservative government in 1868. Next, Gladstone's Liberal government came near to clinching a solution in 1873, but the Bill for affiliation to a Dublin University, along with Trinity College and two of the Queen's Colleges, was defeated by a majority of three in Parliament (and precipitated the fall of the government). A second attempt at affiliation to a Dublin University, this time with the Disraeli government, failed in 1877; and a scheme to unite the Catholic University with Maynooth to form a new university called St Patrick's was also unsuccessful. Finally, in August 1879 Parliament passed the Royal University Act, which abolished the Queen's University (but not the three Colleges), and in its place established the Royal University of Ireland as an examining body entitled to grant degrees. This took place at the very end of Woodlock's long rectorate (1861–79), by which time there were nearly as many professors as students and the Catholic University funds had all but dried up. In 1882, when it was close to extinction, the arts faculty of the Catholic University was reconstituted as University College and made a constituent part of the Royal University of Ireland. A year later the College was taken over by the Jesuits and numbers rose at once. In 1909 University College and the Catholic University Medical School were absorbed into

University College Dublin, which became part of the newly formed National University of Ireland.

Before examining the questions raised at the start of this chapter, it is worth setting the scene by looking at a letter written (anonymously) by Tom Arnold in the *Weekly Register* (5 October 1861) about the obstacles then facing the Catholic University, which identifies five ways in which its growth was inhibited. Though there has been no lack of historians who have tried to explain why the University failed to take off, Arnold's letter merits closer scrutiny as a contemporary attempt—by a former inspector of schools—to explain its lack of success. At the top of Arnold's list is the one single factor that everyone connected with the Catholic University would have agreed upon putting first: namely, the lack of a charter for conferring degrees.[8] More interesting are Arnold's second and third reasons, which were respectively: the absence of 'a Catholic proprietary such as sustains Oxford and Cambridge';[9] and the influence which Trinity exerted over the Irish Catholic gentry and professional classes. What Arnold was alluding to was the low take-up of the University by these social groups, especially in Dublin where the well-to-do families continued to patronise Trinity.[10] Surprisingly, this included even families with close ties to the Catholic University.[11] The reason the professional and upper-middle classes were not won over to the Catholic University is complicated. In part it had to do with their attitude to the British government and their desire to be part of the ruling and educated class; but it was also due to their fractious relationship with the higher clergy—the latter exemplified by Cullen's trenchant opposition to lay involvement in the University project. The fourth difficulty that Arnold mentions was that a university education was not a stipulation for public office or the liberal professions, which meant that there were few who could afford what seemed a luxury.

Arnold's fifth and final explanation for the University's failure has escaped the notice of most historians, but is an important one: it was the lack of understanding of the *purpose* of a university education, and what Arnold calls the 'sheer contentment' parents felt with 'mere collegiate education'[12]—a remark which only becomes clear when set against the educational background of the time. When, in 1840, the University of London gained its charter enabling it to act as an examining body for teaching institutions that wished to affiliate, seven Catholic colleges—six English and one Irish—did so immediately, and others followed soon after.[13] The exams supplied a stimulus for college studies, which were realigned to coincide with the Matriculation and BA syllabuses, and, after 1859, the Intermediate exam. Before the foundation of the Catholic University—and in the absence of any university education suitable for Catholics—the Catholic colleges in the United Kingdom had sought to retain lay boys for higher studies by allowing them to follow the first two years of seminary training, the philosophy course. Tertiary education was most developed at Stonyhurst, which had up to fifty young men (including some from Ireland) aged between seventeen and twenty-one in its 'philosophy department': some studying philosophy proper, some following London University courses, and others completing their education under private tuition.[14] These 'gentlemen philosophers', as they were called, provided colleges like Stonyhurst with a useful stream of income, and naturally the colleges were reluctant to see them leave for the Catholic University—just as educated clergymen like Robert Dunne of St Laurence's were reluctant to surrender their most able pupils to the University. This explains Newman's assessment of the situation, which he confided to the dean of the arts faculty: 'I think we must depend on our own selves, and on none other, under Providence. Affiliated schools will not help us, that is their conductors will not. […] Every school is for itself and no one else. We are our own best friends'.[15]

The Report *of 1859*

In the same way that Arnold's article provides a useful contemporary analysis of the problems faced by the Catholic University, so a report produced not long after Newman's departure reveals much about the state of the University at the time. Cullen had summoned a meeting of the whole episcopate for the summer of 1859 to discuss the governance of the University and the appointment of a new rector, and in advance of the gathering he asked the Senate to compile a report. What resulted was the 150-page *Report on the condition and circumstances of the Catholic University of Ireland*, composed by a committee which analysed in forthright manner every aspect of the University and recommended copious changes, including several bold ones. Published a year after Newman's departure—and two years after his last proper year of residence in Dublin—the *Report* provides a timely verdict on Newman's arrangements, albeit coloured by the difficulties the University was then experiencing. Its authors were six Irishmen—Myles O'Reilly (a lay member of the original University Committee, and one of the subcommittee of three), John O'Hagan (Lecturer in Political Economy), Dr Laurence Forde (Professor of Canon Law), Dr Andrew Ellis (Professor of Surgery), Dr W. K. Sullivan (Professor of Chemistry and Dean of the Faculty of Science) and Dr David Dunne (Professor in Logic and a tutor)—and one Englishman, Tom Arnold (Professor of English Literature and a tutor).

It is clear from their *Report* that the committee members identified strongly with Newman's vision, because the recommendations they made were those they thought would lead to its preservation and consolidation (though, in tinkering with arrangements, the committee inevitably altered the balance of Newman's scheme). They recommended that one of the deans of the collegiate houses be elected from their number and added to the Council, so that he could represent the disciplinary interests of the

University: this was a much-needed modification in the absence of a rector, who would normally have acted as a conduit for the concerns of the heads of house. The committee not only approved the use of tutors, but wanted all the houses to engage their services, and so recommended switching to the system employed at Trinity, where the tutors were officers of the university and so could tutor any student.[16] Nevertheless, they were also keen to retain the custom of 'domestic' tutors and wished each house to have one, the dean taking on the role in the absence of anyone else. In part this was for the sake of discipline: 'Nothing can more effectually tend to secure the cheerful observance of order, than the presence of one who can unreservedly avail himself of the familial opportunities of intellectual intercourse, for the promotion, by example and counsel, of moral discipline.'[17] As for their academic role, the committee members noted that,

> Attendance on Tutors' instructions has never been considered obligatory, and we have reason to believe that the framers of the University attached great importance to the maintenance of this liberty of action on the part of the student. From this opinion we by no means dissent; but we think that habitual and notorious neglect of this most useful of University influences should be understood to operate prejudicially to a young man's claim on the regard and good opinion of the Authorities.[18]

Like Newman, the committee members understood that the questions of living arrangements and discipline were bound together closely. They noted the many advantages of the system of collegiate and licensed houses, not least in providing a variety of styles of living and a family-like atmosphere by means of a common table, but they realised the system was inefficient, especially as there were no economies of scale in the provision of meals. They recommended that in the long run the authorities should provide only rooms, leaving each student, 'under the restrictions necessary to guarantee good order', to arrange board for himself—though the University could consider a 'commons hall' for all students (and staff) along the lines of those established in Germany. The alternative plan they proposed involved a compromise: building residential accommodation and running it in parallel with the collegiate houses.[19] In the short run they suggested that the houses be made self-supporting by a variety of means: abolishing altogether the sliding scale of subsidies, as they maintained 'a fictitious appearance of stability'; the students paying their tuition fees to the tutors directly; and the University paying the salaries of the deans, who would thereby be given greater status, rather than being viewed as 'speculators' on their students. By these means they hoped that the cost of lodging could be brought down to £30 p.a.[20]

At first glance these recommendations might appear as the undoing of Newman's collegiate scheme: but if the University as a whole was considered as a single college (which, in terms of numbers, it effectively was), then the sharing of tutors and a common table amounted to what Newman had originally envisaged for each collegiate house, except that there were supposed to be several.[21] Newman's original scheme had allowed for a gradual increase of student numbers by the creation of additional collegiate houses, ideally with endowments. However, difficult circumstances meant hard choices and the surrender of certain options. Besides the economic drawback of operating small collegiate houses, the authors of the *Report* felt that the collegiate houses had introduced a 'sectional feeling and cliquism', which told against the espirit de corps of the University.[22] But for the medical faculty, which was expanding, the committee had no hesitation in recommending a proper collegiate house for matriculated medical students, following the example of St Luke's.

In matters of discipline the *Report* endorsed what it referred to as the 'most masterly and correct expositions' contained in the fuller, explanatory version of Newman's Rules and Regulations. To Newman's code of behaviour they made just one qualification, for the purpose of clarification: that the guidelines should never be imposed for their own sake, but only with a particular principle in mind. This meant that it was better to declare that certain amusements were prohibited because they were incompatible with the tone and character of the University and with the concentration of mind required for serious study (especially when those habits had not been acquired), than because of the moral dangers involved. This followed Newman's principle that what recommended itself first to the understanding was 'afterwards more easily accepted by the heart'. The committee felt that the indirect enforcement of discipline and the power of a sound and intelligent public opinion were better adapted for university students than any system which consisted entirely in the vigilance of superiors, and 'would be more effective in repressing juvenile extravagance and inclination to irregularities'. Too great a strictness had to be avoided. They felt this principle so strongly that they recommended applying it even to the question of religious observance: practices of piety were better 'enforced by a sense of belonging to an institution where religion was recognised and honoured as its basis, than by a compulsory compliance' by means of detailed rules. In saying as much, and re-stating Newman's policy in their own words, the Senate committee no doubt saw their chance to head off episcopal heavy-handedness.[23]

All but one of the committee were laymen, so it is not surprising that they should have sought to protect the gains won by Newman for the education of those whose duties would lie in the world.[24] Since the University was founded principally for the education of the laity, the committee opined that 'the discipline should fit the lay rather than the ecclesiastical student'. And, they told the bishops (for whom the *Report* was intended), the public had to be satisfied on this point, because false impressions on this front did 'much mischief' to the University. Enlarging on the matter, they explained:

> The public should be made to understand, that the difference between a Catholic University and one in which religion has no place, does not consist in severe discipline, but in blending the knowledge of human sciences with religion, and in training the mind to fit man, not for his temporal destiny only, but for his whole destiny, both temporal and eternal.[25]

In particular the committee felt that the frequency of the sacraments should be 'rather expected than specifically enjoined' on the students. The only specific point on which they questioned the Rules and Regulations was over the requirement for externs to be indoors by 10 pm; mention of the time, they said, should be omitted as it suggested on the one hand that habitually staying out until that hour was reasonable, while on the other it was 'needlessly stringent and certainly inoperative' on other occasions.[26] Overall, in matters concerning 'liberty of action', they felt it was important to try to minimise the points of contrast with other universities—which above all meant Trinity.[27]

Aware of developments at other universities, the committee recognised the growing importance that was being given to sport. The cult of games had emerged as a characteristic feature of British universities (and public schools) towards the end of the 1850s. It was accompanied by an ideology of athleticism, which conferred upon games, especially team sports, the capacity to inspire virtue, develop manliness and form character, and it developed into a simple-minded belief in the value of organised outdoor exercise for producing captains of industry and leaders of empire.[28] In tune with this development, the Senate committee argued that 'Manly sports are the best promoters of discipline, and should be encouraged by the University.'[29] The installation of the billiard table had been beneficial, but more needed to be done, especially at St Patrick's where space for exercise and amusements was limited.

In all likelihood these thoughts on discipline, the education of the laity, and the (general) usefulness of games would have been music to Newman's ears; and the fact that the Senate committee wished to champion this new approach shows that they were largely in agreement with his vision.

Where the committee differed significantly from Newman was on the modifications he had introduced which divided the student body into six or seven categories. One of the committee, Laurence Forde, had previously complained to Cullen about the byzantine complexity of Newman's Rules and Regulations, which had been aggravated by the lack of any explanation: 'Dr. Newman never gave us even one word which would enable us who are expected to be his co-operators the least insight into his views or the drift of the very complicated code which he has presented us with.'[30] It should be noted that these comments pre-dated the statute of 1857, which introduced further subdivisions of interns into 'proper' and 'improper', together with the new distinction between 'residents' and 'non-residents'. The committee regarded the latter distinction as needlessly detailed, since they felt there was no need to recognise non-resident students at all until the University was properly established. 'Less tenable still' was the distinction introduced between interns proper and improper, which they assumed had been introduced as an emergency measure to enable the houses to artificially boost the number of interns so as to qualify for larger subsidies. This was not in fact the principal reason—as Dunne, one of the committee, ought to have known. Unaware that Newman's purpose had been to encourage the externs to become 'quasi interns' (or 'interns improper'), the committee mistakenly concluded that the nomenclature was 'not the expression of any important principle of distinction' and hence not deserving of preservation.[31]

The division between 'intern' and 'extern' was, the committee thought, natural and obvious, yet here too they had strong reservations. In principle they preferred just one class of students, the interns, as they considered that a *residential* university was 'favourable to the maintenance of a correct moral discipline'[32]—especially in a large city, where the student body was too small to impress its distinctive character upon its surroundings, but instead was absorbed into the general population. They cited the example of Louvain, where experience had shown that it would have benefited if admission had been limited to just interns. The committee recognised that if the Catholic University was restricted to interns it needed to bring down the cost of accommodation to match the cheapest living costs outside; and they recognised that exceptions would have to be allowed for students living with their parents. If externs *were* to be allowed, they suggested their number be limited, particularly in the first two years of undergraduate study. Like Newman, they argued that the externs should be under the same obligations as interns as regards attendance at public religious ceremonies and the 'instructions' of the University.

On the question of allowing 'auditors' (i.e. non-matriculated students) to attend lectures, the committee raised two objections: they felt the public should be able to distinguish between them and the externs, whereas they could not; and they thought their presence did not encourage those outside the University to become matriculated students. They recommended that the auditors should not be allowed to attend entire courses, but only specified lectures. As for Newman's termly 'collections', in which the rector, accompanied by lecturers, tutors and deans, examined each student separately, they felt it was a 'valuable and important part' of the assessment process and recommended that its private character be left untouched. Where idleness was apparent, they suggested it be punished with the loss of a term. In keeping with the growing recognition of the principle of meritocracy, the committee wanted *all* the bursaries to be awarded by competitive examination, rather than some being allocated by the bishops, and they expressed a preference for their being distributed *during* the academic year rather than at the beginning.[33] If the current system was to be continued, they wanted the University to have the power to withhold them.

Attached to the Senate *Report* were several appendices, where minority views were aired. In one of them Arnold made three suggestions about the organisation of the two-year undergraduate course leading up to the scholar's exam. He felt that the students were given too much latitude in choosing their books and lectures, and that this 'extreme pliancy' meant that the University pandered to student whims. The sheer number of possible combinations meant, in theory, that thirty students could complete the course by means of thirty different courses of reading. 'Taking young men as they are—for the most part fond of enjoyment, and averse to serious intellectual toil', the system was harmful because it destroyed two powerful inducements to application: the stimulus of companionship, which acted upon those engaged in the same task by making their studies more interesting through sympathy and the exchange of ideas; and the stimulus of emulation. The problem was compounded by admitting students during the academic year, as it became difficult to calculate their 'standing'. Arnold's solution was for the vice-rector to assign each new student to one of the lecturers as his 'college tutor', the allocation being decided by the line of study the student was likely to follow. The college tutor would determine the lectures his student was to attend and exercise a general supervision over his studies during his university career, leaving the 'catechetical instruction' to his collegiate-house or private tutor.[34] Evidently he was proposing a system quite different from Newman's, which entailed all interns and quasi interns being attached to a collegiate house and receiving tuition from the two or three tutors living in or attached to that house.

A separate defect that Arnold identified was the lack of exams for ascertaining merit, as opposed to a minimum standard, and hence lack of motivation for extra exertion. At Trinity, the students were motivated by the possibility of aiming for the honours degree after matriculation, rather than just the pass degree, and the names of successful candidates were posted up in college or published in the press.[35] At the Catholic University, the scholar's exam ascertained only a minimum standard of proficiency. However, Arnold overlooked the distinction that Newman had made between 'satisfactory' and 'meritorious' in the fourth year exams in the arts faculty, which effectively allowed students to work for honours and undertake a deeper study of their subjects; nor did he mention the various prizes that Newman had introduced. While Arnold's recommendation for the introduction of honours at an earlier stage in the course was endorsed by the committee, his other suggestion, on reconfiguring the tutorial system, did not win their approval.

But, apart from Arnold's recommendation about the tutorial system, there was little to separate the committee's views from Newman's: they only really differed in the practical aspects of implementing their shared approach. In some respects, the committee was more unrealistic than Newman (as in their preference for a totally residential university), but in other ways they were more down-to-earth (in tackling the financial viability of the separate residential houses). Overall the committee sought for clarity by cutting away the accretions that had built up as a result of Newman's efforts to steer the University in the desired direction. One of these anomalies was the access to a free education in medicine (and, later, in engineering) which was offered to anyone who had passed through the arts faculty. Intended to boost the arts faculty, it deprived the medical school of much-needed income, a policy which the 'Report of the Sub-committee of Medicine' (appended to the main *Report*) sought to reverse.[36]

At variance with the near-unanimous opinion of the Senate committee was the dissentient voice of James Quinn, the outgoing dean of St Laurence's, who lobbied for drastic changes to the University constitution. Quinn, who had sat on the committee until his elevation to the episcopate, wanted the heads of house to become officers of the University and to rank above the professors, in much the same way as they had in Archbishop Laud's seventeenth-century statutes for Oxford, in which the Hebdomadal Board (the equivalent of the Catholic University's Council) had comprised heads of house, to the exclusion of the professoriate. Quinn was probably unaware that this arrangement had just been abandoned at Oxford, where the reforms introduced in 1854 after the Royal Commission reconstituted the (renamed) Hebdomadal Council, leaving on it just six heads of house. Newman had anticipated this development by deliberately adopting the Louvain model; to change from Louvain to Laudian would, in Newman's opinion, turn the clock back and change the University profoundly. 'In that case it will be simply priest-ridden—I mean persons, who do not know literature and science, will have the direction and teaching. [...] The six heads of house would do all the work'.[37]

More radical still was Quinn's suggestion that the undergraduates be taught in the Catholic colleges throughout the country, the University becoming simply an examining body along the lines of London University. When Ornsby objected to this proposal on the grounds that it surrendered the ancient idea of the university, Quinn retorted that 'the ancient idea was impracticable, on the score of the difficulty as to morals, when youths were congregated in vast masses'.[38] Ornsby was dismayed by Quinn's suggestions and the clerical mentality that underlay them. He had already detected in the proposals contained in the Senate *Report* a tendency to 'ecclesiasticize the institution', because he feared that if externs were discouraged, the University would in all likelihood consolidate itself into one house and become very much a seminary.[39]

One additional, practical recommendation in the *Report* is worthy of note: the suggestion that the Catholic University adapt the charter of the University of Quebec. Founded in Quebec in 1852 as the Université Laval, it had—remarkably—obtained a royal charter the same year,[40] thus becoming the second Catholic university to be founded in modern times. Newman had brought the foundation to public attention in a *Gazette* article in November 1854,[41] and, on Monsell's advice, had referred to the 'Charter lately granted by Government to the Roman Catholic University of Quebec' in his letter to Disraeli petitioning for a royal charter for Dublin.[42] But despite the success of the French Catholic Canadians in gaining a charter from the British government, Laval seems not to have had any impact on the Irish Catholic University, to judge from its almost complete absence from correspondence in Dublin.

The fate of the collegiate houses

Since a central part of Newman's legacy to the University was the system of collegiate houses he had established, any appraisal of the foundational years needs to take into account how the system fared after Newman's departure. An additional reason for considering the fate of the collegiate houses is that it helps us see more clearly what Newman had put in place, and how it contrasted with the standard view of the time. At the end of his last (nominal) year as rector, two of the five houses were operating to capacity: St Patrick's had seventeen students and St Luke's sixteen. The medical house had been opened in late November 1857 and during the 1858/59 session could probably have taken in another ten, if there had been room. As a licensed house its rules were less exacting than those of a collegiate house—but they were enforced, as Dr Henry Tyrrell pointed out in his report to the vice-rector:

1. Each student must be present at mass on all Sundays and holydays of obligation.
2. All must comply with their Easter duty.
3. The hour for breakfast is eight to half-past nine; for lunch, two; for dinner, five; and tea, eight o'clock.
4. Any one absent at these hours, cannot have food prepared for him at any other time.
5. No student may remain out after eleven p.m., except on Saturday, when they may remain till twelve p.m.
6. All students will retire to their respective rooms at half-past ten p.m.
7. No noise or rioting allowed at any time in the house.
8. No spirits of any description allowed to be taken into the house on any occasion.
9. Each student will pay his pension quarterly and in advance.
10. No student can enter for a shorter period than three months, and it is expected he will give at least a month's notice before leaving.
11. As this house was established for industrious students, no one, no matter how well conducted otherwise, can remain in residence unless he applies himself diligently to his studies.[43]

Tyrrell explained that he had little difficulty in keeping order, as the students were grateful for all that had been done for them. He had had to issue several warnings that idleness was incompatible with remaining in the house, but had only parted with one student, whose idle ways threatened to undermine the study habits of the others. He was particularly pleased to remark that the working atmosphere had not only improved over time, but been reflected in the distribution of prizes for medicine, most of which had been awarded to interns of St Luke's the previous April. The terms on which Tyrrell ran the residence were £30 for board, lodging and candles for the nine-month academic year, and this included the cost of all four meals.

Having overseen St Mary's for the summer term of 1859, Gartlan saw no future for it without the return of Newman, even though he realised that closure would signal failure on the part of the University to provide 'for Catholic youth of a higher class'. Spelling out to the bishops his proposals for the collegiate system in his *Vice-Rector's Report* for 1858/59, he argued that the houses should be private voluntary undertakings, not subsidised by the University, and offering board and lodging 'on the model of Surgeon Tyrrell's', with fees of, say, £20, £30, £40 and £50 so as to cater for varying needs. Students not accommodated in these houses should be lodged and boarded on similar terms in families willing to receive them, provided the University had references from clergymen which would guarantee the moral and religious character of these families. To oversee this arrangement, Gartlan proposed the appointment of a Prefect of Residence, who would 'know the inmates of such houses, collegiate and private', and be invested 'with large discretionary powers' so as to 'watch over and protect the lives and morals of those in his parental and economic charge'.[44] The Prefect of Residence, rather than the rector, would appoint the Deans of Residence. Gartlan felt that every effort should be made to allow students to live at home or with relatives, as in his opinion they were more regular than the interns—and he reckoned they could hope for 400–500 such students. He realised that the original intention was that students should reside in collegiate houses, but felt that this was unworkable without being properly endowed and possibly undesirable in a large city like Dublin.

Gartlan's *Report* was completed in June 1859, and would have been read by the Irish bishops before they reconvened for their second meeting that year, in October. By then the bishops would also have had time to digest the Senate's *Report on the condition and circumstances of the Catholic University*. The bishops ignored most of the Senate's recommendations, but they did adopt two concerning the houses: first, by altering the teaching arrangements and resolving 'That a Mathematical Tutor and a Classical Tutor be appointed for the University Students of all the Houses'; and second, by urging 'That the establishment of cheap Boarding Houses in connection with the University be encouraged'.[45] Ornsby's reaction to the first was to tell Newman that the plans 'make a sad botch of your beautiful ideas';[46] as for the second, it was unclear who was to run the desired boarding houses.

Scratton, who (like Ornsby) kept Newman up to date with developments, informed him that the bishops had decided to do nothing for St Mary's and had set themselves against the collegiate houses in their current form. He also revealed that they intended to appoint a board to govern the University which would all but supersede the work of the Council and Senate; in Scratton's opinion, the University had brought this on itself by 'an anarchical use of freedom of action'.[47] The change came about in October 1859, when the bishops met to decide what to do about the Catholic University. In the event they opted to keep the University going, while reducing expenditure, and appointed an Episcopal Board to run it, comprising the four archbishops and eight bishops, two from each of the four provinces. This meant that the bishops had control of everything relating to legislation, expenditure and appointments. In the long run this radically altered the way the University was run, though in the short term there were no wholesale changes as the bishops opined that 'no one should be removed but that remedies should be applied gradually'.[48]

St Mary's was closed down in the summer of 1859, although the University received an offer from Arnold to carry it on, so long as he was furnished with a loan. After his plan was 'smothered' (as Arnold put it) by the authorities, he turned his mind to establishing a house on his own for 'the "nobility and tranquillity, burgomasters and great one-yers", who used to resort to No 6 Harcourt St, while we had a Rector of European reputation'. With a view to advertising himself as a professor at the Catholic University who took in students, he asked Newman for a brief reference 'stating you knew me and could recommend me as a person deserving of parents' confidence'.[49] In his letter of recommendation, based on a draft composed by Arnold, Newman declared that,

> For their intellectual progress and the formation of their minds your name is in various ways a guarantee [...] From what I know of you, I am confident you will watch over the moral interests and personal conduct of any young men who may be entrusted to your care, with yet greater vigilance than that which you would employ to further their intellectual progress.[50]

Though Arnold enlisted one Portuguese nobleman, Count de Villa Real, and had a printed prospectus distributed with *The Rambler*, the plan failed to materialise.

All this was, of course, a far cry from what the Irish bishops had in mind: what they desired were economical houses under clerics, not laymen, and run with the strictness of a seminary. Some idea of the atmosphere at St Patrick's House can be gained from the student ledger for 1858–61, which itemises each resident's petty expenses, lectures attended, and infractions of the house rules. Under Fr Austin O'Loughlin, a former dean and Prefect of the Irish College in Paris, a system of fines operated, which included 2/6 for missing dinner without permission (the most common offence) and a hefty 10/– for being in another student's room after evening prayer. After an incident involving students throwing water onto a policeman from the windows of No. 86, tougher rules were put in place, backed up by a raft of punishments and fines. Habitual non-attendance at Mass and morning prayers now led to forfeiture of scholarships and prizes; absence from dinner without permission incurred a fine of 5/– the first time, and loss of a term if habitual; a similar fine applied for attending the University Mass without cap and gown; and the throwing of water out of any windows was punishable by expulsion.[51]

Though the Carmelites ran a day school which was affiliated to the Catholic University and supplied a trickle of students, in January 1860 Cullen asked the Carmelite Provincial, Thomas Bennet, if he could establish a collegiate house. The Carmelites responded by opening one that November next to their church in Whitefriars Street; a year later, it became the Carmelite College at Terenure, Roundtown, some two miles south-west of St Stephen's Green, but in the summer of 1862 it closed. Why it did so is unclear. It might have proved unattractive to students, or else it may have suffered from the surfeit of places, since two other houses were opened in November 1861: Corpus Christi House at 76 St Stephen's Green and the Medical College[52] at 98 Leeson Street, both under the deanship of the priest Dr John MacDevitt. The Calendar for 1862/63 explains that the Medical College was intended to address the concerns of parents living outside the city who were anxious to secure for their sons 'those safeguards which religion affords against the dangers of a large city'.[53] Its residents were obliged to attend morning and night prayer every day, as well as Mass in the University Church on Sundays; furthermore, they were not allowed to go out after nightfall without permission from the dean. Like the residents of the collegiate houses, students were also expected to frequent the sacraments and follow the devotions recommended to them.

The medical students were also required to take their meals in college, where they could eat cheaply. It is clear that a certain frugality was the order of the day as one of the rules stated, 'Extravagance will not be tolerated, and Students who persist in such a habit will be requested to leave the College.'[54] Annual fees, including lodging and academic fees but excluding hospital fees, were not to exceed £50; students could opt in for private medical tuition at £4 p.a., in addition. An interesting development after Newman's time was that all students were now required to enter the arts faculty; this was to enable them to benefit from a liberal education, while pursuing their medical studies, and become 'thoroughly instructed in the principles of Religion, of Moral Philosophy, etc'.[55] The Calendar explained that, by having an experienced guide during their professional studies, students would be saved from mistakes which inexperienced men were liable to make, mistakes which could seriously affect success in later life. The rector's *Report* for 1862/63 states that of the 108 students in the medical faculty, thirty had begun to attend lectures at St Stephen's Green; that as many as fifty attended the sodality (i.e. confraternity) of our Lady run by the Jesuits, which had just been started in the University Church; and that thirty had resided at the medical house that year.[56]

On 10 March 1863, the day the Prince of Wales (later King Edward VII) married Princess Alexandra at Windsor, an incident occurred at No. 86 that shook the Catholic University and its authorities, and which was all the more unnerving for the prolonged and hostile exposure it received in the press afterwards. To mark the royal wedding the city of Dublin was illuminated that night, and, along with shopkeepers and all, the Catholic University followed suit. The University authorities arranged for illuminations to be displayed on the front of University House which featured the letters 'A. A.', for Albert and Alexandra, and the feathers of the Prince of Wales—but they did not shine out for long, because the students were strongly opposed to the gesture and sabotaged the display. Under student leadership—but quite probably encouraged by professors with nationalist leanings—one of their number, Val Dillon, was hoisted on their shoulders and cut the gas pipe over the door of No. 86, to cheers from the rest.

When the Protestant *Freeman's Journal* claimed that the affair was merely the work of just two or three students, who had been punished, no fewer than thirty-nine of them signed a letter to *The Nation* (28 March), the organ of the Young Ireland movement, declaring that none of them repudiated the deed. The incident had also been reported in *The Times* (16 March), which claimed that the students had defied the Catholic authorities over the illuminations, not once, but twice, and that they were encouraged by two or three professors. More hostile was the Irish press, which spoke of treasonable, irreligious and revolutionary elements within the Catholic University, including the professoriate.[57] To judge from a letter Professor Robertson wrote to Cullen about the affair, there was a good deal of truth in these claims, as Robertson complained that one of his colleagues, who had caused dissension in the University three years earlier, was making the most of the disturbance. The student ringleader was John Patrick McDonnell,[58] who had twice been threatened with expulsion from the University for speaking at the National Brotherhood of St Patrick, a chain of nationalist debating and reading clubs and a front organisation for the secret Fenian Brotherhood. In order to prevent revolutionary principles from taking root within the University, Robertson suggested that, just as Newman used to exact from students a promise to obey the University regulations, so the authorities should now require from them a public promise not to join secret societies.[59]

Although Dillon was sent down by the dean of St Patrick's, fellow students rallied to his side and, by claiming equal responsibility, they forced O'Loughlin to reprieve him—though Dillon then refused to return. Woodlock eventually managed to extract a written apology from the students for their disorderly behaviour and peace (of a kind) was restored. But the worries of the rector continued, as the adverse publicity which persisted throughout 1863 threatened the granting of a charter from the government, and then hundreds of families began a boycott of the University by ceasing their subscriptions to it.[60]

The 'illumination affair' brought Woodlock and Newman into correspondence, as the press had reported that Newman had left the University on account of the anti-English feeling there. Writing to Woodlock, Newman expressed his concern that the University might become as unruly as some of the universities on the European mainland. More confidentially, he told Ornsby 'so gross an act of rebellion ought to be severely visited; nor do I see that there can be any real moral training of youth at the University, if such affronts are offered to authority'. He knew from Ornsby that Cullen and others were preoccupied with opposing Irish nationalism among the young, but Newman felt their approach was misguided. 'You cannot make men believe by force and repression', he told Ornsby; the Church needed to meet the intellectual difficulties of the day. In his own rectorate, when the student population contained a sizeable non-Irish element, 'the national feeling was kept *diluted*, but now it is the genuine high proof whisky and no mistake'.[61] Woodlock was in a difficult situation: he dare not punish too heavily for fear of losing popularity among parents; at the same time, he was not responsible for Cullen's determination to display the illuminations or his policy of breaking with the Young Ireland party. Fortunately, national feeling within the student body was at a lower level three years later when the Prince of Wales visited Dublin and called at No. 86 with the Lord Lieutenant; he was shown inside and cheered by students, who lined the hall, staircase and passages, attired in caps and gowns.

The student troubles of '63 may well have triggered the implementation of drastic measures announced a few months later. Though Corpus Christi House was in its second year and prospering with thirty students, the University Finance Committee reported that the collegiate houses were too expensive to maintain, and the axe fell: the lease on 76 St Stephen's Green was given up at once and the medical house at 98 Leeson Street a year later. The Report of the Finance Committee blamed the collegiate houses for contributing to an average annual loss of £3000, and it recommended that 'pensions' should be made to cover all the boarding expenses. If there was insufficient accommodation available after the closure of the two houses, the Committee recommended that students be allowed to live with families under the supervision of the rector or deans.[62] The loss of 76 St Stephen's Green coincided with the winding up of St Laurence's as a collegiate house, but not Corpus Christi, which moved to 16–17 Harcourt Street, where it shared premises with the secondary school (which now became one of the Catholic University Schools). Corpus Christi and the school cohabited until 1867, when the house was closed down and the school was taken over by the Marist Fathers and moved elsewhere.

After the student disturbance of '63 there was a noticeable tightening up of discipline. A Council of Discipline was formed, comprising the rector and the deans of the houses, for the purpose of ensuring that the externs residing in lodging houses were conforming to the rules and being looked after.[63] At the suggestion of Matthew Quinn, the Council looked at how timetables could be drawn up to allow the medical students to attend lectures in the arts faculty, and how they could arrange for the medical faculty to ensure that these timetables were observed. It was decided that medical students in residence should not be allowed to 'grind' (i.e. employ a private tutor) after dinner, and that the importance of lectures over grinding should be stressed for all, except the fourth-year medics.

Despite appearing to wash their hands of any houses other than St Patrick's and Corpus Christi, the lack of provision did bother the authorities, and to encourage private initiative to take up the slack they inserted a notice in the University Calendar of 1865 which laid down the conditions on which a priest or graduate of the University could set up and run a collegiate house. The conditions advertised were identical to those laid down by Newman ten years earlier; besides stipulating that these houses were an integral part of the University under the rector's overall jurisdiction, the notice stated that the heads of house were charged with the moral and intellectual advancement of their students. That union of moral and intellectual oversight, so emblematic of Newman's approach to education, was spelt out for the aspiring heads: they would be responsible for the 'religious and correct deportment' of their students, for their observing the rules of both house and University, and for their acquitting themselves before professors and examiners. At the same time, the University authorities pointed out that students were also permitted to live in one of the approved lodging houses, which were licensed by the rector and under the inspection of the deans.

Though the capacity of St Patrick's had been reduced in 1862 with the loss of No. 87, it increased in the mid-1860s when students began to double and triple up in rooms.[64] Other than St Patrick's, between 1863 and 1867 interns had the choice of Corpus Christi and St Mary's at Gayfield. For two years St Mary's was under Matthew Quinn but seems not to have been a success, being located away from the city centre, and his brother James (now Bishop of Queensland) tried in vain to get the University to take it over. Under Quinn's successor, Fr E. O'Donohoe, a dispute broke out when the prospectus of St Mary's advertised that it prepared students for the London University external exams; St Mary's was struck off from the list of University houses, but reinstated when O'Donohoe agreed not to advertise the London connection publicly.[65]

After the closure of Corpus Christi in 1867, the only option for medical students wishing to live in collegiate house was to join the younger students at St Patrick's. As this was highly unsatisfactory, Woodlock revived a plan to move the medical school from Cecilia Street to St Stephen's Green, with the aim of bringing the two groups of students together and enabling the medical students to have easier access to lectures at University House; but the proposal did not come to fruition.[66] In 1867, Our Lady's House opened at 89 Leeson Street under the Marist Fathers, but it was essentially a lodging house for seminarians and subject to strict discipline; its students, whether ecclesiastical or lay, were not permitted to leave the precincts other than for lectures without seeking permission from the dean, the Marist priest Dr John Leterrier. When St Mary's closed in 1868, the only alternative to St Patrick's was living with seminarians at Our Lady's.

After receiving complaints about the discipline at St Patrick's, the Episcopal Board decided to clamp down. In March 1871 they imposed on the dean a stringent set of house rules and regulations, and before the new session got under way they warned O'Loughlin that he would be required to give an account of discipline at St Patrick's as part of a commission of enquiry into the state of the University. The changes were another step further away from the student regime Newman had hoped to establish, with its stress on trust and the responsible use of freedom: the new rules introduced a heavily regimented way of life that made the routine at St Patrick's closer to that of a seminary. The rules obliged, rather than expected, the students to attend morning and night prayers (and Mass); formerly students had been 'earnestly recommended' to go to

Confession monthly, whereas it was now laid down that they *had* to go; permission had to be sought if they wanted to accept invitations to dine with friends; except for the summer term, they were not allowed to leave the house after dinner; and the house doors were to be locked at 10.30 pm.

The list of penalties attached to the rules would have confirmed Newman's worst fears, that the University authorities would fall into the hands of narrow-minded men 'who have little other idea of a University than a place for imposing fines ("not above one pound") on those who are slow at lecture'.[67] Fines were specified for attending University Mass without cap and gown (2/6); for missing a lecture without permission (1/–); for each absence from dinner (2/6); and, heaviest of all, for a student found in the room of another after night prayers or with his light on after 11 pm (10/–). Unspecified were the fines for ungentlemanly conduct or for disturbing the house during the time dedicated to lectures and private study (between 9 am and 3 pm). Being out of doors after dinner without permission in the Michaelmas and Lent terms was visited with automatic rustication, and unruly behaviour or irregularity in returning to the house on time with a fine, rustication or expulsion.[68]

The new rules achieved little; two years later, when the Board met to discuss the latest annual report, enquiries were again made into the financial and disciplinary condition of St Patrick's, 'for some time past the only Board House of the University'. The conclusion it reached was that St Patrick's had been badly administered. Austin O'Loughlin, the dean appointed by the archbishops in 1858 (when they usurped Newman's right to nominate the dean), had in the opinion of the Board 'proved himself deficient in the tact, steadiness of purpose and constant supervision, necessary for such an establishment'[69]—but he had been in place for fifteen years and run up a debt to the University of £750! Numbers in St

Patrick's had been declining for some years (twelve in 1867/68, nine in 1870/71, five in 1871/72, and four in 1872/73), and it was felt that its loss of reputation was damaging the University as a whole. The University was by then in a dreadful state: there were few lecturers and one was ill and bankrupt, another irregular in his duties, a third absent and a fourth had been involved in a moral scandal.[70] There were almost no students apart from those attending the medical school, and (as if that were not enough) there were reports that some of them patronised a local brothel.[71]

Having decided that O'Loughlin was insufficiently qualified for a deanship, the Board arranged for him to take over the University Church and offered the running of St Patrick's to the Jesuits. This meant that they accepted responsibility for its administration, financial viability, and the discipline and religious education of its students.[72] Under their direction numbers increased at once: there were fifteen interns and as many externs by the end of the first term; nineteen interns in 1874/75; twenty-three in 1875/76; and twenty-six in 1876/77. But there was a price to pay for the regime change: W. K. Sullivan, the University's leading academic, resigned in the year of the handover, blaming the bishops for wanting to turn the University into a seminary under their control. Worse, he took up the presidency of Queen's College, Cork.

The Episcopal Board disapproved of the mixture of arts faculty and medical students at St Patrick's, which was reported to have acted unfavourably on discipline and studies, and they recommended strongly that only the arts faculty students remain there. The bishops recognised that this was not a problem of O'Loughlin's making, but rather a consequence of the closure of Corpus Christi, and they recommended that a self-supporting house be established for medics under the care of a married medical man, who would act as tutor to the students. A lodging house at 32 Merrion Street was acquired, but the anatomy lecturer who was to oversee it fell ill, and when it opened in January 1874 it failed to attract any of the seventy-five medical students and was closed soon afterwards. Nevertheless, Woodlock remained anxious about solving the problem of providing accommodation for the medics, but was unable to resolve the matter.[73] Anticipating an increase in student numbers, the Board suggested that when new houses were needed they be established by religious communities in or around Dublin with some aid from the University—a plea which received backing from the Pope—but no-one responded to the invitation.

Aftermath

This brief history of the fortunes of the Catholic University and its collegiate houses over the twenty years after Newman's departure is critical for assessing his legacy, for it shows how his scheme was gradually dismantled by men who had not fully grasped what it entailed or how the various parts fitted together. Several of the academic staff, particularly the Oxbridge converts and the members of the medical faculty, were able to enter into his thinking and identify with his approach to the education and formation of the students; but as they left Dublin or were excluded from the government of the University, hope gradually diminished for reviving Newman's scheme. The absence of a rector in the three years after Newman's departure, and thereafter of a vice-rector, was extremely debilitating, and it meant that the University rapidly lost its initial momentum. Once the Episcopal Board replaced the Senate, control of the University and determination of its policies effectively passed into episcopal hands and, in the absence of lay involvement, the University was run on more clerical lines.[74]

The ongoing problems relating to discipline and the provision of accommodation in the period 1858–79 show that the authorities were either unable to find an alternative system to Newman's, or unable to find the people who could make the system work, or both.

Part of the problem was that the lay professoriate was cut off from the Board and effectively excluded from decision-making. On the other hand, Archbishop Cullen and the bishops were preoccupied with the succession of schemes for gaining the all-important charter, and this inevitably diverted their attention. Besides, as Cullen reported to Rome, the Board had decided 'that it would be better for the time being to let things stand and to make gradually the alterations and corrections which seemed necessary but which would cause resentment [...] if done of a sudden'.[75]

In the absence of any official recognition of its courses, other than for medicine, the professoriate found themselves labouring against the odds over academic standards, and the deans of the houses fighting a losing battle over discipline, because the lack of officially-recognised degrees meant that the authorities were unable to use the threat of withholding a degree. As early as 1860 students at the University were being prepared for the London external exams, news of which drew from Newman the remark, 'What can be more disgraceful than its preparing men for the London University!'[76] Yet even Woodlock, at the start of his rectorate, thought London might be a suitable model for the Catholic University, so long as it meant securing recognised degrees.[77] Far less compromising was the preparation of students for the entrance exams of the civil service or the Royal Military Academy at Woolwich, which took place on a small scale throughout the 1860s.

In dealing with the British government and concocting numerous schemes by which the University might secure official recognition and public funding, the Board drafted various constitutions, some of which bore little relation to what Newman had mapped out earlier. In 1865, when pamphlets and schemes about the future of the Catholic University were thick in the air, the academic staff met to discuss the University's predicament and decide how best to safeguard its character. They were unanimous in agreeing that any system of conferring degrees by examination *without* an academic education would be highly prejudicial to the interests of university education in Ireland; more significantly, they thought it highly desirable that the constitution drawn up by Newman and laid before the bishops as the Rules and Regulations should be embodied in any new constitution for the University.[78] This is precisely what happened when, soon afterwards, the Board drew up rules and a constitution. In June 1869 they were formally approved, published and promulgated as the *Constitution and Statutes of the Catholic University of Ireland.*

By ratifying the Rules and Regulations with barely an alteration, the bishops tacitly acknowledged Newman's understanding of how to deal with young men in a university setting.[79] The strange thing was that the document still referred to collegiate houses, their deans and tutors, and the workings of the Senate, even though these were now no longer operational. The fact is that, once the authorities had jettisoned Newman's scheme, they were at a loss as to how to proceed (in what were, of course, exceptionally difficult circumstances); or rather, there was no coherent strategy for governing the University until the Jesuits took over St Patrick's and began to conduct business according to their own long-established college tradition, and with men who knew how to work it.

Since Newman's scheme had not been given time to bed down, it is hard to pass a verdict on it. Newman had hoped that, by nurturing the nascent university and taking care to see it grow in the right direction, it would turn out people who could perpetuate its living tradition. In particular, he hoped that within just a few years some of the first academic crop would become lecturers and, before they settled down and married, would be less expensive to employ than older married ones, thereby solving the problem of supplying inexpensive tutors. After Newman's departure no new tutors were appointed to collegiate houses, other than Augustus Keane at St Laurence's in 1859; and from 1867 reference to tutors in the University Calendar was dropped. Although the distinctive role of tutor (as envisaged by Newman) had been long forgotten, the Board revived the question of tutorial assistance in 1873 when it recognised that a team of tutors and 'grinders' was needed to prepare students for higher-level competitive exams. They discussed whether an obligation to tutor might be attached to some of the scholarships, and whether the rector could be authorised to subsidise the tutorial fees of the more deserving student. Questions that Newman had grappled with in the 1850s, such as the provision of tuition and suitable residential arrangements for medics, continued to surface in the 1880s, and it demonstrates that no workable solution had been found.

At one level, the greatest difficulty the Catholic University faced was a lack of students. This was disguised in the official figures of attendance, which were inflated after 1859 by including those attending the evening lectures.[80] In the mid-1860s it was reckoned that student numbers would have at least trebled if Catholics had not patronised Trinity and the Queen's Colleges,[81] even though the percentage of Catholics at both had been falling for a number of years,[82] possibly the result of warnings from the higher clergy and a drive to encourage Catholic families to support the 'Stephen's Green project'—or 'Dr Cullen's College', the 'Seminary in Stephen's Green' or the 'Ultramontane Establishment', as it was dubbed by the English press. Cullen had come to recognise that the danger for Catholics attending Trinity was not so much its Protestantism as its growing liberalism, which meant that the teaching there had become more dangerous than before. Though the Irish bishops did not denounce Trinity itself, Cullen had no hesitation in telling parents that sending their sons there was like sending them to a town infected with the yellow fever or the plague; that, while many escaped, it meant exposing their souls to the poison of error and heresy, to the loss of faith and to the constant risk of eternal perdition.[83] Yet such was the desperate need for degrees that in 1874 Woodlock proposed the idea of the Catholic University students matriculating and sitting exams at Trinity, but without attending lectures there. The suggestion had four advantages: it would increase numbers at the Catholic University; it would provide a goal for the students and give an impetus to studies; it would remove from Catholic parents the excuse of sending their sons to Trinity; and it would provide the professors with the opportunity of instilling Catholic principles into a greater number of Catholic minds.[84]

Paul Cullen remained the controlling influence behind the Catholic University until his death in 1878. He presided at the six-weekly meetings of the Episcopal Board, which after its enlargement in October 1859 was as much in his pocket as the board of archbishops had been previously. Along with Woodlock, he was its main promoter and spokesman, and on occasions met with students directly. At one prizegiving Cullen told the assembled students that many of them would do well in their careers and give a good account of their faith, yet he advised them to remember that there were three things they must attend to: piety, discipline and study. They must know God and love him; they must acquire a dominion over themselves; and they had to struggle against an inclination to sloth, self-enjoyment and pleasure.[85] Speaking at an inaugural meeting of the Literary and Historical Society, Cullen commented that it was his fervent wish that the same love of knowledge, the same success in study, the same love of the true religion might always animate the society and that its labours might become more and more useful and 'successfully employed in cultivating every portion of the vast field of history and literature'.[86]

Like the medical school, the Literary and Historical Society was flourishing, and from 1868 received grants from the University funds. Several of its auditors (i.e. presidents) went on to distinguish themselves in public life, just as Newman had hoped: Hugh McDermot (auditor in 1858/59) became solicitor-general, attorney-general, then a privy councillor for Ireland; Charles Dawson (auditor in 1867/68)[87] became mayor of Dublin and MP for Carlow; (Sir) George Fottrell (auditor in 1870/71) a political commentator; John Dillon (auditor in 1874/75) the leading nationalist parliamentarian.

The thwarting of lay participation

There has been no shortage of explanations as to why the Catholic University failed to take root and indeed all but withered away. Most relate to factors *extrinsic* to the University, yet there is one explanation which goes deeper and relates to the University itself: it could be described as the thwarting of lay participation. This thwarting operated at various levels: the exclusion of the lay professoriate from sharing in the control and governance of the University; the barring of former students from any involvement in their *alma mater*; the unwillingness to win over the gentry and enlist their support; and the blocking of their rightful contribution to the University's affairs. Not only did the clerical monopoly on the governance of the University stifle growth, but it distorted what life it had, by basing its *modus vivendi* on practices and assumptions that were more akin to the seminary than the education of young men for life in the world.

Woodlock had not been rector long when he identified the exclusion of the laity from any part in the control of the University as a defect that needed to be remedied, and he petitioned the bishops to admit laymen to the Episcopal Board.[88] Seeing that his proposal fell on deaf ears, he compiled a report to convince the bishops of the need to work with the laity. In it, he argued that the enemies of the Faith were exploiting the divisions between clergy and laity to promote what he called the 'Secularisation of education', and alleging that the clergy wanted to arrogate to themselves all control of education.[89] The remedy, Woodlock suggested, was to associate the laity with the University. In many matters of government (such as the salary disputes he was faced with), the laity were better able to resolve practical problems and in doing so would help to relieve the burden on the bishops; besides, the University was in need of their support for both finance and students. His concrete proposal was that the bishops elect twelve laymen by ballot.[90]

The principle of admitting laymen to the University Board was approved at an episcopal meeting in January 1863, and Woodlock was invited to draw up a list of suitable laymen. Cullen, however, was completely opposed to the idea, though he had to disguise his opinion from Woodlock for fear of losing his services. He told Kirby, 'It is not of any great importance to have the laymen in question. They do without laymen in Belgium. We have scarcely any great laymen, who could help to keep up the University, and it is on the body of the people we must rely'.[91] He was reassured to hear that Cardinal Barnabò (the Prefect of Propaganda Fide) had told the Pope that he, Cullen, was against admitting laymen to the Board. At another meeting of the bishops, where all but three spoke in favour of the admission of laymen, he interviewed each bishop separately and used his position as chairman to declare that the arguments against were stronger than those for: the laity, he maintained, were satisfied with things as they were.[92] In passing on the bishops' request to Rome, Cullen was able to water it down by arguing that the matter was of no great concern: the laity did not want a share in the government of the University for its own sake, but because of its current deplorable state. By citing the opposition of Archbishop MacHale to lay participation, he was able to use him as a scapegoat and mask from Woodlock his own opposition to a lay presence on the Board.[93]

Meanwhile Woodlock pressed Rome for an answer, but when the verdict came in May 1864 it was negative.

Somehow Cullen was able to persuade the bishops and Woodlock, who he regarded as 'fanatical about the laity', that Rome was right, arguing that the few laymen interested were unimportant and unwilling to support the University financially or by sending their sons; the people who did support the University were happy with its management by the ecclesiastical authorities.[94] His ability to frustrate the proposal for lay involvement shows how adept Cullen was at manipulation—and why he was distrusted. Determined to maintain a clerical monopoly of education in Ireland, he managed to block the proposal, but without losing Woodlock. In adopting this policy, he must have realised that the price to pay for his insistence on absolute clerical control was the refusal of the one thing the University needed—a charter from the British government allowing it to grant degrees.[95]

The presence of clerics within the professoriate was not the point at issue: during Newman's rectorate there were only two in the arts faculty (William Penny and the l'abbé L. Schürr) and the same number a decade later. But when in 1859 the Episcopal Board became the executive power and assumed the functions of the Senate, the professoriate was confined to internal academic affairs and excluded from the governance of the Catholic University and any policy-making.[96] When the bishops composed a draft charter for the University in 1866, they failed even to seek the opinion of the professoriate, who reacted by expressing their dismay and 'great pain' to Woodlock.[97] Later the same year relations were soured further when the bishops appointed Mgr Patrick Moran, a half-nephew of Cullen, to a chair in Irish History. The appointment drew united protests from all five faculties, who appealed against the appointment and forced the near-defunct Senate to adjudicate according to the statutes.[98]

Of all the professors at the Catholic University, the one who identified most closely with Newman's view on lay involvement and the need of the University for Ireland was the Professor of Chemistry, William Kirby Sullivan. Like several other academics he had been a Young Irelander, but his views had altered.[99] By reputation a leading scientist and a man of wide interests and talents, Sullivan championed the lay cause after Newman's departure. He had come close to resigning in 1858 out of frustration with the bishops, because he felt they had no idea what teaching science meant and of the level of investment it required;[100] the following year he went a step further when Newman's system of government was bypassed and the Council established a department for those attending evening classes, but he withdrew his resignation when the department was discontinued two months later.[101] Then, in April 1859, when there was much squabbling among the University staff, he wrote Newman a far-sighted letter.

> I regret that the admirable basis of a constitution which you laid down, and which now that it was beginning to be understood was giving confidence to the people, had well nigh been abolished. [...] the catholic laity of Ireland, while anxious for separate education upon a religious basis are not satisfied that it would be judicious to hand over the whole education to the clergy without any control by which they could secure a thoroughly efficient secular education. The constitution laid down by you for the university gives or will in time give them that control [...] This is a very serious question and will have much to do with the future history of religion here. I regret that education is not considered from a philosophical point of view, and that in the most critical period of our intellectual and religious history, there is very little thinking upon it [...] I am glad that the constitution of the University—that is the fundamental principle

of it, has been preserved and is perhaps more secure now than before.[102]

Newman replied:

> Certainly, I should be very sorry if any thing occurred so to affect the Statutes, as to deprive the laity of that real and sufficient power in the University, without which it cannot succeed. I consider the body of Professors are so well agreed on this point, that, if they are (as they will be) true to themselves, no mischief will stand a chance of being carried out.[103]

Sullivan had taken a leading part in the negotiations to secure a charter for the Catholic University in 1859, and in March had met with Disraeli. In 1866, when there was a spate of pamphlets about university education in Ireland, Sullivan published his own substantial contribution, entitled *University education in Ireland. A letter to Sir John Dalberg Acton*. There he lamented the fact that the Catholic University was unable to imitate Trinity, whose spirit pervaded all the Protestant schools in Ireland; instead Catholic laymen were faced with the unsatisfactory situation that the 'educational brain' for the Catholic system was the network of ecclesiastical colleges.[104] He attributed the failure of the Catholic University to it being in advance of public opinion (not behind it, as some had claimed, arguing that Newman had merely attempted to revive an outdated medieval system). Indeed, Newman's conception of a university was in advance not only of Catholic *lay* opinion, but of Catholic *clerical* opinion, too, he argued: neither layman nor cleric understood its functions, neither realised how much they needed it. Many priests failed to recognise 'the fundamental difference between lay and ecclesiastical education', because they saw education as the imparting of knowledge rather than the training of the mind and character: the discipline which might produce a good priest would tend to produce a layman lacking the qualities necessary for public life. Furthermore, the clergy were unable to distinguish between a school and a university, because they did not appreciate what a university was for. This mentality was revealed in the way priests were accustomed to speak of the 'rivalry' between Catholic schools and the University—and it was a mentality shared by many laymen, who were accustomed to thinking that university training could be had by remaining at school for an additional year or two.[105] Sullivan argued that the affiliation of these schools to London University only 'multiplies and aggravates the evil results of this serious educational error', as the schools were unable to fulfil the functions of a university, as regards either learning or discipline.[106]

Sullivan's departure in 1873 was a heavy blow for the University, and doubly so in that he was leaving to become President of Queen's College, Cork.[107] In a letter to the politician William Monsell—his parting shot at the Catholic University—Sullivan declared, 'The bishops' ideal of a University is certainly not mine. [...] The bishops want a Seminary or rather a number of Diocesan Seminaries under their absolute control. With them Science and secular learning are naturally secondary objects', and while they spotted dangers to faith in these disciplines, they did not see their 'importance as an element of secular education. [...] They wish besides to impose upon University Students the discipline which in my opinion is even unsuited to a Seminary.' Without proper buildings, money, prestige or degrees, 'with the common sense of the majority in opposition to their system of discipline, with the apathy of a large number of the clergy and bishops and the unconcealed hostility of a considerable number of priests, it is not possible to maintain a central Catholic University in Dublin'. Daily he saw his two goals evaporating: the establishment of 'a great technological Institute and a great free Liberal Catholic University'.[108] As he had told Monsell a fortnight earlier, the laity 'distrust, if they do not absolutely disbelieve, in the capacity of the Irish priests to conduct a good system of lay education'.[109]

Fourteen years earlier, Pollen had moaned about the same tendency he saw in Ireland:

> Is not the religion and its staff in that country really or apparently interested in keeping up a measure of *barbarism*? Are not improvements of land, personal security, intellectual improvement and so forth somewhat dangerous prospects to a body which has held Ireland and kept it religious and even virtuous where these changes have been *kept out*? Is not this the defined and unconscious feeling of the big wigs in respect of our University?[110]

Newman's response was to look at the solution, not the problem: 'As to the University, I really fear that at least some persons already begin, like Frankenstein, to be scared at their own monster.'[111] Despite the difficulties, he tried to encourage Woodlock:

> There is abundance of genius, and varied talent in Ireland to make it a very safe risk indeed to accept the great venture of a real Catholic University. There is talent in the existing body, and other talent (I know well) outside of it which might be brought into it. Men of the width of information, of the varied accomplishments and the vigour of mind, of Professor Sullivan, if not common even in Ireland, still are to be found or to be made.[112]

But Sullivan saw that the departure of the lay professors from the University meant that Catholic higher education would be thrown back into the provincial seminaries. After the collapse of the supplemental charter in 1866, he had reflected bitterly that the loss of each lay professor would cause rejoicing in the camp of the hierarchy, for it had clerical replacements at hand.[113] This might seem exaggerated, but equally strong views were held by clerics who opposed him, such as Cullen's half-nephew Patrick Moran, who wrote: 'The Catholic University, however, had great difficulties to contend against, and not the least is the intrinsic evil of having had a complete set of laymen appointed it professors in the commencement, who now of course look upon it in the light of a monopoly.'[114] Both Moran and Sullivan were, of course, expressing their views in private, which is why they are so robust, but they evidently reflected two opposing mentalities. Renouf wrote more mutedly in a pamphlet for public consumption that a university in which the lay element is powerless 'has *no claim whatever* to the name of a University'.[115]

It might be thought that Sullivan's departure would have caused the episcopate to rethink their attitude, but instead the 'defection' of a layman only served to confirm their view that the laity were not to be relied upon: Scratton, probably the only layman at the University who identified with this way of thinking, saw Sullivan's departure as meaning that they were 'well rid of our worst enemy'.[116] That October the bishops announced a package of reforms in an attempt to persuade the public that the Catholic University was still a viable concern, and among the measures adopted was the decision to include laymen on the Board and the establishment of a finance committee.[117] Ornsby, who had resigned from the University in 1866, returned in 1874 to find that laymen were (ostensibly) about to be co-opted to the Board—a move which delighted Newman[118]—but then saw the plan come to nothing as it was repeatedly postponed; in fact the decision was deferred for as long as the bishops were responsible for governance of the University.[119]

The driving force behind this policy was undoubtedly Cullen, though others shared his views. A key argument underpinning the exclusion of the laity from any control of the University was the contention that the University depended on the diocesan collections and that money was given on the assumption that the episcopate—and they only—could guarantee the Catholic dimension of the project; to give the laity a role in its management would in all likelihood undermine public confidence, with disastrous financial consequences. True, the seminary at Maynooth had from the outset been administered by a board of laity and clergy, but this was the condition imposed by the British government for receipt of an endowment—and, besides, was regarded as a dubious arrangement. Nevertheless, Cullen recognised that if the government granted a charter or an endowment some concessions to lay participation would have to be made, and for this reason he agreed to the gesture of allowing eight laymen to attend the episcopal meeting in August 1863—but not to join the finance committee he formed that year, which comprised himself and two bishops. What is extraordinary is that Cullen managed to convince Woodlock that he was open to lay involvement, when all along he opposed the very idea.[120] As rector, Newman had frequently encountered Cullen's capacity for opaqueness and sensed the lack of complete trust: 'Dr Leahy will trust a man, Dr Cullen will not. Here is the *origo mali*—an Archbishop without trust in anyone. I wonder he does not cook his own dinners.'[121]

In order to boost numbers, Woodlock organised a 'conversazione' in 1869 to which he invited all the professors, preachers, former students and others connected with the University. The event was a success, with around eighty people present, and the guests were shown the manuscripts of Eugene O'Curry, the deceased Professor of Archaeology and Irish History, and other exhibits.[122] But other than this, little was done to harness the goodwill of former students—not, at least, until the University authorities were forced to react when past students entered the public debate about its future. On hearing that present and former students of the University had collaborated on a 'Memorial' which was published in the *Freeman's Journal*, Woodlock suggested to Cullen that they needed a Senate of their own, since otherwise the

University would not receive their sons or their financial backing.[123] They needed to make a great effort to win the support of Catholics from the higher reaches of society, as the little hold they had on the upper classes was fast diminishing; and since the middle classes were loyal, they should start with them.[124] November 1873 saw the publication of the *Memorial addressed by the students and ex-students of the Catholic University of Ireland to the Episcopal Board of the University*. In the final paragraph of the pamphlet the authors declared that they had been encouraged to present their *Memorial* on recalling that Dr Newman had once declared that 'from the co-operation of the Students, with the Superiors of the University, in shaping its future, he looked forward to the creation of a "permanent community of feelings and interest on education and religious subjects, which it will doubtless foster among the educated laity of the country in after life" '.[125]

On being sent the *Memorial* by the former student George Fottrell[126] and informed of its effect, Newman could not but rejoice. In a stirring reply, he wrote:

> One of the chief evils which I deplored in the management of the affairs of the University twenty years ago when I was in Ireland, was the absolute refusal with which my urgent representations were met, that the Catholic laity should be allowed to cooperate with the Archbishops in the work.
>
> As far as I can see, there are ecclesiastics all over Europe, whose policy it is to keep the laity at arms-length; and hence the laity have been disgusted and become infidel, and only two parties exist, both ultras in opposite directions. I came away from Ireland with the distressing fear that there was to be an antagonism, as time went on, between the hierarchy and the educated classes.
>
> You will be doing the greatest possible benefit to the Catholic cause all over the world, if you succeed in making the Univer-

sity a middle station at which clergy and laity can meet, so as
to understand and to yield to each other—and from which,
as from a common ground, they may act in union upon an
age, which is running headlong into infidelity.[127]

Fottrell may well have been inspired by these words when he wrote
to Woodlock with four others—all former officials of the Literary
and Historical Society—to point out that the University was not
successful because its former students were kept out of its government, which meant that they lost interest in it once they left. The
object of the *Memorial* was to bring past students into connection
with it and to show the outside world its benefits: 'Every student
of the University should be a propagandist of its views' and 'should
send other students to its halls'.[128]

Within a few years the ex-students had formed themselves into
the C.U.I. Bono Club, with the aim of taking action on behalf of
the Catholic University.[129] The earliest instance of their efforts
appears to be a circular they issued in 1877 which criticised the
bishops' policy on the future of the University.[130] In the address
composed by the club to mark Newman's elevation to the cardi-
nalate in 1879, he was told that the *Discourses* supplied the lack of
a tradition and effectively acted as the charter for the Catholic
University.

> You have shown that education is a field in which both clergy
> and laity can work together, harmoniously, and without
> jealously, for a common object, and in which both have duties,
> and both have rights, and in establishing this, you [...] have
> rendered valuable assistance to the Catholic Church in her
> struggle for freedom of education throughout the world. [131]

In the early 1870s, Newman composed a lengthy and detailed
memorandum about his connection with the Catholic University.
Reflecting on the lay–clerical divide, he explained that as rector he
had always sought 'to make the laity a substantive power in the

University',[132] but that his attempts to involve them in its financial affairs were repeatedly frustrated by Cullen. He had been confirmed in his thinking by reports he received 'that many of the higher classes of laity would co-operate with the University, were it not for the utter want of confidence they felt in the management of it by the Bishops alone'.[133] He saw the Catholic University as a means to heal the breach between the educated laity and the higher clergy.

> A University, unlike a Seminary or Diocesan College is pre-eminently an institution for the laity, and it may be advantageously used as a means of bringing the educated classes under the just and beneficial influence of the Church. The Bishops ought to be supreme, as the sanctioning, controlling power, and the ultimate authority; but, as the Directors of a bank appoint a Manager [...] so, I conceive, will their Lordships best provide for the interests of the University, and conciliate the laity, if in the management of the current expenses they employ one or two able and zealous men of business to be their Managers.[134]

Entrusting the financial matters of the University to the gentry, whose sons were to be educated there, made sound financial sense, and besides 'would interest them in the University more than anything else'; instead, Newman observed, 'They were treated like good little boys—were told to shut their eyes and open their mouths, and take what we give to them—and this they did not relish.'[135]

This diagnosis of the situation was not something Newman reached after his departure from the University, but was apparent to him during his rectorate, as the following incident shows. In the summer of 1856 a leading article in *The Tablet* by its editor, John Wallis, had sparked off a spirited controversy in the press about the Catholic University and why it languished. Wallis claimed that it had been abandoned both by the 'genteel *Cawtholics*' and by the nationalists who suspected it was becoming, in the hands of Cullen, 'a creature of the State and a propaganda of Whiggery'. Each side suspected that the University favoured the other and therefore neglected it; but as long as Newman was rector, Wallis argued, everyone should support it because he took no part in Irish quarrels.[136] Wallis's analysis of the situation drew from Newman his own diagnosis of the prevailing attitudes, and a different insight. To Newman it seemed that,

> no small portion of the hierarchy and clergy of Ireland think it a mistake and a misfortune that they have any of the upper or middle class among them—that they do but feel awkward when a gentlemen is converted, or shows himself a good Catholic—and in fact, that they think that then only Ireland will become again the Isle of Saints, when it has a population of peasants ruled over by a patriotic priesthood patriarchally.[137]

Since they think 'A gentleman is an evil', and 'The University is for gentlemen', the institution was 'but a provision for perpetu[at]ing and aggravating a recognised evil and nuisance'. Fearing this to be so, Newman thought it impossible that the clergy would take it up wholeheartedly; instead they would only do what Rome compelled them to, with the consequence 'that the University must look out for its friends, its real friends—and must form alliances'.[138] To the editor of *The Rambler*, the organ and mouthpiece of English converts to Catholicism, Newman confided his fear that collisions between the clergy and laity lay ahead: 'The breach between them is fearful—the University may bring it out.'[139]

Two years after leaving Dublin, Newman expressed his suspicions to Ornsby: 'The Irish bishops can command the poorer portion of the community, and through it the *funds* necessary—but they have little or no influence with the classes which provide the *students*—and there has been the hitch.'[140] Hearing in 1861 about the low uptake of students, he commented:

> It is so discouraging to see the educated laity, (lawyers etc) getting more and more separated from the clergy, and tending to a worse state than that of Italy [...] There must be something very wrong somewhere that clergy and laity should have so few sympathies and common thoughts—but we cannot mend matters at our will, and must wait patiently for Providence to do what He has done at other seasons of difficulty for His Church.[141]

Meanwhile he agreed with Ornsby that the exclusion of leading lay Catholics from the government of the University was an anxious matter. The concessions Cullen had appeared willing to make early in Woodlock's rectorate were, in Newman's view, too few; and from across St George's Channel he could detect the jealously towards the laity among Irish ecclesiastics: 'It is creating the evil it fears' —and he, Newman, had been accused of leaning towards Protestantism by protesting against it. The consequence, he noted to Ornsby, was that the gentry would not send their sons to the University and that it would 'become a large school for the middle or sub-middle class'.[142] The situation contrasted with Louvain, where the 'Bishops and clergy and laity *understood the value and the drift* of the Institution'.[143]

Though the failure of the Catholic University has generally been attributed to the lack of a charter (and hence of publicly-recognised degrees) and an endowment, it is telling that Newman thought that, at root, the real problem had more to do with clerical control. This is evident from a letter he wrote to Woodlock in 1868:

> it is *essential* that the Church should have a living presence and control in the action of the University. But still, till the Bishops leave the University to itself, till the University governs itself, till it is able to act as a free being, it will be but

a sickly child, even though it has a charter and an endowment.[144]

When in 1874 Newman heard that the plan of having a mixed board
of bishops and laymen had come to nothing, he expressed his
sadness that the archbishops, being 'not overzealous for laymen',
had not overcome the obstacles. By failing to do so, 'The Bishops
have lost 20 years—and now, after they had such a start, if they
could have used it, Trinity College is in the field to run against them.
It is a very cruel mischance.'[145] And he told the rector, the 'bishops
won't further the University till they trust educated lay Catholics
more'.[146]

* * *

The establishment of the Royal University of Ireland in 1879 did
little to boost student numbers at the Catholic University, nor did
the implementation of a new constitution in 1882 which recast the
Catholic University as a conglomerate of constituent colleges.[147]
One of these was the institution on St Stephen's Green, which now
became known as University College, under the presidency of John
Egan. The College lost £700 during the session 1882/83,[148] even
though it had around thirty students, and Egan resigned at the end.
One reason for the deficit was that the annual collection for the
Catholic University had stopped in 1882; another was that University College did not have the human resources and organisation to
compete with the many schools which now had 'university departments' preparing young men for the degrees of the Royal University.
As it had become clear that the Catholic University was beyond
resuscitation as a corporate institution, Henry Neville, who had acted
as rector from 1879, also resigned in 1883. Unable to find secular
clergy to take on a white elephant, the bishops entrusted the Jesuits
with the management of University College in October 1883.[149]

During its twenty-five years under the Society of Jesus, numbers at the College rose to two hundred and academic successes outstripped those of the three Queen's Colleges.[150] Its success owed a good deal to the supply of well-prepared students from the Jesuits' six thriving secondary schools in Dublin, as well as the transfer of pupils from their recently started university college in Dublin.[151] It also benefitted from an indirect endowment since the Royal University had twenty-six salaried Fellows who acted as examiners, evenly divided between Catholics and Protestants, and all the Catholic Fellows taught at University College.[152] The staff inherited included two of Newman's first appointments, Robert Ornsby and James Stewart, as well as Tom Arnold, who had returned to Dublin; now they served as Fellows of the Royal University. But, despite these appearances of continuity, University College was now operated as a Jesuit institution, which meant that Newman's stamp on it had vanished.

The Catholic University survived notionally as an institution in the person of Gerald Molloy, who had served as vice-rector (1873–83) and Professor of Natural Science under first Woodlock and then Neville before inheriting the rectorship. He occupied rooms at 86 St Stephen's Green until his death in 1906, while the president of University College lived next door at No. 87.[153] 'What is the difference between University College and the Catholic University, seeing that both are in the same building, together with the president of one and the rector of the other?' ran a witticism by John Casey, the Professor of Mathematics. The answer he gave was 'Dr Molloy'[154]—but it is more accurate to say, the rector *plus* the School of Medicine, which was the other surviving part of Newman's Catholic University.

But wholesale changes took place in 1909 which saw the creation of the National University of Ireland, with colleges in Dublin, Galway and Cork, and—as a separate institution—the Queen's University,

Belfast. The School of Medicine, which had continued to expand after Newman's departure, was absorbed into the newly-established University College Dublin,[155] along with the University College of 1882. Though the title of rector of the Catholic University survived, some have argued that while the Catholic University survived *de jure*, it ceased to exist *de facto*; others have argued that University College Dublin, while *de jure* a separate foundation, was *de facto* the lineal successor to University College, which had its roots in the Catholic University.[156] But there were, of course, other points of continuity besides the medical school, such as the Literary and Historical Society; and something of the *genius loci* surely survived, because a good number of the staff appointed to UCD in 1909 had been students during Newman's rectorate.[157] And when the years 1954 and 2004 came round, University College Dublin chose to mark their centenary and 150 years respectively, thereby recognising that John Henry Newman was indeed their founding rector.

Oxford revisited

Having wound up the story of the Catholic University after Newman's departure, we can complete the tale of Newman's practical involvement with higher education by looking briefly at the last three decades of his life back in England. After his departure from Dublin, he continued to take great interest in university education; and on a number of occasions he felt he ought to expand his views on university education—especially over the pressing question faced by English Catholics about attendance at non-Catholic universities. Inevitably, he found himself involved with the university he had severed ties with in 1845, on becoming a Catholic: in fact, developments at his own *alma mater* impinged on his plans for the Catholic University, because, just as it was preparing to receive its first students in the summer of 1854, the Universities Act opened up Oxford and Cambridge to Catholics by removing the religious tests there (except for the MA at Oxford). For the next four decades the question of whether, and under what circumstances, English Catholics could attend a Protestant or non-denominational university was hotly contested. What became known as the 'university question' exercised Catholic minds—and divided the Catholic body.

Although Newman was initially anxious about the effects of the 1854 Act, it soon became apparent that access to the Oxbridge colleges was unaffected, as only a few began to accept Catholics. Nevertheless, two years later he wrote to Bishop Grant of Southwark as he had heard that the bishop intended to give his permission for his ward to go to Oxford. 'I should say that it was a place very dangerous to a young man's faith', he told Grant, 'and though he might be preserved from defection, he might be indelibly stamped with indifferentism, which would be his character through life.' He pointed out that the young man would be saved from this if there was a Catholic hall or college there.

> What is Ireland to me, except the University here is a University for England, as well as for Ireland? I wish to do good, of course, to all Catholics if I can, but to *English* Catholics, as is my duty. I have left England for a while, for what I conceive to be a great *English* interest. But, if I went by my own wishes and tendencies, of course, I would far rather do good to English Catholics in Oxford than in Dublin.

He told Grant that if there was to be a Catholic college in Oxford, 'I am at once loosed from this place'. Meanwhile he feared that Irish as well as English students might transfer to Oxford after a year or two at the Catholic University, 'and make us merely tutors or providers of a Protestant Institution'.[158]

One effect of Newman's departure from Dublin was to aggravate the university question for his countrymen, since any appeal the Catholic University might have had for them now vanished.

Though Newman would undoubtedly have been drawn into the university question in any case, he became directly involved owing to the part he played in another major educational project: the foundation of a school for his convert friends and others who were dissatisfied with provision at the Catholic colleges—which were run as seminaries or by religious orders—and instead wanted a public-school education for their sons. In setting up the first Catholic public school in England, at Edgbaston in Birmingham, and challenging vested interests within the Catholic system of education, Newman and his collaborators encountered great misunderstanding and vehement opposition. Nevertheless, despite the daunting obstacles and an internal crisis that almost destroyed the school in 1861, the Oratory School was soon educating around seventy boys, mainly from the upper reaches of society—and, more significantly, preparing them not for a priestly or religious calling, but for life in the world.[159]

In founding the Oratory School, one of Newman's hopes was to feed the Catholic University with suitably prepared boys. The prospect must have seemed realistic at the outset, since seven of the thirty-eight students in the University's first cohort had previously received tuition at the Birmingham Oratory.[160] But despite his connection with the University and the English presence there, Newman received no support in his strategy from the school promoters or parents, not even from Arnold, who had left Dublin in 1862 to join the school staff: not one Oratory School boy from Newman's time fulfilled his wish, even though a good number came from Ireland.[161] Nor was there much interest in the London University exams: for the majority of Oratory School parents, the only university education they cared for was that provided at the ancient universities. In fact, one of the school's stated aims was to embrace 'the same variety of destinations in life, as are met with and provided for at Eton, Winchester and Rugby',[162] which above all meant preparation for a university education along the lines of Oxford or Cambridge. The problem was that the Catholic Church opposed 'mixed education', and over the following decades the policy hardened, so that 'the school was left in something of a limbo, its basic purpose, to give the pre-university part of a liberal education, being frustrated'.[163] The problem became more acute as the boys at the Oratory School approached university age, and by 1865 Newman noted the effect: the boys at the top of the school 'get slovenly — i.e. for want of a *stimulus*. They have no object before them'.[164]

The problem had been foreseen by the promoters of the Oratory School who, when founding the school, had discussed how a Catholic university might be started in England. Sir John Acton, one of the leading promoters, had envisaged a faculty for the liberal arts growing out of the school. He contended that 'the school must ultimately decide' the university question, 'either by setting up a Catholic university […] or by getting a college at Oxford', and that the pressure to resolve the matter would mount as soon as 'the first generation of boys has been trained to the university level and turned out of Edgbaston'.[165] It was hoped—and almost assumed—that with so much convert talent and energy available, the university question would soon be resolved one way or another. However, the greater complexities of tertiary education meant that there was no equivalent to the commonly shared aspiration for a public school, and instead various schemes emerged. In 1861, Frederick Paley, a convert and former Fellow of St John's College, Cambridge, opened a house for Catholics at his old university and acted as a private tutor for them. Newman, meanwhile, having abandoned hope for an English collegiate house at the Catholic University, turned his mind to the possibility of setting up a college in England which would be affiliated to the Catholic University in the same way that Catholic colleges were affiliated to London University. Although he admitted it would, of course, be '*practically* not a University', he thought that a sufficient number of boys from the leading Catholic schools in England—including the Oratory School—would be enough to give it 'a sort of University character'.[166] He thought that such a college would be attractive, 'if only the great Catholic schools would interest themselves in the subject';[167] but he failed to convince even his own friends.

Newman's chief adviser, James Hope-Scott, expressed a preference for a proper Catholic university and he hoped Newman would lay the foundations for one at Edgbaston. Acton thought along similar lines: the Oratory School would 'create both supply and demand: they [i.e. the Oratory School parents] will feel more than the others the want of a University education and they will furnish one necessary portion of the materials. Here is a basis and an opportunity for the growth of something like a Catholic university such as did not exist in Ireland'.[168] He offered first Newman, then Renouf (the former lecturer at the Catholic University and resident tutor at St Mary's), property and a library so that a start could be made; but neither took up the offer.

Although the number of Catholics entering Oxford and Cambridge was small (about twenty at Oxford in the first decade after the removal of the religious test), between 1863 and 1867 there was a heated debate in Catholic circles over the university question, and it was focused on Oxford and the prospect of establishing a Catholic hall there. Catholics were agreed that Oxford (as well as Cambridge) presented a danger to the faith, as the university was effectively an Anglican seminary; so long as the Protestant upper classes predominated, the atmosphere there was bound to be Protestant. Nevertheless, the converts felt that the real danger to young Catholics was not exposure to High Church views but to intellectual liberalism. The dilemma that presented itself to this social group was that they wished their offspring to mix with the future leaders of English society, but without endangering their faith. In their confusion, some of the converts turned to Newman for guidance.

By 1863 Newman had become convinced that the ideal solution —a Catholic university—was unworkable in England, both for practical considerations and due to his increasing awareness that most Catholics were unable to understand a university in *his* sense of the word.[169] While the plan for a Catholic hall at Oxford had the merit of securing a liberal education, he felt it had a major drawback: the measures likely to be put in place to safeguard faith and morals would make it 'so isolated as not to have the influx of Oxford opinions', and this would encourage Catholics to opt instead for the ordinary colleges, so that the scheme was unlikely to gain ecclesiastical approval. 'The best plan practically' was to continue 'to suffer still young Catholics to go to Oxford' and to introduce a religious body 'to counteract the irreligious spirit of the place'.[170] Newman maintained that while Oxford was dangerous for young men, it was hardly more so than the Royal Military Academy at Woolwich or the University of London, both of which were open to Catholics. The advisability of attendance, he felt, depended on individual circumstances; and he was as much against a general prohibition on Catholics going there—as it would be too great a trial of obedience to some parents—as he was against an indiscriminate and general permission.

The prevailing ecclesiastical view was that attendance at the old universities could not be justified, as the intellectual atmosphere and the social nature of undergraduate life would render all safeguards useless. This view was fortified by the strong stance of influential Oxbridge converts such as H. E. Manning (the future cardinal), W. G. Ward and some of the London Oratorians. But many of the educated laity, particularly converts, inclined to the contrary opinion: that the opportunity to enter fully into national life justified the risk, provided suitable precautions were taken.

As pressure was mounting for coverage of the university question in his *Home and Foreign Review*, Acton withheld an article that proposed allowing Catholics to go Oxford so as to give the scheme for a Catholic university precedence, and he consulted Newman on the matter. The question was certainly a live one. The first issue of the *Dublin Review* under W. G. Ward's editorship (July 1863) contained an article entitled 'The work and the wants of the Catholic Church in England', in which a Catholic university was identified as the third of five 'wants'. The author, no less a figure than Manning, declared that a Catholic university was no Utopian dream, as all the elements were present in the English Catholic body which 'naturally lead up to and demand a University for their completion'.[171] Despite the bold policy advocated in print and Manning's personal desire to find a solution, his scheme was not taken up by Cardinal Wiseman; nor were others that were discussed, such as a Catholic academy in Rome. Meanwhile, Edmund Ffoulkes, an Oxford convert and former vice-principal of Jesus College, began promoting a plan for a Catholic hall at Oxford. The rector of Lincoln had offered to assist him by sponsoring a hall exclusively for Catholics, and Ffoulkes wanted Newman to join his organising committee, which drew mainly from the Catholic aristocracy. But Newman felt unable to support the scheme publicly. Renouf made his own contribution to the debate by issuing a pamphlet, just as he was on the point of leaving Dublin, which argued the case for Catholics to attend halls or colleges at Oxford; it was entitled *University education for English Catholics: a letter to the Very Rev. J. H. Newman, by a Catholic layman* (1864).

At their Low Week meeting in 1864, the bishops decided to reject Ffoulkes's project of a Catholic hall at Oxford. They also agreed that the scheme for a Catholic university was impractical and, despite offering no alternative, instructed the clergy to dissuade Catholic parents from sending their sons to the English universities. The following summer the Bishop of Birmingham, William Ullathorne, offered the Catholic 'mission' (i.e. parish) at Oxford to Newman, who coincidentally had just been given the option on a large central site. Besides wishing to open an Oratory there, Newman now began to look into the feasibility of a Catholic hall. As usual he sought the advice of friends. Some favoured the plan for a Catholic hall, while others told him they preferred to send their sons to one of the colleges. Hope-Scott, however, urged Newman to tread cautiously and test the principle by starting with private houses for a tutor and students. Newman decided to follow this advice, but when he sounded out his bishop, Ullathorne was quick to inform Newman that he would only countenance the plan for an Oratory; and he reminded Newman that he had joined the Irish bishops in asking Rome for a warning against attendance at Oxford and Cambridge, at the time the Catholic University was being founded.

Alarmed at these developments, Manning appealed to Rome for an instruction to prevent more Catholics going to the universities, but Rome responded by directing the bishops to meet again. Prior to their doing so, a slanted questionnaire was sent to a number of graduate converts—but not Newman. Nevertheless, at the episcopal meeting in December 1864 it transpired that only two of the bishops favoured an outright ban on attendance at the universities, and that most preferred to issue a caution on the dangers of attendance. Reflecting on the fact that not one of the thirteen bishops advising the Holy See on the Oxford question had had an English university education, T. W. Allies complained to Newman: 'How many of them care sufficiently for mental culture to give an adequate consideration to the motives determining parents to send their sons to Oxford?'[172] Keenly aware of their parental duties and responsibilities, and eager that their sons should not forfeit an education that would provide access to mainstream national and social life, other converts complained to the bishops directly. Various laymen began to act either individually or collectively, both at home and abroad. One lobbied energetically against a positive prohibition and visited the authorities in Rome; another summoned a meeting of influential laymen in order to draw up an address to Propaganda Fide.[173] While Newman's scope for involvement was severely restricted, on account of his earlier policy and his connection with the Catholic University, he nevertheless felt the question was one which the laity ought to face squarely. The initiative, he believed, would be more effective if it came from those who were immediately involved in the decision.

In February 1865 Propaganda Fide instructed the English bishops to dissuade Catholics from attending non-Catholic universities. Despite this development, Ullathorne again offered the Oxford mission to Newman, and in June 1866 the Birmingham Oratory accepted, on condition that the warning against Oxford was not strengthened. Newman realised that the provision of a strong Catholic presence in Oxford was likely to be considered by many parents as 'a pledge that their children would be protected against the scepticism and infidelity which too notoriously prevail there just now'.[174] It was to avoid this that Propaganda Fide had sanctioned the proposal of an Oxford Oratory dependent on the Birmingham Oratory, with the specific proviso that Newman himself should not reside in Oxford: the intention was to grant Newman sufficient scope to influence Protestants there, but not enough to attract Catholics. Ullathorne, however, withheld this 'secret instruction' from Newman, believing he could get it rescinded. Friends of Newman launched an appeal for the new Oratory church, and within months around £2000 was pledged, mainly from the school promoters. Then in April 1867, when preparations were well under way, the secret ban on Newman was leaked to the press. After agonising over the matter, Newman decided to let the plan lapse.[175] Shortly afterwards Propaganda Fide issued its strongest warning yet, declaring that English Catholics sending their sons to the national universities would be guilty of exposing them to a proximate occasion of grave sin; the bishops were charged to communicate the decision to the faithful through pastoral letters.

Asked by anxious parents for guidance in the face of official strictures, Newman's replies reveal his deep sympathy with the aspirations of youth. He explained to a distressed mother that the declaration was not an outright prohibition but the gravest of warnings, thus a general rule admitting exceptions for very strong reasons.

> It does not do to beat the life out of a youth — the life of aspiration, excitement and enthusiasm. Older men live by reason, habit and self-control, but the young live by visions. I can fancy cases in which Oxford would be the salvation of a youth; when he would be far more likely to rise up against authority, murmur against his superiors, and to become an unbeliever, if he is kept from Oxford than if he is sent there.[176]

The goal of Oxford might be the sole motivation for a youth to work, and avoid idleness and despondency; 'It may make all the difference between his being a useful member of society through life and employing his talents to God's glory, or not'.[177]

In response to repeated promptings from Propaganda Fide (not unlike those to the Irish bishops twenty years earlier) the English bishops appointed a committee in 1871 to study the university question. But Newman had no confidence in the initiative. He told one of the committee that he despaired of any good coming out of these attempts, because 'A University is to make youth "*sensibus perfecti*" [mature in thinking] whereas all we aim at is to keep them "*malitia parvuli*" [babes in evil]—and we think to "overcome the world" by "going out of it" '.[178] What underlay his strong feelings was his conviction that Manning's mind was in the same mould as Cullen's; both men had a broad idea of academic studies, but they would only contemplate an educational endeavour firmly in clerical hands and with strict discipline. When the committee sent him its questionnaire, Newman found himself unable to formulate proper responses on account of differing fundamental assumptions about the nature of education. In attempting to explain his remarks to the questions posed, Newman wrote out a summary of his ideas in what was his most extended commentary on university education since leaving Dublin.

To the first question, which asked whether there were any perceived deficiencies in the provision of liberal education for young Catholic laymen of the higher classes, Newman answered that there was *no* provision: there was nothing available that deserved the name of a liberal education. 'University Education has, properly speaking, no equivalent; what is most like an equivalent in its effect, is for a youth to be well read, well travelled, and well introduced; which the many cannot be, and which is the accident of personal good fortune, not the result of a system.' The second question asked in what ways the current system was deficient. Newman replied that the want was not one of degree, but of kind. The question was based on an assumption—which he refused to grant—that there existed *any* university education in England (provided by Catholics) which was worthy of the name.

> We shall know what University Education is by considering what School is for a boy. Parents send their sons to school because they are in the way, because home instruction is expensive, in order that there may be method in their instruction, — that they may be submitted to discipline — that they may have the stimulus of emulation — and that they may be introduced into the society of their equals, both as a moral preparation for the world, and a formation of character, and also as a means of making acquaintances and friendships which may last through life. It is these latter benefits, so needful for young men, which are provided for by a University. It is a place of residence where youths are brought together from various quarters, and brought into

familiar intercourse and perpetual collision of intellect with a sufficient number of able Professors and Tutors, and of numerous fellow students, candidates together with them for examinations and degrees.[179]

And to guide his reader he enclosed one of the *Discourses* with the relevant passage marked.[180]

The committee's sixth question asked for a response to four concrete proposals: for a central board of examiners on the model of London University; for a system of prizes to raise academic standards at the Catholic colleges; for the foundation of houses of higher studies which might form the nucleus of a future Catholic university; for gaining admission, but without residence, to degrees at Oxford and Cambridge. Newman's response to the underlying fixation with an education driven by exams was terse:

> It is plain that, if a University Education is what I have described it to be, Examinations hold but a subordinate part in it. I have broadly stated in the Discourse enclosed which I have sent you, that a residence without Examinations comes nearer to the idea of a University Education than examinations without residence. Examinations are in this day matters of necessity, and they have their specific use in the training of the intellect. Their prospect keeps youths occupied, and, when frequent, they impart self-confidence, they serve to bring home to a youth what he knows and what he does not, they teach him to bring out his knowledge and to express his meaning clearly—but mere examinations, if they are the first and whole instrument of education, have a special tendency (if I may use very familiar language) [to] promote cramming and create prigs.[181]

For this reason he had more interest in the proposal for houses of higher study than the other three. He refused to be drawn by the question about whether he attached much importance to degrees being recognised by the State; for him, they were only necessary in case there was no other equally powerful stimulus to attract students and encourage study.

Newman was equally frank with the leading layman Lord Howard of Glossop when explaining how he viewed the predicament that Catholics found themselves in.

> We are driven into a corner just now, and have to act, when no mode of action is even bearable. It is a choice of great difficulties. On whole I do not know how to avoid the conclusion that mixed education in the higher schools is as much a necessity now in England, as it was in the East in the days of St Basil and St Chrysostom. Certainly, the more I think of it, the less am I satisfied with the proposal of establishing a Catholic College in our Universities; and I suppose the idea of a Catholic University, pure and simple, is altogether out of the question.[182]

He thought that the bishops should repeal their virtual prohibition of young Catholics attending Oxbridge colleges, and that they should counter 'what can only be tolerated as the least of evils' by placing a strong mission in Oxford. This 'should be a strong religious community, which would act as a support and rallying-point for young Catholics in their dangerous position, commanding their respect intellectually, and winning their confidence, and providing quiet opportunities for their being kept straight both in faith and in conduct'. He gave seven reasons why a Catholic college would not work, and after analysing the problems that at Catholic college would face over discipline, remarked:

> The true and only antagonist of the world, the flesh, and the devil is the direct power of religion, as acting in the Confessional, in confraternities, in social circles, in personal influence, in private intimacies etc etc And all this would be secured by

a strong mission worked zealously and prudently, and in no other way.[183]

Since a large university allowed a student to choose his company, he felt that 'the open University, when complemented by a strong Mission, may be even safer than a close Catholic College'.[184]

In the event, it was not the proposal for houses of study that was adopted but Manning's scheme for a 'Catholic University College', which opened in Kensington, London in 1875. However, it survived only seven years. In the first place Manning's choice of rector was unfortunate, as he turned out to be an incompetent administrator and was forced to resign in 1878; four years later he was suspended from priestly duties for moral reasons. The college also failed because it lacked support: the Jesuits gave the scheme no assistance, the bishops lost interest once it had been opened, and the laity continued to show their preference for Oxford and Cambridge. When Manning invited Newman to participate Newman turned the offer down, officially because of the connection with London University, privately because he feared it would be under too close clerical control. Three years after the demise of the Catholic University College, the warning about Catholic attendance at Oxford was reiterated; but in 1895, after the death of Manning (and Newman), the policy was jettisoned. Although there had been mounting pressure from the laity, the official reason given for the reversal of policy was the assessment that conditions at the universities had changed: Catholic residence was now possible as the moral condition had improved and the Anglican monopoly had been broken.

For many years after Newman's death, those who had known him well must have wondered how it was that all his practical educational endeavours and efforts to guide lay Christians could have come to so little, and that the *Idea* should be considered his sole legacy to the world of education. But now, more than a century later, thanks to the survival of so much archival material, it is becoming evident that this judgement is not tenable. 'That a thing is true, is no reason that it should be said, but that it should be done; that it should be acted upon', Newman wrote;[185] and this applies to those educational truths he discerned and gave life to.

Notes

1   Between 1854 and 1859, 106 students were entered in the books of the Catholic University, excluding the medical students and those attending the evening classes; of these, thirteen came from England or Scotland and fifteen from mainland Europe (Barr, *Paul Cullen*, pp. 221–3). Of the 191 students who registered between 1854 and 1861, 40 came from outside Ireland, i.e. 21%; of the 986 during Woodlock's rectorship (1861–79), 37 came from outside, i.e. less than 4% (Rigney, 'Bartholomew Woodcock', vol. i, p. 326).

2   In 1863 the office of vice-rector was suppressed as an economy measure.

3   Memorandum, n.d., DDA, 45/2–3 (uncatalogued).

4   In addition there were 110 in the medical school and 150 in the evening classes (E. Larkin, *The consolidation of the Roman Catholic Church in Ireland, 1860–1870* (Chapel Hill, 1987), p. 147). In the opening ceremony for the academic year 1862/63 Woodlock read out the names of eleven students whom the staff thought worthy of BA degrees—those who had passed the licentiate—though they merely received certificates (J. J. Hogan, 'The Newman heritage', *Struggle with fortune. A miscellany for the centenary of the Catholic University of Ireland 1854–1954*, ed. M. Tierney (Dublin, 1955), pp. 219–20). Woodlock also referred to BA and MA degrees in his Calendar for 1863.

5   Cullen to Barnabò, 5 December 1861, quoted in Larkin, *Consolidation of the Roman Catholic Church*, p. 147.

6   Cullen to Kirby, 17 November 1861, quoted in Larkin, *Consolidation of the Roman Catholic Church*, p. 146.

7   This was *not* the solution favoured by Newman: he wanted affiliation to the Queen's University, but not incorporation as a college. See Norman, *The Catholic Church and Ireland in the age of rebellion, 1859–1873* (Ithaca, 1965), pp. 199–200; and see p. 315.

8   The first attempt to gain a charter was in the summer of 1858 when Newman wrote on behalf of the professoriate to Disraeli, then Chancellor

of the Exchequer, petitioning for one (*LD*, vol. xviii, pp. 415–16), and Ornsby coordinated the sending of a memorial to him from the professors. This was followed up by proposals from three of the archbishops, who had previously sounded out Disraeli via Monsell.

9   *Weekly Register* (5 October 1861), p. 4.

10   During the mid-1850s the number of Catholics entering Trinity was approximately twenty a year, and this number rose to around twenty-five a year in the 1860s. Most of them were studying for the Bar.

11   Michael Errington, one of the members of the original Catholic University Committee, sent his eldest son George to the Catholic University in 1857, but in 1859 his younger son James went to Trinity. Richard More O'Ferrall, whose brother James was on the Committee, was a constant adviser of Woodlock, but he declined to send his only son to the Catholic University.

12   *Weekly Register* (5 October 1861), p. 4.

13   The Irish college which joined in 1840 was St Patrick's, Carlow. St Kieran's, Kilkenny followed suit in 1844, and St Patrick's, Thurles in 1849 (F. M. G. Willson, *Our Minerva: the men and politics of the University of London, 1836–1858* (London, 1995), appendix II).

14   The story of the Stonyhurst philosophers is told in H. J. A. Sire's *Gentlemen philosophers: Catholic higher studies at Liège and Stonyhurst College, 1774–1916* (Worthing, 1988).

15   Newman to Butler, 19 November 1857, *LD*, vol. xviii, p. 179. Self-reliance was, of course, an important principle with Newman. In the last of six articles on 'The Catholic University' in the *Weekly Register* (13 March 1858) Newman writes: 'we hope that no Catholic University that is or shall be, with its vantage-ground of higher principles, will ever show less self-respect, consistency, and manliness, than Protestant Oxford, in standing on its own sense of right and falling back upon its own resources' (*LD*, vol. xviii, p. 580).

16   The Trinity tutors were essentially lecturers, lecturing to groups of fifteen to twenty-five students for two hours a day. A new system was introduced in 1834 which meant that students were no longer taught just by their own tutor. The division of labour resulted in better lectures, but relations between tutor and pupil were less friendly, and there was less correspondence with the family of the pupil, i.e. the academic gains were offset by a loss of pastoral oversight (*Royal Commission Trinity* (1852), pp. 13–16, 125–6).

17   *Report on the condition and circumstances of the Catholic University of Ireland, presented by a Committee of Senate* (Dublin, 1859), p. 89.

18   *Report on the condition and circumstances of the Catholic University*, p. 21.

19   Woodlock disapproved of the plan for one large collegiate house. One of the six types of residence envisaged at the Queen's Colleges was the 'incorporated hall', founded and endowed for students and recognised by the Colleges, but none had been set up at the time of the Royal Commission, even though the demand existed. At Cork, the authorities estimated that £6000 was the sum required to build a hall without a dining room; at Galway, they estimated that a hall for 100 students would cost £7000 (*Royal Commission Queen's Colleges* (1858), pp. 11–12, 317–18).

20   *Report on the condition and circumstances of the Catholic University*, pp. 79–80. As a consequence of the *Report*, the deans were paid £100 p.a. by the University and the fees at St Patrick's were reduced from £60 to £40 p.a. Board and lodging worked out at £22 p.a. at Belfast and around £42–£44 at Cork and Galway (*Royal Commission Queen's Colleges* (1858), p. 13).

21   Newman, however, feared that the lack of funds was a mere pretext and that 'It may be made an excuse for turning the University into a College, which alone the Bishops understand' (Newman to Ornsby, 16 January 1859, *LD*, vol. xix, p. 19).

22   *Report on the condition and circumstances of the Catholic University*, p. 87.

23   *Report on the condition and circumstances of the Catholic University*, pp. 85–6.

24   The composition of the committee may have influenced two other recommendations: greater investment in science (two were medics); and the commencement of lectures in law (O'Hagan was a barrister, O'Reilly had studied law, and Dunne began training as a barrister shortly afterwards, and lectured in law from 1864).

25   *Report on the condition and circumstances of the Catholic University*, p. 86.

26   The reference to 10 pm appeared in the University Calendar of 1863, but was omitted the following year.

27   *Report on the condition and circumstances of the Catholic University*, pp. 86–7.

28   For a full treatment of this phenomena, see J. A. Mangan, *Athleticism in the Victorian and Edwardian public school* (Cambridge, 1981).

29   *Report on the condition and circumstances of the Catholic University*, p. 87.

30   Forde to Cullen, [1856], quoted in *NU*, p. 508n.

31   *Report on the condition and circumstances of the Catholic University*, pp. 22–3.

32   *Report on the condition and circumstances of the Catholic University*, pp. 23–4.

33   This was the system in place at Trinity, where scholarships were competed for about half-way through the undergraduate course by means of a

competitive examination (McDowell & Webb, *Trinity College Dublin*, pp. 120–1).

[34] Arnold, 'Practical suggestions on the proposed organisation of the undergraduate course in the Faculty of Philosophy and Letters', *Report on the condition and circumstances of the Catholic University*.

[35] The distinction between pass-men and honours-men was introduced at Trinity in 1834 and it meant that the latter read a more varied and extensive course. Those reading for honours had to acquit themselves with distinction in the termly examinations of the pass course in order to qualify for the honours examination (McDowell & Webb, *Trinity College Dublin*, pp. 172–3).

[36] No action appears to have been taken, as the system was still in operation several years later.

[37] Newman to Ornsby, 18 May 1859, *LD*, vol. xix, p. 138.

[38] *LD*, vol. xix, p. 142n. Newman, of course, saw an advantage in having 'vast masses' of students together, so that they could educate each other; discipline was to be achieved by breaking the student body into small collegiate houses.

[39] Ornsby added that if Forde's idea of 'ecclesiastical *fellows*' was taken up, 'it becomes very much of a seminary' (Ornsby to Newman, 30 July 1859, *LD*, vol. xix, p. 187n).

[40] The university developed out of the seminary of Quebec, which had been established in 1668 by François de Laval, the first Bishop of New France. The seminary received a royal charter on 8 December 1852, which granted it the right to confer degrees and created the Université Laval with 'the rights and privileges of a university'—a scheme approved by Pope Benedict XV. Its first rector, the abbé Louis Casault, had visited Europe and studied the university systems there prior to the foundation. According to the terms of the charter, the Visitor was the (Catholic) Archbishop of Quebec, who had the right to veto appointments and regulations; the appointment of the rector lay with the superior of the seminary; and the Council, together with the rector, was to administer the university. The Council was composed of the directors of the seminary together with the three doyen professors of each of the four faculties (theology, law, medicine and the arts); and it was empowered to enact statutes and rules, on the sole condition that they contained nothing contrary to the laws of the United Kingdom or Canada (*Catholic Encyclopedia* (New York, 1910), vol. ix, pp. 47–8).

[41]   In 'State of Seminaries and other schools in the sixteenth century and since' (*CUG* 24 (9 November 1854), p. 191), Newman maintained that the Holy See had shown great confidence in the people of Ireland in recommending to them 'an institution, which it has for centuries rather tolerated as established, than taken the initiative in establishing. The instances of Louvain and Quebec, striking as they are, are less significant, inasmuch as the University of Louvain was only a revival, and the University of Quebec had already existed, or was founded, under the form of a College'. He argued that the three new Catholic universities, Louvain, Quebec, and Dublin, 'suggest to us that a change of policy is in progress at Rome on the subject of methods of education. We are not then concerned in an isolated, experimental, or accidental attempt, but sharing in a great movement, which has the tokens of success in its deliberateness and its extent.'

[42]   Newman to Disraeli, 19 July 1858, *LD*, vol. xviii, p. 416. Monsell had advised Newman on 6 July to 'prepare and sign a document stating the early history, present position, and objects of the Catholic university and praying the government to grant it a charter after the form of that which has recently been granted to the University of Quebec' (*LD*, vol. xviii, p. 401). Newman referred to the granting of a charter to Quebec in 'A charter to the Catholic University', *The Rambler* (1 May 1859).

[43]   H. J. Tyrrell, 'Report on the Medical Lodging House', *The Vice-Rector's Report for the year 1858–1859* (Dublin, 1859), pp. 74–5, DDA, Woodlock Papers, 159/3. The timetable at St Patrick's House during the session 1858/59 included compulsory attendance at morning prayer at 7.30 am and observance of the 'short silence' after night prayer at 10 pm, as well as a specified study time in the evening after tea. The times for meals were virtually identical to those at the medical house (Record of proceedings at St Patrick's House 1858–61, DDA, Woodlock Papers, 106/5).

[44]   The Prefect of Residence was also to act as Prefect of Classes and see that professors and students alike were 'at posts; entering the halls and calling the rolls, as he deems fit' (*The Vice-Rector's Report for the year 1858–1859*, pp. 23–4, DDA, Woodlock Papers, 159/3). At the Queen's Colleges the Deans of Residences had 'the moral care and spiritual charge' of their students, i.e. their co-religionists. They had authority to visit the licensed boarding houses in which their students lived, to give them religious instruction, and to make regulations for the due observance of religious duties and for securing regular attendance at worship. In the case of the Catholic deans, they were to be approved by the local bishop and arch-

bishop. The College registrar was to give the dean the names and addresses of his students; and the dean was supposed to report each session on the general conduct of his students and how they observed College discipline (*Royal Commission Queen's Colleges* (1858), pp. 12, 306).

45 Minute book of the Episcopal Board 1857–79, 19 October 1859, pp. 9, 11–12, UCDA, CU3.

46 Ornsby to Newman, 12 December 1859, *LD*, vol. xix, p. 253n.

47 Scratton to Newman, 22 October 1859, Letter book of University Secretary 1858–60, DDA, Woodlock Papers, 106/112.

48 Cullen to Barnabò, 11 November 1859, *Paul Cullen*, ed. MacSuibhne, vol. ii, p. 302. Cullen told Rome that the Board of twelve had been formed to keep watch and would 'endeavour to introduce good order and the necessary discipline' (*ibid.*, p. 301).

49 Arnold to Newman, 7 November 1859, *Letters of Thomas Arnold*, p. 103. It seems that Arnold was not supported in his second scheme even though Gartlan recommended that, after the closure of St Mary's, professors be given the first option of taking students in so as to attract those of a higher social class.

50 Newman to Arnold, [30] November 1859 [misdated 1857], *LD*, vol. xviii, p. 190. The letter echoes the priorities of Arnold's father, who as headmaster of Rugby placed religious formation first in his priorities, character formation second, and intellectual development third. That Newman really meant what he wrote about Arnold is borne out by a comment that 'for a free and easy quasi Private Tutor or Head of a Lodging House, he [Arnold] would be perfection' (Newman to Monsell, 22 June 1863, *LD*, vol. xx, p. 480).

51 List of fines, 1861, Student ledger of St Patrick's House 1858–61, DDA, Woodlock Papers, 106/5.

52 Why Tyrrell's medical house was closed in the summer of 1861 is a mystery, given that the medical faculty was thriving and the lodging house a success, though the most likely explanation is that the Episcopal Board had decided to replace it with the Medical College.

53 The new Medical College was founded on the model of the Pédagogie des Facultés des Sciences et de Médecine, now existing within the Collége de Marie Thérèse at the Catholic University of Louvain (*Catholic University Calendar*, 1863, p. 29).

54 Bonamy Price of Worcester College had told the Oxford commissioners: 'If every Undergraduate were made to understand that expensive habits were

inconsistent with his College life, and would, if persevered in, lead to his removal, there would soon be a positive change'. Another witness added: 'To correct these evils [of extravagance and idleness] we must make study and not amusement the law of the University' (*Royal Commission Oxford* (1852), pp. 26–7).

55   *Catholic University Calendar*, 1863, p. 30. This development was in keeping with Newman's aims, as one of the four 'immediate objects' he mentioned in 1856 was 'that of securing the moral and liberal education of the Medical Profession' (Memorandum, 20 June 1856, *MC*, p. 147). At the end of Newman's rectorate, in June 1858, David Dunne had started lecturing in philosophy at the medical school.

56   'Report to the Episcopal Board of the Catholic University of Ireland', 1863, DDA, Cullen Papers, 45/4/III(6A).

57   For more details of the affair, see Meenan, *Centenary history*, pp. 15–18; *LD*, vol. xx, pp. 422n, 424n.

58   McDonnell later joined the Irish Republican Brotherhood, a secret oath-bound organisation dedicated to the establishment of an independent Irish republic, and assisted in arms distribution, for which he was jailed. After meeting with Engels and Marx in London, he was appointed to the general council of the First International (*DIB*).

59   Robertson to Cullen, 17 March 1863, DDA, Cullen Papers, 45/4/III(2). In August that year, the bishops condemned the Brotherhood of St Patrick.

60   J. Devoy, *Recollections of an Irish rebel* (Shannon, 1929), p. 16.

61   Newman to Ornsby, 26 January 1863, *LD*, vol. xx, p. 425.

62   Report of the Finance Committee of the Catholic University to the University Board, 1863, p. 2, DDA, Cullen Papers, 45/4/III(7A); Minute book of the Episcopal Board 1857–79, 16 September 1863, UCDA, CU3.

63   At their first meeting in October 1863 it was decided that the externs who did not appear to be conforming to University regulations should be visited, that the dean of the Medical College should compile a report on 98 Leeson Street, and that the dean of St Patrick's should obtain a list of medical students who needed to be reminded about their obligation to attend the University Mass. At a later meeting the Committee decided that excerpts from the Rules and Regulations should be distributed to all externs. Dr MacDevitt's inspection of 98 Leeson Street, which was nominally under his charge, but cared for by a Mr G. Griffin, revealed only a few minor anomalies (Minutes of the Council of Discipline, 1863–64, DDA, Wood-lock Papers, 106/4). The last named is probably Gerald Griffin, who

became a magistrate and was one of the founders of the C.U.I. Bono Club.

64 This is indicated by the students paying for half or a third of a room (Account book of St Patrick's House, 1859–68, DDA, Woodlock Papers, 106/6).

65 O'Donohoe to Woodlock, 19 October 1868; Woodlock to O'Donohoe, 22 October 1868; Woodlock to Cullen, 15 & 19 January 1869; O'Donohoe to Cullen, 6 March 1869; O'Donohoe to Cullen, 8 March 1869, DDA, Cullen Papers, 45/5/IV/(40, 41); 45/5/V/(2); 45/5/VI/(1, 2, 4).

66 Woodlock to Cullen, 2 July 1867, DDA, Cullen Papers 45/5/II(19).

67 Newman to H. Wilberforce, 10 June 1856, *LD*, vol. xvii, p. 259.

68 Rules and Regulations of St Patrick's House (approved by the Episcopal Board on 18 March 1871), Minute book of Episcopal Board 1859–79, 28 March 1871, UCDA, CU3.

69 Minute book of the Episcopal Board 1861–79, [October] 1873, UCDA, CU3. Cullen judged that Loughlin had 'utterly failed' at keeping discipline (E. Larkin, *Roman Catholic Church and the Home Rule Movement in Ireland, 1870–74* (Chapel Hill, 1990), p. 384).

70 Henry Hennessy, the Professor of Natural Science appointed by Newman in 1855, had married a Protestant in a civil ceremony, though the marriage had recently been solemnised after her reception into the Catholic Church (Larkin, *Roman Catholic Church, 1870–74*, p. 370). Previously the bishops had asked the rector to investigate grave reports about the moral character of Hennessy (Minute book of the Episcopal Board 1861–79, 11 October 1871, DDA).

71 A lady reported (to the medical school) that a restaurant in Cecilia Street operated as a brothel and that it was patronised by medical students from the Catholic University (O'Loughlin to Woodlock, 8 May 1873, quoted in Larkin, *Roman Catholic Church, 1870–74*, p. 369). Although there had been great improvements at Oxford, the royal commissioners commented on the existing evils of sensual vice, gambling and extravagant expenditure. They were told that little could be done about 'vice'; prostitution was not widespread in Oxford itself, but London was now within reach of the 'ill-disposed or weak young man' (*Royal Commission Oxford* (1852), p. 23).

72 Before agreeing to take over St Patrick's, the Jesuits asked the Board a number of questions: about their responsibilities with respect to those not living at St Patrick's; about the duties of the Prefect of Discipline and Guardian of Amusements; and about the modifications to be made to the house rules (Minute book of the Episcopal Board 1861–79, 2 December

1873, DDA).

73   Woodlock, Memorandum on Arts studies for Medical Students of the University, 26 February 1874, DDA, Woodlock Papers, 106/21. In this memorandum Woodlock argued that it was necessary to try to persuade parents of the value of combining humanities studies with medical studies.

74   Ornsby told Newman: 'I think the Constitution as you planned it, very much set aside in practice. The senate never meets, and the Rector is supreme in the strictest sense of the word. But the Council assembles as usual, and also the [arts] faculty' (9 January 1862, *LD*, vol. xx, p. 143n).

75   Cullen to Barnabò, 11 November 1859, *Paul Cullen*, ed. MacSuibhne, vol. ii, p. 301. Earlier that year Cullen informed Rome that Newman 'was not able to introduce a sound system of study and discipline in a new institution in Ireland, which needed shaping from the foundations. He nominated a great number of professors, and then let other affairs take their course. It is easy to see that we shall have to start the whole thing afresh' (Cullen to Barnabò, 15 January 1859, quoted in J. H. Whyte, 'Newman in Dublin: fresh light from the archives of Propaganda', *Dublin Review* 483 (Spring 1960), pp. 36–7).

76   Newman to Ornsby, 1 July 1860, *LD*, vol. xix, p. 380.

77   Woodlock to Monsell, 9 July 1861, DDA, Cullen Papers, 45/4/I(7).

78   Memorandum (signed by sixteen academics), 21 November 1865, DDA, Cullen Papers, 45/4/V(17).

79   In *A statement on the university question* (Dublin, 1868, p. 10) Bishops Leahy and Derry maintained that the Irish bishops could not set to work in devising 'a better plan of University Education than that traced out by the master hand of Dr. Newman' (*LD*, vol. xxiv, p. 51n).

80   When the evening classes restarted in April 1858, 105 students enrolled; the following term 179 registered. Thanks to a statute Newman had passed through the Council in January 1857, those attending were able to proceed to degrees. After this promising start, numbers at the evening classes fell, and in 1865 they were discontinued.

81   Speaking in the House of Commons, The O'Donoghue stated that the number of Catholics at other Irish universities was: 22 out of 405 in Belfast; 123 out of 263 in Cork; 78 out of 169 in Galway; 45 out of about 1000 at Trinity—which meant that 268 out of a student population of 1,857 were Catholics (20 June 1865, *Hansard*). These figures are likely to have been underestimates: the figure for Trinity was around 80 (McDowell & Webb, *Trinity College Dublin*, pp. 500, 504).

82   The number of Catholics studying at Trinity between 1829 and 1844 averaged at thirty-two out of 350 on entrance, or 8%. This proportion decreased until the period 1854–59, when it was 6% of the total on entrance. At the Queen's Colleges, there was a steady decrease in the proportion of Catholic students from 36% in 1849 to 23% in 1864 (Statistics at Royal, Endowed, and Erasmus Smith Schools, Queen's and Trinity College, DDA, Cullen Papers, 45/4/VII(28)). The number of Catholics studying at the Queen's Colleges remained at around 135 during the period 1851–57, then it rose to 147 in 1858, 170 in 1859, 205 in 1860 and 238 in 1863 (Robertson Report (1902–3), second appendix, p. 314).

83   Notes of Cullen, n.d., DDA, Cullen Papers, 45/2(17d). To modern ears these words sound extreme, but it needs to borne in mind that at the time a battle was raging at Oxford, which pitted the 'Church party' against those who promoted and encouraged unbridled speculation and the questioning of the tenets of Christianity (M. G. Brock, 'A "plastic structure" ', *The history of the University of Oxford*, vol. vii, pp. 22–33).

84   Woodlock to Cullen, 29 September 1874, DDA, Cullen Papers, 45/6/III(15). There were 185 Catholics at Trinity that year, of whom forty-one had matriculated that session.

85   Notes of Cullen, n.d., DDA, Cullen Papers, 45/2(17e).

86   Notes of Cullen, n.d., [1867], DDA, Cullen Papers, 45/2(17f). According to Meenan (*Centenary history of the Literary and Historical Society*, p. xx), Cullen regarded the society as a 'nest of dissatisfaction' before he changed his tune and spoke at its inaugural meetings.

87   In the year when Dawson was auditor there were twenty-two debates as well as six lectures given by professors (Dawson to Cullen, 15 June 1868, DDA, Cullen Papers, 45/5/III(7)).

88   Minute Book of the Episcopal Board, 11 February 1862, DDA, Woodlock Papers.

89   After discussing the Catholic University at their meeting in August 1859, the bishops released a pastoral letter urging the faithful to continue supporting it. They explained that they were taking control of everything relating to legislation, expenditure and appointments, and that a board for the governance of the University had been selected from their number. Among the reactions against it in the press was one article in the Dublin *Evening Mail* (19 August 1859) entitled 'The old struggle—Priests v. People', which argued that the clergy were trying to put the laity under the absolute control of a foreign authority (Norman, *Catholic Church and*

Ireland, pp. 62, 65–6).

90   Minute Book of the Episcopal Board, 27 January 1863, DDA, Woodlock Papers.

91   Cullen to Kirby, 11 August 1863, quoted in Larkin, *Consolidation of the Roman Catholic Church*, p. 169.

92   Cullen to Kirby, 11 September 1863, quoted in Larkin, *Consolidation of the Roman Catholic Church*, p. 169. Cullen knew from several sources that his opinion was not shared. For example, R. M. O'Ferrall, MP for County Kildare and a lay trustee for Maynooth College, had suggested to Cullen that they ought to imitate the Queen's Colleges by offering scholarships and that the way to do so was for the archbishops to ask the Catholic laity to found them; this would require an alteration to the constitution of the Catholic University so as to admit laymen to participate in its government. 'Many are dissatisfied that there is no lay element in the Govt of the University, such is my feeling, and that it ought to be remedied.' He suggested that Cullen could provide against 'traitors' by keeping a majority of bishops on the Board. O'Ferrall was convinced that if the University was supported by the laity it would be given a charter and other privileges (R. M. O'Ferrall to Cullen, 8 December 1861, *ibid.*, p. 144).

93   Larkin, *Consolidation of the Roman Catholic Church*, pp. 170, 173. Previously Cullen had managed to thwart Newman's scheme for compiling a list of lay patrons for the University, as explained in his letter to Ornsby: 'I quite agree with you in your anxiety about the exclusion of lay Catholics of position and name from the councils of the University. Yet this is the policy which has been recommended to Propaganda from the first. You may recollect that nearly the only alteration that Propaganda made in the details which I put before them, was to hinder me from associating laymen even as *honorary* members' (Newman to Ornsby, 8 November 1861, *LD*, vol. xx, p. 63). See also *AW*, p. 326.

94   Cullen to Kirby, 30 June 1864, quoted in Larkin, *Consolidation of the Roman Catholic Church*, p. 176.

95   Larkin, *Consolidation of the Roman Catholic Church*, pp. 174–9.

96   It may be indicative of the growing clericalisation of the University that in 1865 the names of those on the Board appeared in the University's entry in *Battersby's Catholic Register*—and above those of the academic staff.

97   Woodlock to Cullen, Easter Sunday 1866, DDA, Cullen Papers, 45/4/VIII(25). Eight years earlier, when drafting a letter to Disraeli about a charter, Newman had told the dean of the arts faculty, 'the body of the

Professors should have the *last* word upon it' (Newman to Butler, 20 July 1858, *LD*, vol., xviii, p. 418).

98 A verbatim record of the court proceedings can be found in vol. ii of Professor O'Looney's memoirs (DDA, Woodlock Papers, 124/2). At the time Brian O'Looney occupied the chair of Celtic Studies. The protest against Moran's appointment was unsuccessful; he held chairs in Sacred Scripture and Irish History in the period 1866–70. He later became Archbishop of Sydney and was a severe critic of Newman, describing him as 'a poor theologian, a bad Latinist, [who] knew nothing about Irish history' and as someone who 'regarded with singular distaste everything connected to Irish nationality' ('Cardinal Moran on Newman's Failure in Ireland', *The Catholic Press* (22 July 1909), quoted by C. Barr in ' "An ambiguous awe": Paul Cullen and the historians', *Cardinal Paul Cullen and his world*, ed. D. Keogh & A. McDonnell (Dublin, 2011), p. 416). See also 'Newman's failure in Ireland. Another interview with Cardinal Moran', *The Tablet* 114:3617 (4 September 1909), pp. 381–2, where these comments are repeated almost verbatim.

99 This was the observation of Richard O'Brien, the nationalist historian, who entered the University in the mid-1860s (*DIB*).

100 Sullivan was also shocked by the news of Newman's departure, and he told Ornsby that he only intended to stay on in the expectation that the University would die out in Cullen's hands, so that he could take it on himself (Ornsby to Newman, 3 December 1858, BOA, DP 29).

101 Sullivan complained to Newman that the system which he had put in place might 'be set aside at any time and the Will of a single man substituted', and that as a consequence he was negotiating his departure. The Council had allowed those attending the evening classes to matriculate as members of the University and turned what began as a voluntary work into an obligatory one; the Senate had not been consulted over the new department (Sullivan to Newman, 18 February 1859, *LD*, vol. xix, p. 44n). Newman reacted to this letter by telling Sullivan: 'It will be a great blow, if you leave the University, for I feel you are just the one person who could not be replaced. It would be perfect madness' if the University did not act to prevent his departure (Newman to Sullivan, 19 February 1859, *LD*, vol. xix, p. 44).

102 Sullivan to Newman, 21 April 1859, *LD*, vol. xix, p. 119n.

103 Newman to Sullivan, 29 April 1859, *LD*, vol. xix, p. 119.

104 *University education in Ireland* (London, 1866), pp. 12–13. At the time

around 80% of Catholic boys in secondary education studied at one of the sixty-seven schools or colleges run by priests: twenty-four diocesan seminaries, twenty-eight schools under religious and fifteen schools under secular priests (*ibid.*, p. 9).

[105] In his lengthy account of 'The Catholic University of Ireland' Lambert McKenna SJ emphasises the same points: clergy actually used the term 'university' for schools such as Clongowes, Castleknock and Stonyhurst—and then complained that the Catholic University was doing them harm; while parents kept their sons at school for an extra two or three years because they were unable to appreciate the benefits of a university (*Irish Ecclesiastical Record* 31:724 (April 1928), p. 361).

[106] Sullivan, *University education in Ireland*, pp. 30, 32. Newman would have agreed with all that Sullivan wrote. He said of him: 'his views were large and bold, and I cordially embraced them' (Ward, *The life of Cardinal Newman*, vol. ii, p. 349); he also remarked that he was a 'man of great good sense. All I fear is, that, having no one to agree with, or to grumble to, he may get disgusted' (Newman to Ornsby, 19 January 1859, *LD*, vol. xix, p. 24).

[107] Sullivan had previously offered to implement his plans for a great school of science at the University of Melbourne, but was turned down because he was a Catholic (R. McHugh, 'The Years in Ireland', *A tribute to Newman*, ed. M. Tierney (Dublin, 1945), p. 164)

[108] He also felt that, as a layman, he could not consent to allow the office of university teacher to become, among Catholics, the exclusive privilege of priests (Sullivan to Monsell, 16 June 1873, quoted in Larkin, *Consolidation of the Roman Catholic Church*, pp. 381–2).

[109] Sullivan to Monsell, 1 June 1873, quoted in Norman, *Catholic Church and Ireland*, pp. 193–4.

[110] Pollen to Newman, 5 January 1859, *LD*, vol. xix, p. 8.

[111] Newman to Pollen, 6 January 1859, *LD*, vol. xix, p.10.

[112] Newman to Woodlock, 4 March 1868, *LD*, vol. xxiv, p. 46.

[113] Sullivan to Monsell, 3 May 1867, quoted in Norman, *Catholic Church and Ireland*, p. 241.

[114] Moran to Kirby, 19 July 1866, quoted in Norman, *Catholic Church and Ireland*, p. 233.

[115] *University education for English Catholics: a letter to the Very Rev. J. H. Newman, by a Catholic layman* (London, 1864), p. 5n.

[116] Scratton to Woodlock, 24 September 1873, quoted in Rigney, 'Bar-

tholomew Woodlock', vol. i, p. 367. Another indication that Scratton did not fully identify with Newman's views is a comment of Thomas Arnold to his wife: 'How Newman ever came to appoint him [Scratton], is the mystery to me' (12 January 1859, *Letters of Thomas Arnold*, p. 96).

117 A separate matter from a finance committee was the compilation of the annual report of the accounts of the Catholic University, which was carried out by two auditors, Charles Bianconi and Michael Errington.

118 Newman told the former vice-rector Leahy that he was 'very glad to hear the news about the University' and that Cullen 'had been willing to engage the services of loyal Catholic laymen in the general direction of it and the administration of its finances' (11 April 1874, *LD*, vol. xxvii, pp. 48–9).

119 Larkin, *Consolidation of the Roman Catholic Church*, p. 387.

120 Barr, *Paul Cullen*, pp.199–200; Larkin, *Consolidation of the Roman Catholic Church*, pp. 170–9.

121 Newman to Ornsby, 1 July 1860, *LD*, vol. xix, p. 379.

122 Woodlock to Moran, 26 December 1869, DDA, Cullen Papers, 45/5/VI(15).

123 Woodlock to Cullen, 24 February 1873, DDA, Cullen Papers, 45/5/XIV(3).

124 Woodlock to Cullen, 13 March 1873, DDA, Cullen Papers, 45/5/XIV(17).

125 *LD*, vol. xxvi, p. 394n. The *Memorial* deplored, among other things, the fact that the most recent lecture list did not contain the name of any physical or natural scientist.

126 Fottrell seems to have identified with what Newman sought to achieve in Dublin. In his *Inaugural address delivered before the Literary and Historical Society of the Catholic University of Ireland* (London, 1871), which was on 'The formation of character', Fottrell asked what influence a university ought to have on this formation, and what type of university was best calculated to exercise this influence? Following Newman, he argued that the object of a university was not to make the doctor or lawyer but the man.

127 Newman to Fottrell, 10 December 1873, *LD*, vol. xxvi, pp. 393–4. Newman had first-hand experience of the clergy and laity finding it difficult to work together at the Catholic University: after the first meeting of the Senate, he scribbled a note to Birmingham that the meeting was 'Such a bad experience I don't wish to meet again.' It was priests 'against the rest. It looks like a distinct split [...] *I* can't manage the Priests' (Newman to St John, 16 January 1857, *LD*, vol. xvii, p. 499).

128 Fottrell *et al* to Woodlock, 23 March 1874, DDA, Cullen Papers, 45/6/III(4). Apart from Fottrell (Auditor, 1870/71), the letter was signed

by P. J. O'Connor (Auditor, 1866/67), C. Dawson (Auditor, 1867/68), J. Dillon (Auditor, 1874/75) and one other whose signature is hard to read: it could be that of H. H. MacDermott (Auditor, 1858/59) or R. W. MacDonnell (Auditor, 1865/66).

[129] Besides standing for Catholic University of Ireland, the initials, of course, spell out the first word of the Latin adage *cui bono* which means 'to whose benefit?'.

[130] Circular dated 2 March 1877 signed by C. Dawson, G. Fottrell and J. Dillon on behalf of the C.U I. Bono Club (DDA, Cullen papers, 45/6/VIII(4)).

[131] Address of the C.U.I. Bono Club to Newman, 23 July 1879, *MC*, p. 406.

[132] Newman, 'Memorandum about my connection with the Catholic University', 25 November 1870, *AW*, p. 327. The memorandum is 172 pages long and it is followed by an appendix of 657 pages of letters or excerpts of letters, all but three of which are copied out by Newman himself.

[133] Scratton to Newman, 15 October 1855 (based on a conversation with James More O'Ferrall), quoted in *NU*, p. 366. According to O'Ferrall, there existed a feeling among the Catholic gentry that they were denied their rightful place in the University. His brother Richard said there were Protestants as well as many Catholics who felt that the University had been started with the purpose of 'placing Catholic education entirely in the hands of the clergy, and for the exclusion of the laity from all interference'. Richard was willing to support the University, provided his support was 'taken as a recognition of the right of the laity to a voice in the management of the University' (R. M. O'Ferrall to J. M. O'Ferrall, 5 May 1854, quoted in *AW*, p. 326).

[134] Newman to MacNamara, 29 July 1856, *LD*, vol. xvii, p. 337.

[135] Newman, memorandum, 25 November 1870, *AW*, p. 328.

[136] *The Tablet* (30 August 1856), p. 552.

[137] Newman to Wallis, 23 September 1856, *LD*, vol. xvii, p. 385. It should be noted that this was a private letter and that the irony it contained was not intended for public consumption. Newman's view is expressed even more strongly in a private memorandum: 'I cannot help feeling that, in high circles, the Church is sometimes looked upon as made up of the hierarchy and the poor, and that the educated portion, men and women, are viewed as a difficulty, an encumbrance, as the seat and source of heresy; as almost aliens to the Catholic body, whom it would be a great gain, if possible, to annihilate' (*The living thoughts of Cardinal Newman*, ed. H. Tristram (London, 1946), p. 21).

138 Newman to Wallis, 23 September 1856, *LD*, vol. xvii, pp. 385–6. Though shaken by the strong views expressed, Wallis was persuaded by Newman's analysis of the situation (*LD*, vol. xvii, pp. 386–7n).

139 Newman to Capes, 1 February 1857, *LD*, vol. xvii, p. 514.

140 Newman to Ornsby, 1 November 1860, *LD*, vol. xix, p. 414.

141 Newman to Ornsby, 8 November 1861, *LD*, vol. xx, p. 63.

142 He added that 'the fault and flaw of the whole is, in my judgement, the jealousy of the laity on the part of the ecclesiastics' (Newman to Ornsby, 23 July 1862, *LD*, vol. xx, p. 241). In a similar vein, he spoke to T. W. Allies of 'the same dreadful jealousy of the laity, which has ruined things in Dublin' (30 November 1864, *LD*, vol. xxi, p. 327).

143 Newman to Wiseman, 23 January 1854, *LD*, vol. xvi, p. 27.

144 Newman to Woodlock, 4 March 1868, *LD*, vol. xxiv, p. 46. Emmet Larkin came to the same conclusion, arguing that the real reason why the University was doomed to fail in the long run was because of the refusal to allow lay participation in its governing body (*Consolidation of the Roman Catholic Church*, p. 178; *Roman Catholic Church, 1870–74*, pp. 387–8).

145 Newman to Ornsby, 18 October 1874, *LD*, vol. xxvii, pp. 142–3.

146 Newman to Woodlock, 4 November 1874, *LD*, vol. xvii, p. 151.

147 The new university comprised St Patrick's, Maynooth; Holy Cross College, Dublin; the French College, Blackrock; St Patrick's, Carlow; St Kieran's, Kilkenny; St Ignatius, Dublin; Mount Carmel, Terenure; the Catholic University Medical School; and University College.

148 Robertson Report (1902–3), first appendix, p. 76.

149 The Jesuits had previously administered St Patrick's from 1873 until August 1880.

150 *NU*, p. 494.

151 McKenna, 'The Catholic University of Ireland', pp. 603–4.

152 Although the Fellows were paid £400 and although the Jesuits on the staff gave back their salaries to keep the college going, University College had a deficit of £1500 after one year and £6000 after five years. This was because several of the salaried Fellows were elderly and unable to shoulder much of the teaching load. Out of twenty-six teaching staff and administrators, eight were Jesuits, five of whom were Fellows (Robertson Report (1902–3), first appendix, pp. 76–7).

153 To access their rooms in No. 86, students had to enter No. 87 and use a passage built over the entrance to the University Church.

154 [Society of Jesus], *A page of Irish history: story of University College, Dublin, 1883–1909* (Dublin, 1930), p. 87.

155 In terms of student numbers the Catholic University Medical School was by then the largest of the six medical schools in Ireland.

156 McDowell & Webb, *Trinity College Dublin*, p. 124.

157 M. Tierney, ' "A weary task": the struggle in retrospect', *Struggle with fortune*, p. 5. The first chancellor of the National University was also a former student from Newman's rectorate: William Walsh, the Archbishop of Dublin.

158 Newman to Grant, 7 March 1856, *LD*, vol. xvii, pp. 178–9.

159 For the full story of the foundation and early years of the Oratory School, see P. Shrimpton, *A Catholic Eton? Newman's Oratory School.*

160 Barr, *Paul Cullen*, p. 131.

161 T. W. Allies told Newman that 'no inducement would be strong enough to lead English Catholics of birth and position to send their sons to an Irish university with a chance of bringing back the brogue' (quoted in Jackson, 'John Henry Newman', p. 100n).

162 Oratory School prospectus, 1862, BOA.

163 A. Nash, *Newman's idea of a school* (Woodcote, 1990), p. 4.

164 Newman to Hope-Scott, 28 April 1865, *LD*, vol. xxi, p. 453.

165 Acton to Simpson, 1 January 1862, *The correspondence of Lord Acton and Richard Simpson*, vol. ii (Cambridge, 1973), p. 248.

166 Newman to Acton, 24 April 1862, *LD*, vol. xx, p. 193.

167 Newman to Wynne, 12 September 1862, *LD*, vol. xx, p. 270.

168 Acton to Renouf, 14 November 1862, *Letters of Renouf*, vol. iii, p. 152.

169 Newman told an interested parent that, 'if I had my will, I would have a large Catholic University, as I hoped might have been set up in Dublin, when I went there. But I hold this to be a speculative perfection which cannot be carried out in practice' in England (Newman to Sheil, 22 March 1867, *LD*, vol. xxiii, p. 101). Shortly afterwards he wrote in a 'Memorandum on allowing Catholics to go to the universities', 'I have ever held [...] that the true education is that given in a Catholic University; but at the same time I have ever held, and have said in print, that necessity has no law' (21 April 1867, *LD* xxiii, p. 180).

170 Newman to St John, 26 August 1863 (to which Newman added comments in 1875), *LD*, vol. xx, p. 512.

171 H. E. Manning, *Miscellanies*, vol. i (London, 1877), p. 59.

172 Allies to Newman, 3 December 1864, *LD*, vol. xxi, p. 327n.
173 Rome regarded the United Kingdom as mission territory until 1908, coming under the Sacred Congregation Propaganda Fide (Propagation of the Faith).
174 Newman to Jenkins, 12 December 1867, *LD*, vol. xxiii, p. 383.
175 Although Newman's various schemes for a return to Oxford fell through, he ended up revisiting his *alma mater* in 1878 when he was made the first honorary Fellow of Trinity College. Two years later, when he paid a second visit as a cardinal, he was again invited to Trinity and on this occasion he visited his old rooms.
176 Newman to Lady Simeon, 10 November 1867, *LD*, vol. xxiii, p. 366.
177 Newman to Simeon, 9 December 1867, *LD*, vol. xxiii, p. 381.
178 Newman to Northcote, 18 February 1872, *LD*, vol. xxvi, p. 21. The two phrases in Latin are from 1 Corinthians 14:20; the other quotation is a paraphrase of John 17:15.
179 Newman to Northcote, 23 February 1872, *LD*, vol. xxvi, p. 25.
180 The enclosure was Discourse VI from the *Idea of a university*, with the first paragraph on p. 145 marked in pencil.
181 Newman to Northcote, 23 February 1872, *LD*, vol. xxvi, p. 26.
182 Newman to Howard, 27 April 1872, *LD*, vol. xxvi, p. 75.
183 Newman to Howard, 27 April 1872, *LD*, vol. xxvi, p. 76.
184 Newman to Howard, 27 April 1872, *LD*, vol. xxvi, p. 76.
185 'Unreal words', sermon preached in Advent 1839, *Plain and parochial sermons*, vol. v, p. 45.

8 NEWMAN'S LEGACY

TO WHOM SHOULD the modern university student go in search of wisdom, as well as knowledge? Where should he seek those guiding principles that instruct on the art of living virtuously and happily? What should be uppermost in his mind: the usefulness of the qualification he will gain for his career path,[1] or the sort of person he aspires to become by the end of his course? If the latter, what steps should he take to enable this transformation to take place?

In asking such questions, a student must surely realise that he is not the first to ponder these matters and that there is a long tradition of those who have thought deeply about them. Even to ask these questions entails assumptions about human nature—that we are responsible for the development of our own character—and a realisation that it is by means of cultivating human virtues that ideals and ambitions are achieved. By contrast, those who simply look forward to throwing off the 'shackles' of home and school and to three or four years of pleasure-seeking are squandering their opportunities for personal enrichment in that crucial period of preparation for adulthood and its accompanying responsibilities. In the transitional state of student existence, with its intoxicating mixture of newly-gained independence and relative absence of responsibility, the ordinary undergraduate will at some point reflect on and acquire guiding principles for life, a process which might entail consciously accepting or rejecting the guiding principles of his earlier formative years—or even coming to a judgement on the fact that he did not receive any guiding principles. Those leaving home with a religious faith may well feel the difficulty of living it out in an environment that is hostile to religion without the immediate support of family or school, and perplexed at having to explain to others 'the hope that lies within them' (Peter 3:15). The challenge of standing out from the crowd was mitigated, if not postponed, at the confessional university of the mid-nineteenth century, but Newman was well aware of the need to prepare for life in the world: 'Today a pupil, tomorrow a member of the great world: today confined to the Lives of the Saints, tomorrow thrown upon Babel'.[2]

In 1848 an Oxford don published anonymously his *Ten letters introductory to college residence*. They were intended to smooth the transition from home to school and to alert young men to the fact that they would soon be exposed to the dangers and excesses of student life where many of the constraints of responsibility were absent and the prevailing atmosphere beyond the influence not just of parents, but of the college authorities. These letters express ideas that are remarkably similar to Newman's—which is no surprise, since the two were Oriel Fellows and close friends[3]—and they address the concerns of anxious parents as well as school-leavers. In his two introductory letters, Charles Daman points out to the prospective student that he stood 'at the very threshold of this definite and critical period' of life when he was beginning 'comparative Manhood', with its measure of independence and freedom and its proportionately increased responsibility. The virtues and habits developed in boyhood now had to be built upon, for, Daman told his reader, you are only 'conventionally by courtesy a *Man*, that is a youth, *adolescens*, an inchoate and promissory man'. In his letters the tutor hoped to assist the aspiring undergraduate 'to carry to the utmost your notion, to guide you to the lasting and solid realisation of your wish to be a *man*'.[4]

Daman was a committed Tractarian and in daily contact with Newman. His *Ten letters* were spiritual in tone, encouraging the reader to lead a life of piety and to consider everything *sub specie aeternitatis*, and, much as Newman did, he managed to combine high principle with sound, practical advice. Daman encouraged his reader to consider what it means to be a man, first by dealing with the thinking person, then with the social person, and finally with the ruling or governing person. To become a master of others, the student needed to develop his own higher faculties and become master of himself, which he would do by ordering his time, amusements, reading and companions, to the extent that they were not determined by his college. In his letters, Daman urged that his reader's life should not be merely one of study, but should have the character of devotion too; he gave advice on self-government through keeping to a timetable which would 'form the character'; he counselled him about the companions he should keep; he cautioned him not to single himself out, but to try to accommodate his high principles with his circumstances; and he encouraged him to prepare for university academically by striving for quality rather than quantity of work and by using his vacations well.[5]

Daman and Newman were both attempting to address problems that were prevalent in mid-nineteenth century Britain: some of them are perennial and with us today, others are not. It is by considering their advice intelligently and with a view to context that we can gain from their insights. In retrospect, the various schemes for residential living that Newman recommended for his undergraduates in Dublin might appear overly-ambitious and counter-cultural (or anachronistic), but they do address head-on the call for a smoother transition into what he called the 'dangerous season' of undergraduate life. They also acknowledge that 'nothing is more perilous to the soul than the sudden transition from restraint to liberty'.[6] Above all, Newman was concerned with how best the student should live and how the university should be structured so as to make such living possible; he aimed at optimising the conditions for the flourishing of the individual by allowing for the development of intellectual and moral qualities in a community that functioned like a second home. On one occasion Newman underscored his wish for harmony between collegiate house and home by pointing out to the secretary of the Catholic University, 'Father and Mother have a voice in such [residential] arrangements as my letter implied'.[7]

As I hope the preceding chapters make clear, these were the sort of urgently practical issues that Newman addressed and in his response to them we can see the resourcefulness and the wisdom of one of the great Christian humanists. The story of Newman's pastoral activity in Oxford and Dublin, as it unfolds in both his actions and his writings, speaks to us about many neglected facets of university life. In times like the present, when the undeniable advances in the *organisation* of higher education appear to be offset by a misunderstanding of the *purpose* and role of the university, we need someone like Newman to give us direction and to identify for us the threats to and benefits of true university education. Drawing on a long-established educational tradition and contributing his own insights, Newman challenges us by pointing out where we have gone wrong and what areas we have neglected; and he also unifies our thinking so as to provide a coherent picture of what the university is *about* and what it can accomplish, not only in intellectual but also in moral and indeed spiritual terms.

Rounding out my study in this final chapter will entail three main tasks: evaluating why the Catholic University failed and what lessons can be learned from it; identifying and examining Newman's main pastoral concerns for the University and hence the key strands of his legacy; and assessing his contribution to current thinking and practice in education, while suggesting further ways that this might be sustained. Overall what I trust will emerge is an overview of Newman's guiding principles on the art of student living, which will enable us to ascertain what he would be recommending to us today, were he alive.

The failure of the Catholic University

Reflecting in 1870 on the predicament of the Catholic University and its many problems, Newman concluded that if the Holy See had been better informed it would never have promoted the project in the first place. It had always seemed to Newman that 'a gift of sagacity had in every age characterized' the Holy See, 'so that we might be sure, as experience taught us, without its being a dogma of faith that what the Pope determined was the very measure, or the very policy, expedient for the Church at the time it was determined'; but events in Ireland led him to think that if the Pope had known more about the state of things there, 'he would not have taken up the quarrel about the higher education which his predecessor had left him, and, if he could not religiously have found a way of recognising the Queen's Colleges, then at least he would have abstained from decreeing a Catholic University'.[8]

Newman's reflections on his founding role led him to adjust his human faith in the wisdom of papal government and the policies it chose to pursue—though this made no difference to his faith in the Church itself. For one thing, holding up Louvain as a pattern for the Catholic University to imitate was misleading, for Louvain and Dublin were cities with very different prospects: Belgium was an independent country, whereas Ireland was a subjugated nation; Belgium was prosperous, following closely behind Britain in the Industrial Revolution, while Ireland was wretchedly impoverished; Belgian citizens were equal before the law, whereas in Ireland sectarianism was all-pervasive.[9] Nor must it be forgotten that a number of well-informed Irishmen had strongly advised Newman against attempting the Catholic University in the early 1850s, so obvious did it seem to them that Ireland was not ready for one and that the enterprise was bound to fail.[10] Nevertheless, this does not condemn Newman for attempting to build what they regarded as unbuildable. As regards the University's structure, Newman gladly accepted the model of Louvain as providing an ideal blueprint for its organisation; and although the conception and the implementation of the Catholic University was hedged round with difficulties, Newman still considered it worth attempting—regardless of his later second thoughts.

In his first, introductory university sketch Newman openly acknowledges the difficulties faced by the Catholic University which was 'expected to force its way abruptly into an existing state of society which had never duly felt its absence', rather than gradually evolving over time and 'creating and carrying with it the national sympathy'. The most formidable obstacle, he suggests, lay in the surrounding atmosphere of misunderstanding and prejudice: the University was to be established in the midst of 'a reluctant and perplexed public opinion', and this was not offset by either royal favour or civil approval. Alluding to the Dublin lectures, Newman acknowledges that some misgivings about the enterprise may have arisen from a vision that seemed 'too noble [...] to be possible'.[11] By bringing the Catholic University to Dublin, Newman was attempting to treat the capital of Ireland as a true European capital once more but in doing so he would be thwarted by nationalists on one hand and the clerical-minded on the other, even though a revival of the true Catholic spirit of the European university was central to this project. He displayed finely balanced loyalties and an impressive disinterestedness in combining emphasis on his host land with the broader dimension of the English-speaking world. In this sense, it is tragic that Newman's aspiration 'To respond to the growing importance of Ireland, arising from its geographical position, as the medium of intercourse between the East and the West, and the centre of the Catholicism of the English tongue'[12] should have been thwarted.

Many new schools were founded in the decades after the Great Famine, but the increase in the Irish school population was not matched by a growth in numbers at the Catholic University. The question of numbers is above all one of recruitment, which is a different question from the one of whether what Newman was offering was appealing: to have an appealing offer serves for nothing if one does not appeal to one's audience effectively. Simply because the University was dogged by poor recruitment does not mean that the design of Newman's university was inherently flawed: I would argue, rather, that the design was excellent, and what was flawed was the implementation. If the execution of Newman's design had been conducted more consistently, recruitment would certainly have fared better. If Newman and Paul Cullen had agreed at the outset that recruitment would be one of the major obstacles to success, they might have worked to resolve it. But they did not, and the University failed—despite its promising design.

The previous chapter has shown that the refusal of Paul Cullen to permit more lay participation posed an insuperable difficulty for the University. In mid-nineteenth century Ireland, the balance of leadership of the Catholic body was passing from the gentry and professional classes to clerical leaders and senior clergy; and once it was in the hands of the hierarchy, they were naturally disinclined to relinquish it. The eclipse of lay involvement in education can be seen in the growth of the religious orders and their role in schooling; it was also evident in the marked reluctance of the religious orders to support a venture which was not within their influence. The immediate success of the Jesuits when they took over St Patrick's House in 1873 illustrates this point, as does their success when they were later entrusted with overseeing University College. This more subtle exclusion of the laity from influence in education was instantly recognised by W. K. Sullivan as a setback, and explains why he resigned in 1873.[13]

Though a major part in the failure of the Catholic University may be attributed with some justice to Cullen, it ought to be stressed that the University would not have come into being but for his whole-hearted commitment to the project, nor would Newman have been invited to lead the project.[14] Nevertheless, the very actions by which Cullen paved the way for the foundation were counterproductive, for his heavy-handed manoeuvring and manipulative style of governance alienated many of the clergy and lost vital support for the university project. Cullen's exclusion of the laity from any involvement in the enterprise also scuppered any real hope there might have been of obtaining a royal charter, which would have been a lifeline for the institution, since the British government would only contemplate plans which genuinely involved the laity.[15] Disraeli found Cullen frustrating to deal with in his negotiations in 1867–68 and criticized him severely (under the pseudonym 'Churchill') in his novel *Lothair* (1870).[16]

What is puzzling is that Cullen never faced up to the imprudence inherent in having a part-time rector, even though Newman had drawn attention to this from the outset. Certainly he and Newman differed on how to handle students, but it is unfair to say that all Cullen wanted was a 'glorified Seminary for the laity'.[17] Cullen *was* able to imagine a university along Newman's lines, at least as regards the content and scope of its teaching; but as regards its administration and discipline, his mind was steeped in the workings of the major seminary—which was true, not only of most Irish bishops, but of the episcopate worldwide: they could not envision a university that would not include clerical control of administration and discipline.

But if Cullen was convinced that control of education should lie with the clergy, Newman saw the task as one that should be undertaken with the active cooperation of the laity.[18] This fundamental difference of approach made it impossible for Cullen and Newman to act as effective collaborative partners. Nevertheless, rather than blaming either of these men of action—Cullen or

Newman—for the project's failure, it would be more appropriate to blame the apathy of the upper classes, both in England and Ireland, who ought to have taken a more robust role in supporting *their* university.

By the same token, we should not overlook the contributions of other men besides Cullen and Newman, not least those of the talented Oxbridge converts who threw in their lot with the project and gave it their best. It was a failure for them as well, but it sowed the seeds of future success. There were Irishmen, too, who devoted years of service to the project and were left disappointed, most notably W. K. Sullivan, who understood Newman's insight that the temporal autonomy required for a Catholic university meant that higher education constituted a legitimate sphere of lay influence, and that a university should not only be *supported* by the laity, but should be *run* by them in conjunction with the clergy, thereby 'making the University a middle station at which clergy and laity can meet, so as to understand and to yield to each other'. That this 'middle station' did not emerge confirmed Newman's fear 'that there was to be an antagonism, as time went on, between the hierarchy and the educated classes'.[19]

Newman's short tenure as the founding rector of the Catholic University was a deliberate decision, since he considered that '*my* work would be to *found* various institutions', because 'I do not aspire to the exercise of authority, or rule'.[20] All the institutions that have arisen within the Church, he asserted, 'have their own excellence and do their own service; each is perfect in its kind'. Arguing, as on other occasions, that 'there are two great principles of action in human affairs, Influence and System', he explained that those which flourish and fulfil their mission chiefly by means of *system* are the regular orders; they have the talent of organisation and spread like imperial Rome, not by sentiment or imagination, but by wise policy and the rule of law. Others spread by means of *influence,* the 'admirable spontaneous force, which kept the schools of Athens going'. If there was one Catholic institution which 'caught the idea of the great heathen precursor of the Truth, and has made the idea Christian', Newman thought, then it was the Oratory of St Philip Neri. St Philip had *drawn* men to their duty, instead of commanding them; he had not intended to found a congregation, yet it came about; and when obliged to put it into shape, he shrank from anything that might be restrictive, so that Oratorian houses 'stand like Greek colonies, independent of each other and complete in themselves', and Oratorians are allowed, 'like Athenian citizens, freely to cultivate their respective gifts and to follow out their own mission'. Newman saw a certain providence at play in his being the one to prepare the foundations of a great university. While the task of framing, organising and consolidating was the imperial gift of St Dominic or St Ignatius,

> yet a son of St Philip Neri may aspire without presumption to the preliminary task of breaking the ground [...] of introducing the great idea into men's minds, and making them understand it [...] and show zeal for it; of bringing many intellects to work together for it, and of teaching them to understand each other, and bear with each other, and go on together, not so much by rule, as by mutual kind feeling and a common devotion.[21]

While Newman personally threw himself into the founding of the Catholic University, he was sensible enough to recognize that others must build on the foundation as they saw fit. This long-term outlook also helps to explain his remarkable personal detachment from the University project once he had left Dublin. Despite his having lavished some of his best years on the institution, he disconcerted Robert Ornsby, one of his most loyal friends there, who relayed the news that the authorities were beginning to unravel the constitution he had fashioned so carefully, by telling him: 'I never have been wedded to any view of mine—the great question always is whether a paper constitution will work — and it costs me no trouble to believe that much has to be altered in mine. [...] Internal dissension is the only real evil.'[22] As if to console Ornsby, he wrote soon afterwards to reassure him: 'It does not prove that what I have written and planned will not take effect sometime and somewhere because it does not at once. [...] When I am gone, something may come of what I have done at Dublin'.[23] The Dublin 'disaster' fitted a pattern that was not man's, but of a higher order: 'It is the rule of God's Providence that we should succeed by failure.'[24]

It would, nevertheless, be a mistake to regard Newman's involvement in the Dublin university project merely as a response to a call that he felt honour-bound to accept, instead of a wholehearted commitment to it. In 1872 he told a friend: 'I have, from the very first month of my Catholic existence, when I knew nothing of course of Catholics, wished for a Catholic University'.[25] Nor would it be proper to conclude, as some historians have, that he buckled under the sheer strain of his responsibilities. On the contrary, the facts show that the difficulties he encountered had an energizing effect on him, and that, in the heat of the moment, ideas and plans which had been slowly maturing in his mind were forced into shape. Neither does the University story support the myth that he was a weak administrator or a poor judge of people or events, for he managed almost singlehandedly to bring the institution into being and to assemble a lively, talented common room. It is true that Newman took on too much, though of course his willingness to roll up his sleeves and do all of these vital things himself was admirable. Still, what is admirable is not always practicable. But then, as Aubrey de Vere personally witnessed, the menial tasks that he saw Newman undertake in Dublin 'should have fallen on subordinates, but their salaries it was impossible to provide'.[26]

Assessing Newman's legacy

However exemplary Newman's educational achievements in Dublin might be regarded, it cannot be denied that his influence on the development of the university is almost entirely due to the *Idea*. Yet the *Idea* is about the essence of a university, not its fullness and well-being, and to discern what Newman meant by its *integrity* we need to look at the idea illustrated in history—at the *University sketches*—and in practice—at the Catholic University in Dublin. From Newman's correspondence and university papers there emerges a fuller picture of the educated person, nurtured in his entirety and in his social dimension, and how this might be achieved. The relative failure of the Catholic University and its marginalisation in the history of the university hardly seems an incentive for imitation. Yet without the example of the institution he began and all that it furnishes, the vision he has written about in the *Idea* remains incomplete. The growth of interest in, and studies about, Newman are leading to a widespread appreciation of his insights and contribution to contemporary problems. This book will hopefully form part of that process by filling out Newman's vision for the education and training of the university student: the making of the modern man and woman. By revisiting his responses to the problems of his age, we can learn from his actions, if not his practical solutions, and apply them to our own age, because his high ideals are also suggestive, adaptable, and inspirational.

In an age when all that could be seen were 'naked Universities and naked Colleges',[27] Newman saw clearly that the college–university principle answered a definite and pressing need. After the Oxbridge reforms of the 1850s and 1870s[28]—which were largely welcomed by Newman—a clearer division of labour came about: in the new order, the university stood for the transmission of knowledge and intellectual competence, achieved by means of lectures, laboratory work and exams; the colleges, on the other hand, represented the higher idea of unity of knowledge and the formation of rounded personalities. As Sheldon Rothblatt puts it, 'One kind of institution hearkened back to an organic order of relationships and communities. The other belonged to the same universe of energy that built machines and factories. It was instrumental.'[29] While there are many ways of looking at the complementary functions of college and university (and the different forms each can take), there are no indications that Newman ever had reason to alter his conviction that 'It would seem as if a University seated and living in Colleges, would be a perfect institution, as possessing excellences of opposite kinds.'[30] The consequences of the current-day neglect of the collegiate dimension of university education are evident in their effects: emphasis on technical training and a narrow, skills-based instruction to satisfy the needs of the labour market, at the expense of that more lofty formation which embraces the full measure of what it is to be human. In the long run, Newman's higher vision helps to save us from a reductionist and curtailed vision of humanity.

Newman put great store on the *place* of learning (especially—and ideally—if the university was residential), and on that invisible teacher he called the *genius loci*, since he felt that the right kind of personal character could only be shaped under the right conditions. History added depth to a place, filled it with memory, traditions, connections and responsibilities that could not be ignored; this was the 'transforming power of the hidden but unmistakably vivid influences inhabiting location'.[31] Newman saw clearly what so many fail to see: that the student body in a university shapes intellectual and moral character for better or worse; that the formative interaction between students is often more telling than the mere absorption of information from lecturers; that half the education that really matters in a university is imparted by the students to each other. Studying at university while living at home does not rise to what Newman calls 'the ancient idea of the university'—to say nothing of the various ways of remote learning which largely eliminate the need for personal contact. 'Mutual education, in a large sense of the word,' says Newman, 'is one of the great and incessant occupations of human society, carried on partly with set purpose, and partly not. One generation forms another; and the existing generation is ever acting and reacting upon itself in the persons of its individual members'.[32] This can only take place in a rich, though unsystematic, way in the privileged setting of a university.

For Newman, those who undertake the care of students away from home for the first time have a vital role to play and, by quoting the Gospel phrase *Hospes eram, et collegistis me* (Matthew 25:34) on the dedication page of the *Idea*, he likens their task to that of a corporal work of mercy. He refers to their pastoral responsibilities when speaking of the college as 'a place of residence for the University student, who would then find himself under the guidance and instruction of Superiors and tutors, bound to attend to his personal interests, moral and intellectual'.[33] All this he describes at length in rousing images of security and sanctuary.

What are we to make of Newman's working rule 'that the principal making of men must be by the Tutorial system'? The clearest indication of what Newman meant is illustrated not by anything that happened in Dublin, but by his tutorial row with Edward Hawkins, the provost of Oriel. This, indeed, was even more a matter of principle than the controversy over *Tract* 90, for *Tract* 90 ceased to matter to Newman after he converted (and indeed even before he converted),[34] but he would remain committed to seeing the pastoral charge revived in university education until the day he died. The tutorial row was not accidental; it was one of the greatest rows Newman ever fought. And it was an unavoidable row. Furthermore, the row continues to this day, for it is still being fought by others on Newman's behalf.

In many ways the Oriel common room of Newman's time is a reflection of our own contemporary establishment, which is populated by establishment men such as Hawkins who personify an entirely impoverished view of education and are blind to its deficiencies. Hawkins was acting for an entire academic ethos when he forbade the approach of Newman and his tutorial colleagues Froude and Wilberforce. Newman the educator was looking for something that was absent from the Oxford college system of his day and this is why his pastoral understanding of the tutorial charge meant so much to him.

Newman's daring designs for Oxford came to fruition some fifty years after he and the other Oriel tutors sought to reform the tutorial system in the late 1820s. Looking back from the twenty-first century, it seems perhaps overly ambitious to have attempted to introduce a modified version of the tutorial system into Ireland in the 1850s when the resources were pitiful and the demand non-existent. Yet it should be noted that Newman's aim was to replicate Oxbridge arrangements at a time when tutors were generally young academics who had not long graduated.[35]

So what should we learn from Newman's insistence? Surely it is that personal influence is what gives any system its dynamism: the action of mind on mind, personality on personality, heart on heart—and this is lacking from systems based chiefly on 'distance learning'. And if acquaintance became friendship, all the better since friendship was the privileged way of doing good to someone; 'it requires one to be intimate with a person, to have a chance of doing him good', Newman once told his sister Jemima.[36] All this makes sense on realising that Newman was intent on giving a deep formation to students, a formation which operated at various levels: the intellectual, the moral, the spiritual. In particular it operated on the human and the supernatural levels, according to an understanding that has a long tradition.

In words that are remarkably similar to Newman's, Pope Benedict XVI has argued that the purpose of Catholic education is the promotion of the human person, and that his fundamental needs should be the focus. These needs can only be fulfilled through a rich and living encounter with the deepest truths about God and the human person. If, as Pope Benedict asserts, the family is 'the primary place of "humanisation" for the person and society',[37] then the university hall of residence can surely be regarded as an extension of the family which acts on behalf of parents in offering their offspring a second home. There, habits and character are formed, and personal growth takes place. If the university teaches students how to make a living, then the college teaches them how to live.

Like many great Christian thinkers, Newman had a deep understanding of the scholastic adage *gratia perfecit naturam*, and in various ways grasped the consequences of that interplay between grace and nature which takes place in the baptised person. In his writings he usually takes its workings for granted, though at times he alludes to it directly: 'Let grace perfect nature, and let us, as Catholics, not indeed cease to be what we were, but exalt what we were into something which we were not.'[38] In his last sermon at the Catholic University Church he spoke of St Paul as the shining example of those,

> in whom the supernatural combines with nature, instead of superseding it,—invigorating it, elevating it, ennobling it; and who are not the less men, because they are saints. They do not put away their natural endowments, but use them to the glory of the Giver; [...] Thus they have the same thoughts, feelings, frames of mind, attractions, sympathies, antipathies of other men, so far as these are not sinful; only they have these properties of human nature purified, sanctified, and exalted; and they are made more eloquent, more poetical, more profound, more intellectual, by reason of their being more holy.[39]

Newman does not always make explicit whether he is referring to man in his natural state or as regenerated by grace; sometimes, indeed, his remarks can even be interpreted as referring to both, albeit in different ways. In any case, there is no doubt that much of what he says appeals to those who claim no religious allegiance: they can value his analysis of man on the natural level, even if the idea of grace perfecting nature means nothing to them.

In his celebrated portrait of a gentleman, Newman paints an attractive picture of the educated man who has acquired human virtues with an evident fullness; but for all Newman's admiration of the civility and culture of the refined natural man, he realises that education and formation can simultaneously operate at a higher level in moulding the Christian too. Nevertheless, while educating in a Christian setting, Newman was careful to respect education's inner autonomy; he understood the relationship between education and religion by recognising that 'Knowledge is one thing, virtue is another'.[40] This is why he could claim that 'the University is, we may again repeat, a secular institution, yet partaking of a religious character'.[41] He recognised the harmonious fusion of the secular and religious in the education which was introduced in the twelfth century: 'the germ of the new civilisation of Europe, which was to join together what man had divided, to adjust the claims of Reason and Revelation, and to fit men for this world while it trained them for another'.[42] In the same way he distinguishes in equally stark fashion between a secular university and a fully Christian one:

> A great University is a great power, and can do great things; but, unless it be something more than human, it is but foolishness and vanity [...] It is really dead, though it seems to live, unless it be grafted upon the True Vine [...] Idle is our labour, worthless is our toil, ashes is our fruit, corruption is our reward, unless we begin the foundation of this great undertaking in faith and prayer, and sanctify it by purity of life.[43]

One of Newman's greatest contributions to Christian thinking, and one which guided him in his educational endeavours, concerns the relation of faith and reason in fallen man. He was convinced that the disjunction of academic and moral education was one of the great evils of the age. He saw through the argument that by becoming more knowledgeable, a man would become better morally, while understanding how a people like the English, with no real religious faith to speak of, would resort to such false notions as the supposed moral benefits of knowledge: such an idea, he held, was based on a false understanding of human nature, for it did away with any conception of moral development and neglected the education of conscience. The whole foundation of Bentham's utilitarian University College in London was premised on the idea that knowledge does make men better morally; as early as the 1830s, Newman was a consistent critic of this fallacy of the march of mind.[44] For Newman, the University Church 'symbolized the great principle of the University, the indissoluble union of philosophy with religion'.[45] In 1865, six years after founding the Oratory School in Birmingham, he was able to 'boast' to one of his co-founders that the school really had solved 'the problem of combining a good intellectual education with Catholic morality', which had been the aim from the outset.[46] This is precisely what he had aimed at in Dublin.

In assessing Newman's legacy it is necessary to consider various distortions of it, as these are often used to dismiss Newman's contribution to the university debate. The charge that Newman was incompetent as an administrator has effectively been answered at length in the proceeding chapters, as has the claim that he was wedded to Oxford traditions and advocated little else. Other distortions include a misunderstanding of what he meant by a liberal education and an assumption that his thinking underpinned the 'great books' scheme; the charge that his liberal education is completely unsuited to the modern world and that he was obsessed with social class; that there was no room for women in his male-dominated world; that he opposed research at university or that he thought little of science; and the claim that he is the champion of dissenters and those Catholics who regularly accuse Rome of authoritarianism and overbearing control.

If there is one phrase of Newman's that is most misunderstood, it is 'learning for its own sake'. Many read this and imagine that Newman really was an advocate of Matthew Arnold's liberal idea of education and his 'pursuit of our total perfection by means of getting to know [...] the best which has been thought and said in the world'.[47] It was Arnold's hope that culture—which he was the first to use in its modern use—rather than religion would be the means of humanising an industrial society and of raising its aspirations and giving it moral sensitivity. Newman, of course, regarded such an aspiration as illusory and as hollow as Peel's earlier claim about the moral efficaciousness of reading rooms. When Arnold's essay 'Culture and its enemies' (1867) appeared—which would constitute the first part of *Culture and anarchy* (1869)—the Cambridge philosopher and religious sceptic Henry Sidgwick chided Arnold for trying to enlist Newman's authority in his misguided recommendations for the benefits of culture: 'Newman fought for a point of view which it required culture to appreciate, and therefore he fought in some sense with culture; but he did not fight for culture, and to conceive him combatting side by side with Mr Matthew Arnold is almost comical'.[48]

By advocating an acquaintance with all disciplines and a deep study of a few or one, Newman has been accused of wanting the best of both worlds but of proposing a scheme that would foster neither. In attempting to import Oxford into Ireland[49] and by offering a liberal education instead of a professional training, Newman has also been accused of serving Ireland badly.[50] Most commentators would now side with Fergal McGrath, who argued in his ground-breaking study of the Catholic University that in fact Newman managed to solve the problem of how to combine the interests of all parties: a balance between protecting the initial years for a liberal education and some degree of specialisation in line with future professional studies;[51] preparing those soon to be engaged in the business of life, yet without sacrificing the definiteness and completeness of the academic system or its demands for those to whom knowledge itself is a profession.[52] Many would agree with Alasdair MacIntyre, who draws on Newman in arguing that 'Liberal knowledge transforms us as human beings; it makes us into what we ought to be and need to be if we are to be good human beings.'[53] A liberal education schools the mind in how to make judgments—and this makes one better fitted to take any role. And this is why true liberal education is not impractical, though it looks askance at specialisation.

Newman is regarded by not a few Catholics today as the champion of free-thinking liberals against an overbearing authoritarianism and heavy-handed implementation of Church policy. His 'liberalism' is also admired for his way of dealing with dissent and tolerating the waywardness of youth. But often such comments arise from extrapolations of isolated incidents divorced from their context, and so for a true estimate of his views we need to take in the fuller picture. In the *Imperial intellect* Dwight Culler contends that Newman's approach to the student scene in Oxford had a 'distinctly strained and monastic flavour', whereas in Dublin it was characterised by 'a wonderful lightness and informality'. He explains that this was partly because of experience and maturity; partly because in an unruly Oxford Newman took the hard part of enforcer and in Catholic Dublin the easier role of the humane rector who granted students novel concessions; it was also because in Dublin 'religion was secure of its place'.[54] In both Oxford and Dublin, Newman's liberality was characterised by emphasis on influence and exhortation rather than rules and regulations. In his liberality and in his belief in freedom, not coercion, Newman adopted true liberal ideas, although of course he rejected the false rationalist ideas associated with the liberalism that tore Oxford apart after he departed, a liberalism characterised by scepticism, agnosticism and statism. In all of this he was influenced by St Philip Neri and the non-authoritarian character of the Oratorian rule, which governed by love and mutual charity rather than by rules per se.[55]

That the Catholic University was located in a land torn apart by political divisions was undoubtedly a serious handicap, but there were ways of dealing with the local situation as well as the more general contest taking place across Europe between the champions of the new social order and those of the status quo. While Cullen and other bishops attempted to root out revolutionary elements among the students at the University, Newman wondered what the consequences were likely to be, as he felt uneasy about the way they handled student unrest. More broadly, he felt that the tendency to silence dissentient voices was 'the act of men who are blind to the intellectual difficulties of the day. You cannot make men believe by force and repression.'[56] He was not for humouring incipient Jacobinism in the student body as one might humour high spirits, and it is clear he would have been all for silencing those responsible for protesting against the Prince of Wales's visit, but he wished to replace the older mixture of formality and licence with the right mixture of constraint and liberty.

John Hungerford Pollen, the Professor of Architecture and designer of the University Church, observed Newman at close quarters in Dublin and was won over by a rector who was 'most kind, ever so nice, and full of fun'.[57] A man described by others as having as having 'exercised strict discipline, but always with tact and prudence in the faithful discharge of duty; and [...] treated all with fairness and courtesy' while senior proctor at Oxford, Pollen was well-placed to comment on Newman's ability to match his actions to his words.[58] In a tribute after his death, Pollen declared that 'Newman was very decided as to the *status* of University students. The duty of the Institution in this regard, was to take them when the age of boyhood was over, to discipline and train their faculties; to educate, and not merely to instruct; to prepare them for warfare with the world; to make *men* of them.' This principle was poorly understood in Ireland, whereas for Newman students between 18 and 21 were no longer boys;

> neither was the Institution with its colleges a seminary. It was a gymnasium for the formation of character, and the training of the intellect. It had to exercise its youth in the right use of *moral* restraint; to prepare them for that full liberty which awaited them when University life was ended. They had to learn the right use of liberty as well as the right use of the reasoning powers, and to appreciate the confidence placed in their honour. The fact that such liberty is sometimes abused in the old Universities did not frighten Father Newman. The great value he attached to the kind of discipline he proposed more than outweighed any danger of abuse. And against such danger a Catholic University had safeguards which were lacking in the older institution.[59]

Pollen's tribute also brings out the manner in which Newman identified with young people: 'The late Cardinal's sympathy with the young man was a feature of his character, natural and acquired [...] He felt for their generosity, their hopefulness, the trials, the struggles, the disappointments that might be in store for them in the unknown future'.[60] Mid-nineteenth century Ireland was a time when prim respectability was rising and Irish Catholics began to adopt Anglo-Irish Protestant airs and habits of behaviour, which were influenced by the Evangelical movement.[61] Newman's refusal to bow to the conventions of the time—in Ireland as well as England—in social and Catholic circles shows his clarity of vision and his sensible appreciation of the needs of young people. His comment to Gerard Manley Hopkins, then a lecturer at University College, that, 'If I were an Irishman, I should be (in heart) a rebel',[62] reflected his ability to enter into the hopes, dreams and anxieties of the young—but did not imply that he was wholly sympathetic to Irish revolutionaries.

Newman's practice in Dublin shows he did not set himself against the idea of research, as he tried to ensure that academics at the Catholic University were 'research active'. But he did warn against research becoming the driving force.[63] Michael Oakeshott has articulated Newman's sentiments better than most in the face of the contemporary research ideology:

> A university will have ceased to exist when its learning has degenerated into what is now called research, when its teaching has become mere instruction and occupies the whole of an undergraduate's time, and when those who come to be taught come, not in search of their intellectual fortune but with a vitality so unroused or so exhausted that they wish only to be provided with a serviceable moral and intellectual outfit; when they come with no understanding of manners of conversation but desire only a qualification for earning a living or a certificate to let them in on the exploitation of the world.[64]

When searching for the origins of the contemporary dilemma between research and teaching of the modern university, commentators have sometimes pointed to Humboldt's and Newman's contrasting ideas of a university and see an enduring—even a creative—tension between them. But this contrast actually distorts Newman's point of view, a distortion which can be offset by considering his influence on the Oxford don Mark Pattison, who in the mid-1860s was a prominent figure in the public discussion of the role and organisation of universities. Pattison had entered

Oriel just as Newman's tutorship came to an end and had become
a committed Tractarian, working alongside Newman on several
academic projects; his fame as a tutor at Lincoln College (1843–
55) owed much to the influence of Newman, Froude and Wilberforce, even though it was during this period that he began to drift
into agnosticism. He was convinced of the importance of nurturing
the right relationship between tutor and pupil, taking his pupils on
reading parties and relying above all on Aristotle's *Ethics* in his
teaching. Pattison failed to get elected as rector of Lincoln in 1855,
and turned from teaching to scholarship, visiting German universities and becoming an expert on German education. He returned
to Oxford on his election as rector of Lincoln in 1861.

In his *Suggestions on academical organisation with especial reference
to Oxford* (1868), Pattison argued that universities do not exist merely
for the sake of undergraduate education, but for the sake of culture
and the higher learning, and he became the leading voice for academic
specialisation and the campaign for the 'endowment of research'.
Although he came to see the Oxford colleges as obstacles to these
objectives (he hoped that they might specialise in particular disciplines and be transformed, in effect, into faculties), in many ways he
remained closely identified with the ideas of his former educational
mentor. Like Newman, he held that the promotion of original
research was the responsibility not of universities but of academies
such as the Royal Society, and that learning and intellectual scholarship was the distinctive vocation of the academic.[65] The ambitious
lecture course which T. W. Allies, the Professor of Modern History
at the Catholic University, undertook on Newman's encouragement
and which formed the basis of his major work *The formation of
Christendom* (8 vols, 1865–95), was precisely the sort of scholarship
that Pattison would have applauded.[66]

As well as taking considerable interest in science while at Oxford,
Newman was alive to its growing importance in society and there-

fore its importance for the Catholic University. Nevertheless, he contended that 'a University, after all, should be formally based (as it really is), and should emphatically live in, the Faculty of Arts'.[67] This statement does not contradict his recognition of the importance of science, for he judged that science in his time had not developed sufficiently to act as an ideal subject for training the mind. His instincts in fostering science were backed by the authorities in Rome, who strongly urged him to do all in his power to further the interests of physical science.[68] In his speech to the successful medical students on 14 July 1856 Newman told them, 'It has been too much the custom in these countries to maintain that Catholicism has been prejudicial to abstract science and to success in secular pursuits. It has been said to keep the mind in a sort of childish state, to relax and enfeeble it, to impede it in the investigation of scientific truth'—and it was this 'great delusion' which he hoped to set right.[69]

Newman's understanding of the dynamics of science and its need for autonomy and 'elbow room' are illustrated in four of the ten lectures which make up the second half of the *Idea*.[70] Twenty years before Maxwell opened the Cavendish Laboratory at Cambridge, Newman had set about opening a faculty of science in Dublin: he oversaw the establishment of laboratories for chemistry and physics, ensured that the library was well-stocked with scientific papers and journals, offered valuable scholarships and prizes for those studying science, urged the scientists at the University to undertake research, and helped them do this by starting up *Atlantis*.[71] When the British Association for the Advancement of Science met in Dublin in 1857, he sent delegates to their meetings and welcomed visitors from the conference to the University.[72] And when suggesting ways in which Englishmen of means could help the University, he told a friend: 'let them do a thing which *must* be good, whatever comes of the University, e.g. set up a *school of physical science*; or make us a present of instruments and apparatus'.[73]

It was W. K. Sullivan, Dean of the Faculty of Science,[74] who championed the cause of science on behalf of Newman. He advocated the teaching of physiology, pathology and pharmacy at a time when, outside Edinburgh, they were neglected subjects in the United Kingdom; and in the *Report for 1857/58* he made a lengthy appeal for £20,000 for the science faculty, articulating its urgent need for chairs in botany, zoology, geology and mineralogy. In this he received the rector's full backing.[75] On Sullivan's departure in 1873 there was an outcry about the lack of science teachers at the Catholic University[76] and about its consequent inability to rise to prominence in the country. A memorial entitled 'Science at the Irish Catholic University' published in *The Times* (2 December 1873, p. 7) argued that the neglect of science gave the enemies of the Catholic University the opportunity of accusing the Church of being the enemy of science. It lamented the galling deficiency in scientific education that existed among Irish Catholics.[77]

There is no reference to women at university in any of Newman's schemes for the simple reason that women were only admitted into higher education towards the end of his life, and then only gradually.[78] This raises the problem of how Newman would have reacted to 'mixed education' (understood in the modern sense) and how he would have adapted his thinking and practice. Like that other Christian humanist Thomas More, Newman promoted the education of women in both formal and informal settings, as his considerable correspondence with his female relatives and friends makes clear.[79] In a mixed context he would surely have laid emphasis not just on preparation for adulthood, but for *male* and *female* adulthood; and it can be surmised that while he would have accepted mixed lectures, he would have strongly discountenanced the idea of mixed halls of residence.

Newman today

Anthony Kronman, a professor and former dean of Yale Law School, contends that questions about the meaning of life which were once studied through the Western tradition have been losing their status as a subject of organised academic study and are now pushed to the margins of professional respectability in the humanities. Questions that the humanities once addressed in a public and organised fashion have now been privatised and the authority to address them, he contends, is monopolised by the churches. Like many others, Kronman places the blame on the modern research ideal and on political correctness. Often resorting to apocalyptic language to make their case, academics like Kronman, though they have no sympathy for the role theology once played, have argued that the university has lost its soul.[80]

Meanwhile other philosophers and theologians have taken to exploring the idea of the Christian university by directly thinking through what kind of relationship the university shares or should share with the Church.[81] In addition, some have explored the role of theology itself within the university.[82] Whether discussion is about the plight of the modern university in general or about the Christian or Catholic university or college in particular, to varying degrees those taking part almost inevitably draw on Newman's *Idea of a university*.

In dealing with Newman's legacy it would be a mistake to limit his influence to his educational classic, even if so much of what he wrote there is endlessly suggestive, if not provocative: in fact the theme of education runs through many of his sermons and letters. To try to appreciate his rich understanding of education by reading the *Idea* alone would be impossible. Instead, we should also admire what he achieved in Oxford and Dublin and learn from his efforts to reform education in those two cites, because his achievement shows the extent to which he was able to adapt his thinking to meet the requirements of a very specific time and place, while holding on to what is at the heart of education. His practical engagement shows that he was not just capable of turning out fine phrases and appealing aphorisms, but of setting up, running and reforming educational establishments in ways that are both novel and in keeping with a recognised tradition. Unlike many modern commentators who merely catalogue social ills, Newman diagnoses problems, supplies reasons for why things have gone wrong, and then offers practical remedies.

Newman saw the beginning of post-Enlightenment times, when rationalist ideas were already working their way into society and the university; and it is remarkable how observant he was about contemporary trends and how accurate in his diagnosis of educational policies which distorted the true nature of education. The historian Christopher Dawson comments that 'Newman was the first Christian thinker in the English-speaking world who fully realised the nature of modern secularism and the enormous change which was already in the process of development, although a century had still to pass before it was to produce its full harvest of destruction.'[83] In order to address its shortcomings, Newman sought to get to the root of secularism and understand it, and to discern its manifestations. He identifies the chief dangers of the professorial system which neglects the pastoral or collegiate dimension of education—the system which predominates in the West today—when he asserts, 'These may be called the three vital principles of the Christian student, faith, chastity, love; because their contraries, viz., unbelief or heresy, impurity, and enmity, are just the three great sins against God, ourselves, and our neighbour, which are the death of the soul.'[84] It is easy to see the results in today's students: religious infidelity and indifferentism, sexual licence of every kind, and an unpleasantly narcissistic individualism.

Although Newman believed that nothing could quite take the place of the college, he would not have dismissed the various alternative forms of living arrangements that have filled the vacuum left by its absence: far from it. And while he would have been deeply unhappy with the modern conglomerate, multi-functional university or 'multiversity' which, having dismissed its traditional roles, finds itself struggling for an identity, he was open to alternatives to the traditional university (though he might have been heartened by the failure of the modern university, precisely because that failure throws men back on the fundamental questions that he raises in his *Idea* and elsewhere). He recognized that the alternatives were not ideal, but he saw that they might be inevitable and so in need of shaping. Newman was not a 'traditionalist' in the sense of only admiring institutions of proven reputation; he could be very open to the non-traditional, as in his recognition of the 'virtual' university that is the great city:

> In every great country, the metropolis itself becomes a sort of necessary University, whether we will or no. As the chief city is the seat of the court, of high society, of politics, and of law, so as a matter of course is it the seat of letters also [...] The newspapers, magazines, reviews, journals, and periodicals of all kinds, the publishing trade, the libraries, museums, and academies there found, the learned and scientific societies, necessarily invest it with the functions of a University; and that atmosphere of intellect, which in a former age hung over Oxford or Bologna or Salamanca, has, with the change of times, moved away to the centre of civil government. Thither come up youths from all parts of the country, the students of law, medicine, and the fine arts, and the *employés* and *attachés* of literature. There they live, as chance determines; and they are satisfied with their temporary home, for they find in it all that was promised to them there. They have not come in vain, as far as their own

object in coming is concerned. They have not learned any
particular religion, but they have learned their own particular profession well. They have, moreover, become
acquainted with the habits, manners, and opinions of their
place of sojourn, and done their part in maintaining the
tradition of them. We cannot then be without virtual Universities; a metropolis is such: the simple question is,
whether the education sought and given should be based
on principle, formed upon rule, directed to the highest ends,
or left to the random succession of masters and schools, one
after another, with a melancholy waste of thought and an
extreme hazard of truth.[85]

Newman even suggested that 'the Houses of Parliament and the
atmosphere around them are a sort of University of politics'. While
it would appear 'that every metropolis *is* a University, as far as the
rudiments of a University are concerned', since young men come
in large numbers 'to gain that instruction which will turn most to
their account in after life, and to form good and serviceable connex-
ions',[86] such virtual universities on their own hold out little prospect
of that fullness of education afforded by the college.

Yet mass education at a 'real' (as opposed to a 'virtual') university
does not sit easily with the values and ethos of the collegiate legacy
either. 'There are choices, not experiences, courses in abundance, but
no snapdragon';[87] it allows for, but does not insist upon so many
personal experiences that are wrapped up in the notion of a 'college'.
However, Newman would have pointed out that there are numerous
ways of supplementing and making up for the deficiency. Most
commentators on the Catholic University have assumed that the
collegiate houses Newman established were intended as colleges-
in-the-making, but there is no conclusive evidence to suggest what
he thought the ideal size should be. The Oriel and Trinity he knew
had around sixty or seventy students each, which would make them
nearer in size and atmosphere to some of the permanent private

halls of current-day Oxford. When these halls were reviewed in 2007, the University authorities were forced to recognise the supportive dynamics of these smaller communities, where junior and senior members mix freely over meals and are generally on good terms with one another, and where the possibility exists of spotting problems at an early stage.[88]

Experiments to found collegiate universities have not met with the success that their advocates might have expected. The first attempt in England, the University of Durham, was set up in the early 1830s; but it struggled financially and in numbers for many decades, and since then there has been only one other attempt in Britain, at York. Efforts to establish collegiate universities in the United States have fared little better.[89] The obstacles are formidable, not least the expense and the absence of an established tradition. Any wise university administrator will recognise the extraordinary efforts required at Oxford and Cambridge to make the system work. Nevertheless, there are any number of ways of providing the collegiate support that Newman envisaged, as illustrated by the different forms of student living that he devised in 1857.

While universities nowadays wash their hands of the non-teaching side of student life and outsource the provision of student residences to outside bodies,[90] virtually no-one has challenged the process and asked why. The financial pressures on administrators and the research and teaching pressures on academics are so great that they can spare no thought for such matters. Meanwhile, the inherited notion of what a university education entails is being further whittled down. Newman would have objected strongly—and so, perhaps, will society when it contemplates the damage wrought by the hurried and ill-conceived expansion of higher education. At some point public opinion may challenge the universities and, by asking what conditions are most likely to foster genuine human development, revisit the provision of collegiate houses or their equivalent. These houses play a crucial part in the making of men and women by forming the *whole* student, not just his or her intellectual faculties. A university is an institution, but a college (or its equivalent) creates a family environment which educates the heart, because it forms young people by engendering good dispositions, healthy loyalties and upright affections. Newman's efforts to ensure that this took place were of paramount significance: it is what he meant by 'education, in this large sense of the word'.[91]

Newman witnessed the beginning of that unrestrained quest for professional training and mere technical knowledge, urged by the liberals and utilitarians of his day, and saw an antidote in both a genuinely liberal education and a collegiate education; if a university neglects the residential side then it neglects what it is most dangerous to neglect. Newman inherited the idea that the moral development of the whole person was an essential part of the liberal education associated with Oxford and Cambridge; this education was supposed to form and shape character and inculcate a sense of high responsibility to society. Insofar as it is a place merely for the dissemination of knowledge, a university invariably has a limited effect on the student: the college, aided in its task by the Church, can transform an individual. As Newman commented in the Dublin lectures, 'The world is content with setting right the surface of things; the Church aims at regenerating the very depths of the heart.'[92]

One of the most practical, as well as significant, ideas to emerge from this study of Newman's part in the foundation of the Catholic University in Ireland is the way he sought to associate its non-residential students with the collegiate houses and thereby to substitute for their deficient education. Modern equivalents are obvious: students can fill out their strictly academic education by attending chaplaincies, cultural centres, university residences, and other places which are not driven by examination systems or constrained by bureaucrats, as well as joining university clubs and societies. Yet there is (at least in Britain) a dearth of chaplaincies and university residences along Newman's lines—and, more to the point, the absence is not even noticed. Newman would have drawn attention to this, and argued that there is a need for discipline and training in that art of virtuous living which has been handed down through the generations in order for civilisation to be nourished, renewed and passed on as an integral whole.

Today, financial pressures are causing Oxbridge colleges to adopt cheaper means of preserving the tutorial system; but elsewhere even this luxury cannot be contemplated. Everywhere, contact time is squeezed out by administrators looking to cut corners and costs. But a reaction is beginning to set in: there is a growing concern over how much contact time students have with their lecturers and professors, particularly in the humanities. Surveys which test student satisfaction are becoming the crude mechanism for shaming university faculties into giving greater priority to their teaching commitments by ensuring that academics make themselves available for individual or small-group supervision and introduce more seminars or classes.

On the pastoral front, however, little has changed. More often than not the need for deans of discipline or chaplains—or their modern substitutes, welfare officers and campus psychiatrists—is only perceived *after* a crisis has arisen, and then it can be little more than a form of damage control for authorities loth to appear negligent of the deep human needs of their student body. Even though pastoral care is desperately needed, for students are exposed as never before to the self-destructive temptations of popular culture, only lip service is paid to the quaint idea of 'pastoral wellbeing'. This, surely, is a consequence of a postmodern society where there are no longer shared values and a consensus of what it means to be a well-formed person. In this context, the main hope for a university along Newman's lines is by means of faith-based institutions.

In a public lecture delivered in 2009, Alasdair MacIntyre asserted that 'there are three major issues that put Newman at odds with the contemporary research university's understanding of its mission: its pursuit of highly specialised knowledge, the secular university's understanding of what it is to be secular, and the university's self-justification by appeal to considerations of social utility'.[93] Each of these three denials relates to a central affirmation contained in the *Idea*, and in rejecting these affirmations the modern university contends that Newman's arguments are not just false, but irrelevant. MacIntyre argues that each of these denials betrays a fundamental defect of the modern research university which prevents it from engaging in radical self-criticism and evaluation of its ends. It is because the successful university has lost the ability to think about its purpose and goal that it no longer recognises Newman's arguments. What we need to learn from Newman, says MacIntyre, is 'that undergraduate education has its own distinctive ends, that it should never be regarded as a prologue to or a preparation for graduate or professional education, and that its ends must not be subordinated to the ends of the necessarily specialised activities of the researcher'.[94] In other words, an undergraduate education should be regarded as an end in itself; it is about the making of men.

Mass education has given rise to various forms of 'distance learning', which to varying degrees eliminates much of what lies at the heart of education and can only be achieved in a residential academic community. Despite being an avid reader and a prolific writer, Newman was acutely aware of the dangers of isolated study, even from a strictly academic perspective:

> The general principles of any study you may learn by books at home; but the detail, the colour, the tone, the air, the life which makes it live in us, you must catch all these from those in whom it lives already. [...] we must come to the teachers

of wisdom to learn wisdom, we must repair to the fountain, and drink there. Portions of it may go from thence to the ends of the earth by means of books; but the fulness is in one place alone. It is in such assemblages and congregations of intellect that books themselves, the masterpieces of human genius, are written, or at least originated.[95]

These words will hopefully guide those with responsibility for higher education as the balance between education online and on-campus is tested.

The *Idea* will continue to challenge contemporary thinking on education and to cause discomfort and qualms of conscience to educational administrators. It stresses the importance for a university to teach the *right* things, as opposed to the modern tendency to allow students to choose what they want to study. With further compartmentalisation of subject areas and greater specialisation, Newman's proposal for 'a connected view of things' will prove increasingly attractive; it has already been proposed as a remedy for modern ills by Ian Ker,[96] the leading authority on Newman, and by Alasdair MacIntyre. Perhaps the *University sketches* will reappear on university reading lists, as they are the product of a powerful imagination which was capable of seizing the truth about a long and varied tradition and its relation to the development of European culture. A selection of them regularly formed part of the English course at University College Dublin up to 1924 (and thereafter the *Discourses* were used instead). The warm and popular tone of the *University sketches* contrasts with the severely academic and philosophical tone of the *Discourses*; in that sense the *Sketches* are more accessible, but they rarely match the *Discourses* in literary style and perhaps contain too many historical inaccuracies to warrant inclusion as a set text. Nevertheless, Newman's writings are a sure guide to restoring the modern university to its old function as an essential part of social life in a civilised community in the European tradition.

Despite the contention that a 'Catholic university' represents a contradiction in terms,[97] Newman saw no contradiction in the idea. For him this was not an impossible dream: 'No one doubts, at least I don't, that the true normal condition of things would be a Catholic University for Catholic students', he told William Monsell in 1865.[98] When lines between Catholics and other Christians were drawn as strongly as they were in the mid-nineteenth century, it is perhaps no surprise that Newman expressed his 'great dislike of mixed [i.e. Catholic–Protestant] education',[99] and contended that 'while you have professors of different religions, you never can have a *genius loci*—and the place is no longer a genuine university'.[100] Far from conceding that a Catholic university might be unworkable in an intellectual climate which was inhospitable to Christian truth, Newman considered that it might be easier to do so than in times when society was fully permeated by Catholicism:

> It is one great advantage of an age in which unbelief speaks out, that Faith can speak out too; that, if falsehood assails Truth, Truth can assail falsehood. In such an age it is possible to found a University more emphatically Catholic than could be set up in the middle age, because Truth can entrench itself carefully, and define its own profession severely, and display its colours unequivocally, by occasion of that very unbelief which so shamelessly vaunts itself.[101]

Newman would not therefore discount the possibility of setting up a Catholic university in Britain in the twenty-first century, given the need for one and the untapped promise, but he would question whether there were academics capable of understanding a university in his sense and whether they were willing to work in unison.

The prospects of a Catholic university in Newman's mould in Britain today are good, for a number of reasons. The secular university is academically in crisis; it does not give value for money; it trains the young, but does not educate them. A Catholic university would resurrect the lost idea of collegiality without which no institution of higher education can fully thrive; it would serve Catholics and non-Catholics alike; it would provide coherent, well-coordinated curricula which could serve students whatever they mean to pursue beyond university; it would not thwart the education of the young by requiring them to overspecialise prematurely; and it would prepare students to become proper adults and responsible citizens And for all of these reasons, parents and others interested in revitalizing university education will find Newman's educational ideas in theory and practice of great practical interest.

One of Newman's most significant contributions to Christian thinking is in the formation of the laity; his ideas foreshadowed —and may even have influenced—the teaching of the Second Vatican Council on the laity, though it is hard to identify the intellectual lineage and argue for a *direct* influence. Certainly, an ideal place to see Newman's understanding on the formation of the laity worked out in practice is at the University. His address to the young men of the evening classes on his last full day in Dublin is as fresh and inspiring as it must have been in 1858.

> Gentlemen, I do not expect those who, like you, are employed in your secular callings, who are not monks or friars, not priests, not theologians, not philosophers, to come forward as champions of the faith; but I think that incalculable benefit may ensue to the Catholic cause, greater almost than that which even singularly gifted theologians or controversialists could effect, if a body of men in your station of life shall be found in the great towns of Ireland, not disputatious, contentious, loquacious, presumptuous (of course I am not advocating inquiry for mere argument's sake), but gravely and solidly educated in Catholic knowledge, intelligent, acute, versed in their religion, sensitive of its beauty and majesty, alive to the arguments in its behalf, and aware both of its difficulties and of the mode of treating

them. And the first step in attaining this desirable end is that you should submit yourselves to a curriculum of studies, such as that which brings you with such praiseworthy diligence within these walls evening after evening; and, though you may not be giving attention to them with this view, but from the laudable love of knowledge, or for the advantages which will accrue to you personally from its pursuit, yet my own reason for rejoicing in the establishment of your classes is the same as that which led me to take part in the establishment of the University itself.[102]

Newman had ambitions for the university to regain its position as a centre of influence in society, rather than allow the press to monopolise this function. He recognized that both had a role to play, even if the press was often vulgar, irresponsible and usurpatory. Dissatisfied that the 'authority, which in former times was lodged in Universities, now resides in very great measure in that literary world' of periodicals, whose writers 'can give no better guarantee for the philosophical truth of their principles than their popularity at the moment, and their happy conformity in ethical character to the age which admires them', Newman suggests that a proper university training would provide an antidote to the insatiable 'demand for a reckless originality of thought, and a sparkling plausibility of argument' that periodical literature supplies—and he speaks as someone who wrote for periodicals nearly all his life. Any university training worth its name should stimulate the student's powers into action and prevent a merely passive reception of images and ideas, which so much of the electronic gadgetry now on offer to students promotes.

Let him once gain this habit of method, of starting from fixed points, of making his ground good as he goes, of distinguishing what he knows from what he does not know, and I conceive he will be gradually initiated into the largest and truest philosophical views, and will feel nothing but impatience and disgust at the random theories and imposing sophistries and dashing paradoxes, which carry away half-formed and superficial intellects.[103]

Newman's high aspirations for the role of the university as regards what we now call culture are elaborated in the *Idea*, where he asserts that a university training,

is the great ordinary means to a great but ordinary end; it aims at raising the intellectual tone of society, at cultivating the public mind, at purifying the national taste, at supplying true principles to popular enthusiasm and fixed aims to popular aspiration, at giving enlargement and sobriety to the ideas of the age, at facilitating the exercise of political power, and refining the intercourse of private life.[104]

This sort of service to society might seem improbable in a world where the university has been all but sidelined from the public conversation; but even if this function had not been superseded by the media, it is likely that the university would have merely contributed to the lack of unity in culture and paved the way for postmodernism owing to its own loss of direction. Instead, universities have new roles assigned to them: witness government obsession with the university as an agent of knowledge creation and, in the West, with social mobility. To the extent that the university neglects its role of nurturing well-formed and educated citizens, it will form adults incapable of participating in the institutions of social and political organisation: and that failure is tantamount to an invitation to government abuse, or, worse, tyranny.

Among more recent technological advances, the internet has led to a multiplication of learning experiences and easy access to a new universe of information, which means that the need for unity of knowledge has dramatically increased so as to avoid fragmentation not just of knowledge, but the whole of human life. Universities which are deeply fragmented themselves cannot help here; but those which hold onto a unified understanding of the world might be able to provide public service by ensuring society is culturally leavened by the university. It is worth noting that Newman wrote about the importance of the personal dimension of education and of gaining an overview or 'a connected view'[105] of things precisely at a time when there was an explosion of information through the dissemination of cheap literature and that he did so in order to caution about the use to which it would be put. Though not on the same scale as the internet revolution, the first half of the nineteenth century did witness a profusion of information that was unprecedented, and this lends Newman's words extra weight and applicability.

Newman's attitude to that early manifestation of relativism in the shape of a liberalism which rejected dogma and the objectivity of religious truth, was one of the constants of his adult life and defined his attitudes to public affairs. One of his private letters describes the secularising tendencies he saw at work around him, whose effects were as far-reaching as they were disastrous, and illustrates the difficulties he experienced in countering the drift towards government interference and the growth of the 'nanny state':

> For the last fifty years, since 1827, there has been a formidable movement among us towards assigning in the national life political or civil motives for social and personal duties, and thereby withdrawing matters of conduct from the jurisdiction of religion. Men are to be made virtuous, and to do good works, to become good members of society, good husbands and fathers, on purely secular motives. We are having a wedge thrust into us which tends to the destruction of religion altogether; and this is our misery, that there is no definite point at which we can logically take our stand, and resist encroachment on principle. Such is the workhouse system, such was the Civil Marriage Act. On this

account I looked with jealousy even on Dr Miller's October Hospital Collections; yet it was impossible to refuse to take part in them. The proceedings of the School Board are only a more pronounced form of what really is the Pelagian heresy. Such of course are the Irish Queen's Colleges. Such teetotalism.[106]

It is noteworthy that John Paul II's apostolic constitution on Catholic universities *Ex corde Ecclesiae* (1990) quotes on three occasions from the *Idea of a university*, and each of the three references says something about the general university, not just the Catholic one. First, in dealing with the development of the student as a human person, it says that 'Newman describes the ideal to be sought in this way: "A habit of mind is formed which lasts through life, of which the attributes are freedom, equitableness, calmness, moderation and wisdom".'[107] Secondly, when asserting that a university needs '*to work towards a higher synthesis* of knowledge' and its integration, the constitution points out how 'Newman observes that a University "professes to assign to each study which it receives, its proper place and its just boundaries; to define the rights, to establish the mutual relations and to effect the intercommunion of one and all".'[108] Lastly, the study found that 'It is the honour and responsibility of a Catholic University to consecrate itself without reserve to *the cause of truth*. This is its way of serving at one and the same time both the dignity of man and the good of the Church, which has "an intimate conviction that truth is [its] real ally [...] and that knowledge and reason are sure ministers to faith".'[109] Forming minds in freedom and wisdom; a higher synthesis of knowledge; a consecration to the cause of truth: these are Newman's challenges for the modern makers of men.

Notes

[1]   The obsession of students with their career is seen by one university commentator as paramount to a modern article of faith: 'That a life *is* a

career is for them an article of faith' (A. T. Kronman, *Education's end: why our colleges and universities have given up on the meaning of life* (New Haven, 2007), p. 256).

2   *Idea of a university*, p. 233.

3   Charles Daman, a Fellow (1836–42) and tutor (1837–68) of Oriel, attended several of the tea parties that Newman gave for undergraduates on Monday evenings and regularly dined with him in college. On marrying Emily Hawtrey in 1841 he had to resign his fellowship—but not his tutorship, which he made his life's work.

4   *Ten letters introductory to college residence* (Oxford, 1848), pp. 2, 4, 7, 8. The book is dedicated to S[tephen]. T[homas]. H[awtrey]. his brother-in-law, who was still at Eton. Another book of advice published the same year was Charles Clarke's *Letters to an undergraduate of Oxford*.

5   *Ten letters introductory to college residence*, p. 24. Daman drew on his *Six dialogues touching the nature of man* (1836) when writing about what it is to be a man.

6   'Scheme of Rules and Regulations', 1856, *MC*, p. 115.

7   Newman to Scratton, 21 October 1857, *LD*, vol. xviii, p. 152.

8   Memorandum, 25 November 1870, *AW*, p. 320.

9   *Newman on university education*, ed. R. McHugh (Dublin, 1944), pp. xi–xxi.

10 After re-reading his correspondence of the period 1850–54, Newman concluded that it showed that the plan for the Catholic University was 'to attempt an impossibility' (memorandum, 9 January 1873, *AW*, p. 326). An Irish priest had reported that his bishop had 'the most absolute conviction of its utter impossibility' (George Butler to Newman, 12 February 1854, *LD*, vol. xvi, p. 63n).

11 *HS*, vol. iii, pp. 2–4.

12 Memorandum, 29 April 1854, *MC*, p. 94.

13 In 1861 the proportion of schools under the clergy was 80% and increasing (Sullivan, *University education in Ireland*, p. 9).

14 Cullen invited Newman to become the founding rector in July 1851. In early November Cullen learned that Barnabò would have preferred the archbishop himself to have been president and Newman the director of studies, but by then it was too late to alter things (Larkin, *Making of the Roman Catholic Church*, pp. 124–5).

15 Larkin, *Consolidation of the Roman Catholic Church*, p. 179; *Roman Catholic church*, p. 277.

16 In a single, unmistakable reference to Cullen, Disraeli has a Roman monsignor say: 'We want a statesman in Ireland. We have never been able to find one; we want a man like the cardinal. But the Irish will have a native for their chief. We caught Churchill young, and educated him in the Propaganda; but he has disappointed us. At first all seemed well; he was reserved and austere; and we heard with satisfaction that he was unpopular. But, now that critical times are arriving, his peasant-blood cannot resist the contagion. [...] For the chance of subverting the Anglican Establishment, he is favoring a policy which will subvert religion itself' (*Lothair* (London, 1840), p. 40). This reference was spotted by Colin Barr (*Paul Cullen*, p. 196).

17 C. Butler, *The life and times of Bishop Ullathorne, 1806–1889* (London, 1926), vol. ii, pp. 312–13n.

18 The divide between them is illustrated by their pronouncements on education. In a pastoral letter to the Catholic clergy of Armagh in 1851, Cullen wrote: 'Who else but the pastors of the Church have the mission from Heaven to add the religious element to education? Who else have ever been able to confer this inestimable boon on humanity?' (*The pastoral letters and other writings of Cardinal Cullen*, vol. i, ed. P. Moran (Dublin, 1882), p. 70). In a sermon preached on 19 August 1827, Newman maintained that 'the clergy are not to be considered as controlling education in their own right, but as representatives and instruments of the general body of Christians for whose good God has appointed them to the office of superintendance' ('On general education as connected with the Church and religion', BOA).

19 Newman to Fottrell, 10 December 1873, *LD*, vol. xxvi, p. 394.

20 Newman to Holmes, 25 May 1862, *LD*, vol. xx, p. 200.

21 *HS*, vol. iii, pp. 86–9. Newman ended his last Dublin lecture on the same note, explaining that he could act only in St Philip's way and no other (*Idea of a university*, pp. 238–9).

22 Newman to Ornsby, 1 August 1859, *LD*, vol. xix, p. 187.

23 Newman to Ornsby, 15 December 1859, *LD*, vol. xix, pp. 253–4.

24 Newman to Lord Braye, 29 October 1882, *LD*, vol. xxx, p. 142.

25 Newman to Northcote, 7 April 1872, *LD*, vol. xxvi, p. 58. Several years earlier, when reflecting on his tutoring at Oriel, he wrote: 'My heart was wrapped up in that kind of life' (Newman to H. J. Coleridge, 20 April 1866, *LD*, vol. xxii, p. 218).

26 De Vere, *Recollections*, p. 266.

27 *HS*, vol. iii, p. 229.

[28] The Oxford University Act (1854) ensured that the effective power passed from Convocation, made up by all MAs but dominated by the country clergy, to Congregation, which consisted only in resident MAs; the Hebdomadal Board of heads of house was replaced by an elected Hebdomadal Council (six heads of house, six professors and six others), which took over the executive role; colleges were given the power to remodel their statutes in consultation with commissioners; and non-Anglicans were allowed to matriculate and take a BA. The effect of the Act and subsequent reforms of college statutes was to enhance the influence of college tutors, who began to take over the duties of the private tutors. Another Royal Commission, set up in 1871, enacted further reforms: creating a new class of 'official fellowships' for college tutors and officers, who would be allowed to marry; permitting colleges to give fellowships to university professors; and setting up faculty boards to oversee exams and to coordinate lectures on a university basis.

[29] *The modern university and its discontents*, p. 243.

[30] *HS*, vol. iii, p. 229. See the section 'Between the *Idea* and the reality' in chapter 2 for a discussion of the personal excellences gained within a collegiate university; see the sections on 'The professorial system and its limitations' and 'The collegiate system' in chapter 3 for a treatment of the institutional excellences.

[31] Rothblatt, *The revolution of the dons*, p. 62.

[32] *HS*, vol. iii, pp. 6–7.

[33] *HS*, vol. iii, p. 182.

[34] See Newman to Pusey, 14 November 1865, *LD*, vol. xxii, p. 103.

[35] In 1828 the ages of Dornford, Newman, Froude and Wilberforce were, respectively, thirty-four, twenty-seven, twenty-six and twenty-five; Hawkins was thirty-nine.

[36] 8 February 1829, *LD*, vol. ii, p. 119.

[37] Benedict XVI, Message on World Day of Peace, 2008.

[38] Chapter address, 17 June 1848, *Newman the Oratorian*, p. 221. Different quotations bring out different aspects of the divine order: grace 'has innovated upon nature, not destroying it or suspending it, but bringing it to a higher order' (12 January 1854, *ibid*, p. 276); God 'violates in nothing that original constitution of mind which He gave to man' (*Discourses to mixed congregations* (London, 1849; 1906), pp. 71–2); 'Nature warrants without anticipating the Supernatural, and the Supernatural completes without superseding Nature' (*HS*, vol. iii, p. 79).

39 'St Paul's characteristic gift', sermon preached at the Catholic University Church, 1857, *Sermons preached on various occasions*, pp. 92–3.

40 *Idea of a university*, p. 120.

41 'Architectural description of the University Church', *CUG* 51 (3 April 1856), p. 60.

42 *HS*, vol. iii, p. 152.

43 'The secret power of Divine grace', sermon preached at the Catholic University Church, 28th Sunday after Pentecost, 1856, *Sermons preached on various occasions*, pp. 58–9.

44 While Newman would have admired the attempt at the recently founded New College of the Humanities in London to provide a broader university education and a greater number of 'contact hours', he would have deplored its establishment along Brougham's exclusively secular lines.

45 'What I aimed at', *MC*, p. 290.

46 Newman to Hope-Scott, 28 April 1865, *LD*, vol. xxi, p. 454.

47 *Culture and anarchy*, p. xviii. See endnote 41 in chapter 2 for a longer comparison of Arnold and Newman.

48 Sidgwick, 'The prophet of culture', reprinted in the Oxford World Classics edition of *Culture and anarchy* (Oxford, 1869; 2006), p. 166. These may be strong words, but Sidgwick had discerned that Arnold omitted Newman's stress on the training of the intellect—which Newman designated by phrases like 'culture of the intellect'—and that Arnold merely used religion to serve the purposes of his (vague) notion of culture. Sidgwick's essay 'The prophet of culture' appeared in *Macmillan Magazine* 16 (1867) as a critique of Arnold's essay 'Culture and its enemies', which was published in the *Cornhill Magazine* (July 1867), and in many ways remains the most penetrating of the critiques. I am grateful to Edward Short for bringing this to my attention.

49 His comment to his friend Catherine Froude that it would be strange 'if Oxford is imported into Ireland, not in its members only, but in its principles, methods, ways and arguments' (14 October 1851, *LD*, vol. xiv, p. 389), has been taken too literally by some, whereas it should be seen as an indication that he hoped to renew the battle against liberalism that he once conducted in Oxford.

50 Terence Corcoran taught in the Department of Education at University College Dublin for many years and consistently attacked Newman's educational ideas. His invective is given full force in his introductions to *Newman's theory of liberal education* (Dublin, 1929) and *Newman: selected discourses on liberal knowledge* (Dublin, 1929). Corcoran's views were later

championed by V. A. McClelland in *English Roman Catholics and higher education 1830–1903* (Oxford, 1973).

51   *Newman in Dublin*, p. 21.
52   *NU*, pp. 299–307.
53   Quoted from notes taken by Brian Boyd at the third of five lectures on Newman in the series called 'God, Philosophy, Universities' at the University of Notre Dame on 6 November 2006.
54   *Imperial intellect*, Culler, pp. 165–6.
55   See Placid Murray's *Newman the Oratorian* (pp. 80–1) for a fuller treatment of this.
56   Newman to Ornsby, 26 January 1863, *LD*, vol. xx, p. 425.
57   Pollen to Maria La Primaudaye, 13 May 1855, quoted in Pollen, *John Hungerford Pollen*, p. 253.
58   S. Andrewes, a Christ Church undergraduate, quoted in Pollen, *John Hungerford Pollen*, p. 218.
59   Pollen to Goldie, August 1890, *The Month* 507 (September 1906), pp. 318–19.
60   Pollen to Goldie, August 1890, *The Month* 507 (September 1906), p. 319.
61   L. McRedmond, *Thrown among strangers: John Henry Newman in Ireland* (Dublin, 1990), p. 140.
62   Newman to G. M. Hopkins, 3 March 1887, *LD*, vol. xxxi, p. 195. This may be compared with Newman's query to the President of Maynooth in 1881 as to whether, 'It is a probable opinion and therefore may be acted upon by an individual, that the Irish people has never recognized, rather have and continuously [...] protested against and rejected the sovereignty of England, and have seemingly admitted it only when they were too weak to resist; and therefore it is no sin to be what would be commonly called a rebel' (19 December 1881 (draft), *LD*, vol. xxx, pp. 32–3). See I. Ker's *Biography* (p. 729) for the context of this letter.
63   With hindsight, it seems that in emphasising that the primary purpose of a university is to teach, Newman made a sharper distinction between teaching and research than he intended; after all, his medical school incorporated both functions.
64   M. Oakeshott, 'Idea of a University', 1950, *The voice of liberal learning: Michael Oakeshott on education*, ed. T. Fuller (London, 1989), p. 104.
65   H. S. Jones, *Intellect and character in Victorian England: Mark Pattison and the invention of the don* (Cambridge, 2007), pp. 183, 191, 213. Pattison does not seem to have ever lost his estimation of the importance of that very

Newmanian concept of personal influence. Before the Selborne Commission in 1877, he affirmed that the more advanced education becomes, the more instruction as such is supplanted by 'the direct action of [...] the mind and character of the teacher upon the mind and character of the pupil' (*ibid.*, p. 154). Later, in an article 'What is a college?', he stressed the centrality of personal influence when describing how in higher education, techniques of teaching give way to 'the direct action of intellect on intellect, of character on character—the intellect and character of the teacher upon the intellect and character of the pupil' (*Journal of Education* 4 (1882), p. 71).

[66] Pattison remarked in 1863 that the Tractarians brought about 'a revival of the spirit of learned research' ('Learning in the Church of England', *Essays by the late Mark Pattison*, vol. ii (Oxford, 1889), p. 269).

[67] *Idea of a university*, p. 249. It should be noted that Newman regarded mathematics as part of the arts faculty.

[68] See Newman to Cullen, 17 June 1858, *LD*, vol. xviii, p. 385. 'The establishment of a good School of Science was one of the foremost objects which I kept in view' ('What I aimed at', *MC*, p. 298).

[69] *CUG* 55 (7 August 1856), pp. 116–17.

[70] These are: 'A form of infidelity of the day', 'Christianity and physical science', 'Christianity and scientific investigation', and 'Christianity and medical science'.

[71] Designed to stimulate research and to advertise the University, *Atlantis* kept its readers abreast of scientific advances by means of its abstracts, which reported on scientific developments abroad.

[72] Though the academic input at the BAAS conference was dominated by Trinity College, two scientists from the Catholic University gave papers. In astronomy and meteorology eight papers out of twenty-seven were given by Irishmen, of which five were presented by Henry Hennessy FRS, Professor of Natural Philosophy; in chemistry three papers were given by W. K. Sullivan, Professor of Chemistry and Dean of the Faculty of Science. Sullivan also acted as conference secretary for chemistry and mineralogy.

[73] Newman to Capes, 1 February 1857, *LD*, vol. xvii, p. 513.

[74] It is likely that Newman would have separated the science faculty from the arts faculty if numbers had warranted doing so, but only one student passed his inceptorship in science during Newman's rectorate—and he went on to pass his licentiate in science in 1859.

[75] Newman's final annual report amounted to little more than a covering letter for Sullivan's *Report of the Dean and Faculty of Science of the Catholic*

University, Session 1857–1858, UCDA, 4.G.2/3.

76   Although the University was briefly without a non-medical scientist during 1873, Sullivan was replaced by John Campbell as Professor of Chemistry and Gerald Molloy was appointed as Professor of Natural Science.

77   D. O'Leary, *Roman Catholicism and modern science: religion and science in Victorian Britain* (London, 2006), pp. 31–3. A similar article appeared in the London *Standard* (10 December 1873, p. 5) which was based on the *Memorial addressed by the students and ex-students of the Catholic University of Ireland to the Episcopal Board of the University* (1873).

78   Women were permitted to take degrees in Ireland when the Royal University was formed, but were not allowed to lectures at University College until 1909, when it became part of the National University of Ireland. Several Catholic women's colleges in Dublin taught students for the degrees of the Royal University, and in 1909 these were turned into halls of residence for women. One of the first two women senators at University College Dublin in 1909 was Mary Hayden, daughter of Newman's Professor of Anatomy and Physiology. Women were allowed into Trinity in 1904; before then they could attend the Protestant Alexandra College, which was founded in 1866, and from 1880 they could be taught for degrees from the Royal University.

79   He told his sister-in-law, 'It is one of the best points of this unhappy age, that it has made so many openings for the activity of women' (Newman to Mrs Jane Mozley, 26 February 1884, *LD*, vol. xxx, p. 316).

80   Besides Kronman's *Education's end: why our colleges and universities have given up on the meaning of life* (2008), other examples are W. Readings, *The university in ruins* (1996); H. Lewis, *Excellence without a soul: does liberal education have a future?* (2007); F. Donoghue, *The last professor: the corporate university and the fate of the humanities* (2008); and S. Fish, *Save the world on your own time* (2008).

81   Besides Alasdair MacIntyre's *God, philosophy, universities* (2009), see G. M. Marsden, *The soul of the American university: from Protestant establishment to established non-belief* (1994); P. Gleason, *Contending with modernity: Catholic higher education in the twentieth century* (1995); J. T. Burtchaell, *The dying of the light. The disengagement of colleges and universities from their Christian churches* (1998); G. D'Costa, *Theology in the public square: church, academy, and nation* (2005); S. Hauerwas, *The state of the university: academic knowledges and the knowledge of God* (2007); and J. Smith, *Desiring the kingdom: worship, worldview, and cultural formation* (2009).

82 M. Higton, in *A theology of higher education* (2012), devotes one of his three historical chapters to Newman.

83 'Newman and the sword of the spirit', *The sword of the spirit* (August 1945, p. 1).

84 *HS*, vol. iii, p. 189.

85 *HS*, vol. iii, pp. 13–14.

86 *HS*, vol. iii, pp. 11, 50.

87 Rothblatt, *The modern university and its discontents*, p. 87.

88 *Review of the permanent private halls associated with the University of Oxford* (Oxford, 2007), p. 20. The reviewers also noted their 'financial fragility' and suggested that insufficient numbers in some subject areas meant that the halls could not guarantee the full 'Oxford experience'.

89 The story of these endeavours is told in Alex Duke's *Importing Oxbridge: English residential colleges and American universities* (New Haven, 1996). One of the more remarkable attempts to emulate Oxford took place at Princeton during the presidency of Woodrow Wilson, the future President of the United States. An admirer of Newman's *Idea*, Wilson thought that the primary object of a university was intellectual; that residence in a college would 'fine and refine individual spirits'; that self-education was important; and that teaching should be by means of intellectual companionship. There were three phases to Wilson's plan: a reorganisation of the curriculum; the establishment of a modified tutorial (or preceptorial) system; and the remodelling of Princeton on a system of residential colleges. The first was straightforward to achieve. The second resulted, in 1905, in weekly meetings with preceptors who were chosen for their gentlemanly and companionable qualities so that they could influence the students beyond the academic sphere—but by 1925 the preceptorial system was abandoned. Most difficult of all was the creation of colleges as this meant contending with a well-established club system (Duke, *Importing Oxbridge*, pp. 81–3). See also A. Grafton, 'Precepting: myth and reality of a Princeton institution', *Princeton Alumni Weekly* 103:11 (March 12, 2003), pp. 16–19.

90 In 2011 the University of Reading announced that it had decided to outsource the running of its student accommodation to a private company (*Times Higher Education Supplement*, 5 May 2011).

91 Journal, 21 January 1863, *AW*, p. 259.

92 *Idea of a university*, p. 203.

93 'The very idea of a university: Aristotle, Newman and us', *British Journal of Educational Studies* 57:4 (December 2009), p. 350. This was the second

annual John Henry Newman lecture, given at St John's College, Oxford on 9 June 2009.

94 'The very idea of a university: Aristotle, Newman and us', p. 362. Earlier in his lecture (p. 350), MacIntyre remarks that while contemporary universities justify their existence to students, donors and governments by being a cost-effective means of providing skilled labour and research that leads to economic growth, Newman, by contrast, argues that 'the activities that contribute to the teaching and learning of a university have goods internal to them that make those activities worthwhile in themselves'.

95 *HS*, vol. iii, p. 9. Here, in 'What is a university?' (*HS*, pp. 6–17), Newman argues at length that a university is still a place for personal teaching even in age of books and periodicals—an argument that would still hold up in the age of the internet.

96 This is one of the themes in Ker's lecture at Harvard Law School on 29 September 2010 entitled 'John Henry Newman's *Idea of a university*. A classic for our times?' A video of this lecture can be accessed at <http://www.law.harvard.edu/news/2010/10/21_ker.html>.

97 In his *Suggestions on academic organisation, with special reference to Oxford* (1868, p. 301), Mark Pattison asserted that 'Catholic schools there may be, but a Catholic university there cannot be'.

98 Newman to Monsell, 12 January 1865, *LD*, vol. xxi, p. 384. He likewise told Woodlock, 'A Catholic University, recognised as such by the State, is [...] the normal instrument of high education and of literary and scientific proficiency within the pale of the Church' (23 February 1868, *LD*, vol. xxiv, pp. 40–1).

99 Newman to Denison, 2 November 1858, *LD*, vol. xviii, pp. 500–1. Newman wrote this two days before he left Ireland for the last time.

100 Newman to Monsell, 3 February 1853, *LD*, vol. xv, p. 283. A different version of this letter runs: 'Where professors, or where students, are of distinct religions among themselves, there will be no genius loci, or at least no healthy genius. Religion will be either altogether excluded as a latent element—or else you will have a number of small sectarian clubs, each representing its own religious tenets, and brim full of the odium theologicum' (*LD*, vol. xxxi, p. 34*). According to John Jackson ('John Henry Newman', p. 104), during Newman's rectorate there were a significant number of Protestants in the medical school: one academic and between fifteen and twenty students.

101 *Idea of a university*, pp. 382–3.

[102] 'Discipline of mind', 2 November 1858, *Idea of a university*, pp. 486–7.

[103] Preface, *Idea*, pp. xix–xxii.

[104] *Idea of a university*, pp. 177–8.

[105] *Idea of a university*, p. 134.

[106] Newman to Longman, 28 May 1878, *LD*, vol. xxviii, pp. 363–4.

[107] *Ex corde Ecclesiae*, note 23, which quotes from the *Idea of a university*, pp. 102–3.

[108] *Ex corde Ecclesiae*, section 16; and note 23, which quotes from the *Idea of a university*, p. 457.

[109] *Ex corde Ecclesiae*, section 4, which quotes from the *Idea of a university*, p. xi.

APPENDIX I

Extract from the Idea of a university (1873) on the effect of a university education

I T IS THE education which gives a man a clear conscious view of his own opinions and judgments, a truth in developing them, an eloquence in expressing them, and a force in urging them. It teaches him to see things as they are, to go right to the point, to disentangle a skein of thought, to detect what is sophistical, and to discard what is irrelevant. It prepares him to fill any post with credit, and to master any subject with facility. It shows him how to accommodate himself to others, how to throw himself into their state of mind, how to bring before them his own, how to influence them, how to come to an understanding with them, how to bear with them. He is at home in any society, he has common ground with every class; he knows when to speak and when to be silent; he is able to converse, he is able to listen; he can ask a question pertinently, and gain a lesson seasonably, when he has nothing to impart himself; he is ever ready, yet never in the way; he is a pleasant companion, and a comrade you can depend upon; he knows when to be serious and when to trifle, and he has a sure tact which enables him to trifle with gracefulness and to be serious with effect. He has the repose of a mind which lives in itself, while it lives in the world, and which has resources for its happiness at home when it cannot go abroad. He has a gift which serves him in public, and supports him in retirement, without which good fortune is but vulgar, and with which failure and disappointment have a charm.[1]

Note

[1]   *Idea of a university,* p. 178.

APPENDIX II

T HE TRUE GENTLEMAN in like manner carefully avoids whatever may cause a jar or a jolt in the minds of those with whom he is cast;—all clashing of opinion, or collision of feeling, all restraint, or suspicion, or gloom, or resentment; his great concern being to make every one at their ease and at home. He has his eyes on all his company; he is tender towards the bashful, gentle towards the distant, and merciful towards the absurd; he can recollect to whom he is speaking; he guards against unseasonable allusions, or topics which may irritate; he is seldom prominent in conversation, and never wearisome. He makes light of favours while he does them, and seems to be receiving when he is conferring. He never speaks of himself except when compelled, never defends himself by a mere retort, he has no ears for slander or gossip, is scrupulous in imputing motives to those who interfere with him, and interprets every thing for the best. He is never mean or little in his disputes, never takes unfair advantage, never mistakes personalities or sharp sayings for arguments, or insinuates evil which he dare not say out. From a long-sighted prudence, he observes the maxim of the ancient sage, that we should ever conduct ourselves towards our enemy as if he were one day to be our friend. He has too much good sense to be affronted at insults, he is too well employed to remember injuries, and too indolent to bear malice. He is patient, forbearing, and resigned, on philosophical principles; he submits to pain, because it is inevitable, to bereavement, because it is irreparable, and to death, because it is his destiny. If he engages in controversy of any kind, his disciplined intellect preserves him from the blundering discourtesy of better, perhaps, but less educated minds; who, like blunt weapons, tear and hack instead of cutting clean, who mistake the point in argument, waste their strength on trifles, misconceive their adversary, and leave the question more involved than they find it. He may be right or wrong in his opinion, but he is too clear-headed to be unjust; he is as simple as he is forcible, and as brief as he is decisive. Nowhere shall we find greater candour, consideration, indulgence: he throws himself into the minds of his opponents, he accounts for their mistakes. He knows the weakness of human reason as well as its strength, its province and its limits. If he be an unbeliever, he will be too profound and large-minded to ridicule religion or to act against it; he is too wise to be a dogmatist or fanatic in his infidelity. He respects piety and devotion; he even supports institutions as venerable, beautiful, or useful, to which he does not assent; he honours the ministers of religion, and it contents him to decline its mysteries without assailing or denouncing them. He is a friend of religious toleration, and that, not only because his philosophy has taught him to look on all forms of faith with an impartial eye, but also from the gentleness and effeminacy of feeling, which is the attendant on civilization.[1]

Note

[1] *Idea of a university*, pp. 209–10.

APPENDIX III

A UNIVERSITY EMBODIES THE principal of progress, and a College that of stability; the one is the sail, and the other the ballast; each is insufficient in itself for the pursuit, extension, and inculcation of knowledge; each is useful to the other. A University is the scene of enthusiasm, of pleasurable exertion, of brilliant display, of winning influence, of diffusive and potent sympathy; and a College is the scene of order, of obedience, of modest and persevering diligence, of conscientious fulfilment of duty, of mutual private services, and deep and lasting attachments. The University is for the world, and the College is for the nation. The University is for the Professor, and the College for the Tutor; the University is for the philosophical discourse, the eloquent sermon, or the well contested disputation; and the College for the catechetical lecture. The University is for theology, law, and medicine, for natural history, for physical science, and for the sciences generally and their promulgation; the College is for the formation of character, intellectual and moral, for the cultivation of the mind, for the improvement of the individual, for the study of literature, for the classics, and those rudimental sciences which strengthen and sharpen the intellect. The University being the element of advance, will fail in making good its ground as it goes; the College, from its Conservative tendencies, will be sure to go back, because it does not go forward. It would seem as if a University seated and living in Colleges, would be a perfect institution, as possessing excellences of opposite kinds.[1]

Note

1 'Abuses of the colleges. Oxford', *HS,* vol. iii, pp. 228–9. The original sketch
  was entitled 'Abuses of the collegiate system' (*CUG* 29, 14 December 1854).

APPENDIX IV

Extract from Newman's 'Scheme of Rules and Regulations' (1856) on how to manage a university residence

I T IS ASSUREDLY a most delicate and difficult matter to manage youths, and those lay youths, in that most dangerous and least docile time of life, when they are no longer boys, but not yet men, and claim to be entrusted with the freedom which is the right of men, yet punished with the lenience which is the privilege of boys. In proposing rules on this subject, I shall begin with laying down, first, as a guiding principle, what I believe to be the truth, that the young for the most part cannot be driven, but, on the other hand, are open to persuasion and to the influence of kindness and personal attachment; and that, in consequence, they are to be kept straight by indirect contrivances rather than by authoritative enactments and naked prohibitions. And a second consideration of great importance is, that these youths will certainly be their own masters before many years have passed, as they were certainly schoolboys not many months ago.

A University residence, then, is in fact a period of training interposed between boyhood and manhood, and one of its special offices is to introduce and to launch the young man into the world, who has hitherto been confined within the school and the playground. If this be so, then is it entrusted with an office as momentous as it is special; for nothing is more perilous to the soul than the sudden transition from restraint to liberty. Under any circumstances it is a serious problem how to prepare the young mind against the temptations of life; but, if experience is to be our guide, boys who are kept jealously at home or under severe schoolmasters, till the very moment when they are called to take part in the business of the world, are the very persons about whom we have most cause to entertain misgivings. They are sent out into the midst of giant temptations and perils, with the arms, or rather with the unarmed helplessness, of children, with knowledge neither of self nor of the strength of evil, with no trial of the combat or practice in sustaining it; and, in spite of their good feelings, they too commonly fail in proportion to their inexperience. Even if they have innocence, which is perhaps the case, still they have not principle, without which innocence is hardly virtue. We could not do worse than to continue the discipline of school and college into the University, and to let the great world, which is to follow upon it, be the first stage on which the young are set at liberty to follow their own bent. So proceeding, we should be abdicating a function, and letting slip the opportunities, of our peculiar position.

It is our duty and our privilege to be allowed to hold back the weak and ignorant a while from an inevitable trial;—to conduct them to the arms of a kind mother, an Alma Mater, who inspires affection while she whispers truth; who enlists imagination, taste, and ambition on the side of duty; who seeks to impress hearts with noble and heavenly maxims at the age when they are most susceptible, and to win and subdue them when they are most impetuous and self-willed; who warns them while she indulges them, and sympathizes with them while she remonstrates with them; who superintends the use of the liberty which she gives them, and teaches them to turn to account the failures which she has not at all risks prevented; and who, in a word, would cease to be a mother, if her eye were stern and her voice peremptory. If all this be so, it is plain that a certain tenderness, or even indulgence[1] on the one hand, and an anxious, vigilant, importunate attention on the other, are the characteristics of that discipline which is peculiar to a University. And it is the necessity of the exercise of this elastic Rule, as in a good sense of the term it may be called, which is the great difficulty of its governors.[2]

It is easy enough to lay down the law and to justify it, to make your rule and keep it; but it is quite a science, I may say, to maintain a persevering, gentle oversight, to use a minute discretion, to adapt your treatment to the particular case, to go just as far as you safely may with each mind, and no further, and to do all this with no selfish ends, with no sacrifice of sincerity and frankness, and with no suspicion of partiality.[3]

Notes

[1] The earlier version has 'laxity of rule' for 'indulgence'.

[2] In the first version this sentence read as follows: 'And it is the necessity of the exercise of this "Lesbian Canon", as the great philosopher calls it, which is the great difficulty of the governors of such an institution.'

[3] 'Scheme of Rules and Regulations submitted to the Council in April 1856', *MC*, pp. 114–17. This was eventually incorporated into and published as *Constitution and Statutes of the Catholic University of Ireland*, 1869 (DDA 45/5/V(4)).

APPENDIX V

Extract from Newman's 'Scheme of Rules and Regulations' (1856) on the role of the college tutor

I T WILL BE prudent in him to anticipate, in the case of many of his charge, little love of study and no habit of application, and, even in the case of the diligent, backwardness and defective or ill-grounded knowledge. Towards them, as well as towards the studious and advanced, he will have to address himself according to the needs of each. He will select for them their course of reading, recommend them the lectures which they are to attend, and the books and subjects which they are to present for examination.

As to the more promising, he will superintend their reading. He will set them off, for instance, in private informal lectures and conversations, at the commencement of new and difficult authors. He will then let them go a while, and bid them bring him their difficulties. He will keep his eye upon them, and from time to time examine them, take them in hand again when they come to more difficult portions, and bring to their notice points which would otherwise escape them. He will direct them to works in illustration of their subject, help them with analyses and abstracts, or teach them how to make them; and, as their examination draws near, he will go over the ground again with them, and try them to and fro in their books.

On the other hand, in the case of the backward, he will ascertain their weak points, and set them on remedying them. He will force upon them the fact of their want of grounding and other defects, and, without annoying them, will be jealous and importunate on the subject in proportion to their indisposition to amend. He will try to keep them up to the mark of the Professors' Lectures which they attend, and prevent them from showing ill there. As to the idle, he will be in [the] practice of sending for them, will ask them if they have prepared to-morrow's lectures, oblige them to come at a certain hour for examination in them, treating them throughout with good-humour, but with the steadiness of a superior. In like manner, he will bring before them their approaching examination, confront them with the disgrace of failure, and impress upon them their ever-accumulating loss of time, and the extreme difficulty of making up for it.

All this involves a real occupation on the part of the Tutor, but it is close rather than great, and continual rather than continuous; it does involve, however, a sustained solicitude, and a mind devoted to his charge. And because of the serious importance, and the really interesting nature of the office, when understood and entered into, and again, of the difficulty some persons have in understanding it, its duties have here been drawn out somewhat in detail. The way to a young man's heart lies through his studies, certainly in the case of the more clever and diligent. He feels grateful towards the superior, who takes an interest in the things which are at the moment nearest to his heart, and he opens it to him accordingly. From the books which lie before them the two friends are led into conversation, speculation, discussion: there is the intercourse of mind with mind, with an intimacy and sincerity which can only be when none others are present. Obscurities of thought, difficulties in philosophy, perplexities of faith, are confidentially brought out, sifted, and solved; and a pagan poet or theorist may thus become the occasion of Christian advancement. Thus the Tutor forms the pupil's opinions, and is the friend, perhaps the guide, of his after life. He becomes associated with the pupil's brightest and pleasantest years, and is invested in the hues of a past youth.

In this idea of a College Tutor, we see that union of intellectual and moral influence, the separation of which is the evil of the age. Men are accustomed to go to the Church for religious training, but to the world for the cultivation both of their hard reason and their susceptible imagination. A Catholic University will but half remedy this evil, if it aims only at professorial, not at private teaching. Where is the private teaching, there will be the real influence.

To fulfil this idea, however, the Tutor must have no part in the College discipline, nor any academical authority over his pupils. Should he be invested with these additional duties, he will often find it expedient to commit the Tutorial care of certain of his pupils to externs [i.e. outside Tutors]; on the principle on which the offices of Ruler and Confessor are separated in Religious communities.[1]

Note

[1] 'Scheme of Rules and Regulations submitted to the Council in April 1856', *MC*, pp. 117–20.

Select biographies of promoters of and staff at the Catholic University

Allies, Thomas William (1813–1903), was educated at Eton and Wadham College, Oxford, where he became a Fellow. While an Anglican curate, he made a deep study of the Catholic Church and its educational systems in France, Germany and Italy on several tours abroad, and in 1850 he became a Catholic. He acted as secretary to the sub-committee on the organization of the Catholic University in 1851, and was appointed Professor of Modern History in 1855; though he resigned shortly afterwards, because of a dearth of students, the lecture course he prepared under Newman's encouragement formed the basis of his voluminous *The formation of Christendom* (8 vols, 1865–95). He was Secretary of the Catholic Poor School Committee for the period 1853–90 and actively promoted Catholic elementary education in England, in the process setting up three teacher training colleges. A small dapper man with a pugnacious disposition, he was known among friends as 'bantam cock'. (*ODNB*)

Anderdon, William Henry (1816–90), a nephew of Henry Edward Manning, was educated privately, attended King's College London, and then studied at Oxford, first at Balliol, then at University College. While at Oxford, he lived in considerable style, keeping a horse and holding memorable breakfast parties, but later as an Anglican curate he was known for his poverty. He became a Catholic in 1850, was ordained three years later, and lectured on rhetoric at Ushaw. For the period 1856–63 he was dean of the Catholic University Church, where his sermons drew large congregations; he acted as provisional pro-vice-rector in September 1858, and during the first two terms of 1858/59 he was dean of St Mary's, where he fell out with Newman over a disciplinary affair. He wrote a number of heavily didactic historical novels, the best-known being *The adventures of Owen Evans* (1863), a tale of the conversion to Roman Catholicism of a marooned Welsh sailor, which was nicknamed the 'Catholic Crusoe'. He also wrote three books on Luther and contributed articles to the *Dublin Review, The Month,* and the *Weekly Register.* (*ODNB*)

Arnold, Thomas (1823–1900), the second son of Thomas Arnold, the famous headmaster of Rugby School, was educated at Rugby School and University College, Oxford. He worked for the Colonial Office before becoming an inspector of schools in Tasmania in 1850, where he married Julia Sorrell; they eventually had nine children. In 1856, to the horror of his wife, he entered the Catholic Church, and resigned his inspectorship. That year Newman appointed him Professor of English Literature at the Catholic University, where his lectures formed the basis of *A manual of English literature* (1862), which saw seven editions in the author's lifetime; he also acted as a tutor in classics at St Patrick's and St Mary's, and was the only non-Irishman on the committee which compiled the *Report on the condition and circumstances of the Catholic University of Ireland* (1859). In 1862 he left Dublin to become the senior classics master at Newman's Oratory School in Birmingham, but in 1865 he left the school—and the Church—to become a tutor in Oxford. He published a translation and edition of *Beowolf* (1876), but ruined his academic career at Oxford by returning to the Catholic Church. After living off journalism and examining for the civil service commission, he returned to Dublin, at Newman's encouragement, to become Professor of English at University College, the renamed arts faculty of the Catholic University. He continued teaching until his death, once marking an undergraduate essay by the young James Joyce, as well as working alongside Gerard Manley Hopkins, who was Professor of Classics. (*DIB, ODNB*)

Bennet, Thomas, was educated at Louvain University and became the provincial of the Calced Carmelites in Ireland, acting for a time as the vice-president of All Hallows. He became dean of the Carmelite House of Our Lady of Mount Carmel when, in 1855, the older students of the Carmelite secondary school became members of the Catholic University.

However, less than a dozen students joined the University. Bennet attempted to open a separate collegiate house in 1861, but it closed a year later.

Bianconi, Charles (1786–1875), was born in Italy and came to Ireland when aged fifteen. He was an astute businessman and made a fortune as the founder of Ireland's public transport system. Bianconi was naturalised in 1831 and became a friend and supporter of Daniel O'Connell. He had many contacts in government circles, took an active part in the civic affairs of Clonmel, and was elected mayor in 1844 and in 1845; during the Famine he took care of the tenants on his own estate and gave employment to others. In 1863 he was appointed deputy lieutenant of the county of Tipperary. Bianconi served on the original Catholic University committee and was one of the two auditors of the University accounts, as wells as advising Newman and Cullen on financial matters connected with the University. (*DIB, ODNB*)

Butler, Edward (d. 1902), was educated at Trinity College Dublin and became Chief Inspector of the National Board of Education, but gave up the position (and accepted a drop in salary) to become Professor of Mathematics at the Catholic University in 1854. He was the first dean of the arts faculty. In 1859 he was appointed Principal of the Training Department for teachers at Marlborough Street, Dublin, by the Commissioners of National Education and left the Catholic University.

Casey, John (1820–91), was a self-educated mathematician who entered Trinity College Dublin as a student when he was thirty-eight after a career in teaching. He was elected a member of the Royal Irish Academy in 1866, and in 1873 turned down a professorship at Trinity for one at the Catholic University. On account of his work in geometry—twenty-five papers and six books—he was elected a member of the London Mathematical Society, a Fellow of the Royal Society of London, a member of the Société Scientifique de Bruxelles and of the Société Mathématique de France. He taught at St Stephen's Green until his death. (*DIB, ODNB*)

Crofton, Morgan William (1826–1915), was educated at Trinity College Dublin where he was a gold medallist in mathematics and physics. From 1849 to 1852 Crofton occupied the chair of natural philosophy (physics) at the newly founded Queen's College, Galway. He was received into the Catholic Church by Newman in 1851, and examined at the Catholic University in 1856/57, though he turned down Newman's invitation to become the University Observer (i.e. astronomer) and a tutor in mathematics. For many years he taught at the Royal Military Academy, Woolwich, where he worked with J. J. Sylvester. He made significant contributions to mathematics in the areas of geometrical probability and integral calculus, and was on the council of the London Mathematical Society. In 1882 he became one of the Catholic Fellows of the Royal University of Ireland. (*DIB, ODNB*)

Cryan, Robert (1826–81), was appointed Professor of Anatomy and Physiology at the Catholic University in 1855, having been a lecturer in anatomy and physiology at Carmichael School, Dublin. He was a member of the Royal College of Physicians and of the Royal College of Surgeons. When the president of Queen's College Cork claimed in the press that there was little difference between Cork and the Catholic University, because the latter admitted Protestants too, Cryan wrote to clarify the matter (*Freeman's Journal*, 21 November 1856).

Cullen, Paul (1803–78), entered Carlow College when he was fourteen, and three years later moved to the Irish College in Rome where he lived for the next thirty years. He was a model student who studied an impressive range of subjects and won many prizes. After his ordination, Cullen taught in Rome and became rector of the Irish College, which grew in his time from under twenty to nearly sixty seminarians. He became the official agent in Rome of the Irish bishops, which meant that he was privy to all Irish ecclesiastical business carried out at Rome. He returned to Ireland in May 1850 as archbishop of Armagh and apostolic delegate of the Pope, and from 1852 was archbishop of Dublin. Cullen was the driving force behind the Catholic University, and it was he who selected Newman as the founding rector. The University was one of

Cullen's pet projects until his death, though his energies were employed in many areas as he sought to reorganise the Irish Church. Cullen outmanoeuvred Archbishop MacHale in a struggle that lasted a decade and became the dominant figure in the Irish Church, but it came at a price to his reputation; in 1858 Cullen had a physical and mental breakdown which took him seven months to recover from. In 1866 he was created the first cardinal of Ireland and served on several Roman Congregations. (*DIB, ODNB*)

Dunne, David Basil (1828?–92), gained doctorates in philosophy and theology at the Irish College in Rome, but did not become a priest. He was appointed a lecturer in logic at the Catholic University in 1854 and acted as tutor at St Patrick's. He began lecturing in the Catholic University Medical School in June 1858 and, after training as a barrister, became Professor of Law and Logic. Dunne married in 1855 and had five children. In 1879 he displaced Scratton as Secretary when the Catholic University became part of the Royal University. He was a much-liked lecturer and tutor, and had great admiration for Newman, with whom he kept in touch after his departure from Dublin.

Dunne, Robert (1830–1917), the younger brother of David, was educated at the Irish College, Rome where he gained his doctorate. Back in Dublin he taught at St Laurence's School, succeeding James Quinn as dean of St Laurence's House. He joined Quinn in Brisbane in 1861 and on his death became the second bishop—and first archbishop—of Brisbane. (*Australian dictionary of biography*)

Ellis, Andrew (1792–1867), the son of a gentleman farmer in Wicklow, was appointed surgeon to St Mary's Hospital, Dublin in 1821 and that year began lecturing on anatomy. He became Professor of Surgery at the medical school in Cecilia Street in 1837; when it closed in 1854, he helped Newman acquire it for the Catholic University. The leading Catholic surgeon of his day, he was made Professor of the Theory and Practice of Surgery at the Catholic University Medical School when it opened in 1855. He published several books, including *Lectures and*

observations on clinical surgery (1846), and was a member of the Royal
College of Physicians.

Errington, Michael (*c*.1810–74), from a Yorkshire family, married a
sister of R. M. O'Ferrall and settled in Dublin and purchased estates in
Tipperary. His brother George was Archbishop of Trebizond and
Cardinal Wiseman's coadjutor. He was one of the eight laymen co-opted
onto the Catholic University Committee at the Synod of Thurles (1850)
and was on the subcommittee for finance (which met only once). His
son George entered the Catholic University and resided at St Mary's in
1858/59. The following year he sent his younger son James to Trinity
College Dublin.

Flanagan, Terence (1817?–59), a cousin of the Oratorian priest John
Flanagan, studied for eighteen months at Trinity College Dublin, and then
worked for three years at an engineering office. He was the chief engineer
of several railway lines: one around Blackburn, one from Antwerp to
Rotterdam, and another from Lisbon to Cintra. He was elected a member
of the Institute of Civil Engineers. In 1850 Newman chose him as the
architect for the Oratory house in Birmingham, and in 1855 he appointed
him as Professor of Civil Engineering at the Catholic University.

Flannery, Michael (1818–91), was Professor of Moral Theology at All
Hallows, 1845–51, and vicar general of Killaloe, 1853–59. At Cullen's
indication, he was appointed dean of St Patrick's House at the Catholic
University in 1854 and remained there until he became coadjutor bishop
of Killaloe in 1858, succeeding a year later. He was not suited to running
St Patrick's as he had little idea of how to manage students. As a bishop
he threw himself into his work, which was considerable in the post-
famine years, and within four years he was burnt out; he moved to Paris
in 1863 for health reasons, while his diocese was managed by three
consecutive coadjutor bishops until his death in Paris.

Forde, Laurence (1820–70), was educated at the Irish College, Rome,
where he completed doctorates in philosophy and theology. After serving

as Cullen's chaplain, he became Professor of Theology at the Irish College, Paris. At Cullen's wish, he was appointed Professor of Canon Law at the Catholic University, though initially there were no students to teach. In January 1857 he substituted as vice-rector when Dr Leahy was ill, but Newman found him impossible to deal with. Moreover, he was unpopular and had little understanding of Newman's idea of a university, and when Cullen tried to make Forde the vice-rector, Newman effectively blocked the appointment; he told a friend, 'I should be a traitor to the University if I concurred in such a choice'. Forde became one of the three vicar-generals of the diocese of Dublin.

Gartlan, James Francis (1804–68), went to the Irish College, Salamanca at the age of fifteen and gained his doctorate there; after four years as a curate in Ireland he returned to the College as rector. Against his inclinations, he stepped in as vice-rector of the Catholic University in November 1858, and left on the arrival of the new rector in April 1861.

Godwin, Thomas ('Frederic'), was a servant of Frederick Faber at Elton and followed him to the Birmingham Oratory. For several years he was an Oratorian lay-brother, before moving to Dublin and acting as the house manager of St Mary's House, 1854–59. He returned to England, married and set up a milk shop.

Hayden, Thomas (1823–81), had a Protestant father and a Catholic mother who was related to the Duke of Wellington. He was Professor of Anatomy and Physiology at the Catholic University from 1855 until his death; he was also the physician at the Mater Misericordiae Hospital from its foundation, and had a private practice too. Known as 'gentle Thomas' on account of his courtesy and charm, he contributed articles to medical journals and to *Atlantis*, and was vice-president of the College of Physicians in Ireland, 1875–77; his major book on *Diseases of the heart and aorta* (1875) broke new ground. He lived in the fashionable Merrion Square, where he entertained regularly. His daughter Mary Theresa was the academic historian and campaigner for women's causes, who was the only female founder-member of the senate of the new National University of Ireland in 1909. (*DIB*)

Hennessy, Henry (1826–1901), brother of the politician and colonial administrator Sir John Pope Hennessy, received an excellent education in classics, modern languages and mathematics at Cork, but was deprived of a university education on account of being a Catholic. He was librarian at Queen's College, Cork from 1849 until 1855, when he was invited by Newman to become Professor of Natural Philosophy at the Catholic University, charged with the task of setting up a physics laboratory. Though the plans fell through, he published many original and valuable papers in British and foreign scientific journals in terrestrial physics, meteorology, and climatology, and devised several mechanical inventions. While at the Catholic University he published *On the study of science in its relation to individuals and society* (1858); *On the freedom of education* (1859); and *The relation of science to modern civilisation* (1862). He was elected a Fellow of the Royal Society in 1858, and was the vice-president of the Royal Irish Academy, 1870–73. Although he was active in trying to promote the study of science among Catholics, he transferred his services to the Royal College of Science, Dublin in 1874 and acted as its dean in 1880 and 1888. (*DIB, ODNB*)

Hope-Scott, James Robert (1812–73), was the son of the governor of the Royal Military Academy, Sandhurst and MP for Linlithgowshire. He was educated at Eton and Christ Church, Oxford, and became a Fellow of Merton, where he was a keen Tractarian and a close friend of Newman's. In the 1840s he helped to rescue St Columba's, the 'infant Eton or Winchester' in County Meath, for the Irish Protestants, which William Monsell and Lord Adare had founded; and along with Gladstone he helped to found Glenalmond College in Scotland. In 1847 Hope married a grand-daughter of Sir Walter Scott, and on the death of his brother-in-law inherited Abbotsford and assumed the name Hope-Scott. In 1851 he was received into the Catholic Church, and followed by his wife and other relations. That year he was approached by Cullen about setting up the Catholic University, and told him: 'First get Newman.' Hope was Newman's constant adviser on a whole range of matters, including the Catholic University. In recognition of his 'early researches and the munificence of his later deeds'—his £5000 was the largest gift to the University—Newman dedicated to him *Office and works of universities* (1856), the collected volume of his university sketches. (*ODNB*)

Kavanagh, James William (1818–86), a Senior Inspector of the National Board of Commissioners and author of *Mixed education: the Catholic case stated* (1859), was appointed Professor of Mathematics at the Catholic University in 1859; he continued on the staff until 1882, and also served as an Examiner for the Irish Education Board.

Kelly, Matthew (1814–58), taught for two years at the Irish College in Paris, then at Maynooth, where he became Professor of Ecclesiastical History. He published several Irish historical texts including *A calendar of Irish saints* (1857). He was appointed vice-rector of the Catholic University in September 1858, but died on 30 October that year. (*DIB, ODNB*)

Leahy, Patrick (1806–75), was educated at the classical day school in Thurles, then entered Maynooth, being ordained in 1833. Leahy served on the original University Committee at a time when he was vicar-general of Cashel and president of St Patrick's, Thurles. He was one of the subcommittee of three which drew up plans for the initial organisation of the Catholic University, and he became Professor of Exegetics and the first vice-rector, while also acting as parish priest of Cashel—with an indult from Rome allowing him to reside for much of the year in Dublin. On becoming bishop of Cashel in 1857, he resigned the vice-rectorship. In 1866 and 1867 he acted on behalf of the Irish Catholic bishops in negotiating with Lord Mayo, the chief secretary for Ireland, over the proposed endowment of the Catholic University. A man of great courtesy and dignity, he acted as a buffer between the dictatorial Cullen and the wary episcopate. (*DIB, ODNB*)

Lewis, David (1814–95), was educated at Jesus College, Oxford, where he became a Fellow and vice-principal. He was the curate of the University Church of St Mary the Virgin during Newman's last years as vicar, and became a Catholic shortly after Newman. He lived in Dublin for a while, married the daughter of Lord Methuen, and moved to Brussels, where he acted as the official correspondent between the Catholic University in Dublin and the Catholic University in Louvain.

Lyons, Robert Spencer Dyer (1826–86), was the son of the mayor of Cork, Sir William Lyons. He studied medicine at Trinity College Dublin and became a member of the Royal College of Surgeons in Ireland. He went out to the Crimea as pathologist-in-chief in 1855, where he reported on diseases in the trenches; later that year he was appointed Professor of Physiology and Pathology at the Catholic University. He wrote widely on subjects in medicine, education, and forestry: of note are *A handbook of hospital practice* (1859); *Intellectual resources of Ireland: supply and demand for an enlarged system of Irish university education* (1873); *Forest areas in Europe and America* (1884). A Young Irelander in his youth, Lyons served on Gladstone's Commission in 1870 to inquire into the treatment of Irish political prisoners in English goals, and became a Liberal MP for Dublin, 1880–85. He married the daughter of D. R. Pigot, Chief Baron of the Exchequer in Ireland. (*DIB, ODNB*)

MacCarthy, Denis Florence (1817–82), studied for the priesthood at Maynooth, before switching to law at Trinity College Dublin. He was called to the Irish Bar, but then devoted himself to literature. He was a prominent Young Irelander, contributing regularly to *The Nation* and writing on the history and religion of the Irish, and on ballad poetry. Most of MacCarthy's original work and his translations from Spanish, German, French, Italian, Greek and Latin poetry were published in periodicals. He was appointed Professor of Poetry and English Literature at the Catholic University in 1854, resigning (possibly for reasons of health) in 1856. He wrote an *Early life of Shelley* (1872), and was elected a member of the Real Academia of Spain in recognition of his work in translating the plays of Calderón. (*DIB, ODNB*)

McCarthy, James J. (1806–82), a friend of Pugin and the architect of many Irish churches, was appointed Professor of Architecture at the Catholic University in 1857. He published *Suggestions on the arrangements and characteristics of parish churches* (1851) and wrote on the principles of ecclesiastical architecture in *Duffy's Irish Catholic Magazine,* and became known as the 'Irish Pugin'. (*DIB, ODNB*)

MacDevitt, John (b. 1834), entered the Irish College, Rome in 1852, and after ordination joined the staff of All Hallows. He was dean of Corpus Christi House during the period 1861–67 and had oversight for the Medical School residence. He contributed to the debate on higher education with a pamphlet entitled *University education in Ireland and 'Ultramontanism'* (1866).

MacDermott, Robert (1829–59), was educated at Clongowes Wood and studied classics at Trinity College Dublin, before studying medicine. He was appointed Professor of Material Medica (i.e. Pharmacology) at the Catholic University in 1855 and had the reputation of being the best lecturer of his day.

MacHale, John (1791–1881), was the first modern Irish bishop to be educated entirely in Ireland. He became Archbishop of Tuam in 1834 and denounced the national system of primary education, which had been established by the government in 1831, for being subversive of the faith of Irish Catholics; and in 1840 he publicly endorsed the movement launched by Daniel O'Connell for the repeal of the Act of Union. By 1845 MacHale was, after Daniel O'Connell, the most popular man in Ireland. A political radical known as the Lion of the West, his stance was pugnacious and his tactics confrontational. MacHale was an uncompromising champion of the poor and underprivileged, and the combination of his stand on social justice with his commitment to cultural and political nationalism explains why he was idolized in his own day. Once dominant within the Irish Church, he was totally isolated within the hierarchy by the end of his life. As one of the four archbishops, he was theoretically in control of the Catholic University, but as Cullen had a fully supportive archbishop and the casting vote, MacHale's presence was futile. After the first meetings of the University Committee he did his best to obstruct Cullen's every move. (*DIB, ODNB*)

Marani, Augustus Caesar (b. *c*.1815), a supporter of Young Italy, was educated at the Jesuit College and University in Modena, Italy, before coming to Ireland. He became Professor of Italian at Trinity College Dublin and acted as a private tutor. In 1854 he accepted Newman's invitation to the chair of Italian and Spanish at the Catholic University, and he stayed on after Newman's departure.

Monsell, William (1812–94), first baron Emly, was educated at Winchester and Oriel College, Oxford. He was MP for Limerick, 1847–74, and from 1855 held various offices in the Liberal government, though he never reached the cabinet. Along with William Sewell and Lord Adare, whose sister he married, he helped to found St Columba's in County Meath for the Irish Protestants. He became a Catholic, and together with Hope-Scott and Manning advised Cullen in 1851 about the Catholic University. Although he had no official attachment to the Catholic University, he and Newman exchanged many letters about it; and after Newman's departure, he acted energetically for the University to gain a charter and endowment, most notably in the scheme Gladstone brought forward in 1873. Newman dedicated to him *Lectures and essays on university subjects* (1859), the second half of the *Idea*, as 'a memorial of work done in a country which you so dearly love, and in behalf of an undertaking in which you feel so deep an interest'. A regular contributor to *The Rambler*, he was a close friend of the French liberal Catholic leader Montalembert. He was the second vice-chancellor of the Royal University of Ireland. (*DIB, ODNB*)

O'Curry, Eugene (1796–1862), was educated at home and worked on his father's farm. After a brief spell as a schoolmaster, then at a mental hospital, he started to work for the historical and topographical section of the Irish Ordnance Survey. In the process of cataloguing and transcribing Irish manuscripts for Trinity College Dublin, the Bodleian Library Oxford and the British Museum, he established his reputation as an authority on Irish language and history. He was elected to the Royal Irish Academy in 1851, and in 1854 Newman appointed him Professor of Irish History and Archaeology at the Catholic University. The lectures he gave there in 1855/56 were published at the University's expense as *Lectures on the manuscript materials of ancient Irish history* (1861). A later series of *Lectures on the manners and customs of the ancient Irish* (3 vols, 1873), was posthumously published by W. K. Sullivan. During his lifetime he published in *Atlantis*, the University's academic journal. His joint work with John O'Donovan on Irish legal manuscripts was published posthumously as the *Ancient laws and institutes of Ireland* (6 vols, 1865–1901). O'Curry's industry and profound learning have ensured him a prominent place in the history of Irish studies. (*DIB*, *ODNB*)

O'Ferrall, James More (1802–76), was born into an Irish landed family. He was one of the eight laymen on the Catholic University Committee and one of the three laymen on the financial committee, which met only once. He was a member of the Royal Commission investigating Maynooth (1853–55), and later became a Commissioner of National Education. He did not marry.

O'Ferrall, Richard More (1797–1880), elder brother of James, was a prominent figure in the struggle for religious and civil liberty and an MP during the periods 1830–47 and 1859–65, holding office in 1835 as Lord of the Treasury. He gave up his seat in Parliament in 1847 to become Governor of Malta, but resigned in 1851 after refusing to work under the Prime Minister Lord John Russell, as he had carried the Ecclesiastical Titles Act. He was a lay trustee of Maynooth and urged those in control of the Catholic University to allow the laity a greater say in its running. He was a constant adviser to Newman's successor, Woodlock, though he declined to send his son to the University.

O'Hagan, John (1822–90), was a graduate of Trinity College Dublin and qualified as a barrister, becoming a Justice of the High Court. A poet and noted Young Irelander, he wrote patriotic songs and contributed to *The Nation*. Newman appointed him a lecturer in Political Economy at the Catholic University in 1854, though he declined a salary, and the two became close friends. When the Council of the Catholic University met for the first time in November 1855, Hagan acted as dean of the faculty of law. He was a good scholar and published in *Atlantis*. O'Hagan became commissioner to the Board of National Education in 1861, and in 1881 Gladstone appointed him Chief Judicial Commissioner for the Irish Land Commission. He married a daughter of Thomas, later Lord, O'Hagan. (*DIB, ODNB*)

O'Loughlin, Austin, was for many years Prefect and dean of the Irish College in Paris. He succeeded Flannery as dean of St Patrick's House in 1858, became the financial secretary of the Catholic University a year later, and succeeded Anderdon at the University Church. The episcopal board removed him from St Patrick's in 1873 for incompetence, but he stayed on at the University Church.

O'Reilly, Edmund Joseph (1811–78), was educated at Clongowes Wood before studying for the priesthood, first at Maynooth then at the Irish College, Rome, where he made friends with Cullen. After gaining a doctorate in theology, he held the chair of theology at Maynooth until 1851, when he asked to become a Jesuit. His revised *Catechism of Scripture history* (1852) and theological lectures at the Jesuit college of St Beuno's in Wales led Newman to appoint him Professor of Dogmatic Theology at the Catholic University, though he did not draw a salary for the first three years, as there were no students. Newman regarded him as 'one of the first theologians of the day' and wanted to him to be made the pro-vice-rector in 1857. In 1859 he was withdrawn from the University and was appointed superior of a new Jesuit retreat at Milltown, near Dublin, where he remained for the rest of his life. (*DIB, ODNB*)

O'Reilly, Myles (1825–80), was born in Ireland and educated at Ushaw. He graduated from the University of London and gained an LLD from Rome, then returned to Ireland where he assumed the part of a country gentleman who bred horses and prize cattle. He was a member of the original Catholic University Committee and one of the subcommittee of three which drew up plans for the initial organisation of Catholic University. He acted as examiner in classics at the Catholic University, agreed to lecture in the philosophy of law, and was one of the authors of the *Report on the condition and circumstances of the Catholic University of Ireland* (1859). O'Reilly joined the Louth rifles militia, holding a captain's commission, then entered the papal army with the rank of major and was appointed to command the Irish brigade; in September 1860 the battalion of St Patrick gallantly defended Spoleto against Piedmontese troops, but was forced to surrender. On his return to Ireland, he was elected MP for County Longford, 1862–79, and was a prominent speaker in Parliament on Irish, military and educational matters. He wrote pamphlets and articles on the question of university education, and on renouncing his seat in Westminster was appointed assistant commissioner of intermediate education. (*DIB, ODNB*)

Ornsby, Robert (1820–89), studied at Lincoln College, Oxford and became a Fellow of Trinity College. He was a college lecturer in rhetoric, a private tutor for four or five years, and held the university office of Master of the Schools. Newman considered him 'an excellent man' and thought highly of him academically, having examined him at Oxford. Ornsby took Anglican orders, and in 1847 became a Catholic; his wife followed him a year later. Ornsby moved to Dublin, where he assisted Frederick Lucas in editing *The Tablet*. He was appointed Professor of Latin and Greek and a tutor in classics at the Catholic University in 1854, where he stayed until 1866, keeping Newman up to date with developments after his departure. After a spell as tutor to the fifteenth Duke of Norfolk, Ornsby returned to his old post in Dublin in 1874, and in 1882 became a Fellow of the Royal University of Ireland. He published *The Greek Testament, from Cardinal Mai's edition of the Vatican Bible, with notes, chiefly philological and exegetical* (1860) and *Memoirs of James Robert Hope-Scott* (2 vols, 1884). (*ODNB*)

Penny, William Goodenough (1815–c.85), was educated at Westminster School and Christ Church, Oxford, where he gained the top mark in his year in mathematics and became a Student (i.e. a Fellow). He took

Anglican orders, but became a Catholic in 1848 and joined Newman at Littlemore, Maryvale then Rome, where he was ordained. He left the Oratory in 1851 (but not the priesthood), and remained a good friend of Newman. Newman invited him to a tutorship in mathematics at the Catholic University, and a year later he became the University Catechist; in 1856 he succeeded Newman as dean of St Mary's House, but resigned after two years. Penny succeeded Butler as Professor of Mathematics, 1860–73. He was a popular tutor and lecturer, and took a great interest in student sport, acting as a rowing coach and umpire.

Pollen, John Hungerford (1820–1902), was the great-great-nephew of Pepys and the nephew of the architect C. R. Cockerell. After an education at Eton and Christ Church, Oxford, he became a Fellow of Merton and came under the influence of the Tractarians. In the summer of 1847 Pollen travelled to France with T. W. Allies in order to discover how the Catholic Church dealt with the poorest parts of the community, before they moved on to Italy and Germany. Pollen was an Anglican curate at St Saviour's, Leeds, but turned down a wealthy living to become a Catholic in 1852; thereafter he devoted himself to art and architecture. In 1855 he became Professor of Fine Arts at the Catholic University; he married that year and settled in Dublin. He worked closely with Newman on the building of the University Church, and became one of Newman's most devoted friends. Pollen's lectures on art in 1856 were later published in *Atlantis*. In 1857 he moved to London, where he had a large family. In various commissions he worked with and befriended the Pre-Raphaelites Edward Burne-Jones, J. E. Millais and D. G. Rosetti. Pollen became assistant keeper at the South Kensington (now the Victoria and Albert) Museum, 1863–76, then acted as private secretary to the Marquis of Ripon, who had become a Catholic and, in 1880, was appointed viceroy of India. In 1889 Pollen helped to found the United Arts and Crafts Guild. (*DIB, ODNB*)

Quinn, James (1819–81), studied under Cullen at the Irish College in Rome, where he first met Newman. After his ordination he became the first head of St Laurence O'Toole's School, Dublin. When it was affiliated to the Catholic University in 1854, Quinn became the dean of St

Laurence's House until 1859, when he was consecrated the first bishop of Brisbane. His episcopate was marked by disputes arising from his authoritarian style and tendency to micro-manage his diocese; his efforts to encourage Irish immigration caused sectarian hostility, which was aggravated by his quip that the colony might yet be called 'Quinn's land'. Despite the initial warmth between them, Quinn and Newman did not get on well together in Dublin. (*DIB, Australian dictionary of biography*)

Renouf, Sir Peter le Page (1822–97), of an old Guernsey family, was educated at Pembroke College, Oxford and came under the influence of the Tractarians. He became a Catholic in 1842 and, after teaching at Oscott, acted as private tutor to the son of the comte de Vaulchier, traveling with the family and continuing his studies. In 1854 he was appointed lecturer in French at the Catholic University and his tutee entered as a student; a year later he became Professor of Ancient History, then Professor of Oriental Languages and began his studies in Egyptology. Renouf published several articles in the University journal *Atlantis*; he joined Newman and Sullivan to edit the journal in 1859, and in 1862 and 1863 replaced Newman as its literary editor. After Newman's departure, he hoped to take Catholic pupils at Oxford, but instead became an inspector of Catholic schools, 1864–85. He contributed to the liberal Catholic *Home and Foreign Review*, edited by Acton, and briefly served as a sub-editor; later he contributed to its successor, the *North British Review*. He opposed the defining of papal infallibility, and his pamphlet about it was put on the Index, but he remained in the Church after the First Vatican Council, while remaining in contact with those who left, such as Döllinger and his brother-in-law Franz Brentano. He became a member of the Society of Biblical Archaeology in 1872 and contributed to its publications as well as publishing *An elementary grammar of the Egyptian language* (1875), and served as its president from 1887 to his death. In 1886 he was appointed Keeper of the Egyptian and Assyrian Antiquities at the British Museum, where he carried on the work of arranging, modernizing, and enlarging the Egyptian and Assyrian collections. His most important work was *The book of the dead* (1890); his shorter works were republished under the supervision of his widow as *The life-work of Sir Peter Le Page Renouf* (4 vols, 1902–7). He was knighted in 1896. (*ODNB*)

Robertson, James Burton (1800–77), was born to a Scottish Presbyterian father, an estate owner in Grenada, and a Catholic mother. He was educated at St Edmund's Ware, trained in law and was called to the Bar, but moved to France to study literature, philosophy and theology under the direction of Lamennais. He published a translation of Schlegel's *Philosophy of history* (2 vols, 1835), which sold tens of thousands of copies, and between 1836 and 1854 was an assiduous contributor to the *Dublin Review* and other periodicals. He spent seventeen years in Belgium and Germany and published a translation of Möhler's *Symbolism* (2 vols, 1843); this and his work on Schlegel gained him a European reputation. In 1855 he was appointed Professor of Geography and Modern History at the Catholic University to which was added English literature in 1862. He was the butt of student jokes on account of his eccentricities, but respected for his immense learning; he was a regular visitor to 6 Harcourt Street, where Newman lived. He published two sets of *Public lectures delivered before the Catholic University of Ireland*, the first on ancient and modern history (1859), the second on modern history and biography (1864). There followed *Writings of Chateaubriand, and on the Illuminati, Jacobins, and Socialists* (1864); *Lectures on the life, writings, and times of Edmund Burke* (1869); and a translation of Hergenröther's *Anti-Janus* (1870), with an introduction on the history of Gallicanism. He received a civil pension of £90 p.a. in recognition of his services to English literature and in 1873 was made a doctor in philosophy by Pope Pius IX. (*DIB, ODNB*)

Scott, William Henry (1819–59), the son of a Staffordshire baronet, was educated at Rugby School, became a scholar at Trinity College, Oxford and then a Fellow of Brasenose, 1844–50. He took Anglican orders, but became a Catholic in 1854. The following year he joined the Catholic University as a tutor in classics at St Mary's House, moving to St Patrick's in 1857. He acted as an examiner on two occasions, and in 1858/59 he became the University's first Public Examiner.

Scratton, Thomas (1821–95), studied at Christ Church, Oxford and took Anglican orders. He became a Catholic in 1850 and three months later tried his vocation at the Birmingham Oratory, but left within a year. Although unsure about how well he would get on with others, Newman appointed him Secretary to the Catholic University, where he remained until the reorganisation in 1879. Newman declined to support his application for the post of Secretary to the newly established Royal University, nor later for a professorship in classics; Scratton sued the Irish bishops and obtained £300 in compensation for his dismissal. Newman found him a difficult character and regretted appointing him: he was unpopular, eager for a prominent position, gossiped, and tried to undermine Newman, whose educational ideas he did not grasp. Three of Scratton's daughters became nuns.

Stewart, James (c.1816–91), was educated at Marischal College, Aberdeen, and Trinity College, Cambridge. He took Anglican orders, acted as a schoolmaster for six years at Houghton-le-Spring, then as a tutor and curate in Suffolk. On becoming a Catholic in 1849 he went to teach in Mauritius, returned to England in 1852 and became a tutor again. Newman appointed him lecturer in Ancient History at the Catholic University, then Professor of Greek and Latin languages, 1857–91. In 1882 he became a Fellow of the Royal University of Ireland.

Sullivan, William Kirby (*c.*1821–90), a native of Cork, studied chemistry under von Liebig at Giessen, Germany, where he completed his doctorate. While chemist to the Museum of Irish Industry in Dublin, he investigated ways of using the industrial resources of Ireland and published *The manufacture of beetroot sugar in Ireland* (1851). He was appointed Professor of Theoretical and Practical Chemistry at the newly-founded School of Science Museum in 1854 and retained some of his duties when he was appointed Professor of Chemistry and Dean of the Faculty of Science at the Catholic University in November 1855. He championed Newman's idea of a university and cherished the hope that the University would become a preeminent centre for science, but his hopes were thwarted, first by Newman's resignation, then by the attitude of the Irish bishops. He strongly opposed the gradual clericalisation of the University, and threatened his resignation several times:

Newman told him, 'It will be a great blow, if you leave the University, for I feel you are just the one person who could not be replaced.' When the opportunity arose, Sullivan took a leading part in the negotiations with the government for a charter and endowment, and wrote *University education in Ireland. A letter to Sir John Dalberg Acton* (1866). Besides his scientific papers, he became a competent Gaelic scholar and an accomplished philologist, and edited E. O' Curry's *Lectures on the manners and customs of the ancient Irish* (3 vols, 1873) for publication; he also edited the University journal *Atlantis* (1858–59, 1862–63, 1870). He became secretary of the Royal Irish Academy, then Professor of Theoretical Chemistry at the Royal College of Science, founded in 1867. When the Jesuits were given the running of St Patrick's House in 1873, he resigned in protest and took up the presidency of Queen's College, Cork. There he actively promoted its science departments. He married the sister of Henry Hennessy and they had five children. (*DIB*)

Tyrrell, Henry (1833–79), was educated at Clongowes Wood and the Original School of Medicine, Dublin. He was a surgeon first at the Jervis Street Hospital, then at the Mater Misericordiae Hospital; in 1855 Newman appointed him one of the Demonstrators in Anatomy at the Catholic University Medical School. He was proactive in setting up St Luke's House, the residence for medical students, and acted as its dean.

Vere, Aubrey Thomas de (1814–1902), was born on the family estate of Curragh Chase, Adare, the third son of Sir Aubrey de Vere and Mary Rice, sister of the first Lord Monteagle. He was privately tutored then studied metaphysics and theology at Trinity College Dublin, though he did not proceed to holy orders. He visited Oxford in 1838 and met Newman, whom he described as a 'youthful ascetic of the middle ages'; and in 1839 he visited Cambridge, where he discovered an entirely different intellectual climate at the Apostles club. In 1841 he met Wordsworth, by then poet laureate, and was invited to his extended household in the Lake District, where he fitted in easily. De Vere published *The Waldenses and other poems* (1842) and *The search after Proserpine and other poems* (1843). He also became a friend of Browning,

Carlyle and Tennyson. From his involvement in famine relief and emigration schemes after the potato blight of 1846 came his study of the Anglo-Irish political economy, *English misrule and Irish misdeeds* (1848), where he called for systematic emigration from a rural society that was uneconomic, as well as the redevelopment of agriculture along efficient lines. In 1851 he and H. E. Manning made a study of St Thomas Aquinas and Dante, and on their way to Rome de Vere became a Catholic, despite the warnings of Carlyle. Newman appointed him Professor of Political and Social Science at the Catholic University in 1855, but having no students de Vere resigned in 1858. The lectures he prepared at the Catholic University were published in substance in *Essays, chiefly literary and ethical* (1889). De Vere never married and spent the rest of his life at the family home, writing poetry and essays on Irish political questions. (*DIB, ODNB*)

Walford, Edward (1823–97), was captain of school at Charterhouse and a scholar at Balliol College, Oxford. He taught at Tonbridge for a year, then spent three years as a private tutor preparing pupils for Oxford. He became a Catholic in 1853 and acted as an examiner for the Catholic University in 1855 and 1858, and briefly took on some tutoring at St Patrick's House, but preferring biographical and antiquarian work he left the University to work in publishing and journalism. He returned to the Church of England in 1860, became a Catholic again in 1871, only to return to the Church of England a year before his death.

Woodlock, Bartholomew (1819–1902), was educated at Clongowes Wood and studied for the priesthood at the Roman Seminary. On his return to Ireland he was appointed Professor of Dogmatic Theology at All Hallows on its opening in 1842, and became president in 1854. He left in 1861 to become the rector of the Catholic University, which had been without a head since Newman's departure in 1858. His rectorship began with great promise, but after only two years cuts had to be made and the fortunes of the University gradually dwindled. When he resigned in 1879, on being appointed Bishop of Armagh, the University was in a parlous state, despite his great personal abilities, energy and vision. (*DIB*)

Select biographies of students at the Catholic University

Barnewall, Sir Reginald Aylmer (1838–1916), was the posthumous son of the ninth baronet, who fought at Waterloo and belonged to one of the oldest Irish families. He joined St Mary's House in 1854 and left in 1857, having passed the scholar's and inceptor's exams; Newman describes him as 'sharp and a good scholar'. Reginald visited Newman in Birmingham in 1860 and again in 1870; he did not marry.

Bethell, Augustus Philip (1838–1912), became a Catholic as a boy. After attending Ushaw, he entered the Catholic University as an intern at St Mary's House in 1855, and in 1857 succeeded his elder brother as president of the Historical, Literary and Aesthetical Society. Augustus tried his vocation at the Birmingham Oratory in 1860 and was ordained in 1863, but left the Oratory and worked as a priest for the diocese of Southwark, where he became a canon in 1887.

Bethell, Henry Slingsby (1836–1908), became a Catholic in 1850, three years after his mother and shortly before his father, who practised as a solicitor in London. His uncle, Sir Richard Bethell, became the attorney-general in 1856, then reached the Woolsack as Lord Westbury in 1861. Henry was educated at Eton, Oscott and Ushaw, before he entered St Mary's House in 1855. He is the first recorded president of the Historical, Literary and Aesthetical Society (in 1856/57). His success in winning a prize from the government-sponsored School of Science Applied to the Arts was much publicised by the Catholic University; he also won university prizes for English verse and criticism. He joined the engineering business set up by his father, who patented a diving apparatus and a process for preserving timber from decay, and later lived abroad, dying in Rome.

Bowden, Henry George (1836–1920), son of Henry Bowden by his first wife, was educated at Eton, 1848–52, and played for the football and cricket XIs. He was received into the Catholic Church at Gibraltar in 1852 and became a private pupil of Robert Ornsby in Dublin, entering the Catholic University as an extern of St Mary's House in 1854. On leaving he joined the Rifle Brigade, and a year later transferred to the Fusilier Guards, where he served for eleven years. On leaving the army in 1867 he joined the London Oratory and was ordained a priest in 1870; he was provost there during the periods 1889–92 and 1903–7.

Bretherton, John (1839–78), son of Peter Bretherton, who had a horse and carriage business in Birmingham, entered the Catholic University in 1856, after being educated at Yvetot in France. He was expelled from St Mary's House by Anderdon in 1859, then transferred to St Patrick's, where he was tutored by Tom Arnold.

Dawson, Charles (1842–1917), was born in Limerick. He entered the Catholic University in 1864—O'Shea says it was earlier—and was auditor of the Literary and Historical Society for the session 1867/68. He became high sheriff of Limerick in 1876–77 and lord mayor of Dublin in 1882 and 1883, and later became MP for Carlow, 1880–85.

de la Pasture, Charles Edward (1839–1923), was the second son of the marquise de la Pasture, who had become a Catholic with her three children in 1850, ten years after the death of her husband, a lieutenant in the 18th Hussars. Charles joined the Catholic University from Downside in January 1855 and entered St Mary's House; he obtained his licentiate with honours in 1858 and in 1915 received an honorary LLD from the National University of Ireland. He joined the English Jesuits in 1863 and served at their church in Bournemouth from 1884 until his death.

Dillon, John (1851–1927), studied at the Catholic University from 1865 to 1870, and was treasurer of the Literary and Historical Society in 1869/70 and auditor in 1874/75. After an apprenticeship with a cotton broker in Manchester, he entered the Medical School in 1878, obtaining his degree from the Royal College of Surgeons, but soon became a follower of Parnell and entered Parliament. He was imprisoned several times, and was eventually one of the leaders of the Irish Nationalist Party until its extinction in 1918. (*DIB, ODNB*)

Duke, Victor (1835–72), one of eight children of William Duke, a well-known doctor at St Leonard's, became a Catholic in 1846 along with his parents and siblings. He stayed at the Birmingham Oratory in the autumn of 1853 and entered St Mary's House in January 1855, winning a university prize for Greek in 1855. On leaving the Catholic University, he returned to Birmingham to begin his novitiate in 1856, but left a year later.

Errington, (Sir) George (1839–1920), was the eldest son of Michael Errington, one of the eight laymen co-opted onto the Catholic University Committee. He joined St Mary's House from Ushaw in November 1857 and was the only resident remaining at the end of Lent Term 1859; he left when St Mary's House closed down that summer. George succeeded to his father's estates and became a magistrate and MP for County Longford, 1874–85. He was sent to the Vatican by Gladstone to give information about the Irish nationalist movement, and in 1885 was created a baronet. (*DIB*)

Farfan, José Manuel (1836–80), of St Joseph, Trinidad, was a member of an important Spanish Trinidadian Creole family. After spending five years at Ushaw, he entered St Mary's House in 1855, and left the following summer, after taking the scholar's exam, to study civil engineering in Paris. He started work as an engineer in Spain (using a contact of the father of Augustus and Henry Bethell) on the construction of a railway from Valencia to Ponferrado, then acted as chief engineer for the construction of a railway near Barcelona, before he returned to Trinidad, where he entered the government service. In 1880 he carried out a survey of parts of the colony to ascertain what new roads were required to be opened by the government.

Fottrell, (Sir) Charles (1849–1925), was auditor of the Literary and Historical Society in 1871. His *Inaugural address delivered before the Literary and Historical Society of the Catholic University of Ireland* (1871) followed closely Newman's ideas about the university being a place for the formation of character. He was the moving force behind the *Memorial addressed by the students and ex-students of the Catholic University of Ireland to the Episcopal Board of the University* (1873); he was also heavily involved in the founding of C.U.I. Bono Club, the society for former students of the Catholic University.

Fraser, Henry Thomas (1838–1904), the fourth son of the eleventh Lord Lovat, studied at Downside, then entered St Mary's House, 1855–57. He became Colonel of the first battalion of the Scots Guards.

Gallwey, Patrick Francis, entered St Patrick's in November 1854. He was awarded a university prize for mathematics in December 1855, and as an engineering student was successful in passing the entrance exams for the College of Military Engineering at Woolwich in 1856.

Green, Michael John, attended the Catholic University during the period 1857–59. A volunteer in St Patrick's Battalion of the Papal army, he was a corporal during the battle of Spoleto in 1860 and won a Papal honour for performing an act of heroic valour under the eyes of his commanding officer, Major Myles O'Reilly. He became a barrister and legal-commissioner under the Land Act.

Hardman, John Bernard (1843–1913), was the son of the leading Birmingham Catholic who owned an ecclesiastical metalwork and stained glass firm and worked with Pugin. He was educated at Oscott, tutored at the Birmingham Oratory, then attended the Catholic University, where Ornsby was his tutor. He became a partner in his father's firm in 1867 and played a part in local government, becoming a member of the Birmingham municipal council.

Keane, Augustus Henry (1833–1912), was born and educated at Cork. He was awarded a scholarship at the Catholic University and became an intern of St Patrick's, where he won prizes for Greek criticism, an English essay, and Latin prose; he obtained his licentiate in 1858 and then became a tutor at St Patrick's. After publishing a *Handbook of the history of the English Language* (1860), and after working as a journalist, he began his life's work of registering and classifying almost every known language, and using the data to work out a system of ethnology. He edited Stanford's *Compendium of geography* and, besides many papers in academic journals, published *Ethnology of the Egyptian Sudan* (1884), *The Lapps, their origin, affinities ... and customs* (1885), *Eastern geography: a geography of the Malay peninsula, Indo-China, the eastern archipelago, the Philippines and New Guinea* (1887), *Ethnology* (1896), *The early chartered companies* (1896), *Asia* (1896), *Africa* (1898), *Man, past and present (1899)*, *The Boer States: land and people* (1900), *The world's peoples: a popular account of their bodily and mental characters (1908)* He was made Professor of Hindustani at University College, London in 1882 and a Fellow of the Royal Geographical Society.

Kerr, Francis Ernest (1840–84), third son of Lord Henry Kerr, became a Catholic in 1852. From Stonyhurst, he went to the Catholic University at the age of fourteen as an extern 'accidentally lodging with Newman'. He served in the Rifle Brigade and was governor of the military prison at Malta. In 1870 he married the eldest daughter of Robert Monteith.

Kerr, Lord Ralph (1837–1916), third son of the seventh Marquis of Lothian, became a Catholic in January 1854 and spent the rest of the year at the Birmingham Oratory. He entered St Mary's House that November and was tutored by Newman. He joined the army and became Colonel of the 10th Hussars, enjoying a distinguished army career, mainly in India. From 1891 to 1896 he was major-general commanding the Curragh, in Ireland. He married Lady Anne Fitzalan Howard, daughter of the fourteenth duke of Norfolk; their only son, Philip Kerr, eventually became the eleventh Marquis of Lothian and was the British Ambassador at Washington.

Ligne, Prince Charles de (1837–1914), was the son of Eugène, eighth Prince de Ligne by his third wife Hedwig, Princess Lubomirska. Eugène, who was President of the Belgian Senate, 1852–78, and one of the most powerful financiers in Europe, sent Prince Charles and his younger brother to St Mary's House in 1856. On leaving, Charles entered the French diplomatic service as an attaché at Vienna. He married in 1876 and settled at the family château at Antoing.

Ligne, Prince Edouard de (1839–1911), younger brother of Charles, entered St Mary's House in 1856 and left with Count Zamoyski at the end of November 1858 after a dispute with Scratton and Anderdon. He joined the papal army and took part in the campaign for the defence of the papal states, being decorated in the process. He married Augusta Cunningham, daughter of the sixth baron of Milncraig, in 1866; after her death, he married Princess Eulalie Dorothée.

MacDermot, Hugh Hyacinth O'Rorke (1834–1904), was educated at home until he entered Maynooth at the age of eighteen with the priesthood in mind. Two years later, he attended the Catholic University on a medical scholarship nominated by the Bishop of Achonry. He won university prizes for his poetry, criticism and English verse, and was president of the Historical, Literary and Aesthetical Society in 1858/59. While at the University he began studying law, being admitted to the King's Inns in 1857. He was called to the Bar in 1862, became a Queen's Counsel in 1877 and was engaged for the leading political cases in the west of Ireland. On the death of his father he became 'The MacDermot'. Gladstone appointed him Solicitor General for Ireland in 1885 and Attorney General and a Privy Councillor for Ireland in 1892. He married twice and had eight sons. (*DIB, ODNB*)

McDonnell, Joseph Patrick (1846–1906), enrolled at the Catholic University in 1860 or 1861. He joined the National Brotherhood of St Patrick, a chain of nationalist debating and reading clubs, and was twice threatened with expulsion for giving lectures at the NBSP. He actively opposed the visit of the Prince of Wales in 1863, and later joined the Irish Republican

Brotherhood and assisted in arms distribution, for which he served a prison sentence. After a meeting with Engels and Marx in London he was appointed to the general council of the First International. (*DIB*)

Maunsell, Thomas (1839–1937), was one of the first students of the Catholic University Medical School, having been schooled at St Laurence's, and sat on the first committee of the Historical, Literary and Aesthetical Society. He joined the British Army in 1860, serving in the Burma and Chitral campaigns, and became surgeon-general in 1895; he was made a Companion of the Order of Bath. He retired in 1899, and in 1911 founded what became the Guild of Catholic Doctors, on account of which he was decorated with the papal Cross of Honour. In 1915 he received one of the honorary degrees conferred by the National University of Ireland on those who 'during their student days, for conscientious reasons, refrained from attending Institutions where they could have obtained a University Degree, and in place thereof, resorted to the Catholic University of Ireland, which was unable to grant them that privilege'.

Molloy, James Lynan (1837–1909), was born in Ireland and educated at St Edmund's Ware, 1851–55, along with his brother Bernard, who later became an MP. He won a classical scholarship to the Catholic University in 1855 and was a resident at St Patrick's. He was vice-president of the Historical, Literary and Aesthetical Society in 1856/57, and also showed considerable musical ability, singing during the Holy Week services. After graduating in 1858, he continued his studies in London, Paris and Bonn, and was called to the Bar in 1863. He became secretary to the British Attorney-General, Sir John Holker, but from 1865 he turned to composing songs and became one of most successful songwriters of his generation. He brought out a collection of Irish tunes entitled *Songs of Ireland* (1873); in all he wrote around a hundred songs, including 'Kerry Dance' and 'Thady O'Flynn'. Molloy composed an operetta, *The students' frolic*, to a libretto by Arthur Sketchley; though it was not successful, the melody of one of the songs, 'Beer, beer, beautiful beer', became extremely popular as 'The Vagabond', with words by C. L. Kenney. His one work of prose, *Our autumn holiday on French rivers* (1874), is said to have inspired R. L. Stevenson's *An inland voyage* (1878). In 1889 he was made private chamberlain to Pope Leo XIII. (*DIB, ODNB*)

Mulholland, John (or 'Jack'), was at Stonyhurst for six years before being nominated for a medical burse at the Catholic University in 1856, joining St Patrick's. He was secretary of Historical, Literary and Aesthetical Society in 1856/57 and won the criticism prize in 1858 for 'A critical comparison of the respective merits of Shakespeare and Æschylus as tragedians, with reference chiefly to the plays of Macbeth and Agamemnon'. He died of consumption when young.

O'Connell, Daniel (1839–72), was the eldest son of John O'Connell, MP and chief political assistant of his father, the Liberator. The grandson received a free place at the Catholic University when it opened, but Newman was not in favour of giving a free place to his younger brother as Daniel had 'not done us credit'. Nevertheless Daniel was awarded a prize for an essay on the Conversion of Ireland. He was drowned while sailing in Dublin Bay.

O'Meagher, Ernesto (b. 1837), son of the Irish journalist Patrick O'Meagher, who worked in Madrid and Paris as the special correspondent for *The Times*, and his wife, Adélaïde *née* de Brumont, was born in Spain and educated in Madrid and Paris. He entered the Catholic University in 1855, winning a scholarship in 1856, and later studied at the University of Paris; he also studied civil engineering at the University of London. He subsequently returned to his native San Sebastian, where he taught English and French.

O'Shea, John Augustus (1839–1905), entered the Catholic University in 1856, nominated to a medical bursary by the Bishop of Kildare, and stayed at St Patrick's for three years. In 1859 he moved to London and became a journalist, working for *The Irishman* and the London *Standard*. He was the *Standard* correspondent for the Franco-Prussian War, when he was captured by the French and nearly executed as a spy; he was in the siege of Paris and in Spain during the Carlist War of 1872; and he reported the famine in Bengal in 1877. He was a long-standing member of the staff of *The Universe,* and in 1885 he became president of the Southwark Irish Literary Club, an important centre for the Gaelic revival in London. He wrote several volumes of stories and an autobiography. His memoir *Roundabout recollections* (2 vols, 1892) devotes a whole chapter to life at the Catholic University. (*DIB, ODNB*)

O'Shea, William Henry (1840–1905), the only son of a Limerick solicitor, was educated at Oscott, and entered St Mary's House in January 1856. He proved a troublesome resident and left at the end of the summer term for Trinity College Dublin. Soon afterwards, his father purchased a commission for him in the 18th Hussars, where William lived extravagantly, largely at his family's expense. In 1867 he married the youngest daughter of Rev. Sir John Page Wood, and in 1880 became MP for County Clare. His wife's relations with Parnell led to the divorce proceedings in 1890 which brought Parnell's political career to a close. (*DIB, ODNB*)

Ryder, (Sir) George Lisle (1838–1905), second son of George Ryder, was a godson of Newman. He was educated at the Birmingham Oratory, then Ushaw, before entering St Patrick's in January 1855. He was withdrawn that summer and sent to Ushaw. He became Chairman of the Board of Customs in 1899, and was made a KCB in 1901.

Ryder, Henry (Ignatius) Dudley (1837–1907), the eldest son of George Ryder, spent six months at St Mary's House before he was withdrawn in July 1855. He joined the Birmingham Oratory, taking the name Ignatius, and became the superior after Newman's death.

Seager, Osmund (1843–1920), was the son of Charles Seager, an Oxford convert who had lived at the 'house for young writers' in Oxford, lectured in Hebrew, and was described by Newman as a 'man of original mind, thoroughly earnest, and deeply pious' as well as 'eccentric in his manners and ways'. Osmund studied for four years at the Jesuit college at Metz before entering the Catholic University; he lived at St Mary's House during the session 1857/58. Osmund became an assistant principal at the Admiralty and was a member of the Hammersmith Board of Guardians and their representative on the Metropolitan Asylums Board.

Throckmorton, John (1840–1918), was the third surviving son of Sir Robert Throckmorton, MP for Berkshire and eighth baronet, and Elizabeth Acton, sister of Cardinal Acton and aunt of Sir John Acton. John arrived at St Mary's House in 1858 from Downside in order to prepare for the entrance exams for the Royal Military Academy at Woolwich.

Thynne, Frederick (1838–81), eldest son of Lord Charles Thynne, was educated at Ushaw, and entered the Catholic University in April 1855, but was encouraged to leave a few weeks later after disgracing himself. He became an officer in the army.

Vaulchier, Louis, vicomte de (1837–1910), was the only child of the comte and grandson of the marquis de Vaulchier, to whose title he succeeded. His mother died when he was young and he was brought up strictly by his maternal grandmother. In 1846 the family took on Peter le Page Renouf as his tutor. Renouf and Louis entered St Mary's House in November 1854, as tutor and lecturer and as student respectively, where they remained for three years. Louis won an English essay prize in 1855. He left the Catholic University in 1857, studied law at the Sorbonne, and in 1861 dedicated his thesis to Newman 'as a slight token of gratitude and respect to one who has been so consistently kind to me'. In 1866 he married Marie Anatole Alix de Raincourt. He served as an officer in the 55th regiment during the Franco-Prussian, was wounded in battle, and made a Chevalier of the Légion d'honneur. He was editor of the review *Annales franc-comtoises*, and in 1891 was elected a member of the Académie de Besançon.

Walsh, William Joseph (1841–1921), the son of a Dublin watchmaker and jeweller, studied at St Laurence's and entered the Catholic University in 1856, where he studied for two years on a mathematical exhibition, leaving after taking the scholar's exam. He proceeded to Maynooth and, after he was ordained, taught dogmatic and moral theology there until he became the president. He became Archbishop of Dublin in 1888 and for the next quarter of a century was the dominating personality of the Church in Ireland; a champion of Catholic educational interests, he was made the first chancellor of the National University of Ireland in 1909. (*DIB, ODNB*)

White, John Patrick (Jasper) (1840–92), son of John White, a wealthy Jamaica estate owner, was educated at Stonyhurst and arrived at St Mary's in March 1857. He later joined the British Army and served overseas, reaching the rank of Lieutenant-Colonel. In 1861 he married Emily MacMahon (d. 1906); of their seven children, his son Thomas became a Jesuit and two daughters, Eileen and Emily, became nuns in England.

Zamoyski, Count Etienne (1837–99), son of Count Zdzislaw Zamoyski (1810–1855), came from a family from Austrian Poland, living in exile in France. He joined St Mary's House in 1856 and was expelled in December 1858, though he returned to take his exams in January 1859. He transferred to London University, married Zofia Potocka in 1879 and became a member of the Sejm of Polish Galicia; he was a known economic activist. He died in Paris.

BIBLIOGRAPHY

ARCHIVAL SOURCES

1. Dublin Diocesan Archives

a) Cullen Papers

45/2 Catholic University, undated documents

45/3 Catholic University, 1850–60

> VI(22) Prospectus for the Catholic University Medical School, 17 August 1855
>
> VI(26) *Catholic University of Ireland, Calendar for 1855–56* (Dublin: J. F. Fowler, 1855)
>
> VI(27)Prospectus for the Catholic University School of Engineering, 1855–56
>
> IX *Irish Catholic University Prospectus, 1858–59* (Dublin: J. F. Fowler, 1858)
>
> IX *Catholic University of Ireland, Calendar for 1858–59* (Dublin: J. F. Fowler, 1858)

45/4 Catholic University, 1861–66

> I(1) *Catholic University of Ireland, Calendar for 1861* (Dublin: J. F. Fowler, 1861)
>
> I(1) Catholic University. Report by the Dean of the Medical Faculty on the Condition of the School buildings etc, 1861
>
> III(6A) 'Report to the Episcopal Board of the Catholic University of Ireland', 1863
>
> III(7A) 'Report of the Finance Committee of the Catholic University to the University Board', 1863
>
> V(7) 'Report to the Episcopal Board of the Catholic University of Ireland', 1865

45/5 Catholic University, 1867–73

V(4) *Constitution and Statutes of the Catholic University of Ireland* (Dublin: Catholic University of Ireland, 1869)

XIII(4) 'Report on the present condition of the Catholic University', 1873

45/6 Catholic University, 1873–78

II(7) 'Report on the Catholic University', 1874

IV(2) 'Report on the Catholic University', 1875

VI(7) 'Report on the Catholic University', 1876

X(2) 'Report on the Catholic University', 1878

45/7 Catholic University, 1878–81

45/8 Catholic University, 1882–85

45/9 Catholic University, various papers

b) Woodlock Papers

106/1 Catholic University bank book, 1854–1873

106/2 Account book of St Patrick's House, 1861–63

106/4 Minutes of the Council of Discipline, 1863–64

106/5 Student ledger of St Patrick's House 1858–61

106/6 Accounts book of St Patrick's House, 1859–68

106/7 Catholic University accounts ledger, 1856–60

106/20 *Faculty of Science outline of course of studies and exams* (Dublin: J. F. Fowler, 1857)

106/103 'Report on the Catholic University', 1877

106/112 Letter book of University Secretary, 1858–60

159/3 *The Vice-Rector's Report for the year 1858–1859* (Dublin; J. F. Fowler, 1859)

Catholic University accounts ledger, 1854–55

Minute Book of the Episcopal Board of the Catholic University, 1861–79

Report on the Present Condition of the Catholic University (1873)

2. Oratory of St Philip Neri, Birmingham

A3.8 Memorandum relating to the Catholic University

A34.2 Catholic University, Formal and Documental, incl. University Journal

A6.15 Memorandum Book about College Pupils

C.6.26 University correspondence, 1856–57

C.7.3 Letters and papers belonging to rectorship, 1851–58

> No 25 Testimonials, applications & salaries of professorship
>
> No 29 Dean's houses 1858–1859, St Mary's House
>
> No 30 Dean's houses 1854–1858/59, St Patrick's House
>
> No 31 Dean's houses 1855–57, St Laurence's House
>
> No 32 University publications
>
> No 44 Residence, externs, etc., 1856–58
>
> No 47 Scratton letters, 1852–64
>
> No 49 Letters, Ireland, 1854
>
> No 50 Letters, Ireland, 1855

'On popular mistakes as to the object of education', sermon preached on 8 January & 27 August 1826

'On general education as connected with the Church and religion', sermon preached on 19 August 1827

3. University College, Dublin

a) Archives

CU1 Minute book of the Catholic University Committee, 1850–56

CU3 Minute book of Episcopal Board, 1857–79

CU4 Minutes of the Council of the Faculty of Philosophy and Letters, 1856–78

CU6 Student Register, 1854–79

CU10 University Transactions, 1854–80

CU11 Letter book of University Secretary, 1854–55

b) Special collection

34.G.2/1 *The Irish Catholic University, Calendar for 1858-59* (Dublin: J. F. Fowler)

15.J.1-5 *The Irish Catholic University, Calendar for 1863, 1865, 1866-67, 1867-68, 1869* (Dublin: J. F. Fowler)

34.G.2/5 *Report by the Dean of the Medical Faculty on the condition of the school buildings, etc.* (Dublin: J. F. Fowler, 1861)

4.G.2/3 *Report of the Dean and Faculty of Science of the Catholic University, Session 1857–1858* (Dublin: J. F. Fowler, 1858)

34.G.2/2 *Report on the condition and circumstances of the Catholic University of Ireland, presented by a Committee of Senate, July 1859* (Dublin: J. F. Fowler, [1859])

48.O.1/1 *Rules and Regulations of the Historical, Literary, and Æsthetical Society* (Dublin: J. F. Fowler, 1857)

Subject catalogue of the Library of the Catholic University of Ireland, 3 vols, Dublin, [1858–186?]

PRINTED SOURCES

'A' [Arnold, T.], letter to *Weekly Register* (5 October 1861)

——, *Passages in a wandering life* (London: Edward Arnold, 1900)

——, *Letters of Thomas Arnold the younger, 1850–1900*, ed. J. Bertram (London: OUP, 1980)

Atlantis, a register of literature and science conducted by members of the Catholic University 1–9 (1858–59, 1860, 1862–63, 1870)

Battersby, W. J., *Battersby's registry for the Catholic world for 1845(–56)* (Dublin, 1844–56)

——, *Battersby's Catholic Directory, Almanac, and Registry for 1857 (–64)* (Dublin, 1857–63)

Bristed, C. A., *Five years in an English university* (New York: G. P. Putnam & Son, 1852)

[Capes, J. M.], 'Catholic and Protestant collegiate education', *The Rambler* (December 1848), pp. 235–41

[———], 'The duties of journalists: Catholic and Protestant education', *The Rambler* (January 1849), pp. 325–31

[———], 'The Catholic University: its difficulties and prospects', *The Rambler* (February 1857), pp. 83–98

[———], 'Ireland's opportunity', *The Rambler* (September 1857), pp. 161–72

[———], 'The Catholic University of Ireland', *The Rambler* (May 1860), pp. 1–10

Catholic University Gazette 1–55 (1854–56)

Constitution and Statutes of the Catholic University of Ireland, (Dublin: Catholic University of Ireland, 1869)

Cullen P., *Paul Cullen and his contemporaries: with their letters from 1820–1902*, 5 vols, ed. P. MacSuibhne (Naas: Leinster Leader, 1961–74)

[Daman, C.], *Ten letters introductory to college residence* (Oxford, 1848)

de Vere, A., *Recollections of Aubrey de Vere* (New York: Edward Arnold, 1897)

Fottrell, G., *Inaugural address delivered before the Literary and Historical Society of the Catholic University of Ireland* (London, 1871)

[Gartlan, J.], *Vice-Rector's Report for the year 1858–1859* (Dublin; J. F. Fowler, 1859)

Gorman, W. G., *Converts to Rome: a biographical list of the more notable converts to the Catholic Church in the United Kingdom during the last sixty years* (London: Sands & Co., 1910)

The Irish Catholic University, Calendar for 1855 (–1869) (Dublin: J. F. Fowler, 1855–56, 1856–57, 1858–59, 1861, 1863, 1864, 1865, 1866–67, 1867–68, 1869)

The Irish Catholic University, Prospectus 1858–59 (Dublin: J. F. Fowler, 1858)

Martin, J., *The address of the Committee of the Synod of Thurles to the Catholics of Ireland reviewed and the objections to the Queen's Colleges considered* (Dublin: J. McGlashan, 1850)

[Mozley, H.], *Family adventures* (London, 1852)

Mozley, T., *Reminiscences: chiefly of Oriel College and the Oxford Movement*, 2 vols (London: Longman, Green & Co., 1882)

'A' [Newman, J. H.], 'Hints to religious students at College', *The Christian Observer* 22 (October 1822), pp. 623–6

'Catholicus' [——], 'The Tamworth Reading Room', letters to *The Times* (February 1841); reprinted in *Discussions and arguments on various subjects* (1872; London: Longmans, Green & Co., 1891), pp. 254–305

——, *Loss and gain. The story of a convert* (1848; London: Longmans, Green & Co., 1872)

——, *Lectures on the present position of Catholics in England* (1851); ed. A. Nash (Leominster: Gracewing, 2000)

——, *University sketches. Text of 1856*, ed. M. Tierney (Dublin: Browne & Nolan, [1952])

——, *The rise and progress of the universities and Benedictine essays* (1856); ed. M. K. Tillman (Leominster: Gracewing, 2001)

——, 'The Catholic University', *Weekly Register* (23 & 30 January, 6 & 13 February, 6 & 13 March 1858); reprinted in *LD*, vol. xix, pp. 565–83

——, 'On consulting the faithful in matters of doctrine', *The Rambler* (July 1859), pp. 198–230; reprinted in *On consulting the faithful in matters of doctrine*, ed. J. Coulson (London: G. Chapman, 1961)

——, 'Charter to the Catholic University', *The Rambler* (May 1859), pp. 125–6

——, 'The Catholic university', *The Rambler* (July 1859), p. 257

'H. O.' [——], 'Seminaries of the Church', *The Rambler* (September 1860), pp. 398–401; reprinted in *LD*, vol. xix, pp. 554–7

——, *Apologia pro vita sua* (1865; London: Longmans, Green & Co., 1908)

——, *An essay in aid of a grammar of assent* (1870; London: Longmans, Green & Co., 1898)

——, *Sermons preached on various occasions* (1870; London: Longmans, Green & Co., 1898)

——, *Historical sketches*, vol. iii (1872; London: Longmans, Green & Co., 1909)

——, *The idea of a university: defined and illustrated 1. in nine discourses delivered to the Catholics of Dublin, 2. in occasional lectures and essays addressed to the members of the Catholic University* (1873; London: Longmans, Green & Co., 1907); ed. I. T. Ker (Oxford: Clarendon, 1976)

——, *My campaign in Ireland, Part 1: Catholic University reports and other papers*, ed. W. Neville (Aberdeen [Ireland]: A. King & Co., 1896)

——, *Addresses to Cardinal Newman with his replies*, ed. W. P. Neville (London: Longmans, Green & Co., 1905)

——, *John Henry Newman: autobiographical writings*, ed. H. Tristram (London: Sheed & Ward, 1956)

——, *Newman the Oratorian: his unpublished Oratory papers*, ed. P. Murray (Dublin: Gill & Macmillan, 1969)

——, *The letters and diaries of John Henry Newman*, 32 vols, ed. C. S. Dessain *et al.* (London: T. Nelson, 1961–72; Oxford: Clarendon Press, 1973–2008)

——, *Newman on university education*, ed. R. McHugh (Dublin: Browne & Nolan, 1944)

Pattison, M., *Memoirs* (1885; London: Centaur, 1969)

Pollen, J. H., letter to Fr Goldie, August 1890, *The Month* (September 1906), pp. 318–20

O'Shea, J. A., *Roundabout recollections*, 2 vols (London: Ward & Downey, 1892)

[Renouf, P.], *University education for English Catholics: a letter to the Very Rev. J. H. Newman, by a Catholic layman* (London: Burns & Lambert, 1864)

——, *The life work of Sir Peter le Page Renouf*, ed. W. H. Rylands, G. Maspero & E. Neville (Paris: Leroux, 1907)

——, *The letters of Peter le Page Renouf (1822–1897)*, 4 vols, ed. K. J. Cathcart (Dublin: UCD Press, 2003)

Report and evidence upon the recommendations of Her Majesty's Commissioners for inquiring into the state of the University of Oxford, presented to the Board of Heads of Houses and Proctors (Oxford: OUP, 1853)

Report by the Dean of the Medical Faculty on the condition of the school buildings, etc. (Dublin: J. F. Fowler, 1861) [UCD, spec. coll. 34.G.2/5]

Report of Her Majesty's commissioners appointed to inquire into the management and government of the College of Maynooth, the discipline and course of studies pursued therein, British Parliamentary Papers, 1855, vol. xxii

Report of Her Majesty's commissioners appointed to inquire into the progress and condition of the Queen's Colleges at Belfast, Cork, and Galway: with minutes of evidence, documents, and tables and returns, British Parliamentary Papers, 1858, vol. xxi

Report of Her Majesty's commissioners appointed to inquire into the state, discipline, studies and revenues of the University and colleges of Oxford: together with the evidence, and an appendix, British Parliamentary Papers, 1852, vol. xxii

Report of Her Majesty's commissioners appointed to enquire into the state, discipline, studies and revenues of the University of Dublin and of Trinity College, together with appendices, containing evidence, suggestions, and correspondence, British Parliamentary Papers, 1853, vol. xlv

Report of the Dean and Faculty of Science of the Catholic University, Session 1857–1858 (Dublin: J. F. Fowler, 1858) [UCD, spec. coll. 34.G.2/3]

Report of the Royal Commission on University Education in Ireland (Robertson Report), British Parliamentary Papers, 1902–3, vols xxxi–ii

Report on the condition and circumstances of the Catholic University of Ireland, presented by a Committee of Senate, July 1859 (Dublin: J. F. Fowler, [1859]) [UCD, spec. coll. 34.G.2/2; also DDA]

Robertson Report, see *Report of the Royal Commission on University Education in Ireland*

Rules and Regulations of the Historical, Literary, and Æsthetical Society (Dublin: J. F. Fowler, 1857) [UCD, spec. coll. 48.0.1/1]

Sullivan, W. K., *University education in Ireland. A letter to Sir John Dalberg Acton* (London: Ridgways, 1866)

SECONDARY SOURCES

Addington, R., *The idea of the Oratory* (London: Burns & Oates, 1966)

Allies, M. H., *Thomas William Allies* (London: Burns & Oates, 1907)

Allitt, P., *Catholic converts: British and American converts turn to Rome* (Ithaca: Cornell University Press, 1977)

Altholz, J. L., *The Liberal Catholic movement in England: the 'Rambler' and its contributors, 1848–1864* (Montreal: Palm Publishers, 1962)

Arthur, J. & Nicholls, G., *John Henry Newman.* Continuum library of educational thought, vol. xviii (Continuum: London, 2007)

Ashton, R., *Victorian Bloomsbury* (New Haven: Yale University Press, 2012)

Barr, C., *Paul Cullen, John Henry Newman, and the Catholic University of Ireland, 1845–1865* (Gracewing: Leominster, 2003)

Bergonzi, B., *A Victorian wanderer: the life of Thomas Arnold the younger* (New York: OUP, 2003)

Blehl, V. F., *John Henry Newman: a bibliographical catalogue of his writings* (Virginia: University Press of Virginia, 1978)

Blum, C. O., 'Newman's collegiate ideal', *Pro Ecclesia* 17:3 (2008), pp. 310–25

Bottone, A., *The philosophical habit of mind: rhetoric and person in John Henry Newman's Dublin writings* (Bucharest: Zeta books, 2010)

Briel, D., 'The idea of a university', *Wisdom and holiness, science and scholarship*, ed. M. Dauphinais & M. Levering (Florida: Sapientia Press, 2007), pp. 1–16

Brockliss, L. W. B., 'The European University in the age of Revolution, 1789–1850', *The history of the University of Oxford*, vol. vi, ed. M. G. Brock & M. C. Curthoys (Oxford: OUP, 1997), pp. 77–145

——, 'In search of the new Newman', *Oxford Magazine* 319 (Hilary Term 2012), pp. 4–6

Budd, D. & Hinds, R. (eds), *The Hist and Edmund Burke's Club: an anthology* (Dublin: Lilliput Press, 1997)

Butler, C., 'Newman and modern education', *Downside Review* 70 (1952), pp. 259–74

Caterson, S., *The idea of a residential college. Image and reality from John Henry Newman to Harry Potter and 'the social network'* (Monash University, 2011)

Chapman, M., 'Newman and the Anglican idea of a university', *Journal for the history of modern theology* 18:2 (October 2011), pp. 212–27

Chavasse, P., 'Newman and the laity', *Newman today*, ed. S. L. Jaki (San Francisco: Ignatius Press, 1989), pp. 49–78

Collini, S., *What are universities for?* (London: Penguin, 2012)

Coolahan, J., *Irish education: its history and structure* (Dublin: Institute of Public Administration, 1981)

Coulson, J., 'Newman's idea of an educated laity—the two versions', *Theology and the university: an ecumenical investigation*, ed. J. Coulson (Baltimore: Helicon Press, 1964), pp. 47–63

Culler, A. D., *The imperial intellect: a study of Newman's educational ideal* (New Haven: Yale University Press, 1955)

Curthoys, M. C., 'The "unreformed" colleges', *The history of the University of Oxford*, vol. vi, ed. M. G. Brock & M. C. Curthoys (Oxford: OUP, 1997), pp. 146–73

—— & Day, C. J., 'The Oxford of Mr Verdant Green', *The history of the University of Oxford*, vol. vi, ed. M. G. Brock & M. C. Curthoys (Oxford: OUP, 1997), pp. 268–86

——, 'The colleges in the new era', *The history of the University of Oxford*, vol. vii, ed. M. G. Brock & M. C. Curthoys (Oxford: OUP, 2000), pp. 115–58

Dale, P. A., 'Newman's "The idea of a university": the dangers of a university education', *Victorian Studies* 16:1 (September 1972), pp. 5–36

Davies, M., 'Newman and education: some questions for today', *Newman and Education*, ed. M. Davies (Rugeley: Spode House, 1980), pp. 4–20

Davis, H. F., 'Our idea of a university in 1952', *Some centenary addresses on Newman's Idea of a university*, ed. H. J. Parkinson (London: Newman Association, 1953), pp. 1–17

——, 'Newman, Christian or humanist?', *Blackfriars* 37:441 (December 1956), pp. 516–26

——, 'Newman on educational methods', *Dublin Review* 472 (winter 1956–57), pp. 101–13

Doolin,W., 'Newman and his medical School', *Studies: an Irish quarterly review* 42 (1953), pp. 151–68

Duke, A., *Importing Oxbridge: English residential colleges and American universities* (New Haven: Yale University Press, 1996)

Engel, A. J., *From clergyman to don: the rise of the academic profession in nineteenth-century Oxford* (Oxford: Clarendon Press, 1983)

Erb, P., 'Newman and the idea of a Catholic university', *Aquinas centre of theology. Occasional papers on the Catholic intellectual life*, ed. P. L. Reynolds & S. Glaze (Atlanta: Emory University, 1997)

Fleischacker, D., 'The development of Newman's idea of a university education, 1851–1858', PhD, Catholic University of America, 2004

Foister, S., *Cardinal Newman 1801–1890: a centenary exhibition* (London: NPG, 1990)

Gaughan, J. A., *Newman's University Church. A history and guide* (Dublin: Kingdom, 1997)

Gilley, S., *Newman and his age* (London: Darton, Longman & Todd, 1990)

——, 'What has Athens to do with Jerusalem? Newman, wisdom and the *Idea of a university*', *Where shall wisdom be found? Wisdom in the Bible, the Church and the contemporary world*, ed. S.C. Barton (Edinburgh: T&T Clark, 1999), pp. 155–68

——, 'Life and writings', *The Cambridge companion to John Henry Newman*, ed. I. Ker & T. Merrigan (Cambridge: CUP, 2009), pp. 1–28

Graham, G., *Universities: the recovery of an idea* (Thorverton: Imprint Academic, 2002); reprinted as part of *The institution of intellectual values. Realism and idealism in higher education* (Exeter: Imprint Academic, 2005)

Harvie, C., *The lights of liberalism. University liberals and the challenge of democracy 1860–86* (London: Allen Lane, 1976)

Hauerwas, S., 'How Christian universities contribute to the corruption of youth', *Christian existence today. Essays on church, world and living between* (North Carolina: Labyrinth Press, 1988), pp. 237–52

——, *The state of the university: academic knowledges and the knowledge of God* (Oxford: Blackwell, 2007)

Higton, M., *A theology of higher education* (Oxford: OUP, 2012)

Hochschild, J. P., 'The re-imagined Aristotelianism of John Henry Newman', *Modern Age* 45 (Fall 2003), pp. 333–42

Hodgson, P., *Newman and science* (Oxford: Corpus Christi College, 1998)

Hopkins, C., *Trinity. 450 years of an Oxford college community* (Oxford: OUP, 2005)

Horwood, T., 'The rise and fall of the Catholic University College, Kensington, 1868–1882', *Journal of Ecclesiastical History* 54: 2 (April 2003), pp. 302–18

Jackson, J., 'John Henry Newman: the origins and application of his educational ideas', PhD, Leicester University [?], 1968 [BOA]

Jones, H. S., *Intellect and character in Victorian England: Mark Pattison and the invention of the don* (Cambridge: CUP, 2007)

Kane, E., 'John Henry Newman's Catholic University Church in Dublin', *Studies: an Irish quarterly review* 119 (Summer/Autumn 1977), pp. 105–20

——, 'John Henry Newman's Catholic University Church revisited', *Artefact* 1 (Autumn 2007), pp. 6–27

Ker, I. T., 'Did Newman believe in the idea of a Catholic university?', *Downside Review* 93:310 (January 1975), pp. 39–42

——, 'Newman the teacher', *Newman and education*, ed. M. Davies (Rugley: Spode House, 1980), pp. 32–41

——, *John Henry Newman: a biography* (Oxford: Clarendon Press, 1988)

——, *The achievement of John Henry Newman* (London: Collins, 1990)

——, 'Newman's *Idea of a university*. A guide for the contemporary university?', *The idea of a university*, ed. D. Smith & A. K. Langslow (London: Jessica Kingsley, 1999)

——, ' "Not ... as equal, but ... one of his subjects": John Henry Newman's perception of the archbishop of Dublin', *Cardinal Paul Cullen and his world*, ed. D. Keogh & A. McDonnell (Dublin: Four Courts Press, 2011), pp. 277–88

Kerr, C., *The uses of the university* (Cambridge Massachusetts: Harvard, 1963)

Kerr, D., 'Dr Quinn's School and the Catholic University, 1850–67', *Irish Ecclesiastical History* 108 (1967), pp. 89–101

——, *A nation of beggars? Priests, people and politics in famine Ireland, 1842–1852* (Oxford: Clarendon Press, 1994)

Kronman, A. T., *Education's end: why our colleges and universities have given up on the meaning of life* (New Haven: Yale University Press, 2007)

Larkin, E., *The making of the Roman Catholic Church in Ireland, 1850–1860* (Chapel Hill: University of North Carolina Press, 1980)

——, *The consolidation of the Roman Catholic Church in Ireland, 1860–1870* (Chapel Hill: University of North Carolina Press, 1987)

——, *The Roman Catholic Church and the Home Rule Movement in Ireland, 1870–1874* (Chapel Hill: University of North Carolina Press, 1990)

Lefebvre, P., 'John Henry Newman tuteur: tradition, rupture, developpement 1826–1831', DEA, Ecole Doctorale des Etudes Anglophones, Paris, 2004

Luce, J. V., *Trinity College Dublin. The first 400 years* (Dublin: TCD Press, 1992)

Lyons, F. S. L., *Ireland since the famine* (London: Weidenfeld & Nicolson, 1971)

MacIntyre, A., 'Catholic universities: dangers, hopes, choices', *Higher learning and Catholic traditions*, ed. R. E. Sullivan (Indiana: Notre Dame, 2001), pp. 1–21

——, 'The end of education: the fragmentation of the American university', *Commonweal* 133:18 (October 2006), pp. 10–14

——, *God, philosophy, universities: a selective history of the Catholic philosophical tradition* (Maryland: Rowman & Littlefield, 2009)

——, 'The very idea of a university: Aristotle, Newman and us', *British Journal of Educational Studies* 57:4 (December 2009), pp. 347–62; *New Blackfriars* 91:1031 (2010), pp. 4–19

Markwell, D., 'John Henry Newman and the denominational university college today', *'A large and liberal education': higher education for the 21st century* (Melbourne: Australian Scholarly Publishing, 2007)

Maskell, D. & Robinson, I., *The new idea of a university* (London: Haven books, 2001)

Mason, P., *The English gentleman: the rise and fall of an ideal* (London: A. Deutsch, 1982)

Matthew, H. C. G., 'Noetics, Tractarians, and the reform of the University of Oxford in the nineteenth century', *History of Universities* 9 (1990), pp. 195–225

Maxwell, C., *A history of Trinity College, Dublin, 1591–1892* (Dublin: University Press, 1946)

McCarthy, M. J. F., *The Irish Roman Catholic University and the Jesuits* (London: Hodder and Stoughton, 1908)

McCartney, D., *UCD: a national idea. A history of University College Dublin* (Dublin: Gill & Macmillan, 1999)

McClelland, V. A., *English Roman Catholics and higher education, 1830–1903* (Oxford: Clarendon Press, 1973)

McDowell, R. B. & Webb, D. A., *Trinity College Dublin 1592–1952: an academic history* (Cambridge: CUP, 1952)

McHugh, R., 'The Years in Ireland', *A tribute to Newman*, ed. M. Tierney (Dublin: Browne & Nolan, 1945), pp. 144–71

McGrath, F., *Newman's university: idea and reality* (London: Longmans, Green & Co., 1951)

——, *The consecration of learning. Lectures on Newman's 'Idea of a university'* (Dublin: Gill & Son, 1962)

——, *Newman in Dublin* (Dublin: CTSI, 1969)

McKenna, L., 'The Catholic University of Ireland', *Irish Ecclesiastical Record* 31:723–6 (March–June 1928), pp. 225–45; 351–71; 482–90; 589–605

McRedmond, L., *Thrown among strangers: John Henry Newman in Ireland* (Dublin: Veritas, 1990)

Meenan, F. O. C., *Cecilia Street: the Catholic University Medical School, 1855–1931* (Dublin: Gill & Macmillan, 1987)

Meenan, J. F. (ed.), *Centenary history of the Literary and Historical Society of University College, Dublin, 1855–1955* (Tralee: Kerryman, [1956])

Moberly, W., *The crisis in the university* (London: SCM Press, 1949)

Morrissey T. J., *Towards a national university: William Delany SJ (1835–1924)* (Dublin: Wolfhound Press, 1983)

Mulcahy, D. G., 'Personal influence, discipline, and liberal education in Cardinal Newman's Idea of a university', *Newman-Studien* 11 (1980), pp. 150–8

Newsome, D., *Godliness and good learning: four studies on a Victorian ideal* (London: John Murray, 1961)

——, *Two classes of men: Platonism and English Romantic thought* (London: John Murray, 1974)

——, *The convert cardinals: John Henry Newman and Henry Edward Manning* (London: John Murray, 1993)

——, *The Victorian world picture* (London: John Murray, 1997)

Nockles, P., 'An academic counter-revolution: Newman and Tractarian Oxford's idea of a university', *History of universities* 10 (1991), pp. 137–97

——, 'Lost Causes and ... impossible loyalties: the Oxford Movement and the University', *History of the University of Oxford*, vol. vi, ed. M. G. Brock & M. C. Curthoys (Oxford: OUP, 1997), pp. 195–267.

——, 'Newman and Oxford', *John Henry Newman in his time*, ed. P. Lefebvre and C. Mason (Oxford: Family Publications, 2007)

——, 'Oriel and the making of John Henry Newman—his mission as college tutor', *Recusant History* 29:3 (May 2009), pp. 411–21

——, 'Oriel and religion, 1800–1833', *Oriel College: a history*, ed. J. Catto, (Oxford: OUP, 2013), pp. 291–327

——, 'A house divided: Oriel in the era of the Oxford Movement, 1833–1860', *Oriel College: a history*, ed. J. Catto, (Oxford: OUP, 2013), pp. 328–70

Norman, E. R., *The Catholic Church and Ireland in the age of rebellion, 1859–1873* (Ithaca: Cornell University Press, 1965)

——, *The English Catholic Church in the nineteenth century* (Oxford: Clarendon Press, 1984)

O'Duffy, E. (ed.), *A college chorus. A collection of humorous verses by students of University College, Dublin, from the pages of 'St. Stephen's' and 'The National Student'* (Dublin: Martin Lester, [1935?])

Ornsby, R., *Memoirs of James Robert Hope-Scott*, 2 vols (London: John Murray, 1884)

Palfreyman, D. (ed.), *The Oxford tutorial: 'thanks, you taught me to think'* (Oxford: OxCHEPS, 2001)

Pelikan, J., *The idea of a university: a re-examination* (London: Yale University Press, 1992)

Pereiro, J., *'Ethos' and the Oxford Movement: at the heart of Tractarianism* (Oxford: OUP, 2008)

Pollen, A., *John Hungerford Pollen, 1820–1902* (London: John Murray, 1912)

Prickett, S., 'Polyphany, the idea of education, and social utility', *Education! Education! Education! Managerial ethics and the law of unintended consequences*, ed. S. Prickett & P. Eskinne-Hill (Thorverton: Imprint academic, 2002), pp. 85–101

Rannie, D. W., *Oriel College* (London: F. E. Robinson, 1900)

Readings, W., *The university in ruins* (London: Harvard University Press, 1996)

Reilly, S. M. P., *Aubrey de Vere: Victorian observer* (Dublin: Clonmore & Reynolds, 1936)

Rigney, W. J., 'Bartholomew Woodlock and the Catholic University of Ireland 1861–79', 2 vols, PhD, University College Dublin, 1995

Roberts, J. M., 'The idea of a university revisited', *Newman after a hundred years*, ed. I. Ker & G. Hill (Oxford: Clarendon Press, 1900), pp. 193–222

Rothblatt, S., *The revolution of the dons: Cambridge and society in Victorian England,*(London: Faber & Faber, 1968)

——, *Tradition and change in English liberal education* (London: Faber & Faber, 1976)

——, 'An Oxonian "idea" of a university: J. H. Newman and "well-being"', *The history of theUniversity of Oxford,* vol. vi, ed. M. G. Brock & M. C. Curthoys (Oxford: OUP, 1997), pp. 287–305

——, *The modern university and its discontents: the fate of Newman's legacies in Britain and America* (Cambridge: CUP, 1997)

——, 'Loss and gain: John Henry Newman in 2005', *The university and society: from Newman to the market. Conference on shaping the future of university education,* ed. A. Lavan (Dublin: UCD, 2006), pp. 15–34

Rutler, G. W., 'Newman's idea of a Catholic university', *Newman today,* ed. S. L. Jaki (San Francisco: Ignatius Press, 1989), pp. 95–120

Sanderson, J. M. (ed.), *The universities in the nineteenth century* (London: Routledge & Kegan Paul, 1975)

Searby, P. (ed.), *A history of the University of Cambridge,* vol. iii 1750–1870 (Cambridge: CUP, 1992)

Slee, P., 'The Oxford idea of a liberal education 1800–1860: the invention of tradition and the manufacture of practice', *History of Universities* 7 (1988), pp. 61–87

Short, E., *Newman and his contemporaries* (London: T&T Clark, 2011)

Shrimpton, P. A., 'John Henry Newman and the Oratory School, 1857–72: the foundation of a Catholic public school by converts from the Oxford Movement', PhD, London University, 2000

——, *A Catholic Eton? Newman's Oratory School* (Leominster: Gracewing, 2005)

Sire, H. J. A., *Gentlemen philosophers: Catholic higher studies at Liège and Stonyhurst College, 1774–1916* (Worthing: Churchman, 1988)

[Society of Jesus], *A page of Irish history: story of University College Dublin, 1883–1909* (Dublin: Talbot, 1930)

Sparrow, M., *Mark Pattison and the idea of a university* (London: CUP, 1967)

St. Stephen's. A record of university life 1:1–7 (June 1901–June 1902)

Stockley, W. F. P., *Newman, education and Ireland* (London: Sands, 1933)

Stork, R. A. P., 'John Henry Newman and the laity', STD, Lateran University, Rome, 1966

Tapper, T. & Palfreyman, D., *Oxford and the decline of the collegiate tradition* (London: Woburn Press, 2000)

Tierney, M., 'Catholic University', *A tribute to Newman*, ed. M. Tierney (Dublin: Browne & Nolan, 1945), pp. 172–206

——, 'Newman's doctrine of university education', *Studies: an Irish quarterly review* 42:166 (summer 1953), pp. 121–31

——, (ed.), *Struggle with fortune. A miscellany for the centenary of the Catholic University of Ireland 1854–1954* (Dublin: Browne & Nolan, 1955)

Trevor, M., *Newman: the pillar of the cloud* (London: Macmillan, 1962)

——, *Newman: light in winter* (London: Macmillan, 1962)

——, *The Arnolds: Thomas Arnold and his family* (London: Bodley Head, 1973)

Tristram, H., *Newman and his friends* (London: John Lane, 1933)

——, 'London University and Catholic education', *Dublin Review* 199 (October 1936), pp. 269–82

Vale, M. D., 'Origins of the Catholic University of Ireland, 1845–1945', *Irish Ecclesiastical Record* 1039, 1041, 1042 (July, October, December 1954), pp. 1–16, 152–64, 226–41

Walsh, W. J., *The Irish university question, addresses at the Catholic University School of Medicine and Blackrock College* (Dublin: M. H. Gill, 1890)

Ward, W., *The life of John Henry, Cardinal Newman*, 2 vols (London: Longmans, Green & Co., 1912)

Warner, D. B., 'John Henry Newman's idea of a Catholic academy: contributions from his life and works towards a theology of education, with reference to recent documents of the Catholic Church', PhD, Open University, 2001

Wheeler, T. S., 'Life and work of William K. Sullivan', *Studies. An Irish quarterly* 34:133 (March 1945), pp. 21–36

Whyte, J. H., 'Newman in Dublin: fresh light from the archives of Propaganda', *Dublin Review* 483 (Spring 1960), pp. 31–9

INDEX

The connection of individuals to the Catholic University is indicated in bold italics: adviser, agent, caretaker, catechist, chaplain, co-founder, committee member, dean (of collegiate house), examiner, financial auditor, professor (or lecturer), rector, secretary, student, tutor, vice-rector.

Bianconi, Charles **committee,**
   financial auditor 447, 521
Birmingham Oratory 41–4, 59–
   60, 185–6, 190, 207, 213–14,
   237, 277, 292, 308, 325, 362,
   428
Blackstone, William xxxvi
Blount, Michael 323
Bowden, Henry **student** 190, 196,
   221, 542
Bowden, John 4, 7–9
Bowden, Elizabeth 191, 200
Bowyer, George 204
Boyd, Brian xliii, 163, 498
Bristed, Charles: *Five years in an*
   English university 249–51
British Critic, The 40, 225
Brougham, Lord 74–6
Browning, Oscar 244
Brownson, Orestes 90
Buck, Victor du 288
Burke, Edmund 222, 237, 284
Butler, Edward **professor** 245,
   302, 325, 338–40, 521
Butler, Joseph: *Analogy of religion*
   21, 36, 255

Cambridge University 33, 37, 50,
   51, 52, 121–3, 135–6, 168,
   224, 244, 249–52, 285, 314,
   420–33, 477, 484
Capes, J. M. 322
Casey, John **professor** 419, 521

Catholic emancipation 55–6,
   68–9, 78, 110–11, 177, 179,
   267–9, 288, 408, 474
Catholic University, Ireland
   academic
      academic dress 159–60, 273,
         289
      admissions 174, 180, 182,
         214–15, 219, 242, 294,
         306, 309, 381
      Atlantis 252, 283, 477
      Catholic University Gazette
         67, 90, 118–19, 151, 238,
         242, 246–52
      degrees 87, 216, 218, 248–9,
         266, 313–15, 323–4,
         372–3, 400–3, 406, 417,
         434
      evening classes 217, 225–6,
         407, 434, 442, 489
      examinations 88–89, 95,
         140, 146–7, 152, 174,
         180–1, 195, 197–9, 209–
         211, 215, 235, 243, 255,
         266–8. 309, 316, 324,
         354, 381–4, 401–3, 515–
         16
      faculties 60–1, 113, 162,
         204–5, 208–9, 242–5,
         406
      lecturers and professors 61–
         3, 93, 147–51, 209–11,
         231, 234, 243–5, 381–2,
         401
      library 89, 154, 207, 234, 477
      museum 89

science 7, 38, 60, 89, 162, 200–3, 222, 253, 407–9, 476–8

training the intellect xxv, 40, 48, 63, 72–3, 78, 151–2, 173, 181, 253, 317, 379, 409, 431, 474, 477, 497

tutorial system 14–38, 62–5, 87–91,128, 146–54, 157–9, 195, 206, 209, 211, 243–4, 249–52, 299–310, 317–18, 335–43, 466–7

publications

Apologia pro vita sua 30

Bartholomew's Eve 7

Historical (or University) sketches vol. iii 108, 119–20, 125–39, 242, 255, 458, 464, 487, 510

Idea of a university xxv, xliii, 66–80, 120, 493, 505, 507–8

Loss and gain: the story of a convert 44

Sermons preached on various occasions 290

'The Tamworth reading room' 40, 75–6, 105

Tract 90 41, 466

The Undergraduate 7–8, 31, 256–7

Nicholas, George 3

Noetics 11–15, 225

Northcote, James 150

Notre Dame University xxvii, 163

Oakeshott, Michael 475

O'Brien, Richard *student* 445

O'Connell, Daniel, the 'Liberator' 83, 219

O'Connell, Daniel, grandson of the 'Liberator' *student* 181–2, 231, 548

O'Curry, Eugene *professor* 240–1, 360, 412, 530–1

O'Donohoe, E. *dean* 395–6

O'Ferrall, James More *adviser* 92, 98, 223, 448, 531

O'Ferrall, Richard 92, 435, 444, 448, 531

Ogle, James 9, 47

O'Hagan, John *professor* 224–5, 280, 375, 436, 531–2

O'Hagan, (Lord) Thomas 204

O'Looney, Brian *professor* 445

O'Loughlin, Austin *dean* 342, 389, 392, 396–8, 532

O'Meagher, Ernest *student* 189, 548

Oratory of St Philip Neri xli, 41–2, 207, 462, 473

see Birmingham Oratory; London Oratory

Oratory School, Birmingham xiii, 180, 422–4, 470

Oriel College, Oxford 10–41, 63, 99, 225, 454, 482, Plates 1, 2

common room 11, 15, 467

tutorial reforms 15–32, 64–5, 88, 137–8, 466–7

Lightning Source UK Ltd.
Milton Keynes UK
UKOW04f0635161114

241666UK00002B/14/P